SECOND-LANGUAGE WRITING IN THE COMPOSITION CLASSROOM

A Critical Sourcebook

SECOND-LANGUAGE WRITING IN THE COMPOSITION CLASSROOM

A Critical Sourcebook

EDITED BY

Paul Kei Matsuda
University of New Hampshire

Michelle Cox
University of New Hampshire

Jay Jordan
Pennsylvania State University

Christina Ortmeier-Hooper
University of New Hampshire

Published in cooperation with the
National Council of Teachers of English

BEDFORD / ST. MARTIN'S   Boston • New York

For Bedford / St. Martin's

Executive Editor: Leasa Burton
Editorial Assistant: Katherine Bouwkamp
Associate Editor, Publishing Services: Ryan Sullivan
Senior Production Supervisor: Dennis J. Conroy
Production Associate: Matthew P. Hayes
Project Management: DeMasi Design and Publishing Services
Text Design: Anna Palchik
Cover Design: Donna L. Dennison
Composition: Macmillan India, Ltd.
Printing and Binding: RR Donnelley & Sons Company

President: Joan E. Feinberg
Editorial Director: Denise B. Wydra
Editor in Chief: Karen S. Henry
Director of Marketing: Karen Melton Soeltz
Director of Editing, Design, and Production: Marcia Cohen
Manager, Publishing Services: Emily Berleth

NCTE Stock No. 42923
Published in cooperation with the
National Council of Teachers of English
1111 W. Kenyon Road
Urbana, Illinois 61801-1096
www.ncte.org

Library of Congress Control Number: 2005934832

Manufactured in the United States of America.

1 0 9 8 7 6
f e d c b a

For information, write: Bedford/St. Martin's, 75 Arlington Street,
Boston, MA 02116   (617-399-4000)

ISBN: 0-312-44473-7
EAN: 978-0-312-44473-0

Acknowledgments

*Acknowledgments and copyrights are continued at the back of the book on pages
413–14, which constitute an extension of the copyright page.*

ACKNOWLEDGMENTS

First and foremost, we would like to thank Bedford/ St. Martin's, its staff members, and president Joan E. Feinberg for agreeing to make this resource available to composition teachers who wish to learn more about working with second-language writers. We are especially indebted to Leasa Burton, executive editor, who saw the value of this project from early on and provided ongoing support and guidance throughout the process. Katherine Bouwkamp, editorial assistant, provided us with invaluable editorial help at crucial moments. We also thank Sara Eaton Gaunt, development editor for English, for listening to the idea of this book and putting us in touch with Leasa. In addition, Linda DeMasi, project manager, was extremely helpful with the final details.

We are also grateful to the National Council of Teachers of English for supporting this project and for copublishing this book. Zarina Hock, director of book publications and senior editor, has been especially supportive of this sourcebook and other similar initiatives to provide resources for teachers who work with second-language writers.

Our reviewers for this project—Kevin Eric DePew, Helen Fox, Kate Mangelsdorf, Susan K. Miller, and Duane Roen—were invariably supportive and provided many useful comments that helped us refine the project. Thank you.

We also thank the authors, editors, and publishers of the works that appear in this book. These publications have been valuable to the field of second-language writing, and we hope that this collection will help them reach a wider audience of composition teachers.

Finally, we thank our families—Aya and Kana Matsuda; Matt, Gaven, and Quinn Cox; Tom, Sean, and Zachary Hooper; and Stefanie Rehn Jordan and Davis Jordan—for their support and love. Without them, this book would not be here.

CONTENTS

INTRODUCTION

The first-year composition classroom is no longer the kind of monolingual space it once was. In the nineteenth century, when higher education was highly exclusive, the college student population was relatively linguistically homogenous — at least on the surface (Matsuda). In the late nineteenth century and throughout the twentieth century, colleges and universities opened their doors to a wider variety of students, and the demographics in higher education began to reflect the growing cultural and linguistic diversity of the larger society. Part of this demographic shift has included increasing numbers of second-language writers[1] in our classrooms and across our campuses. As of 2004, over a half million international students were studying at U.S. colleges and universities (Institute of International Education). Even though that number has declined somewhat during the last few years as post-9/11 restrictions have made it more difficult for international students to study in the United States, many colleges and universities continue to recruit internationally. Furthermore, international students are not the only second-language writers to study in this country. The 2000 U.S. Census reports show that there are 3.5 million foreign-born U.S. residents between the ages of 19 and 24, along with 5.5 million English language learners (ELLs) in U.S. public schools (U.S. Department of Commerce; U.S. Department of Education).

Prompted by these current demographic shifts and by institutional initiatives to increase diversity and diversity-related awareness, many college teachers are beginning to reconsider the implications of their instructional practices for students who come from various ethnic, cultural, and linguistic backgrounds. Those who teach composition courses are no exception. In the field of composition studies, the interest in second-language writers is part of larger pedagogical and research trends. Studies of multiculturalism, plurality, alternative rhetorics, and hybridized discourses all speak to a changing sense of how composition instructors see and value language and writing.

These are not necessarily new trends, either. In 1974, the Conference on College Composition and Communication (CCCC) released its statement, *Students' Right to Their Own Language*, which asserted the value of students' dialects and charged teachers with learning about and respecting them. Since then, issues of diversity have been prominent in discussions in composition studies. And especially since the early 1990s, these discussions have increasingly included concerns about meeting the needs of second-language and linguistic minority students, as attested by the increasing number of sessions at CCCC and the National Council of Teachers of English (NCTE) on second-language writing. In 2001, CCCC and NCTE acknowledged these interests by adopting the "CCCC Statement on Second-Language Writing and Writers," which formally recognized the growing number of second-language writers in U.S. institutions, observing that "second-language writers have become an integral part of higher education, including writing programs" (p. 10 in this volume).

Yet despite the growing presence of second-language writers and the increased awareness of second language writing issues in academia, many conscientious teachers continue to feel underprepared to work with them. This discomfort may be due to the fact that composition scholarship overall has been rather slow to reflect the influx of second-language writers in composition classrooms. It may also be due to the lack of availability of graduate composition courses on second-language writing and the lack of inclusion of this area in teacher preparation. Additionally, many composition teachers may continue to feel disconnected from second-language writers: since many institutions have English as a Second Language (ESL) programs and second-language specialists, compositionists may feel that second-language writers would be better served exclusively by those specialists. And in some programs, placement procedures may separate second-language writers from native-English-speaking (NES) writers before these students reach composition classrooms.

However, second-language writers do find their way into composition classrooms for complex reasons. Some campuses may have a shortage of second-language specialists and second-language–dedicated sections, which effectively forces students into mainstream composition courses. Where there are sufficient sections of second-language writing, those courses may be remedial and/or noncredit bearing, which discourages many students from taking that option. Students may be advised into composition sections based on assessments of their oral proficiency, which is often an inaccurate predictor of experience and comfort with writing in English. Furthermore, the very definition of what it means to be an ESL writer can vary greatly, depending on institutional definitions and students' experiences with that term, leading students to reject ESL courses as stigmatized. As the line separating ESL and NES becomes blurred, so too does the line between second-language writing and composition pedagogies. Second-language students in first-year composition continue to encounter curricula, assignments, and assessment practices that are not designed with their needs and abilities in mind, and even the most conscientious of composition teachers often have not been given access to the background or resources to make their instructional practices more compatible with their students.

As a response to these challenges, this collection of articles provides a foundation in second-language writing for composition professionals. The five major sections in this book represent a sample of research involving second-language students in various settings over the last fifteen years. The first section, "Situating Second-Language Writing within Composition Studies," provides a backdrop to how second-language writing and writers fit into the broad field of composition studies. The second section, "Second-Language Writers: Definitions and Complexities," includes articles that describe the characteristics and needs of various categories of second-language writers, including international visa students and resident students. Section three, "Shifting Our Theoretical Framework," presents articles that provide a critical response to classroom interactions in culturally and linguistically diverse classrooms. Section four, "Rethinking Curriculum Design," features articles that challenge traditional strategies of writing instruction in light of the increasing linguistic and cultural diversity in composition classrooms. Section five, "Responding to and Assessing Second-Language Writing," presents articles that analyze the implications of teacher response and assessment and provide suggestions for these integral practices. In addition, a final section provides recommended readings that expand on the issues each section introduces. It also lists more readings on topics that, due to space constraints, are not covered in this collection but are relevant to the needs of second-language writers and their teachers.

Of course, composition professionals as well as instructors across the disciplines encounter second-language writers not just in the first-year course but in a variety of settings—from writing centers to writing-intensive or "writing across the curriculum" classes. The different contexts those settings represent add complexities to many of the issues covered here. However, this collection focuses on the first-year course because, despite debates about what the content of the course should be and despite calls from some prominent scholars in composition studies (see especially Crowley) to abolish it as a requirement, it persists as a gateway for the vast majority of students to higher-level work in most academic disciplines. It also persists as a site where composition instructors learn their first lessons in how to teach writing. Thus, first-year composition provides a continuous opportunity for students to negotiate both interpersonal and academic situations through writing and for teachers to refine their pedagogies as the student population continues to change.

Chapters included in this collection present various theoretical and methodological perspectives, including historical studies, reflections on teaching practices, and qualitative and quantitative studies. Broadly speaking, this collection represents a critical approach to second-language writing. The articles included provide practical information about how to address various issues, but they and this collection overall do so from the perspective that the assumptions that guide composition professionals' interactions with second-language students are just as important as the interactions themselves. That is, the *why* is just as crucial as the *what* and *how* in determining the best methods of addressing second-language writers' needs and abilities, especially since more and more students defy simple categories. Several scholars in the fields of composition studies, second-language writing, and applied linguistics have argued that critical and pragmatic considerations in teaching culturally and linguistically diverse students ought to be closely allied (Benesch; Canagarajah; Gilyard; Pennycook). By addressing practical concerns in a critical framework, this collection seeks to encourage such an alliance.

The field of second-language writing has grown exponentially over the last few decades. Given the expanding scope of the field and the growing number of publications on the topic, no single collection can provide a comprehensive treatment of research in the field. A major goal of this volume is to provide starting points for composition teachers who wish to add to their understanding of second-language writers and second-language writing instruction.

NOTES

1. In the fields of second-language studies, a number of terms are used to refer to multilingual writers. We often see "English as a Second Language" (ESL), "English Speakers of Other Languages" (ESOL), "English Language Learners" (ELL), "bilingual students," "multilingual students," and "second-language" (L2) students. Each of these terms comes with its own history, some more contended than others. In recent years, "English Language Learners" (ELLs) has been the term used by educational policy makers at the national level, but many scholars ask, When does a person stop being an English language learner? What is the bar-level of expertise? Furthermore, "ESL" and "ESOL" are often seen as negative markers that stay with students long after they have exited from formal programs. For our purposes, the editors of this collection have decided to use "second-language students" and "second-language writers" as our terms of choice, in keeping with the "CCCC Statement on Second-Language Writing and Writers." However, we also acknowledge the limitation of those terms, since many second-language writers are indeed third and fourth language speakers and writers.

WORKS CITED

Benesch, Sarah. *Critical English for Academic Purposes: Theory, Politics, and Practice.* Mahwah, NJ: Erlbaum, 2001.

Canagarajah, A. Suresh. *Critical Academic Writing and Multilingual Students.* Ann Arbor: U of Michigan P, 2002.

"CCCC Statement on Second-Language Writing and Writers." *College Composition and Communication* 52.4 (2001): 669–74.

Crowley, Sharon. *Composition in the University: Historical and Polemical Essays.* Pittsburgh: U of Pittsburgh P, 1998.

Gilyard, Keith. *Let's Flip the Script: An African American Discourse on Language, Literature, and Learning.* Detroit: Wayne State UP, 1996.

Pennycook, Alastair. "Vulgar Pragmatism, Critical Pragmatism, and EAP." *English for Specific Purposes* 16.4 (1997): 253–69.

Students' Right to Their Own Language. Spec. issue of *College Composition and Communication* 25.3 (1974): 1–32.

Institute of International Education. "Open Doors 2004: International Students in the U.S." *IIE Network* (10 Nov. 2004). 4 Dec. 2004 <http://opendoors.iienetwork.org/?p=50137>.

Malone, Nolan, Kaari F. Baluja, Joseph M. Costanzo, and Cynthia J. Davis. *Census 2000 Brief: The Foreign-Born Population 2000.* Dec. 2003. Census Bureau, U.S. Department of Commerce. 4 Dec. 2004. <http://www.census.gov/prod/2003pubs/c2kbr-34.pdf>.

Matsuda, Paul Kei. "The Myth of Linguistic Homogeneity in U.S. College Composition." *College English* (forthcoming).

U.S. Department of Education. Office of English Language Acquisition, Language Enhancement, and Academic Achievement for Limited English Proficient Students. *English Language Learners and the U.S. Census 1990–2000.* Washington, DC: U.S. Department of Education, 2002.

PART ONE

Situating Second-Language Writing within Composition Studies

Introduction to Part One

In the early 1990s, second-language writing emerged as an interdisciplinary field situated at the crossroads between second-language acquisition and composition studies. These two disciplines often present very different perspectives on "good" writing, pedagogy, and research. For second-language writers who found themselves somewhere in the middle of those crossroads, these disciplinary divisions have also meant having to make difficult choices about identity, placement, and academic achievement. And the truth is that the needs of second-language writers are still unmet in many colleges and universities. Given this, how do we work toward a more inclusive understanding of second-language writers and their writing within the field of composition? This section explores some of the issues and challenges that we face as our classrooms and students become more linguistically and culturally diverse. It also seeks to understand what historical events, trends, and administrative responses have brought us to the current condition. The section begins with the "CCCC Statement on Second-Language Writing and Writers." It then presents two essays that put the issues raised by the statement into historical perspective and also complicate that perspective by examining a particular gap in the way writing programs often address second-language writers.

The "CCCC Statement on Second-Language Writing and Writers," adopted by CCCC in 2000 and endorsed by Teachers of English to Speakers of Other Languages (TESOL) in 2001, is a formal recognition that second-language writers and second-language writing pedagogy are a part of the composition classroom. It contends that compositionists have a professional responsibility to understand the needs of an increasingly linguistically and culturally diverse group of students and to develop instructional practices to meet those needs. The statement provides writing programs and composition instructors with a road map for instruction, assessment, and class size. Furthermore, it advocates for increased teacher preparation and support for writing instructors who have second-language writers among their students. The statement, as with other CCCC statements, can serve as a powerful tool for instructors and writing program administrators who advocate on behalf of second-language writers at their institutions. In this collection, it serves to provide an important overview of issues and definitions that should guide our understanding of second-language writers and their writing.

If the CCCC statement provides the overview, then the essay that follows by Paul Kei Matsuda, "Second-Language Writing in the Twentieth Century: A Situated Historical Perspective," puts those issues and definitions into a historical context. The reality of composition courses today is that many second-language writers and their writing instructors find themselves at a disciplinary crossroads between ESL programs and first-year writing programs. These are often two programs administered by different departments and administrators with different sets of objectives, teaching practices, and research. But this crossroads is not a new phenomenon; it is part of a historical legacy, a "disciplinary division of labor," as Matsuda describes. First published in 2003, this essay charts the development of second-language writing as a discipline and provides the necessary historical work that helps explain why these divisions exist and how compositionists can address the complexities second-language writers introduce into the classroom. Matsuda argues that existing historical narratives about second-language writing that simply catalogue major pedagogical approaches are often inadequate in providing a broader sense of how second-language writers and writing fit into our collective understanding of composition.

While Matsuda examines the disciplinary gap between composition studies and second-language acquisition from a historical perspective, the third article, "Bilingual Minorities and Language Issues in Writing: Toward Professionwide Responses to a New Challenge" by Guadalupe Valdés, complicates that narrative by examining the impact of those divisions on language minority students. Originally published in 1992, Valdés's article explores the complex and varied characteristics of "bilingual minority students" and the increasing presence of these students in composition courses (pp. 31–70 in this volume). Valdés argues that the "compartmentalization" of composition and second-language writing has a direct impact on instructors' ability to meet the needs of students. She notes that the English composition profession "includes two large and distinct areas of interest and expertise": teaching second-language students and teaching mainstream native-English-speaking students (p. 32). She complicates these divisions further by describing subsets within the group of native-English-speaking students—most notably basic writers and speakers of underprivileged varieties of English. Yet second-language students remain on the margins, distinctly apart from these subsections and disengaged from the professional landscape of many composition teachers. Her descriptions of these bilingual minority students illustrate the difficulty of placing second-language writers into writing courses, and how the divisions between composition and second-language studies often leave students falling through the cracks.

If Valdés's article was a call to action for professionals in the fields of composition and second-language studies, scholarship in recent years has provided a growing response to that call. With the creation of the disciplinary infrastructure such as the *Journal of Second Language Writing*, the biennial Symposium on Second Language Writing, the Committee on Second Language Writing at CCCC, and the Second Language Writing Interest Section at TESOL, second-language writing specialists have worked to build an ongoing repertoire of pedagogy, theory, and research that seeks to bridge the divides between composition and second-language studies. Yet many of the issues and challenges that are discussed in this section still remain unresolved. As more and more second-language writers enter colleges and universities, compositionists face new challenges in terms of assessment, placement, and curriculum design. Increasingly, composition instructors and second-language specialists need to work together in order to work with these students in whatever classroom they find themselves. Writing program administrators, researchers, and teachers can no longer linger on their respective sides of the disciplinary divide.

1 CCCC *Statement on Second-Language Writing and Writers*

PART ONE: GENERAL STATEMENT

The Conference on College Composition and Communication (CCCC) recognizes the presence of a growing number of second-language writers in institutions of higher education across North America. As a result of colleges and universities actively seeking to increase the diversity of the student population, second-language writers have become an integral part of higher education, including writing programs.

Second-language writers are found in writing programs at all levels — from basic writing and first-year composition to professional writing and writing across the curriculum — as well as in writing centers. Although providing additional linguistic support in the forms of intensive language programs and special second-language sections of writing courses may be helpful they will not remove the responsibility of writing teachers, researchers, and administrators to address second-language issues because the acquisition of a second language and second-language literacy is a time-consuming process that will continue through students' academic career and beyond.

Second-language writers include international visa students, refugees, and permanent residents as well as naturalized and native-born citizens of the United States and Canada. Many of them have grown up speaking languages other than English at home, in their communities, and in schools; others began to acquire English at a very young age and have used it alongside their native language. To many, English may be the third, fourth or fifth language. Many second-language writers are highly literate in their first language, while others have never learned to write in their mother tongue. Some are even native speakers of languages without a written form.

Second-language writers — who have come from a wide variety of linguistic, cultural, and educational backgrounds — may have special needs because

From *College Composition and Communication* 52.4 (2001): 669–74.

the nature and functions of discourse, audience, and persuasive appeals often differ across linguistic, cultural, and educational contexts. Furthermore, most second-language writers are still in the process of acquiring syntactic and lexical competence—a process that will take a lifetime. These differences are often a matter of degree, and not all second-language writers face the same set of difficulties. While some native speakers of English may face similar difficulties, those experienced by second-language writers are often more intense.

For these reasons, we urge writing teachers and writing program administrators to recognize the regular presence of second-language writers in writing classes, to understand their characteristics, and to develop instructional and administrative practices that are sensitive to their linguistic and cultural needs. We also urge graduate programs in writing-related fields to offer courses in second-language writing theory, research, and instruction in order to prepare writing teachers and scholars for working with a college student population that is increasingly diverse both linguistically and culturally.

We also stress the need for further investigations into issues surrounding second-language writing and writers in the context of writing programs. Since those issues permeate all aspects of writing theory, research, and instruction—from textual features and composing processes to collaborative strategies and writing assessment—we encourage scholars and researchers of writing to include second-language perspectives in developing theories, designing studies, analyzing data, and discussing implications.

PART TWO: GUIDELINES FOR WRITING PROGRAMS

Placement

Decisions regarding the placement of second-language writers into writing courses should be based on students' writing proficiency rather than their race, native-language background, nationality, or immigration status. Nor should the decisions be based solely on the scores from standardized tests of general language proficiency or of spoken language proficiency. Instead, scores from the direct assessment of students' writing proficiency should be used, and multiple writing samples should be consulted whenever possible. Writing programs should work toward making a wide variety of placement options available—including mainstreaming, basic writing, and second-language writing as well as courses that systematically integrate native and nonnative speakers of English. Furthermore, writing programs should inform students of the advantages and disadvantages of each placement option so that students can make informed decisions.

Assessment

Writing prompts for placement and exit exams should avoid cultural references that are not readily understood by people who come from various cultural backgrounds. To reduce the risk of evaluating students on the basis of their cultural knowledge rather than their writing proficiency, students should be given several writing prompts to choose from when appropriate. The scoring of second-language texts should take into consideration various aspects of writing (e.g., topic development, organization, grammar, word choice), rather than focus only on one or two of these features that stand out as problematic.

Class Size

Since working with second-language writers often requires additional feedback and conference time with the instructor, enrollments in mainstream writing classes with a substantial number of second-language writers should be reduced; in classes made up exclusively of second-language writers, enrollments should be limited to a maximum of 15 students per class.

Credit

Second-language sections of composition courses should be offered for credit that can be used toward satisfying the writing requirement. Second-language writing courses prerequisite to required composition courses should be offered for credit that can be used toward satisfying the foreign-language requirement and should receive the same credit accorded other prerequisite composition courses.

Teacher Preparation

Any writing course—including basic writing, first-year composition, advanced writing, and professional writing as well as second-language writing courses—that enrolls any second-language writers should be taught by a writing teacher who is able to identify and is prepared to address the linguistic and cultural needs of second-language writers.

Teacher Support

Writing programs should offer pre-service and in-service teacher preparation programs in teaching second-language writing. Writing programs should also provide resources for writing teachers, including textbooks and readers on the teaching of second-language writing as well as reference materials such as dictionaries and grammar handbooks for language learners. Moreover, writing programs should encourage—and offer incentives for—writing teachers to attend workshops on teaching second-language writers that are presented at professional conferences such as CCCC and Teachers of English to Speakers of Other Languages (TESOL).

PART THREE: SELECTED BIBLIOGRAPHY

Belcher, Diane, and George Braine, ed. *Academic Writing in a Second Language: Essays on Research and Pedagogy*. Norwood, NJ: Ablex, 1995.

Braine, George. "Starting ESL Classes in Freshman Writing Programs." *TESOL Journal* 3.4 (1994): 22–25.

Candlin, Christopher N., and Ken Hyland, ed. *Writing: Texts, Processes and Practices*. New York: Longman, 1999.

Connor, Ulla. *Contrastive Rhetoric: Cross-Cultural Aspects of Second-Language Writing*. New York: Cambridge UP, 1996.

Ferris, Dana, and John S. Hedgcock. *Teaching ESL Composition: Purpose, Process, and Practice*. Mahwah, NJ: Erlbaum, 1998.

Fox, Helen. *Listening to the World: Cultural Issues in Academic Writing*. Urbana, IL: NCTE, 1994.

Hamp-Lyons, Liz, ed. *Assessing Second Language Writing in Academic Contexts*. Norwood, NJ: Ablex, 1991.

Harklau, Linda, Kay M. Losey, and Meryl Siegal, ed. *Generation 1.5 Meets College Composition: Issues in the Teaching of Writing to U.S.-Educated Learners of ESL*. Mahwah, NJ: Erlbaum, 1999.

Hillenbrand, Lisa. "Assessment of ESL Students in Mainstream College Composition." *Teaching English in the Two-Year College* 21.2 (1994): 125–29.

Kroll, Barbara. "The Rhetoric/Syntax Split: Designing a Curriculum for ESL Students." *Journal of Basic Writing* 9.1 (1990): 40–55.

Leki, Ilona. *Understanding ESL Writers: A Guide for Teachers*. Portsmouth, NH: Heinemann-Boynton/Cook, 1992.

Leki, Ilona, and Tony Silva, ed. *Journal of Second Language Writing*. New York: Elsevier.

Martino, Marta. "Issues in ESL: Give Credit Where Credit Is Due." *College ESL* 2.1 (1992): 20–22.

Matsuda, Paul Kei. "Composition Studies and ESL Writing: A Disciplinary Division of Labor." *College Composition and Communication* 50.4 (1999): 699–721.

——. *Second Language Writing Research Network Forum*. Dept. of English, Purdue University. <http://icdweb.cc.purdue.edu/~silvat/forum/>.

——, and Tony Silva. "Cross-Cultural Composition: Mediated Integration of US and International Students." *Composition Studies* 27.1 (1999): 15–30.

Severino, Carol, Juan C. Guerra, and Johnnella E. Butler, ed. *Writing in Multi-cultural Settings*. New York: MLA, 1997.

Silva, Tony. "Toward an Understanding of the Distinct Nature of L2 Writing: The ESL Research and Its Implications." *TESOL Quarterly* 27.4 (1993): 657–77.

——. "An Examination of Writing Program Administrators' Options for the Placement of ESL Students in First Year Writing Classes." *Writing Program Administration* 18.1/2 (1997): 398–428.

——. "Toward the Ethical Treatment of ESL Writers." *TESOL Quarterly* 31 (1997): 359–63.

Silva, Tony, Colleen Brice, and Melinda Reichelt, ed. *Annotated Bibliography of Scholarship in Second Language Writing: 1993–1997*. Stamford, CT: Ablex, 1999.

Silva, Tony, and Paul Kei Matsuda, ed. *On Second Language Writing*. Mahwah, NJ: Erlbaum, 2001.

——, ed. *Landmark Essays on ESL Writing*. Mahwah, NJ: Erlbaum, 2001.

Tannacito, Dan J. *A Guide to Writing in English as a Second or Foreign Language: An Annotated Bibliography*. Alexandria, VA: TESOL, 1995.

Tucker, Amy. *Decoding ESL: International Students in the American College Classroom*. Portsmouth, NH: Heinemann-Boynton/Cook, 1995.

Valdés, Guadalupe. "Bilingual Minorities and Language Issues in Writing." *Written Communication* 9 (1992): 85–136.

The Executive Committee of the CCCC approved the Statement on Second-Language Writing and Writers in November 2000. The statement was also endorsed by the TESOL Board of Directors at their February 2001 meeting.

Members of the CCCC Committee on Second Language Writing are: Paul Kei Matsuda, Chair; Akua Duku Anokye; Christine Pearson Casanave; Helen Fox; Tony Silva; Guadalupe Valdés; and Bob Weissberg.

2

Second-Language Writing in the Twentieth Century: A Situated Historical Perspective

PAUL KEI MATSUDA

Existing historical accounts of studies in second-language (L2) writing, which began to appear in the 1990s, usually begin with the 1960s and catalogue pedagogical approaches or emphases (e.g., Leki, 1992; Raimes, 1991; Silva, 1990).[1] It is not historically insignificant that many researchers see the 1960s as the beginning of the field, that they focus on pedagogical approaches or emphases, and that historical accounts began to appear in the 1990s because these accounts embody a set of assumptions about the disciplinary and epistemological status of second-language writing. That is, these accounts tend to position second-language writing as a subfield of second-language studies and present the primary responsibility of second-language writing researchers as the development of pedagogical knowledge in the service of advancing the field. Yet, a broader view of the history seems to suggest the limitations of these assumptions. Although it is true that writing issues began to attract serious attention from L2 specialists only in the 1960s, historical evidence suggests that L2 writing instruction did not suddenly become an issue in the 1960s (Matsuda, 1999). Furthermore, the rise of historical consciousness in the early 1990s seems to indicate that the nature of second-language writing studies began to change around that time.

My goal in this chapter is to provide an understanding of the dynamics of the field of second-language writing by considering its development from a broader, interdisciplinary perspective. Specifically, I will be examining how this academic specialty has been shaped by the interdisciplinary relationship between composition studies and second-language studies. Understanding the historical context of the field is important both for researchers and teachers because our theoretical and pedagogical practices are always historically situated. Without knowing the context in which certain theories or pedagogical strategies developed, we will not be able to apply them or modify them in other contexts or in light of new theoretical insights. Without an understanding

From *Exploring the Dynamics of Second Language Writing*. Ed. Barbara Kroll. New York: Cambridge UP, 2003. 15–34.

of the history, we may continue to use pedagogical strategies that are no longer appropriate for the changing student population or dismiss some useful ideas or practices for the wrong reasons. In other words, this historical chapter tries to enhance second-language writing teachers' understanding of the existing theoretical and pedagogical insights.

THE GENESIS OF SECOND-LANGUAGE WRITING ISSUES

Writing was neglected in the early years of second-language studies possibly because of the dominance of the audiolingual approach in the mid-twentieth century. As I have argued elsewhere (Matsuda, 2001), however, the neglect of writing in second-language studies goes even further back, namely, to the rise of applied linguistics in the late nineteenth century. Early applied linguists of that era sought to apply, quite literally, the findings of scientific linguistics—which has until fairly recently focused almost exclusively on spoken language—in the realm of language teaching. Reacting against the perceived dominance of "writing" in L2 learning (i.e., literary texts in such "dead" languages as Latin), the intellectual leaders of early applied linguistics in Europe—most notably, phoneticians Henry Sweet (1899/1964) and Paul Passy (1929)—argued that phonetics should be the basis of both theoretical and practical studies of language (i.e., linguistics *and* applied linguistics) and that the spoken form of language should take precedence over the written form. For the most advanced language learners, the use of free composition—or the production of extended written discourse by reproducing previously learned materials—was recommended as a more desirable alternative to then-traditional translation exercises. However, priority was given to spoken language because writing was defined merely as an orthographic representation of speech and because letter writing was considered to be the highest literacy need for most people.

The view of language teaching as an application of scientific descriptive linguistics—with a strong emphasis on the primacy of spoken language—became influential in many parts of the world. For this reason, writing did not become an important component of L2 teaching until fairly recently. The neglect of written language was most conspicuous in the United States between the 1940s and the 1960s, when the view of language as speech was institutionalized through the work of Leonard Bloomfield and Charles C. Fries.

The Rise of L2 Studies in U.S. Higher Education

Although U.S. higher education institutions began to enroll a significant number of international English as a Second Language (ESL) students starting in the late nineteenth century, the teaching of ESL did not receive serious attention until the 1940s. At this time, the potential threat of totalitarianism coming into Latin American countries made the teaching of English to people from those nations a matter of national security for the United States, especially given their geographic proximity. To provide English instruction and develop pedagogical materials for those Spanish-speaking students, the English Language Institute (ELI), the first intensive language program of its kind, was created at the University of Michigan in 1941 with Charles C. Fries as its director. After World War II, the ELI expanded its scope to provide instruction for international students from other countries.

The curriculum at the Michigan ELI reflected the influence of Sweet's work as well as Fries's strong commitment to the application of descriptive linguistics (Allen, 1973). The production of extended written discourse was not one of the instructional goals of the ELI because Fries (1945), like Sweet, assumed that students would be able to write once they mastered the structure and sounds of a language. Although written script was sometimes used, it was usually to facilitate the learning of spoken language through the use of printed materials developed at the ELI. The ELI also provided professional preparation in the teaching of ESL, contributing to the creation of intensive English programs across the nation (modeled on the ELI) as well as the professionalization of the field of *teaching* ESL (hence TESL) in the United States and abroad. The teaching of writing, however, was not a significant part of the ESL teacher's preparation at least until the late 1950s.

In the context of foreign language teaching, this development was paralleled by the work of Leonard Bloomfield. Because of his strong commitment to the application of linguistics to the teaching of language—which was inspired by the work of Sweet (1899/1964) and Otto Jespersen (1904), among others—his pedagogy, which he had begun to develop as early as 1914, focused exclusively on spoken language. Parallel to these developments, reading had been the primary goal of instruction in the foreign language teaching community since the early twentieth century. Only in the 1940s was Bloomfield's *Outline Guide for the Practical Study of Foreign Languages* (1942) adopted by the Intensive Language Program of the American Council of Learned Societies as well as by the Army Specialized Training Program (ASTP).

Later, the ASTP Method—which was informed by Bloomfield's pedagogical work—and Fries's oral approach were consolidated to form what came to be known as the audiolingual approach; this became influential in both ESL and foreign language classrooms. However, the presence of an increasing number of international ESL students in higher education and required college composition courses led to the emergence of instruction in second language writing in U.S. higher education institutions.[2]

L2 Issues in English Departments

In English departments, which had been offering required first-year composition courses since the late nineteenth century, L2 writing instruction first became a serious concern. After World War II (1939–1945), the number of international students in the United States began to increase rapidly, especially at research institutions. Between 1940 and 1950, the number rose from 6,570 to 29,813 (Institute of International Education, 1961). No longer able to ignore the presence of non-native speakers, teachers and administrators of composition began to create special sections of freshman English courses. Although some institutions labeled these courses remedial, others considered them equivalent to composition courses required of native-English speakers and awarded ESL students college credit for such courses.

Reflecting the increasing recognition of the instructional problem, L2 writing instruction became a significant issue at annual meetings of the Conference on College Composition and Communication (CCCC), which was established in 1949 as the primary professional forum at which teachers and scholars gathered to discuss the field. During the 1950s, ESL panels and workshops at CCCC were attended by composition teachers as well as ESL teachers. Many second-language specialists at CCCC recommended the use of materials developed at the Michigan ELI because no other available textbooks for L2 learners were informed by linguistic perspectives. Although these materials were intended for the teaching of spoken language in intensive programs, they were targeted to L2 students, in contrast to available composition textbooks that had been developed for L1 students.

In the late 1950s, concern with L2 writing issues began to shift gradually from composition studies to second-language studies. The professionalization of second-language teachers, prompted by the creation of the Michigan ELI and other teacher preparation programs, led ESL specialists to argue that L2 students should be taught only by trained specialists (now that such training was available). As a result, many composition specialists of the time lost interest in ESL issues. By the mid-1960s, attendance at ESL sessions of CCCC had become so small that at the 1966 meeting the discouraged members of the ESL workshop decided not to meet there again. In the same year, a new organization was founded to serve the needs and interests of L2 specialists in general: TESOL (Teachers of English to Speakers of Other Languages). Consequently, writing issues were divided into L1 and L2 components, and L2 writing issues came to be situated almost exclusively in second language studies—or more specifically, in the area of Teaching English as a Second Language (TESL). Thus, the *disciplinary division of labor* between composition studies and second-language studies was firmly established.[3]

SECOND-LANGUAGE WRITING AS A SUBDISCIPLINE OF TESL

With the continuing increase of international students in U.S. higher education and the creation of the disciplinary division of labor between L1 and L2 composition, preparing international ESL students for required first-year composition courses became an important responsibility for ESL teachers in intensive English programs, which were usually external to college curricula.[4] In other words, the intensive English program began to assume a remedial role in relation to the composition program. When second-language writing instruction became part of ESL programs in the early 1960s, however, ESL teachers were not specifically prepared for the new responsibility because their professional preparation, if any, focused almost exclusively on teaching the spoken language. It was clear to many that a pedagogy in second-language writing was needed for intermediate ESL students who had completed the oral component of the program but who were yet not prepared for first-year composition courses. For this reason, second-language writing emerged as a "subdiscipline" (Ferris & Hedgcock, 1998, p. 5) of TESL with a strong pedagogical emphasis. A number of pedagogical approaches were proposed, each representing a different conception of the nature of writing,[5] several of which are discussed briefly.

Writing as Sentence-Level Structure

In response to the gap between the need to prepare ESL students for free composition—or the production of "an original discourse . . . about some given subject matter" (Erazmus, 1960, p. 25)—and the lack of writing pedagogy, ESL specialists attempted to extend the application of existing principles of second language pedagogy (i.e., the oral approach and the audiolingual approach) to the teaching of second language writing. Edward Erazmus, who at the time was a staff member of the Michigan ELI, attempted to reintroduce the use of free composition exercises as a way of developing fluency in writing. He also suggested the application of Kenneth Pike's tagmemics as an invention heuristic, which later became influential in the field of composition studies. However, arguments for free composition exercises were dismissed as "naive traditional views" by those who, from the perspective of contrastive linguistics and a behavioral theory of learning, believed that "any free, random, hit-or-miss activity" should be "eliminated wherever possible, so that errors arising from the native-to-target language transfer can be avoided" (Pincas, 1962, p. 185). Instead, the use of controlled composition, an approach that focused on sentence-level structure, was proposed. Informed by a behavioral, habit-formation theory of learning, controlled composition consisted of combining and substitution exercises that were designed to facilitate the learning of sentence structures by providing students with "no freedom to make mistakes" (Pincas, 1982, p. 91).

The limitation of controlled composition soon became clear, however, because sentence-level grammar exercises did not help students to produce original sentences, let alone free composition. For this reason, the use of guided composition, which provided less rigid structural guidance, was devised. In its broadest conception, guided composition "includes any writing for which students are given assistance such as a model to follow, a plan or outline to expand from, a partly-written version with indications of how to complete it, or pictures that show a new subject to write about in the same way as something that has been read" (Pincas, 1982, p. 102). Despite some efforts to provide empirical support for fluency over accuracy (e.g., Brière, 1966), a consensus seemed to have emerged that "composing—writing beyond the sentence—must be guided or controlled" (Slager, 1966, p. 77). Although the teaching of sentence-level structure continues to be a concern in many ESL writing classrooms, its place in writing pedagogy has been a controversial issue (see Ferris, 1999; Truscott, 1996, 1999).

Writing as Discourse-Level Structure

Neither controlled nor guided composition provided adequate preparation for free composition, however, because both focused almost exclusively on sentence-level structures. Observing the discrepancy between students' ability to produce grammatically correct sentences and the ability to achieve "logical organization" as judged by native-English-speaking (NES) readers, Robert B. Kaplan (1966) argued that the problem stemmed from the transfer of L1 structures beyond the sentence level. He was especially influenced by composition specialist Francis Christensen, whose "Generative Rhetoric of the Paragraph" (1965) extended the analysis of linguistic structure to the level of the paragraph. Drawing on the principles of contrastive analysis and the Sapir-Whorf hypothesis, Kaplan suggested that paragraph structures, like sentence structures, were language and culture specific, a founding principle of the field of contrastive rhetoric (discussed more fully in Connor, 2003). Kaplan's suggestion led to a realization that "writing is much more than an orthographic symbolization of speech; it is, most importantly, a *purposeful selection and organization of experience*" (Arapoff, 1967, p. 33).

The emphasis on "rhetoric," narrowly defined as the organizational structure, came to be conceived of as an intermediate step between controlled or guided exercises at the sentence level and free composition at the other extreme. In the 1980s, the development of discourse analysis and text linguistics in the United States and Europe provided various theoretical and methodological frameworks for investigating written discourse systematically, and researchers began to examine structures of written discourse in various languages and their possible influences on L2 texts. Alternative explanations for L2 textual structures were also explored, and the notion of contrastive rhetoric came to be defined less deterministically. In recent years, contrastive rhetoric research has evolved into a field of research of its own, encompassing more than just the organizational structure of written discourse (see Connor, 1996, 2003; Panetta, 2001). Yet implications of contrastive rhetoric research in the context of the second-language writing classroom remain a point of contention (see Kubota, 1998; Leki, 1991; Matsuda, 1997).

Writing as Process

Until well into the 1970s, the teaching of second-language writing focused mostly on the features of L2 written text—orthography, sentence-level structure, and discourse-level structure—and the way L2 student texts deviated from the L1 norm. In the late 1970s and the 1980s, however, a number of developments in both composition studies and second-language studies prompted second-language writing teachers and researchers to consider factors other than properties of the texts themselves. In composition studies, the interest had begun to shift from textual features to the *process* of writing itself, with researchers from various philosophical and methodological orientations investigating the processes underlying the production of written discourse (e.g., Emig, 1971; Flower & Hayes, 1981).[6]

The notion of writing as process was introduced to L2 studies by Vivian Zamel (1976), who argued that advanced L2 writers are similar to L1 writers and can benefit from instruction emphasizing the process of writing. Rather than the view of writing as a reproduction of previously learned syntactic or discourse structures, the process-based approach emphasized the view of writing as a process of developing organization as well as meaning. Invention strategies, multiple drafts, and formative feedback—both by the teacher and by peers—also became important parts of writing instruction in many L2 writing classrooms. Although some L2 teachers—following Hairston (1982) and others in composition studies—enthusiastically promoted the process-based approach, characterizing its arrival as a paradigm shift (e.g., Raimes, 1983b), others warned against its uncritical acceptance (e.g., Horowitz, 1986; Susser, 1994). The applicability in the L2 context of pedagogical practices that had been developed for L1 writers also came to be questioned, and researchers began to examine L2 writing processes to see how they were similar to *and* different from L1 processes (for overviews of L2 writing process research, see Krapels, 1990; Sasaki, 2000; Silva, 1993).

Writing as Language Use in Context

The introduction of writing as process was paralleled by a development in second-language studies—that is, English for Specific Purposes—which considered language and writing in the specific context of their use (see Johns & Dudley-Evans, 1991) as well as the development of English for Academic Purposes (EAP) (see Jordan, 1997), a major emphasis prompted by an increase of composition courses designed specifically for international ESL students in English-dominant countries. This movement was also fueled by the demand for writing instruction for a growing number of nonnative-English-speaking graduate students, particularly in the United States.

If instruction that was specific to the context of language use was to be provided, an understanding of the various contexts of writing first had to be developed. For this reason, EAP researchers began to describe various aspects of writing in relation to their specific context of use, including features of academic genre (for a review, see Johns, 2003) and academic writing needs as well as tasks that are required in courses across the discipline. The reconceptualization of errors in light of their effects on a native-English-speaking academic audience has also taken place as part of this focus (see Frodesen & Holten, 2003). As a result of these developments, ESL writing courses at many institutions were reconceived as preparation for writing in academic discourse communities rather than as remediation for required composition courses, although the ability of language teachers to provide domain-specific language instruction has been questioned by some teachers (see Spack, 1988).

The Limitations of Pedagogical Focus

These pedagogical approaches, which were based on differing conceptions of writing, emphasize different aspects of second-language writing, but they are by no means mutually exclusive. As Raimes (1983a) writes, few teachers are "so devoted to one approach as to exclude all others" (p. 11). Yet in the professional literature, these approaches have often been pitted against one another, resulting in "a rather unproductive approach cycle" that did not "encourage consensus on important issues, preservation of legitimate insights, synthesis of a body of knowledge, or principled evaluation of approaches" (Silva, 1990, p. 18). Further aggravating the situation was the lack of professional preparation opportunities in the teaching of L2 writing. Until fairly recently, few post-baccalaureate professional preparation programs in TESL or related fields offered a course in second-language writing. With few opportunities for professional preparation, teachers of L2 writing often relied on textbooks as their source of pedagogical knowledge coupled with their own classroom experience for most of their preparation in the field. Thus, textbooks and teacher "lore" (North, 1987) were their preparation. However, as Raimes (1986) has pointed out, "new theories and approaches are . . . often slow to find their way into practice" because of the influence of "the oppositions in the field" as well as "publishing and marketing demands" (p. 157).

ESL WRITING ISSUES IN COMPOSITION STUDIES IN NORTH AMERICA

While ESL writing pedagogy and research flourished in second-language studies, ESL writing issues were conspicuously absent from composition studies for many years because of the disciplinary division of labor (Matsuda, 1998, 1999). Although there were some exceptions, ESL concerns were virtually nonexistent in composition studies between the mid-1960s and the late 1970s. In the meantime, the ESL student population in U.S. higher education continued to grow, as reflected in the annual Open Doors Reports issued by the Institute of International Education. The number of ESL writers was further increased by the advent of open admissions policies in the 1960s and the 1970s, which brought in numbers of immigrant ESL students who had previously been excluded from higher education.

Although the quantity of intensive English programs was also increasing, composition instructors in general continued to face the challenge of working with ESL writers because the number of institutions enrolling international ESL students far outnumbered those that offered special ESL programs. Even when ESL programs were available, L2 writers' "written accent"—L2 textual features that deviated markedly from L1 texts—would not often disappear after a few months of instruction. As a result, many international ESL students seeking a baccalaureate degree—in many cases after completing intensive language courses—were placed in basic writing courses before becoming eligible to enroll in required first-year composition courses.

The field of basic writing,[7] a subfield of composition studies, emerged in the 1970s as a result of open admissions policies at many urban institutions — most notably, the City University of New York (CUNY) — and brought a significant number of traditionally excluded groups of students to U.S. higher education. Although basic writing was concerned with all students who were enrolled in basic writing courses, its primary focus was "native-born" rather than "foreign-born" students because of the differing needs of the two groups. Some institutions, such as Hunter College, created separate courses for NES basic writers and ESL students, but many institutions, because of the lack of resources, placed ESL writers into basic writing courses that were taught by teachers with little or no preparation in working with ESL writers. Thus, the placement of ESL writers in basic writing classes became a point of contention. Many argued that ESL and basic writers should be taught separately because of their differing needs; others — especially those who had background in both ESL and writing — argued that they could be taught together profitably.[8]

Contrary to popular belief that L1 composition influences L2 composition but not the other way around, some insights from second-language studies have been applied to L1 composition studies as a way of addressing the needs of NES basic writers. For instance, Mina Shaughnessy, a pioneer in the field of basic writing, suggested that "many of the techniques developed in foreign language teaching seem to be applicable to basic writing" (1976, p. 162) because basic writers, "however different their linguistic backgrounds, are clearly colliding with many of the same stubborn contours of formal English . . . that are also troublesome to students learning English as a second language" (1977, p. 92). For this reason, a number of basic writing specialists suggested the application in basic writing instruction of theoretical and pedagogical insights from second-language studies, including error analysis, vocabulary lists, and controlled composition. Shaughnessy (1977) also tried to improve writing teachers' attitudes toward basic writers by adapting "the view a teacher is more likely to have toward a foreign student learning English" (p. 121). As a result, "writing as a second language" came to the fore as a metaphor for characterizing the difficulties NES writers faced in learning to produce the type of formal writing required in higher education. However, the goal of these borrowed practices usually was to meet the needs of NES basic writers rather than to help ESL writers in basic writing programs (Matsuda & Jablonski, 2000).

Nevertheless, basic writing specialists, with their strong commitment to helping traditionally excluded students gain access to higher education, also welcomed the discussion of ESL issues in their publications. For instance, the *Journal of Basic Writing* (*JBW*), established in 1975 and published by CUNY, has featured a number of articles concerning ESL writers. In 1985, the *JBW* officially announced the inclusion of ESL as a topic of interest, and articles focusing on ESL writing increased rapidly. The interest in ESL issues was so intense that in 1991 *College ESL*, also published by CUNY, was established as a journal that focused on "urban immigrant and refugee adults in college and pre-college settings" (editorial policy). The publication of this new journal was significant because it created additional space to discuss issues surrounding the traditionally neglected population of immigrant and refugee ESL writers. Yet it may also have reinforced the disciplinary division of labor between composition studies and second-language studies, as the number of ESL-related articles in the *JBW* dropped noticeably after the founding of *College ESL* (Matsuda, 2003).

Although intensive English programs and basic writing courses served a remedial role, composition teachers continued to face the challenge of working with ESL writers because a few semesters of additional language instruction would not usually allow them to achieve native-like writing proficiency. For this reason, ESL issues once again became an issue in composition studies in the late 1970s. As L2 writing issues became more visible and as teachers and researchers from both composition studies and second-language studies became involved in second-language writing research, the disciplinary boundary between the two became increasingly blurred. Although the collaborative efforts of L1 and L2 specialists have resulted in various publications, and although CCCC has recently adopted an official statement concerning second language writing and writers in North American college composition programs (CCCC Statement on Second-Language Writing and Writers, 2001), more efforts need to be made to fully integrate L2 writing issues into composition studies (Matsuda, 1999; Silva, Leki, & Carson, 1997).

THE EMERGENCE OF AN INTERDISCIPLINARY FIELD

As the exchange of insights between composition studies and second-language studies has increased, researchers have come to recognize the complexity and multidisciplinary nature of second-language writing research and teaching. For instance, Johnson and Roen (1989) point out that a "broader, multidisciplinary base is important in examining issues in L2 writing" because "no single theory from a single discipline can account for the complex and interacting social, cultural, cognitive, and linguistic processes involved" (p. 3). Kroll (1990) also writes that "for those engaged in teaching second-language [writers], what is needed is both a firm grounding in the theoretical issues of first and second language writing *and* an understanding of a broad range of pedagogical issues that shape classroom writing instruction" (p. 2; italics mine). Consequently, second language writing evolved into an interdisciplinary field of inquiry situated in both composition studies and second-language studies simultaneously.

With second-language writing recognized as a legitimate field, the number of studies examining it has increased exponentially. Research articles on second-language writing issues have become increasingly visible in journals such as *College ESL, English for Specific Purposes, Language Learning,* and *TESOL Quarterly*. Some journals in composition studies—such as *College Composition and Communication, Teaching English in the Two-Year College, WPA: Writing Program Administration,* and *Written Communication*—have also begun to feature articles related to L2 writing. An increasing number of dissertations are now being devoted to second-language writing. Only about a half dozen dissertations on L2 writing were written in the 1960s and about thirty in the 1970s, but this number rose to more than 150 in the 1980s and well over 300 in the 1990s. As the number of studies increased, the shortage of outlets for publication became apparent and the field began to develop its own disciplinary infrastructure to facilitate the creation and dissemination of knowledge about second-language writing.

In response to the "explosion of interest in research on composing in a second language" (Leki & Silva, 1992, p. iii), the *Journal of Second Language Writing* was established in 1992, indicating "the maturing of scholarly communication in the field" (Tannacito, 1995, p. v). The number of books on second language writing also increased, including monographs (e.g., Connor, 1996; Fox, 1994; Johns, 1997; Li, 1996; Pennington, 1996; Rodby, 1992; Swales, 1990; Tucker, 1995) and edited collections (e.g., Belcher & Braine, 1995; Connor & Johns, 1990; Harklau, Losey, & Siegal, 1999; Kroll, 1990; Severino, Guerra, & Butler, 1997; Silva & Matsuda, 2001b) as well as collections of reprinted articles (e.g., DeLuca et al., 2002; Leeds, 1996; Silva & Matsuda, 2001a; Zamel & Spack, 1998). Textbooks for second-language writing teachers also began to appear (Campbell, 1998; Ferris & Hedgcock, 1998; Grabe & Kaplan, 1996; Hyland, 2002; Leki, 1992; Reid, 1993). With the increase of scholarship in the field, bibliographic sources focusing on second-language writing have also become available. *A Guide to Writing in English as a Second or Foreign Language: An Annotated Bibliography* (Tannacito, 1995) features annotations of articles, books, and conference presentations that were published before 1994. Since 1993, the *Journal of Second Language Writing* has been providing annotated bibliographies of recent related scholarship on a regular basis. A five-year compilation of this bibliography has also been separately published (Silva, Brice, & Reichelt, 1999). In addition, Polio and Mosele (1998) have developed an online bibliography that focuses on the teaching and learning of writing in second languages other than English.

Several conferences focusing solely on second-language writing issues have been held, each resulting in an edited collection of essays and research reports. The first of these conferences, called Second Language Acquisition and Writing: A Multi-Disciplinary Approach, took place in the summer of 1996 at the University of Southampton (United Kingdom). Papers from that conference appear in Archibald and Jeffrey (1997). Additional edited collections resulting from recent conferences include papers from the Ohio State Conference on Reading-Writing Connections (Belcher & Hirvela, 2001) and papers from the first Symposium on Second Language Writing held at Purdue University (Silva & Matsuda, 2001b). The Symposium on Second Language Writing has now become a biennial event. In addition to specialized conferences, presentations and workshops focusing on second-language writing issues have become increasingly visible at related conferences, such as those of the American Association for Applied Linguistics, the Conference on College Composition and Communication, and Teachers of English to Speakers of Other Languages, among others.

Opportunities for professional development have also increased in recent years. In the latest edition of *The Directory of Professional Preparation Programs in TESOL in the United States and Canada, 1999–2001* (Garshick, 1998), an increasing number of professional preparation programs in TESOL have indicated the availability of coursework in second-language writing or writing in general. A few programs are even beginning to offer a specialization in second-language writing that integrates coursework in both composition studies and second-language studies. At a number of institutions—such as Indiana University of Pennsylvania, Northern Arizona University, Purdue University, the University of Toronto/Ontario Institute for the Studies in Education, and the University of New Hampshire—second-language writing specialists work closely with doctoral students, contributing to the development of the next generation of second-language writing teachers, researchers, and teacher educators.

Another important sign of maturity for second-language writing as a field is the existence of metadisciplinary discourse—or self-conscious inquiries into its nature and history (Matsuda, 1998). Metadisciplinary discourse may include, for example, the discussion of methodology (e.g., Goldstein, 2001; Polio, 2001, 2003), history (e.g., Matsuda, 1999, 2001; Raimes, 1991; Silva, 1990), interdisciplinary relations (e.g., Atkinson & Ramanathan, 1995; Matsuda, 1998; Matsuda & Jablonski, 2000; Santos, 1992; Silva, Leki, & Carson, 1997), and ideological and political issues (e.g., Benesch, 1993, 2001; Santos, 1992, 2001), as well as personal reflections on professional growth (e.g., Belcher & Connor, 2001; Blanton & Kroll, 2002; Kroll, 2001), and the general discussion of the status of the field (e.g., Atkinson, 2000; Kaplan, 2000; Santos, Atkinson, Erickson, Matsuda, & Silva, 2000).

Thus far, the field has focused mostly on issues that are specific to the needs of international ESL students in U.S. higher education because of the historical circumstances surrounding the origin of second-language writing; more recently, however, there has been an increasing attention to immigrant and refugee students in North America (e.g., Harklau, Losey, & Siegal, 1999).[9] This is not to say that research in contexts other than U.S. higher education or second languages other than English has not taken place. As Reichelt (1999) points out, there is a growing body of literature on foreign language writing in the United States that draws on both L1 and ESL composition research. An increasing number of studies have also examined L2 writing instruction outside the United States (e.g., Tarnopolsky, 2000), with many such studies coming out of Hong Kong and Japan. Unfortunately, these studies are often circulated locally and tend to remain unknown to researchers and teachers in other countries. The lack of interaction among scholars and teachers in various sites is problematic: just as theories of writing derived only from first language writers "can at best be extremely tentative and at worst totally invalid" (Silva, Leki, & Carson, 1997, p. 402), theories of second-language writing derived only from one language or one context are also limited. For second-language writing instruction to be most effective in various disciplinary and institutional contexts, it needs to reflect the findings of studies conducted in a wide variety of instructional contexts as well as disciplinary perspectives.

DIRECTIONS FOR THE FUTURE

The field of second-language writing, which initially arose in reaction to immediate pedagogical concerns in U.S. higher education, has undergone a number of disciplinary and epistemological shifts to become an interdisciplinary field of inquiry with its own body of knowledge about the nature of second language writing and writing instruction. In addition, to facilitate and guide the development of knowledge, the field has developed its own disciplinary infrastructure and metadisciplinary discourse. Yet second-language writing should not become completely independent from other fields that are also concerned with language and writing. Severing interdisciplinary ties would be counterproductive because the field does not have its own instructional domain; that is, L2 writing courses or programs are almost always situated in broader programs or departments, such as applied linguistics, composition studies, education, foreign languages, linguistics, and TESL. To maintain the field's ability to affect pedagogical decisions in a wide variety of institutional contexts, L2 writing teachers and researchers should continue to draw on and contribute to other domains of knowledge that may influence L2 writing instruction; in other words, the field of second-language writing should be seen as a *symbiotic field* (Matsuda, 1998). As such, it can and should continue to provide an evolving discourse community in which specialists from various related fields can come together to discuss common issues and concerns—the nature of second-language writing and writing instruction in various institutional contexts—and to negotiate differences in theoretical, ideological, and methodological perspectives.

NOTES

1. Silva (1990) is an exception in that he begins his history from the 1940s.

2. For a personal perspective on the influence of the "Michigan approach" as it related to the teaching of writing in the 1960s, see Blanton (2002).

3. For a detailed discussion of ESL issues at CCCC and the creation of the disciplinary division of labor between L1 and L2 writing, see Matsuda (1999).

4. The interest in the teaching of ESL writing was not limited to the United States. While no other institutions placed so much emphasis on first-year composition courses as was found in U.S. higher education, growing skepticism about the audiolingual approach in the professional literature prompted second language teachers in other countries to explore different approaches to the teaching of writing.

5. For different perspectives on the development of pedagogical approaches or emphases, see Blanton (1995), Ferris and Hedgcock (1998), Leki (1992), Raimes (1991), Reid (1993), and Silva (1990).

6. For a succinct overview of L1 process pedagogy, see Tobin (2001).

7. The term "basic writing" first became popularized in the 1970s as an alternate for the term "remedial writing." Courses for L1 students with weak writing skills are also sometimes labeled "developmental writing." Such courses are considered below the level of freshman composition.

8. For an overview of placement options for ESL writers, see Silva (1994).

9. Kaplan (2000) contends that studies of issues related to L2 writing outside the United States have existed since the early part of the twentieth century, although, as Atkinson (2000)

points out, they have not had a significant impact on the formation of the field of second language writing as "an organized academic field" (p. 318).

REFERENCES

Allen, H. B. (1973). English as a second language. In T. A. Sebeok (Ed.), *Current trends in linguistics: Linguistics in North America* (Vol. 10, pp. 295–320). The Hague: Mouton.

Arapoff, N. (1967). Writing: A thinking process. *TESOL Quarterly, 1*(2), 33–39.

Archibald, A., & Jeffrey, G. (Eds.). (1997). *Second language acquisition and writing: A multidisciplinary approach.* Southampton, UK: The University of Southampton.

Atkinson, D. (2000). On Robert B. Kaplan's response to Terry Santos et al.'s "On the future of second language writing." *Journal of Second Language Writing, 9,* 317–320.

Atkinson, D., & Ramanathan, V. (1995). Cultures of writing: An ethnographic comparison of L1 and L2 university writing/language programs. *TESOL Quarterly, 29,* 539–568.

Belcher, D., & Braine, G. (Eds.). (1995). *Academic writing in a second language: Essays on research and pedagogy.* Norwood, NJ: Ablex.

Belcher, D., & Connor, U. (Eds.). (2001). *Reflections on multiliterate lives.* Clevedon, UK: Multilingual Matters.

Belcher, D., & Hirvela, A. (Eds.). (2001). *Linking literacies: Perspectives on L2 reading/writing connections.* Ann Arbor: University of Michigan Press.

Benesch, S. (1993). ESL, ideology, and the politics of pragmatism. *TESOL Quarterly, 27,* 705–717.

Benesch, S. (2001). Critical pragmatism: A politics of L2 composition. In T. Silva & P. K. Matsuda (Eds.), *On second language writing* (pp. 161–172). Mahwah, NJ: Lawrence Erlbaum.

Blanton, L. L. (1995). Elephants and paradigms: Conversations about teaching L2 writing. *College ESL, 5* (1), 1–21.

Blanton, L. L. (2002). As I was saying to Leonard Bloomfield: A personalized history of ESL/writing. In L. L. Blanton & B. Kroll et al., *ESL composition tales: Reflections on teaching* (pp. 135–162). Ann Arbor: University of Michigan Press.

Blanton, L. L., & Kroll, B., et al. (2002). *ESL composition tales: Reflections on teaching.* Ann Arbor: University of Michigan Press.

Bloomfield, L. (1942). *Outline guide for the practical study of foreign languages.* Special Publications of the Linguistic Society of America. Baltimore: Linguistic Society of America.

Brière, E. J. (1966). Quantity before quality in second language composition. *Language Learning, 16,* 141–151.

Campbell, C. (1998). *Teaching second-language writing: Interacting with text.* Boston: Heinle & Heinle.

CCCC Statement on Second-Language Writing and Writers. (2001). *College Composition and Communication, 52,* 669–674.

Christensen, F. (1965). A generative rhetoric of the paragraph. *College Composition and Communication, 16,* 144–156.

Connor, U. (1996). *Contrastive rhetoric: Cross-cultural aspects of second-language writing.* New York: Cambridge University Press.

Connor, U. (2003). Changing currents in contrastive rhetoric: Implications for teaching and research. In B. Kroll (Ed.), *Exploring the dynamics of second language writing* (pp. 218–241). Cambridge, UK: Cambridge University Press.

Connor, U., & Johns, A. M. (Eds.). (1990). *Coherence in writing: Research and pedagogical perspectives.* Alexandria, VA: TESOL.

DeLuca, G., Fox, L., Johnson, M. A., & Kogen, M. (Eds.). (2002). *Dialogue on writing: Rethinking ESL, basic writing, and first-year composition.* Mahwah, NJ: Lawrence Erlbaum.

Emig, J. (1971). *The composing process of twelfth graders.* Urbana, IL: National Council of Teachers of English.

Erazmus, E. (1960). Second language composition teaching at the intermediate level. *Language Learning, 10,* 25–31.

Ferris, D. (1999). The case for grammar correction in L2 writing classes: A response to Truscott (1966). *Journal of Second Language Writing, 8,* 1–11.

Ferris, D., & Hedgcock, J. (1998). *Teaching ESL composition: Purpose, process, and practice.* Mahwah, NJ: Lawrence Erlbaum.

Flower, L., & Hayes, J. R. (1981). A cognitive process theory of writing. *College Composition and Communication, 22,* 365–387.

Fox, H. (1994). *Listening to the world: Cultural issues in academic writing.* Urbana, IL: National Council of Teachers of English.

Fries, C. C. (1945). *Teaching and learning English as a foreign language.* Ann Arbor: University of Michigan Press.

Frodesen, J., & Holten, C. (2003). Grammar and the ESL writing class. In B. Kroll (Ed.), *Exploring the dynamics of second language writing* (pp. 141–161). Cambridge, UK: Cambridge University Press.

Garshick, E. (Ed.). (1998). *The directory of professional preparation programs in TESOL in the United States and Canada, 1999–2001.* Alexandria, VA: TESOL.

Goldstein, L. (2001). For Kyla: What does the research say about responding to ESL writers? In T. Silva & P. K. Matsuda (Eds.), *On second language writing* (pp. 73–89). Mahwah, NJ: Lawrence Erlbaum.

Grabe, W., & Kaplan, R. B. (1996). *Theory and practice of writing: An applied linguistic perspective.* London: Longman.

Hairston, M. (1982). The winds of change: Thomas Kuhn and the revolution in the teaching of writing. *College Composition and Communication, 33,* 76–88.

Harklau, L., Losey, K. M., & Siegal, M. (Eds.). (1999). *Generation 1.5 meets college composition.* Mahwah, NJ: Lawrence Erlbaum.

Horowitz, D. (1986). Process, not product: Less than meets the eye. *TESOL Quarterly, 20,* 141–144.

Hyland, K. (2002). *Teaching and researching writing.* Harlow, England: Longman.

Institute of International Education. (1961). *Handbook on international study: For foreign nationals.* New York: Institute of International Education.

Jespersen, O. (1904). *How to teach a foreign language.* (Sophia Yhlen-Olsen Bertelsen, Trans.). London: Allen and Unwin.

Johns, A. M. (1997). *Text, role, and context: Developing academic literacies.* New York: Cambridge University Press.

Johns, A. M. (2003). Genre and ESL/EFL composition instruction. In B. Kroll (Ed.), *Exploring the dynamics of second language writing* (pp. 195–217). Cambridge, UK: Cambridge University Press.

Johns, A. M., & Dudley-Evans, T. (1991). English for specific purposes: International in scope, specific in purpose. *TESOL Quarterly, 25,* 297–314.

Johnson, D., & Roen, D. H. (Eds.). (1989). *Richness in writing: Empowering ESL writers.* New York: Longman.

Jordan, R. R. (1997). *English for academic purposes. A guide and resource book for teachers.* New York: Cambridge University Press.

Kaplan, R. B. (1966). Cultural thought patterns in inter-cultural education. *Language Learning, 16,* 1–20.

Kaplan, R. B. (2000). Response to "On the future of second language writing," Terry Santos (Ed.) et al. *Journal of Second Language Writing, 9,* 317–320.

Krapels, A. R. (1990). An overview of second language writing process research. In B. Kroll (Ed.), *Second language writing: Research insights for the classroom* (pp. 37–56). New York: Cambridge University Press.

Kroll, B. (Ed.). (1990). *Second language writing: Research insights for the classroom.* New York: Cambridge University Press.

Kroll, B. (2001). The composition of a life in composition. In T. Silva & P. K. Matsuda (Eds.), *On second language writing* (pp. 1–16). Mahwah, NJ: Lawrence Erlbaum.

Kubota, R. (1998). An investigation of L1–L2 transfer in writing among Japanese university students: Implications for contrastive rhetoric. *Journal of Second Language Writing, 7,* 69–100.

Leeds, B. (Ed.). (1996). *Writing in a second language: Insights from first and second language teaching and research.* New York: Longman.

Leki, I. (1991). Twenty-five years of contrastive rhetoric. Text analyses and writing pedagogies. *TESOL Quarterly, 25,* 123–143.

Leki, I. (1992). *Understanding ESL writers: A guide for teachers.* Portsmouth, NH: Boynton/Cook.

Leki, I., & Silva, T. (1992). From the editors. *Journal of Second Language Writing, 1*(1), iii–iv.

Li, X. (1996). *"Good writing" in cross cultural context.* Albany: SUNY Press.

Matsuda, P. K. (1997). Contrastive rhetoric in context: A dynamic model of L2 writing. *Journal of Second Language Writing, 6,* 45–60.

Matsuda, P. K. (1998). Situating ESL writing in a cross-disciplinary context. *Written Communication, 15,* 99–121.

Matsuda, P. K. (1999). Composition studies and ESL writing: A disciplinary division of labor. *College Composition and Communication, 50,* 699–721.

Matsuda, P. K. (2001). Reexamining audiolingualism: On the genesis of reading and writing in L2 studies. In D. Belcher & A. Hirvela (Eds.), *Linking literacies: Perspectives on L2 reading/writing connections* (pp. 84–105). Ann Arbor: University of Michigan Press.

Matsuda, P. K. (2003). Basic writing and second language writers: Toward an inclusive definition. *Journal of Basic Writing, 22*(2), 67–89.

Matsuda, P. K., & Jablonski, J. (2000). Beyond the L2 metaphor: Towards a mutually transformative model of ESL/WAC collaboration. *Academic Writing, 1.* http://aw.colostate.edu/ articles/matsuda_jablonski2000.htm.

North, S. M. (1987). *The making of knowledge in composition: Portrait of an emerging field.* Upper Montclair, NJ: Boynton/Cook.

Panetta, C. G. (Ed.). (2001). *Contrastive rhetoric theory revisited and redefined.* Mahwah, NJ: Lawrence Erlbaum.

Passy, P. (1929). *La phonétique et ses applications.* Cambridge, UK: International Phonetic Association.

Pennington, M. (1996). *The computer and the non-native writer: A natural partnership.* Cresskill, NJ: Hampton Press.

Pincas, A. (1962). Structural linguistics and systematic composition teaching to students of English as a foreign language. *Language Learning, 7,* 185–195.

Pincas, A. (1982). *Teaching English writing.* London: Macmillan.

Polio, C. (2001). Research methodology in second language writing research: The case of text-based studies. In T. Silva & P. K. Matsuda (Eds.), *On second language writing* (pp. 91–115). Mahwah, NJ: Lawrence Erlbaum.

Polio, C. (2003). Research on second language writing: An overview of what we investigate and how. In B. Kroll (Ed.), *Exploring the dynamics of second language writing* (pp. 35–69). Cambridge, UK: Cambridge University Press.

Polio, C., & Mosele, P. (1998). *References on the teaching and learning of foreign language writing focusing on languages other than English.* Center for Language Education and Research, Michigan State University. http://polyglot.cal.msu.edu/clear/writing/.

Raimes, A. (1983a). *Techniques in teaching writing.* New York: Oxford University Press.

Raimes, A. (1983b). Tradition and revolution in ESL teaching. *TESOL Quarterly, 17,* 535–552.

Raimes, A. (1986). Teaching ESL writing: Fitting what we do to what we know. *The Writing Instructor, 5,* 153–166.

Raimes, A. (1991). Out of the woods: Emerging traditions in the teaching of writing. *TESOL Quarterly, 25,* 407–430.

Reichelt, M. (1999). Toward a more comprehensive view of L2 writing: Foreign language writing in the U.S. *Journal of Second Language Writing, 8,* 181–204.

Reid, J. M. (1993). *Teaching ESL writing.* Englewood Cliffs, NJ: Regents/Prentice Hall.

Rodby, J. (1992). *Appropriating literacy: Writing and reading in English as a second language.* Portsmouth, NH: Boynton/Cook.

Santos, T. (1992). Ideology in composition: L1 and ESL. *Journal of Second Language Writing, 1,* 1–15.

Santos, T. (2001). The place of politics in second language writing. In T. Silva & P. K. Matsuda (Eds.), *On second language writing* (pp. 173–190). Mahwah, NJ: Lawrence Erlbaum.

Santos, T., Atkinson, D., Erickson, M., Matsuda, P. K., & Silva, T. (2000). On the future of second language writing: A colloquium. *Journal of Second Language Writing, 9,* 1–20.

Sasaki, M. (2000). Toward an empirical model of EFL writing processes: An exploratory study. *Journal of Second Language Writing, 9,* 259–291.

Severino, C., Guerra, J. C., & Butler, J. E. (Eds.). (1997). *Writing in multicultural settings.* New York: Modern Language Association.

Shaughnessy, M. P. (1976). Basic writing. In G. Tate (Ed.), *Teaching composition: 10 bibliographical essays* (pp. 137–167). Fort Worth, TX: Texas Christian University Press.

Shaughnessy, M. P. (1977). *Errors and expectations: A guide for the teacher of basic writing.* New York: Oxford University Press.

Silva, T. (1990). Second language composition instruction: Developments, issues, and directions in ESL. In B. Kroll (Ed.), *Second language writing: Research insights for the classroom* (pp. 11–23). New York: Cambridge University Press.

Silva, T. (1993). Toward an understanding of the distinct nature of L2 writing: The ESL research and its implications. *TESOL Quarterly, 27,* 657–677.

Silva, T. (1994). An examination of writing program administrators' options for the placement of ESL students in first year writing classes. *WPA: Writing Program Administration, 18*(1–2), 37–43.

Silva, T., Brice, C., & Reichelt, M. (1999). *Annotated bibliography of scholarship in second language writing: 1993–1997.* Stamford, CT: Ablex.

Silva, T., Leki, I., & Carson, J. (1997). Broadening the perspective of mainstream composition studies: Some thoughts from the disciplinary margins. *Written Communication, 14,* 398–428.

Silva, T., & Matsuda, P. K. (Eds.). (2001a). *Landmark essays on English as a second language writing.* Mahwah, NJ: Lawrence Erlbaum.

Silva, T., & Matsuda, P. K. (Eds.). (2001b). *On second language writing.* Mahwah, NJ: Lawrence Erlbaum.

Slager, W. R. (1966). Controlling composition: Some practical classroom techniques. In R. B. Kaplan (Ed.), *Selected conference papers of the Association of Teachers of English as a Second Language* (pp. 77–85). Los Angeles: National Association for Foreign Student Affairs.

Spack, R. (1988). Initiating ESL students into the academic discourse community: How far should we go? *TESOL Quarterly, 22,* 29–51.

Susser, B. (1994). Process approaches in ESL/EFL writing instruction. *Journal of Second Language Writing, 3,* 31–47.

Swales, J. (1990). *Genre analysis: English in academic and research settings.* New York: Cambridge University Press.

Sweet, H. (1964). *The practical study of language.* London: Oxford University Press. (Original work published 1899).

Tannacito, D. J. (1995). *A guide to writing English as a second or foreign language: An annotated bibliography of research and pedagogy.* Alexandria, VA: TESOL.

Tarnopolsky, O. (2000). Writing English as a foreign language: A report from Ukraine. *Journal of Second Language Writing, 9,* 209–226.

Tobin, L. (2001). Process pedagogy. In G. Tate, A. Rupiper, & K. Schick (Eds.), *A guide to composition pedagogies* (pp. 1–18). New York: Oxford University Press.

Truscott, J. (1996). The case against grammar correction in L2 writing classes. *Language Learning, 46,* 327–369.

Truscott, J. (1999). The case for "the case against grammar correction in L2 writing classes": A response to Ferris. *Journal of Second Language Writing, 8,* 111–122.

Tucker, A. (1995). *Decoding ESL: International students in the American college classroom.* Portsmouth, NH: Boynton/Cook.

Zamel, V. (1976). Teaching composition in the ESL classroom: What we can learn from research in the teaching of English. *TESOL Quarterly, 10,* 67–76.

Zamel, V., & Spack, R. (Eds.). (1998). *Negotiating academic literacies: Teaching and learning across languages and cultures.* Mahwah, NJ: Lawrence Erlbaum.

3

Bilingual Minorities and Language Issues in Writing: Toward Professionwide Responses to a New Challenge

GUADALUPE VALDÉS

*D*iversity and *multiculturalism* are the fashionable words of this new decade. Their use throughout the programs of most pedagogically oriented professional meetings, for example, reflects a concern about and an interest in the changing population of this country. Unfortunately, in many instances, the words *diversity* and *multiculturalism* are being used imprecisely and perhaps primarily because they are fashionable and politically correct.

In and of itself, political correctness is not a problem. Moreover, in the case of the English composition profession in particular, the deep commitment of many of its members to the education of nonmainstream students has been well established. Many serious efforts have been made by the members of organizations such as NCTE, CCCC, and MLA to gain an understanding of issues and questions having to do with the writing of non-English-background students. Talking about diversity and inviting members of minority groups to address professional organizations at annual meetings is an important attempt to exchange information and to gain insights into these new areas of concern.

Discussions about diversity and multiculturalism, however, even for truly well-intentioned groups of professionals, are only a first step. Teaching the new population of this country, especially students who come from non-English-speaking backgrounds, will involve much more than "celebrating" cultural differences. Addressing the needs of these students will demand carefully planned pedagogical solutions based on an understanding of their unique characteristics.

For English composition professionals, working effectively with diverse students will require extensive knowledge about this new minority population. Very specifically, teaching non-English-background students must be based on a deep understanding of the nature of societal bilingualism and on an examination of existing views about writing and the development of

From *Written Communication* 9.1 (1992): 85–136.

writing for bilingual individuals. It will demand a critical evaluation of the profession's own capacity to work with nonnative English-speaking students, and it will necessitate asking hard questions about the consequences of using approaches that were designed for native speakers with developing bilingual writers.

The purpose of this article is to contribute to the efforts currently being made by the English composition profession to explore the role that it will play in working with diverse students from multicultural backgrounds. In particular, my objective is to describe for the profession the singular characteristics of the bilingual minority students who are now entering community colleges, colleges, and universities and to explore the questions that stem from these students' presence in regular English composition courses intended for native speakers.

In order to provide a framework for this discussion, I will first argue that the English composition profession must become aware that it is currently divided into a series of compartments. I will point out that this compartmentalization or specialization is based on views about the characteristics of the student population in this country that may be both seriously outdated and inaccurate. More important, I will suggest that the persistence of such compartmentalization will directly affect the ways in which the profession will respond to present and future student needs.

I will devote the second section of this article to a description of minority bilingualism. I will present a general overview of the field and introduce key concepts that are relevant to both practitioners and researchers in the field of English composition. In the final section, I will review trends in current scholarship in the area of second-language writing, identify a series of existing lacunae in our knowledge about the writing of functional bilinguals, and present an outline of issues and questions that need to be explored by mainstream researchers. Throughout the article, I will argue that unless we emphasize the importance of bilingual issues within the writing profession and particularly the significance of the questions that stem from the very nature of bilingualism, many individuals will continue to view language minority students as a problem that is exclusively the domain of a small group of specialists outside the mainstream of the English composition field.

THE COMPARTMENTALIZATION OF THE ENGLISH-TEACHING PROFESSION

As is the case with a number of their fields and professions, the English-teaching profession is divided into several different groups and segments. As Figure 1 illustrates, the profession includes two large and distinct areas of interest and expertise. These two areas are the teaching of English to native speakers of English and the teaching of English to speakers of other languages.

As shown in Figure 1, the two compartments are of unequal size. The larger of the two compartments focuses on native English-speaking students. The smaller compartment is concerned with students who are not yet fully functional in the English language. The fact that these two areas are quite different can perhaps be best appreciated by examining the membership of

FIGURE 1.   Compartments within the English Composition Profession

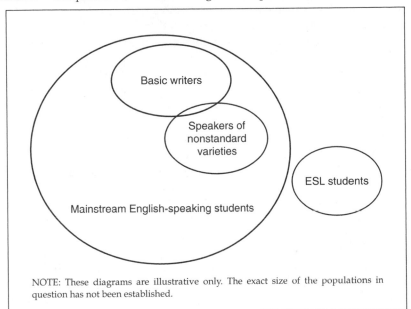

NOTE: These diagrams are illustrative only. The exact size of the populations in question has not been established.

professional organizations. Individuals who focus on the teaching of English to native speakers generally belong to organizations such as NCTE (National Council of Teachers of English) and CCCC (Conference on College Composition and Communication). Individuals, on the other hand, who focus on the teaching of English to nonnative speakers of English are generally members of TESOL (Teachers of English to Speakers of Other Languages) or NABE (National Association of Bilingual Education). Even though there are segments within CCCC and NCTE that specialize in the writing of nonmainstream students, these two organizations are not generally known for their expertise on matters related to the teaching of English to students from non-English-speaking backgrounds.

Figure 1 also shows that the largest group of English composition professionals focuses on the native English-speaking population, and most of this group's attention is directed at "mainstream" students, that is, at students who are native speakers of nonstigmatized or standard varieties of English. Much attention is also given to basic writers and to students who are speakers of nonstandard varieties of English. As I have conceptualized the compartments in this figure, students who are primarily monodialectal speakers of Black English, Appalachian English, and the like would be placed in the compartment dealing with speakers of nonstandard varieties. On the other hand, bidialectal students who can already speak and write mainstream English in addition to their own variety of English would be placed outside of this compartment. Some would still be in the basic writer section, but others would be placed in regular mainstream English classes. Within this larger compartment, it is possible for even bidialectal students to experience problems.

As Farr and Daniels (1986, chap. 3) pointed out, research on writing and most of the theories underlying current practice have been developed with a focus on a mainstream and native-speaking population.[1]

As Figure 1 also illustrates, nonnative-speaking students are seen as separate from students considered to have native-speaker competencies and as the province of specialists who have been trained to teach them English. The important point here is that, because of the way the compartments are structured within the profession, when nonnative English-speaking students leave the ESL compartment, they must move directly into the native-speaker domain. There is no other compartment for them to enter. Once out of ESL, nonnative students enroll in classes with native speakers. Whether placed in the basic skills or nonmainstream English compartments, these new speakers of English are expected to compete with individuals who come into English composition courses with native-speaking strengths and abide by the standards set for them. Generally, very little systematic accommodation is made to the essential nature of the difference between these students and their native-speaking peers.

As I will argue in this article, this position is inadequate in that it fails to take into consideration the complexities of bilingualism per se and in particular the special characteristics of American minority bilingualism. In my view, the existing compartmentalization, which is in evidence whenever issues of diversity or multiculturalism are discussed, results in a view of the nature of writing and the teaching of composition that can be potentially harmful to a large segment of the population of this country.

AMERICAN MINORITY BILINGUALISM

The Study of Bilingualism

The study of bilingualism is a complex and multifaceted area of inquiry. The literature on the subject is extensive and encompasses work carried out on both individual and societal bilingualism from the perspectives of linguistics, sociolinguistics, and psycholinguistics. So vast indeed is the subject that reviews of the literature on bilingualism as a whole (e.g., Appel & Muysken, 1987; Baetens-Beardsmore, 1982; Grosjean, 1982; Hakuta, 1986; Hamers & Blanc, 1989; and Romaine, 1989) are produced only in book-length form. Full treatments of the field of bilingualism generally include examinations of the various definitions of the term *bilingualism*, descriptions of different kinds and types of individual bilingualism, descriptions of the characteristics of the languages of various types of bilingual speakers, discussions about the problems involved in the measurement of bilingualism, syntheses of research conducted on bilingual communities of different types around the world, syntheses of research documented on information processing in individual bilinguals, and overviews of the relationship between education and bilingualism. Partial treatments of the field and collections of research articles generally focus on particular subdomains such as American societal bilingualism (e.g., Ferguson & Heath, 1981; McKay & Wong, 1988); information processing in bilingual individuals (e.g., Albert & Obler, 1978; Vaid, 1986); childhood bilingualism (e.g., Bialystok, 1991; Garcia, 1983; Homel, Palij, & Aaronson, 1987); bilingualism and ethnic identity (e.g., Fishman, 1989; Gudykunst, 1988); bilingualism and education (e.g., Cummins & Swain, 1986; Skutnabb-Kangas, 1981; Skutnabb-Kangas & Cummins, 1988; Spolsky, 1986); and first-language attrition among bilinguals (e.g., Seliger & Vago, 1991).

In general, students of bilingualism have attempted to answer such questions as how and why do individuals become bilingual? how are bilinguals different from monolinguals? how do individuals function in two languages? and how can bilingualism be measured? Beginning with the work of Weinreich (1953/1974), research on bilingualism has been carried out by more and more researchers in many different settings around the world.[2]

From the work conducted to date, we now know that bilingualism is a widespread natural phenomenon that has come about in different places for different reasons and that factors such as movement of peoples, military conquest, and the expansion of religious practices have resulted in the acquisition of a second language (L2) by certain groups of people.[3] We also know that, depending on the particular characteristics of the language contact,[4] individuals who acquire another language in addition to their first and who use both languages in the course of their everyday lives vary in their productive and receptive abilities in both languages. Certain individuals develop high productive and receptive abilities in both the oral and the written modes; and still others develop no productive control of either mode. Individuals who manifest only receptive abilities in the spoken language are known as receptive or passive bilinguals. Individuals who manifest productive abilities are known as productive bilinguals.[5]

In general, the research on bilingualism has concerned itself primarily with the study of the spoken language. Most studies have focused on *bilingualism* as opposed to *biliteracy*. The reasons for this focus are many. Some of these reasons have to do with the contexts in which bilingualism occurs,[6] and others have to do with the particular theoretical interests of linguists, sociolinguists, and psycholinguists who carried out this research. For a long period of time, for example linguists were interested primarily in understanding how one language system used by a bilingual influenced the other system. They sought to describe this influence at the phonological, morphological, and syntactic levels and ordinarily viewed the spoken language as primary.

Sociolinguists, on the other hand, attempted to answer the question who speaks what language to whom and why? This emphasis on spoken interaction defined the scope of most studies. With the exception of Fishman's classic study *Language Loyalty in the United States* (1966), in which he documented the existence of ethnic language newspapers and presses in this country, few individuals sought to describe language maintenance among bilinguals by focusing on their ability to read and write the ethnic language.

Biliteracy was also of little interest to psycholinguists. These researchers were typically interested in how bilingual individuals processed information using two language systems rather than in the modality (written or oral) of the information. For example, experiments carried out with bilinguals assumed the presence of biliterate skills and often used single words flashed on a screen as stimuli (e.g., Lambert, 1955). Conclusions, however, about bilingual dominance based on experiments using the written mode assumed that processing the written language did not differ in important ways from processing the oral language.

An interest in biliteracy in conjunction with bilingualism has been recent. In general, this research and pedagogical focus stems from an expanding concern about the education of linguistic minorities all over the world. Existing work, therefore, on the development of productive and receptive abilities in the written language in each of a bilingual's two languages has been carried out by researchers of different disciplinary backgrounds in an attempt to determine how best to educate children who are not speakers of a societal language. The principal question for these researchers has involved the choice of the language in which children should first be taught to read. Much of this research has led to the conclusion that early instruction through the mother tongue results in greater gains in reading achievement in the societal language.[7] In the United States, these conclusions have been the subject of intense debate.[8] For the most part, however, regardless of the researcher's preference with respect to school language, work on biliteracy has focused on young children in the early stages of acquiring a second language. In addition, this research has most often focused on the development of reading skills. With few exceptions (e.g., Ammon, 1985; Edelsky, 1982, 1983, 1986; Hudelson, 1981), researchers have only recently begun to examine the development of abilities related to the production of written language by bilingual children.

In spite of its limitations, research conducted in response to the problems faced by children who do not speak the language of the schools has led to important theoretical contributions. The work carried out by Cummins (1979a, 1979b, 1980, 1981), for example, suggests that literacy skills acquired in one of a bilingual's two languages transfer successfully to the other language. According to Cummins, if the first language (L1) of a bilingual is well established, literacy skills developed in this language will transfer easily to the second language. Conversely, if skills are not developed in the first language, acquiring academic-level reading and writing skills in their second language will be difficult for many bilingual children.

In sum, research conducted on the nature of bilingualism has mainly concentrated on the study of the oral mode. Even though some attention has more recently been given to the examination of biliterate abilities among bilinguals by linguists, sociolinguists, and psycholinguists (e.g., McLaughlin, 1987; Segalowitz, 1986), we do not have available a body of research about the role, function, and development of these abilities in bilingual societies. Attempts to summarize and review current knowledge relating to literacy and bilingualism tend, unfortunately, to be based on a superficial and incomplete understanding of the nature of bilingualism. As the following section will make clear, the greater part of the research currently being carried out has focused on the development of productive and receptive abilities in the written mode in a very distinct type of bilingual individual.

Bilingual Individuals: Elective versus Circumstantial Bilingualism

Although no universal agreement exists about what key categories or dimensions should be used in the description of bilingualism, most researchers have divided bilinguals into two fundamental categories: elective bilinguals and circumstantial bilinguals.[9]

Elective bilinguals are individuals who choose to become bilingual, who seek out either formal classes or contexts in which they can acquire a foreign language (i.e., a language not spoken ordinarily in the communities in which they live and work), and who continue to spend the greater part of their time in a society in which their first language is the majority or societal language. The bilingualism of such elective bilinguals has also been referred to as "additive bilingualism" because these individuals are in a position of adding another language to their overall linguistic competence in a context in which their first language still remains the language of greater prestige and dominant usage.

Monolingual English-speaking Americans who learn French in foreign language classes, for example, are elective bilinguals. They remain bilingual by choice even when they travel to French-speaking countries in order to perfect their French. In contrast with circumstantial bilinguals, elective bilinguals put themselves in "foreign" settings for the principal purpose of expanding their language ability. They generally do not intend to live in the foreign country permanently and thus have no "real" need to use their new language in order to survive.

Students from other countries who study English in school and who then come to this country for advanced study are also elective bilinguals. For the most part, they intend to return to their countries to practice their chosen profession and are in the United States only to obtain an education. Many of these foreign students are members of the upper and middle classes and have been educated well in their first language. They have elected to learn and use English in order to further their position in their countries upon their return.

Circumstantial bilinguals, on the other hand, are individuals who, because of their circumstances, find that they must learn another language in order to survive. As Haugen (1972, p. 310) put it, they are individuals whose first language does not suffice to carry out all of their communicative needs. Because of the movement of peoples and/or because of changes in political circumstances (e.g., immigration, conquest, shifting of borders, establishment of postcolonial states), these individuals find themselves in a context in which their ethnic language is not the majority, prestige, or national language. In order to participate economically and politically in the society of which they are a part, therefore, such persons must acquire some degree of proficiency in the societal language.

Circumstantial bilingualism has sometimes been referred to as subtractive bilingualism because the condition of adding the societal language as a second language frequently leads to a loss of the first language. Because of the strong pressures exerted by the majority society and the lack of prestige of the original language, for these individuals, the condition of bilingualism is a temporary one that often results in the gradual abandonment of L1.[10] Bilingual American minorities are, by definition, circumstantial bilinguals. They are forced by circumstances to acquire English, and they do so in a context in which their own first languages are accorded little or no prestige by the larger society. Whether they acquire English in formal settings (i.e., in voluntary ESL classes) or in natural interactions with English speakers, they are fundamentally different from elective bilinguals, that is, from persons who study foreign languages strictly by choice. While immigrant bilinguals have a choice of not acquiring English, the consequences of their not doing so have far more direct consequences on their daily lives than do decisions made by elective bilinguals when they elect to learn or not to learn a second language.

The fundamental difference between elective and circumstantial bilinguals has to do, then, not just with conditions in which languages are acquired, but also with the relationship between groups of individuals. Elective bilinguals become bilingual as individuals. The groups to which they belong have little to do with their decision to become speakers of another language. Circumstantial bilinguals, on the other hand, are generally members of a group of individuals who as a group must become bilingual in order to participate in the society that surrounds them.[11]

The principal characteristics of these two types of bilingualism are summarized in Table 1.

Types of Bilingual Individuals and Bilingual Communities

Because of the complexity of circumstantial bilingualism, one cannot easily classify bilingual individuals using one or two key variables such as "first language learned" or "language spoken in the home," as criteria. Individual circumstantial bilingualism can only be understood within the framework of societal bilingualism, that is, by taking into account the place and function of the two languages in question in the lives of particular groups of bilingual individuals who primarily share with each other the fact that they are not monolingual. The specific experiences of different individuals in using one or the other of their two languages will have a direct impact on the development of their functional ability in each language as well as their linguistic competence in both languages. Factors such as the arrival and presence of new immigrants, the background of these persons (e.g., education, social class), existing attitudes of established members of the community toward

TABLE 1.   Elective versus Circumstantial Bilingualism

Elective Bilingualism	*Circumstantial Bilingualism*
1. Elective bilingualism is characteristic of individuals.	1. Circumstantial bilingualism is generally characteristic of groups of people.
2. Individuals choose to learn a nonsocietal language and create conditions (e.g., enrolling in language classes) that help bring such learning about.	2. Group members respond to circumstances created by movement of peoples, conquest, colonization, immigration, and the like. A second language is learned because the first language does not suffice to meet all of the group's communicative needs.
3. Communicative opportunities are artificially created in a classroom setting or sought specifically by learners. Some individuals may seek greater integration with the target language community. Such efforts are initiated by the language learner and may include marriage, residence abroad, and so on.	3. Communicative needs may relate to either survival (minimal contact with the majority society) or success (ability to function totally in the majority society). Not everyone in the community will have the same communicative needs.
4. In the U.S., elective bilinguals are generally middle class. Occasionally, working class students are also successful in foreign language classes. Working class bilinguals who acquire a second language in schools or neighborhoods because they frequently interact with recent immigrant populations are also encountered.	4. In the U.S. circumstantial bilinguals include both indigenous groups (American Indians) and immigrant groups. Among immigrant groups, there may be individuals of different class backgrounds depending on the characteristics and history of the original group. The Vietnamese group in the U.S., for example, includes persons from urban upper-class backgrounds as well as persons of peasant background.
5. In the U.S., foreign students who come here to study from overseas are elective bilinguals. Children raised in families where two languages are spoken may be considered elective bilinguals if the circumstances requiring the use of two languages are created deliberately by the parents and are not present in the surrounding societal context outside the home.	5. Circumstantial bilinguals include immigrants and original residents of territories conquered or colonized. Children raised in families where two languages are spoken are considered circumstantial bilinguals if the circumstances requiring the use of two languages also exist outside of the home.

TABLE 1.   (Continued)

Elective Bilingualism	Circumstantial Bilingualism
6. For most elective bilinguals who study or use a second language for limited periods of time, their first language will remain their stronger language.	6. Circumstantial bilinguals will, over time, become stable bilinguals whose two languages play complementary roles in their everyday lives. For most domains, topics, and styles, circumstantial bilinguals (even those whose two languages are very strong) will have a momentarily stronger language. This momentarily stronger or preferred language (Dodson, 1985) is one in which an individual feels a greater facility or capacity for efficient communication given the specific topic, speakers, and function in question.

these immigrants, and the opportunities for revitalizing the ethnic language play a large role in the retention or loss of this language by individual speakers. Elements such as the presence of other immigrant groups in the same community and the perceived need to use the societal language as a lingua franca will also influence significantly the degree to which community members use this language frequently. The language used for religious practice, for carrying out business transactions, for entertainment (e.g., availability of movies and television in immigrant languages) will also affect the rate of acquisition of the societal language as well as the maintenance of the ethnic language.[12]

Many of these same elements and other similar factors may be present repeatedly in the community at different times. Particular bilinguals will be affected by these factors to a greater or lesser degree depending on their individual circumstances. Thus, one individual might be affected by the presence of new immigrants in adolescence, be involved in activities that only require English during his or her twenties, and later marry (for the second time) a newly arrived immigrant from the home country. These different factors, then, will be reflected in the relative frequency with which he or she uses each of the two languages over the course of his or her life and the facility that he or she develops to discuss specific topics in each language.

More important, however, at any given moment, this same bilingual will reflect a sense of greater functional ease (not necessarily an awareness of such an ease) in one or the other of his or her languages, depending on his or her experience in similar contexts, with similar speakers, with similar topics or similar functions. Indeed, some researchers (Dodson, 1985) have suggested that for any given interaction or function, all bilinguals have a momentarily stronger language. Whether it is possible for them to choose to function in that "stronger" language for that particular interaction depends on the circumstances in which they find themselves.

Individual bilingualism that results from real use of and experience with two languages is highly complex and variable. While at the macro-level, one may be able to generalize about group tendencies or experiences, at the micro-level, one cannot make assumptions about the relative strengths and proficiencies of a bilingual's two languages based on one or two factors about his or her background and experiences. Factors such as language spoken in the home, age of arrival in the U.S., first language spoken, and even language used most frequently can predict little about a bilingual's relative strengths in each language. Two bilinguals, for example, who share each of the above characteristics may, nevertheless, have had experiences and contacts that resulted in very different strengths and weaknesses (e.g., strategic proficiency, linguistic proficiency, lexical range) in each of their languages.

In the United States, circumstantial bilingualism is generally the product of language contact that comes about as a result of immigration. However, this type of bilingualism also developed when territories (e.g., tribal lands inhabited by Native Americans, former Mexican territories such as the states of Texas, New Mexico, Arizona, and California) were taken over by English-speaking populations. Most American circumstantial bilinguals, therefore, acquire their two languages within the context of a minority or immigrant community of which they are a part. Both the nature and the type of language proficiency that individuals acquire and develop in these communities depend on such factors as generational level, age, occupation, opportunity for contact with speakers of English, and exposure to English media.

The acquisition of English by new immigrants depends both on the nature of the community in which they settle and on the amount of exposure they have to English in their everyday lives. First generation immigrants, for example, can become quite fluent in English after a brief period of residence in this country, especially if they have had previous exposure to the formal study of English before emigrating to the United States. It is also possible that depending on their place of residence and the number of bilinguals and monolinguals they interact with, they will fluctuate in their control and comfort in using the new language over the course of their lives. For most first generation bilinguals who arrive in this country as adults, however, the immigrant language remains dominant.

This is not necessarily the case for second generation immigrants. Ordinarily, English exerts a strong pressure involving both prestige within the immigrant community and access to the wider community's rewards. Generally, by the end of their school years, second generation immigrants develop a greater functional ease in English for dealing with most contexts and domains outside of the home and immediate community. Once again, there can be many differences between individuals of the same generation. Both the retention of the immigrant language and the acquisition of English depend on the opportunities available for use. In diglossic communities,[13] these individuals will have little access to a full repertoire of styles and levels of language. Because the immigrant language tends to become a language of intimacy and informality, their competence in this language may soon be outdistanced by their competence in English.

This same phenomenon, that is, the outdistancing of the immigrant language by English, is also observed in the area of literacy. By the end of the school years (even when the first three may have been supported by mother-tongue teaching), most immigrant bilinguals will have developed what skills they have in both reading and writing primarily in English. Pressures from the wider society, lack of opportunities for using the written immigrant language, and the limited availability of reading materials in these languages result in English language literacy rather than in a bilingual and biliterate profile.

The same generalizations made about first and second generation bilinguals can be made for third and fourth generation bilinguals. As in the case of second generation bilinguals, much variation occurs within generations, and this variation depends on the access to both English and the immigrant language. Numerous factors can influence both immigrant language retention and immigrant language loss for different individuals. According to Fishman (1964), it is generally the case, however, that by the fourth generation, immigrants become monolingual in English, the language of the majority society.

Incipient Circumstantial Bilingualism versus Functional Circumstantial Bilingualism[14]

Except for simultaneous bilinguals, that is, individuals who acquire two languages as a "first" language, most American circumstantial bilinguals acquire their ethnic or immigrant language first and then acquire English, this country's majority or societal language. The period of acquisition of the second language is known as incipient bilingualism.

As Figure 2 indicates, for different individuals, the period of incipient bilingualism varies, but it is normally followed by stages of stable functional bilingualism, that is, by stages at which these individuals can interact effectively with native speakers of the second language in order to carry out a broad range of communicative activities.

The length of the period of incipient bilingualism appears to depend on a number of factors, such as age at time of first exposure to the second language, amount of exposure to the second language, attitudes toward the second language, and individual personality characteristics. An individual, for example, who lives in a bilingual community but has no access to monolingual speakers of the majority language or few opportunities to hear English will logically go through a very long period of incipient bilingualism and may indeed never arrive at a period of stable functional bilingualism.[15]

The characteristics of functional bilingualism also vary. For a given bilingual, this stage may be characterized by the ability to use a very broad range of styles and levels in both languages, including the second language, or it may

FIGURE 2.   Stages of Incipient and Functional Bilingualism

Bilingual 1	Incipient stage	Functional stage
Adult learner Good access to L2 speakers	4 years	Remains L1 preferrent in all domains Can function in L2 in most contexts and domains
Bilingual 2	Incipient stage	Functional stage
Child learner	2 years	Becomes L2 preferrent in all domains Avoids using L1 L1 features still reflected in L2 production
Bilingual 3	Incipient stage/limited functional stage	
Adult learner Limited or sporadic access to L2	10 years Remains L1 preferrent Interacts primarily with monolingual speakers of L1 or with bilingual speakers	

be restricted to a set of very limited communicative and/or linguistic abilities in the second language. What is clear, however, is that the English of very few of these bilinguals will be identical to the English of English-speaking mono-linguals. Their nonnative origins may be evident at a number of different levels. Nevertheless, the important point here is that no matter how many features remain that are nonnative-like, there is a point at which an individual must be classified as a functional bilingual rather than as an incipient bilingual.

If one takes the view that incipient bilinguals are the responsibility of ESL programs and that functional bilinguals are beyond such instruction, the focus of the English composition teaching profession changes as in Figure 3. In this figure, the "mainstream" student population now includes a large number of functional bilinguals. These individuals are outside the formal ESL compartment and have spilled over into the realm of mainstream instructors. As will be noted, some bilingual students will be considered basic writers. The nonnative quality of their writing will be interpreted as signaling inexperience with writing. Other bilingual students will be seen to have problems in their mastery of standard English and will be placed in the compartment dedicated to helping nonstandard speakers to write in mainstream English. Still others will simply be placed among regular composition students. Ideally, as should be the case with bidialectal students who have already mastered the standard dialect, functional bilingual students would simply be seen as part of the mainstream population. Their particular problems and needs would be well known to all composition instructors.

Currently, however, the mainstream profession is not structured to address the needs of "diverse" learners outside the compartments designated for them. Ordinarily instructors of "regular" composition classes will have some knowledge about the language characteristics of nonmainstream

FIGURE 3.   The Place of Incipient and Functional Bilinguals within Existing Compartments

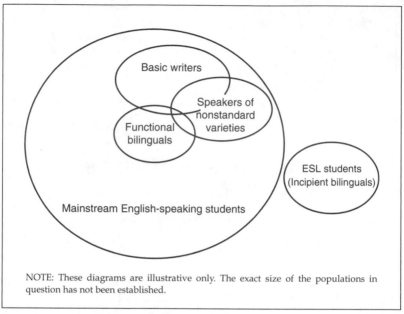

NOTE: These diagrams are illustrative only. The exact size of the populations in question has not been established.

English speakers but will have little background in the topic of language differences associated with bilingualism. They have not been trained to evaluate the writing of non-English-background students and to determine what kinds of instruction they need.

ESL VERSUS MAINSTREAM: WHO BELONGS WHERE?

The question of how long an individual can be considered a "language learner," placed in the ESL compartment, and seen as an incipient bilingual is a complex one. While most scholars in the field of second language acquisition agree that second language learning is not identical to first language learning and that the key difference is the fact that a second language is generally not acquired "perfectly," scholars have not yet developed criteria for evaluating when a given individual can be considered to have passed from the incipient or learning stage of bilingualism to the fully developed stage.

A number of students of language acquisition hold that in a "first" language, language learning continues throughout a lifetime and that for "second" language learning, conditions are similar. In this sense, then, bilingual individuals as well as monolingual individuals would be considered language learners beyond the point at which they have acquired all or most of the linguistic structures of the language. They would be considered to continue to learn language as they become more educated, acquire a range of speaking and writing styles, and add to their vocabulary for example.

I, however, would argue that in trying to establish how long nonnative speakers of a language can be considered "learners" or "acquirers" of essential competencies or proficiencies of a target language,[16] comparisons with native speakers are not useful. Research has shown that not all second language learners continue to learn or acquire the various different kinds of competencies until they reach native-like abilities. For reasons not clearly understood, even though most functional bilinguals can achieve native-like control of many levels of a second language, they will still continue to use learner-like features of the language in certain expressions. The use of such learner-like features in bilinguals is known as fossilization. Fossils (nonnative-like features) appear to remain in these individuals' second language production even after many years of constant exposure to and use of a second language and often in spite of direct instruction designed to eradicate these features. Fossilization may occur at the phonological, morphological, syntactic, discourse, and pragmatic levels.

To complicate matters further, highly bilingual and even monolingual speakers from a given ethnic group will speak what is called a contact variety of English. These individuals have learned English in communities from speakers of "imperfect" English who were themselves functional bilinguals. This imperfect English containing nonnative-like features over time can become part of the variety of English spoken in the bilingual community. It is this variety that is acquired even by children who are raised as monolingual speakers of the language. For example, in Mexican American communities, monolingual speakers of English often speak a Spanish-influenced variety of English that is characterized particularly by the use certain non-English-like phonological features. Metcalf (1979) referred to the English spoken in such communities as *Chicano English* and argued that it is spoken not by learners of the language but by "people whose native language is a special variety of English with a Spanish sound to it" (p. 1).

The result of the existence of different varieties of immigrant-language-influenced English is that, when teachers see, for example, a piece of writing produced by a student whose first language is not English, it is difficult for them to determine whether nonnative-like features present in the writing are the result of incipient bilingualism (learning still formally in progress), the result of functional bilingualism containing many fossilized elements, or characteristic of a contact variety of English.

The distinction is important for teachers of composition because in the first case if the student is an incipient bilingual he or she could be assigned once again to the ESL specialist. But if the student is a stable, functional bilingual, it is doubtful that direct instruction in English morphology or syntax will result in the elimination of these "foreign" or nonnative-like features.

To date, because of the lack of information available about the nature of bilingualism within the field of mainstream English-language writing, many instructors expect that once the ESL or incipient stage of language learning is completed, non-English-background students will be able to write very much like native speakers of English. Because they are now technically outside the

ESL compartment, mainstream standards are applied, and not surprisingly, many such students fail to meet these standards.

If the instructor is tolerant, if he or she is committed to valuing both content and form, functional bilinguals will not suffer. They will not be penalized for not being native speakers. If the instructor is not tolerant, however, or if he or she has no knowledge about the nature of bilingualism, students are likely to receive low grades or to be sent back to the ESL compartment to classes and instruction that in terms of the development of their English-language proficiency can no longer do anything for them. The problem is illustrated in Figure 4. As Figure 4 demonstrates, the very same evidence, that is, the obvious nonnative quality of students' written production, may lead both practitioners and researchers to very different conclusions. Differences in production between different types of functional bilinguals are subtle, and pedagogical approaches as well as theories about composition pedagogy for these students are nonexistent.

In order to illustrate this point, let us examine two samples of compositions produced by individuals who were technically beyond the ESL stage. Both of the samples have been taken from the work carried out by Yorio (1989) who, in his study of idiomaticity and second-language writing, found that, even after 5

FIGURE 4.   Nonnative-like Writing: Possible Diagnoses and Solutions

Diagnoses	Evidence	Conclusion	Solution	Instruction
Diagnosis 1 Student is an incipient bilingual	English is non-native-like Many grammatical "errors" present	Student is a learner of English	Send to ESL	A. English grammar B. Mechanics
Diagnosis 2 Student is a Type 1 functional bilingual	Produces L1-influenced English "Errors" are systematic but different across students	Student is a functional bilingual Production includes fossilized elements	Treat as mainstream	A. Practice in editing own writing B. Instruction in identifying "fossilized" usages
Diagnosis 3 Student is a Type 2 functional bilingual or student is a monolingual speaker of a contact variety of English	Produces L1-influenced English "Errors" are systematic and similar across students	Student is a functional bilingual He or she is (also) a speaker of a contact variety of English	Treat as speaker of nonstandard variety of English	A. Compare characteristics of contact variety with standard written English B. Instruction in correcting non-standard features

to 6 years of residence in this country, having exited ... nd having used English as a sole medium of instruction, no ... still had problems producing writing that displayed native-lik ...

As these samples illustrate, Yorio's writers failed ... entionalized language consistently, that is, language that was ... tic. Contrary to what is generally believed to happen with yo ... rding to Yorio, older learners appear not to learn prefabricatec ... ns easily. As will also be appreciated in these samples, this v ... rized by what Yorio terms a "non-phonological 'accent.'" Of th ... s:

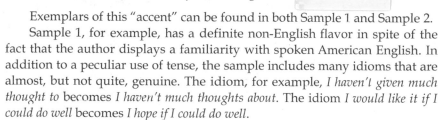

> Idiomaticity is a non-phonological "accent," not ... e to
> surface language errors, but to a certain undefine ... any
> frustrated composition teachers define as "I don' ... rong
> with this, but we just don't say that in English."

Exemplars of this "accent" can be found in both Sample 1 and Sample 2.

Sample 1, for example, has a definite non-English flavor in spite of the fact that the author displays a familiarity with spoken American English. In addition to a peculiar use of tense, the sample includes many idioms that are almost, but not quite, genuine. The idiom, for example, *I haven't given much thought to* becomes *I haven't much thoughts about*. The idiom *I would like it if I could do well* becomes *I hope if I could do well*.

Sample 2, while much more sophisticated in both organization and form, also reflects the same type of nonphonological accent. It is again the idioms, the prefabricated phrases and routines, that appear to be just slightly off. The idiom *for their own good* becomes *for the good of them*. The idiom *was being taken care of fine* becomes *was being taking care fine*. In this sample, in particular, the writer appears to have a strong control of English grammar. His or her "errors" are limited to those phrases that Yorio considers to be conventionalized and preformulated.

SAMPLE 1.

(Korean speaker, 18 years old, 6 years' residence in New York City, English medium of instruction in high school)

I haven't much thoughts about plans for weekend. On Saturday I'd work. Have a part-time job at the Bronx doing salesman and manager at a Wine and Liquor store. I can't make any plans on the Saturday, except working.

On Sunday I always go to a church and I spend time all day at the church. But not this weekend because I have a very important exam is coming up next week. So I'd stay home do my study. No matter what happens tomorrow, I'd not miss the baseball game. This Sunday there is the National League Championships finals. Also I'm big fan of the footballs. Anyway good luck to both teams. I'm very excited about it. I hope if I could do well on the exam.

NOTE: These samples were taken from Yorio (1989).

SAMPLE 2.

(Spanish speaker, 6 years' residence in the United States, Writing Assessment Test Score 6)

I agree with the idea that women are working more today for the good of them and for the economy, but it is not good for the children of working mothers.

From my experience it is clear that mothers with children can't work, because children will suffer and they will feel isolated and abandoned. A mother should provide to her children love, care protection, and time, but if she is a working mother, she won't have time to provide her kids all those mention above. For example, my mother placed my little brother in a Day Care Center to go to work. My brother was being taking care fine for the two first week, but a month later he got sick. He had some kind of disease on his stamach, the doctor said that he was not getting the right amount of food per day. Either he was eating too much or not enough. After he was released from the hospital, my mother took care of him, he started to do fine.

From my observation of others, I believe that mothers should stay home. They should not go out to work for the good of their own children.

For example, my cousin has 3 beautiful daughters. They are in a school few blocks away from their house. They ages are six, seven and eight. One day she was tired of being indoor all of the time. She decided to get a job. She found a job. The three little girls were taking care of themselves. The oldest one used to supervise the younger. But one day when they were open their apartment door, a man who was coming upstairs saw those three little girls. He got into the apartment with them. He raped them, and he robbed all of what he could from the apartment. When my cousin came from work, she saw what haf happen she almost died.

In conclusion, mothers should be more aware of their children. If they decided to go to work they should get a good babysitter; otherwise, they should stay home taking care of their children. Children are the future men, so they need care, time, love and security. If you are mother please don't go out to work. Stay with your children. They need you more than anything else.

Unfortunately, as Yorio himself admitted, such conventionalized or preformulated idiomaticity is hard to define or describe. Nevertheless, following Pawley and Syder (1983), Yorio (1989) defined native-like selection as "the ability of the native speaker routinely to convey his meaning by an expression that is not only grammatical but also native-like" (p. 66). Native-like fluency, on the other hand, is "a native speaker's ability to produce fluent stretches of spontaneous connected discourse." Native-like selection requires that an individual choose from among a number of grammatical and correct paraphrases, elements that are both natural and idiomatic.

What this suggests for researchers and practitioners in the field of composition is that the learning of automatic and conventional phrases, of collocations, and of idiomaticity is complex. Even bilinguals who are native-like in their fluency may be most unnative-like in their selection and in their use of conventionalized language. Problems of selection or idiomaticity are particularly salient in written language.

From my own study of the writing of nonnative writers,[17] I would maintain that it is problems of this nature that most affect functional bilinguals enrolled in classes with native speakers. A great deal of the writing produced by such bilinguals appears to be almost native-like. Certainly the basic grammatical rules have been acquired, yet it is also obvious that the nonnative quality remains.

What should be done? Should such students be sent back to ESL? Will more instruction in English structure solve the problem? This solution may not be particularly effective. Indeed, I would argue that in the case of the writer of Sample 2, additional instruction in formal grammar and even in the totality of English language idioms would not result in more native-like production. The fact of the matter is that the writing of most or many functional bilinguals will be characterized by such a lack of total idiomatic control. In spite of much instruction at the ESL stage of their schooling and in spite of the efforts made by functional bilinguals to edit their own writing, their writing will not be indistinguishable from that of native speakers.

The questions for professionals in the area of composition are many: How should mainstream teachers deal with such students? Should they view them as regular mainstream writers? Should they be viewed as basic writers? Should the same assumptions about sound pedagogical approaches made for mainstream writers inform the teaching of writing to bilingual students? How will functional bilinguals be affected by current popular practices, such as writing across the curriculum,[18] writing to learn, and the like? Will they be penalized for the nonnative quality of their writing? And will they be penalized unfairly?

In the case of idiomaticity and selection, we can maintain that it is to date poorly understood and that it is only now beginning to be investigated by students of bilingualism. However, the point to be made is a larger one. Idiomaticity is only one example of the kind of difference between native and nonnative English speakers that composition professionals may find impossible to interpret without background and training in the area of circumstantial functional bilingualism. This, in turn, also suggests that the English composition profession must begin to see itself as a profession that is seriously concerned with the deeper and more complex realities of diversity.

RESEARCH IN WRITING IN ENGLISH AS A SECOND LANGUAGE (ESL)

In order to understand the problems confronted by functional bilinguals when writing in a second language, both practitioners and researchers must begin to examine current research and to identify directions and priorities for further study. The following overview is presented from this perspective.

Existing research on non-English-background writers has concentrated almost exclusively on ESL writers, that is, on students who are still enrolled in ESL programs. As might be expected, language-teaching professionals involved in the teaching of English in this country (ESL professionals) have been directly affected by the new writing emphasis. Students exiting from ESL courses are now being expected to write well in English and even to compete with their English monolingual peers using standards established for writing in English as a native language rather than a second language.

As a result of pressure felt by ESL professionals about the new demands placed on their students, much research has been carried out and continues to be carried out on second language writing. This research includes work on such topics as business letter writing in English, French, and Japanese (Jenkins & Hinds, 1987); the revising and composing strategies of young children learning to write in English (Urzua, 1987); responses to student writing (Zamel, 1985); the composing processes of advanced ESL students (Zamel, 1983); cultural differences in the organization of academic texts (Clyne, 1987); the composing processes of unskilled ESL students (Jones, 1985; Raimes, 1985, 1987); writing development in young bilingual children (Edelsky, 1982, 1983, 1986); the development of appropriate discourse organization (Mohan & Lo, 1985); the development of temporality in native and nonnative speakers (McClure & Platt, 1988); invention preferences of advanced ESL writers (Liebman-Kleine, 1987); and the development of pragmatic accommodation (Stalker & Stalker, 1988). Recently, several collections of articles (e.g., Johnson & Roen, 1989; Kroll, 1990) have focused exclusively on the writing of ESL students.

Characteristics of the Research

In comparison to the work that has been carried out on the writing of American students whose first language is English, relatively little research has been carried out on writing in English as a second language. Moreover, because a number of fields are concerned about second language writers (e.g., the ESL teaching profession, the ESP [English for special purposes] teaching profession, the foreign language-teaching profession, and bilingual educators), research carried out within the traditions of these various subfields has remained compartmentalized and has failed to yield a coherent view of the development of writing skills in individuals who are in the process of acquiring a second language. These four fields have had even less to say about the development of writing skills in functional bilinguals who are beyond the incipient stages of bilingualism.

Consequently, even though some research on writing has been carried out from these different perspectives, until recently the tendency had been for this research to respond to immediate concerns within the particular subfield in question and in many cases to either ignore research carried out on the writing of mainstream students or to follow its models slavishly. A study of early research on writing that focused on Hispanic-background students (Valdés, 1989), for example, revealed that work on these bilingual students was largely concerned about negative interference between students' two languages. More important, however, the majority of the research conducted on these non-English-background students did not assess the actual language proficiency of the students in question. Students were grouped together and labeled "limited-English-speaking," "Spanish surnamed," "ESL students," but seldom were any attempts made to determine whether these individuals were indeed similar. The result of this tendency is that little information is available about the relationship between actual language proficiency and writing.

Even with these limitations, however, work carried out in the late 1970s and early 1980s addressed a number of key areas. What emerges from existing work is a growing sense that learning how to write in a second language may involve much more than simply learning how to avoid interference from the native language. Work carried out from a number of directions argues for a perspective on second language writing that takes into account what we know about basic and skilled writers who are native speakers of English, that attempts to understand in what ways second language writers are different from these native language writers, and that looks closely at the actual writing process of second language learners as they write.

Two examples of work that has examined the growth and progress of ESL writers in comparison to native-speaking writers are the studies carried out by Edelsky (1982, 1983, 1986) and by Mohan and Lo (1985). Specifically, the work carried out by Edelsky documented ways in which young children use writing skills and perceptions about writing that they had already developed in their first language as they begin to write in English. This work suggests that, for children, some aspects of learning about writing conventions in English parallels some of the aspects encountered in the study of early writing in a first language. Work carried out by Mohan and Lo argued that rather than assuming that organizational "problems" in the writing of second language learners are due to interference or negative transfer, researchers should consider explanations that take into account how appropriate discourse organization grows and matures in native speakers.

Work in this direction is particularly important because it suggests that second language learners cannot be expected to grow in their writing abilities in English in ways that are very unlike the patterns of growth generally exhibited by native speakers of English. Even though exact stages and patterns of growth have not been described for native English-language writers, work carried out on both basic and expert writers and writers and writing in general (e.g., the work analyzed and discussed by Hillocks, 1986) offers a good point of departure. For example, given what we know about the differences between basic writers and skilled writers, if L2 writers are young or basic writers in addition to being second language learners, they will probably progress somewhat along the lines that developing basic writers progress on their way to becoming good writers. One might expect, then, that the writing of second language learners might display a number of features typical of basic writers that have little or nothing to do with transfer from their first language.

Taking a developmental view has important implications for the analysis of the writing of second language learners. It implies, for example, that conclusions about first language transfer at the level of discourse for inexperienced writers may be more complex than early researchers in this area suggested. Even though the work carried out by Choi (1988), Clyne (1987), Hinds (1980, 1983), Jenkins and Hinds (1987), Kaplan (1966), and Matalene (1985) was valuable in suggesting that "accents" could exist at the discourse level, much more may be involved than simple cross-linguistic transfer. "Unexpected" discourse characteristics in the writing of beginning writers (those who have no experience writing in their first language) may not actually be discourse transfer, but simply the product of beginning writing development.

Obviously, a developmental perspective based on knowledge about mainstream writers makes an assumption about parallels to be found between first and second language writers. The expectation is that important similarities exist between the stages of writing growth and sophistication of young native-speaking writers of English and those of English language learners who are learning to write in their second language. This expectation is shared by a number of researchers who have already examined this assumption and have sought to study it in a number of different ways. McClure and Platt (1988), for example examined the development of temporality in written narratives in young native and nonnative children and found that although the pattern of use of temporality was similar, nonnative children exhibited a developmental lag. This study offered support for the view that there are similarities between native and nonnative writers, even though the latter may lag behind the former.

Other researchers, while focusing less on sequences of growth, have also compared first and second language writers. Liebman-Kleine (1987) examined the invention preferences of advanced ESL students in order to discover how like or unlike native speakers they might be in these preferences. She concluded that, unlike native speakers, ESL students found systematic heuristics unsuccessful because these techniques depend to a large extent on linguistic abilities. Similarly, ESL students found open-ended exploratory writing only moderately helpful. Stressing the fact that words are not cheap for writers who are writing in a second language, Liebman-Kleine suggested a significant difference between first and second language writers. In the first case, writers have highly developed linguistic abilities in the language in which they are writing, but in the second case they do not.

Other comparisons of native and nonnative speakers and their writing include a study of pragmatic accommodation (Stalker & Stalker, 1988), a study of orienting skills of natives and nonnatives (Scarcella, 1984), and a study of cohesion and coherence (Connor, 1984). Seen as a body, these studies suggest that there are both similarities and differences between natives and nonnatives. Certain expected differences (e.g., cohesion density) were not found (Connor, 1984), but other differences (e.g., limited comparative ability to orient their readers) were indeed found (Scarcella, 1984). Even though one may conjecture that nonnative writing abilities will develop following a sequence similar to that of native writers, the research on differences and similarities between these two groups of individuals suggests that limitations in linguistic ability cannot be overlooked. *development, patterns of essays diff*

Important insights about this question, that is, about the relationship between language limitations and writing, have been provided by the research carried out on the composing processes of second language learners (e.g., Jones, 1985; Raimes, 1985, 1987; Zamel, 1983). Zamel (1983), for example, found that advanced ESL students "attend to language-related concerns only after their ideas have been delineated" (p. 165). Similarly, unskilled ESL students in Raimes's study (1985) did not edit very often in the course of writing and could not be grouped neatly in their behaviors according to level of language proficiency. Raimes found few similarities between her subjects and the basic writers studied by Perl (1979). Finally, Jones (1985) found that the use of what Krashen termed "the monitor" (conscious grammatical knowledge) as a filter or editor in writing did not lead to improved writing.

In sum, research on the composing process of nonnative English language has focused primarily on students who can still be classified as incipient bilinguals. Moreover, many of the studies cited above have investigated the writing of elective and noncircumstantial bilinguals—foreign students who have been educated in their own countries and who have elected to enroll in American universities—rather than American bilingual minority students. Given the vast differences between the nature of these two groups' bilingual experience, it is unclear how much one can generalize from such studies to the study of bilinguals who have had very little access to education in their first language.

BREAKING OUT OF COMPARTMENTS: DIRECTIONS FOR FUTURE RESEARCH

Rethinking divisions within professional associations and breaking out of compartments is not a simple task for any group. For the English composition profession, in particular, restructuring its focus in order to make bilingual minority students a professionwide concern for both researchers and practitioners will present many challenges. One of the first steps in facing these challenges must be the involvement of mainstream researchers in the study of the writing of fluent functional bilinguals. Without the involvement of mainstream researchers, without a profound interest by these individuals in the examination of issues they might once have considered to be "out of their fields of expertise," the study of diverse populations will continue to be considered the exclusive property of minority researchers or of a small number of specialists.

Even though research on writing on mainstream populations has increased greatly in the last several years, the same is not true about the research currently being carried out on the writing of minority populations. When such research is carried out, moreover, it is often unrelated to current theories about writing and writing instruction. In this final section of the article, I have included an outline of a number of research directions focusing on the writing of bilingual minority students. In compiling this outline, I have taken the position that research on bilingual minority writers must begin at the beginning;

that is to say, it must begin by asking how and whether such bilingual students actually experience problems in writing. By limiting my assumptions, I hope to suggest that, to some degree, the writing of minority bilinguals must be studied independently of the writing of mainstream individuals. While a number of areas require comparisons between mainstream and minority students, the research on mainstream writers cannot serve as a point of departure for most of the research carried out on bilingual writers. Rather, such research must stem from an understanding of both bilingualism *and* writing.

The Writing of Bilingual Minority Students: Issues and Questions

An outline of issues dedicated to the examination of the writing of bilingual individuals in this country must include questions and directions of relevance to the study of the two different populations identified above: circumstantial bilinguals (minority group members who have acquired or are acquiring English) and elective bilinguals (majority group members [English speakers] who are studying or learning languages other than English as foreign languages). Although one could argue that the writing of both groups can be studied under the general heading of writing in a second language, the differences between the backgrounds of the two populations are so fundamental that a single agenda would either exclude a series of concerns relevant to the study of circumstantial bilinguals or include a variety of questions irrelevant to the study of elective bilingualism and writing.

The research directions presented here will be limited to the study of the writing of bilingual minority students in this country. Although much within this agenda can apply to bilingual individuals of many different types, I leave to others the tasks of developing an outline of research directions that addresses writing in a second language among majority group individuals. Specifically, this preliminary listing of research topics is organized to respond to four key questions.

1. What kinds of writing instruction are bilingual minority students generally exposed to?
2. In what ways is the writing of bilingual minority students treated as a problem by mainstream teachers?
3. What is the impact of language factors on the writing of incipient bilinguals and of fluent/functional bilinguals?
4. What is the influence of background factors on the writing of bilingual minority students?

In the remainder of this section, I will discuss each of these four questions and suggest a number of subquestions in each area.

1. What Kinds of Writing Instruction Are Bilingual Minority Students Generally Exposed To?   Before we can determine whether problems experienced in writing by bilingual minority students occur because they are both bilingual and minority students, we must investigate the writing instruction that these students generally receive. In this article, I have argued that the English composition field is divided into two main compartments. What we do not know is what type of instruction bilingual minority students are generally exposed to in each compartment. Given the realities of ESL programs—which frequently are heavily grammar oriented—and the tendency for "low ability" students to be placed in remedial or basic skills classes, it is possible that bilingual students actually receive little instruction in writing. Descriptive research is needed that helps us understand what happens to these students at the elementary, secondary, and postsecondary levels. We need information about how fluent functional bilinguals who first enter college perform on writing placement tests, about what kinds of effects different methods of assessment have on different kinds of bilinguals, and on the relationship between previous writing instruction at the high school level and success in college. Before we can understand why students arrive at the college level with what appear to be limited writing abilities, we must study their high school experiences carefully. We must ascertain how much bilingual minority students write as compared with majority students who are both college and non-college bound. We must discover when they begin to write, what they are expected to write, and how often they are required to write during the course of their school lives.

We must also investigate the quality of the instruction these students receive. For example, are the English teachers most concerned about and interested in writing normally assigned to the honors English classes, or do they principally teach in schools populated with middle-and upper-middle-class students? What happens in the lower tracks? What are the attitudes of these instructors toward their students? What are the general trends, across the country, at the elementary, junior high school, and high school levels for teaching writing to bilingual minority students as compared with the teaching of writing to majority, mainstream students? Are writing-across-the-curriculum models mainly implemented with mostly mainstream students labelled high ability? How are the approaches used with the different groups similar? How are they different? And most important, can differences in instruction explain differences in outcomes?

Currently, little is known about whether process-oriented instruction has been used with these students, how successful it has been, and how it has been adapted to the bilingual capabilities of these individuals. We do not know whether approaches often advocated for use with mainstream students will be effective with the special category of students of interest. Research on how well process-oriented activities work must be carried out. We must determine, for example, how bilingual minority students of different language proficiencies profit from the use of such activities as brainstorming, free writing, peer response groups, and prewriting activities. We need to investigate what the best methods are to teach these students to plan, to set goals, and to think about the reader when writing.

Much work has been carried out in the area of instruction of majority students. One cannot assume, however, that methods and approaches that have been effective with this group will automatically be successful with students of very different backgrounds. Systematic research must be carried out in this area in order to identify effective and adaptable approaches.

2. In What Ways Is the Writing of Bilingual Minority Students Treated as a Problem?   Recent interest in writing has responded to a vocal national concern about students' writing skills and about the teaching of writing in American schools. In the public mind, the nation is in the midst of a "writing crisis," and much attention has been given to addressing the problems associated with that crisis. Given the concern about educating the increasingly diverse student population of this country, a large segment of the public also believes that if mainstream middle-class students have problems writing, the problems faced by minority bilingual students must be even greater.

Even though researchers studying mainstream students have perhaps never seriously investigated the extent of the "writing crisis," it is important that research on the existence and the nature of the writing "problem" for bilingual minorities be carried out systematically. Minimally, we must investigate whether the writing of these students is actually a problem or whether it is simply treated as a problem by researchers and practitioners. Of the total articles and research reports that I recently examined on the writing of one of the large bilingual minority groups in this country,[19] I found only a few articles (e.g., Ford, 1984, McArthur, 1981; Merrill, 1976) that attempted to determine whether the writing of mainstream students and bilingual minority students is actually different, whether it is responded to differently by teachers and evaluators when ethnic identity is masked, and whether differences, if present, go beyond the surface level. Studies are needed in which the writing of mainstream students is compared to that of different types of bilinguals (e.g., fluent, English-dominant individuals; fluent, Spanish-dominant individuals; limited English-speaking, Spanish-dominant bilinguals; and incipient bilinguals with and without previous writing experience in their own languages). Analyses of these writing products must go beyond the examination of errors and must include organizational features as well. Profiles and composites of the writing of different types of bilinguals based on these analyses must then be compiled.

Once solid descriptions or composite samples of the writing of both monolingual and bilingual students of different types are available, we must determine what features of each composite appear to affect its evaluation. Do mechanical errors of a specific type affect teachers and evaluators more than other errors? Are those errors perceived as more "foreign"? Is there a tendency for such "foreign" errors to blind evaluators to other aspects of the writing? Do similar features occur in the writing of bilingual students from different language backgrounds? Are responses the same or different if teachers are told that authors are members of one minority group as opposed to another? Are the same features considered salient for evaluating the writing of students from different backgrounds? Do teachers of other subjects re-spond in the same way as English teachers and teachers of composition?

Clearly the dimensions of the writing "problem" for bilingual minority students must be established. We cannot carry out research on its causes if the problem remains vague and undefined or if discussions of the nature of the difficulties or problems are based not on real data, but on contrastive analyses of two systems. A fundamental task for researchers, then, will be to provide accurate descriptions of the writing of bilingual minority students *of different types* and to ascertain how this writing is evaluated (accepted or not accepted) by various individuals who may be in a position of making judg-ments about these students' writing.

We must carefully document the effects and consequences of the new emphasis on writing for bilingual minority students. We must determine, for example, if either perceived or actual difficulties in writing result in low grades. Are these grades lower than those obtained by majority students with similar writing problems? Do these problems result in tracking? Is writ-ing used to place students in different classes? Is writing used to place students in homogeneous "ability" groups within the same class? Do these problems af-fect students' success in the use of writing outside of the school context? Do they fare well or poorly in classes in which essay examinations are required? Are they able to write college-admissions essays? Do poorly written essays affect their acceptance to college?

Clearly, in order to understand how significant the problem is, we must also investigate what effect the new writing emphasis has had and will have on students in general. We need to examine how what is seen as a lack of adequate writing skills in one environment affects students' success in the broader context of everyday living. This broader context includes other classes, other domains in which writing is used, and the real world of work and survival.

In the case of minority students, this information is particularly impor-tant. If, for example, research determines that a deficiency in writing skills correlates highly with low achievement and lack of vocational success for bilingual minority students, can it be concluded that improved writing abili-ties would change this pattern? Is it the case that the writing "problem" is separable from the rest of the academic and societal difficulties of these stu-dents?

As important as writing is, we must not lose sight of the fact that factors such as overagedness (perhaps caused by retention), ineffective schooling, segregated schooling, low socioeconomic background, tracking, and the like also have a significant impact on low achievement and college eligibility. Re-search is needed that allows us to determine if there are ways of breaking the cycle of failure for these students. Success in learning how to write, success in using writing for self-disclosure and for self-expression, success in communi-cating through writing how much is learned or understood in class, and suc-cess in being considered a "good writer" by teachers may indeed influence students' total school performance. It is important to investigate, however, whether the process or practice of writing itself contributes to students' success uniquely, or whether any other subject or area in which students experience success could be used with the same results.

The academic difficulties faced by bilingual minority students are many, and the causes of these general difficulties are complex and poorly understood. Even though a deficiency in writing skills may contribute to these difficulties, learning to write, by itself, will not change the reality that many of these students face on an everyday basis. Writing researchers must be aware that any research done on writing alone that is not directly grounded in the academic and personal experiences of the minority students in question will contribute little to our understanding of the actual value of writing for these students, of the other factors that influence their academic success, and of the approaches that could be taken to break long-established patterns and expectations. Interesting as the theoretical questions relating to the writing of these students may be, educational researchers must not lose sight of the fact that practical solutions are desperately needed.

3. What Is the Impact of Language Factors on the Writing of Incipient and Fluent/Functional Bilinguals?   Assuming that writing is a problem for bilingual minority students, that it is a serious problem and one much beyond that experienced by mainstream majority students, and assuming also that one could separate writing from the other academic problems encountered by minority students, the research priority would then be to examine the possible "causes" of the perceived problem.

Because one of the principal differences between mainstream students and bilingual minority students is that the latter are bilingual, the relationship among levels of language proficiency, types of bilingualism, and the development of writing ability need to be investigated. However, most studies conducted to date that address language factors and writing in bilingual minority students have tended to focus on interference (negative language transfer) between the immigrant language and English. Few studies have investigated the process or the practice of writing as each relates to such areas as the nature of bilingualism, bilingual processing, or second language acquisition.

In spite of the fact that bilingual individuals differ in levels of language proficiency, range in each language, and functional ability in each language, most of studies that I reviewed for the project on the writing of Hispanics failed to measure the language competencies or proficiencies of the groups investigated. Bilingual groups were generally poorly chosen and described by researchers and included Spanish-surnamed students, students enrolled in bilingual education programs, or students enrolled in ESL, without regard to differences in proficiency and ability among individuals. I suspect that other bilingual groups have been treated similarly by researchers.

The research topics and questions to be listed and discussed next are dependent on the measurement and description of the language abilities and proficiencies of the students investigated. I must again emphasize that research on bilingual minority students that attempts to understand how language factors affect writing cannot be considered valid if the language abilities/proficiencies of these students are not measured or described in some detail.

For this discussion, circumstantial bilingual individuals have been divided into two large groups: incipient bilinguals (individuals who are in the process of acquiring a second language and who cannot yet be considered fully fluent in English) and fluent, functional bilinguals. As will be recalled from the discussion of bilingualism, both categories necessarily include a wide variety of individuals who possess different levels of proficiency in different language modes (i.e., in speaking, listening, reading, and writing) and different strengths in each mode.

A. The Writing of Incipient Bilinguals.   The investigation of the writing of incipient bilinguals presents opportunities for researchers to study how skilled English language writing grows and develops in different groups of language learners depending on their age, their background in writing in their original language, their levels of oral fluency in English, the exposure to written English models, and their exposure to writing instruction. Research on bilingual students of various ages whose backgrounds in reading and writing in their first language vary is critical, as is research on nonliterate adults.

Research is needed, for example, on incipient bilinguals of various ages who have already acquired writing skills in their first language. This may include students in transitional bilingual education programs or students who have moved to this country after having attended school for 1 or more years in their own countries. For these individuals, we need to determine what their perceptions about writing are, what they believe the purposes of writing include, how they view the relationship between speech and writing, and what they consider to be "good" writing. Much has been said about the differences between the edited written register of a language and its spoken registers. What do individuals schooled in other countries know about this distinction? Can these bilinguals recognize the differences between spoken and written registers in English? Are they capable of using a spoken level of English that is similar to the written standard? If they are proficient only in the informal, casual, and intimate levels of English, what happens when they attempt to write academic prose? Do they tend to "think" in their first language? Do they automatically reproduce the rhetorical and syntactic properties of the edited written standard that they know well in their own language and then attempt to translate into English? We need to determine what the results of these attempts are. When is negative transfer from L1 more likely to occur? When negative transfer does occur, what are its causes? Does it result from an insufficient familiarity with organization conventions? with English spelling conventions, with English syntax? Does it result from an entirely different way of conceptualizing the task, or from the fact that the student is attempting to translate and is using L1 syntax and organization as a basis?

What approaches can be developed to sort out these various possibilities? How aware are individual students of how they write and of the writing process itself?

To date, most research on incipient bilinguals schooled initially in their home language has taken the position that their writing will be contaminated by features of their L1. Instruction, then, is directed at getting them to avoid such contamination by either "thinking in English," editing their own writing using key grammar rules, or adapting writing models considered "good" writing for their own use. Very little attention has been given to what students bring with them, to the understandings they already have about the written language, to the skills they may have already developed, and to the ways in which they can be taught to use their first language strategically in learning to write in English.

The research questions outlined above, if pursued, would do much to establish important points of departure for teaching to learners' strengths and for critically examining all instructional approaches that presuppose little or no knowledge or awareness of writing on the part of these individuals.

The development of writing abilities should also be studied among non-literate, adult incipient bilinguals. In this particular case, studies can focus on how "naive" adults (as compared to children) uncover various aspects of the written language. These studies can help us understand how this process differs if the written language is L1 as opposed to L2, how the process differs if adults have been exposed to print previously, and how it differs if members of their immediate family (i.e., children, spouse) are also in the process of acquiring the English language and skills in reading and writing. In carrying out such research, the relationship between L2 development and its different stages and general characteristics must be taken into account.

The importance of this research, especially when compared with studies carried out on young incipient bilinguals, is that it can allow us to determine how age contributes or fails to contribute to both the process of acquiring a second language and the process of learning to write. It can also shed light on the impact of utility, the actual practical application of these abilities, on both the learning and the use of the written language.

In sum, the investigation of the writing of incipient bilinguals presents opportunities for researchers to study the relationship between the stages and levels of second language proficiency and the process of learning to write. Important comparisons can be made across stages of proficiency, age, background, previous exposure to the written language, and the like, that can contribute to our understanding of positive and negative language transfer, the use of L1 as a strategy in learning to write L2, the sequence of development of writing abilities in different types of incipient bilinguals, and the relationship between spoken language proficiency and control over the academic register in both its oral and written modes.

B. Questions Investigating the Writing of Fluent/Functional Bilinguals. Contrary to the claims made often by such groups as English Only and US English, an increasingly large number of members of ethnic minority groups can be classified as English dominant.[20] Because of their exposure to English, some of these English-dominant bilinguals will be indistinguishable from their monolingual peers in every type of oral exchange. What is interesting for writing researchers is that, given these fluent bilinguals' control, command, and proficiency in English, it is not unlikely that in some cases the writing of such bilinguals would be equally indistinguishable from that produced by their same-age and background monolingual peers. Research on these kinds of cases would reveal much about the relationship between bilingualism and writing.

As in the case of incipient bilinguals, research on fluent/functional bilinguals must include the measurement and description of the language abilities and proficiencies of the students investigated. It must also include research on different types of bilinguals who differ in general background and exposure to writing. While specific research foci would differ, questions such as the following would make up the core of a research agenda on fluent/functional bilinguals. Are there "expert" bilingual writers? Assuming that there are expert bilingual writers, how do these writers go about the process of writing? Do they write in both of their languages? What is the same and what is different about the products they produce in different languages? What is the same and what is different about the products they produce in different languages? What is the same and what is different in the processes used to compose in the two languages? What is the difference between expert monolingual writers and expert bilingual writers?

How do bilingual individuals actually go about writing? Are their strategies based on one language? On both languages? Do the strategies used differ in different kinds of bilinguals? How does exposure to the written language in L1 affect the process of writing for different types of bilinguals? What is the relationship between writing tasks and writing processes?

We need descriptions of the written products of fluent/functional bilinguals of various types, information about the qualities and features of products written for different purposes and under different conditions, and analyses of the relationship between writing tasks and writing products. We also need information about the approaches currently being used to assess the writing of bilingual students.

It may be bilingualism per se that causes problems for students, but it may also be that length of exposure to writing and writing conventions is more closely linked to writing difficulties. Perhaps a certain length of exposure to the written language in either L1 or L2 is required before any benefits are reflected in students' writing. Perhaps there are significant differences between students who learned to write in their second language before they learned to write in their native language and those who learned to write in L1 before writing in L2.

Understanding how the processes of revising and editing work for fluent bilinguals is essential. We need investigations of when and how these individuals revise their drafts, how L1 and L2 are used in revising and/or editing by different types of bilinguals, and how grammatical rules are used in both of these processes. And, in the light of instructional approaches that emphasize writing to learn, we also need studies of the connections between writing and learning for different types of bilinguals. In what ways does writing improve learning for bilingual students? What kinds of writing have what kinds of effects? In what ways and at what levels of proficiency does writing frustrate or interfere with student learning?

As the list of questions above has undoubtedly made clear, in order to be complete, research on the writing of fluent/functional bilinguals must encompass the investigation of questions that have already been examined in monolingual writers. The question of whether the language factor is a cause of the "problems" experienced by bilingual minority students can be understood only if it is studied in both incipient and fluent bilinguals of as many different types as possible and compared with what is currently known about writing "problems" of monolingual individuals.

In addition, however, the study of the writing of fluent/functional bilinguals can contribute to a more complete understanding of the nature of writing and the process of writing in general if researchers take the perspective that, as opposed to what is commonly believed, there are expert bilingual writers, writers who have learned how to capitalize on the strengths of their two languages and from whom much can be learned.

The question of how and whether language factors such as age of acquisition, degree of proficiency, and exposure to writing in L1 affect the ways in which students write, their attitudes toward writing, the sequence in which skilled writing develops, is a complex one. As the discussion of needed research has attempted to illustrate, the questions and issues to be considered go much beyond a superficial view of such frequently researched areas as first language interference. They go much beyond the study of student performance on specific writing tasks and require the careful description of the language characteristics of the students being investigated. I must emphasize that without such descriptions, what is being investigated cannot contribute to our understanding of how language factors actually affect the process of writing, writers themselves, and those evaluating the writing of such writers.

4. What Is the Influence of Background Factors on the Writing of Bilingual Minority Students?   In trying to identify the causes of the writing problems experienced by bilingual minority students, a number of researchers have suggested that background factors may also play a significant role in defining how these students approach writing in general. Among the documents I examined for my work on the writing of Hispanic bilinguals, for example, several studies (e.g., Galvan, 1985; Gonzalez, 1982; Rigg, 1985; Rodriguez, 1977; Seale, 1976; Shuman, 1983; Trevino, 1976; Trueba, 1987) took the position that students encounter difficulties in writing because what they are asked to do in the classroom is not relevant or connected to their cultural background or to their daily lives.

The possibility of attributing writing difficulties experienced by non-mainstream students to cultural and background factors is an attractive one. In many ways, it lets both students and instructors off the hook. If a student appears to be having problems writing persuasive essays, for example, it seems plausible to suggest that these problems stem from a lack of experience with reasoned arguments in his or her household or that the existence of cultural traditions discouraging the expression of personal opinion are responsible for the student's performance.[21]

In point of fact, however, before such statements can be made validly, research on background factors and their influence on writers must be carried out on different groups and compared with similar studies of mainstream students, their families, and their communities. For example, it is easy to believe that the American middle class is made up of individuals who are highly literate and who use writing regularly in the course of their everyday lives, both at home and at work; however, it is becoming increasingly clear that the demands made by writing in educational institutions are unlike those made normally for most individuals. Except for families in which there are persons who make their living writing (e.g., college professors, writers, newspaper people, etc.), most mainstream children do not grow up in households where the functions and uses of writing match those found in the school and in the classroom.

The question, then, for those concerned with the study of bilingual minority students is, how does the gap for these students compare with the gap for mainstream students? Does the magnitude of the gap depend on the class or educational background of the family as it does for mainstream students? Does it depend on whether their communities of origin were or were not highly literate in particular ways? What does bridging the gap (of whatever magnitude) involve?

We need studies that focus on exactly how writing fits into the lives of both mainstream and minority families and communities. We need to understand what "ordinary" individuals (not those who write in their professions) write, how they write, what they write, and why. Before we paint a picture of minority families in which the absence of books leads us to the conclusion that members of the family seldom write, we must spend time observing these families closely as they go about their business. We must be aware, however, that seeing exactly how writing is used among specific groups of people may take a very long time. Even when long-term observational studies on the uses and functions of writing in specific families and communities are conducted and compared with studies of mainstream populations, there is still a danger of either overstating the impact of background factors or of minimizing their importance. Moreover, the notions that make up the construct of "background factors" are often fuzzy. Almost anything can be attributed to cultural differences.

In spite of this danger, however, a need clearly exists for studies that will allow us to understand how rules of interaction in a particular culture, how role relationships, and how traditions governing appropriate expression of feelings or beliefs have an impact on students when they write. We must seek to understand, for example, how a student's perception of his or her intended reader (e.g., teacher, other students, self) and the cultural traditions governing interactions with such individuals influence the manner in which the student develops an argument, persuades, or defines. If the intended reader is assumed to be the teacher, for example, how do bilingual minority students from different cultural backgrounds write for such a reader? Do they limit how they argue, what they recount, what they explain because the teacher is the sole audience? Do they consider certain kinds of writing (e.g., persuasion) to be inappropriate for addressing an instructor? Do they believe that certain kinds of narrative and narrative sequence are required for recounting events to different individuals (e.g., an inferior, a superior, a peer)? What about mainstream students? Are their cultural, familial, and personal rules of communication in harmony with expressing an opinion strongly, with explaining, with narrating? Do nonminority students also find problems in using certain kinds of writing? How are minority and nonminority students alike or different in this respect?

The relationship between speech and writing must also be taken into account in the study of the impact of background factors on writing. It cannot be assumed, for example, that because a student fails to develop coherent arguments in writing, that he or she also lacks the ability to structure such arguments in interactive settings orally using one or both languages. Before one suggests that the ability to structure discourse of a specific type is beyond the capabilities or experiences of students, it is important that a study be made of the discourse organization in question as it occurs in normal interaction using the spoken language.

In comparison to investigating language and/or writing instruction as causes of students' problems, the investigation of background factors is much more difficult. Many subtle issues must be taken into account, most of which have not been investigated thoroughly. In addition, without information about the same background factors in mainstream populations and the impact of these factors on "good" writers, we will not be able to determine whether bilingual minority students are better, worse, or the same at overcoming limitations and at developing strategies for learning how to write well. What we do know is that even without much evidence, the writing of bilingual minority students is currently believed to be affected significantly by family background and by cultural values. However, much caution needs to be exercised in attributing to cultural background what may be, in fact, the effect of a combination of factors, all of which have a significant effect on writing and the writing process.

TOWARD PROFESSIONWIDE RESPONSES TO THE NEW CHALLENGE OF DIVERSITY

In order to break down compartments now existing within the profession, composition specialists must begin to see the "new" student population not as a special group destined to disappear quickly into the mainstream but as a population that will significantly change the character of the entire student community in this country. Tomorrow's mainstream student group will be made up of what we consider today to be "diverse" students.

The position I have taken here is that research on bilingual minority writers must be carried out by mainstream researchers as well as minority researchers and viewed as a legitimate focus of activity. Such research must be based on a good understanding of the nature of bilingualism and on long-term familiarity with research on the nature of writing. In my opinion, research on the writing of fluent/functional bilinguals, besides contributing to our understanding of how and whether language factors result in writing problems, also presents opportunities for researchers to expand the present focus on monolingual individuals that now dominates writing research to include a focus on persons who function comfortably and effectively in more than one language. The significance of this shift in focus will be evident to those concerned about the development of a theory of writing in the broadest sense. The fact is that theories about the nature of writing, writing development, the uses of writing, and the process of writing, cannot be said to correspond to external reality broadly if these theories do not account for the experiences of over half of the world's population, the half that can be placed along the bilingual continuum and classified as fluent and functional in two languages.

The study of the writing of fluent minority bilinguals, then, can be approached from two different perspectives: the perspective that limits its focus to the investigation of minority bilinguals and their success or failure in writing as a basis for problem solving as well as the perspective that views the study of bilingual individuals as a means of more fully understanding the very nature of writing. The first perspective is concerned primarily with improving writing skills in minority bilinguals. It is concerned with how this population differs from monolingual populations only to the degree that it contributes to improving writing instruction and writing practice for minority bilinguals. The second perspective has a more theoretical orientation and is based on the assumption that, by using bilingual individuals to study questions of major theoretical interest, it will be able to strengthen the explanatory power of existing theories about the process and practice of writing in general. Both perspectives are of key importance to the profession if it is truly dedicated to addressing the needs of the new diverse population of students.

Bilingual individuals and their writing will continue to present challenges to the profession in the many years to come. It is time for compartmentalization between and within professions to end and for "mainstream" researchers and practioners to begin to address these challenges.

NOTES

1. In stating that the majority of the attention of the English composition profession has been aimed at speakers of nonstigmatized varieties of English, I do not mean to imply that there has been little interest in the writing of nonmainstream writers. Work carried out, for example, by

Cronnell (1983, 1984), Farr Whiteman (1981), Farr and Janda (1985), and Wolfram and Whiteman (1971) on writing and dialect differences is well known to many members of the profession. In addition, the publication of work by Brooks (1985) and Farr and Daniels (1986) by NCTE has made evident that the English profession has made serious efforts at addressing the needs of nonmainstream students.

2. Prior to the work carried out by Weinreich (1953/1974) on bilingualism in Switzerland, some research had been carried out on bilingualism in the Americas. Haugen (1956) summarized this early work in a bibliography and research guide.

3. For an excellent discussion of these factors, see Wardhaugh (1987).

4. Two languages are said by Weinreich (1953/1974) to be "in contact" when they are used alternately by the same speakers. More recently, Appel and Muysken (1987) have broadened this definition. According to these researchers, two languages are in contact when through force of circumstances, speakers of one language must interact with speakers of another in the course of their everyday lives.

5. In theory, for each of his or her two languages, a bilingual individual could develop productive control (the ability to speak) and receptive control (the ability to understand) of the spoken language. He or she could also develop both productive control (the ability to write) and receptive control (the ability to read) of the written language.

6. For example, in some cases, individuals who have become bilingual have been speakers of languages that have no written form. This was the case with most groups of native Americans in this country. In other instances, conquering groups have imposed the use of the conquering language for all official written interaction and have discouraged the use of other written languages. In still other instances, people who have moved from one country to another have had little access to written materials in their first language. Moreover, they have been schooled only in the societal language of the new country. Because such conditions and others like them were generally present in most language contact situations, many scholars who studied a particular bilingual society took for granted the fact that, given the limitations of access, biliteracy would not be likely to be highly developed. They did not spend much time describing or documenting the results of these limitations in the productive or receptive written language skills of bilinguals.

7. This research includes work carried out in many different countries around the world. A good review of some of this work and these findings is contained in Dutcher (1982).

8. For an overview of this debate, see Cazden and Snow (1990), Crawford (1989), Hakuta (1986), and Imhoff (1990).

9. The terms *elective bilingualism* and *circumstantial bilingualism* were proposed in Valdés and Figueroa (1994) instead of the terms *natural* and *elite/academic bilingualism* that have been used by others (e.g., Baetens-Beardsmore, 1982; Paulston, 1977; Skutnabb-Kangas, 1981).

10. The abandonment or retainment of the first language by circumstantial bilinguals is much more complex than I have outlined here. Numerous factors such as geographical proximity of the original sending community, large number of speakers, ethnic identity, literacy, and emotional attachment to the first language contribute to language maintenance. Other factors such as small number of speakers, high social and economic mobility in the majority society, and denial of ethnic identity contribute to language shift. For a listing of these factors, see Conklin and Lourie (1983, pp. 174–175) and Grosjean (1982, p. 107). An overview of the theoretical perspectives guiding research in the area of language shift and maintenance in bilingual societies is found in Fishman (1964).

11. It is important to note that the categories *elective bilingual* versus *circumstantial bilinguals*, while helpful, are not always mutually exclusive. For example, an individual whose circumstances demand that he or she acquire a second language may choose or elect to study this language in a formal setting. Similarly, an elective bilingual may decide to reside permanently in a setting wherein he or she is "forced" by circumstances to acquire levels of language not within the school-developed range. These distinctions, however, are useful for differentiating between two very different circumstances under which individuals initially come into contact with a language other than their first.

12. For a review of the very large number of studies that have established the claims made here, see chapter 2 of Romaine (1989) and chapters 5, 6, and 7 of Hamers and Blanc (1989).

13. According to Fishman (1965, 1972), diglossic communities are those in which one language or one variety of language is used for all formal (high) functions (e.g., interacting with official agencies, the presentation of formal speeches, the education of children, etc.) and the other language or variety is used for all informal (low) functions. In American immigrant communities, it is generally the case that English is considered appropriate for formal exchanges (political rallies, business meetings, announcements, sermons, and lectures) and the immigrant language is

used within the home and community. As a result, U.S. born persons of immigrant background will seldom have the opportunity to hear the immigrant language used for the high or formal functions. Thus (except for radio and television where available in immigrant languages), they will have no models for this register of language and will not develop this level of language.

14. As opposed to the use of the term *functional* in the study of literacy, within the field of bilingualism, the term has no negative connotations. A functional bilingual is considered to be not a minimally competent bilingual but an individual who can function, that is, actually use his or her language in real-life interaction.

15. The terms *mature bilingualism* and *steady-state bilingualism* have also been proposed by Hyltenstam and Obler (1989) to distinguish between the period in which individuals are becoming bilingual and the period when individuals can be considered to have acquired their second language.

16. A number of researchers, for example, Canale and Swain (1980), have suggested that these proficiencies or competencies include linguistic competence, sociolinguistic competence, strategic competence, and discourse competence. More recently, Bachman (1990) has proposed an even more complex model of communicative language ability.

17. My work on nonnative writers has been carried out primarily in the development of text materials for Spanish language majors in foreign language departments. The texts produced as a result of 14 years' experience in teaching advanced composition courses to both native and nonnative Spanish-speaking students in the same classroom include *Composición: Proceso y síntesis* (Valdés, Dvorak, & Hannum, 1989; Valdés, Hannum, & Dvorak, 1984) and *Español escrito: Curso para hispanohablantes bilingües* (Valdés & Teschner, 1978, 1984). Recently, I have completed work (Valdés, Haro, & Echevarriarza, 1992) on the development of writing proficiencies in English monolingual students at different levels of study of the Spanish language.

18. Concern about such matters has recently been expressed by McPherson (1991). McPherson worries that untrained teachers in history or horticulture may insist on a set of "misunderstood and arbitrary 'rules' that good writing teachers have long ago abandoned" (p. 87).

19. During the years 1986 to 1988, I conducted a project funded by the Center for the Study of Writing at the University of California, Berkeley entitled "Identifying Priorities in the Study of Hispanic Background Students: A Synthesis and Interpretation of Available Research." The results of this work are reported in Valdés (1989).

20. For discussion of the growing English dominance among immigrant groups, see Veltman (1983). An excellent overview of the increasing English monolingualism among the largest of the bilingual minority groups, the Hispanics, is found in Solé (1990).

21. Even though I have not found arguments such as these directly articulated in the literature, these types of judgments are implied in most of the work that focuses on "cultural" differences. I have, however, encountered the direct statement of these kinds of hypotheses among well-intentioned doctoral students who have sought my advice in proposing the verification of their conjectures as a dissertation topic.

REFERENCES

Albert, M., & Obler, L. (1978). *The bilingual brain*. New York: Academic Press.
Ammon, P. (1985). Helping children learn to write in English as a second language: Some observations and hypotheses. In S. Freedman (Ed.), *The acquisition of written language: Revision and response* (pp. 65–84). Norwood, NJ: Ablex.
Appel, R., & Muysken, P. (1987). *Language contact and bilingualism*. London: Edward Arnold.
Bachman, L. F. (1990). *Fundamental considerations in language testing*. Oxford: Oxford University Press.
Baetens-Beardsmore, H. (1982). *Bilingualism: basic principles*. Clevendon, Avon: Multilingual Matters.
Bialystok, E. (1991). *Language processing in bilingual children*. Cambridge: Cambridge University Press.
Brooks, C. (1985). *Tapping potential: English and language arts for the black learner*. Urbana, IL: National Council of Teachers of English.
Canale, M., & Swain, M. (1980). Theoretical bases of communicative approaches to second language teaching and testing. *Applied Linguistics, 1,* 1–47.
Cazden, C. B., & Snow, C. E. (Eds.). (1990). English plus: Issues in bilingual education [Special Issue]. *Annals of the American Academy of Political and Social Science, 508.*
Choi, Y. H. (1988). Text structure of Korean speakers' argumentative essays in English. *World Englishes, 7*(2), 129–142.
Clyne, M. (1987). Cultural differences in the organization of academic texts. *Journal of Pragmatics, 11,* 211–247.

Conklin, N. F., & Lourie, M. A. (1983). *A host of tongues: Language communities in the United States.* New York: Free Press.

Connor, U. (1984). A study of cohesion and coherence in English as a second language students' writing. *Papers in Linguistics, 17,* 301–315.

Crawford, J. (1989). *Bilingual education: History, politics, theory, and practice.* Trenton, NJ: Crane.

Cronnell, B. (1983). Dialect and writing: A review. *Journal of Research and Development in Education, 17*(1), 58–64.

Cronnell, B. (1984). Black English influences in the writing of third and sixth grade black students. *Journal of Educational Research, 77*(4), 233–236.

Cummins, J. (1979a). Linguistic independence and the educational development of bilingual children. *Review of Educational Research, 49,* 895–897.

Cummins, J. (1979b). Cognitive academic language proficiency, linguistic interdependence, the optimum age question and some other matters. *Working Papers on Bilingualism, 19,* 197–205.

Cummins, J. (1980). The cross-lingual dimensions of language proficiency: Implications for bilingual education and the optimal age issue. *TESOL Quarterly, 4,* 175–187.

Cummins, J. (1981). The role of primary language development in promoting educational success for language minority students. In California State Department of Education (Ed.), *Schooling and language minority students: A theoretical framework* (pp. 3–49). Los Angeles: Evaluation, Dissemination and Assessment Center.

Cummins, J., & Swain, M. (1986). *Bilingualism in education: Aspects of theory, research and practice.* New York: Longman.

Dodson, C. J. (1985). Second language acquisition and bilingual development: A theoretical framework. *Journal of Multilingual and Multicultural Development, 5*(6), 325–346.

Dutcher, N. (1982). *The use of first and second languages in primary education: Selected case studies* (Rep. No. 504). Washington, DC: World Bank.

Edelsky, C. (1982). Writing in a bilingual program: The relation of L1 and L2 tests. *TESOL Quarterly, 16*(2), 211–228.

Edelsky, C. (1983). Segmentation and punctuation: Developmental data from young writers in a bilingual program. *Research in the Teaching of English, 17*(2), 135–156.

Edelsky, C. (1986). *Habia una vez: Writing in a bilingual program.* Norwood, NJ: Ablex.

Farr, M., & Daniels, H. (1986). *Language diversity and writing instruction.* New York: ERIC Clearinghouse on Urban Education.

Farr, M., & Janda, M. A. (1985). Basic writing students: Investigating oral and written language. *Research in the Teaching of English, 19*(1), 62–83.

Farr Whiteman, M. (1981). Dialect influences in writing. In M. Farr Whiteman (Ed.), *Variation in writing: Functional and linguistic-cultural differences* (pp. 153–166). Hillsdale, NJ: Lawrence Erlbaum.

Ferguson, C. A., & Heath, S. B. (1981). *Language in the USA.* Cambridge: Cambridge University Press.

Fishman, J. A. (1964). Language maintenance and language shift as a field of inquiry: A definition of the filed and suggestions for further development. *Linguistics, 9,* 32–70.

Fishman, J. A. (1965). Who speaks what language to whom and when? *La Linguistique, 2,* 67–68.

Fishman, J. A. (1966). *Language loyalty in the United States.* The Hague: Mouton.

Fishman, J. A. (1972). Societal bilingualism: Stable and transitional. In A. S. Dil (Ed.), *Language in sociocultural change: Essays by Joshua Fishman* (pp. 135–152). Stanford, CA: Stanford University Press.

Fishman, J. A. (1989). *Language and ethnicity in minority sociolinguistic perspective.* Clevedon, Avon: Multilingual Matters.

Ford, C. E. (1984). The influence of speech variety on teachers' evaluation of students with comparable academic ability. *TESOL Quarterly, 18*(1), 25–40.

Galvan, M. (1985). *The writing processes of Spanish-speaking, bilingual/bicultural graduate students: An ethnographic perspective.* Unpublished doctoral dissertation, Hofstra University, Hempstead, NY.

Garcia, E. E. (1983). *Early childhood bilingualism.* Albuquerque: University of New Mexico Press.

Gonzalez, R. D (1982). Teaching Mexican-American students to write: Capitalizing on culture. *English Journal, 71*(7), 20–24.

Grosjean, F. (1982). *Life with two languages.* Cambridge, MA: Harvard University Press.

Gudykunst, W. B. (1988). *Language and ethnic identity.* Clevedon, Avon: Multilingual Matters.

Hakuta, K. (1986). *Mirror of language: The debate on bilingualism.* New York: Basic Books.

Hamers, J. F., & Blanc, M.H.A. (1989). *Bilinguality and bilingualism.* Cambridge University Press.

Haugen, E. (1956). *Bilingualism in the Americas: A bibliography and research guide.* University, AL: University of Alabama Press.

Haugen, E. (1972). The stigmata of bilingualism. In A. S. Dil (Ed.), *The ecology of language* (pp. 307–324). Stanford, CA: Stanford University Press.

Hillocks, G. (1986). *Research on written composition: New directions for teaching.* Urbana, IL: National Conference on Research in English and ERIC Clearinghouse on Reading and Communication Skills.

Hinds, J. (1980). Japanese expository prose. *Papers in Linguistics, 13,* 117–158.

Hinds, J. (1983). Contractive rhetoric: Japanese and English. *Text, 3*(2), 183–195.

Homel, P., Palij, M., & Aaronson, D. (1987). *Childhood bilingualism: Aspects of linguistic, cognitive, and social development.* Hillsdale, NJ: Lawrence Erlbaum.

Hudelson, S. (1981). An introductory examination of children's invented spellings in Spanish. *NABE Journal, 6*(2–3), 53–67.

Hyltenstam, K., & Obler, L. K. (1989). Bilingualism across the lifespan: An Introduction. In K. Hyltenstam & L. Obler (Ed.), *Bilingualism across the lifespan: Aspects of acquisition, maturity and loss* (pp. 1–12). Cambridge: Cambridge University Press.

Imhoff, G. (1990). *Learning in two languages: From conflict to consensus in the reorganization of schools.* New Brunswick, NJ: Transaction Publishers.

Jenkins, S., & Hinds, J. (1987). Business letter writing: English, French and Japanese. *TESOL Quarterly, 21*(2), 327–349.

Johnson, D. M., & Roen, D. H. (1989). *Richness in writing: Empowering ESL students.* London: Longman.

Jones, S. (1985). Problems with monitor use in second language composing. In M. Rose (Ed.), *When a writer can't write* (pp. 96–117). New York: Guilford Press.

Kaplan, R. B. (1966). Cultural thought patterns in inter-cultural education. *Language Learning, 16,* 1–20.

Kroll, B. (1990). *Second language writing.* Cambridge: Cambridge University Press.

Lambert, W. (1955). Measurement of the linguistic dominance of bilinguals. *Journal of Abnormal and Social Psychology, 50,* 197–200.

Liebman-Kleine, J. (1987). Teaching and researching invention: Using ethnography in ESL writing classes. *ELT Journal, 41*(2), 104–111.

Matalene, C. (1985). Contractive rhetoric: An American writing teacher in China. *College English, 47*(8), 789–808.

McArthur, D. L. (1981). *Bias in the writing of prose and its appraisal.* Los Angeles: University of California, Los Angeles, Center for the Study of Evaluation and Assessment. (ERIC Document Reproduction Service No. ED 217 073).

McClure, E., & Platt, E. (1988). The development of the expression of temporality in the written English narratives of monolingual American and bilingual Mexican pupils. *World Englishes, 7*(2), 197–210.

McKay, S. L., & Wong, S. C. (1988). *Language diversity: Problem or resource?* New York: Newbury House.

McLaughlin, B. (1987). Reading in a second language: Studies with adult and child learners. In S. Goldman & H. Trueba (Ed.), *Becoming literate in English as a second language.* Norwood, NJ: Ablex.

McPherson, E. (1991, February). Reply by Elizabeth McPherson. *College Composition and Communication, 42,* 87.

Merrill, C. (1976, January). *Contrastive analysis and Chicano compositions.* Paper presented at the Conference on College English and the Mexican American, Edinburg, Texas. (ERIC Document Reproduction Service No. ED 136 291).

Metcalf, A. A. (1979). *Chicano English.* Arlington, VA: Center for Applied Linguistics.

Mohan, B. A., & Lo, W. A. (1985). Academic writing and Chinese students: Transfer and developmental factors. *TESOL Quarterly, 19*(3), 515–534.

Paulston, C. B. (1977). Theoretical perspectives on bilingual education. *Working Papers on Bilingualism, 13,* 130–177.

Pawley, A., & Syder, F. H. (1983). Two puzzles for linguistic theory: Native-like selection and native-like fluency. In J. Richard & R. Schmidt (Ed.), *Language and communication.* New York: Longman.

Perl, S. (1979). The composing processes of unskilled college writers. *Research in the Teaching of English, 13,* 317–336.

Raimes, A. (1985). What unskilled ESL students do as they write: A classroom study of composing. *TESOL Quarterly, 19*(2), 229–258.

Raimes, A. (1987). Language proficiency, writing ability, and composing strategies: A study of ESL college writers. *Language Learning, 37,* 439–467.

Rigg, P. (1985). Petra: Learning to read at 45. *Journal of Education, 1,* 129–139.

Rodriguez, R. J. (1977, March–April). *Awareness of multicultural language and learning styles research: An urging.* Paper presented at the annual meeting of the Conference on College Composition and Communication, Kansas City, MO.

Romaine, S. (1989). *Bilingualism.* Oxford: Basil Blackwell.

Scarcella, R. (1984). How writers orient their readers in expository essays: A comparative study of native and non-native English writers. *TESOL Quarterly, 18*(4), 671–688.

Seale, J. (1976, October). *Mexican-American folklore: An approach to the research paper.* Paper presented at the annual meeting of the South Central Modern Language Association, Dallas, TX.

Segalowitz, N. (1986). Skilled reading in a second language. In J. Vaid (Ed.), *Language processing in bilinguals: Psycholinguistic and neuropsychological perspectives* (pp. 3–19). Hillsdale, NJ: Lawrence Erlbaum.

Seliger, H. W., & Vago, R. M. (1991). *First language attrition.* Cambridge: Cambridge University Press.

Shuman, A. (1983). Collaborative literacy in an urban multiethnic neighborhood. *International Journal of Sociology of Language, 42,* 69–81.

Skutnabb-Kangas, T. (1981). *Bilingualism or not: The education of minorities.* Clevedon, Avon: Multilingual Matters.

Skutnabb-Kangas, T., & Cummins, J. (1988). *Minority education: From shame to struggle.* Clevedon, Avon: Multilingual Matters.

Solé, Y. R. (1990). Bilingualism: Stable or transitional? The case of Spanish in the United States. *International Journal of the Sociology of Language, 84,* 35–80.

Spolsky, B. (1986). *Language and education in multilingual settings.* San Diego, CA: College Hill Press.

Stalker, J. W., & Stalker, J. C. (1988). A comparison of pragmatic accommodation of nonnative and native speakers in written English. *World Englishes, 7,* 119–128.

Trevino, A. D. (1976, January). *Designing a non-remedial freshman composition course for Mexican-Americans.* Paper presented at the Conference on College English and the Mexican American, Edinburg, TX. (ERIC Document Reproduction Service No. ED123 914).

Trueba, H. T. (1987). Organizing classroom instruction in specific sociocultural contexts: Teaching Mexican youth to write in English. In S. R. Goldman & H. T. Trueba (Ed.), *Becoming literate in English as a second language* (pp. 235–252). Norwood, NJ: Ablex.

Urzua, C. (1987). You stopped too soon: Second language children composing and revising. *TESOL Quarterly, 21*(2), 279–304.

Vaid, J. (1986). *Language processing in bilinguals: Psycholinguistic and neuropsychological perspectives.* Hillsdale, NJ: Lawrence Erlbaum.

Valdés, G. (1989). *Identifying priorities in the study of Hispanic background students: A synthesis and interpretation of available research* (Final Report to OERI). Berkeley: University of California, Berkeley, Center for the Study of Writing.

Valdés, G., Dvorak, T., & Hannum, T. (1989). *Composición: Proceso y síntesis.* (2nd ed.). New York: Random House.

Valdés, G., Hannum, T., & Dvorak, T. (1984). *Composición: Proceso y síntesis.* New York: Random House.

Valdés, G., & Figueroa, R. A. (1994). *Bilingualism and testing: A special case of bias.* Norwood, NJ: Ablex.

Valdés, G., Haro, P., & Echevarriarza, M. P. (1992). The development of writing abilities in a foreign language: Contributions towards a general theory of L2 writing. *Modern Language Journal, 76*(3), 333–352.

Valdés, G., & Teschner, R. V. (1978). *Español escrito: Curso para hispanohablantes bilingües.* New York: Scribner.

Valdés, G., & Teschner, R. V. (1984). *Español escrito: Curso para hispanohablantes bilingües* (2nd ed.). New York: Scribner.

Veltman, C. (1983). *Language shift in the United States.* Berlin: Mouton.

Wardhaugh, R. (1987). *Languages in competition.* Oxford: Basil Blackwell.

Weinreich, U. (1974). *Languages in contact.* The Hague: Mouton. (First edition published 1953)

Wolfram, W., & Whiteman, M. (1971). The role of dialect interference in composition. *Florida Foreign Language Reporter, 9*(1–2), 34–38, 59.

Yorio, C. (1989). Idiomaticity as an indicator of second language proficiency. In K. Hyltenstam & L. K. Obler (Ed.), *Bilingualism across a lifespan: Aspects of acquisition, maturity and loss* (pp. 55–72). Cambridge: Cambridge University Press.

Zamel, V. (1983). The composing processes of advanced ESL students: Six case studies. *TESOL Quarterly, 17*(2), 165–187.

Zamel, V. (1985). Responding to student writing. *TESOL Quarterly, 19*(1), 79–101.

Second-Language Writers: Definitions and Complexities

Introduction to Part Two

The spectrum of second-language writers is broad and nuanced. Many second-language students come to the United States from wholly foreign educational backgrounds, while others may be immigrants or refugees who have spent some time in the United States before matriculating. There are also bilingual minority students, as addressed by Guadalupe Valdés in the previous section, who may have been born in the United States but raised in families and communities where English was not the dominant language. Some of those students may identify themselves as second-language learners or English speakers of other languages (ESOL), but others may reject those labels. The articles in this section begin to define the spectrum of second-language writers that may be found in first-year composition classes, but they also address the difficulties and challenges that often arise from these definitions and categories. The section begins with Joy Reid's "'Eye' Learners and 'Ear' Learners: Identifying the Language Needs of International Student and U.S. Resident Writers," originally published in 1998. Reid describes the different ways U.S. resident and international second-language students have learned English and the implications of their different learning styles on their writing. As Reid explains, U.S. resident second-language writers are often "ear" learners, who learn English through immersion in various elements of everyday U.S. culture. These students are very familiar with popular U.S.-related topics, have strong oral fluency, and are comfortable with U.S. school systems. On the other side of Reid's spectrum are "eye" learners, international visa students who are deemed "well-educated," "literate and fluent in their first language," and who learned English primarily through formal foreign language instruction abroad. They are described as "eye" learners because "they have learned English principally through their **eyes**, studying vocabulary, verb forms, and language rules" (p. 79 in this volume). Depending on the approach used in their foreign language courses, these students may have limited experience with writing in English. Reid explores implications of these differences for writing instruction and the varying levels of assistance that may be available for students who reflect these differences.

Yuet-Sim D. Chiang and Mary Schmida add further depth to the spectrum of second-language writers by addressing the importance of language identity and ownership. Their article, "Language Identity and Language Ownership: Linguistic Conflicts of First-Year University Writing Students," is part of a 1999 edited collection entitled *Generation 1.5 Meets College Composition* (Harklau, Losey, and Siegal) — an influential text in both second-language writing and composition that focuses on the experiences of immigrant students who complete parts of their education both in the United States and in other countries. Chiang and Schmida examine the "multi-layered" nature of language and identity. They found that many children of immigrants feel conflicts between their "linguistic identity and linguistic ability," which influence the labels they attach to themselves, such as "bilingual" and "native speaker" (p. 93). The students in Chiang and Schmida's study do not feel ownership of English language or U.S. culture, and they often feel that their continued depiction and placement as a "linguistic minority" by university instructors and administrators perpetuates this belief, leaving them marginalized in the classroom and the university.

The issue of how students are positioned by their teachers also resonates in the next article in this section, Linda Harklau's "From the 'Good Kids' to the 'Worst': Representations of English Language Learners across Education Settings," first published in 2000. Harklau explores the experiences of immigrant students as they move from high school to college, particularly in terms of how they are positioned and represented by their teachers in different institutional settings. She observes how the high school teachers in her study tended to view students as "hard-working." Yet when the same set of students entered their first year of college, they were often viewed as "resistant" by their college instructors. Students adopted these images of themselves, which impacted their attitudes toward learning in the two different educational contexts. Harklau argues that writing teachers need to be aware of how students form their identities as English language learners, as well as of students' backgrounds and experiences, in designing curricula and in interacting with students in the classroom.

This section concludes with Awad El Karim M. Ibrahim's critical ethnographic study of African youths in a Franco-Ontarian high school in Canada and their identification and adoption of Black English Vernacular (BEV) and American hip-hop culture. Originally published in 1999, "Becoming Black: Rap and Hip-Hop, Race, Gender, Identity, and the Politics of ESL Learning" draws attention to the political dimensions of identity and second-language writing instruction. Ibrahim explores how African students, with their own distinctive linguistic and cultural backgrounds, may enter overdetermined social spaces in which they are unproblematically constructed as "Black." In turn, Ibrahim argues that it is "no coincidence" that the African students then begin to modify their behavior and assimilate the expectations of the dominant group, taking up rap, hip-hop, and BEV forms. He contends that these acts represent students' desire "to belong to a location, a politics, a memory, a history, and hence a representation" (p. 134). For composition instructors, these acts help us to reconsider our responses to second-language writers and to think about what it means for them to adapt, assimilate, or reject the various cultural identities that are available within a pluralistic culture.

In the end, each of these articles argues for a deeper understanding of second-language writers and their identities. It is imperative that composition instructors acknowledge and examine how classroom behaviors and writing experiences are affected by and influence students' negotiations of different social contexts in constructing their identities.

4

"Eye" Learners and "Ear" Learners: Identifying the Language Needs of International Student and U.S. Resident Writers[1]

JOY REID

Students differ, and the educational background differences among second-language students in ESL writing classrooms can be especially diverse. Student writing by nonnative speakers of English often contains unusual, and sometimes puzzling, language structures, and the rhetorical needs of those ESL students may also demonstrate a wide range of needs. Fortunately, many teacher resources have focused on teaching ESL writing (cf. Belcher & Braine, 1995; Brock & Walters, 1993; Fox, 1994; Leki, 1992; Kroll, 1990; Reid, 1993; Swales & Feak, 1994). The context for this discussion, however, is the differences between writing by (1) U.S. resident students for whom English is a second (or third or fourth) language and (2) students who have come from non-English-speaking countries to study at postsecondary institutions in the U.S. Generally speaking, these two groups of ESL students have learned their English differently, and so their language problems have different sources and different solutions.

Before beginning this discussion, I believe it is necessary to emphasize that just because this chapter concentrates on writing *problems* by ESL students, that need not be the most important focus of the ESL writing teacher. With structured practice, teacher intervention, and revision, student fluency and confidence in their writing skills often increase; language errors decrease, and rhetorical frameworks develop accordingly (cf. Cohen & Cavalcanti, 1990; Ferris, 1997; Jacoby et al., 1995; Li, 1996). Therefore, the concentration on ESL student error in this chapter does not rest in my belief that error is the overriding consideration for the teacher or the student, but rather that it is frequently a source of puzzlement and frustration for both.

U.S. RESIDENT ESL WRITERS

At one end of the continuum of nonnative English speakers is the refugee student whose parents have fled political upheaval for the U.S. or sent the

From *Grammar in the Composition Classroom: Essays on Teaching ESL for College-Bound Students.* Patricia Byrd and Joy M. Reid. New York: Heinle, 1998. 3–17.

children ahead to live with relatives or even strangers. Such students are usually orally fluent in their first language, but due to limited or interrupted schooling, they may not be fully literate in that language. These students have learned English by being suddenly immersed in the language and culture of the U.S. Specifically, they have acquired English principally through their **ears**: They listened, took in oral language (from teachers, TV, grocery clerks, friends, peers), and subconsciously began to form vocabulary, grammar, and syntax rules, learning English principally through oral trial and error.

Usually, these students have graduated from U.S. high schools, have had some tutoring—often fragmented—in ESL "pullout" programs when they first entered school, and have been accumulating U.S. culture for a number of years. They have relatively developed English oral fluency and listening skills, and they understand the slang, the pop music, the behaviors, and the "cool" clothes of the schools they attend. Their background knowledge of life in the U.S. is, in many cases, both broad and deep: Their personal experiences have made them familiar with class structures and expectations; they have opinions on current controversies and issues; and they recognize cultural references to, for instance, television programs, cartoon humor, and advertising. However, their reading skills may be hampered by limited understanding of the structures of the English language, and/or a lack of literacy, and/or lack of reading experience. Their writing displays the conversational, phonetic qualities of their "ear-based" language learning, as well as the use of their self-developed language "rules" that may, upon examination, prove to be overgeneralized or false. Below is a writing sample from a Vietnamese student that is typical of the writing done by many U.S. resident students. The in-class essay was written in response to a written text (about students having jobs while in college) during her first day in a first-year university composition course.

> The main ideas of the Article is saying that *because of* working while going to School reduces the G.P.A. of students. Some of the Reasons *while* students gettings jobs is because of Advertisements and personnal luxuries that the students needed during School.
>
> What the Article is saying is true about students getting lower grade in school, while working. But if we try to put strict rules on College curriculas and stopping Television advertising, it wouldn't help *much*. Because almost all students know *what they're doing to themselves*. Students are awared of the lower grades they're getting but *there are more to it, then* just *because* of Work. I agree, that when you get a job, your hour of studying *reduces*. After coming home from work you felt tired and only wanted to put School *words* aside. I have this experiences in the past myself. It does reduced my G.P.A., but I'm not blaming it on T.V. advertising or *anything else*.

Three general areas of error bear examination here. First, there are numerous mistakes in inflection (e.g., verb endings, plurals: note the underlined words).[2] Some of these errors might occur because the student's first language is not highly inflected, as English is, and Vietnamese does not have auxiliary verbs (*to be, to have, did/does*). Consequently, the student might question whether to add a plural *-s* to *grade* or *work*, and might not suspect that *are* is needed before *getting* in the second sentence. In addition, even if the student had been tutored in English, it's quite possible that subject-verb agreement in English may not be a fully developed concept, nor agreement between demonstrative pronouns (*this/that*) and nouns. These errors may therefore be "development" (i.e., with practice, the student will learn and produce the correct usage) or "fossilized" (i.e., the student will have to unlearn the deeply acquired and practiced error, then relearn the correct form, a more difficult and time-consuming process).

It is probable, however, that many of the verb tense errors occur more from "ear-learning" than from first-language transference. That is, because the English verb tense system is complex—a single sentence, and certainly a single paragraph, may contain several verb tenses—and because these students have listened to the language rather than studied it, they may not even recognize the mistakes. Moreover, because the mistakes they make may not have interfered with their ability to communicate orally, they may have structured rules for verb use that will seem idiosyncratic to the teacher. Think, for example, of a sentence a student in my class wrote recently: *The students are taken their time*. Then try reading the Vietnamese student's paragraph (p. 77 in this volume) aloud, attending to the possibility of slurring or unstressed final syllables that are not articulated, and thinking about how this student may have learned her verbs.

Second, the student has made some vocabulary mistakes and has used some idiomatic expressions (correctly or incorrectly) that indicate her immersion in U.S. culture (see the italicized words and phrases). During a conference, this student indicated that she had never noticed the word *why*; instead, she thought that *why* and *while* were the same word (*while*) with different meanings—because the *l* in *while* is not pronounced. "Like lot of English words," she said. Idiomatic language used by this student, which might be unknown to international students who have studied English as a foreign language, include *it wouldn't help much, what they're doing to themselves*, and *anything else* (although an international student might write *any other reason*). The use of *Because of* is an oral insertion that would probably not be noticed in a conversation. Following are are some other authentic examples of U.S. resident ESL writers mixing informal idioms into their writing because, like many native English writers, they do not understand levels of formality in English writing.

- Young **folks** usually get a better **kick out of** trips than older people.
- which is imperative **to hang around** a large number of friends
- they will want **to take off ASAP**.
- **Guys** like Neil Bush are destroying the American future.
- when you spend time with **a couple** of your close friends.

Finally, the seemingly arbitrary capitalization needs analysis. When I asked the student why she capitalized *Article* and *School*, she told me that she had learned that all nouns had to be capitalized. Of course, she did not know very much about nouns, but she did her best. She had later added the (correct) rule about capitalizing "I," though she found that English rule peculiar and intimidating because capitalizing "I" made her "stand out too much" in her writing.

INTERNATIONAL STUDENT WRITERS

At the opposite end of the continuum from U.S. resident ESL students are international students who have chosen to attend postsecondary schools in the U.S., in much the same way that U.S. college students spend a semester or a year "abroad." Many of these nonimmigrant, visa-holding students come from relatively privileged and well-educated backgrounds. They are literate and fluent in their first language, and they have learned English in foreign language classes. That is, they have learned English principally through their **eyes**, studying vocabulary, verb forms, and language rules.

These students know, understand, and can explain English grammar; they have usually learned grammar through methodologies that focus on rule learning. Often their reading skills are substantial. Usually, however, their listening and oral skills are hampered by lack of experience, nonnative English-speaking teachers, and the culture shock that comes from being immersed in a foreign culture, the language of which sounds like so much "noise," so different from their studied English language. Their writing skills are often also limited because their prior English education has not provided opportunities for composed writing, preferring instead exercises in written grammar or answering reading questions in single sentences (Leki, 1992). Below is an e-mail from a native Spanish speaker who has spent some time in the past studying in the U.S., but who is now in his native country, Chile.

Dear Rolf Turner:

Thanks you in asking my question.

In memorian I am study models of regression and multivariates data for my **tessis academic** deductive in productivity and quality *"just and time"* in **management industrial**, (my carrer) in complexity with n variables **incidents operationals** and costs, this new study is cassual, and important help for our country chile and United States of America in potentials **management strategic**. Before studied T.U. industrial control my investigation in data standars in **control of qualyty final** in cocesa (cobre cerrillos s.a. chile) associate with Phelps Dodge in EEUU. I am not expert in statisticals but know ideas in mejority **methods productivity multivariates** in industries.

We might investigate three major areas of language error in this sample. First, interference from this writer's first language is visible in the false cognates: words that are close (but not exact) in meaning and used in both Spanish and English (underlined in the paragraph). For example, *en memorian* means *to remind you* in Spanish. In addition, the boldfaced phrases indicate the use of Spanish word order, in which (1) the adjective follows the noun (*qualyty final* instead of *final quality*), and (2) adjectives in Spanish are appropriately inflected (*operationals incidents*, a plural adjective for the plural noun).

Next, the structure "*Before studied* . . ." also demonstrates the transference of Spanish rules into English. Spanish allows a subject not to be named in a sentence if that subject is understood. Finally, the writer gives three examples of English use that demonstrate a lack of understanding about U.S. idioms and culture. He uses *asking* for *answering*; instead of writing *Thank you for* or *Thanks to you*, he writes *Thanks you*; and he attempts an idiom (*just in time*) — which may well be an "ear error" gained during his earlier U.S. studies.

CAVEATS: BETWEEN THE EXTREMES

Between the two ends of the continuum are immigrant students whose families have chosen to come to the U.S., and/or whose education in their first language has been substantial, and/or whose first language may not have a written language, and/or who may have studied English as a foreign language for a relatively limited period of time before they arrived in the U.S. Also along the continuum are international students who have come to the U.S. to study because they have not been successful in their own educational systems, and/or whose study of both their first language and English has been limited.

There are also differences within the differences: parental attitudes toward education that include the belief that women should not attend college; a prior education system that values rote memorization and/or teacher-centered classrooms in which students do not participate orally; a culture that values reflective thought or cooperation above the analysis and competition valued in many U.S. classrooms. And there are individual student differences in personality, learning styles, learning strategies, and motivation (Reid, 1993, 1995).

Finally, more caveats about this chapter. First, I need to point out that although this chapter focuses on linguistic and rhetorical writing problems, some ESL student writing will equal and surpass writing by native English speakers (NES). Many ESL writers will have little need of English language development; their writing problems may differ from NES writing problems in type, but the quality or sophistication of the writing may well be comparable.

I also need to distinguish between generalization and stereotype. In this chapter, I discuss two general kinds of students; I write about typical problems of students from different language and cultural backgrounds. However, I am keenly aware that while many stereotypes begin with a grain of truth, individual students differ widely in their educational backgrounds, their unique approaches to learning, and their levels of proficiency. Therefore, it is essential to approach each student as an individual, and to identify each student's needs.

INITIAL IDENTIFICATION

For the teacher of an ESL writer, discovering whether that student is a U.S. resident or an international student is the first step in identifying the student's needs and formulating an assistance plan. The process is simple: Ask the student for background information so that appropriate resources and support for the student can be recommended. Sample questions that might be asked via a written survey or an oral interview (whichever is best for the student's English language proficiency and comfort level) include those listed in Table 1.

It may also be important to discover more background information about the ESL writers. Follow-up questions for resident and international students alike are included in Table 2.

TABLE 1.   Sample Survey/Interview Questions to Identify ESL Student Writer's Language Background

1. Is English your second (or third or fourth) language? _____
   - What is your first language? _____
   - List your previous schooling
     - in your first language: grade ____ through grade ____
                                  total years ____
     - in English: grade ____ through grade ____
                                  total months/years ____
2. Did you graduate from a U.S. high school? Yes ____ No ____
3. If the answer to the last question is

No	*Yes*
(*Usually* indicates an international student)	(*Usually* indicates a U.S. resident)
• TOEFL score _____	• high school attended _____
• TOEFL section scores:	• graduated in what year _____
listening _____	• ESL classes taken
structure/written expression ____	____ hours each week
reading _____	in grades ____ to ____
TWE _____	• was your first language
• full-time English language study:	schooling interrupted?
Yes ____ No ____	Yes ____ No ____
If yes, where? _____	If yes, how long? _____
how long? _____	• fluency in first language (high, medium, or low)
	speaking & listening _____
	reading _____
	writing _____

TABLE 2.   Sample Follow-Up Questions for ESL Student Writers

1. How did you learn English?

	a lot	some	a little	none
• studying grammar				
• listening to English speakers				
• practicing with language tapes				
• reading English literature				
• watching U.S. movies				
• watching U.S. television				
• other: _____				

2. How would you evaluate your English language proficiency?

	excellent	very good	average	poor
• speaking				
• listening				
• reading				
• writing				
• grammar				

U.S. RESIDENT ESL WRITERS

Investigation

Resident students may provide more complete information if the surveys are administered orally, allowing the students to use their English speaking proficiency. Results of the surveys will differ according to students' prior experiences. For example, a U.S. resident who has studied several years in U.S. public schools, and who has had constant language support through an excellent ESL program, will probably have the necessary skills to succeed in college or university work with minimal external support. In contrast, the writing of a student who has attended only the last year or two of U.S. high school, along with some classroom study of English prior to arrival, may have a combination of international and resident errors that make solutions to writing problems more complex.

Moreover, resident ESL writers who are fluent and literate in their first languages will acquire written English more easily than students who are not fully literate in their first languages. And students whose educations have been interrupted (by war, flight, refugee camps, and the like) may also be older and may have problems external to language learning that impact their ability to learn more English. Finally, students who have attended U.S. schools for a significant period of time but whose formal ESL education has been spotty are often doubly disadvantaged. Orally fluent, they have developed (perhaps unconsciously) language "rules," some of which must be identified, unlearned, and relearned if they are to become successful academic writers. In the meantime, they are saddled with prior experiences of failure, and their reading as well as their writing skills may be limited.

Assistance

U.S. resident students have many resources for assistance on college or university campuses. First, they have direct access to federally funded student programs on the campus for help and tutoring (and perhaps test accommodation) in writing, reading, and math. The student (or the teacher) can contact those offices for short- and long-term assistance, and the teacher can require that the students seek this assistance. Often the support offered by these offices provides the necessary scaffolding and encouragement that resident students need to achieve successful learning experiences.

It is possible that the campus personnel are not adequately trained to help ESL writers, but that training is available through the college or university intensive English language program, the English Department, or through written materials. The books and articles in Table 3 will prove helpful resources for teachers and tutors. In addition, teachers or tutors who need information about the rules of English grammar might consult the resources in Table 4.

TABLE 3.   Resources for Teachers and Tutors

- Bates, Linda; Lane, Janet; and Lange, Ellen. 1993. *Writing Clearly: Responding to ESL Compositions.* Boston: Heinle & Heinle.
- Carson, Joan, and Leki, Ilona (Eds.). 1993. *Reading in the Composition Classroom.* Boston: Heinle & Heinle.
- Connor, Ulla, and Kaplan, Robert B. 1987. *Writing across Languages: Analysis of L2 Text.* Reading, MA: Addison-Wesley.
- Fox, Helen. 1994. *Listening to the World: Cultural Issues in Academic Writing.* Urbana, IL: National Council of Teachers of English.
- Johnson, Donna, and Roen, Duane. 1989. *Richness in Writing: Empowering ESL Students.* New York: Longman.
- Kroll, Barbara. 1990. The rhetoric/syntax split: Designing curriculum for ESL students. *Journal of Basic Writing* 9 (1), 40–55.
- Kroll, Barbara. 1991. Teaching writing in the ESL context. In *Teaching English as a Second or Foreign Language* (2nd Ed.) (Marianne Celce-Murcia, Ed.), pp. 245–263. Boston: Heinle & Heinle.
- Leki, Ilona. 1992. *Understanding ESL Writers. A Reference for Teachers.* New York: St. Martin's Press.
- Li, Xiao-Ming. 1996. *"Good Writing" in Cross-Cultural Context.* Albany: State University of New York.
- Reid, Joy. 1993. *Teaching ESL Writing.* Englewood Cliffs, NJ: Prentice Hall-Regents.
- Scarcella, Robin. 1990. *Teaching Language Minority Students in the Multicultural Classroom.* Englewood Cliffs, NJ: Prentice Hall.

TABLE 4.   English Grammar Resources

- Byrd, Patricia, and Benson, Beverly. 1989. *Improving the Grammar of Written English: The Editing Process*. Belmont, CA: Wadsworth.
- Byrd, Patricia, and Benson, Beverly. 1992. *Applied English Grammar*. Boston: Heinle & Heinle.
- Celce-Murcia, Marianne, and Larsen-Freeman, Diane. 1998. *The Grammar Book: An ESL/EFL Teacher's Course*. Rowley, MA: Newbury House.
- Frodesen, Jan, and Eyring, Janet. 1993. *Grammar Dimensions: Form, Meaning, and Use* (Book Four). (Diane Larsen-Freeman, Series Ed.) Boston: Heinle & Heinle.
- Master, Peter. 1996. *Systems in English Grammar: An Introduction for Language Teachers*. Englewood Cliffs, NJ: Prentice Hall-Regents.

INTERNATIONAL STUDENTS

Investigation

In contrast to U.S. residents, many international students can provide the teacher with actual data that will help analyze their writing problems. Most will have taken the TOEFL (Test of English as a Foreign Language), an examination that is required for admission at most U.S. colleges and universities. At present the test is a multiple-choice examination designed and administered world-wide each month by the Educational Testing Service (ETS), the same educational corporation that administers the SAT, GMAT, and LSAT. An overall TOEFL score of 550 or above often indicates that the student is ready for full-time postsecondary work; a score below 500 usually indicates that the student should be taking intensive English language courses.

TOEFL section scores can also be quite revealing. The three section scores on the TOEFL indicate general proficiency in listening, grammar, and reading skills; those scores are reported in double digits, but by adding a zero to a section score, you can compare it with the overall TOEFL score. For example, a section score of $55 \rightarrow 550$ indicates that a student has adequate language proficiency in that language skill. However, while students from different language backgrounds may have similar overall TOEFL scores, their section scores may differ, indicating potential problems in U.S. classes. For instance, often Asian students will score well on grammar and reading (e.g., $58 \rightarrow 580$), but less well on listening skills (e.g., $45 \rightarrow 450$). These students may be able to keep up with university reading assignments, but they may have problems understanding lectures or working with other students. In contrast, Arabic students may score higher on the listening section and lower in the reading section; these students may seem fluent during class discussions, but they may have substantial problems completing reading assignments. Table 5 summarizes TOEFL examination scores.

Several times a year, the Test of Written English (TWE) is added to the TOEFL exam; the TWE is a direct test of student writing and is evaluated holistically by experienced writing teachers at large scoring sessions held in California. The maximum score is 6; a score of 4.5 or better usually means

TABLE 5.   TOEFL Examination Scores

Typical Admission Scores at U.S. Colleges and Universities[a]

	Undergraduate Students	Graduate Students
Unconditional Admission	525	550
Provisional Admission	500	525

Sample TOEFL Section Scores

Listening	55 → 550	(Add a zero to
Grammar	50 → 500	compare with
Reading	45 → 450	overall TOEFL
		score)

Overall TOEFL Score (average of three section scores) → **500**

Test of Written English (TWE)
- administered with the TOEFL exam several times a year
- scored from 1 to 6 (including 1.5, 2.5 etc.)
- typical admission TWE score: 4 to 4.5

[a]The Educational Testing Service does not provide recommended admission scores for the TOEFL. Rather, it encourages admissions officers and department faculty to set those scores at individual campuses.

that the student can do postsecondary written work.[3] Scores lower than 4 suggest that those students may need intensive work in U.S. academic writing. Unfortunately, many international students will not have a TWE score, either because it is not offered on every TOEFL examination or because they chose not to take it. And many postsecondary institutions still do not require the TWE as a viable admissions tool.

Another variable in international students' preparation may be attendance in an intensive English language program, either prior to their arrival in the U.S. or in a U.S.-based program. If students have studied ESL in the U.S., they may have encountered the rhetoric of academic English writing and so may be relatively proficient in presenting written ideas; the concepts of topic sentence, supporting detail, and essay structure may be familiar to them. For students who have studied English prior to their arrival, even intensively, the rhetorical principles of academic writing may not be information that they have encountered, much less practiced (Leki, 1992).

Assistance

Generally speaking, international students are not eligible for federal assistance although some colleges and universities do not discriminate (or simply do not know the differences between the two types of students). However, international students who have had prior experience with an intensive En-glish language program on or near the campus have access to previous teachers in that program, and those teachers have knowledge of other campus options. In addition, because of their prior English language study, international students are usually capable of using a handbook or a dictionary to

TABLE 6.   ESL Handbooks[a]

- Asher, Allen. 1993. *Think about Editing: A Grammar Editing Guide for ESL Writers*. Boston: Heinle & Heinle.
- Byrd, Patricia, and Benson, Beverly. 1994. *Problem/Solution: A Reference for ESL Writers*. Boston: Heinle & Heinle.
- Fox, Len. 1992. *Focus on Editing: A Grammar Workbook for Advanced Writers*. New York: Longman.
- Heinle & Heinle. 1996. *The Newbury House Dictionary of American English*.
- Lane, Janet, and Lange, Ellen. 1993. *Writing Clearly: An Editing Guide*. Boston: Heinle & Heinle.
- Raimes, Ann. 1992. *Grammar Troublespots: An Editing Guide for Students* (2nd ed.) Englewood Cliffs, NJ: Prentice-Hall Regents.

[a]Of course, the resources for teachers and students listed in Tables 3 and 4 are also relevant for teachers of international students and those students themselves, and the handbooks listed here (Table 6) may be used with success by some U.S. resident students.

check their errors and to expand their knowledge of English grammar and mechanics. However, because handbooks for native speakers of English do not address ESL problems effectively, I suggest the resources in Table 6.

ALL ESL STUDENT WRITERS

Other campus resources that are available to all ESL student writers (and usually assist students free of charge) include the campus writing center (or writing laboratory). The writing center is a valuable resource that will support ESL writers throughout their postsecondary careers, so students should be encouraged to investigate and use this resource. Moreover, paid tutors, often accessible through the international student services/education office, the intensive English language program, or the MA TESL/TEFL program, can provide necessary support for ESL writers.

NES friends can also serve as editors and language informants (Healy and Bosher, 1992). I advise my ESL students about appropriate approaches to such assistance:

- Never expect a friend to write, revise, or rewrite your paper.
- Sit with your NES friend and learn from him/her.
  - Identify specific problems.
  - Ask specific questions.
  - Draw conclusions and learn!
- Ask politely for assistance; don't demand.
- Offer a friendly trade, such as
  - pizza for proofreading, or
  - sharing language and cultural information.
- Give thanks with a smile.

TABLE 7.   ESL Writing Textbooks

- Leki, Ilona. 1995. *Academic Writing: Exploring Processes and Strategies* (2nd ed.). New York: St. Martin's Press.
- Mlynarczyk, Rebecca, and Haber, Steven. 1996. *In Our Own Words: A Guide with Readings for Student Writers*. New York: St. Martin's Press.
- Reid, Joy. 1988. *The Process of Composition* (2nd ed.). Englewood Cliffs, NJ: Prentice Hall-Regents.
- Spack, Ruth. 1996. *Guidelines: A Cross-Cultural Reading/Writing Text* (2nd ed.). New York: St. Martin's Press.
- Swales, John, and Feak, Christine (1994). *Academic Writing for Graduate Students: A Course for Nonnative Speakers of English*. Ann Arbor: University of Michigan Press.
- Weissberg, Robert, and Buker, Suzanne. 1990. *Writing Up Research: Experimental Research Report Writing for Students of English*. Englewood Cliffs, NJ: Prentice Hall-Regents.

It is, of course, possible for ESL students to abuse the help from friends; teachers may question how much of the draft actually "belongs" to the student. While the issue is real, the pedagogical aim is valid, and safeguards can be instituted to check for ESL student involvment:

- briefly conference with both the ESL student and the NES friend near the beginning of the semester to ensure that both fully understand the process;
- assign frequent in-class writing (formal and informal) to discern whether the ESL student is actually learning;
- require the student to write regular memos to the teacher describing the friendly tutoring sessions, identifying and evaluating the changes made, and
- journal/learning log entries analyzing what was learned during the tutoring sessions;
- ask the student to write a memo on the final draft that describes the changes made from previous drafts.

Finally, for the many resident and international student writers whose rhetorical background is limited, the resources cited in Table 7 can help. First-year composition textbooks for NES writers may not address the differences in rhetorical presentation of materials between ESL students' cultural/educational backgrounds and U.S. academic prose. However, there are materials written for ESL writers that explain U.S. academic rhetoric and provide adequate practice for the students.

CONCLUSION

The discussion in this chapter does not mean to suggest that ESL student writers are any less capable cognitively than other postsecondary students. Indeed, learning and using a second language, attending and participating in classes in another language, and writing for an audience with different linguistic, rhetorical, and cultural expectations are extremely challenging tasks. Moreover, ESL students are not typical "basic writers"; for example, many international students' educational backgrounds have provided them with substantial grammar and reading skills, and they are often successful students who have fine coping skills. They need information and practice in specific areas of academic prose such as content and organization. Many U.S. residents have only limited (and often incorrect) ideas about English grammar and written communication. Yet they may have significant cultural background from their prior school experiences, and their bicultural, bilingual lives make them unique.

NOTES

1. For more information about student learning styles, including information about cultural differences and lesson plan development, as well as several learning styles instruments, see *Learning Styles in the ESL/EFL Classroom* (Ed., J. Reid, 1995). Boston: Heinle & Heinle.

2. Each of these comments has been taken from *Teaching English as a Second or Foreign Language* (Ed., M. Celce-Murcia, 1991, 2nd Ed.). Boston: Newbury/Heinle & Heinle.

3. For a thorough discussion of grammar clusters in U.S. academic writing, see Chapters 2–4 in *Grammar in the Composition Classroom: Essays on Teaching ESL for College-Bound Students* (Byrd & Reid, 1998).

4. Each of these samples is taken from one of the four textbooks in the *Looking Ahead* series (Series Eds., Joy Reid and Patricia Byrd, 1998). Boston: Heinle & Heinle. The explanations and grammar exercises have been taken from *Applied English Grammar* (Patricia Byrd and Beverly Benson, 1992). Boston: Heinle & Heinle.

REFERENCES

Belcher, D., & Braine, G. (Eds.). (1995). *Academic writing in a second language: Essays on research and pedagogy*. Norwood, NJ: Ablex.

Brock, M., & Walters, L. (Eds.). (1993). *Teaching composition around the Pacific Rim*. Clevedon, UK: Multilingual Matters.

Byrd, P., & Reid, J. M. (1998). *Grammar in the composition classroom: Essays on teaching ESL for college-bound students*. Boston: Heinle & Heinle.

Celce-Murcia, M. (Ed.). (1991). *Teaching English as a second or foreign language* (2nd ed.). Boston: Newbury House/Heinle & Heinle.

Cohen, A., & Calvalcanti, M. (1990). Feedback on compositions: Teacher and student verbal reports. In B. Kroll (Ed.), *Second language writing: Research insights for the classroom* (pp. 155–177). Cambridge: Cambridge University Press.

Ferris, D. (1997). The influence of teacher commentary on student revision. *TESOL Quarterly, 31*(2), 315–339.

Fox, H. (1994). *Listening to the world: Cultural issues in academic writing*. Urbana, IL: National Council of Teachers of English.

Healy, D., & Bosher, S. (1992). ESL tutoring: Bridging the gap between curriculum-based and writing center models of peer tutoring. *College ESL, 2*(2), 25–32.

Jacoby, S., Leech, D., & Holten, C. (1995). A genre-based developmental writing course for undergraduate ESL science majors. In D. Belcher & G. Braine (Eds.), *Academic writing in a second language: Essays on research and pedagogy* (pp. 351–373). Norwood, NJ: Ablex.

Kroll, B. (Ed.). (1990). *Second language writing: Research insights for the classroom*. Cambridge: Cambridge University Press.

Leki, I. (1992). *Understanding ESL writers. A reference for teachers*. New York: St. Martin's Press.

Li, X. (1996). *"Good writing" in cross-cultural context*. Albany: State University of New York Press.

Reid, J. (1993). *Teaching ESL writing*. Englewood Cliffs, NJ: Prentice Hall-Regents.

Reid, J. (1995). *Learning styles in the ESL/EFL classroom*. Boston: Heinle & Heinle.

Reid, J., & Byrd, P. (Series Eds.). (1998). *Looking ahead* (Vols. 1–4). Boston: Heinle & Heinle.

Swales, J., & Feak, C. (1994). *Academic writing for graduate students: A course for non-native speakers of English*. Ann Arbor: University of Michigan Press.

5

Language Identity and Language Ownership: Linguistic Conflicts of First-Year University Writing Students

YUET-SIM D. CHIANG AND MARY SCHMIDA

How can I give myself an American identity if I cannot even feel connected to the American language itself? By saying connected, I mean the feeling of owning the language and, therefore having full authority over it. It does not matter how frequently I use English, somehow I can never feel that I own it.

—HAI NGUYEN

I am a native speaker of English because English is the language I know best.

—PETER MACK

I communicated with my sisters at home only through English in the midst of mom yelling, "Speak Korean! Are you Korean?"

—JANE KIM

Now, the only time I speak Vietnamese is to my parents. Unfortunately, I don't talk to them much, only when necessary; it's not very often that I speak their native tongue. I speak English fluently now and this is the reason why I don't talk to my parents very often.

—CHRISTINE NGUYEN

Recently, a body of research has emerged that views language and literacy acquisition from a broad-based sociocultural perspective; a perspective that seeks to explain success or failure of learning from within a social and political context in which the language learning occurs (Lantolf, 1996; Peirce, 1995; Rampton, 1995; Siegal, 1996). It is within this theoretical framework that we align ourselves.

From *Generation 1.5 Meets College Composition: Issues in the Teaching of Writing to U.S.-Educated Learners of ESL.* Ed. Linda Harklau, Kay M. Losey, and Meryl Siegal. Mahwah, NJ: Erlbaum, 1999. 81–96.

Our study is somewhat different than those conducted by researchers before us, however, in that this study deals *not* with immigrant populations learning the language of the dominant society, but with U.S. born children of immigrant parents who must define and negotiate the boundaries of language and identity.

Despite this new trend in considering the construction of identity in language and literacy acquisition, however, there is still a shortage of research-based studies that specifically examine the conflicting constructions of English literacy, language identity, and native language loss among speakers of non-English language background (NELB). The lack of study is not coincidental; rather, we argue that it is a culmination of several factors that include: (a) the traditional and unchallenged division of native and nonnative speakers, (b) an oversimplification of English learning at the college level into arbitrary categories such as (mainstream) English and English as a second language (ESL), and (c) a lack of theoretical discussion of the literacy practices of language users caught on the language borderlands of these three subcategories.

Although the linguistic gaps between first language (L1) learning and native language loss have been documented by linguists at a macro level, and acknowledged by leading Asian American writers (e.g., Fong-Torres, 1994; Tan, 1989) at a personal level, the social, cultural, and emotional tensions of the disharmony have yet to be framed carefully within the theoretical and pedagogical frameworks of applied linguistics studies.

THE STUDY

The Institution: College Writing Programs

This year-long study was conducted during the fall semester 1995 and the spring semester 1996 within the College Writing Programs (CWP) at the University of California (UC), Berkeley, where both researchers were instructors. The aim and scope of the CWP, as stated in the college writing handbook, is to help students ground their own literacy within the demands of the larger language community, while simultaneously helping them to develop fluency and control over their own language skills. In both the reading and writing activities, students' language experiences are an integral part of the classroom discourse. This six unit, one-semester course, College Writing 1A, fulfills the Subject A requirement as well as English 1A. Students who pass this course with a C or better may enroll directly in an English 1B course.

All freshmen entering the UC, Berkeley, must fulfill an English proficiency requirement which is called the Subject A requirement. Students can meet the Subject A requirement before coming to Berkeley by passing the university's writing proficiency Subject A essay exam, which involves reading a short selection and writing an essay within 3 hours. Students who receive a combined score of 6 or below (out of a possible 12 points) must take College Writing 1A.

The Participants

In the state of California, the Asian population of NELBs is predicted to increase from 5.2 million in 1976 to 8.3 million in 2000, a jump of 36% (Oxford-Carpenter, Pol, Lopez, Stupp, Gendell, & Peng, 1984). Within the CWP, where this study was conceived and conducted, Asian American students make up approximately 56% of the student population (Simons, Perrow, Stritikus, Schmida, & Ponte, 1997). Because of these figures, this study was limited to Asian American students.

Although statistically it appears that the Asian population has maintained its home language (50% of the Asian American students in our study reported that they speak their ethnic language at home, vs. only 15% of the Chicano students), these categories do not tell the true story. It was through student interviews that the reality of language loss and the tension between linguistic identity and language ability emerged.

Research Questions

This study focused on the following questions:

1. How are the boundaries among English literacy, language identity, cultural identity, and native (heritage) language loss manifested, defined, and maintained?

2. What are the social, cultural, and emotional consequences/implications of the phenomena of language use and language identity for this particular linguistic group?

3. How do NELB students negotiate between the borders of English language use and L1 (e.g., Chinese) identity?

4. What is the impact of the disharmony among language use, language identity, and language ownership on their development as English language users?

Stages of Study

This study was conducted in two main stages. Stage 1 consisted of pretesting the survey questions that came out of an analysis of students' literacy experiences from Chiang's class. This student information was gathered over a period of two academic years (1995 and 1996) by compiling students' "Literacy Life History" essays, writing in which students examine their own literacy journeys. *Literacy journey* in this context refers to the students' relationships with literacy and language, both written and spoken. Twenty-five questions were posed to the students as writing prompts in this assignment, and included both open-ended questions (Writing is:____; English is:____;) as well as more directed questions (When were you first aware of using language? Who were the people involved? What is good writing?). The survey questions were later refined and then administered to the larger group of 471 students enrolled in any of the 14 sections of College Writing 1A.

The answers given by the students in the large survey were examined and from those, 20 randomly selected students who reported that they were Asian American were chosen to participate in individual open-ended interviews with the researchers. These taped interviews lasted anywhere from 1 to 2½ hours.

DATA ANALYSIS

Data analyzed consisted of responses from surveys from this section (termed *general response 1*), students' written responses in the survey, detailed transcriptions from the 20 interviews, and students' writing portfolios.

Method of Analysis

The constant comparative method outlined in Bogdan and Biklen (1982) was used in the analysis of the collected data. The constant comparative method allowed for the delimiting of the ongoing hypotheses in which tentative theories were generated and which, in turn, were either rejected or supported by the collected data, for example, surveys versus literacy biographies versus personal essays versus interviews.

Data collected from the program-wide written survey were coded quantitatively when appropriate; the open-ended survey and interview questions were coded according to themes that emerged from the students' responses. Themes included such categories as: emotional attachment to English, dominance of English in society, notions of what it means to be a nonnative or a native speaker of a language, code-switching, English as a tool, bilingualism, definitions of self, and cultural and linguistic bonds to a language.

Of the students surveyed, 60% of the Asian American students reported that they were nonnative English speakers (NNES), and 91% reported they were bilingual according to their responses on the survey. Interestingly, although 91% of the students designated themselves as bilingual, only 37% reported they spoke both their ethnic (heritage) language and English at home. And among the 40% of the Asian American students who labeled themselves as native speakers of English, only 28% of those same students reported learning English as a first language. What this points to is that 12% of the 40% of students who labeled themselves as native speakers of English actually began speaking English as a *second* language (L2), not as a first language. Perhaps these students label themselves as native English speakers because they think that their primary language — the language of school and economic success in the United States — is and has been English.

RESEARCH FINDINGS

"The act of learning language[,] is also learning the culture through language. The semantic system which he is constructing becomes the primary mode of transmission of the culture" (Halliday, 1975, p. 66).

The scope of this chapter does not allow us to address the multilayered issues of language, identity, and literacy that have emerged from the study. Instead, we devote our discussion to a dominant theme captured in the study; namely, the conflicts between linguistic identity and linguistic ability, and how these conflicts are manifested in students' self-definitions of the following categories: bilingual identity versus bilingual literacy, native versus nonnative speaker, and cultural identity versus linguistic identity.

Bilingual Identity versus Bilingual Literacy

By the students' own definition, a *bilingual individual* is one who *identifies* with a language other than English. In other words, their self-definition does not necessitate an ability to speak, read, and write in their heritage language, but rather a traditional cultural *affiliation* with the heritage language. Throughout the study, we note that the students' self-definition is not grounded in a clear or competent ability to speak the ethnic language; instead, it is informed by a sense of cultural identification as the following attests:

> WONG: I find it hard to speak to my grandparents, because I don't speak it [Chinese] anymore, and so I can't communicate with them what I want to.
>
> RESEARCHER: Why is that important to you?
>
> WONG: I just think it is. I guess the most important reason is I want to be able to talk with my grandparents . . . and I remember a time when it was really easy for me to talk to [my grandmother]. Now, if I try to say the words, I have a very strong English accent and it's kind of a shock that I didn't realize I was losing my Chinese so quickly, but I was. I want to get it back, trying to get at least the sound right.

In fact, in many instances, language for these students is being used as a synonym for culture. This double-edged consciousness—culture as language—operates at a very complex level, often forcing students to position themselves as in between worlds in spite of the publicly self-proclaimed bilingual identity. The following excerpts capture the dilemma many students feel in terms of language use and the positionality of their two worlds:

> *Excerpt 1:*
>
> STUDENT: You either speak really good English or you're kind of in between.
>
> RESEARCHER: What do you mean by "you're kind of in between"?
>
> STUDENT: It's like me. I can't really speak really well in English. Like right, you know? But I can't do really good in Chinese either. So I'm kind of in between.
>
> *Excerpt 2:*
>
> RESEARCHER: You wrote in the written response that you're "bilingual." What do you mean by this?
>
> WONG: I don't know if I am really bilingual because I don't really bond with— I don't really connect with the English culture. American culture. I'm kind of

in between, I guess. I don't really speak [Chinese] that well, therefore I'm non-native Chinese. But language and the culture are kind of connected, I think.

RESEARCHER: Do you consider yourself bilingual?

WONG: To a point.

RESEARCHER: To an extent?

WONG: Yeah. But I think more English 'cause I don't use Chinese on a regular basis. . . . I don't feel emotionally attached to it, but sometimes I feel guilty when I don't . . . But I feel I should be Chinese. I, like I said, when I, I think in English. It's so, it's easy. When I think in Chinese, I have to think for a while. It's hard . . . I never really thought in Chinese for really anything . . . I feel like a, like a, you know if I were to use a term, a bamboo. Like um, yellow on the outside and white on the inside.

It seems that for this group of linguistic minorities, the collapsing of language and culture into one category allows them to name their allegiance to their ethnic heritage without impeding their linguistic ability in English. However, this seemingly benign conceptualization is problematic for it raises crucial questions of the core and essence of being literate. What these students are experiencing seems to be serious disjunctures between the way they conceptualize their linguistic identities. That is, on the one hand, they are not fully comfortable with speaking, reading, or writing their heritage language, whereas on the other hand, they are not fully integrated into the culture of mainstream, academic English by the virtue of the label, linguistic minority. Although at ease with their ethnic culture, these students do not possess the full linguistic facility to participate fully as members of a cultural group, particularly so if we view language learning as a transmitter of culture. Their inability to have full participation at the cultural level is captured in the following excerpt:

SOO KIM: The only time I can talk to my parents is when I speak Konglish or in broken English.

RESEARCHER: When you talk about family problems, is English used then? Or Korean? In conflicts, what language is used?

SOO KIM: Um. I think English is used when dealing with family problems and with other people. But if I have a problem, I'll talk with them in both Korean and English. Because sometimes I feel like when I talk to them in Korean, I can really get their attention. You know, really grasp hold of them when I talk in Korean because it's their whole language. Maybe it'll penetrate their psyche or something, you know.

RESEARCHER: What happens when you try to do so but you do not have adequate vocabulary and terms and all that?

SOO KIM: I have to speak English. I find myself doing that. I would just start talking in English.

RESEARCHER: So then you have a combination of both?

SOO KIM: Yeah. But that doesn't happen too often. I can usually talk to my parents in basic Korean most of the time.

RESEARCHER: What do you mean by basic Korean?

SOO KIM: Just non-complicated vocabulary. There's nothing complicated. Just regular phrases, conversational dialogue, that kind of thing. Nothing complicated.

RESEARCHER: So for complicated or complex concepts, you use English?

SOO KIM: Yes. I use English, yeah. I just ask them how to say it in Korean.

If, as Halliday (1975, p. 66) posited, "the act of learning language [is] also learning the culture through language. The semantic system which [the student] is constructing becomes the primary mode of transmission of the culture," and if indeed the semantic system is the primary mode of transmission of the culture, it raises questions of whose culture, and whose semantic systems are being privileged in English learning.

Another dominant thread is that these students identify with their heritage language, even if they do not speak it (indeed, they *all* reported that they were bilingual). It is as if by claiming the language, they claim a linguistic identity that perhaps exists in their minds, but not in their tongues. Even as they assert that they are native speakers of English, they are also asserting that they are bilingual (even if their heritage language use is devoid of any language transactions involving complex negotiations). One student said, "I am a Chinese American. So, I guess I'm bilingual," as if one begets the other, or vice versa. Language exists in the mind; for these students, it remains there, and they identify with it by considering themselves "bilingual" even when their bilingualism is not supported by a clear literacy competence (indeed, most of the students reported that they cannot read or write in their heritage language).

What is most troubling is that although school literate in English, these very students are not able to fully "bond" with the language because of the ways in which they perceive speakers of English in relation to themselves (as "they," "them," and the "other"). And although they feel connected to their home culture, they are not able to connect with it linguistically, often needing to resort to "konglish," "vietnamish," "chinglish," "broken English" or "English substitutions." More often than not, their linguistic lack in the heritage language compelled them to simplify the naming of their complex realities to simple or broken English. They are faced with the double whammy of having a cultural home language in which they have the culture but not the full linguistic ability, and with English (for many a home and school language) in which they have the linguistic ability (however varying it is) but not the culture that, according to the students, means mainstream culture.

NATIVE VERSUS THE NONNATIVE ENGLISH SPEAKER

The constant waverings in the bilingual identification also seem to complicate the way students define themselves in terms of the native speaker identification. Although a majority of the students interviewed were either born here or came to the United States at a preschool age, and in spite of the clear documentation (indeed, UC Berkeley undergraduates are from the top 12% of California schools) that they could only read and write English, many of them did not claim the native-speaker identity. The following three excerpts are typical of the spectrum of student responses when asked to elaborate on their native or nonnative affiliation:

Excerpt 1:

CHAN: A native speaker—to me, I think it's somebody who can speak English very well. I mean, it doesn't matter where you were born. A couple of my friends came here when they were small and they speak English perfectly. So shouldn't that be native? . . . I don't really know how to define myself. Am I a native speaker of English, too?

RESEARCHER: How would you define a nonnative speaker?

CHAN: Nonnative speakers. Hmm. Are they supposed to be less of an English speaker? Do they speak not as well as the people that are born here? I think that language is basically your culture, by your family. So when you're not born here, I think you don't speak well, maybe. Maybe that's how they define it. Nonnative: You're not born here and you don't speak as well because you don't culturally, like, bond.

Excerpt 2:

RESEARCHER: How do you define the "native" speaker?

NGUYEN: It [English] is just the way they speak in America.

RESEARCHER: And what about Vietnamese?

NGUYEN: My native language.

RESEARCHER: What does the term nonnative speaker mean to you?

NGUYEN: A person that English wasn't their first language.

RESEARCHER: And how about when you hear the word "native English speaker"?

NGUYEN: Like, they constantly use English, and I think, like, their first language.

RESEARCHER: Are you a native or a nonnative speaker of Vietnamese?

NGUYEN: I'm not sure. I don't know. [pause] I think I'm a nonnative 'cause my Vietnamese isn't that great.

RESEARCHER: And what about English?

NGUYEN: I think I'm native.

For many of these students, despite their sometimes contradictory ambivalence in the native and nonnative categories, we discovered that when questioned about their "thinking" language, English predominates:

SHUN: I think the native speaker is probably either English was your first language or English is a language you're fluent at. But native sounds like to me, it's your first language. But that's complicated because I actually learned Korean first. . . . Then I took on English and then my fluency in

English took off, whereas with Korean, it just gradually . . . I don't know. It's complicated.

RESEARCHER: So you consider yourself a nonnative speaker of English?

SHUN: I don't think so. Probably because I'm so fluent at it. So if I said I was a nonnative speaker, it would sound funny because I would say, "Wait. But I speak it fluently." So I can't be. It just contradicts itself.

With other students, the ambivalence is less defined even as they "other" the native speaker:

RESEARCHER: So what is a native speaker?

CHENG: I . . . I'm not sure. It's like other people in class, when they have to speak English, they have to think first right? So, their original language is like their natural instinct; that's how it is for me. English is, it's natural. I think in English.

These identification labels that the students create illustrate their dissatisfaction with the inherent binary categories with respect to their bilingual identity, which force them to categorize their identity into an either–or sort of framework, when in fact they may not perceive it in such clear-cut distinctions. At the beginning of the interview, Cheng talks about her bond to the Chinese culture, and how she understands it better than she understands U.S. culture. Dominating her literacy narrative is the self-imposed nonnative speaker. However, when asked to define a native speaker, she answers, "I'm not sure." In fact, her linguistic identity dramatically turns around when she talks about the "natural instinct" and how to her, "English is natural." Cheng even goes further to say that she "thinks in English" even as she holds on to a nonnative identity. It is as if to say that she could not be a native speaker of English because of her more primal bond to Chinese. Many of the students said that they hear the heritage language spoken at home, between parents and grandparents, or at family gatherings, and that because of this they feel a connection to the language. It seems that regardless of their linguistic inability to fully communicate with the language, the students' emotional connection to the heritage language remains deep and complex.

Another point of interest is that with some students, the native speaker label comes not by conscious choice, but by default as the following responses attest:

SHENNIE: I describe myself as a native English-speaking student because I was born and educated under the U.S. system. The English I've learned in public schools was the same for both White and non-White students, regardless of the home language.

LEE: I think I'm a native speaker of English because I'm proficient in it even though I learned a language before hand [meaning Taiwanese] but there's a cultural language which is Chinese; it's like my language that I can always be at, I can always like, I can always revert back to, because it is, it is innate in me in some ways, you know. . . . But to me a native language is a language that you continually speak, that you write an essay on it. You know like I just wrote an essay for College Writing and, and there's no way I could have put those ideas into Chinese. So, and that's why I like, just creating ideas and creating new thoughts is like what I think is a native language just because that's how you advance.

So despite the fact that these students use English to create "ideas" and "new thoughts" and that English is primary in their lived realities, they still distance themselves from English, often times reducing it to "a tool." "English is a great tool, a tool you know, tool for me that I use as a language, and you know, to write my papers and stuff like that, useful things" (Wong, Interview 1). And that despite the fact they could not read, write, and can barely speak in their heritage language, these students still see it as their bond to their cultural roots: "Chinese to me is uh, in the essence, it is me."

Perhaps because of their difficulty in labeling their own linguistic abilities, many of these students refer to English-speaking people, and the English-speaking world, in terms of "other." Although most of the students were born in this country, and English is primary in their lived realities, they are unable to fully assert themselves as native speakers. In fact, to many of these students, native speakers are the Americans, the "they" and the "them." Although English-dominant, these students are not as ready to identify with the language, in terms of the native label, as they perhaps do with their heritage language, although many are not speakers of that language.

BLURRED BOUNDARIES: REVISIONING THESE STUDENTS

The varying contradictions in students' definitions of bilingual identity, bilingual literacy, and their ambivalence toward defining themselves as a native versus a nonnative speaker raise some important questions of the way literacy experiences of linguistic minorities are defined. Our students do not neatly fit into clean-cut categories such as mainstream English speaker, ESL speaker, or bilingual students. Neither does it seem that their literacy journeys are duly served by the arbitrary and ill-challenged categories of language minority students, ESL, and international students.

Category 1: Mainstream English Speakers

The students we interviewed shared many of the literacy needs and orientations of mainstream students — literacy as an act of making meaning, literacy as an act of self-definition, and literacy as a way to engage with the world even as they are tagged with the nonnative English-speaking label. That many resisted enrolling in a nonnative English-speaking section (an option available to ESL students), and that all our students interviewed were from the native English-speaking section further attest to their mainstream affiliation. For many of the students, the reality is that English is more than a functional tool, or an L2; in many aspects, it is their primary language.

Although the needs of these students cannot be adequately addressed under the mainstream English speakers category, ironically, they are as mainstream as can be. The students we have are considered the model students. They are enrolled in three or four other classes in addition to their college writing class, and are successful in meeting the academic demands of the university. These are the students who are seen as having made it; whose education is smooth sailing, whose relationship with the English language has gotten them all As.

Paradoxically, another indication of their primary affiliation to English (part of the mainstream linguistic identity) is in their struggle with their linguistic and cultural loyalties. Perhaps, had these students not had such a primary and emotional bond with English, they would not have been so split in their struggles with, contradictions, and uncertainties about their cultural and linguistic identities.

Category 2: Language Minorities

The label *language minority* is used to group and homogenize language learners of non-English language background. The underlying sociopolitical assumption is that these "linguistic minorities" do not speak English as a primary language. Instead, what is often assumed in this reductionist term is that English is an add-on, that is, students are assumed to have primary affiliation with their heritage language—be it Spanish, Vietnamese, Cantonese—and a lesser/secondary affiliation with English. The complex juxtaposition of home language and the primacy of English in their lived realities is eclipsed by the term *language minority*.

The student responses suggest that English and the students' heritage tongue are not viewed in competition with one another. Home language and school language (i.e., English) are felt to coexist comfortably at various levels; English is understood to work in parallel with their mother tongue.

Indeed, although many of our students may be termed as *language minorities*, their literacy journey indicates that English is really their primary language even when they seem to flip flop between the two languages. The primacy of English reverberates throughout their literacy narratives. Significant, too, is the use of English when students articulate their need to combine two languages to express their complex thoughts:

> For everyday, routine speech, I would think in Chinese when I want to speak Chinese, and in English when I want to think in English. For abstract thinking, I would think in English or most of the time, and in Chinese for concepts that are not readily expressed by English. Therefore, when I "flip-flop" between Chinese and English, I am relying on *both* at the same time in order to help express my ideas.

Yet, in as much as these students are aware of that need to combine the heritage and the learned/school language, their sense of their own language deficiency plagues their journey, as the following excerpts revealed:

Excerpt 1:

Therefore, I do not have a well-founded mastery of either language but a superficial knowledge of both languages, with each language being only capable in expressing my basic thoughts. (It is only when I combine the two languages that I can express my complex thoughts.)

Excerpt 2:

Because I do not have a solid language foundation in one language, I will have trouble communicating my complex ideas with using one language. [i.e., Chinese and English]. . . . As a result, my weak language foundation affects my learning and writing English or Chinese.

Category 3: ESL Speaker

The biggest assumption (and perhaps the most homogenized category) is that of ESL. The embedded hierarchy indicates the secondary importance of English in relation to the native tongue. In other words, because English is their second language, students are assumed to have difficulties with the language. As noted by Reyes, "in classrooms and schools, as in larger societal structures, educators and policymakers are conditioned to ignore differences and to treat them as deficiencies" (Reyes, 1992, p. 437). The educational society expects them to make ESL mistakes; they are expected to stumble over the English language for it is not their native tongue. Students in our study often internalize this ill-defined assumption even when their affiliation to English is primary rather than secondary. And this internalization often leads them to see themselves as incapable of owning the language as captured in the following:

I am unsure about writing. I am confused. I am frustrated. I think I will never become a good writer because I am Asian. It is excusable for me not to be good at writing. I am not supposed to be good anyway. People expect me to be geared toward science and math. This expectation gives me an excuse to avoid writing. "People don't expect me to do well anyway," or "Why bother? I will never learn how to speak and write like natives," I always say to myself.

It is further assumed that they have their first or native tongue to fall back to. Whereas they are not expected to have English mastery because it is their second tongue, they are presumed to have mastery in their native tongue. In many instances, this may be the case, but this is not true for all our students. Almost without exception, each expressed great difficulties in using their native or mother tongue:

Because I learned both languages at a relatively early age, I spoke both English and Cantonese without any accent. However, my Cantonese vocabulary was limited to that of a five-year-old.

To compensate for their linguistic limitations in the heritage language, many students either resorted to keeping their thoughts simple so they have enough words to express them, or to the use of broken English to keep up communication when speaking to family members, or to combining English with the heritage language such as in "konglish," "vietnamish," or "chinglish." As Jane Kim describes in one of her portfolio pieces:

> I communicated with my sisters at home only through English in the midst of my mom yelling "Speak Korean! Aren't you Korean?" Then I would start to break out in "Konglish" whenever my mom was nearby. I felt my English had to compensate for what I lacked in my knowledge of Korean. Although I don't speak Korean with a heavy accent, it's still difficult to communicate in the language. My vocabulary is very limited and my reading and writing power is very weak.

> Many people are surprised that I can speak as well as I can for someone who has practically lived in America all her life. I'm still saddened at the fact that I can't communicate to my parents the same way my sisters are able. If I talk to my mom, it's usually just simple questions I need to ask her; otherwise I'd ask my sisters to ask for me.

Characterizing Jane Kim's English as her second language does not capture the full complexity of her linguistic experience. Kim's experiences with language and literacy, particularly in the home context, seem to depict someone who turns to English for stability and a sense of self.

Therefore, a further limitation in the ESL characterization is that English is really the primary medium students use to articulate their complex realities. They depend on it to help them weave in and out of their everyday communication interactions. Their race and/or ethnicity does not preclude them from relying on English to express their multifaceted realities and to make the necessary transitions between home and school.

CONCLUSIONS

What we strive to do in this chapter is to highlight the cultural and linguistic web of home language and English for students from NELB. Essentially, we hope that the insights of their multifaceted experiences provoke language educators to question and think beyond the narrow confines of a monolithic English ideology, and reorientate themselves to the sociocultural politics of English literacy in a multicultural and multilingual world.

In addition, we wish to suggest the following educational implications.

- The need for language teachers to be adequately trained and professionally prepared to recognize and attend to the increasingly blurred cultural and linguistic boundaries of linguistically diverse students. Whereas categories like ESL, bilingual, and linguistic minority do indeed serve to delineate some students, these categories are inadequate when it comes to capturing the literacy journey of students whose lived realities often waver between cultural and linguistic borderlands.

- The urgency to reexamine the categorization of native versus nonnative students and reconceptualize the labels. As our study has indicated, the nonnative labels are neither adequate in capturing the complexities of their literacy experiences, nor resonant in representing their paralleling cultural and linguistic ties to English and their heritage language. Perhaps the overarching question should be less whether these linguistically diverse students are native or nonnative, but rather how primary English fits their literacy and linguistic identity. The reorientation will not only serve in recentering the primacy of English literacy as an act of constructing one's social, cultural, and political place in the world, but it will also heighten the role of English as a world language.

- The need for greater interaction and exchanges among leaders of National Council of Teachers of English, Teachers of English to Speakers of Other Languages, National Association of Bilingual Education, and World Englishes and their obligation to provide more informed and cross disciplinary insights into the multiplicity of English learning in a pluralistic world. With the increasing dominance of English across the world, it is no longer sufficient to work within the narrow paradigms and specificities contained within each linguistic field. Instead, researchers need to view commonalties and contradictions and come up with new insights and models formed from multiple perspectives. This kind of interdisciplinary model will add to a fuller understanding of the literacy journey of a diverse student population.

- The need to not only acknowledge but accommodate the intersections of race, culture, and ethnicity in the sociopolitical constructions of English literacy. As pointed out by Peirce (1995), which our study supports, "the individual language learner is not ahistorical and unidimensional but has a complex and sometimes social identity, changing across time and space" (pp. 25–26).

ACKNOWLEDGMENTS

Preparation of this chapter was supported in part by a major grant from the National Council of Teachers of English "Grant-in-Aid" and by College Writing Programs, UC–Berkeley.

REFERENCES

Bogdan, R., & Biklen, S. (1982). *Qualitative research for education: An introduction to theory and methods.* Boston: Allyn & Bacon.

Fong-Torres, B. (1994). *The rice room: Growing up Asian American. From number two son to rock 'n roll.* New York: Hyperion.

Halliday, M. A. K. (1975). *Learning how to mean: Explorations in the development of language.* London: Edward Arnold.

Lantolf, J. (1996). SLA theory building: Letting all the flowers bloom! *Language Learning, 46,* 713–749.

Oxford-Carpenter, R., Pol, L., Lopez, D., Stupp, P., Gendell, M., & Peng, S. (1984). *Demographic projections of non-English language background and limited English proficient persons in the United States to the year 2000 by state, age, and language group.* Rosslyn, VA: National Clearing House for Bilingual Education.

Peirce, B. N. (1995). Social identity, investment, and language learning. *TESOL Quarterly 29*(1), 9–31.

Rampton, B. (1995). *Crossing: Language and ethnicity among adolescents.* New York: Longman.

Reyes, M. (1992). Challenging venerable assumptions: Literacy instruction for linguistically different students. *Harvard Educational Review, 62*(4), 427–446.

Siegal, M. (1996). The role of learner subjectivity in second language sociolinguistic competency: Western women learning Japanese. *Applied Linguistics, 17*(3), 356–382.

Simons, H., Perrow, M., Stritikus, T., Schmida, M., & Ponte, E. (1997). *Participating in academic conversation: An evaluation of college writing.* Unpublished report, University of California at Berkeley.

Tan, A. (1989). *The Joy Luck Club.* New York: Putnam.

6

From the "Good Kids" to the "Worst": Representations of English Language Learners across Educational Settings

LINDA HARKLAU

As Nayar (1997) has pointed out, the generic label *ESL* has been applied to a wide variety of different populations, instructional goals, and student needs, and some of these populations are more researched than others. In the context of U.S. K–12 education, processes of English language learning are best documented in the elementary grade levels. In contrast, in spite of a growing body of recent research (see, e.g., Davidson, 1996; Faltis & Wolfe, 1999; Fu, 1995; Harklau, 1994; Lucas, 1997; Lucas, Henze, & Donato, 1990; Mace-Matluck, Alexander-Kasparik, & Queen, 1998), secondary-school-level immigrant and bilingual students may be "the most underrepresented, understudied group of students in the United States" (Faltis, 1993, p. 2). Too little is known about how these English language learners take on the simultaneous challenges of managing high school content-area academics, learning a new language, and coming of age in U.S. society. Moreover, increasing numbers of immigrant ESL students educated in U.S. secondary schools are discovering that getting through high school is often inadequate in itself to secure a prosperous future in their adopted country. Rather, in a postindustrial economy in which three quarters of all jobs will require some postsecondary education (U.S. Department of Labor, 1991), students find that a major function of U.S. high schools is to serve as a prelude for and gateway into college.

Nonetheless, if ESL students at the secondary level are an underresearched population, work on their transition from high school into college is virtually nonexistent. There is a significant lack of communication and articulation between secondary and postsecondary institutions in the United States, and colleges are inconsistent in the data they collect and the policies they enact regarding ESL students who enter higher education by way of U.S. secondary schools (see, e.g., ESL Intersegmental Project, 1997). U.S.-educated immigrants and bilingual students may not even be acknowledged as a special population, and many colleges appear to confound them with international

From *TESOL Quarterly* 34.1 (2000): 35–67.

students (Gray, Rolph, & Melamid, 1996). The difference between these populations is becoming abundantly clear to college ESL educators, however, as they work to tailor instruction to students with vastly different sorts of academic and life experience in the United States and abroad (see, e.g., Harklau, Losey, & Siegal, 1999; Reid, 1997).

The lack of research on the growing population of adolescent and young adult ESL students in U.S. high schools and colleges provided the impetus for the study described in this article. Its initial purpose was to describe how one group of U.S. immigrant students negotiated the changing academic and linguistic demands of the transition from secondary to postsecondary education. As the study progressed, I found that the very same ESL students who had been considered "the good kids" in high school, the ones praised and admired by their teachers, subsequently came to be characterized as underachieving and difficult students in their college ESL classes. The institutional label *ESOL student*[1] and the meanings given to it became an increasingly salient issue, and I found that the ways in which students' identities were constructed in these two different educational institutions played a crucial role in students' transition from high school to college.

The finding that learners' identities affected their experience in school is consistent with the work of other researchers, who have increasingly called on the construct of *learner identity* to understand classroom learning. Drawing variously from critical theory, social practice, and poststructuralist approaches, recent contributions have emphasized the role of sociocultural context in language teaching and learning (see, e.g., Angélil-Carter, 1997; Duff & Uchida, 1997; McKay & Wong, 1996; Norton, 1997; Peirce, 1995; Rampton, 1995; Thesen, 1997; Toohey, 1998). Much of this work has taken place in educational institutions, exploring how schools categorize and position students with identities; how classroom curricula, social organization, and interactions serve to reinforce or contest these categories; and how students accommodate, resist, and counter identities imposed on them (see, e.g., Thesen, 1997; Toohey, 1998).

Drawing on work in this vein, this article begins from the premise that identities are locally understood and constantly remade in social relationships. Thus, even though an identity label such as *ESOL student* may seem self-evident, its meanings are in fact constantly renegotiated and reshaped by particular educators and students working in specific classrooms, institutions, and societies. At the same time, even if sociocultural categories of culture and identity are viewed as intrinsically unstable and heterogeneous and therefore problematic (see, e.g., Atkinson, 1999), it is important to account for the ubiquity of such categories and how they come to appear so stable, homogeneous, and taken-for-granted in a given context. In this article, I highlight the role of representation in accounting for the dynamics through which vastly different images of English language learners' backgrounds and experiences come to be embodied in the same designation of *ESOL student* across educational institutions.

Representation refers here to the images, archetypes, or even stereotypes of identity with which students are labeled. I argue that representations result from constant attempts to hold a heterogeneous and ever-evolving social world still long enough to make sense of it. Whereas identities may be multiple, fragmentary, and subject to constant change, representations are temporary artifacts that serve to stabilize and homogenize images of identities. Because the processes that give rise to representations are largely out of conscious awareness, the tendency is to accept representations such as that of ESOL students as relatively unchanging and self-evident even though, as this article illustrates, they are in fact locally shaped and continually re-created.

Representation is employed here to explain the dynamics through which vastly different images of English language learners' backgrounds and experiences come to be embodied and applied to the very same individuals across educational institutions, and how such images are constantly re-created and resisted at the institutional level through classroom interactions among teachers and students. Drawing on year-long ethnographic case studies of immigrant students' transitions from an urban U.S. secondary school to a community college ESOL program, I illustrate the interplay between student and teacher agency and wider societal representations of language and ethnicity in re-creating institutional representations in each setting. I show how the representation of what it meant to be an ESOL student in these particular students' high school facilitated favorable classroom conditions for learning, whereas the dominant representation of ESOL students in their subsequent community college experience led to increasing student resistance and inimical relationships with educators. I argue that the notion of representation lends useful insight in understanding how labels given to students in classrooms and institutions have consequences for students' classroom behavior and ultimately for students' motivation or *investment* (Peirce, 1995) in English and academic learning.

REPRESENTATION AND SOCIAL CONSTRUCTION OF ESOL STUDENT IDENTITY

Sociologists, anthropologists, and historians have long contended that classrooms and educational institutions play a prominent role in the identity formation of language minority students in immigrant-receiving countries such as the United States (see, e.g., Olneck, 1995). Likewise, researchers and theorists within L2 studies have suggested that prevalent images of immigrants and linguistic minority groups are conveyed in the curriculum in North American educational settings and that such images have significant effects on the intertwined processes of student identity formation and learning. For example, several scholars have posited that schools perpetuate prevalent societal images of immigrants and minority groups through a *hidden curriculum* of schooling (Auerbach, 1995; McGroarty, 1985; Tollefson, 1989). They contend that the hidden curriculum functions as a means of socializing immigrants to take on certain roles and positions in society (e.g., consumer, worker, tenant). Likewise, Cummins (1997) has suggested that the negotiation of identity among educators and students plays a central role in achievement. Cummins hypothesizes that the images of teachers' roles and students' identity manifested in classroom interactions often reflect oppressive power relations in the broader society, leading subordinated social groups to feel ambivalence and insecurity in regard to cultural identity. However, he also believes that these images can be altered in classroom interactions among educators and students that explicitly challenge power relations in the broader society.

The notion that dominant societal images of students' identities are not simply mirrored in classroom processes is echoed by other researchers, who cast classroom practices and social structure as mutually constitutive in shaping students' identity and achievement. For example, in a study of ESOL students' experiences in mainstream elementary classrooms, Toohey (1998) shows how school and classroom organization and interaction served to socialize immigrant children into the prevalent institutional and societal image of learners as individuals who independently negotiate classroom life and achievement. Toohey emphasizes that it is largely through classroom practices that are "so commonplace in classrooms as to be almost invisible" (p. 77) that prevalent societal assumptions about learner identity are communicated and re-created; for example, conventional classroom seating arrangements reinforce the notion that learning is an individual endeavor. Thus, Toohey (following Mehan, 1993) concludes that classroom practices both exhibit and generate social structures.

Recent poststructuralist perspectives on second language acquisition (SLA) have further amplified the reciprocity of social context and individual interactions in forging learners' identities. In particular, this work has emphasized the fluidity and instability of resulting identities. For example, several studies have documented the multiple, contradictory, and locally contingent nature of identity categories that are constructed by and for learners (see, e.g., Angélil-Carter, 1997; McKay & Wong, 1996; Peirce, 1995; Siegal, 1996). Another approach has employed learners' experience as a means of critiquing identity categories themselves (Kubota, 1999; Leung, Harris, & Rampton, 1997; Rampton, 1995; Thesen, 1997), examining notions of identity prevalent in particular social contexts and exposing their socially constructed nature and homogenizing effects.

Less explored in this work is why notions of identity appear to be so stable, unitary, and self-evident in a given context in spite of their multiplicity and constant flux or why identity categories such as *ESOL student* remain omnipresent and seemingly indispensable even when regarded as problematic. This article builds on poststructuralist perspectives on SLA by proposing the concept of representation as a means of accounting for how apparently unchanging and homogeneous categories of institutional and societal identity emerge from the highly unstable, disjunct, and interactionally rendered processes of identify formation by English language learners. Although varying theoretical perspectives on the term exist (see Hall, 1997; hooks, 1992;

Rattansi, 1995; Weedon, 1997, pp. 24–26), by representation here I mean seemingly static, commonsense categorical perceptions of identity prevalent in particular sociocultural, historical, and institutional settings. The notion of representation is rooted in the premise that human beings make meaning through a process of sorting perception and experience into relational categories. Identities—one's own and others'—in this view are relational categories that are embedded in and inextricable from the diffuse yet powerful influence of broader social forces, or *discourses*, in any given setting (Foucault, 1979). Discourses do not impose meaning deterministically or monolithically but rather direct and limit what may be seen as normal, commonsense, or *appropriate* (Fairclough, 1995). In this fashion, they exert influence on the categories through which individuals make sense of their social worlds and thus on how individual teachers and students construe the category of English language learner within particular institutions and classrooms.

Because they are constantly re-created and reshaped in particularistic processes of social interaction, identities such as *ESOL student* are relational categories that are always context specific, multiple, and in constant flux. Far from being self-evident, these identities embody myriad meanings depending on contextual factors, such as whether English is the socially dominant language (Nayar, 1997). It is through representation that teachers and students create images or archetypes of ESOL students that have the effect of fixing meaning, lending fleeting identities the sense of normalcy, common sense, and timelessness in a particular social setting. Representations are thus artifacts of meaning-making processes that are inherently retrospective—they look backward, attempting to capture ephemeral identities—and conservative—they attempt to homogenize and preserve identities that are always multiple and always changing (Rattansi, 1995). I argue that these sorts of archetypes or representations of ESOL learner identity inevitably exist in all institutional settings (and in all classrooms) in which students are educated. Prevalent institutional representations promote certain views of learner identity, making these views seem self-evident and unchanging—just the way ESOL students are—while limiting recognition of other views of students or of heterogeneity among them.

Power figures prominently in the exercise of representation because it can lend a greater sense of authority and sense of reality to some representations than to others. Because the teaching and learning of English take place amid asymmetric relations of power between teachers and students in the classroom and between majority and minority in the broader society, educators are more able than their students to impose their perspectives and viewpoints as commonsense. Thus, educators' representations of ESOL student identity are more likely to be reflected and reproduced in broader institutional discourses than their students' are. However, because individuals also have agency, the view of representation forwarded here suggests that institutional images of ESOL students are not simply handed down monolithically and deterministically; rather, students and educators constantly appropriate, reshape, and contest and resist them even as they re-create them in the course of classroom interaction.

The notion of representation thus allows a means to account for the presence of seemingly stable social categories of identity in a manner that is neither a priori nor deterministic. In this article, I illustrate the dynamic process through which representations of learner status are re-created and resisted across two institutional settings and argue that predominant institutional representations of what an ESOL student is have direct and material consequences for learning paths. I show how such archetypes can be so implicitly assumed and normalized that their locally situated and socially constructed nature becomes evident only in crossing from one educational setting to another. Like Thesen (1997), I utilize the transition from secondary to postsecondary education as a means of illuminating *identity in movement* and the changing identity categories encountered when crossing institutional settings. By contrasting the classroom experiences of three immigrants in two U.S. educational contexts, one an urban secondary school and the other a community college, I show how the seemingly self-evident identities of ESOL students in each setting were in fact socially constructed and rendered static through a process of representation. Moreover, I describe the mutual roles of educators, students, and broader curricular, institutional, and societal forces in simultaneously re-creating and resisting prevalent representations of what it means to be an ESOL student. I show how representations have direct effects on classroom behavior and achievement in both settings, keeping students engaged in language and academic learning in high school and turning them away in the community college.

METHOD

This article is based on three year-long ethnographic case studies of language minority students.[2] Initial fieldwork in the study took place at an ethnically diverse urban high school (approximately 60% Black, 30% White, and 10% Latino and Asian American students). Students participating in the study were enrolled in a science and technology magnet program at the school that was generally regarded as one of the district's best and most competitive. Students receiving ESOL instruction represented 45 of the school's approximately 950 students. Of these, students from Southeast Asia predominated, although some also came from Haiti, Ukraine, Puerto Rico, Turkey, Taiwan, China, and Bosnia. The three participants (Aeyfer, Claudia, and Penny;[3] see Table 1) were recruited from college-bound high school seniors identified by the ESOL teacher among her present and former students at the school.

This study adopts an ethnographic perspective (Green & Bloome, 1997), in which theories of culture and inquiry practices derived from anthropology inform case study methodology (regarding qualitative case study methodology, see Davis, 1995; Merriam, 1998). Qualitative case studies provide a particularly effective means of organizing inquiry into the experiences of learners who traverse multiple classroom settings with multiple instructors,

TABLE 1.   Case Study Profiles

	Student		
	Aeyfer	*Claudia*	*Penny*
Home language	Turkish	Vietnamese	Cantonese, Vietnamese
Years in U.S. when study began	6	10	7
High school courses	English 12, General Physics, Sequential Math 2A, Computer Applications	English 12, French I, Economics, General Physics, Sequential Math III, Computer Graphics	English 12, General Physics, Pre-Calculus I, Computer Applications, Economics
College courses	ESOL 213 Reading and Vocabulary, ESOL 203 Writing, Travel and Tourism 101, TVL 213 Domestic Ticketing	ESOL 103 Reading and Vocabulary, ESOL 104 Writing and Grammar, Sociology, College Algebra, Community First Aid and Safety/ CPR for the Professional Rescuer	ESOL 184 Grammar, ESOL 103 Reading and Vocabulary, ESOL 101 Writing, Sociology 101

such as the U.S. high school and college students described here. As is typical in qualitative case study research, three main sources—interviews, observation, and written documents—formed the basis of data collection and analysis (Merriam, 1998, p. 137).

Data Collection

Tape-recorded interviews 30–50 minutes long were conducted with each case study participant at the school at 2- to 4-week intervals in January–June, during the students' senior year of high school. The interviews were loosely structured. At each interview, the students were asked to recount recent class activities and assignments in each of their classes. I prepared follow-up interview questions as I reviewed classroom observations, teacher interviews, students' work, and students' comments in previous interviews.

Each of the students' teachers was contacted by telephone or in person before the classroom observations and asked to comment specifically on the case study students' performance in their classes and more generally on their experiences with ESOL students. Teachers also made time in their busy schedules to speak with me before or after observed classes or at lunchtime, and these interviews ranged from 10 to 50 minutes in length. Before the student interviews began, I formally interviewed the students' ESOL teacher twice for over an hour regarding the case study students and language minority students' experience at the school, and these interviews were tape-recorded and transcribed. I also kept in contact with the teachers informally as the semester progressed to talk about the students and emerging data themes. In addition, two 50-minute interviews were conducted with the students' two English teachers, one jointly and another separately. In addition to their classroom teachers, the school's writing resource teacher and Claudia and Aeyfer's counselor were interviewed. I also met with various students and faculty on a few occasions in 1995 and 1996.

Each student's classes were observed throughout 2 full school days, and field notes were recorded. In all I spent 10 full school days at the school during the spring semester of the students' senior year in high school. In addition, I spent over 30 class periods in interviews and on a number of other less formal occasions visited with students at the school during breakfast, returned schoolwork, made interview appointments, or checked in on teachers and administrators. Other informal contact with teachers took place in the teacher's lounge, where I spent time between interviews.

Written documents are a crucial data source in advanced levels of the U.S. educational system, in which reading and writing are tightly integrated into classroom communication and language use (Alvermann & Moore, 1996). Accordingly, completed schoolwork (some of which predated the interviews), including class handouts, essays, tests, note packets, and assigned readings, were solicited at every student interview and again after final examinations concluded. These materials were photocopied and returned to students. Textbook chapters corresponding to material covered on the days students were observed were photocopied. The ESOL teacher also provided portfolios of students' written work across the curriculum collected over the course of middle school and high school.

Although all three of the case study students eventually hoped to earn 4-year baccalaureate degrees, they decided to enter a community college in the vicinity in order to gain vocational credentials in dental hygiene (Claudia, Penny) and travel and tourism (Aeyfer) while earning associate degrees. The college was a state-sponsored institution offering 2-year degree programs. It was a modern facility of 12 interconnected buildings surrounded by vast commuter parking lots. With an enrollment of approximately 13,700, it featured a growing ESOL program serving 250 students from over 30 countries, with recent Southeast Asian and Eastern European immigrants predominant. Data collection at the college paralleled that in high school. In all, the data reflect over 50 formal interview sessions with students and instructors as well as over 25 other informal interviews with students' instructors, 10 days of high school classroom observations and over 50 hours of community college classroom observations, and over 5,000 pages of written materials collected from students and from the study sites over the course of the year in which the study took place.

Data Analysis

As is typical in qualitative research and particularly ethnographic approaches (see, e.g., Bogdan & Biklen, 1998), the data were analyzed inductively and recursively throughout the project. Initial data analysis through coding and analytic memoing served to generate further questions to be explored and to identify emergent thematic elements. Data across cases and sources were subjected to triangulation in search of confirming, disconfirming, and altering initial themes. In interviews with the students at the conclusion of the study, I verified findings with them. The students also received all manuscripts resulting from the study.

In keeping with the theoretical framework utilized here, I note that the description here, like all ethnographic descriptions, is itself an interpretation or representation (Ramanathan & Atkinson, 1999; Van Maanen, 1995). Given the paucity of work on the student's perspective in L2 research (Leki, 2001; Rampton, 1995; Thesen, 1997), I set out to represent this perspective. Had I chosen to focus on teachers' perceptions, this account would no doubt be considerably different. Nevertheless, although the interpretive lens attempted to privilege students' views, this account has come to focus on institutional and educators' perspectives in interaction with those of their students, or what Thesen (1997) has termed "the tensions between the labelers and the labeled" (p. 488).[4] In addition, like any researcher, I am a positioned subject who is "prepared to know certain things and not others" (Rosaldo, 1989, p. 8), and I am inexorably subject to the very social and institutional forces that I interpret here.

HIGH SCHOOL: "THE KIDS WITH DETERMINATION"

Students at the case study students' high school had elected to participate in its particularly rigorous academic program (including 4 years each of math, science, and computer programming courses). Thus, language minority students at the school were probably a somewhat select group, possessing higher-than-average degrees of ability and motivation. Their small number at the school as well as the single ESOL teacher's high profile as a student mentor and advocate seemed to contribute to a pan-ethnic category of ESOL student identity in spite of considerable heterogeneity in ethnicity and in socioeconomic and educational background. Immigrant students at the school seemed to be viewed primarily as affiliated with and the responsibility of the ESOL program and teacher. For example, the ESOL teacher reported that she was routinely called in by other teachers, counselors, and administrators to deal with any issues arising about language minority students at the school whether they were in ESOL or not. As she put it, "If it's a fight, a pregnancy, or an award, they just come and get me" (I, February 10, 1993).[5] During observations, a chemistry teacher inquired about an absent student by asking the ESOL teacher, "Where's your Cambodian today?" (FN, January 26, 1994). A sense that ESOL students were regarded as and regarded themselves as a group was also borne out by the school's Bilingual Club. The club was an extracurricular organization consisting mostly of language minority students at the school who organized presentations and field trips together. Additionally, for a number of reasons, including the tracking system, the logistics of ESOL class scheduling, and the ESOL teacher's hand-scheduling of some students into classes where teachers were most likely to be sympathetic towards non-native speakers of English, Aeyfer, Claudia, and Penny had attended the same schools and many of the same classes together since they had arrived in the United States.

Even though they might have been distinguished at the high school by their affiliation with the ESOL teacher and program, the case study students spent the vast majority of their high school careers in mainstream content-area courses alongside native speakers. In fact, two of the three students (Claudia and Aeyfer) were not enrolled in ESOL at all in their senior year. None of the three had spent more than one of their six class periods per day in ESOL for several years. Thus most of these students' classroom interactions and identity construction in high school derived from participation in mainstream classrooms. Several layers of representations of ESOL status in these classrooms were apparent in classroom observations, written communication, and interviews with teachers and case study students.

"An Inspiration for Everyone"

A prevailing institutional representation seemed to draw on broader U.S. societal "Ellis Island" images of immigrants leaving their homes, enduring financial and emotional hardships, and through sheer perseverance succeeding in building a better life for themselves in America. In the context of the high school, these images informed a representation of ESOL students as hardworking, highly motivated students who had triumphed over adversity. The strongest expression of this sentiment came from Claudia and Aeyfer's English teacher. In interviews, he observed, "These students have such determination. It's incredible." He said that he admired ESOL students, asserting that "they're an inspiration for EVERYONE, they really are." "They just perform well. The drive and desire, I mean, it's just unbelievable" (I, March 29, 1994). Although this teacher's opinion was perhaps the most emphatic, most of the students' teachers commented favorably on ESOL students' motivation and school performance as a whole. Clearly, many of the students had experienced hardship and did work hard. But even though the representation of immigrants as determined, hardworking, and even inspirational students may have seemed like just a commonsense social observation to students and teachers, there was considerable evidence that students and teachers collaboratively regenerated and perpetuated this representation of identity, primarily through the relating of personal stories and through their classroom comportment.

Personal Stories.   In classrooms such as English, where journals and essays were common practices, students and teachers seemed to make occasions for the telling and retelling of personal stories about the difficulties students had faced and overcome as immigrants to the United States. Aeyfer's English class, for example, featured a pictorial autobiography project. The cover of Aeyfer's autobiography featured the potent image of her sitting between two flags, one Turkish and one U.S. In her narrative, Aeyfer related that she was forced to leave school and begin a job as an apprentice hairdresser in her last year in Turkey. She wrote that she prayed to Allah to send her to school, a dream that she could only attain because her family came to America (D, English, March 15, 1994). Aeyfer's autobiography drew an outpouring of sympathy, support, and admiration from her teacher. His comments in the margins included "Wonderful," "I'm proud of you," "Your writing is very perceptive," and "You do very well. You are a smart young lady." In an interview her teacher commented on how much her story had moved him, marveling that because "she wasn't able to go to school," "her DREAM was to go to school" (I, March 29, 1994). In an interview discussing this project, Aeyfer both proudly and sheepishly noted, "I guess he was reading it to classes!" (I, April 11, 1994) and said that her autobiography had inspired a question on the midterm asking students whether they felt that they valued school or took it for granted. Aeyfer was complimented by the attention she received: "I was like, 'This is my thing!' . . . I felt good" (I, April 11, 1994). As Cummins (1997) has observed, teachers' and students' roles are mutually constituted, and in this example mutually ennobling representations of teacher and ESOL student identity are perpetuated through a cooperative process, with educators implicitly represented in student text as fulfillers of immigrant dreams and ambitions and the student cast in turn by her teacher as a model of how to overcome hardship and obstacles to succeed.

This example would be unremarkable if it were an isolated instance. However, although more prosaic writing did appear in the case study students' compositions (e.g., Penny's discussion of her favorite movie [D, English, September 9, 1993]; Claudia's story about what happened when she came home with a bad grade in math [D, English, April 29, 1994]), many of the students' writing assignments seemed to be oriented toward particular genres of personal writing—autobiographies, leave-taking stories, stories about hardships they had endured as immigrants, and essays about customs and holidays in their countries of origin. This sort of writing by ESOL students appears to be widespread. For example, Fu (1995) reports very similar genres of personal writing in her study of immigrant high school students. As Fu amply documents, the representation of ESOL student identity appropriated from broader societal images of immigrants and manifested in these stories and essays has undoubted benefits. Students in this study found these sorts of writing assignments highly motivating for the most part. The assignments provided links between school and personal experience and encouraged the students to take pride in their unique status as immigrants. They provided the students with opportunities to express heartfelt feelings and thoughts and to cast themselves and their experiences in a positive light for their teacher audience. In many ways, then, these assignments were emotionally positive experiences for students, helped cement social relationships with teachers, and at the same time acted to reinforce the representation of ESOL student identity already prevalent in the school.

However, the origins and motivations of students' production of tales of immigrant hardship and success were complex and more than a simple matter of self-expression and self- (and teacher) affirmation. Such stories were enmeshed in issues of personal disclosure and student-teacher power relationships. For example, although the sentiments expressed in Aeyfer's autobiography may have been genuine, at the same time her teacher was perhaps unaware that Aeyfer had been asked to produce virtually the same narrative by at least two previous teachers and had probably received similar reactions (D, ESL, 1992; I, January 19, 1995). In fact, the power of such narratives to arouse sympathy and admiration created significant incentives for students to disclose such narratives even when not explicitly solicited by teachers. For example, in response to the fairly broad and open-ended essay prompt, "Give an account of an event that actually happened or that you imagined," Claudia told the story of how she had been singled out for harassment by U.S.-born peers as a newcomer in elementary school (D, English, November 9, 1993).

These stories carry at least the potential for students to essentialize themselves as a cultural "other" in order to secure teachers' sympathy and support. Leki (1995), for example, relates the story of a Taiwanese student attending a U.S. university who incorporated her identity as an outsider in virtually every academic writing assignment she was given, commenting, "I am Chinese. I take advantage." Significantly, the school's ESOL teacher was the only one at the high school who regularly and explicitly discussed with me factors in ESOL students' background besides immigrant status, such as class, gender, and family circumstances. She was also the only teacher who articulated concern about the perils of overgeneralizing about individuals based on their backgrounds, noting that "each time you think you sort of have a profile of what the family situation probably is based on a few indicators, I find out that it's—I really can't make that assumption" (I, March 29, 1994). Thus, although immigrant narratives seemed to contribute for the most part to a favorable representation of ESOL students at the school, the representation by its very nature also tended to essentialize and homogenize student identity within the institution.

Classroom Behavior.   A second major means through which ESOL students collaborated in their teachers' construction of them as persevering, model students was classroom behavior. For example, Claudia and Penny attended class more regularly than U.S.-born peers, a seemingly trivial detail but one highly valued by the high school teachers. In senior classes, where teachers routinely reported absenteeism rates up to 50%, Penny missed only three school days all year, and she had had perfect attendance in her junior year. In observations, none of the three exhibited the cat-and-mouse or adversarial classroom behavior often seen in their U.S.-born adolescent peers. They were consistently diligent and attentive in the classroom. This is not to say that ESOL students viewed their teachers less critically than their peers did. Claudia, for example, was not hesitant to tell me what she thought about her economics class—"I hate that class! I HATE the teacher!" (I, February 8, 1994)—or to observe of another teacher, "He's so WEIRD!" (I, March 28, 1994). Still, they tended not to demonstrate such attitudes overtly in classes. As Claudia put it, "I just sit there and listen" (I, February 8, 1994). The immigrant students in this study also seemed to be freer with displays of appreciation of and even affection for their teachers than the U.S.-born adolescents at the school did. For example, Penny ended a note to her ESOL teacher with, "One more thing I have to say to my sweet teacher—THANK YOU" (D, ESL, November 13, 1990).

The contrast between U.S.-born and immigrant students' behavior was rendered even more distinct when immigrants were placed in low-track classes, a frequent occurrence because of an inflexible statewide tracking system for high school students. ESOL students regularly reported days when only two of their classmates attended class or when those who attended were napping. When surrounded by U.S.-born peers half-jokingly referred to as "lunatics" and "parolees" by a teacher (I, June 21, 1994), immigrants found it relatively easy to appropriate the representation of the hardworking, diligent immigrant to portray themselves as exemplary students. One teacher enthusiastically reported, for example, "They're showing up. They're doing the best they can" (I, April 20, 1994). Another teacher noted favorably that Penny completed her work before her (frequently off-task) U.S.-born peers (FN, March 9, 1994). On-task behavior and perseverance had come to be an intrinsic part of the representation of immigrant students, and teachers expressed surprise when students did not conform to the representation. Penny's English teacher, for example, related that her senior English class had become listless and that students often stared off into space the last few weeks of school. But she noted that she became truly alarmed when "She [Penny] was getting that way, and I said, 'Oh no! Even my GOOD kid's bad now!'" (I, June 21, 1994).

"They Struggle"

The perseverance that was part of the prevailing institutional representation of immigrant students at the high school may have been regarded as admirable, but it was simultaneously construed as a possible indication of a lack of innate ability. Aeyfer's counselor, for example, commented that she "has to work hard" and portrayed her as "sticking it out" in high school. Likewise, the same counselor commented that Claudia's high grades came from "pure determination and lots of time" (I, June 16, 1994). Another teacher remarked of Aeyfer, "She struggled in high school" (I, April 19, 1994). Although educators may have seen immigrants' effort and diligence in school as commendable, the same effort and diligence also led them to doubt students' linguistic and academic capabilities. Some invoked a deficit model of bilingualism when discussing students' academic performance. Situated in a predominantly monolingual society in which SLA research itself has tended to cast learner status as "fundamentally stigmatized" (Firth & Wagner, 1997; Rampton, 1995, p. 292) and in an educational context where English was the exclusive medium of instruction, it is unsurprising that some teachers cast these students' ability to communicate in two languages not as a special talent or strength but rather as a disability, emphasizing what immigrant students could not do relative to monolingual, standard English speakers. One teacher, for example, commented, "It must be like somebody who's very bright and has a stroke. And can't express themselves" (I, June 21, 1994).

Nor did teacher and institutional representations of immigrants as model students necessarily imply a high estimation of their academic ability. Some teachers clearly held high opinions of the students' academic potential. Claudia and Aeyfer's English teacher, for example, consistently commented that ESOL students did not have any weaknesses and that he had no doubt that they were going to be very successful (I, March 29, 1994; April 20, 1994). However, like the college faculty Zamel (1995) surveyed, other educators at the high school seemed to conflate English proficiency with cognitive ability, questioning ESOL students' intellects. Aeyfer's math teacher observed that the motivation and discipline of ESOL students was usually quite high but that concepts sometimes "give them trouble" (FN, April 29, 1994). Likewise, another teacher commented, "They'll be successful because they are very motivated, but I have no idea of what their natural ability is" (I, June 15, 1994). Speaking of one ESOL student's performance on a standardized state writing competency test, the same teacher asserted, "She had trouble — and it's not brain surgery . . . some of them have trouble just organizing. That is more of an analytic skill" (I, June 15, 1994). Perhaps because teachers viewed these perceived students' deficits sympathetically, the students seemed largely unaware that there was some question about their linguistic and academic abilities. For their part, the students spoke of their bilingualism matter-of-factly or as a talent. Aeyfer, for example, regarded her bilingualism as a significant asset in fulfilling her goal of making a career in the Turkish tourism industry (I, April 21, 1994). She also spoke proudly of her studies in Quranic Arabic literacy (I, October 19, 1994). Similarly, Penny reported that her family had gone to some lengths, including hiring private tutors, to ensure that she was literate in her native Chinese[6] as well as in English (I, March 17, 1994).

Thus, in spite of considerable variation in curricula, experiences, orientation, and relationships among educators and immigrant students, there nonetheless seemed to be institutional consistencies in the representation of ESOL students' status at the high school. The prevailing representation of well-behaved, hardworking, persevering students at the school was shaped by and served to reinforce broader societal notions about the immigrant experience. It led to generally supportive and cordial relationships with teachers and positive evaluations of ESOL students' classroom performance even in the face of evidence to the contrary. For example, Aeyfer's physics teacher rated her "attitude" and "behavior" as excellent in his class (D, physics, November 2, 1993) even though he commented on a progress report that she needed to treat lab work more seriously, read assigned material, and do all assigned work; even though she had done poorly on a quiz and a test; and even though he rated her participation and organization as only satisfactory. The prevailing representation of immigrant students at the school was neither consistent nor unequivocally positive, however. It intrinsically held the potential to essentialize and even stereotype immigrant students at the school and, embedded in broader U.S. societal discourses, it cast students' bilingualism only as a deficit in English. Nevertheless, because the representation held many affirming elements for how they were viewed academically and socially at the school, students continually invoked and re-created it in the course of classroom interactions with their teachers. The representation of ESOL students as persevering through the hardships of immigration thus played a role in keeping students engaged in classroom learning, and in that sense it was ultimately consequential for the ways in which ESOL students' academic and linguistic learning took place in high school.

COLLEGE: "THE WORST OF AMERICAN STUDENTS' HABITS"

Claudia, Penny, and Aeyfer enrolled at an urban community college the following fall. Through collegewide entrance placement tests, each was identified as a nonnative speaker of English. They were directed to the ESOL program, where they were further tested and placed in one of four levels of intensive reading-vocabulary, writing, and grammar classes. Each of the case study students was placed in low-intermediate- to advanced-level courses (see Table 1), and these ESOL courses dominated their schedules in their first semester in college. Although they were each allowed to take one to three introductory-level college courses (e.g., Introduction to Sociology, Travel and Tourism 101), their *ESOL student* label became the primary determinant of their program of study. Because ESOL classes had not formed a significant portion of their secondary school course work, the fact that the community college positioned the students first and foremost as in need of ESOL constituted a significant contrast from the way that they had been constructed in high school. This in itself was not unwelcome to them, however. Students initially expressed eagerness to begin their college careers with ESOL classes. Penny, for example, thought that ESOL would help her acclimate to college-level academic work (I, May 19, 1994). Aeyfer even asserted that taking ESOL was her main objective in college, saying, "I really need to get my English more. I don't care about the other stuff. I care, but not as much" (I, May 18, 1994).

Each of the case study students' classes included 1–3 students identified by teachers and students as long-term U.S. residents and U.S. high school graduates. The rest of the classes, typically 10–15 students, consisted mostly of recent adult immigrants who had received all of their previous secondary and postsecondary education abroad (I, program director, May 26, 1994). Even though faculty were clearly mindful of and concerned about the needs of the long-term resident U.S. high school graduates in their classes, the curriculum and teacher talk were in many ways still oriented to the majority of students in the program—newcomers to the United States who had been educated abroad. This orientation gave rise to particular institutional and programmatic representations of ESOL students that carried significant assumptions about students' need for cultural orientation, about students' cultural experiences and affiliations, about the origins of and appropriate instruction for students' English language features, and about students' *cultural capital* (Bourdieu, 1977) deriving from educational background and social class. Walking into college ESOL classes, the students in this study found themselves viewed in ways that not only were discontinuous with the predominant representation of their identity as ESOL students in high school but also seemed to cast their experiences with U.S. schooling and society in an unfavorable light.

"Acculturation to Life in America"

Because most of the community college students were new to the United States, the prevailing representation of ESOL student identity depicted students as in need of socialization into U.S. college norms and behavior as well as to life in U.S. society more broadly. The curriculum in ESOL classes reflected this image of students as cultural novices. For example, the goals of the ESOL program as written by one of the teachers for a collegewide presentation included not only instrumental academic and linguistic goals, such as "through language study [the program] opens the door to a college degree program" and "better communication," but also goals related to cultural orientation: "acculturation to life in America" and "personal growth" (FN, November 16, 1994). These goals in themselves are unremarkable—Nayar (1997), for example, notes that they are frequently the province of ESOL programs in immigrant-receiving countries. These goals, however, were diametrically opposed to the case study students' self-perceptions and expectations as seasoned school-goers and residents of the United States. When I asked Claudia about the goals, she commented of the latter two, "What does this got to do with the college, anyway? That's just my opinion" (I, December 8, 1994).

Perhaps because institutional and programmatic discourses constructed acculturation as a student need and a program responsibility, many of the ESOL instructors at the community college assumed a caregiver persona in the classroom. For example, they often policed students' behavior. The syllabus for Penny's ESOL writing course featured a lengthy section on students' classroom conduct, including "Class attendance is mandatory. Students should not schedule appointments during class hours. . . . A successful student is one who regularly completes his/her homework. . . . Eating, drinking or other distracting behavior will not be permitted" (D, writing, September 7, 1994). Some instructors prohibited students from wearing baseball caps or chewing gum in their classes. Aeyfer's reading teacher shushed students when they spoke out of turn. The same instructor often fell into a caregiver or foreigner-talk register signaled by exaggerated intonation contours and frequent imperatives; for example, "That's RIGHT. Ve:ery go:od"; "Put those eyes down. Skim quickly. Got it?" or "Read it for us, Jerry" (FN, December 6, 1994; December 9, 1994).

Many newcomer students no doubt welcomed the explicit socialization and guidance provided by the ESOL instructors. However, the case study students contrasted their ESOL classes with the considerably enhanced autonomy and self-determination they experienced in regular college classrooms. They all noted that college instructors, unlike high school teachers, no longer monitored or policed their academic and classroom conduct. Either students did the work, or they failed. This ethos was reflected on syllabi, such as the one for Penny's sociology course, which in contrast to the ESOL course syllabi made no mention of classroom behavior aside from one statement about mandatory attendance and participation (D, sociology, autumn 1994). Observations of these classrooms similarly recorded no comments by instructors about students' conduct, in spite of the prevalence of eating, chewing gum, and wearing baseball caps. As long-term U.S. residents and citizens, the case study students became ambivalent about the ESL instruction, which appeared to question their ability to function autonomously in college or in the United States at the very same time in their lives when U.S. society conferred expectations of increased autonomy and recognition as high school graduates and adults.

Because the prevalent institutional representation of ESOL students and the behavior of many of the newcomers led ESOL instructors to expect compliance with and even gratitude for the social orientation they provided in classes, the independence of U.S.-educated students often struck teachers as lack of cooperation and rudeness. One teacher, for example, noted that the students she had problems with were always the ones who had gone to high school in the United States (I, November 16, 1994). Although the teachers varied in their views of the socialization needs of newcomers and long-term residents,[7] the prevailing representation of ESOL students as newcomers and cultural novices led to significant similarities in socialization practices in ESOL classrooms and a corresponding similarity in long-term resident students' resistance to them throughout the semester.

"Your Country"

As the high school classes had, and for much the same reasons, college ESOL classes elicited narratives about immigration from students' personal experience. Claudia, for example, was asked to write an "arrival story" as one of her first ESOL writing assignments (D, writing, September 8, 1994). As in high school, the elicitation of such stories tapped into broader U.S. beliefs about the nobility and pathos of immigration. In fact, Penny was even assigned a reading about Ellis Island (D, reading, November 17, 1994). And much as in high school, these stories were privileged over other, perhaps more mundane or universal aspects of their experience.

Unlike the situation in high school, however, long-term U.S. residents were surrounded by classmates whose formative life experiences and education had taken place outside the United States. The programmatic representation of ESOL students at the community college was also reinforced by an international student archetype, common in U.S. college-level ESOL materials and textbooks, that likewise assumed that ESOL students have grown to adulthood abroad. This representation overlooked the multiple cultural affiliations of long-term resident students. Instead, curricula and teacher talk in college ESOL courses tended to position students as outsiders through discourses presuming a mutually exclusive "United States" and "your country." For example, students were frequently assigned to write about their country of origin on topics such as "my hometown," "homeless people in your country," " 'low'- or 'high'-class foods in your country" (D, Penny, writing, November 1, 1994; reading, October 4 and December 8, 1994), "a holiday of your culture," "my country—a great place to visit," and "problems of students in my country" (D, Claudia, writing, September 8 and November 21, 1994; FN, November 17, 1994).

These assignments and the assumptions underlying them seemed unproblematic for students recently arrived in the United States. In fact, newcomers actively sought out occasions to talk about their countries in college ESOL classrooms. Long-term residents' cultural experiences and affiliations, however, were by no means that simple. For one thing, their lives and cultural identities were situated in the multiethnic, urban U.S. social milieu in which they had grown to adulthood. Their ethnic affiliations were grounded at least as much in a culturally hybrid immigrant community as in their natal countries. Recollections of what the assignments assumed to be their countries were colored by a separation long in time and distance. For example, in response to the composition assignment "Return Home," Penny wrote such a detached and speculative composition that her teacher was prompted to inquire, "Have you ever had this experience?" (D, writing, October 6, 1994). She wrote back, "I have left my country since 1987. I have lived in the United States for seven years. I believed my country changed a lot. I haven't go back to country yet, but some of my cousins went back to visit and they told me somethings had changed" (D, writing, October 16, 1994).

The very assumption that Vietnam was still Penny's home (or at least her only home) was a dubious one. Penny, who had just become a U.S. citizen, reported that she had few relatives or friends left in Vietnam (I, December 2, 1994). Likewise, Claudia reported that when she visited Vietnam after 9 years in the United States, her Vietnamese relatives regarded her as an American, simultaneously a status symbol and somewhat distancing (I, September 28, 1994). As long-term U.S. residents who knew the ropes, the case study students also felt a separation from and perhaps a certain superiority to the newcomers in their classes. Penny seemed to pity newcomers, commenting that "the English is not really good," and said that she had helped a newcomer classmate with a report because "he would be—like, appreciate it if we share, you know? So I do it with him" (I, November 16, 1994). Claudia told me flatly that she would not associate with newcomers from Vietnam in her classes, contending that newer Vietnamese immigrants were not as self-disciplined or hardworking (I, October 17, 1994).

If they were not pure cultural exemplars of those other places, neither did these students feel themselves to be wholly affiliated with the White, middle-class version of culture that they and their teachers referred to generically as "American." They were neither or both depending on time and context, something that the dualistic representations of culture prevalent in their classes did not easily allow. For example, the students' writing on topics comparing the United States with their natal country shows constant shifts in pronominal usage and cultural perspective. Penny wrote in a composition on shopping, "In *my* culture *we* go to the market to buy food every morning. Not like *here, we* shop once a week" (italics added; D, reading, October 4, 1994). Similarly, when Claudia was telling me about a visit to Vietnam, I was struck by her easy alteration between frames of reference, between "in my country" and "because we're American," affiliations and referents that shifted constantly as she discussed different settings and participants (I, September 28, 1994). The dualistic framing of most of the curricula and teacher talk in these classrooms simply could not account for such complexity.

Thus, the prevailing institutional representation of ESOL students as adult newcomers implicitly presumed pure exemplars of other cultures and languages, and in doing so, it led to the neglect or implicit devaluation of the hybridity and multiplicity of U.S. high school graduates' ethnic affiliations in the college's ESOL curriculum. One can see that these U.S. high school graduates might find the predominant representation of ESOL student identity alienating and even a bit insulting. Although these students had been able to draw on broader societal representations of the hardships and perseverance of immigrants in high school in order to construct favorable representations of themselves, in college they were in effect out-newcomered and out-othered by their classmates.

"You Are Starting to Do This on Instinct"

Students and the community college ESOL teachers soon found themselves in conflict because of the curriculum's implicit representations of ESOL students as inexperienced users of English and related assumptions about the transient and erasable nature of nonnative speaker language features. This representation overlooked students' considerable previous experiences, academically and otherwise, with English. For example, students were assigned to read a novel and subscribe to a newspaper on the assumption that they were not accustomed to extensive reading in English. However, after several years attending English-medium schools in an English-dominated society, U.S. high school graduates were quite comfortable reading in English. In fact, English was the only language in which Claudia was literate. The lack of recognition given to these students' considerable experience with English language texts led to resistance in college ESOL classes. For example, while her teacher lectured the class on how to locate stories in sections of the newspaper, Penny could be seen flipping to her horoscope and local department store ads, a small but telling act of resistance as well as a more authentic act of newspaper reading than the class exercises (FN, November 8, 1994).

Grammar instruction in the college's ESOL classes also presumed that students' language features were simply the result of lack of experience with English. Although the students in the study had received some explicit grammar instruction in middle school and high school from ESOL and writing teachers, most of their language learning had taken place as part of their immersion in an English-medium schooling environment. As a result, they had a keen implicit understanding of English form and usage. When Claudia's grammar teacher asked the class why a sentence was ungrammatical, Claudia simply replied, "It sounds stupid" (FN, November 17, 1994). However, because their understanding of English form and function was largely intuitive, they tended to perform poorly on exercises or tests that required them to identify and label parts of speech or be familiar with metalinguistic terminology (see Ferris, 1999; Reid, 1997). Unfortunately, the ESOL program's placement tests and curricula tended to presume exactly those sorts of knowledge. Penny's performance on the program's diagnostic test—a commercially published, standardized multiple-choice, grammar-oriented measure designed for nonnative speakers of English—resulted in her placement in a low intermediate grammar class that began with a review of present tense verb usage. Given Penny's 6 years in the United States, it is unsurprising that her teacher was soon noting that she should have been placed higher (I, October 31, 1994) and that Penny was complaining, "some:times, it's very boring, you know?" (I, October 5, 1994). Likewise, Claudia's grammar teacher once lectured the class, "You know, I think a lot of you are starting to do this on instinct. That's good, but we shouldn't get carried away" (I, November 15, 1994). The statement was telling in its presumptions that students were starting from rule-based instruction and only then applying it to productive use and that they were only beginning to develop intuitions about language use. In fact, Claudia, who had been in the United States for a decade, may have been learning rules for things that she had done "on instinct" for years.

In daily, subtle ways, the curriculum and teacher talk in college ESOL classrooms denied these immigrants ownership of English. A telling example comes from a teacher's comment on a composition Penny wrote in response to a reading about an immigrant who does not want to speak his native language in class with friends. At the bottom, the teacher wrote, "How much time do you speak English compared to your language?" (D, reading, October 31, 1994). In a very real sense, English was just as much Penny's language as Chinese or Vietnamese was. The representation of these ESOL students as novices in English in spite of their considerable accomplishments in the language led the immigrants to counter with classroom displays of self-assured expertise and boredom. In my classroom observations of Claudia's grammar and writing class, for example, she unabashedly worked on her homework assignments as her teacher lectured, looking up ever so casually from the book from time to time to call out answers to his questions. On one occasion she answered and then loudly declared, "I learned that in seventh grade" (FN, November 15, 1994). She handed in one assignment with a flourish 5 minutes after it had been assigned, as if to say, "See how easy these are for me?" (FN, November 17, 1994). Claudia also made it clear to her teacher that she regarded language assignments as busy work, doing the minimum necessary to complete them. For example, on an exercise about clause connectors, she used *since* for every sentence. Because the teacher did not specify which connectors to use, she technically fulfilled the assignment requirements. Nevertheless, she drew her teacher's ire and a C on the assignment (FN, November 17, 1994).

"She Knows What the Teacher Wants"

Many newcomers in the college program arrived as "privileged" students (Vandrick, 1995) with significant amounts of cultural capital (Bourdieu, 1977) — relatively privileged social status and educational backgrounds — in their native countries. Moreover, both teachers and students regarded the educations these students had received abroad as having been more rigorous than the educations received by U.S. high school graduates. As Aeyfer observed, "When you are, like, in the fifth grade [in Turkey], you know the [U.S.] high school math. The highest, the regent one. When you are in the high school, you know the COLLEGE stuff!" (I, May 18, 1994). The socioeconomic and educational background of these internationally educated students had become normative in the representation of ESOL students within the institution, much as it has in U.S. college-level TESOL research and pedagogy.

As a result, even though the community college was itself part of the U.S. educational system, U.S. schooling and the immigrants who were products of it were stigmatized and seen as comparatively lacking. Two instructors asserted, for example, that immigrants were lacking in cognitive academic language proficiency (CALP; see Cummins, 1981) as a result of their U.S. high school education (I, October 26, 1994; FN, November 16, 1994). Claudia and Penny's reading teacher asserted that U.S. high school graduates seemed to assimilate the worst from U.S. high schools. She felt that teachers had to provide "structure" to such students, implying a relative lack of motivation (I, November 10, 1994). Claudia's composition teacher lamented that a group of Vietnamese American male students would pass the course "because they've been here awhile, but that is a big part of their problem." The teacher told me that he could not imagine teaching American students fresh out of high school, then paused as he realized, "But maybe I am" (I, November 17, 1994).

Although the college ESOL teachers acknowledged that their students behaved in much the same way as their U.S.-born peers did (in fact, as noted above, they often behaved better), teachers clearly disapproved of their behavior as well. Thus, ironically enough, teachers implicitly rejected the very Americanness of students' educational backgrounds in favor of the class and educational backgrounds of students educated abroad. For their part, the case study students recognized and sometimes resented the favoritism shown toward newcomers in their classes. Aeyfer, in particular, voiced her frustration: "You know that girl? Who was talking mostly? . . . She knows, you know, what she [the teacher] wants" (I, January 19, 1995). Aeyfer complained that such students dominated class discussions and the teacher's attention. In fact, she reported several heated exchanges with her teacher on the issue of differential treatment of U.S. high school graduates over the semester (see Harklau, 1999, for elaboration).

Resistance

In many ways, then, the representation of ESOL students that immigrants encountered in the community college ESOL program did not reflect their backgrounds and experience, and because of this mismatch the students often found themselves cast as deficient. As a result, resistance soon began surfacing in all the case study students and escalated over the course of the semester. It was not that the students set out to dislike ESOL classes or that they took pleasure in complaining. On the contrary, they were often hesitant to say anything negative, making noncommittal remarks such as "She's ni:ice" (I, November 16, 1994) when asked about their teachers or classes. Many forms of resistance were subtle. Aeyfer made a point of declaring to her reading teacher that she seldom read the assigned newspaper (FN, December 6, 1994), but she told me later in an interview that she had read it frequently and enjoyed it (I, January 19, 1995). During my observations, Penny spent most of her writing and grammar classes listlessly fidgeting, kicking her foot, and putting her head on her desk (FN, October 31, 1994; November 2, 1994). Claudia and Aeyfer conspicuously forgot to bring their books to classes (FN, November 10, 1994; December 6, 1994).

Other forms of resistance were manifest. Already in September, Claudia had begun a refrain of "I just think this class is BORING" and "I don't want to take those class!" (I, September 28, 1994). She soon shared that sentiment with her teachers, which surely won her no favors. In fact, she joked, "That's why I continue to take it [ESOL]!" (I, December 8, 1994). Similarly, Aeyfer's teachers consistently remarked that although she had begun the term with high motivation and had completed all of her assignments, as the semester progressed her work had deteriorated, and she had begun to miss class and assignments. One teacher commented, "She doesn't seem to have the spark and enthusiasm that she did at the beginning" (I, December 6, 1994). From her perspective, Aeyfer was trying to simply tolerate her classes until they ended. She commented, "It's hard! I keep quiet, you know? She [the teacher] KNOWS I don't like that class" (I, November 16, 1994). As the students withdrew or made more overt demonstrations of resistance to the received representations of their identities cast for them within college ESOL classrooms, the students' resistance—that is, their failure to mirror the representation—in turn served for the teachers as increasing confirmation of their original assessments of and previous experiences with U.S. high school graduates as implicitly deficient.

It is easy to see why the community college's ESOL teachers did not welcome these comparatively ill-behaved and combative students in their classes. The faculty clearly recognized that they had a problem with disaffection and resistance among U.S. high school graduates. As skillful and experienced instructors, they were concerned about long-term residents' performance in their program and sought out more effective ways to teach them. However, many did not appear to recognize the extent to which the very representations of English language learners in their classroom talk and curricula were implicated in resistance. Some of the teachers, especially two who had been high school teachers themselves, were aware of how differently these students were viewed and treated in their program than they had been in high school. One, for example, acknowledged that students were "used to feeling successful" in high school (FN, May 6, 1995). However, instructors often seemed to believe that U.S. high school graduates' resistance and acting out in their classrooms stemmed from intrinsic surliness or poor command of classroom etiquette rather than from the dissonance students experienced in the dominant institutional representation of their experience. Even when teachers appeared to recognize the interconnections of representation and resistance among immigrants in their classes, they faced a number of constraints on their ability to respond or make instructional adjustments, including a heavy workload, isolation within the college, and the need to balance among various student constituencies.

By the end of their first semester in ESOL classes, these students' resistance to alienating representations of their identities had become complete rejection. Claudia had consulted with friends and had discovered the little-advertised fact that ESOL courses were not compulsory—that is, students could simply choose to bypass the sequence and register for first-year composition. Aeyfer had made the same discovery and also planned to bypass the program, commenting, "I think I need more ESOL classes . . . but I don't want to go in there anymore." She added "I got sick and tired of learning English" (I, January 19, 1995).

IMPLICATIONS

In the classroom language learning experiences of long-term U.S. residents across two institutional settings, significant differences emerge in how the seemingly self-evident term *ESOL student* is constructed and understood.

Informed in part by broader U.S. societal discourses regarding the immigrant experience, the representation of ESOL students that held sway in the case study students' high school was one of enduring emotional and material hardships in order to strive, through education, for a better life in the United States. Although the same perseverance that was seen as ennobling also cast doubt on immigrants' linguistic and perhaps even innate cognitive abilities, the largely positive ways in which the representation depicted ESOL students academically and socially were significant enough to foster its continual reappropriation by students and educators at the high school.

On the other hand, *ESOL student* meant something considerably different in the students' community college ESOL program. With a student body consisting mainly of new arrivals who brought with them significant, often socially privileged educational and life experience outside the United States, and reinforcement from college ESOL textbooks and pedagogical literature favoring a similar archetype, the college's prevalent representation in many ways implicitly overlooked or devalued the resources and skills of U.S. high school graduates and cast them as deficient. Because the backgrounds and characteristics of the majority of students in the program in some ways matched the dominant representation and because of the asymmetric power relations between teachers and students in the classroom, the representation of the privileged newcomer prevailed, setting in motion ever-deepening cycles of resistance on the part of long-term resident students, teacher sanctions in the classroom, and the students' eventual rejection of college ESOL instruction. Thus, prevalent institutional and programmatic representations of what it means to be an ESOL student had material effects on students' motivation and classroom experiences in both settings, confirming the integral role the schools play in the intertwined processes of English language learning and academic achievement.

The workings of representation illustrated in this article provide one means of exploring seemingly stable and unitary identity categories in social contexts such as educational institutions within a poststructural framework positing identities to be inherently dynamic, contradictory, and partial. The study also lends support to Thesen's (1997) and Norton's (1997) observations regarding the productivity of learner transitions in revealing the socially constructed nature of identity categories. Similar to language minority students in British educational contexts as described by Leung et al. (1997) and by Rampton (1995), the learners described here did not fit neatly into prevailing images of ethnic and linguistic identity in U.S. society and educational institutions, particularly at the college level, where international students often remain the implicit archetype in research and curriculum planning. It is precisely these students' marginality in existing representations or labels of ethnolinguistic identity (e.g., *L2 learner, language minority student*) that makes their experiences compelling; in a sense, their characterization becomes a window into prevailing discourses of the institutions they enter. It is only in looking at the same individuals across institutional settings that the contextual particularity and homogenizing effects of representations of identity such as *ESOL student* are made clear. What appear to be commonsense or self-evident conceptualizations from within a classroom or program can be seen as prevailing institutional representations, forged in broader processes of social interaction and meaning making and manifested in educators' and students' perceptions, classroom talk, and curricula.

It would be easy to think of the representations of immigrant student identity described here as the foibles of teachers other than ourselves or institutions other than our own (from which we are thankfully free), but to do so would miss the point. Because these representations are understood at the level of common sense, they are largely implicit and not easily open to examination. I do not believe that the educators I have depicted here were any less perceptive, compassionate, or skilled than educators elsewhere. Rather, they were subject to the same discourses and social and institutional forces that tended to position students in certain ways. From the theoretical perspective forwarded here, representation is inevitable. It is an artifact of the discursive processes through which teachers and students make sense of the social world, processes that operate at a level that is seemingly self-evident and taken for granted. Like the teachers and students in this study, we cannot operate outside of the meaning-making effects of discourses and our own social positioning. And although representations give the effect of fixing meaning, they are not deterministic and are subject to continual change and revision. Students' and educators' agency — the fact that we can and do take action as individuals — means that we are continually re-creating and reshaping notions of identity in the course of classroom interaction.

Because institutional representations are arguably at the heart of how entering students are placed and evaluated in college language programs, they have significant educational implications. U.S. high school graduates from minority language backgrounds are placed variously in college intensive English programs, ESOL academic skills sequences, regular composition programs, basic writing sequences, or academic assistance sequences depending on the specific practices of the postsecondary institution they enter. Institutional representations of language minority students — how students' non-English language backgrounds are construed by colleges and universities — affect the configuration of programs, placement measures and evaluation, and exit tests. This study lends support to Thesen's (1997) call for greater institutional and educator awareness of how students' identities are shaped by institutional labels. It also indicates a need to constantly reexamine how program configurations and placement measures are chosen, and what is taken for granted in those choices. This study also points out the need for TESOL educators to engage students in an explicit dialogue on how and why program and placement decisions are made. As the study concluded, such an effort was already underway in the community college ESOL program described here. Through ongoing discussions, the faculty had identified a need to explain the rationale for ESOL placement to long-term U.S. residents and citizens and to address students' heterogeneity in background, experience, and outlook more explicitly in the classroom. Instructors had also begun working to reorient their curriculum to better acknowledge and draw on the life experience and expertise brought by long-term U.S. residents and citizens into their classes.

This study dealt with particular students in particular contexts. Because "the contextual ground of education is always shifting" (Dyson, 1997, p. 179), the significance of case studies such as these lies not so much in specific prescriptions for practice as in their heuristic value—in the ongoing conversation they initiate regarding ESOL students' identity formation in educational settings and in their capacity to help us as TESOL professionals "attend to the world a bit differently" (p. 179). Understanding the nature of these fundamental processes of cultural identity formation is vital in order to recognize that we are never entirely immune from nor entirely subject to the societal positionings of ourselves or our students, and that things we do in the classroom not only serve to teach language but also serve to shape our students' attitudes toward schooling and their very sense of self.

ACKNOWLEDGMENTS

I would like to thank Claudia, Penny, Aeyfer, Hanh, and Marianne for their immeasurable help and guidance throughout the study and beyond. I am also grateful to the teachers and institutions described here for opening their classrooms and sharing their insights, to Ana Ramos-Pell for her assistance during the study, and to Bettie St. Pierre, Meryl Siegal, Joan Kelly Hall, and anonymous reviewers for comments on earlier drafts of the article.

NOTES

1. I use *ESOL* to refer to English language teaching and learning throughout this article, in keeping with usage where the study took place.

2. The study began with five case studies. One student eventually decided not to enroll in college. College data from a case study student who attended a different college are not included in this analysis.

3. All names are pseudonyms.

4. I thank Carol Chapelle for this insight.

5. Coding conventions are as follows: I = interview; FN = field notes; D = document. Extracts from documents are identified by subject (e.g., English, physics).

6. Although Penny's family was from Vietnam and Penny spoke Vietnamese, the family was ethnic Chinese and spoke Cantonese at home.

7. Gender, for example, seemed to play a significant role in the degree to which teachers sanctioned students' classroom behavior or used a caregiver register, for example.

REFERENCES

Alvermann, D. E., & Moore, D. W. (1996). Secondary school reading. In R. Barr, M. L. Kamil, P. Mosenthal, & P. D. Pearson (Eds.), *Handbook of reading research* (Vol. 2, pp. 951–983). Mahwah, NJ: Erlbaum.

Angélil-Carter, S. (1997). Second language acquisition of spoken and written English: Acquiring the skeptron. *TESOL Quarterly, 31,* 263–287.

Atkinson, D. (1999). TESOL and culture. *TESOL Quarterly, 33,* 625–654.

Auerbach, E. R. (1995). The politics of the ESL classroom: Issues of power in pedagogical choices. In J. W. Tollefson (Ed.), *Power and inequality in language education* (pp. 9–33). New York: Cambridge University Press.

Bogdan, R. C., & Biklen, S. K. (1998). *Qualitative research for education: An introduction to theory and methods.* Boston: Allyn & Bacon.

Bourdieu, P. (1977). Cultural reproduction and social reproduction. In J. Karabel & A. H. Halsey (Eds.), *Power and ideology in education* (pp. 487–511). New York: Oxford University Press.

Cummins, J. (1981). The role of primary language development in promoting educational success for language minority students. In California State Department of Education (Ed.), *Schooling and language minority students: A theoretical framework* (pp. 3–49). Los Angeles: California State University, Evaluation, Dissemination, and Assessment Center.

Cummins, J. (1997). Minority status and schooling in Canada. *Anthropology and Education Quarterly, 28,* 411–430.

Davidson, A. L. (1996). *Making and molding identity in schools: Student narratives on race, gender, and academic engagement.* Albany, NY: SUNY Press.

Davis, K. A. (1995). Qualitative theory and methods in applied linguistics research. *TESOL Quarterly, 29,* 427–453.

Duff, P. A., & Uchida, Y. (1997). The negotiation of teachers' sociocultural identities and practices in postsecondary EFL classrooms. *TESOL Quarterly, 31,* 451–486.

Dyson, A. H. (1997). Children out of bounds: The power of case studies in expanding visions of literacy development. In J. Flood, S. B. Heath, & D. Lapp (Eds.), *Handbook of research on teaching literacy through the communicative and visual arts* (pp. 167–180). New York: Simon & Schuster/Macmillan.

ESL Intersegmental Project. (1997). *California pathways: The second language student in public high schools, colleges, and universities.* Glendale: California TESOL.

Fairclough, N. (1995). *Critical discourse analysis: Papers in the critical study of language.* New York: Longman.

Faltis, C. J. (1993). Editor's introduction: Trends in bilingual education at the secondary school level. *Peabody Journal of Education, 69,* 1–5.

Faltis, C., & Wolfe, P. (Eds.). (1999). *So much to say: Adolescents and ESL.* New York: Teachers College Press.

Ferris, D. R. (1999). One size does not fit all: Response and revision issues for immigrant student writers. In L. Harklau, K. Losey, & M. Siegal (Eds.), *Language minority students, ESL, and college composition* (pp. 143–157). Mahwah, NJ: Erlbaum.

Firth, A., & Wagner, J. (1997). On discourse, communication, and (some) fundamental concepts in SLA research. *Modern Language Journal, 81,* 285–300.

Foucault, M. (1979). *Discipline and punish: The birth of the prison.* New York: Vintage Books.

Fu, D. (1995). *My trouble is my English: Asian students and the American dream.* Portsmouth, NH: Boynton/Cook.

Gray, M. J., Rolph, E., & Melamid, E. (1996). *Immigration and higher education: Institutional responses to changing demographics.* Santa Monica, CA: RAND.

Green, J., & Bloome, D. (1997). Ethnography and ethnographers of and in education: A situated perspective. In J. Flood, S. B. Heath, & D. Lapp (Eds.), *Handbook of research on teaching literacy through the communicative and visual arts* (pp. 181–202). New York: Simon & Schuster/Macmillan.

Hall, S. (1997). The work of representation. In S. Hall (Ed.), *Representation. Cultural representations and signifying practices* (pp. 13–64). London: Sage/Open University.

Harklau, L. (1994). ESL and mainstream classes: Contrasting second language learning contexts. *TESOL Quarterly, 28,* 241–272.

Harklau, L. (1999). Representing culture in the ESL writing classroom. In E. Hinkel (Ed.), *Culture in second language teaching and learning* (pp. 109–130). New York: Cambridge University Press.

Harklau, L., Losey, K., & Siegal, M. (Eds.). (1999). *Generation 1.5 meets college composition: Issues in the teaching of writing to U.S.-educated learners of English as a second language.* Mahwah, NJ: Erlbaum.

hooks, b. (1992). *Black looks: Race and representation.* Boston: South End Press.

Kubota, R. (1999). Japanese culture constructed by discourses: Implications for applied linguistics research and ELT. *TESOL Quarterly, 33,* 9–35.

Leki, I. (1995). Coping strategies of ESL students in writing tasks across the curriculum. *TESOL Quarterly, 29,* 235–260.

Leki, I. (2001). Hearing voices: L2 students' experiences in L2 writing courses. In T. Silva & P. K. Matsuda (Ed.), *On second language writing* (pp. 17–28). Mahwah, NJ: Erlbaum.

Leung, C., Harris, R., & Rampton, B. (1997). The idealised native speaker, reified ethnicities, and classroom realities. *TESOL Quarterly, 31,* 543–560.

Lucas, T. (1997). *Into, through, and beyond secondary school: Critical transitions for immigrant youths.* Washington, DC: Center for Applied Linguistics/Delta Systems.

Lucas, T., Henze, R., & Donato, R. (1990). Promoting the success of Latino language-minority students: An exploratory study of six high schools. *Harvard Educational Review, 60*, 315–340.

Mace-Matluck, B. J., Alexander-Kasparik, R., & Queen, R. M. (1998). *Through the golden door: Educational approaches for immigrant adolescents with limited schooling.* Washington, DC: Center for Applied Linguistics/Delta Systems.

McGroarty, M. (1985). Images of the learner in English language texts for adults: From citizen to consumer. *Issues in Education, 3*, 13–30.

McKay, S. L., & Wong, S. C. (1996). Multiple discourses, multiple identities: Investment and agency in second-language learning among Chinese adolescent immigrant students. *Harvard Educational Review, 66*, 577–608.

Mehan, H. (1993). Beneath the skin and between the ears: A case study in the politics of representation. In S. Chaiklin & J. Lave (Eds.), *Understanding practice: Perspectives on activity and context* (pp. 241–268). New York: Cambridge University Press.

Merriam, S. B. (1998). *Qualitative research and case study applications in education* (2nd ed.). San Francisco: Jossey-Bass.

Nayar, P. B. (1997). ESL/EFL dichotomy today: Language politics or pragmatics? *TESOL Quarterly, 31*, 9–37.

Norton, B. (1997). Language, identity, and the ownership of English. *TESOL Quarterly, 31*, 409–429.

Olneck, M. R. (1995). Immigrants and education. In J. A. Banks & C. A. M. Banks (Eds.), *Handbook of research on multicultural education* (pp. 310–327). New York: Macmillan.

Peirce, B. N. (1995). Social identity, investment, and language learning. *TESOL Quarterly, 29*, 9–31.

Ramanathan, V., & Atkinson, D. (1999). Ethnographic approaches and methods in L2 writing research: A critical guide and review. *Applied Linguistics, 20*, 44–70.

Rampton, B. (1995). *Crossing: Language and ethnicity among adolescents.* New York: Longman.

Rattansi, A. (1995). Just framing: Ethnicities and racisms in a "postmodern" framework. In L. Nicholson & S. Seidman (Eds.), *Social postmodernism: Beyond identity politics* (pp. 250–286). New York: Cambridge University Press.

Reid, J. M. (1997). Which non-native speaker? Differences between international students and U.S. resident (language minority) students. *New Directions for Teaching and Learning, 70*, 17–27.

Rosaldo, R. (1989). *Culture and truth: The remaking of social analysis.* Boston: Beacon Press.

Siegal, M. (1996). The role of learner subjectivity in second language sociolinguistic competency: Western women learning Japanese. *Applied Linguistics, 17*, 356–382.

Thesen, L. (1997). Voices, discourse, and transition: In search of new categories in EAP. *TESOL Quarterly, 31*, 487–512.

Tollefson, J. W. (1989). *Alien winds: The reeducation of America's Indochinese refugees.* New York: Praeger.

Toohey, K. (1998). "Breaking them up, taking them away": ESL students in Grade 1. *TESOL Quarterly, 32*, 61–84.

U.S. Department of Labor, Secretary's Commission on Achieving Necessary Skills. (1991). *What work requires of schools: A SCANS report for America 2000.* Washington, DC: U.S. Government Printing Office.

Van Maanen, J. (1995). An end to innocence: The ethnography of ethnography. In J. Van Maanen (Ed.), *Representation in ethnography* (pp. 1–35). Thousand Oaks, CA: Sage.

Vandrick, S. (1995). Privileged ESL university students. *TESOL Quarterly, 29*, 375–380.

Weedon, C. (1997). *Feminist practice and poststructuralist theory* (2nd ed.). Cambridge, MA: Blackwell.

Zamel, V. (1995). Strangers in academia: The experiences of faculty and ESL students across the curriculum. *College Composition and Communication, 46*, 506–521.

7 Becoming Black: Rap and Hip-Hop, Race, Gender, Identity, and the Politics of ESL Learning

AWAD EL KARIM M. IBRAHIM

The problem of the twentieth century is the problem of color-line," asserted Du Bois (1903, p. 13). If this is so, what are the implications of this prophetic statement for L2 learning and second language acquisition (SLA)? At the end of the 20th century, when identity formation is increasingly mediated by technological media, who learns what, and how is it learned? How do differently raced, gendered, sexualized, abled, and classed social identities enter the process of learning an L2? In a postcolonial era when postcolonial subjects constitute part of the metropolitan centers, what critical pedagogy is required in order not to repeat the colonial history embedded in the classroom relationship between White teachers and students of color? Finally, at a time when North American Blackness is governed by how it is negatively located in a race-conscious society, what does it mean for a Black ESL learner to acquire Black English as a second language (BESL)? In other words, what symbolic, cultural, pedagogical, and identity investments would learners have in locating themselves politically and racially at the margin of representation?

This article is an attempt to answer these questions. Conceptually, it is located at the borderline between two indistinguishable and perhaps never separable categories of critical discourses: race and gender. The article addresses the process of *becoming Black*, in which race is as vital as gender, and articulates a political and pedagogical research framework that puts at its center the social being as embodied subjectivities that are embedded in and performed through language, culture, history, and memory (Dei, 1996; Essed, 1991; Gilroy, 1987; Giroux & Simon, 1989; Ibrahim, 1998; Rampton, 1995). As an identity configuration, becoming Black is deployed to talk about the *subject-formation project* (i.e., the process and the space within which subjectivity is formed) that is produced in and simultaneously is produced by the process of language learning, namely, learning BESL. Put more concretely, becoming Black meant learning BESL, as I show in this article, yet the very process of

From *TESOL Quarterly* 33.3 (1999): 349–69.

BESL learning produced the epiphenomenon of becoming Black. I have argued elsewhere (Ibrahim, 1998) that to become is historical. Indeed, history and the way individuals experience it govern their identity, memory, ways of being, becoming, and learning (see also Foucault, 1979, pp. 170–184). To address questions of pedagogy in this context therefore requires attending to and being concerned with the linkages among the self, identity, desire, and the English(es) that students invest in.

BACKGROUND

This article is part of a larger ethnographic study (Ibrahim, 1998) that made use of the critical frames[1] just described and the newly developed methodological approach called *ethnography of performance*. The latter argues that social beings *perform* (Butler, 1990), at least in part, their subjectivities, identities, and desires in and through complex semiological languages, which include anything that cannot produce verbal utterances yet is ready to speak: the body, modes of dress, architecture, photography, and so on (see Barthes, 1967/1983; Halliday & Hasan, 1985). The research, which took place in an urban, French-language high school in southwestern Ontario, Canada, looks at the lives of a group of continental Francophone African youths[2] and the formation of their social identity. Besides their youth and refugee status, their gendered and raced experience was vital in their *moments of identification*: that is, where and how they saw themselves reflected in the mirror of their society (see also Bhabha, 1994). Put otherwise, once in North America, I contend, these youths were faced with a *social imaginary* (Anderson, 1983) in which they were already Blacks. This social imaginary was directly implicated in how and with whom they identified, which in turn influenced what they linguistically and culturally learned as well as how they learned it. What they learned, I demonstrate, is *Black stylized English* (BSE), which they accessed in and through Black popular culture. They learned by taking up and repositioning the rap linguistic and musical genre and, in different ways, acquiring and rearticulating the hip-hop cultural identity.

BSE is Black English (BE) with style; it is a subcategory. BE is what Smitherman (1994) refers to as *Black talk*, which has its own grammar and syntax (see Labov, 1972). BSE, on the other hand, refers to ways of speaking that do not depend on a full mastery of the language. It banks more on *ritual expressions* (see Rampton, 1995, for the idea of rituality) such as *whassup* (what is happening), *whadap* (what is happening), *whassup my Nigger*, and *yo, yo homeboy* (very cool and close friend), which are performed habitually and recurrently in rap. The rituals are more an expression of politics, moments of identification, and desire than they are of language or of mastering the language per se. It is a way of saying, "I too am Black" or "I too desire and identify with Blackness."

By Black popular culture, on the other hand, I refer to films, newspapers, magazines, and more importantly music such as rap, reggae, pop, and rhythm and blues (R&B). The term *hip-hop* comprises everything from music (especially rap) to clothing choice, attitudes, language, and an approach to culture and cultural artifacts, positing and collaging them in an unsentimental fashion (Walcott, 1995, p. 5). More skeletally, I use hip-hop to describe a way of dressing, walking, and talking. The dress refers to the myriad shades and shapes of the latest *fly gear*: high-top sneakers, bicycle shorts, chunky jewelry, baggy pants, and polka-dotted tops (Rose, 1991, p. 277). The hairstyles, which include high-fade designs, dreadlocks, corkscrews, and braids (Rose, 1991, p. 277) are also part of this fashion. *The walk* usually means moving the fingers simultaneously with the head and the rest of the body as one is walking. *The talk*, however, is BSE, defined above. Significantly, by patterning these behaviors African youths enter the realm of becoming Black. Hence, this article is about this process of becoming and how it is implicated in BSE learning.

In this process, the interlocking question of identification and desire is of particular interest. It asks the following: Who do we as social subjects living within a social space desire to be or to become? And whom do we identify with, and what repercussions does our identification have on how and what we learn? This question has already been dealt with in semiology (Barthes, 1967/1983; Eco, 1976; Gottdiener, 1995), psychoanalysis (Kristeva, 1974; Lacan, 1988), and cultural studies (Bhabha, 1994; Grossberg, Nelson, & Treichler, 1992; Hall, 1990; Mercer, 1994). I have not yet seen it raised, let alone incorporated seriously, in ESL and applied linguistics research. For instance, Goldstein (1987) focuses on the linguistic features of Black English as found in the speech of a group of Puerto Rican youths in New York City. However, she does not address the issue of what it means for Puerto Rican youths to learn Black English. What investment do they have in doing so? And what roles, if any, do race, desire, and identification have in the process of learning? Instead, Goldstein offers a very meticulous syntactico-morphological analysis. One approach does not rule out the other, but I strongly believe that it would be more fruitful for ESL pedagogy and that the nature of SLA would be better understood if both were located within a sociocultural context. Language, Bourdieu (1991) argues, has never been just an instrument of communication. It is also where power is formed and performed based on race, gender, sexuality, and social-class identity. My work differs from Goldstein's study in that it moves toward a cultural, political, and stylistic analysis.

In what follows, I discuss the research's guiding propositions, contentions, and questions and look at how I as the researcher am implicated in the research and the questions I ask. This is followed by a description of the methodology, site, and subject of my research. I then offer examples of African youths' speech in which BSE can be detected to demonstrate the interplay between subject formation, identification, and BESL learning. I also offer students' reflections and narratives on the impact of identification on becoming Black. Centralizing their everyday experience of identity, I conclude with some critical pedagogical (Corson, 1997; Peirce, 1989; Pennycook, 1994) and didactic propositions on the connections between investment, subjectivity, and ESL learning. Beginning with the premise that ESL learning is locality, I ask the following: If local identity is the site where we as teachers and researchers should start our praxis and research formulations (Morgan, 1997; Norton, 1997; Rampton, 1995), then I would contend that any pedagogical input that does not link the political, the cultural, and the social with identity and, in turn, with the process of ESL learning is likely to fail.

My central working contention was that, once in North America, continental African youths enter a *social imaginary*: a discursive space or a representation in which they are already constructed, imagined, and positioned and thus are treated by the hegemonic discourses and dominant groups, respectively, as Blacks. Here I address the White (racist) everyday communicative state of mind: "Oh, they all look like Blacks to me!" This positionality, which is offered to continental African youths through netlike praxis[3] in exceedingly complex and mostly subconscious ways, does not acknowledge the differences in the students' ethnicities, languages, nationalities, and cultural identities. Fanon (1967) sums up this netlike praxis brilliantly in writing about himself as a Black *Antillais* coming to the metropolis of Paris: "I am given no chance, I am overdetermined from without. . . . And *already* [italics added] I am being dissected under White eyes, the only real eyes. I am *fixed* [italics added]. Having adjusted their microtomes, they objectively cut away slices of my reality" (p. 116).

In other words, continental African youths find themselves in a racially conscious society that, wittingly or unwittingly and through fused social mechanisms such as racisms and representations, asks them to racially fit somewhere. To fit somewhere signifies choosing or becoming aware of one's own being, which is partially reflected in one's language practice. Choosing is a question of agency; that is, by virtue of being a subject, one has room to maneuver one's own desires and choices. That is, although social subjects may count their desires and choices as their own, these choices are disciplined (Foucault, 1979) by the social conditions under which the subjects live. For example, to be Black in a racially conscious society, like the Euro-Canadian and U.S. societies, means that one is expected to be Black, act Black, and so be the marginalized Other (Hall, 1991; hooks, 1992). Under such disciplinary social conditions, as I will show, continental African youths express their moments of identification in relation to African Americans and African American cultures and languages, thus becoming Black. That they take up rap and hip-hop and speak BSE is by no means a coincidence. On the contrary, these actions are articulations of the youths' desire to belong to a location, a politics, a memory, a history, and hence a representation.

Being is being distinguished here from *becoming*. The former is an accumulative memory, an experience, and a conception upon which individuals interact with the world around them, whereas the latter is the process of building this conception. For example, as a continental African, I was not considered Black in Africa; other terms served to patch together my identity, such as *tall*, *Sudanese*, and *basketball player*. However, as a refugee in North America, my perception of self was altered in direct response to the social processes of racism and the historical representation of Blackness whereby the antecedent signifiers became secondary to my Blackness, and I retranslated myself: I became Black.

METHOD

Site

Between January and June 1996, I conducted a critical ethnographic research project[4] at Marie-Victorin (MV),[5] a small Franco-Ontarian intermediate and high school (Grades 7–13). MV had a school population of approximately 389 students from various ethnic, racial, cultural, religious, and linguistic backgrounds. Although it is a French-language school, the language spoken by students in the school corridors and hallways was predominately English; Arabic, Somali, and Farsi were also spoken at other times. The school had 27 teachers, all of whom were White. The school archives show that until the beginning of the 1990s, students were also almost all White, except for a few students of African (read Black) and Middle Eastern descent.

For over 6 months, I attended classes at MV, talked to students, and observed curricular and extracurricular activities two or three times per week. Because of previous involvement in another project in the same school for almost 2 years, at the time of this research I was well acquainted with MV and its population, especially its African students, with whom I was able to develop a good relationship.

Being the only Black adult with the exception of one counselor and being a displaced subject, a refugee, and an African myself had given me a certain familiarity with the students' experiences. I was able to connect with different age and gender groups through a range of activities, initially "hanging out"[6] with the students and later playing sports with various groups. I was also approached by these students for both personal guidance and academic help. Because of my deep involvement in the student culture, at times my status as researcher was forgotten, and the line between the students and myself became blurred; clearly, we shared a safe space of comfort that allowed us to speak and engage freely. This research was as much about the youths themselves and their narration of their experiences as it was about my own; in most cases, the language itself was unnecessary to understand the plight of the youths and their daily encounters, both within MV and outside its walls.

Significantly, at the time of this research, students (or their parents) who were born outside Canada made up 70% of the entire school population at MV. Continental Africans constituted the majority within that figure and, indeed, within MV's population in general, although their numbers fluctuated slightly from year to year. However, with the exception of one temporary Black counselor, there was not one teacher or administrator of color at the school. Despite this fact, the school continued to emphasize the theme of unity within this multicultural and multiethnoracial population. The slogan that the school advertised, for instance, was *unité dans la diversité* (unity in diversity). This discourse of unity, however, remained at the level of abstraction and had little material bearing on the students' lives; it was the Frenchness of the school that seemed to be the capital of its promotion. That is, the French language, especially in Canada, represents a form of extremely important *symbolic capital*, which, according to Bourdieu (1991), can be the key for accessing *material capital*—jobs, business, and so on. Given their postcolonial educational history, most African youths in fact come to Franco-Ontarian schools already possessing a highly valued form of symbolic capital: *le français parisien* (Parisian French).

Participants and Procedure

My research subjects encompassed these youths and part of a growing French-speaking continental African population in Franco-Ontarian schools, which I refer to as *Black Franco-Ontarians*. Their numbers have grown exponentially since the beginning of the 1990s. The participants varied, first, in their length of stay in Canada (from 1–2 to 5–6 years); second, in their legal status (some were immigrants, but the majority were refugees); and, third, in their gender, class, age, linguistic, and national background. They came from places as diverse as Democratic Republic of Congo (formerly Zaire), Djibouti, Gabon, Senegal, Somalia, South Africa, and Togo. With no exception, all the African students in MV were at least trilingual, speaking English, French, and a mother tongue or L1,[7] with various (postcolonial) histories of language learning and degrees of fluency in each language.

On my return to MV in January 1996 to conduct my research, I spent the first month talking to and spending time with male and female African youths of different age groups, with their permission as well as their parents' and the school administration's. I attended classes, played basketball, volleyball, and indoor soccer, and generally spent time with the students. After a month, I chose 7 boys and 5 girls (see Table 1) for extensive ethnographic observation inside and outside the classroom and inside and outside the school and interviewed all 16. Of the 7 boys, 6 were Somali speakers (from Somalia and Djibouti), and 1 was Ethiopian. Their ages ranged from 16 to 20 years. The 5 girls were all Somali speakers (also from Somalia and Djibouti), aged 14 to 18 years.

I conducted individual interviews as well as two focus-group interviews, one with the boys and one with the girls. All interviews were conducted on the school grounds, with the exception of the boys' focus-group interview, which took place in one of the student residences. The students chose the language in which the interviews were conducted: Some chose English, but the majority chose French. I translated these interviews into English. The only Black counselor and the former Black teacher were also interviewed. The interviews were closely transcribed and analyzed. I consulted school documents and archives and occasionally videotaped cultural and sport activities; on two occasions, I gave tape recorders to students in order to capture their interactions among themselves (Rampton, 1995).

TABLE 1. Background of Participants Quoted in the Article

Name	Gender	Age	Grade	Country of Origin	Other Information
Amani	F	16	11	Somalia	Very active politically and culturally; organized Black History Month activities and wrote a theatrical play for the occasion; did not hesitate to speak her mind even before the highest official in the school's administration
Asma	F	16	11	Djibouti	Was considered one of the beauties of the school; was one of the school's most popular students; was proud of her mastery of French
Aziza	F	18	13	Somalia	Had a sister and two brothers at MV; came from a well-to-do, almost bourgeois family
Hassan	M	17	12	Djibouti	Although born in Ethiopia, presented himself as a Djiboutian as he grew up in Djibouti; was politically active; was considered by school administration and peers as an elder; received several social and academic awards
Jamal	M	18	12	Djibouti	Had dropped out of school for a period of time; at the time of the interview was holding a job while going to school part-time; was host of a local radio show airing rap in English and French
Juma	M	19	12	Senegal	Lived in the house where the focus-group interview with the boys was conducted; learned the Somali language by living with Somali students
Mukhi	M	19	12	Djibouti	Was quiet but held strong opinions; was one of the school's best basketball players
Najat	F	14	9	Djibouti	Came to Canada when she was 8 years old; lived with her single mother and her sister, who used to attend MV but transferred to an English-language school

TABLE 1.   (Continued)

Name	Gender	Age	Grade	Country of Origin	Other Information
Omer	M	18	12	Ethiopia	As an elder, spoke on behalf of African students before the school administration; was sought out for guidance by students
Sam	M	19	12	Djibouti	Had been at the school since Grade 7; was considered the "Michael Jordan" of the basketball team and "the rapper" of the school
Samira	F	16	11	Djibouti	Was popular; organized a fashion show
Shapir	M	17	12	Somalia	Had dropped out of school for one term; was taking advanced courses while enrolled in a co-op program

FINDINGS

Becoming Tri- or Multilingual: Sites and Sides of ESL Learning

Most Francophone African youths come to a Canadian English-speaking metropolis, such as Vancouver or Winnipeg, because their parents happen to have relatives in that city. I asked Hassan why his parents had considered moving to an English-speaking city as opposed to Quebec, a French-speaking province.

> First of all, we had relatives who were here. Yes, secondly, because there is French and English. It is more the relative question because you know when you go to a new country, there is a tendency to go towards the people you know. Because you don't want to adventure in the unknown; and you can't have, you also want to get help, all the help possible to succeed better. (individual interview, French)[8]

In this context, in which English is the medium of everyday interaction, African youths are compelled or expected to speak English in order to be understood and in order to perform simple daily functions like negotiating public transport and buying groceries. In the following excerpt, Aziza recounts her early days, when her competence in speaking English was limited:

> If I want to go to the boutique, I have to speak to the guy [she called him *monsieur*] in English because he doesn't speak French. If I go to the shop to buy clothes, I have to speak in English, you see. It is something that you have to do; you have to force yourself. In the early days, I used to go with my sister because my sister spoke English. So I always took her

with me. Then I had to go by myself because she was not always going to be by my side. I had to speak, I had to learn to speak English so I can help myself, and I can you know, I can deal with anything, you see. So, in other words, you are obliged, it is something you can't escape from. Because the society is Anglophone, the country is Anglophone, the services are in English, you see, that's why. (individual interview, French)

For the youths, the inescapability of interacting in English translates into a will to learn English rapidly. Popular culture, especially television, friendship, and peer pressure, all hasten the speed of learning. The African students felt peer pressure especially in their early days in the school, when they were denigrated for not speaking English. Franco-Ontarian students, Heller (1992, 1994) explains, use English in their everyday interaction, especially outside class. If African students want to participate in schoolwide as well as in- and out-of-class activities, they have no option but to learn English. Once learned, English becomes as much a source of pride as it is a medium of communication, as Asma explained:

If you don't speak English, like in my Grade 7, "Oh, she doesn't speak! Oh, we are sorry, you can explain to her, she doesn't understand English, *la petite.*[9] Can you?" They think that we are really stupid, that we are retarded, that we don't understand the language. Now I know English, I speak it all the time. I show them that I understand English [laughs], I show them that I do English. <u>Oh, I got it, it gives me great pleasure.</u>[10] (group interview, French)

Asma addresses, first, the teacher's condescending manner of speech on realizing that Asma did not speak English. Undoubtedly, this condescension leads to more pressure on Asma and African students in general to learn English. Secondly, her narrative addresses the threshold desire of a teenager who wants to fully participate in dominant markets and public spaces. Her inability to speak English, which would allow her to make friends, obstructs full participation. Yet making friends, and even learning English, is influenced by the popular imaginary, representation, and culture: television. I asked students in all of the interviews, "Où est-ce que vous avez appris votre anglais?" (Where did you learn English?). "Télévision," they all responded. However, within this *télévision* is a particular representation—Black popular culture—seems to *interpellate*[11] (Althusser, 1971) African youths' identity and identification. Because African youths have few African American friends and have limited daily contact with them, they access Black cultural identities and Black linguistic practice in and through Black popular culture, especially rap music videos, television programs, and Black films. Following is a response to my query about the last movies a student had seen:

NAJAT: I don't know, I saw *Waiting to Exhale* and I saw what else I saw, I saw *Swimmer*, and I saw *Jumanji*; so wicked, all the movies. I went to *Waiting to Exhale* wid my boyfriend and I was like "men are rude" [laughs].

ASMA: Oh believe me I know I know.

NAJAT: And den he [her boyfriend] was like, "no, women are rude." I was like we're like fighting you know and joking around. I was like, and de whole time like [laughs], and den when de woman burns the car, I was like, "go girl!" You know and all the women are like, "go girl!" you know? And den de men like khhh. I'm like, "I'm gonna go get me a popcorn" [laughs]. (individual interview, English)

Besides showing the influence of Black English in the use of *de, den, dat,* and *wicked* as opposed to, respectively, *the, then, that,* and *really really good,* Najat's answer shows that youths bring agency and social subjectivities to the reading of a text. These subjectivities, importantly, are embedded in history, culture, and memory. Two performed subjectivities that influenced Najat's reading of *Waiting to Exhale* were her race and gender identities. Najat identified with Blackness embodied in a female body; the Black/woman in burning her husband's car and clothes interpellates Najat.

Another example in a different context demonstrates the impact of Black popular culture on African students' lives and identities. Just before the focus-group interview with the boys, *Electric Circus*, a local television music and dance program that plays mostly Black music (rap/hip-hop, reggae, soul, and rhythm and blues) began. "Silence!" one boy requested in French. The boys started to listen attentively to the music and watch the fashions worn by the young people on the program. After the show, the boys' code switched among French, English, and Somali as they exchanged observations on the best music, the best dance, and the cutest girl. Rap and hip-hop music and the corresponding dress were obviously at the top of the list.

The moments of identification in the above examples are significant in that they point to the process of identity formation that is implicated in turn in the linguistic norm to be learned. The Western hegemonic representations of Blackness, Hall (1990) shows, are negative and tend to work alongside historical and subconscious memories that facilitate their interpretations by members of the dominant groups. Once African youths encounter these negative representations, they look for Black cultural and representational forms as sites for positive identity formation and identification (Kelly, 1998). An important aspect of identification is that it works over a period of time and at the subconscious level. In the following excerpt, Omer addresses the myriad ways in which African youths are influenced by Black representations.

Black Canadian youths are influenced by the Afro-Americans. You watch for hours, you listen to Black music, you watch Black comedy, Mr. T,[12] the *Rap City*, there you will see singers who dress in particular ways. You see, so. (individual interview, French)

Mukhi explored the contention of identification by arguing that

We identify ourselves more with the Blacks of America. But, this is normal, this is genetic. We can't, since we live in Canada, we can't identify ourselves with Whites or country music, you know [laughs]. We are going to identify ourselves on the contrary with people of our color, who have our lifestyle, you know. (group interview, French)

Mukhi evokes biology and genetic connection as a way of relating to Black America, and his identification with it is clearly stated. For all the students I spoke to, this identification was certainly connected to their inability to relate to dominant groups, the public spaces they occupied, and their cultural forms and norms. Black popular culture emerged as an alternative site not only for identification but also for language learning.

"A'ait, Q7 in the House!"[13]

For the students I interviewed, rap was an influential site for language learning. The fact that rap linguistic performance was more prevalent in the boys' narratives than in the girls' raises the question of the role of gender in the process of identification and learning.

On many occasions, the boys performed typical gangster rap language and style, using language as well as movement, including name calling. What follows are just two of the many occasions on which students articulated their identification with Black America through the recitation of rap linguistic styles.

SAM: One two, one two, mic check. A'ait [aayet], a'ait, a'ait.

JUMA: This is the rapper, you know wha 'm meaning? You know wha 'm saying?

SAM: Mic mic mic; mic check. A'ait you wonna test it? Ah, I've the microphone you know; a'ait.

SAM: [laughs] I don't rap man, c'mon give me a break. [laughs] Yo! A'ait a'ait you know, we just about to finish de tape and all dat. Respect to my main man [pointing to me]. So, you know, you know wha 'm mean, 'm just represen'in Q7. One love to Q7 you know wha 'm mean and all my friends back to Q7 . . . Stop the tapin' boy!

JAMAL: Kim Juma, live! Put the lights on. Wardap. [students talking in Somali] Peace out, wardap, where de book. Jamal 'am outa here.

SHAPIR: Yo, this is Shapir. I am trying to say peace to all my Niggers, all my bitches from a background that everybody in the house. So, yo, chill out and this is how we gonna kick it. Bye and with that pie. All right, peace yo.

SAM: A'ait, this is Sam represen'in AQA [. . .] where it's born, represen'in you know wha 'm mean? I wonna say whassup to all my Niggers, you know, peace and one love. You know wha 'm mean, Q7 represen'in for ever. Peace! [rap music]

JAMAL: [as a DJ] Crank it man, coming up. [rap music] (group interview, English)

Of interest in these excerpts is the use of BSE, particularly the language of rap: "respect to my main man," "represen'in Q7," "peace out, wardap," "'am outa here," "I am trying to say peace to all my Niggers, all my bitches," "so, yo, chill out and this is how we gonna kick it," "I wonna say whassup to all my Niggers," "peace and one love." On the other hand, when Shapir offers "peace to all" his "Niggers," all his "bitches," he is first reappropriating the word *Nigger* as an appellation that is common in rap/hip-hop culture. That is, friends, especially young people, commonly call a Black friend *Nigger* without its traditional racist connotation. Second, however, Shapir is using the sexist language that might exist in rap (Rose, 1991). These forms of sexism have been challenged by female rappers like Queen Latifa and Salt-N-Pepa and were critiqued by female and male students. For example, Samira expressed her dismay at the sexist language found in some rap circles:

> OK, hip-hop, yes I know that everyone likes hip-hop. They dress in a certain way, no? The songs go well. But, they are really really, they have expressions like fuck, bitches, etc. Sorry, but there is representation. (group interview, French)

Here, Samira addresses the impact that these expressions might have on the way society at large perceives the Black female body, which in turn influences how it is represented both inside and outside, rap/hip-hop culture. Hassan as well expressed his disapproval of this abusive language: "Occasionally, rap has an inappropriate language for the life in which we live, a world of violence and all that" (individual interview, French).

In rap style, one starts a performance by "checking the mic": "One two, one two, mic check." Then the rapper either recites an already composed lyric or otherwise "kicks a freestyle," displaying the spontaneity that characterizes rap. The rapper begins the public performance by introducing herself or himself with a true or made-up name ("Yo, this is Shapir") and thanking her or his "main man," or best friend, who often introduces the rapper to the public. Specific to gangster rap, one represents not only oneself but a web of geophysical and metaphorical spaces and collectivities that are demarcated by people and territorial spaces: "represen'in Q7," "a'ait, this is Sam represen'in AQA." At the end of the performance, when the recitation or freestyle is completed, again one thanks the "main man" and "gives peace out" or "shad out" (shouts out) to the people.

The boys were clearly influenced by rap lyrics, syntax, and morphology (in their broader semiological sense), especially by gangster rap. In learning ESL in general and BSE in particular through music, Jamal used significant strategies, including listening, reading, and repeating: He was listening to the tunes and lyrics while reading and following the written text. Acting as a DJ, he then repeated not only the performer's words and expressions but also his accent.

Depending on their age, the girls, on the other hand, had an ambivalent relationship with rap, although they used the same strategies as Jamal in learning English through music. For example, during a picnic organized by a group of males and females, the females listened to music while following the written text and reciting it (complete with accents) along with the singer. The girls' choice of music (including songs performed by Whitney Houston and Toni Braxton) differed in that it was softer than that chosen by the boys and contained mostly romantic themes.

For the most part, the older females (16–18 years old) tended to be more eclectic than the younger ones in how they related to hip-hop and rap. Their eclecticism was evident in how they dressed and in what language they learned. Their dress was either elegant middle class, partially hip-hop, or traditional, and their learned language was what Philip (1991) calls *plain Canadian English*. The younger females (12–14 years old), on the other hand, like the boys, dressed in hiphop style and performed BSE.

In spite of their ambivalent relationship to rap and hip-hop, I detected the following three features of BE in both the older and the younger girls' speech:

1. the absence of the auxiliary *be* (19 occasions, e.g., "they so cool" and "I just laughing" as opposed to *they are so cool* and *I am just laughing*);

2. BE negative concord (4 occasions; e.g., "all he [the teacher] cares about is his daughter you know. If somebody just dies or if I decide to shoot somebody you know, he is *not* doing *nothing* [italics added]"; the expression would be considered incorrect in standard English because of the double negative); and

3. the distributive *be* (4 occasions, e.g., "I be saying dis dat you know?" or "He be like 'Oh, *elle va être bien*' [she's going to be fine]").

These BE markers are both expressions of the influence of Black talk on the girls' speech and performances of the girls' identity location and desire, which they apparently ally with Blackness. (For a description of BE features, see Goldstein, 1987; Labov, 1972.)

Performing Acts of Desire

I have identified rap and hip-hop as influential sites in African students' processes of becoming Black, which in turn affected what and how the students learned. Their narratives also show that the youths were quite cognizant of their identification with Blackness and the impact of race on their choices. In the following conversation, Mukhi reflected on the impact of rap (as just one among many other Black popular cultural forms) on his life and the lives of those around him:

> AWAD: But do you listen to rap, for example? I noticed that there are a number of students who listen to rap eh? Is . . .
>
> SAM: It is not just us who listen to rap, everybody listens to rap. It is new.
>
> AWAD: But do you think that that influences how you speak, how . . .
>
> MUKHI: *How we dress, how we speak, how we behave* [italics added]. (group interview, English)

The linguistic patterns and dress codes that Mukhi addresses are accessed and learned by African youths through Black popular culture. As I have noted, these patterns and codes do not require mastery and fluency. Indeed, they are performative acts of desire and identification. As Amani contended,

We have to wonder why we try to really follow the model of the Americans who are Blacks. Because *when you search for yourself, search for identification, you search for someone who reflects you, with whom you have something in common* [italics added]. (group interview, French)

Hassan supported Amani as follows:

HASSAN: Yes yes, African students are influenced by rap and hip-hop because they want to, yes, they are influenced probably a bit more because it is the desire to belong may be.

AWAD: Belong to what?

HASSAN: To a group, belong to a society, to have a model/fashion [he used the term *un modèle*]; you know, the desire to mark oneself, the desire to make, how do I say it? To be part of a rap society, you see. It is like getting into rock and roll or heavy metal. (individual interview, French)

Hence, *one invests where one sees oneself mirrored.* Such an investment includes linguistic as well as cultural behavioral patterns. In an individual interview, Hassan told me it would be unrealistic to expect to see Blackness allied with rock and roll or heavy metal, as they are socially constructed as White music. On the other hand, he argued emphatically that African youths had every reason to invest in basketball—which is constructed as a Black sport—but not hockey, for example.

CONCLUSION: IDENTITY, DISCIPLINE, AND PEDAGOGY

Analogously, the desire on the part of African youths, particularly the boys, to invest (Norton, 1997) in basketball is no different from their desire to learn BESL. Learning is hence neither aimless nor neutral, nor is it free of the politics of identity. As I have shown, an L2 learner can have a marginalized linguistic norm as a target. But why would these youths choose the margin as a target? What is their investment and politics in doing so? And what role, if any, do race, gender (sexuality), and differences in social class play in their choices? In other words, if youths come to the classrooms as embodied subjectivities that are embedded in history and memory (Dei, 1996), should we as teachers not couple their word with their world (Freire, 1970/1993)?

Clearly, my perspective is an interdisciplinary one that may have raised more questions than it has satisfactorily answered. However, my intention has been to ask new questions that link identity, pedagogy, politics, investment, desire, and the process of ESL learning by borrowing from cultural studies. I have discussed how a group of continental African youths were becoming Black, which meant learning BESL. Becoming Black, I have argued, was an identity signifier produced by and producing the very process of BESL. To become Black is to become an ethnographer who translates and looks around in an effort to understand what it means to be Black in Canada, for example. In becoming Black, the African youths were interpellated by Black popular cultural forms, rap and hip-hop, as sites of identification. Gender, however, was as important as race in what was being chosen and translated, and by whom and how it was chosen and translated.

Choosing the margin, I emphasize, is simultaneously an act of investment, an expression of desire, and a deliberate counterhegemonic undertaking. The choice of rap especially must be read as an act of resistance. Historically, rap has been formed as a voice for voicelessness and performed as a prophetic language that addresses silence, the silenced, and the state of being silenced. It explores the hopes and the human, political, historical, and cultural experience of the *Black Atlantic* (Gilroy, 1993). As Jamal argued,

> Black Americans created rap to express themselves; how do I say it? Their ideas, their problems, [and] if we could integrate ourselves into it, it is because rappers speak about or they have the same problems we have. (individual interview, French)

Such problems may include human degradation, police brutality, and everyday racism (Anthias & Yuval-Davis, 1992; Essed, 1991).

If learning is an engagement of one's identity, a fulfillment of personal needs and desires (of being), and an investment in what is yet to come, any proposed ESL pedagogy, research, or praxis that fails to culminate in these will quite obviously not draw in the youths described in this article and is therefore bound to be unsuccessful, if not plainly damaging. Identity, as re- and preconfigured here, governs what ESL learners acquire and how they acquire it. What is learned linguistically is not and should not be dissociable from the political, the social, and the cultural. Hence, to learn is to invest in something (e.g., BESL) that has a personal or a particular significance to who one is or what one has become. Because language is never neutral, learning it cannot and should not be either. Thus we as teachers must, first, identify the different sites in which our students invest their identities and desires and, second, develop materials that engage our students' raced, classed, gendered, sexualized, and abled identities.

I therefore identify and propose rap and hip-hop (and Black popular culture in general) as curriculum sites where learning takes place and where identities are invested. In the language of antiracism education (Dei, 1996; hooks, 1994), this proposition is, on the one hand, a call to centralize and engage marginalized subjects, their voices, and their ways of being and learning and, on the other, a revisit to this question: In the case of African youths, whose language and identity are we as TESOL professionals teaching and assuming in the classroom if we do not engage rap and hip-hop? That is, whose knowledge is being valorized and legitimated and thus assumed to be worthy of study, and whose knowledge and identity are left in the corridors of our schools? To identify rap and hip-hop as curriculum sites in this context is to legitimize otherwise illegitimate forms of knowledge. As Bourdieu (1991) shows, wittingly or unwittingly, schools sanction certain identities and accept their linguistic norm by doing nothing more than assuming them to be the norm; we as teachers should remember that these identities are raced, classed, sexualized, and gendered.

However, because rap and hip-hop are also historical and social productions, they are as much sites of critique as they are sites of hope. As noted, rap and hip-hop are not immune to, for example, sexism (and homophobia; see also Rose, 1991). Therefore, they should not be readily consumed but should be critically framed, studied, and engaged with. To be able to do so, however, teachers need first to be in tune with popular culture, for television, music, newspapers, and other media—not the classroom—are increasingly the sources from which students learn English. Second, teachers who are unfamiliar with popular culture should engage the Freireian notion of *dialecticism*, in which their students can become their teachers. In practical terms, this might mean planning activities in which students explain to the teacher and to the rest of the class what rap and hip-hop are and what they represent to the students.

Rap and hip-hop are also sites of hope and possibility: the hope that all learners (from dominant groups or others) can be introduced to and be able to see multiple ways of speaking, being, and learning. In the case of African students, in particular, rap and hip-hop are sites of identification and investment. To introduce them in the classroom, to paraphrase Freire (1970/1993), is to hope to link their world, identities, and desires with their word. To put it more broadly, maybe the time has come to close the split between minority students' identities and the school curriculum and between those identities and classroom pedagogies, subjects, and materials.

ACKNOWLEDGMENTS

I thank Loreli Buenaventura, Alastair Pennycook, and the anonymous reviewers for their comments and feedback.

NOTES

1. Although I do not directly cite them, my work is greatly influenced by other critical discourses, especially postcolonial (see Ashcroft, Griffiths, & Tiffin, 1995) and cultural studies (see Grossberg, Nelson, & Treichler, 1992). In fact, I see this article as a hopeful inauguration of a long dialogic journey between the encompassing field of cultural studies and the fields of ESL, applied linguistics, and SLA.

2. By *continental African*, I mean Africans from the continent Africa, as opposed to *diasporic African* (the populace of African descent that does not live in Africa, e.g., African Americans). I use *youths* interchangeably with *students, boys, girls, males*, and *females*, given their arbitrary nature as a social construct.

3. I understand *praxis* as a moment, a borderland of the intersection of discourse, action, and representations (Freire, 1970/1993, chap. 3). These representations and borderlands are mutually dependent and shoulder one another to create a web of meaning that can be deciphered only when all the strings are pulled together.

4. For Simon and Dippo (1986, p. 195), *critical ethnographic research* is a set of activities situated within a project that seeks and works its way towards social transformation. This project is political as well as pedagogical, and who the researcher is and what his or her racial, gender, and class embodiments are necessarily govern the research questions and findings. The project, then, according to Simon and Dippo, is "an activity determined both by real and present conditions, *and* certain conditions still to come which it is trying to bring into being" (p. 196). The assumption underpinning my project was based on the assertion that Canadian society is "inequitably structured and dominated by a hegemonic culture that suppresses a consideration and understanding of why things are the way they are and what must be done for things to be otherwise" (p. 196).

5. All names are pseudonyms.

6. Staying somewhere to familiarize oneself with the place, its people, and their ways of being in that space. In the school, these sites are informal, such as hallways, the schoolyard, the school steps, the cafeteria, and the gymnasium, where the people in them are comfortable enough to speak their minds.

7. *Mother tongue* is the first-acquired language whereas L1 is the language of greatest mastery. One's mother tongue can be one's L1, but one can also have an L1 that is not one's mother tongue. This is quite common in postcolonial situations.

8. Each extract is followed by the type of interview (individual or group) and the language in which it was conducted. The following transcription conventions are used:

underlined text	English spoken within French speech or French spoken within English speech
[ ]	Explanation or description of speaker's actions
[. . .]	Text omitted

9. A disparaging expression commonly used to patronize and belittle.

10. In another context, Asma argued that one reason for wanting to speak English is that "I didn't want people talking behind my back. I wanted to so badly learn English to show them that I could do it [laughs]. And to speak English like they do. And I am really really I'm happy I did that. I'm very proud of myself" (group interview, French).

11. The subconscious ways in which individuals, given their genealogical history and memory, identify with particular discursive spaces and representations and the way this identification participates hereafter in the social formation of the Subject (identity).

12. Host of a local rap music television program called *Rap City*, which airs mostly U.S. rap lyrics.

13. *A'ait* = all right; *Q7* = the clique to which the students belong; *in the house* = present.

REFERENCES

Althusser, L. (1971). *Lenin and philosophy and other essays*. London: New Left Books.
Anderson, B. (1983). *Imagined communities: Reflections on the origin and spread of nationalism*. London: Verso.
Anthias, F., & Yuval-Davis, N. (1992). *Racialized boundaries*. London: Routledge.
Ashcroft, B., Griffiths, G., & Tiffin, H. (Eds.). (1995). *The postcolonial studies reader*. New York: Routledge.
Barthes, R. (1983). *Elements of semiology*. New York: Hill & Wang. (Original work published 1967)
Bhabha, H. (1994). *The location of culture*. London: Routledge.
Bourdieu, P. (1991). *Language and symbolic power* (G. Raymond & M. Adamson, Trans.). Cambridge: Polity Press.
Butler, J. (1990). *Gender trouble: Feminism and the subversion of identity*. New York: Routledge.
Corson, D. (1997). Critical realism: An emancipatory philosophy of applied linguistics? *Applied Linguistics, 18*, 166–188.
Dei, G. J. S. (1996). *Anti-racism education: Theory and practice*. Halifax, Canada: Fernwood.
Du Bois, W. E. B. (1903). *The souls of black folk*. New York: Penguin Books.
Eco, U. (1976). *A theory of semiotics*. Bloomington: Indiana University Press.
Essed, P. (1991). *Understanding everyday racism*. Newbury Park, CA: Sage.
Fanon, F. (1967). *Black skin, white masks*. New York: Grove Weidenfeld.
Foucault, M. (1979). *Discipline and punish: The birth of the prison* (A. Sheridan, Trans.). New York: Vintage Books.
Freire, P. (1993). *Pedagogy of the oppressed*. New York: Continuum. (Original work published 1970)
Gilroy, P. (1987). *There ain't no black in the Union Jack: The cultural politics of race and nation*. London: Hutchinson.
Gilroy, P. (1993). *The Black Atlantic: Modernity and double consciousness*. London: Routledge.
Giroux, H. A., & Simon, R. (1989). Popular culture as a pedagogy of pleasure and meaning. In H. A. Giroux & R. Simon (Eds.), *Popular culture, schooling, and everyday life* (pp. 1–29). Boston: Bergin & Garvey.
Goldstein, L. (1987). Standard English: The only target for nonnative speakers of English? *TESOL Quarterly, 21*, 417–438.
Gottdiener, M. (1995). *Postmodern semiotics*. Oxford: Blackwell.
Grossberg, L., Nelson, C., & Treichler, P. (Eds.). (1992). *Cultural studies*. New York: Routledge.
Hall, S. (1990). Cultural identity and diaspora. In J. Rutherford (Ed.), *Identity, community, culture, difference* (pp. 222–237). London: Lawrence & Wishart.

Hall, S. (1991). Ethnicity: Identity and difference. *Radical America, 13*(4), 9–20.

Halliday, M. A. K., & Hasan, R. (1985). *Language, context, and text: Aspects of language in a social-semiotic perspective*. Oxford: Oxford University Press.

Heller, M. (1992). The politics of codeswitching and language choice. *Journal of Multilingual and Multicultural Development, 13*, 123–142.

Heller, M. (1994). *Crosswords: Language, education and ethnicity in French Ontario*. Berlin: Mouton de Gruyter.

hooks, b. (1992). *Black looks*. Boston: South End Press.

hooks, b. (1994). *Teaching to transgress: Education as the practice of freedom*. London: Routledge.

Ibrahim, A. (1998). *"Hey, whassup homeboy?" Becoming black: Race, language, culture, and the politics of identity. African students in a Franco-Ontarian high school*. Unpublished doctoral dissertation, Ontario Institute for Studies in Education of the University of Toronto, Canada.

Kelly, J. (1998). *Under the gaze: Learning to be Black in White society*. Halifax, Canada: Fernwood.

Kristeva, J. (1974). *La révolution du langage poétique* [Revolution in poetic language]. Paris: Lautréament et Mallarmé.

Labov, W. (1972). *Language in the inner city: Studies in the Black English vernacular*. Philadelphia: University of Pennsylvania Press.

Lacan, J. (1988). *The seminars of Jacques Lacan*. New York: Norton.

Mercer, K. (1994). *Welcome to the jungle: New politics in Black cultural studies*. New York: Routledge.

Morgan, B. (1997). Identity and intonation: Dynamic processes in an ESL classroom. *TESOL Quarterly, 31*, 431–450.

Norton, B. (1997). Language, identity, and the ownership of English. *TESOL Quarterly, 31*, 409–429.

Peirce, B. N. (1989). Toward a pedagogy of possibility in the teaching of English internationally: People's English in South Africa. *TESOL Quarterly, 23*, 401–420.

Pennycook, A. (1994). *The cultural politics of English as an international language*. London: Longman.

Philip, M. N. (1991). *Harriet's daughter*. Toronto, Canada: Women's Press.

Rampton, B. (1995). *Crossing: Language and ethnicity among adolescents*. London: Longman.

Rose, T. (1991). "Fear of a Black planet": Rap music and Black cultural politics in the 1990s. *Journal of Negro Education, 60*, 276–290.

Simon, R. I., & Dippo, D. (1986). On critical ethnography work. *Anthropology and Education Quarterly, 17*, 195–202.

Smitherman, G. (1994). *Black talk: Words and phrases from the hood to the amen corner*. Boston: Houghton Mifflin.

Walcott, R. (1995). *Performing the postmodern: Black Atlantic rap and identity in North America*. Unpublished doctoral dissertation, Ontario Institute for Studies in Education of the University of Toronto, Canada.

PART THREE

Shifting Our Theoretical Framework

4/24/07:
questions

1) Do we mark ESL errors
   in students' original
   poems? ("Balloon fly high" —
   narration, not exhortation)

2) ESL instr. at EVC — S-V agreement
   (is "localized")
   is not serious error — doesn't
   interfere w/ meaning like
   fragment or run-on ?!!

Introduction to Part Three

What does it mean for composition, as a field, to become more aware of the classroom as a linguistically and culturally pluralistic space? While, in a sense, this is the question that this entire collection addresses, this section focuses on the theoretical implications of seeing second-language students not at the margins of our classrooms, but at the heart—a shift in perspective that seriously challenges the way that writing instruction is imagined and practiced.

The first article in this section, Tony Silva's "On the Ethical Treatment of ESL Writers," first published in 1997, shows us the steps that must be taken to move second-language writers out of the shadows of our field's consciousness. In this article, Silva lays out a course of action for making composition programs and classrooms more equitable for ESL students—from placing students in more appropriate instructional contexts, to providing writing instruction that is more appropriate for second-language writers, to assessing second-language writing more fairly. Silva invites compositionists to not only see second-language writers as an integral part of composition programs, but to take steps that address the unique challenges second-language writers face in higher education.

In shifting our view of the composition classroom as culturally and linguistically diverse, we recognize that this space has long been imagined as monocultural and monolingual. Vai Ramanathan and Dwight Atkinson's "Individualism, Academic Writing, and ESL Writers" highlights these tacit cultural underpinnings of composition pedagogy. Their article, first published in 1999, demonstrates how North American cultural assumptions about the relationship between the individual and society lie beneath the surface of much composition practice and pedagogy, especially in relation to the importance of a writer's voice, peer review, critical thinking, and textual ownership. Ramanathan and Atkinson argue that these ideas and practices "assume culturally specific norms of thought and expression" that many second-language writers do not share (p. 160 in this volume). One of the implications of their article is that second-language writers must often negotiate these cultural aspects of composition curricula, which may not even be visible to teachers themselves.

Wei Zhu's "Interaction and Feedback in Mixed Peer Response Groups" describes a research study that explores the complications of peer review, a commonly assigned composition activity that requires students to negotiate difference. Originally published in 2001, Zhu's study provides important insights into how second-language and NES students interact in peer response groups. Zhu found that all of the students in her study provided global feedback to their peers' writing, but that second-language students' oral participation was relatively limited. In addition, they tended to exercise less control over conversations and were often interrupted by their NES peers. However, the second-language students in the study gave valuable feedback — especially written feedback — thus suggesting the benefit of expanding feedback types and opportunities in "mixed" groups. As the demographics of the composition classroom come to mirror these "mixed" groups, the implications of Zhu's study will speak to more aspects of composition pedagogy.

"Understanding Critical Writing," the first chapter of A. Suresh Canagarajah's 2002 monograph, *Critical Academic Writing and Multilingual Students*, lays out a new framework for understanding pedagogical approaches to cultural and linguistic difference. Canagarajah uses the terms *difference-as-deficit*, *difference-as-estrangement*, and *difference-as-resource* to refer to the different stances that can be taken in relation to the linguistic and cultural differences between ESL and NES students. Canagarajah describes difference-as-deficit as an approach that identifies ESL students' linguistic and cultural differences in relation to their NES peers as places where ESL students are lacking. This approach leads to pedagogy that seeks to convert second-language writers to North American cultural and linguistic norms. The difference-as-estrangement approach swings the pendulum in the other direction to view all linguistic and cultural difference as untouchable and in need of protection from change. As Canagarajah comments, on the surface, this pedagogy appears "egalitarian," as it recognizes and honors the differences the student's cultural and linguistic background represents, but, in practice, this approach may lead to pedagogy that traps second-language students in their cultural and linguistic pasts. The third approach, difference-as-resource, is the model that Canagarajah ultimately argues for, as this model can lead to pedagogy that encourages second-language students to use their linguistic and cultural differences as resources from which to critique, resist, and negotiate academic literacies.

This section concludes with "Should We Invite Students to Write in Home Languages? Complicating the Yes/No Debate" (2003), which was cowritten by eleven scholars who represent a wide range of disciplines, including composition studies, second-language acquisition, sociolinguistics, and literacy studies. Janet Bean and her co-authors pick up on Canagarajah's difference-as-resource approach to advocate for shifting composition instructors' attention from the question of whether students should write in their mother tongues to *"when and under what conditions"* (p. 226, italics in original) linguistic diversity can be welcomed in the composition classroom. They point out the benefits of encouraging students — even NES students — to use their home languages at different points in the writing process to facilitate "cognitive fluency," but they warn against forcing students to do so, especially where students' home languages are stigmatized (pp. 232, 234).

Ultimately, Bean et al. suggest, as do other articles in this collection, that composition instructors need to find specific opportunities to invite second-language students to utilize their full range of linguistic resources, while not singling out these students. A pedagogy that welcomes linguistic and cultural pluralism, rather than denies or tokenizes difference, enriches composition curricula for all students.

8 On the Ethical Treatment of ESL Writers

TONY SILVA

As ever-increasing numbers of nonnative speakers of English enroll in 1st-year writing classes in colleges and universities in North America, questions about how to deal with these students have become more frequent, important, and urgent. In an attempt to address some of these questions, researchers who focus on L2 writing have generated a fairly large body of scholarship and commentary on a great number of relevant theoretical and practical issues. However, I believe that one area that needs further exploration is the matter of the ethics (that is, a system or code of conduct) employed in the treatment of ESL writers. Therefore, I would like to present my thinking on this issue, which is based on the notion of respect, for it is my belief that an instructional program that does not respect its students is primed for failure and almost certain to engender resentment. In this article, I draw on my understanding of the existing L2 writing research as well as my own experience in teaching ESL writers and administering ESL writing programs. My aim is not to preach or to attempt to reveal any transcendent truths but to provoke thought and discussion.[1]

In my view, there are four basic ways in which ESL writers need to be respected: they need to be (a) understood, (b) placed in suitable learning contexts, (c) provided with appropriate instruction, and (d) evaluated fairly.

UNDERSTAND ESL WRITERS

First, those who would deal with ESL writers need to recognize that these writers may be very different from their native English-speaking (NES) peers in important ways. ESL writers come, of course, from many different cultures, rhetorical traditions, and linguistic backgrounds and may bring with them distinct strategies for learning and writing.

The results of the relevant research suggest that, in general, ESL writing is distinct from and often simpler and less effective (in the eyes of NES judges)

From *TESOL Quarterly* 31.2 (1997): 359–63.

than that of their NES peers. ESL writers' composing processes seem constrained in some salient ways. Because they are not writing in their native language, they may plan less, write with more difficulty owing to a lack of lexical resources, reread what they write less, and exhibit less ability to revise in an intuitive manner—on the basis of what "sounds" right.

At the discourse level, ESL writers' texts often do not meet the expectations of NES readers. Their texts frequently exhibit distinct patterns of exposition, argumentation, and narration; their orientation of readers has been deemed by some to be less appropriate and acceptable, and they sometimes manifest a distinct pattern and less facility in their use of certain cohesive devices.

In terms of lower level linguistic concerns, ESL writers' texts typically exhibit a style of writing that is simpler than that of NES writers. ESL writers' sentences often include more coordination, less subordination, less noun modification, and fewer passives. As language learners, ESL writers usually use shorter words and less specific words and generally manifest less lexical variety and sophistication. (See Silva, 1997, for a fuller account of this research and its findings.)

It is important to note that ESL writers may also be very different from one another; that is, ESL writers comprise a very heterogeneous population. For example, there are international students (in a country to study and then return home), immigrants (in a country to stay), and resident bilinguals (who were in a country all the time). Recognizing these differences and understanding their nature and implications for writing instruction is, in my view, the basis for the ethical treatment of ESL writers.

PROVIDE SUITABLE LEARNING CONTEXTS

Second, those who would deal with ESL writers need to recognize that these differences may call for special instructional contexts. First, I believe it is necessary to offer ESL writers as many placement options as possible. According to their abilities and preferences, they should be given the choice of enrolling in mainstream composition classes, basic writing classes, sheltered ESL classes, or classes designed to accommodate both native and nonnative speakers of English. (See Silva, 1994, for a further discussion of placement issues.) Regardless of which placement option is chosen, it is crucial for teachers to be knowledgeable about and have experience in working with ESL writers. (An open mind, a tolerance of difference, and an interest in other cultures is necessary but by no means sufficient here.) It is likewise essential to consider that curricula, materials, and practices that are successful with NES writers may not necessarily be successful with their ESL peers, that the unreflective adoption of mainstream composition materials may seriously disadvantage ESL writers by assuming knowledge that they do not possess (Who is your favorite character on television and why?) or expecting a familiarity or proficiency with rhetorical notions (reader-based writing, directness), linguistic notions (syntactic and lexical variety), conventional notions (citation and quotation), and strategic notions (drafting and revising) that they may not share with their NES teachers and peers.

Teachers must also recognize that working with ESL writers may require more time and effort than working with native English speakers. In my view, these additional requirements need to be met by requiring fewer writing assignments or, preferably, enrolling fewer students in classes. The courses ESL writers take must also be credit bearing and fulfill requirements, like foreign language classes for NES students.

Provide Appropriate Instruction

Third, those who deal with ESL writers must provide appropriate instruction, which, in my view, should explicitly recognize students as intelligent human beings and unique individuals with their own views and agendas and their own interesting stories to tell, not as blank slates for teachers to inscribe their opinions on nor as buckets to be filled with their teachers' worldly wisdom. Furthermore, ESL writers should not be subjected to bait-and-switch scams. If they enroll in courses with titles like Introductory Writing or Freshman Composition, I believe it is certainly reasonable for them to expect and to get courses that focus primarily if not exclusively on writing, as opposed to such interesting and important yet inappropriate topics such as peace education, conflict resolution, environmental concerns, political issues, particular ideologies, literature, critical thinking, cultural studies, or some other cause célèbre du jour, and use writing merely as an add-on or reinforcement activity. I am not suggesting here that teachers conceal their personal interests or political views from their students — this is unrealistic and perhaps impossible; I am suggesting that these interests and views should neither control nor become the curriculum.

But then what are teachers to teach? Some would say that writing courses are merely skill-building courses that have no inherent content, that composition teachers need to bring in content from some other discipline or link their class with a content course to have something to teach. I respectfully disagree. I feel that there is an abundance of information about writing that teachers can and should share with ESL writers. Much can and needs to be said about rhetorical, linguistic, conventional, and strategic issues and about the distinct nature of writing in an L2 and its implications for these issues. (See David, Gordon, & Pollard, 1995, for a similar argument in the context of mainstream writing instruction.)

But then what are students to write about? It seems to me most reasonable and motivating to have students (individually or as a group) choose their own topics, those in which they have a sincere interest and some intellectual and emotional investment. In my experience, asking ESL writers to write on topics of their own choice often results in texts that are well informed, skillfully crafted, very persuasive, and incredibly moving — I am thinking, in particular, of a piece on the public's lack of understanding of and often inappropriate response to those afflicted with autism, a paper written by a young

Chinese woman majoring in psychology who had helped raise her autistic younger brother. In short, I suggest that students be given control of the why and what of writing and that teachers focus on the how, where, and when, on facilitating rather than controlling student writing. (See Leki, 1991/1992, for a description of an innovative introductory writing curriculum that accommodates such student choice.)

EVALUATE FAIRLY

Fourth, those who deal with ESL writers must evaluate their writing fairly, in both mass and classroom testing contexts. They need to understand that second language acquisition is a slow and gradual process and that expecting ESL students' writing to be indistinguishable in terms of grammar from that of their NES counterparts is naive and unrealistic. Teachers also need to recognize that ESL writers' rhetorical differences may be manifestations of their cultural backgrounds and not cognitive or educational deficiencies. (For particularly cogent overviews of contrastive rhetoric research see Connor, 1996; Grabe & Kaplan, 1989; Leki, 1991.) Testers need to provide writing prompts and contexts that do not disadvantage ESL students. (See Kroll & Reid, 1994; Reid & Kroll, 1995, for a lucid and comprehensive discussion of this issue.) Finally, it is important to understand that acceptable performance in one's classes (including writing classes) means more than the results of any writing test, no matter how well constructed.

In summary, to show ESL writers the respect they are due, to treat them ethically, it is necessary to (a) understand how they are different from their NES counterparts and from each other and to try to accommodate these differences; (b) provide them with instructional options and ESL-friendly teachers, curricula, and materials; (c) offer instructional programs that focus on writing and students' interests; and (d) judge students' writing in an informed and equitable manner. To do less is to work against the retention and success of nonnative speakers of English in institutions of higher learning.

NOTE

1. Although I draw upon the work of others in this paper, the position I present is my own; that is, I am not trying to imply that the people I cite necessarily agree with my views.

REFERENCES

Connor, U. (1996). *Contrastive rhetoric: Cross-cultural aspects of second language writing.* New York: Cambridge University Press.

David, D., Gordon, B., & Pollard, R. (1995). Seeking common ground: Guiding assumptions for writing courses. *College Composition and Communication, 46,* 522–532.

Grabe, W., & Kaplan, R. (1989). Writing in a second language: Contrastive rhetoric. In D. Johnson & D. Roen (Eds.), *Richness in writing: Empowering ESL students* (pp. 263–283). White Plains, NY: Longman.

Kroll, B., & Reid, J. (1994). Guidelines for designing writing prompts: Clarifications, caveats, and cautions. *Journal of Second Language Writing, 3,* 231–255.

Leki, I. (1991). Twenty-five years of contrastive rhetoric: Text analysis and writing pedagogies. *TESOL Quarterly, 25,* 123–143.

Leki, I. (1991/1992). Building expertise through sequenced writing assignments. *TESOL Journal, 1*(2), 19–23.

Reid, J., & Kroll, B. (1995). Designing and assessing effective classroom writing assignments for NES and ESL students. *Journal of Second Language Writing, 4*, 17–41.

Silva, T. (1994). An examination of writing program administrators' options for the placement of ESL students in first year writing classes. *Writing Program Administration, 18*, 37–43.

Silva, T. (1997). Differences in ESL and native-English-speaker writing: The research and its implications. In J. Butler, J. Guerra, & C. Severino (Eds.), *Writing in multicultural settings* (pp. 209–219). New York: Modern Language Association.

9   *Individualism, Academic Writing, and ESL Writers*

VAI RAMANATHAN AND DWIGHT ATKINSON

The eminent language socialization researcher Shirley Brice Heath has described marked differences in the ways individuals are conceptualized and socialized across cultural groups in the U.S.:

> [Mainstream, middle-class Americans] view infants as individuals and orient them to see themselves as individuals who have the right and obligation to voice their judgments against those of others, so long as they respect rules and roles in doing so. . . . [But] many sociocultural groups traditionally orient their young to group membership and adherence to age and gender roles rather than to individual status. Community-valued institutions, such as the church, may underscore age and gender roles as well as particular or literal readings of written materials. Any interpretation that sets up the views of the individual against those of the group or of those in authority may be widely discouraged or even punished. . . . Hence it is clear that students from many minority communities will be at a disadvantage in classrooms and on certain types of tasks that expect their thinking, as demonstrated through oral and written language, to bear certain characteristics. As the research on cooperative learning has clearly demonstrated, some cultural groups place much higher value on learning in groups and the downplaying of individual displays of knowledge than in other groups (Kagan, 1986; Slavin, 1983). (Heath, 1991, pp. 12–14)

In contrast to the "mainstream U.S." view of the individual described by Heath, a British-Chinese research team derived the following generalizations from their recent, in-depth study of language education in the People's Republic of China (PRC):

> Seeing such classes, with communicative approaches in mind and an uncomfortable feeling that memorising is rote learning, Western teachers might deplore the lack of interaction and individualisation, the absence of creativity and self-expression, or dearth of personal interpretation

From *Journal of Second Language Writing* 8.1 (1999): 45–75.

and experiential learning. Chinese counterparts would draw attention to the large class size, the importance of discipline, the significance of giving children necessary knowledge, the pressures of the curriculum and exam system. They might remark on the role of students' individual learning and preparation at home, on how teachers stress meaning and understanding before recitation and learning, on how students who attend with concentration do indeed interact with teacher and text, in their minds. They could point out that every Chinese child is an individual with different abilities and needs, but that in Chinese society — and in the classroom — the priorities are that each person must be part of a group or community; learning interdependency, co-operation and social awareness; becoming oneself in relation to significant others; expressing that which is socially shared rather than individually felt; creating on the basis of mastery rather than discovery. (Cortazzi & Jin, 1996, pp. 177–178)

Over the past 20 years, varying cultural "ideologies of the individual" have been convincingly established by researchers from a wide variety of fields, including anthropology, education, linguistics, psychology, and sociology.[1] In this study, we explore some of the implications of such variation for the teaching of university writing to non-native writers of English.

There has been a notable increase of non-native writers in traditionally L1 U.S. university writing classes in recent years, with mixed results (Atkinson & Ramanathan, 1995; Braine, 1996; Santos, 1992). Recent research also suggests that various pedagogical concepts and practices emanating from the teaching of L1 writing assume culturally specific norms of thought and expression which non-mainstream writers of English may have little social training in and thus real difficulty accessing. These principles and practices (and some of their critics) include: process writing (e.g., Delpit, 1988; Inghilleri, 1989; Kalantzis & Cope, 1993; Scollon, 1991; Trimbur, 1994); peer review (e.g., Allaei & Connor, 1990; Carson & Nelson, 1994, 1996; Nelson & Carson, 1998; Connor, 1996; Linden-Martin, 1997; Zhang, 1995); and "critical thinking" (Atkinson, 1997; Fox, 1994; Gee, 1990; Heath, 1991; Ramanathan & Kaplan, 1996b).

In this article we focus on four principles and practices of U.S. university writing pedagogy in which the ideology of individualism appears to be strongly, if tacitly, implicated. The main principle we discuss is "voice," but we also deal with the peer review process, critical thinking, and textual ownership. We then briefly address some recent critiques of cross-cultural writing research, arguing that they themselves are based on the very ideology of individualism problematized in this article, and finally conclude by defending cross-cultural writing research as an important and necessary contribution to the teaching of L2 writing.

VOICE AND INDIVIDUALISM

Before Defining Voice

A metaphorical notion of "voice" or something like it seems to exist in, if not pervade, mainstream U.S. society, although it is not clearly recognized as such. In this sense it appears to operate as part of a *social practice* (e.g., Atkinson, 1997; Gee, 1990)—a widely if tacitly held and approved concept, on the basis of which social members partly view and define themselves and one another, and by which they thereby facilitate the carrying-on of everyday life. The core notion underlying this social practice seems to be that, as individuals, we all have essentially private and isolated inner selves, which we give outward expression to through the use of a metaphorical "voice."

Evidence that such a concept of metaphorical voice exists and is important in U.S. society can be found in its frequent occurrence in the mass media and popular culture. To give but two examples: A recent *New York Times Magazine* article (Smith, 1997, p. 22) reported of the popular singer/songwriter/ producer known as Babyface that: "His defining work must be the 'Waiting to Exhale' soundtrack; Babyface's singing never appears on it, yet his voice is everywhere apparent"; and a brochure recently received by one of us in the mail began: "Introducing *DoubleTake*—the new 'literary-visual' magazine where the world's finest writers, documentary photographers, and new voices gather to reveal to you their most personal, heartfelt work." Such examples can be multiplied endlessly, as the syndicated columnist William Safire showed in a 1992 column. There, Safire satirically examined the metaphorical use of "voice" in U.S. society, finding that it extended even to the personification of inanimate objects, as in the following from a car advertisement: "This confident new Audi has a distinct voice" (Safire, 1992, p. 14).

One interesting aspect of this broad metaphorical notion of voice is that it does not automatically refer to linguistic communication. This is indicated in two of the examples already given—cars obviously can't talk but still manage to express themselves (even "distinct[ly]"!) in the Audi ad, and Babyface's "voice" comes through loud and clear while being nowhere literally represented on the soundtrack. Safire quotes the playwright Sam Shepard to this same effect in comparing "voice" to "style" in their more literary manifestations: "Style is the outer trappings. . . . But a voice is almost without words. . . . It's something in the spaces, in between" (Safire, 1992, p. 14).

Still, the most common use of this metaphorical notion of voice appears to involve linguistic (or near-linguistic) communication. And when it does, it seems to be slanted toward a particular ideology or worldview of such communication—one in which the individual is foregrounded and valorized. "Voice" in this sense is seen to represent linguistic behavior which is *clear, overt, expressive,* and even *assertive* and *demonstrative*. That such uses of voice are grounded in a particular communicative ideology is suggested by a growing body of work on communicative styles across cultures (see Atkinson, 1997 for a partial review). This research indicates that a broad range of the world's peoples conventionally adopt models and norms of communication that are almost diametrically opposed to the one just described, in that they foreground the *subtle, interpretive, interdependent, non-assertive,* and even *nonverbal* character of communicative interaction.

Ishii and Bruneau (1994), for instance, review research which points to just such a model of communication among many Japanese, one in which silence is in some sense the preferred norm, and where language is judged and valued more for what it *doesn't* directly express — for what it leaves up to the interpretive activity of the interlocutor or audience — than for what it tries to make clear and overt (see also Barnlund, 1975; Carson, 1992; Clancy, 1986; Fischer & Teigo, 1968; Hinds, 1987; Ito, 1980; Loveday, 1982; Nitobe, cited in Barnlund, 1975, p. 133; and Yamada, 1997 for similar findings regarding Japanese communicative style. Basso, 1972; Crago, 1992; and Scollon & Scollon, 1981 provide parallel descriptions of communicative style among North American Indian groups). Likewise, Harklau (1994) found that "perhaps the single most salient aspect" of her observations of Chinese immigrant students in the mainstream U.S. high school classrooms she studied ethnographically was "their reticence and lack of interaction with native speaking peers" (p. 251), a reticence nearly equaled in their lack of verbal engagement with the teachers in these classes. Such behavior was justified by one of the immigrant students, originally from Taiwan, in the following terms (the student begins by stating a Chinese proverb and then explicates it):

> "Being quiet is gold and vigorously debating is silver." Being quiet is considered polite and intelligent because only the insecure ones need to prove themselves smart by talking loud. For that reason the school [in Taiwan] wanted the students to keep quiet in the classroom.[2]

In sociocultural contexts where such views are widely shared — and they have sometimes been said to be held by a "world-majority" (Fox, 1994) — the notion of individualist voice would seem to make little sense. This, then, is a first way in which we would claim that there is much cultural in the concept of voice.

Defining Voice

L1 and some L2 compositionists have used "voice" in a variety of ways.[3] The most common and longest-standing usage (cf., Bowden, 1995) is as a more active alternative to personal "style" (see Harklau & Schecter, 1996) or "presence," as *that which individuates a writer from all other writers, as evidenced in that writer's texts.* Donald Stewart, one of its original proponents, defined written voice in just this way:

> Your authentic voice is that authorial voice which sets you apart from every living human being despite the common or shared experiences you have with many others. (Stewart, 1972; cited in Bowden, 1995, p. 175)

Bowden (1995) has described the historical genesis of the notion of written voice as part of the larger 1960's and 1970's reaction to social and educational systems that were emphasizing the impersonal over the personal, the technological over the natural — systems that had themselves arisen partly in response to the Soviet launching of the Sputnik in 1957 and the Cold War. Written voice was born, then, out of the counterculture movement of the late 1960's and 1970's, with its goals of liberation from traditional social bonds, enhanced self-exploration, and, among other things, a more humanistic academics.

Bowden attributes three fundamental characteristics to the original "personal" or "authentic" view of written voice. First, it is (almost by definition) *inward-centered*—it is fundamentally about having contact with one's essential "inner self." In this sense, this version of voice is seen as part of a "neo-romantic" movement in education—as manifested within L1 composition by the "expressivist" or "vitalist" school of Ken Macrorie, Peter Elbow, Donald Murray, and others, and described by Berlin (1987, 1988).

Second, it assumes the *primacy of oral over written communication*. That is, like the related metaphorical, notion, "tone," voice suggests that writing is in some sense displaced or deficient speech. At the least, it appears to suggest that speech is more natural than writing—that whereas one's unique inner self is often easily expressible orally, the same cannot be said for writing. The great orality-versus-literacy debates of the last 30 years have sometimes been phrased in similar terms: Walter Ong (1982, cited in Bowden, 1995, p. 185), for example, has written that "[S]peech is inseparable from our consciousness." Closer to home, Elbow (1981, p. 288) states: "Voice . . . is what most people have in their speech but lack in their writing—namely, a sound or texture—the sound of 'them.'"

Third and finally, Bowden points out that the notion of personal written voice has a distinctly literary flavor. Thus, the prototypical examples of a clear personal voice given by Elbow (e.g., 1981, ch. 25) and others are often taken from literary works, and both the concept itself and the pedagogies that foster it tend to advantage students who are strong in the personal, creative-writing mode. Trimbur (1994, p. 110; see also Li, 1996) has made substantially this same point:

> the canniest among [the students in the expressivist process-oriented classroom] recognized that sincerity and authenticity of voice were the privileged terms of symbolic exchange. . . . If process teachers were reading what they took to be a direct and unmediated prose of personal experience, the most successful students were hard at work constructing the authorial persona of self-revelatory personal essays written in a decidedly non-academic style. To put it another way, the irony of process pedagogy is that teachers' desire to operate outside oppressive institutions and avoid the errors of the past only reinstituted the rhetoric of the belletristic tradition at the center of the writing classroom.[4]

As might be imagined, the original notion of written voice as the expressive potential of a unique individual has been widely critiqued on a number of fronts. In many cases, these critiques come out of movements and theories of writing (e.g., social constructivism) which were not yet known in composition studies when the voice metaphor made its original appearance. Alternative views of voice emanating from these movements include Lisa Ede's (1989) concept of "situational voice," which also has clear precedents in classical rhetoric:

> Just as you dress differently on different occasions, as a writer you assume different voices in different situations. If you're writing an essay about a personal experience, you may work hard to create a strong

personal voice in your essay. . . . If you're writing a report or essay exam, you will adopt a more formal, public tone. (1989; cited in Bowden, 1995, p. 175)

This situational view of voice also has close parallels with a major tenet of post-structuralist thought—that people have, by their very nature, multiple instead of unitary personalities or *subjectivities* (e.g., Foucault, 1980; Pennycook, 1996).

But perhaps the most influential alternative version of written voice has been derived from the work of Mikhail Bakhtin (e.g., 1986), the Russian literary and linguistics scholar. His notion of *heteroglossia,* the idea that all language-in-use is made up of bits and pieces in effect borrowed from other language users and infused with their intentions (to put it oversimply), has suggested to some composition scholars that a writer's voice is inevitably multiple and intertextual (e.g., Yancey, 1994). In his own development of the theory, however, Bakhtin moved beyond this view, stating—in true dialectical style—that a language user must appropriate the other, prior voices inhabiting his or her language, in Bakhtin's words "populat[ing] it with his own intention" (1986, quoted in Yancey, 1994, p. xiii).

Individualist Expression and Voice

Questions regarding the nature of written voice in relation to the individual—and the meaning and appropriate expression of individuality itself—point to our major concern with at least its more "expressivist" manifestations in teaching writing to non-native speakers (NNS) of English. If it is true that the notion of the individual varies substantially across cultures, as has been widely described and argued (see, Markus & Kitayama, 1991 and Atkinson, 1997 for partial reviews), then a concept of written voice that centrally assumes the expression of a "unique inner self" may be problematic for some NNSs.

In a major review of the literature on conceptions of self across cultures, Markus and Kitayama (1991) distinguish cultural views which they term "independent" versus "interdependent" construals of self. As they describe these contrasting conceptions:

> In many Western cultures, there is a faith in the inherent separateness of distinct persons. The normative imperative of this [i.e., U.S.] culture is to become independent from others and to discover and express one's unique attributes (Johnson, 1985; Marsella et al., 1985; J. G. Miller, 1988; Shweder & Bourne, 1984). Achieving the cultural goal of independence requires construing oneself as an individual whose behavior is organized and made meaningful primarily by reference to one's own internal repertoire of thoughts, feelings, and action, rather than by reference to the thoughts feelings, and actions of others. . . . In contrast, many non-Western cultures insist . . . on the fundamental connectedness of human beings to each other. A normative imperative of these cultures is to maintain this interdependence among individuals (De Vos, 1985; Hsu, 1985; Miller, 1988; Shweder & Bourne, 1984). Experiencing interdependence

entails seeing oneself as part of an encompassing social relationship and recognizing that one's behavior is determined, contingent on, and to a large extent organized by what the actor perceives to be the thoughts, feelings, and actions of others in the relationship. (pp. 226–7)[5]

Numerous studies of language socialization have shown how children are socialized to such differing versions of selfhood basically from day one. Clancy (1986), for example, describes in detail the daily routine by which Japanese mothers inculcate in their children the twin social norms of empathy and conformity—arguably the two most important social skills in modern Japanese society. Empathy training is effected, for example, by constantly attributing feelings to others (including even inanimate objects) in order to mold socially appropriate responses. Thus, toys are often pointedly described by mothers as "pitiful" (i.e., to be felt sorry for—*kawaisoo* in Japanese) when their children treat them roughly. Conformity training takes place when mothers indicate that their childrens' speech or actions are socially deviant, for instance by calling the unwanted behavior "strange" (*okashii* or *hen*, words that carry deep significance as tools of socialization and social control in Japanese society—Hendry, 1986) or "scary" (*kowai*).

In a second socialization study, Scollon and Scollon (1981) describe how, following middle class U.S. child-rearing practices, they socialized their infant daughter, Rachel, to take an individualist and more or less "objective" position in the course of her daily activities—to see herself as in some sense separated from the flow of social life. As a result, at two years of age Rachel commonly "fictionalized herself"—referring to herself in the third person and using conventional story structures, reading prosody, and literate performance frames to narrate her own activities. This was in sharp contrast to the highly involved narrative approaches taken by the Athabaskan children she often played with, including those who were much older.

Other cross-cultural socialization research (e.g., Caudill & Weinstein, 1974; Heath, 1983, 1991; Matsumori, 1981 cited in Clancy, 1986, p. 218; Ochs, 1992; Ochs & Schieffelin, 1984; Schieffelin & Ochs, 1986) suggests how American middle class mothers go to great lengths to tacitly aid in constructing the identity of "autonomous individual" for their children. Child development researchers as far back as Piaget realized that "individual independence is a social fact, a product of civilization" (Piaget, 1928/1977, cited in Rogoff, 1991, p. 34).

Regarding, more specifically, differing expressions of self across cultures in writing, Scollon (1991) investigated the extreme difficulties his Taiwanese university EFL writers were having with the Elbow-based process approach he adopted in the classroom. On the basis of both the cross-cultural/ anthropological literature treating notions of self in Chinese cultural contexts and his own empirical research (Scollon & Scollon, 1991), Scollon came to the general conclusion that:

the stance of self-expression set by such writers as Elbow is so productive in North America because it is so squarely based on the western,

> individualist sense of self. For the same reason this stance is all but un-
> intelligible to Chinese writers; at least it was to my students at Ching
> Yi. (p. 4)

More specifically, according to Scollon, his students appeared to adopt a
view of self in their writing very similar to Markus and Kitayama's "interdependent" norm—one which "is not highly assertive, but seeks to accommodate others and in return receives enduring social support" (Chu, 1985,
quoted in Scollon, 1991, p. 4). This approach made it all but impossible for
the students to operate successfully under a process-based pedagogy,
because:

> the writing process asks of the writer that he or she take the rhetorical po-
> sition of an autonomous, rational mind, untroubled by the inconsisten-
> cies of the phenomenal world and equally untroubled by the push and
> pull of human arrangements. This is a persona which western students
> are all too ready to adopt; to them it seems a natural intuition. (p. 11)

Scollon's students, on the other hand, were:

> not writing primarily to express [themselves] but for the purpose of be-
> coming integrated into a scholarly community. The purpose of student
> writing [in Taiwanese Chinese culture] is to learn to take on a scholarly
> voice in the role of commentator on the classics and on the scholarship
> of others. One is writing to pass on what one has received. (p. 7)

The notion of written voice, then, that Scollon found relevant in describing this community is the diametric opposite of the one commonly assumed
by "personal voice" advocates, most notably Elbow himself (e.g., 1981, ch. 25,
1994a).

A second study bearing on self and voice in writing across cultures is Li's
(1996) semi-ethnographic account of what constitutes "good writing" in U.S.
and PRC schools. Li asked high school writing teachers from both countries
to do three things. First, she asked four teachers (two from each country) to
select exceptionally well-done personal essays by their own or other students
and to comment on what made them so good. She then circulated the different essays (in translated form, where appropriate) and their choosers' comments among the other teachers, asking for their reactions to both. Finally,
she sent a subset of the essays to a larger group of 45 teachers (23 Chinese
and 22 American), along with an open-ended survey querying their judgments in order to confirm the evaluations and their justifications she had earlier received from the group of four.

Although Li identified differences of judgment within the cultural
groups in regard to particular essays, her major finding was that, in general,
each group held distinct and divergent underlying principles of evaluation.
The single greatest difference—and that on which all other differences depended, according to Li—concerned what each group saw as the wider
function of school-based writing. For the Chinese teachers, such writing represented:

the acquisition and dissemination of an honorable way of life that con-
forms to certain established moral codes. Good writing, therefore,
should carry a positive, or more desirably, a profound moral message;
never mind whether it be a mere reiteration of a popular witticism or
what parents or teachers have preached to the writer. (p. 90)

For the U.S. writing teachers, on the other hand:

[t]he primary function of writing . . . is the exploration and expression
of "self." As Jane [an American teacher] expounded eloquently, "It is
very important for writers to deal with life, to reflect, to look into themselves and the meaning of their lives. That's the whole purpose of writing as far as I am concerned." . . . Repetition of a known moral dictum
is to [these teachers] slavishly following the convention at the expense of
one's intellectual independence. (p. 91)

Not surprisingly, Li also found that the U.S. teachers put great emphasis
on the notion of personal voice in student writing, given that "good writing
should demonstrate the writer's unique perspective on life" (p. 93). These
teachers stressed that language which sounded "phony" or "too literary"
marked the writing as inauthentic — that the author had "moved far away
from his natural voice" (p. 93). In contrast, "the notion that students should
find their unique voice in their writing seemed an alien notion" (p. 93) to the
Chinese teachers.

In a third study with implications for the expression of self and voice in
writing across cultures, Ho (1998) investigated the English language learning
strategies of technological university students in Taiwan. Interviewing 20 proficient EFL writers regarding their strategies for learning to write well in
English, Ho found that, overwhelmingly, they stressed memorization and
imitation over other strategies, and that these preferred strategies accorded
with internalized social definitions of good writing in Chinese. In characterizing the latter, Ho (1998, p. 227) states:

The most dominant type of essay for writing classes, for [university]
joint entrance examinations, and for civil service examinations in Taiwan is the argumentative essay containing four parts or paragraphs.
The topic of an argumentative essay is often a quotation from a classical
text or a saying of an ancient sage. The student/writer is expected to
paraphrase the quotation or the saying, argue for it, and conclude with
remarks which support the validity of the concepts and beliefs presented in the quotation or saying and which demonstrate his or her
conformity to traditional Chinese values. . . . Elegant, polished style
is very much valued in this kind of writing, for it indicates that the
writer is versed in Chinese literature and the classics and has memorized many classic [sic] texts and four-character Chinese idioms. Being
able to quote sentences from ancient texts and use idioms skillfully is
considered one of the most valuable characteristics of a good writer. As
Scollon (1991) has indicated, "The Chinese student is not writing primarily to express himself or herself. . . . One is writing to pass on
what one has received." (p. 7)

In accordance with this culturally defined model of good writing, Ho's interviewees described their preferred approaches to writing and learning to write better in English in terms like the following—terms which closely echoed these students' descriptions of how they wrote essays in Chinese:

STUDENT 3: I memorize beautiful phrases and sentences included in dictionaries, hoping that I may use them in future writing tasks. . . . I quote or cite others' sentences and turn to others' essays for assistance and reference and turn to handouts containing famous quotations, axioms, and proverbs for reference in writing. (p. 232)

STUDENT 4: I consider it important to memorize sentences to write better. . . . If the English teacher required me to write a long English essay . . . I would turn to famous sayings and sentences derived from famous writers and essays on the same topic. I would imitate what other people say and use their sentences in my essays. I would at most change a single word but I would not change the main frame or structure. . . . If my English teacher required me to write long English essays, I would use famous sayings, proverbs, and quotable phrases quite often, just as I use them very often in writing Chinese essays, for I consider they are essential in writing Chinese and English essays. (p. 234)

STUDENT 12: I have the habit of memorizing beautiful sentences, and my memory bank now contains more and more quotable sentences. When writing an English essay, I will use them directly in the essay. . . . If I happen to remember a proverb or saying or a well-put quotation I will try my best to use it in my English essay. I will produce many sentences which are related to that saying, proverb, or quotation or even distort my original intended meaning or plan just to use that proverb or saying or quotation. (p. 233)

STUDENT 19: I consider it very helpful and useful in reading English essays to learn how authors write. A lot of sentences can be taken from model essays to use in your own writings. . . . I will turn to textbooks and broadcasting English magazines [i.e., magazines designed to accompany popular English-language radio shows] for imitation and reference. I turn to them to look for patterns I can use in writing. I turn for reference and imitation to English articles or essays dealing with topics similar to or related to the one I am dealing with. I study English essays and articles to help me to perform better in writing exams and writing assignments. (p. 233)

As Ho insists, these are not simply acontextual learner/writer strategies innovated by a few students at a single university. Rather, he concludes that "[t]heir emphases on imitation and memorization and their turning to other essays and articles for reference and imitation have their origins in their prior educational experiences and their cultural background" (p. 231). While Ho does not mention written voice per se in his analysis, his study does provide a good sense of how proficient Taiwanese EFL learners/writers envision the task of English writing in a university setting and suggests the relative lack of importance—or more accurately, the irrelevance—of strong expressions of an individualist self and personal voice in this activity.

But perhaps the most compelling evidence for widely differing notions of individuality across cultures, and their implications for written voice, comes from the personal stories of those who have attempted to transplant themselves from one culture to another that is widely distant. Fan Shen (1989), a PRC immigrant to the U.S., for example, tells of his stuggles with English composition on arriving in this country — struggles which eventually necessitated his "creating a new self," as he puts it. To his teachers' constant encouragement to "Be yourself," "Just write what you think," Shen responds:

> In order to write good English, I knew that I had to be myself, which actually meant not to be my Chinese self. It meant that I had to create an English self and be *that* self. And to be that English self, . . . I had to accept the way a Westerner accepts himself in relation to the universe and society. (p. 461)

As for how Shen defined his "Chinese self":

> the image or meaning that I attached to the word "I" or "myself" was . . . different than that of my [American] English teacher. In China, "I" is always subordinated to "We" — be it the working class, Party, the country, or some other collective body. Both political pressure and literary tradition require that "I" be somewhat hidden or buried in writings and speeches; presenting the "self" too obviously would give people the impression of being disrespectful of the Communist Party in political writings and boastful in scholarly writings. The word "I" has often been identified with another "bad" word, "individualism," which has become a synonym of selfishness in China. . . . As a result, even if I had brilliant ideas [as a scholar], the "I" in my papers always had to show some modesty by not competing with or trying to stand above the names of ancient and modern authoritative figures. . . . I had even committed what I can call "reverse plagiarism" . . . when I was in middle school: willfully attributing some of my thoughts to "experts" when I needed some arguments but could not find a suitable quotation from a literary or political "giant." (p. 460)

From this starting point, Shen initially went about the rather challenging task of "creating a new self" by doing such things as imagining himself reborn in a new body with its head on upside down, or crawling out of "my old identity, the timid humble, modest Chinese 'I,'" and creeping into my new identity (often in the form of a new skin, or a mask), the confident, assertive, and aggressive English "I" (p. 462). In his classroom writing, Shen set about making intentional — and what he considered "pompous" and "immodest" — displays of individuality in his papers, for example by using "I" whenever possible and deleting quotations from other authors. Eventually, after considerable frustration and difficulty, Shen became more comfortable with his new "self." Despite this apparently happy outcome, however, we would simply ask at this point: How realistic is it to regularly expect or demand of our NNS students that they basically *become someone else?* Might not the notion of personal voice, at least, for some of them in some sense *require* that? And where does this place such students vis à vis those who have received "personal voice training" with their mother's milk, so to speak, and practiced it daily for the intervening twenty or so years? A growing number of case studies of NNS and bilingual students struggling and not infrequently failing in U.S. universities and colleges (e.g., Belcher, 1994; Fox, 1994; Johns, 1991; Schneider & Fujishima, 1995) reveal that laboring under such exteme cultural-academic demands does not always produce happy outcomes or desirable results. In the heartfelt words of a Nepalese student quoted by Fox (1994, p. 109):

> What is the process, what is the way we can change so radically here [in the U.S. university] so that we can be accepted, so that we can gain recognition? . . . Foreign students have been getting recognition from the ways they have been thinking and communicating and writing in their previous settings. And all of a sudden they lose all that. You can't imagine what happens to these people! They become very irritated. Very much miserable.

Peer Reviewing and Individualism

A second realm in the writing classroom in which conflicts regarding the presentation of an individualist self seem apparent is the peer review process. Peer review has on the whole been regarded as beneficial in L2 writing instruction, inasmuch as it provides student writers with added motivation for revision (Koch, 1982; Hedgcock & Lefkowitz, 1992) and encourages anticipating the expectations of otherwise-absent readers (Mittan, 1989). However, it has also been criticized for having a tacit basis in various social practices that may not extend beyond the bounds of mainstream American culture (e.g., Allaei & Connor, 1990; Carson & Nelson, 1994; Carson & Nelson, 1996; Nelson & Carson, 1998; Connor, 1996; Linden-Martin, 1997; Zhang, 1995).

One such American mainstream social practice is individualism. While peer review sessions are seemingly set up as group activities — in which peers comment on one anothers' essays in groups — they serve, in actuality, as mechanisms through which the individual is substantially fronted (Berlin, 1987; Carson, 1992; Carson & Nelson, 1994, 1996; Spigelman, 1998). Thus, group members are expected to comment on why particular elements of an individual's essay are effective or lacking and are encouraged to support these views with examples from the essay itself. By laying out what they think about a piece of writing and why, reviewers are also expected to express themselves individualistically, and so to develop their own critical writing/revising skills. The author likewise participates in the group on the assumption that she or he will take away whatever comments have been given for the purpose of *individual* improvement, as made clear by Elbow (1973, p. 126, italics in original):

> At first . . . you depend on all this feedback you are getting: you wonder how you wrote anything before without it. But after a while you

don't care about it so much. . . . [I]nstead of letting the standards of the readers call the shots for you, gradually you come to make your own decisions as to what is good and bad, and use the responses of others to help you fulfill *your own* goals, not their goals.

NNS writers—at least those from cultural backgrounds where more interdependent views of the individual are normative and who thus have been socialized to value group relations very highly—may for these reasons experience conflicts in the peer review context; out of a sense of identification with and concern for other group members, reviewers are more likely to say what they believe will not disrupt the group (Allaei & Connor, 1990; Carson & Nelson, 1996). Matsumoto (1988) clearly states the basic notion underlying this claim in describing Japanese norms of politeness:

> A Japanese generally must understand where s/he stands in relation to other members of the group or society, and must acknowledge his/her dependence on the others. Acknowledgment and maintenance of the relative position of others, rather than preservation of an individual's proper territory, governs all social interactions. (Matsumoto, 1988, p. 405)

Likewise, in a study of recent PRC school textbooks, Lin (1993) quotes a 1990 textbook to support her claim that "the texts always point out that the collective interest is most important" (p. 5):

> We young people have to nourish collective consciousness and to learn to deal correctly with the relationship between personal interests and collective interests. When they are in conflict, we should consciously place collective interests first and personal interests second. If it is necessary that we have to sacrifice personal interests, we should have the courage to give up all, including ourselves, to protect collective interests. (*Citizenship*, 1990, cited in Lin, 1993, p. 5)[6]

Peer review group members socialized to such views, then, may be more likely to say what they think will not threaten the positive "face" of their peers (Allaei & Connor, 1990; Carson & Nelson, 1996) than responding "from the heart," as it were. According to Miyoshi (1989, p. 39), for example, "discussion and criticism . . . imply dissent and protest, which most [Japanese people] seem eager to avoid."[7]

In a recent empirical study, Carson and Nelson (1996; see also Nelson & Carson, 1998) found that students from the PRC and Taiwan had a difficult time usefully commenting on their peers' essays.[8] In comparing these students with their native Spanish-speaking classmates, Carson and Nelson discovered that the former were reluctant to criticize others' essays partly out of a need to preserve the peers' face and maintain group harmony, but also because they did not feel that they had enough authority to do so. One Chinese student voiced her reluctance in this regard in the following terms:

> I think a lot and then realize that I'm not a critic, I'm just a reader, I read something, I cannot say, "Oh the writer is wrong". . . . [Being a critical reader] I don't think is a good idea. Because I think every time

I read something, he give me the information. But we don't have the right to judge it—especially for this essay—because we have different ideas. (p. 12)

A second manifestation of interdependent views of self therefore also seems to be operating in the peer review process for students from cultural contexts that favor them: Cultures oriented to more interdependent representations of self appear to emphasize the relatively strict observance of social hierarchies (Chao, 1994; Nakane, 1970; Roland, 1988; S. Scollon, 1989). When asked to critique others' work, these students may find it less natural than do some of their counterparts (and certainly than do many native English-speaking U.S. students) because it implies assuming a higher-status role with someone who is really a peer. Scollon (1991), Powers and Gong (1995), and Rao (1996) maintain as much for native Chinese-speaking students in discussing the Confucian origins of social structure in Chinese cultural contexts: Confucian precepts mandate that each person occupy their proper place in society and behave accordingly, without disrupting the social order.

CRITICAL THINKING AND INDIVIDUALISM

Another important concept used in the writing classroom in which individualism seems to play a central role is critical thinking. According to Ramanathan and Kaplan (1996b) and Atkinson (1997), what is commonly and unproblematically referred to as critical thinking is in fact ill-defined and implicit, more in the nature of a social practice (as defined briefly above; see Atkinson, 1997; Gee, 1990 for more extended definitions) than a well-articulated and straightforward educational concept.[9] Atkinson (1997, p. 80) explicitly connects the social practice of critical thinking with individualism:

Cultures that view individuals as primary units appear to permit—and even depend on—relatively unconstrained individual activity and expression. Where such individual activity exists, individual conflict and competition seem to be inevitable. Notions of the primacy of the individual and their consequences underlie the social practice of critical thinking at a fundamental level: the very concept of "critical" presupposes that individual conflict and dissensus are a social reality, if not a tool for achieving socially desirable ends, while "thinking"—at least in a western context—assumes the locus of thought to be within the individual.

Scollon (1995; Scollon & Scollon, 1995) and Pennycook (1996) trace the genealogy of a form of literacy (called "essayist literacy" by Gee [1990] and Scollon & Scollon [1981]) from its original roots in the valorization of the individual (versus God) in Renaissance humanism and Enlightenment rationalism, through the Romantic period, up to its various manifestations in present-day academic writing. This approach to written discourse "places a high value on individual autonomy [and] rationality . . . [a]long with . . . a now familiar group of characteristics, often inaccurately attributed to literacy, of analysis, originality, decontextualization, and objectivity" (Scollon, 1995, p. 25).

Based on her decade-long ethnographic work with three different social groups in the Piedmont Carolinas, Heath (1983; 1991, pp. 12–13) describes the induction into the social practice of critical thinking that mainstream U.S. children receive as part of their primary socialization:

> Mainstreamers view infants as individuals and orient them to see themselves as individuals who have the right and obligation to voice their judgments against those of others, so long as they respect rules and roles in doing so. . . . Through questioning, they test their propositions [about the nature of the world] on their parents, who value their children's display of knowledge about the world. . . . 2-year-olds move from a world of all no's to the abundant questioning and sharing of experiences of 3- and 4-year-olds. Much of the early book reading and game playing that mainstream parents do with their children encourages youngsters to compare, complement, and supplement the information of the books they read. As they reach 8 to 10 years of age, they take up activities sponsored by community organizations. . . . At home and in community based activities, youngsters learn to display knowledge, consider its relevance for action, and challenge the ideas of others in gradually molded acceptable verbal forms. Hence, without explicit teaching about the need to approach information from others conditionally, mainstream children learn in their everyday worlds acceptable ways to express their skepticism. . . . But these children learn more than this on their way to becoming critical thinkers; they learn to think about how they will argue their position, with more evidence than just their own previous experience. They learn that they must separate their experience from the proposition or general principle they wish to maintain; and they must, more often than not, structure their argument while in the midst of receiving information from others. Mainstream, literate-oriented families prepare their children to disengage from their own experience to attend to general argumentative principles by modeling talk about the language of argument within households (e.g., "But that doesn't make sense. You just said X. You can't now say Y!"). These redundant, repetitive, and multiply reinforced ways of socializing mainstream children as individual knowers and verbal contestants provide the bedrock discourse forms that sustain what schools define as critical thinking. The irony is that those who can practice them in school, more often than not, have to *learn* them outside school—through family and community life. [Note: Paragraph breaks in original not reproduced here]

The import of Heath's final sentence becomes clearer when we consider that the other two social groups she studied—working class African Americans living in the same town and white millworkers living in the surrounding countryside—took approaches to socializing their children that varied markedly from the one described here. Further, in neither of the two non-mainstream groups did the children's socialized skills mesh with those sponsored in the schools they attended, leading to disproportionately high rates

of school failure among them. Heath's description of mainstream U.S. socialization practices has been confirmed by the work of other researchers (e.g.,
Scollon & Scollon, 1981, reviewed in part above; Taylor, 1983).

In the realm of teaching composition, U.S. university composition programs frequently place strong emphasis on the development and use of students' critical thinking skills (Atkinson & Ramanathan, 1995), as represented
at all levels: institutional "thought styles" (Fleck, 1979), public justifications,
new instructor training, syllabi, curricula, and teachers' pedagogical practices. Composition textbooks written primarily for L1 students but used
frequently with L2 writers also reflect a similar emphasis (Ramanathan &
Kaplan, 1996a, 1996b), encouraging students to take one side on issues such
as gun control, animal rights, and TV violence, and to argue strongly and as-
sertively for their position (see Johns, 1991; McKay, 1989 for students having
trouble writing on such topics). Students are expected to analyze the situation critically, convincingly support their opinions, anticipate and defend
against counter-arguments, and judiciously weigh various kinds of evidence
that may strengthen their positions. All these points, it will be noticed, also
have direct implications for developing and asserting one's individuality: articulating individual stances and decisions on such issues, sharpening one's
own stand against (sometimes-hypothetical) others that disagree, and empowering one's individual point of view with whatever resources of evi-
dence/support that can be brought to bear. Such approaches have frequently
been found to be problematic for L2 writers from more interdependently oriented cultural backgrounds (e.g., Cadman, 1997; Choi, 1988; Fox, 1994;
Kobayashi, 1984a, 1984b, and Oi, 1984, all cited in Silva, 1993).

As has been argued elsewhere (Ramanathan & Kaplan, 1996a, 1996b),
such assignments are based on at least the following assumptions, all of which
appear to be foundational in middle class/mainstream U.S. culture: (1) that
the survival of a democracy depends partly on raising critical questions
about social issues (Cederblom & Paulsen, 1987); (2) that the U.S. public
should be prepared to take decisions on such issues; and (3) that these are areas around which honest disagreement is possible (McPeck, 1981). Laudable
though these goals may be, the implications they have for students from
more interdependently oriented cultures are significant in that these students
do not necessarily share appropriate cultural frames or assumptions, particularly where strongly voicing their views may violate sociocultural norms
based on overall consensus and the relative avoidance of personal disagreement and social discord (e.g., Atkinson & Ramanathan, 1995; Cadman, 1997;
Fox, 1994; Li, 1996; Matsumoto, 1988; Shen, 1989).

TEXTUAL OWNERSHIP AND INDIVIDUALISM

The phrase "textual ownership" encompasses such issues as plagiarism, the
documentation of sources, and authorship. It also raises—albeit in not so obvious ways—issues regarding the nature of learning, memory, culture, and attitudes toward the language being used as a source, as well as widely differing

conceptions of the individual (Bowden, 1996; Duranti, 1993; Pennycook, 1994b, 1996; Scollon, 1995).

In general, U.S. educators see instances of plagiarism as violations of honor and morals, and normally sympathetic teachers are often turned into angry and self-righteous guardians of truth by them (Kolich, 1983). This view is predicated on cultural assumptions that many in the U.S. share: Texts are their authors' personal property, and helping oneself to a text without permission from the author amounts to stealing. Such views are clearly evident across the academy, though they may take on even greater urgency in the teaching of composition. Many if not most composition textbooks, for instance, have sections on how to document sources, the importance of doing so, and the dangers of plagiarism (Kroll, 1988). Thus, the popular freshman writing textbook *Writing Arguments* (Ramage & Bean, 1994) describes plagiarism as "nothing less than cheating and theft [which] . . . demands serious punishment" (p. 283), and offers the following reasons for citing one's sources:

> (1) It reflects your own honesty and seriousness as a researcher; (2) it enables the reader to find the source of the reference and read further and sometimes to verify that the source has been correctly used; (3) it adds the authority of experts to your arguments. (p. 283)

Descriptions such as these — and there are many like them — reveal how seriously practitioners of composition want students to regard the importance of "individual expression," and the gravity of borrowing others' language and passing it off as one's own.

While such views may indeed be justified in an individualistically oriented culture, they are based on a complex web of cultural assumptions that may not transfer well beyond cultural boundaries. Writing partly in the context of Hong Kong's university system, Pennycook (1994b) suggests some of the cultural complexities:

> Plagiarism needs to be understood relative to the context of the concept (i.e., Western academic concepts of authorship, knowledge, and ownership), the context of the students (their cultural and educational backgrounds), the context of the institution (the demands of English-medium institutions in a colonial context), the context of the specific tasks required (assumptions about background knowledge and language ability), and the context of the actual use and "misuse" of text (the merits and demerits of the actual case of textual use). (p. 278)

This quotation is taken from Pennycook's response to Deckert's (1993) study wherein the latter tested 211 native Hong Kong university students on their knowledge of plagiarism by having them rate six passages based on a newspaper article. Interpreting his results, Deckert concluded that there was little consensus among his students regarding the occurrence of plagiarism. Pennycook then administered the same six passages to 22 native and nonnative speaker colleagues at the English Centre at Hong Kong University, finding that their answers varied almost as much as those of Deckert's subjects. From this and other evidence, Pennycook surmised that "if students cannot recognize plagiarism, then they are unlikely to be helped much by teachers who cannot recognize it either" (p. 278).

The issue of plagiarism goes far beyond being able to recognize particular instances of it, however. It is integrally tied to cultural notions of effective learning and knowing, as well as to how cultures view individuality and its appropriate expression (Ballard & Clanchy, 1991, ch. 2; Currie, 1997; Fox, 1994; Scollon, 1991). In interdependently oriented cultural contexts like India, for example, both home-based and school-based educational practices — early socialization and literacy training, formal assessment procedures, teaching methodologies, pedagogical practices, and the worldviews of teachers, parents, and other "authority figures" — reinforce the centrality of memorization at an everyday level. In the home, for instance, Brahmin male children (and in the case of the first author at least, female children as well) are supposed to have memorized particular Sanskrit chants and mantras and are expected to rehearse and produce them on particular (religious) occasions. In the school, the importance of memorizing is reinforced when the child is expected to produce various kinds of factual information from memory, most especially in essay-type exams where accurate factual recall and rote production — including the production of whole previously memorized essays — are highly evaluated. At almost all levels of education, then, and certainly still at the undergraduate level students are heavily involved in memorizing texts and information in order to demonstrate academic competence and achieve academic success.[10]

What constitutes successful learning in more interdependently oriented cultures is therefore often likely to differ from its counterpart in more independently oriented ones. Students socialized to the requirements of the former learn to write not so much to present an original, strong, individual self, but to show how much they have internalized of the transmittable traditions of their cultures (Scollon, 1991). At least in the case of India, they learn to align themselves with traditional (and sometimes non-traditional) texts by being able to reproduce them since the degree to which one can do so is often more highly valued than writing something "new." The various statements made by Ho's (1998) subjects reported above in the section entitled "Voice and Individualism," as well as the findings reported there of Scollon (1991) and Li (1996), suggest that very similar approaches are highly valued in Chinese cultural contexts (see also Carson, 1992; Cortazzi & Jin, 1996; Fox, 1994).

CONCLUSION: INVISIBLE PEDAGOGY, INDIVIDUALISM, AND THE ROLE OF CROSS-CULTURAL WRITING RESEARCH

A number of educational researchers (e.g., Atkinson, 1985; Bernstein, 1973; Delpit, 1988; Inghilleri, 1989; Kalantzis & Cope, 1993) have developed the concept of a "hidden pedagogy" in exploring the generally subpar performance of some sociocultural groups in Anglo-American and Australian schools. They relate this hidden pedagogy to the implicit, apparently non-directive nature of educational ways of acting and being that are covertly based on middle-class, mainstream social practices and are enshrined and publically justified in a "progressivist" pedagogy and philosophy of education. Thus, according to Kalantzis and Cope (1993, p. 57):

> Lisa Delpit argues that progressivism's apparent anti-authoritarianism is a cultural hoax—a cultural product of a White liberalism which, underneath, is as authoritarian as any. . . . Here veiled, rather than explicit commands are used to enforce adult authority. 'Would you like to do this next, Betty?' [Middle-class] White children in American schools know that this means they are expected to do something but to [non-middle-class] Black children this means the . . . teacher has abdicated authority, so the class reacts accordingly. The problem for Black students is misreading the cues of an alien discourse.

One important manifestation of this invisible pedagogy that has been investigated in some depth by researchers is process writing (Delpit, 1988; Gilbert, 1989; Inghilleri, 1989; Kalantzis & Cope, 1993). They point out that the non-directive teacher behavior, inductive learning (including the ability to induce organizational structure in the process of writing—Inghilleri, 1989), and discovery and assertion of self that are supposed to go on in the expressivist process-writing classroom really advantage those who have been socialized into these practices from an early age according to a highly child-centered, middle-class form of socialization.

Likewise, the concepts discussed in the present paper—voice, peer reviewing, critical thinking, and textual ownership—would seem to have a common grounding in the invisible pedagogy of progressivist education. Their underlying basis in individualism, as manifested in the all-important progressivist principle of developing autonomous, self-actualized individuals, is in fact at the core of progressivism (Pennycook, 1997). Thus, Cope and Kalantzis (1993, p. 58) see an intimate connection between educational progressivism and the metaphor of personal voice: "The motivation in progressivism . . . is based entirely on the individual's voice, the individual's sense of destiny." Similarly, Ramanathan and Kaplan (1996b) connect the development of critical thinking as an important educational goal in the U.S. to the influence of John Dewey, a major influence on educational progressivist thought.

It is also fruitful in this regard to view recent critiques of cross-cultural writing research (Raimes, 1998; Raimes & Zamel, 1997; Spack, 1997; Zamel, 1997) from the standpoint of a progressivist philosophy of education that valorizes individualism above all else. According to Spack (1997, p. 772), for example:

> [T]eachers and researchers need to view students as individuals, not as members of a cultural group, in order to understand the complexity of writing in a language they are in the process of acquiring.

Numerous questions might immediately be posed in response to this comment—some with no direct relationship to an underlying progressivism, but which are nonetheless crucial to ask: Why, for example, exclude *any* potentially relevant knowledge at all that might help us to help our students? Isn't the teaching of L2 writing already complex enough without automatically ruling certain kinds of potentially helpful information out of court? More directly related to individual-centered progressivism are the questions: What is it that leads one to juxtapose cultural group membership and individuality? Why does individuality need to be pared down to something acultural? Shouldn't a mature, sophisticated, multicultural understanding of individuals take their culturality fully into account, instead of denying or avoiding it? What is the import of this statement if not the opposite extreme of attempting to reduce all individuals to cultural types—reducing individuals to *a*cultural types?

A likely answer, to our way of thinking, can be found in an important corollary of progressivist approaches in education—universalism (Ellsworth, 1989; Pennycook, 1997). By ruling cultural influence and knowledge out of the picture one becomes able to assume that *everyone is like me*—in the sense of believing that, while we may have different preferences and make different choices, we must all basically think of ourselves in relation to society in more or less the same way, i.e., individualistically. Thus, while we are all individuals, we are all individuals on the same basic plan—our basic individualism is not at issue.

In his work on ideology and composition teaching, Berlin (1988, p. 486) identifies a similar universalizing assumption as the core of "expressivist" (or, in Berlin's terms, "expressionist") writing pedagogy:

> The underlying conviction of expressionists is that when individuals are spared the distorting effects of a repressive social order their privately determined truths will correspond to the privately determined truths of all others: my best and deepest vision supports the same universal and external laws as everyone else's best and deepest vision. Thus, in *Writing Without Teachers* Elbow admits that his knowledge about writing was gathered primarily from personal experience, and that he has no reservations about "making universal generalizations upon a sample of one" (p. 16). Murray is even more explicit in his first edition of *A Writer Teaches Writing*: "the writer is on a search for himself. If he finds himself he will find an audience, because all of us have the same common core. And when he digs deeply into himself and is able to define himself, he will find others who will read with a shock of recognition what he has written" (p. 4).

Advocates of progressivism, of which expressivist writing pedagogy is in large part a manifestation, therefore make the tacit assumption that *everyone is fundamentally like us, so everyone must want what we want.* Or, to formulate it differently: Everyone is an individual, *but they are individuals on our terms.* Surely, this is not a principle that will help us to understand NNSs *on their terms*, or that will allow us to use this understanding to help students negotiate the complex demands of academic literacy in North American, British, or Oceanic universities.

What *will* help—and what much cross-cultural writing research has so far contributed to and will continue to contribute to—is a complex, multidimensional understanding of individuals-in-context. The twenty or so years of socialization and education into particular ways of knowing and being in the world that international undergraduates bring with them to "Western" anglophone universities should not be considered insignificant or ruled out of court, any more than it should be mistaken for the full measure of the person. What we know about cultures and their varying approaches to knowing, meaning, and being should not be feared and denied. Rather it should be seen as integral to personhood, part and parcel of the individuality of the living, breathing, thinking, feeling, laughing and crying human beings that we meet everyday in our classrooms.

In closing her study of what constitutes "good writing" in U.S. and PRC schools, Li (1996, p. 127) expresses what she believes to be the practical outcome of her project. We too would like to close with Li's statement, since it captures for us the vitally important educational role of much cross-cultural writing research:

> To make judicious judgment about the sources of students' problems [and, we would add, strengths and coping strategies] . . . writing teachers should acquaint themselves with students' native cultures. . . . I hope this study on "good writing" in cross-cultural context serves to stretch the imagination of educators in both countries to understand the cultural bias in the standards many of them so rigorously maintain, without having to go through the troublesome experience of Fan Shen.

ACKNOWLEDGMENTS

For their valuable comments and much-appreciated assistance during the writing of this paper, we would like to thank Diane Belcher, Linda Harklau, Alan Hirvela, Iping Ho, Kay Losey, Terry Santos, Meryl Siegal, and Isabelle Thompson.

NOTES

1. This body of research would require a separate article—or quite possibly a book—to review. Studies which we cite elsewhere in this article include: Bellah, Madsen, Sullivan, Swidler, and Tipton, 1985 in sociology; Markus and Kitayama, 1991 in psychology; Atkinson, 1997; Carson, 1992; Clancy, 1986; Crago, 1992; Heath, 1983, 1991; Matsumoto, 1988; Ramanathan, 1996b; Schieffelin and Ochs, 1986; Scollon, 1991, 1995; Scollon and Scollon, 1981, 1995 in linguistics, education, and anthropology; Ishii and Bruneau, 1994 in communication studies; and Shen, 1989; Li, 1996 in composition studies. Atkinson, 1997; Carson, 1992; Markus and Kitayama, 1991; and Schieffelin and Ochs, 1986 provide partial reviews of this research.

As is well-known, the concept of "culture" has come in for a large amount of criticism in recent years (see Ramanathan & Atkinson, 1999, for a brief summary of criticisms). While we have sympathy for such viewpoints, particularly where they serve to correct earlier views of culture(s) as monolithic, static, essentialist, and all-encompassing, they also indicate to us a pendulum-like swing toward the opposite extreme—*that there is basically no such thing as culture.* In fact, as is often the case in such matters, a middle-ground position on culture seems far more tenable; i.e., an understanding of culture in terms of the tendencies, ideologies, and socializable patterns and practices of social groups that may indeed be resisted and subverted to the benefit of individuals—but the normalizing power of which is also acknowledged and affirmed by such resistant acts, which may also incur real individual costs. Significantly, many of the critics of "culture" themselves seem to partake of a view similar to our middle-ground position (e.g., Clifford, 1986; Gupta & Ferguson, 1997), as indicated by their refusal to dispense with the notion altogether.

For present purposes, we therefore define culture/s as "bodies of knowledge, structures of understanding, conceptions of the world, . . . collective representations" (Schieffelin & Ochs, 1986, p. 166), social practices and tendencies, and group ideologies through which, by virtue of participating in, one is marked as a member of a social group, or discourse (Gee, 1990).

2. See the strikingly similar comment of Kato (1972, reported in Barnlund, 1975, p. 89): "In Japan, speech is not silver or copper or brass—it is scrap." The import of this comment, if not the precise metallurgic imagery, is virtually identical to that of the student quoted by Harklau. Many similar quotations (e.g., Cortazzi & Jin, 1996, p. 190) appear in the literature.

3. At least two major attempts—Yancey (1994) and Elbow (1994b)—have recently been made to sort out the various definitions and conceptions of "voice" as it is used in L1 composition theory and practice. While these are clearly important efforts, we are more interested in this paper in the subtle social-practice nature of the concept—and its problematic availability to L2/language minority writers—than we are with attempts to promote (and perhaps reify) the notion by resolving conflicting views.

4. Trimbur's statement seems also to address the apparent contradiction—pointed out to us first by Meryl Siegal—that the affinity with oral communication implicated in Bowden's second characteristic of personal voice is at odds with her third point, its distinctly literary flavor. Like Trimbur, Li (1996, pp. 124–5) points out that the "natural" qualities of "strongly voiced" prose favored by the American teachers in her cross-cultural study were in fact anything but natural—that they involved taking on a particular literary persona with studied casualness at its core.

5. Despite their own attempts to qualify its categorical nature, Markus and Kitayama's characterization effectively establishes independent versus interdependent views of self as binary opposites. For us, they more accurately represent opposite ends of a continuum, and cultural ideologies and social practices rather than absolute cultural categories (see note 1, above). Thus, variation in this regard within and across particular social groups and individual members of larger cultures is certainly possible (and always to be expected) without threatening the larger generalization that, overall, demonstrable cultural differences may exist. The quotation from Heath (1991) beginning this article points to variation across U.S. social groups in norms for the expression of individuality, while Belcher (1997) suggests intracultural gender variation in this area. It is partly for these reasons that language socialization researchers such as Heath (e.g., 1983), Ochs and Schieffelin (e.g., 1984), and Ron and Suzanne Wong Scollon (e.g., 1981) use terms such as "mainstream" or "middle class" American culture rather than referring to "American culture" or "U.S. culture" in general. Any description of a whole culture is obviously a blunt instrument, but that by no means invalidates the point that there *are* widely-held cultural norms within social groups and among peoples with closely shared histories—in short, that *people do live culturally*.

6. Bellah, Madsen, Sullivan, Swidler, and Tipton's (1985) characterization of middle class U.S. individualism provides a useful contrast to Li's and Matsumoto's formulations:

> We [Americans] believe in the dignity, indeed the sacredness, of the individual. Anything that would violate our right to think for ourselves, judge for ourselves, make our own decisions, live our lives as we see fit, is not only morally wrong, it is sacrilegious. Our highest and noblest aspirations, not only for ourselves, but for those we care about, for our society and for the world, are closely linked to our individualism. (p. 142)

7. These comments, of course, should in no way be taken to suggest that Japanese or Chinese people do not hold views representing their personal opinions. An important distinction is in fact made in Japanese language, thought, and communicative practice between *honne*—one's true opinion, basically—and *tatemae*—what it is appropriate to say in social circumstances (Doi, 1973). Hu's (1944, cited in Scollon, 1995, p. 14) *miànzi* versus *lian* contrast in Chinese would seem to capture something of the same basic distinction.

8. Although this study is based on a small sample—Carson and Nelson videotaped 18 peer-response group sessions involving 11 international students over a period of six weeks, and then conducted in-depth interviews (using the videotapes to prompt recall and discussion) involving three L1 Chinese speaking and two L1 Spanish speaking participants—we believe that the results accord with a body of practical knowledge that is widely shared by L2 writing practitioners (e.g., Allaei & Connor, 1990) and to that extent is generalizable. All research ultimately depends for its validation on a community of practice (see, for example, Latour & Woolgar, 1986; Latour, 1987; Mishler, 1990), and such validation is particularly important in the case of situated/qualitative

research of the type performed by Carson and Nelson (Ramanathan & Atkinson, 1999; Mishler, 1990).

9. As made clear in our earlier work on critical thinking (Atkinson, 1997; Ramanathan & Kaplan, 1996b), attempting to give discrete definitions of notions that function substantially as social practices is tricky, inevitably reductive and reifying, and quite possibly misguided. Nonetheless, for the purposes of the present paper we would suggest that definitions of critical thinking focusing on the skills underlying conventional "Western" academic skepticism and rationality (e.g., McPeck, 1981) are probably as close as one can get to an accurate definition of this particular social practice, at least when discussing critical thinking in relation to formal schooling. Obviously, there are proponents of particular brands of critical thinking theory and pedagogy that vary more or less widely from this one who would find our definition problematic (e.g., Benesh, 1993); some of these alternative possibilities are covered in Atkinson (1997, p. 74, note 3).

10. According to Schiffman (1996, pp. 171–2), the emphasis on memorization in modern Indian society has roots in the powerful hold of oral traditions (though we would add that these are oral traditions that have existed in many cases in complex symbiotic relationships with sophisticated literate traditions for thousands of years):

> [A] cornerstone of Indian linguistic culture is surely the reliance on orality and the elaboration of complicated methods of oral transmission of language. This continues to be one of the hardest facts about Indian linguistic culture for outsiders to the tradition to accept, because it contradicts their theoretical notions of what is possible and what is not possible. . . . This ability to memorize things seems to be highly valued in the culture in many ways, and can be observed in many other contexts, for example, the recent press reports of a young Indian man, Rajan Mahadevan, who, having already memorized the value of π to 31,811 places, has now declared his intention to memorize it (the value of π) to the millionth place. It is hard to imagine another culture on earth where anyone would even want to do this: In Indic culture it seems not at all extraordinary.

REFERENCES

Allaei, S. K., & Connor, U. (1990). Exploring the dynamics of cross-cultural collaboration in writing classrooms. *The Writing Instructor, 10,* 19–28.

Atkinson, D. (1997). A critical approach to critical thinking in TESOL. *TESOL Quarterly, 31,* 71–94.

Atkinson, D., & Ramanathan, V. (1995). Cultures of writing: An ethnographic comparison of L1 and L2 university writing/language programs. *TESOL Quarterly, 29,* 539–568.

Atkinson, P. (1985). *Language, structure and reproduction: An introduction to the sociology of Basil Bernstein.* London: Methuen.

Bakhtin, M. (1986). *Speech genres and other late essays.* (C. Emerson & M. Holquist, Eds.). Austin: University of Texas Press.

Ballard, B., & Clanchy, J. (1991). *Teaching students from overseas: A brief guide for lecturers and supervisors.* Sydney: Longman Chesire.

Barnlund, D. C. (1975). Communication styles in two cultures: Japan and the United States. In A. Kendon, R. M. Harris & M. R. Key (Eds.), *Organization of behavior in face-to-face interaction* (pp. 427–456). The Hague: Mouton.

Basso, K. H. (1972). 'To give up on words': Silence in Western Apache culture. In P. P. Giglioli (Ed.), *Language in social context.* (pp. 67–86). Harmondsworth, UK: Penguin Books.

Belcher, D. (1994). The apprenticeship approach to advanced academic literacy: Graduate students and their mentors. *English for Specific Purposes, 13,* 23–34.

Belcher, Diane. (1997). "An Argument for Nonadversarial Argumentation: On the Relevance of the Feminist Critique of Academic Discourse to L2 Writing Pedagogy." *Journal of Second Language Writing, 6* (1): 1–21.

Bellah, R. N., Madsen, R., Sullivan, W. M., Swidler, A., & Tipton, S. M. (1985). *Habits of the heart: Individualism and commitment in American life.* Berkeley: University of California Press.

Benesch, S. (1993). Critical thinking: A learning process for democracy. *TESOL Quarterly, 27,* 545–547.

Berlin, J. A. (1987). *Rhetoric and reality: Writing instruction in American colleges, 1900–1985.* Carbondale, IL: Southern Illinois University Press.

———. (1988). Rhetoric and ideology in the writing class. *College English, 50,* 477–494.

Bernstein, B. (1973). Class and pedagogies: Visible and invisible. In *Class, codes and control,* vol. 3: *Towards a theory of educational transmissions.* (2nd rev. ed., pp. 116–151) London: Routledge and Kegan Paul.

Bowden, D. (1995). The rise of a metaphor: "Voice" in composition pedagogy. *Rhetoric Review, 14,* 173–188.

——. (1996). Stolen voices: Plagiarism and authentic voice. *Composition Studies, 24,* 5–18.

Braine, G. (1996). ESL students in first-year writing courses: ESL versus mainstream classes. *Journal of Second Language Writing, 5,* 91–107.

Cadman, K. (1997). Thesis writing for international students: A question of identity? *English for Specific Purposes, 16,* 3–14.

Carson, J. (1992). Becoming biliterate: First language influences. *Journal of Second Language Writing, 1,* 37–60.

Carson, J., & Nelson, G. (1994). Writing groups: Cultural issues. *Journal of Second Language Writing, 3,* 17–30.

——. (1996). Chinese students' perceptions of ESL peer response group interaction. *Journal of Second Language Writing, 5,* 1–19.

Caudill, W., & Weinstein, H. (1974). Maternal care and infant behavior in Japan and America. In T. S. Lebra & W. P. Lebra (Eds.), *Japanese culture and behavior: Selected readings* (pp. 225–276). Honolulu: University of Hawaii Press.

Cederblom, J., & Paulson, D. (1987). *Critical reasoning.* Belmont, CA: Wadsworth Publishing Company.

Chao, R. (1994). Beyond parental control and authoritarian parenting style: Understanding Chinese parenting through the cultural notion of training. *Child Development, 65,* 1111–1119.

Chu, G. (1985). The changing concept of self in contemporary China. In A. Marsella, J. Anthony, G. DeVos, and F. L. K. Hsu (Eds.), *Culture and self: Asian and western perspectives.* (pp. 252–277). New York: Tavistock Publications.

Clancy, P. M. (1986). The acquisition of communicative style in Japanese. In B. B. Schieffelin & E. Ochs (Eds.), *Language socialization across cultures.* (pp. 213–250). Cambridge: Cambridge University Press.

Clifford, J. (1986). Introduction: On partial truth. In J. Clifford & G. E. Marcus (Eds.), *Writing culture: The poetics and politics of ethnography* (pp. 1–26). Berkeley: University of California Press.

Connor, U. (1996). *Contrastive rhetoric: Cross-cultural aspects of second-language writing.* Cambridge: Cambridge University Press.

Cope, B., & Kalantzis, M. (Eds.) (1993). *The powers of literacy: A genre approach to teaching writing.* Pittsburgh: University of Pittsburgh Press.

Cortazzi, M., & Jin, L. (1996). Cultures of learning: Language classrooms in China. In H. Coleman (Ed.), *Society and the language classroom* (pp. 169–206). Cambridge: Cambridge University Press.

Crago, M. (1992). Communicative interaction and second language acquisition. *TESOL Quarterly, 26,* 487–506.

Currie, P. (1997). Staying out of trouble: Apparent plagiarism and academic survival. *Journal of Second Language Writing, 7,* 1–18.

Deckert, G. (1993). Perspectives on plagiarism from ESL students in Hong Kong. *Journal of Second Language Writing, 2,* 131–148.

Delpit, L. (1988). The silenced dialogue: Power and pedagogy in educating other people's children. *Harvard Educational Review, 58,* 280–298.

Doi, T. (1973). *The anatomy of dependence.* Tokyo: Kodansha International.

Duranti, A. (1993). Beyond Bahktin, or the dialogic imagination in academia. *Pragmatics, 3,* 333–340.

Ede, L. (1989). *Work in progress: A guide to writing and revising.* New York: St. Martin's.

Elbow, P. (1973). *Writing without teachers.* New York: Oxford University Press.

——. (1981). *Writing with power: Techniques for mastering the writing process.* New York: Oxford University Press.

——. (1994a). What do we mean when we talk about voice in texts? In K. B. Yancey (Ed.), *Voices on voice: Perspectives, definitions, inquiry* (pp. 1–35). Urbana, IL: National Council of Teachers of English.

——. (Ed.) (1994b). *Landmark essays on voice and writing.* Davis, CA: Hermagoras Press.

Ellsworth, E. (1989). 'Why doesn't this feel empowering?' Working through the repressive myths of critical pedagogy. *Harvard Educational Review, 59,* 297–324.

Fischer, J. L., & Teigo, Y. (1968). The nature of speech according to Japanese proverbs. *Journal of American Folklore, 81,* 34–43.

Fleck, L. (1979). *Genesis and development of a scientific fact.* Chicago: University of Chicago Press.

Foucault, M. (1980). *Power/knowledge: Selected interviews and other writings, 1972–1977.* (Edited by C. Gordon). New York: Pantheon Books.

Fox, H. (1994). *Listening to the world: Cultural issues in academic writing.* Urbana, IL: National Council of Teachers of English.

Gee, J. (1990). *Sociolinguistics and literacies: Ideology in discourses.* Pittsburgh: Falmer Press.

Gilbert, P. (1989). *Writing, schooling and deconstruction.* London: Routledge and Kegan Paul.

Gupta, A., & Ferguson, J. (1997). *Culture, power, place: Explorations in critical anthropology.* Durham, NC: Duke University Press.

Harklau, L. (1994). ESL versus mainstream classes: Contrasting L2 learning environments. *TESOL Quarterly, 28,* 241–272.

Harklau, L. A., & Schecter, S. R. (1996). Sociocultural dimensions of voice in non-native language writing. In L. Bouton (Ed.), *Pragmatics and language learning* (Vol. 7, pp. 141–152). Urbana: University of Illinois Press.

Heath, S. B. (1983). *Ways with words: Language, life, and work in communities and classrooms.* Cambridge: Cambridge University Press.

———. (1991). The sense of being literate: Historical and cross-cultural features. In R. Barr, M.L. Kamil, P.B. Mosenthal, & P.D. Pearson (Eds.), *Handbook of reading research* (Vol. 2, pp. 3–25). New York: Longman.

Hedgcock, J., & Lefkowitz, N. (1992). Collaborative oral/aural revision in foreign language writing instruction. *Journal of Second Language Writing, 1,* 255–269.

Hendry, J. (1986). *Becoming Japanese: The world of the pre-school child.* Manchester, UK: Manchester University Press.

Hinds, J. (1987). Reader versus writer responsibility: A new typology. In U. Connor & R.B. Kaplan (Eds.), *Writing across languages: Analysis of L2 text.* (pp. 141–152). Reading, MA: Addison-Wesley Publishing Company.

Ho, I. (1998). Relationships between motivation/attitude, effort, English proficiency, and sociocultural educational factors and Taiwan technological university/institute students' English learning strategy use. Unpublished dissertation, Auburn University.

Hu, H. C. (1944). The Chinese concept of "face." *American Anthropologist, 46,* 45–64.

Inghilleri, M. (1989). Learning to mean as a symbolic and social process: The story of ESL writers. *Discourse Processes, 12,* 391–411.

Ishii, S., & Bruneau, T. (1994). Silence and silences in cross-cultural perspective: Japan and the United States. In L. A. Samovar & R. E. Porter (Eds.), *Intercultural communication: A reader.* (7th edition). (pp. 246–251). Belmont, CA: Wadsworth Publishing Company.

Ito, K. (1980). Towards an ethnopsychology of language: Interactional strategies of Japanese and Americans. *Bulletin of the Center for Language Studies* (Kanagawa University, Yokohama) *3,* 1–4.

Johns, A. (1991). Interpreting an English competency examination: The frustrations of an ESL science student. *Written Communication, 8,* 379–401.

Kalantzis, M., & Cope, B. (1993). Histories of pedagogy, cultures of schooling. In B. Cope & M. Kalantzis (Eds.), *The powers of literacy: A genre approach to teaching writing.* (pp. 38–62). Pittsburgh: University of Pittsburgh Press.

Koch, R. (1982). Syllogisms and superstitions: The current state of responding to writing. *Language Arts, 9,* 464–471.

Kolich, A. (1983). Plagiarism: The work of reason. *College English, 45,* 141–148.

Kroll, B. (1988). How college freshmen view plagiarism. *Written Communication, 5,* 203–221.

Latour, B. (1987). *Science in action.* Cambridge, MA: Harvard University Press.

Latour, B., & Woolgar, S. (1986). *Laboratory life: The construction of scientific facts.* Princeton, NJ: Princeton University Press.

Li, X. (1996). *"Good writing" in cross-cultural context.* Albany, NY: SUNY Press.

Lin, J. (1993). *Education in post-Mao China.* Westport, CT: Praeger.

Linden-Martin, M. (March, 1997). Hesitancy working with a peer: Comparison of two studies, 1995 and 1996. Paper presented at TESOL Convention, Orlando, FL.

Loveday, L. (1982). Communicative interference: A framework for contrastively analysing L2 communicative competence exemplified with the linguistic behaviour of Japanese performing in English. *International Review of Applied Linguistics, 20,* 1–16.

Markus, H. R., & Kitayama, S. (1991). Cultures and the self: Implications for cognition, emotion, and motivation. *Psychological Review, 98,* 224–253.

Matsumoto, Y. (1988). Reexamination of the universality of face: Politeness phenomena in Japanese. *Journal of Pragmatics, 12,* 403–426.

McKay, S. (1989). Topic development and written discourse accent. In D. M. Johnson & D. H. Roen (Eds.), *Richness in Writing: Empowering ESL students.* (pp. 253–262). New York: Longman.

McPeck, J. E. (1981). *Critical thinking and education.* New York: St. Martin's Press.

Mishler, E. (1990). Validation in inquiry-guided research: The role of exemplars in narrative studies. *Harvard Educational Review, 60*, 415–442.

Mittan, R. (1989). The peer review process: Harnessing students' communicative power. In D. Johnson & D. Roen (Eds.), *Richness in writing.* (pp. 207–219). New York: Longman.

Miyoshi, M. (1989). Thinking aloud in Japan. *Raritan, 9*, 29–45.

Nakane, C. (1970). *Japanese society.* Harmondsworth: Penguin Books.

Nelson, G. L., & Carson, J. G. (1998). ESL students' perceptions of effectiveness in peer response groups. *Journal of Second Language Writing, 7*, 113–131.

Ochs, E. (1992). Indexing gender. In A. Duranti & C. Goodwin (Eds.), *Rethinking context: Language as an interactive phenomenon.* (pp. 335–358). Cambridge: Cambridge University Press.

Ochs, E., & Schieffelin, B. (1984). Language acquisition and socialization: Three developmental stories and their implications. In R. A. Shweder & R. A. LeVine (Eds.), *Culture theory: Essays on mind, self and emotion.* (pp. 276–320). Cambridge: Cambridge University Press.

Ong, W. (1982). *Orality and literacy: The technologizing of the word.* New York: Routledge.

Pennycook, A. (1994a). *The cultural politics of English as an international language.* London: Longman.

———. (1994b). The complex contexts of plagiarism: A reply to Deckert. *Journal of Second Language Writing, 3*, 277–284.

———. (1996). Borrowing others' words: Text, ownership, memory, and plagiarism. *TESOL Quarterly, 30*, 201–230.

———. (1997). Cultural alternatives and autonomy. In P. Benson & P. Voller (Eds.), *Autonomy and independence in language learning.* (pp. 35–53). London: Longman.

Powers, J., & Gong, G. (1995). East Asian voice and the expression of cultural ethos. In K. B. Yancey, (Ed.), *Voices on voice: Perspectives, definitions, inquiry* (pp. 202–225). Urbana, IL: National Council of Teachers of English.

Raimes, A. (1998). Teaching writing. *Annual Review of Applied Linguistics, 18*, 142–167.

Raimes, A., & Zamel, V. (1997). Response to Ramanathan and Kaplan. *Journal of Second Language Writing, 6*, 79–81.

Ramage, J., & Bean, J. (1994). *Writing arguments.* New York: Macmillan.

Ramanathan, V., & Kaplan, R. B. (1996a). Audience and voice in current composition textbooks: Implications for L2 student-writers. *Journal of Second Language Writing, 5*, 21–34.

———. (1996b). Some problematic "channels" in the teaching of critical thinking in current L1 composition textbooks: Implications for L2 student-writers. *Issues in Applied Linguistics, 7*, 225–249.

———. (1997). Response to Raimes and Zamel. *Journal of Second Language Writing, 6*, 83–88.

Ramanathan, V., & Atkinson, D. (1999). Ethnographic approaches and methods in L2 writing research: A critical guide and review. *Applied Linguistics, 20*, 1, 44–70.

Rao, Z. (1996). Reconciling communicative approaches to the teaching of English with traditional Chinese methods. *Research in the Teaching of English, 30*, 458–471.

Rogoff, B. (1991). *Apprenticeship in thinking: Cognitive development in social context.* New York: Oxford University Press.

Roland, A. (1988). *In search of self in India and Japan: Toward a cross-cultural psychology.* Princeton: Princeton University Press.

Safire, W. (1992). The take on voice. *New York Times Magazine*, June 28, p. 14.

Santos, T. (1992). Ideology in composition: L1 and ESL. *Journal of Second Language Writing, 1*, 1–15.

Schieffelin, B. B., & Ochs, E. (1986). Language socialization. *Annual Review of Anthropology, 15*, 163–191.

Schiffman, H. F. (1996). *Linguistic culture and language policy.* London: Routledge.

Schneider, M., & Fujishima, N. (1995). When practice doesn't make perfect: The case of a graduate ESL student. In D. Belcher & G. Braine (Eds.), *Academic writing in a second language.* (pp. 3–22). Norwood, NJ: Ablex.

Scollon, R. (1991). Eight legs and an elbow: Stance and structure in Chinese English compositions. In *Launching the literacy decade: Awareness into action. Proceedings of the Second North American Conference on Adult and Adolescent Literacy. Multiculturalism and citizenship* (pp. 1–14). Toronto: International Reading Association.

———. (1995). Plagiarism and ideology: Identity in intercultural discourse. *Language in Society, 24*, 1–28.

Scollon, R., & Scollon, S. (1981). *Narrative, literacy, and face in interethnic communication.* Norwood, NJ: Ablex.

Scollon, R., & Scollon, S. W. (1991). Topic confusion in English-Asian discourse. *World Englishes, 10*, 113–125.

———. (1995). *Intercultural communication: A discourse approach.* Oxford: Blackwell.

Scollon, S. (1989). Literacy and face relations in teaching English in China. In S. Chang (Ed.), *A collection of papers presented in the Sixth Conference on English Teaching and Learning in the Republic of China* (pp. 195–204). Taipei: Crane.

Shen, F. (1989). The classroom and the wider culture: Identity as a key to learning English composition. *College Composition and Communication, 40,* 459–466.

Silva, T. (1993). Toward an understanding of the distinct nature of L2 writing: The ESL research and its implications. *TESOL Quarterly, 27,* 657–677.

Smith, R. J. (1997). The soul man of suburbia. *New York Times Magazine,* January 5, pp. 22–27.

Spack, R. (1997). The rhetorical construction of multilingual students. *TESOL Quarterly, 31,* 765–774.

Spigelman, C. (1998). Habits of mind: Historical configurations of textual ownership in peer writing groups. *College Composition and Communication, 49,* 234–255.

Stewart, D. (1972). *The authentic voice: A pre-writing approach to student writing.* Dubuque, IA: Brown.

Taylor, D. (1983). *Family literacy: Young children learning to read and write.* Exeter, NH: Heinemann.

Trimbur, J. (1994). Taking the social turn: Teaching writing post-process. *College Composition and Communication, 45,* 108–118.

Yamada, H. (1997). *Different games, different rules: Why Americans and Japanese misunderstand each other.* New York: Oxford University Press.

Yancey, K. B. (Ed.). (1994). *Voices on voice: Perspectives, definitions, inquiry.* Urbana, IL: National Council of Teachers of English.

Zamel, V. (1997). Toward a model of transculturation. *TESOL Quarterly, 31,* 341–352.

Zhang, S. (1995). Reexamining the affective advantage of peer feedback in the ESL writing class. *Journal of Second Language Writing, 4*(3), 209–222.

10 *Interaction and Feedback in Mixed Peer Response Groups*[1]

WEI ZHU

1. INTRODUCTION

During the last two decades, peer response in which students critique and provide feedback on one another's writing in small groups has captured the attention of many writing teachers and researchers in both first (L1) and second (L2) language settings. The interest in peer response is reflected in the numerous journal publications as well as conference colloquiums and presentations devoted to the topic. The enthusiasm for peer response is not difficult to understand, considering the strong theoretical support for and claims made about peer response. Supported by theories emphasizing the social nature of language, learning, knowledge-making, and writing (Berlin, 1987; Bruffee, 1984, 1993; Vygotsky, 1962, 1978), peer response seems to hold considerable promise as a viable tool in writing instruction at multiple levels. Its potential to help students develop audience awareness and improve writing through negotiating peer feedback is particularly appealing.

To date, writing research has examined various issues related to peer response in first as well as second/foreign language classrooms. One strand of research has focused on the impact of peer response on students' revision and quality of writing (Chaudron, 1983; Connor & Asenavage, 1994; Graner, 1987; Hedgcock & Lefkowitz, 1992; Herrington & Cadman, 1991; Mendonca & Johnson, 1994; Nelson & Murphy, 1993; Nystrand & Brandt, 1989). Results, however, are largely mixed. Another line of research, perhaps spurred by mixed results on peer response, has examined the effects of training students for peer response tasks (Berg, 1999; Hacker, 1996; Stanley, 1992; Zhu, 1995). In these studies, students are trained and helped to develop strategies for peer response, and results are overwhelmingly positive in both L1 (Hacker, 1996; Zhu, 1995) and L2 settings (Berg, 1999; Stanley, 1992). More specifically, trained peer response is found to (a) result in more and better quality peer feedback and peer talk (Hacker, 1996; Stanley, 1992; Zhu, 1995), and (b) increase student engagement and interaction during peer response (Stanley, 1992; Zhu, 1995).

From *Journal of Second Language Writing* 10.4 (2001): 251–76.

Peer response involves students working together and interacting with one another. Given this, it is not surprising that a major line of research has investigated peer response processes, focusing on student interaction and negotiation (Freedman, 1992; Gere & Abbott, 1985; Lockhart & Ng, 1995; Nelson & Murphy, 1992; Sommers & Lawrence, 1992; Spear, 1988; Villamil & De Guerrero, 1996). Studies along this line of research have examined oral and/or written feedback generated during peer response, often with a particular interest in peer talk during the response process. Researchers working in the L1 context have examined peer interaction and feedback by analyzing turn-taking behaviors and amount and functions of peer talk and by inspecting the different aspects of writing addressed by peer comments (e.g., Freedman, 1992; Gere & Abbott, 1985; Sommers & Lawrence, 1992; Spear, 1988). For example, Sommers and Lawrence (1992) found that female students talked less and were interrupted more than male students in groups that did not receive specific guidelines for conducting peer group sessions. In another study, Gere and Abbott (1985) examined peer response talk by 5th, 8th, and 11th grade students. Transcripts of peer group discussions were first coded into idea units and subsequently coded in terms of language functions (inform, direct, or elicit), area of attention (writing or group), and specific focus (process, content, form, or context). Gere and Abbott found that the highest proportion of the idea units fell under the "inform" function, involving students informing peers about the content of writing. Idea units that directed peers with regard to the writing process (e.g., revisions to be made) were second in number.

Second language writing researchers have also examined interaction and feedback during peer response, addressing issues concerning language functions of peer utterances, aspects of writing attended to by students, reader stances, and group dynamics (Lockhart & Ng, 1995; Mangelsdorf & Schlumberger, 1992; Mendonca & Johnson, 1994; Nelson & Murphy, 1992; Villamil & De Guerrero, 1996). For example, Lockhart and Ng (1995) analyzed transcripts of 27 L2 response dyads and identified 4 types of reader stances during peer response: authoritative, interpretive, probing, and collaborative. They also found differences across the stance types with respect to language functions performed and aspects of writing attended to by the students during peer response. For example, while readers with authoritative and interpretive stances performed the "give opinion" function (evaluation of writing) more, those with probing and collaborative stances performed the "give information" (e.g., insights and examples) function more.

Research in the L2 setting has also addressed issues specifically related to L2 peer response. One issue concerns the unique challenges associated with peer interaction in the L2 setting, given the cultural and linguistic variables involved (Carson & Nelson, 1994, 1996; Nelson & Carson, 1998). Because second language learners must comment on peer writing in a language in which they are still developing reading and communicative skills, and because second language learners must accommodate the different communication styles of peers from different cultures (Allaei & Connor, 1990) and cope with "different attitudes toward working in groups and different expectations concerning group norms" (Nelson & Murphy, 1992, p. 173), peer response in the L2 setting may be particularly challenging.

L1 and L2 peer response studies focusing on student interaction and feedback have shed considerable light on several aspects of peer response, including (a) how groups function, (b) how students perform peer response and comment on peer writing, (c) what characterizes successful peer response groups, and (d) what factors may affect peer interaction. They also suggest possible areas for intervention during peer response training. Most studies, however, have focused on response groups composed exclusively of native speakers or of second language learners. Few studies have investigated feedback and interaction in mixed peer response groups, those groups composed of both native speakers and second language learners. Yet peer response involving both native speakers and second language learners merits closer examination than that accorded by existing research because such research can shed further light on the peer response process and therefore inform implementation of peer response in composition classrooms. Compared to peer response groups composed of native speakers or second language learners exclusively, mixed groups are unique in that group members seem to bring differing levels of linguistic and cultural/pragmatic skills to peer response tasks. The native speakers have acquired their first language, and thus, to a large extent, can be assumed to be equipped with the basic oral skills necessary for peer interaction. Second language learners, on the other hand, are still in the process of developing language skills in their L2. Although there are considerable individual differences (e.g., some L2 learners have native-like or near-native communicative competence in L2), and although oral skills are only one kind of skills needed for successful peer response,[2] native speakers generally seem to be at an advantage in oral interaction because of the stronger language-related skills they possess. This situation in mixed peer response groups differs from that in groups composed of native speakers only, in which all participants seem to have acquired language-related skills for peer response, and also from that in groups composed of second language learners only, in which all participants are developing skills in the language used to conduct peer response.

Besides their uniqueness, the increasing presence of mixed peer response groups in college writing classes in English-dominant countries also warrants examination of these groups. With the steady growth of the foreign student population on US campuses (Davis, 1998), it is not unusual to see English as a Second Language (ESL) students enroll in mainstream freshman writing or technical writing courses in which peer response is an integral component. Given that peer response constitutes an important channel for providing and receiving feedback on writing in these courses, it would be useful to investigate how this channel is utilized by native speakers and ESL students.

The study reported below aimed at extending existing peer response research and set out to examine student interaction and feedback in mixed peer response groups. More specifically, interaction was examined in terms of participants' turn-taking behaviors and language functions performed during peer response. The specific research questions addressed were:

1. What are the turn-taking behaviors of native and non-native English speakers during peer response?

2. What are the language functions of native and non-native speakers' utterances during peer response?

3. What similarities and/or differences exist concerning native and non-native speakers' comments on different aspects in peer writing?

In the sections below, I will first describe the research context and methodology. Then, I will report the findings and suggest some possible implications of the findings for writing instruction and future research.

2. METHODOLOGY

2.1. Participants and Context

Participants in this study were 11 students in 3 peer response groups in 2 freshman composition classes at a medium-sized comprehensive university in the southwest of the United States. Eight participants were native speakers of English, and three were non-native English speakers. Group 1 consisted of four students, two males and two females. One was a female student from Malaysia. Group 2 consisted of four students, two males and two females. One was a male student from Spain. Group 3 consisted of three students, all male. One was a student from Greece. All three ESL students were recent arrivals in the US at the time of data collection: the Greek and Spanish students had arrived several weeks prior to the study, and the Malaysian student had arrived several months before the study started. Specific TOEFL scores of the three ESL students were not available, but all three had satisfied the university admission requirement of a minimum of 500 on the TOEFL. The freshman writing course was one of the first courses the ESL students were taking at the university. The two freshman composition classes were taught by two different instructors, and peer response was an integral component of writing instruction in both classes. Both instructors emphasized the writing process, and at least one draft was required of each out-of-class assignment. Four native speakers (two in Group 1 and one each in Groups 2 and 3) said that they had done peer response before; one ESL student (from Malaysia) said she had taken a pre-university intensive English course in which peer response was used.

2.2. Research Approach

This study adopted a case study approach. Stake (1998) defines a case as a "functioning specific" (p. 87), a system with boundaries. A case may be an individual, a class, or a "communicative interaction in a particular situation" (Johnson, 1992, p. 76). In the present study, three small group interactions were inspected, and each interaction as a bounded system included the interaction activity itself as well as the tool involved in the interaction: the response sheets. The case study approach, with its focus on naturally occurring phenomena, was chosen because it is compatible with the purpose of the study and the phenomenon examined. The present study aimed at investigating peer interaction in natural classroom contexts, and, as Johnson (1992) points out, communicative interaction is "well suited to a case study research approach" (p. 83). Further, a case study approach was adopted because it is flexible and can involve qualitative or quantitative data or both. By examining three small group interactions, this study represents what Stake calls a "collective case study," as "it is believed that understanding them will lead to better understanding, perhaps better theorizing, about a still larger collection of cases" (p. 89).

2.3. Peer Response Procedure

At the beginning of the semester, students in both classes viewed a video titled "Beginning Writing Groups" (Wordshop Productions, 1991) and had a class discussion on the purpose of peer response. Students, however, did not receive additional training on peer response. In both classes, instructors used ice-breaking activities to help students become comfortable with group discussions before the initial peer response session. For example, one instructor used a group activity in which group members had to discuss and decide who could leave the island to get help when a group of people was stranded on an island. The specific procedures followed in the peer response sessions were the same in both classes. Students were asked to bring copies of their drafts to class for group members, who would then critique the drafts in class. The instructors provided a simple set of guidelines orally prior to peer response. Students were told to consider the strengths and weaknesses in peer writing and to provide specific suggestions for revision. They were also encouraged to engage in the give-and-take of peer response: to ask questions and seek clarifications when something was not clear. Students were told to provide oral as well as written feedback on peer writing. The peer response procedure consisted of two main components. In each group, the writer first read aloud his/her essay while peers followed along on copies of the essay. Then, peers commented on the paper and provided suggestions for revision. Students were provided with response sheets to record written feedback (for sample response sheets, see the Appendix) and were instructed to fill out the response sheets in class and give them to the writers at the end of the response session. Students' oral discussions of the papers were audiotaped.

The peer response groups examined in this study were selected according to three criteria. First, because the focus of the study was on interaction and feedback in mixed peer response groups, each group had to have an ESL student and at least two native speakers.[3] Second, each group had to have critiqued at least one essay written by a native speaker and one by a non-native speaker. This criterion was necessary because students did not always bring their drafts to the peer response sessions, and therefore, mixed peer response groups did not always discuss native as well as ESL essays in a particular response session. Third, in each group, students had to have turned in the response sheets so that written feedback could be examined. ESL students' first language backgrounds and gender did not constitute criteria for group selection although these variables could potentially influence group interaction.

2.4. Data and Data Analysis

Data analyzed for the purpose of this study included transcripts of tape-recordings of peer discussions of six papers as well as students' written comments on peer writing recorded on the response sheets. Each group discussed two papers, one written by a native speaker and one written by the non-native speaker in the group. If a group discussed more than one essay written by native speakers, discussion of the first essay was selected. Note that in each group, the ESL student functioned as a reader and writer, respectively, in the two discussions.

Transcripts were examined for specific aspects of interaction. First, students' turn-taking behaviors were examined, and turns taken by each participant were numbered and counted. Each participant in the following brief excerpt was considered to have taken one turn.

WRITER: What did you guys think?

READER: One strength of your paper was that you used a lot of details. All those details made the story very interesting.

Turns serving back-channeling purpose such as "Okay" and "Alright" were excluded from analysis given that most analysts did not accept "murmurs of assent" as real turns (Coulthard, 1985). Initiation of discussion and interruptions were examined as part of the turn-taking behaviors. Interruptions occurred when another speaker disrupted the current speaker before the current speaker could finish his or her turn.

The functions of participants' utterances indicate how participants critique peer writing and convey feedback; therefore, an examination of the language functions of peer talk can provide considerable insight into interaction during peer response. Transcripts of student discussions were first coded in terms of idea units. Gere and Abbott (1985) define idea units as "brief spurts which reflect the speaker's object of consciousness. These spurts are idea units, and their boundaries are marked by intonation . . . by pauses, and by syntax" (p. 367). Each speaking turn consists of one or more idea units. For example, the turn "Oh, yes, this is wonderful content. I enjoyed reading it" consists of two idea units. In the present study, turns serving back-channeling purpose exclusively such as "Okay" and "Yeah" were not counted as idea units. I first segmented the transcripts into idea units and then asked a second reader, with whom I had discussed the concept of "idea unit" and gone over examples of idea units using transcripts not analyzed in this study, to check my segmentation of the transcripts. The second reader indicated places of disagreement on the transcripts. We agreed on 94% of the segmentations, and instances of disagreement were resolved through discussion.

Once idea units were identified, the function of each unit was coded based on an adapted version of Stanley's (1992) coding scheme. Stanley's coding scheme was chosen because it provides more specific information about peer interaction by coding the reader's (the respondent's) and writer's comments separately, thus making it possible to examine the functions of student utterances in terms of reader and writer roles. Also, Stanley's system appears to be adequate and efficient. The coding scheme encompasses a sufficiently wide range of specific language acts with a limited number of categories. In Stanley's study, which examined the impact of training for peer response, seven categories were used for the reader role (Pointing, Advising, Collaborating, Announcing, Reacting, Eliciting, Questioning) and three for the writer role (Responding, Eliciting, Announcing). Adaptation of Stanley's scheme for this study occurred in two ways: appropriate categories were added (e.g., Elaborating, Hedging, Confirming, and Justifying), and definitions of several categories were modified (e.g., Announcing, Reacting, and Eliciting). One category Stanley used to categorize reader comments, "Collaborating," was not observed in the discussions analyzed for this study and was therefore dropped. Also, "Announcing," a category Stanley used to code writer comments, was not used in the present study because no instances of "Announcing" were observed in the writers' remarks. The coding categories used for this study are presented below and illustrated with examples from transcripts of peer discussions analyzed for this study.

Reader roles

Pointing: Readers point to specific parts of the text when responding. For example, "Like right here, you say the elderly should not be sent to the nursing home."

Advising: Readers make general or specific suggestions. For example, "Give a picture about their lives."

Announcing: Readers "walk through" the essay, identify a problem, or explain their reactions to the essay. For example, "You mentioned something about atmosphere, and then it kind of got lost."

Reacting: Readers respond to the essay or other readers' comments by providing evaluative remarks. For example, "I thought it was very well written."

Eliciting: Readers elicit feedback explicitly from the writer or other group members. Feedback can center on a particular essay or the peer response process. For example, "What do you have to say?" (Reader A to Reader B).

Questioning: Readers ask questions of the writer or other participants. For example, "What are their values?"

Elaborating: Readers clarify a previous comment by giving examples. For example, "Like maybe why you like that one better than some other one or something?" (following a previous comment "compare to that one.")

Hedging: Readers soften the tone of the critique using phrases such as "I don't know."

Confirming: A reader confirms the writer's or another reader's interpretation of his/her comments or indicates agreement with the writer or other readers. For example, "Wait, yeah, it's just that one teacher." (responding to a comment by a peer "I thought we didn't have to talk about others' learning styles.")

Justifying: Readers defend their comments by giving reasons. For example, "I thought he (the instructor) was talking about learning styles, teaching styles, how you adapt." (responding to the peer comment "I thought we didn't have to talk about others' learning styles.")

Writer roles

Responding: Writer reacts to readers' comments. For example, "Alright, I see what you are saying."

Eliciting: Writer elicits feedback explicitly. For example, "What did you guys think?"

Clarifying: Writer explains intentions or brings in extra information to help the reader understand what has been written. For example, "We were in this place, and my mom and I had a deal."

I first coded the transcripts using Stanley's scheme and noted necessary adaptations of the scheme so that all data could be accounted for. Then, I revised the coding scheme based on categories identified through initial coding. Another reader and I coded the transcripts independently using the adapted scheme and were able to agree on 82% of the utterances coded. Disagreement was resolved through discussion.

Participants' written feedback was analyzed to examine the different aspects of writing addressed in peer comments. Written feedback was used for two reasons. First, participants in this study were explicitly instructed to record their comments on the response sheets and give the response sheets to the writers at the end of the response session. Thus, written feedback constituted an important component of the peer response process and deserved examination. Second, a comparison of participants' written comments with their oral feedback revealed that participants did not always discuss all of their written comments during oral response. This was particularly true for the ESL students (more information on this is provided in the Results section).

Students' written comments were coded as "evaluative," "global," and "local." A comment referred to a general remark or a statement, question, or suggestion concerning an aspect in peer writing. It often corresponded to a sentence or phrase, and in some cases, the sentence or phrase might be followed by further elaborations. Evaluative comments referred to those comments which expressed readers' *overall evaluation* of peer writing. For example, "I really like your paper" or "Excellent."[4] Global comments referred to those comments which addressed discourse-level concerns of writing such as support for main ideas, development of ideas, and organization of writing. For example: "Describe the situation a little more." Local comments referred to those comments which addressed sentence-level concerns of writing. For example, "Change little mistakes."

Another reader and I coded students' written comments and agreed on all the comments coded.

3. RESULTS

To illustrate the peer response processes in the three groups and provide a context for interpreting the results pertaining to the research questions, I first present a description of the discussions that occurred in the three groups. Each participant was assigned a pseudonym in the description below.

In Group 1, three native speakers, John, Lucy, and Tom, and an ESL student from Malaysia, Maznah, first discussed Maznah's paper, which compared and contrasted how the elderly people were treated in two different cultures. John opened the discussion by commenting on the good examples Maznah used in her writing; Lucy agreed with John but indicated that she would like more clarifications. Tom indicated that he would like more details. The group members also talked about word choice in the essay. The group then discussed Tom's essay, which compared the prices and qualities of different music CDs. Lucy opened the discussion by stating what she liked about the essay, and John also commented on the strengths of the essay. At this point, Maznah commented that she did not understand what the essay was about until she read the main part, implying that the introduction did not provide a clear enough direction. Her comment, however, was interrupted by the writer, Tom. Lucy concluded the discussion by giving advice on a couple of sentence-level issues.

Group 2 consisted of Melissa, Jack, Linda, and an ESL student from Spain, Jose. The assignment asked each student to compare his/her learning style with the teaching style of a particular teacher. Melissa opened the discussion of Jose's paper by commenting on the strengths of the paper and providing advice on revisions. Jack then pointed out the problem of repetition in Jose's paper and asked questions about how Jose adapted to other teachers' teaching styles. Linda added to this discussion by giving a specific idea for revision, asking Jose to explain why he liked a particular teacher's style better. After hearing Linda's comment, Jose asked how he could incorporate the ideas in revision. Jack responded to Jose's question, but his response triggered a discussion about the assignment, which constituted the major chunk of the remaining discussion. Students discussed whether or not they needed to discuss others' learning styles and teaching styles. Melissa said that they needed to focus on one teacher only, and she and Linda gave suggestions as to how Jose could compare his learning style to the teaching style of an instructor.

Melissa opened the discussion of Jack's paper by saying that the paper was well written and then commented that the paper provided a list of definitions of learning styles, which Jack perhaps could connect together. She also mentioned that her understanding of the assignment was different from Jack's but felt that the essay was well written. Linda echoed Melissa's comment and said that there seemed to be two papers in Jack's essay. She softened her criticism by mentioning the consistent good quality of Jack's writing. The rest of the discussion consisted of an exchange between Jose and Jack. Jose asked Jack about his learning style, and seemed to be ready to comment on the paper when he was interrupted by Jack. Jose concluded his comments by saying that everything seemed to be okay.

Group 3 was composed of two native speakers of English, Steve and Tim, and an ESL student from Greece, Andreas. The assignment required students to describe a situation and reflect on it. Steve initiated the discussion of his own paper by inviting feedback. Tim responded to Steve's invitation by commenting on the good use of details and asking a few questions. He suggested that Steve focus more on one central idea. The ESL student, Andreas, then started sharing his feedback. He also commented on the use of details and pointed out that Steve did not write much about the subject. Andreas prompted Steve to reflect more on what he observed.

The discussion of Andreas' essay involved the two respondents, Steve and Tim, each taking a turn and reporting feedback back to Andreas. There was no interaction between the respondents, nor was there interaction between the respondents and Andreas, the writer. Steve and Tim said that Andreas' essay was interesting and suggested that Andreas describe more and attend to grammar errors.

With this knowledge of the peer response processes in the three groups, let's turn to the results concerning the three research questions posed earlier.

Question 1. What are the turn-taking behaviors of native and non-native English speakers during peer response?

Turns participants took during peer response were examined. Table 1 presents the number of turns taken by the participants. Please note that all the readers of the ESL essay in each group were native speakers, and readers of the native essay in each group included the ESL student and the other native speakers except the writer. As shown in Table 1, there was some variation both within and across groups concerning the number of turns taken. However, except for the ESL writer in Group 3 (Andreas from Greece), all participants took turns during peer discussion although the number of turns taken by each participant differed.

The turn-taking behaviors of native and non-native speakers were examined according to the specific roles they played during peer response: as the writer and as the reader (respondent). As writers, the three ESL students took a total of 5 turns while the three native speaker writers took a total of 16 turns, three times more than the ESL writers. That the ESL writer in Group 3 (Andreas) did not take any turns certainly contributed to the gap between the ESL and the native English-speaking writers with respect to the number

TABLE 1.   Number of Turns Taken by Native and Non-native Speakers during Peer Response

Group	Number of turns on ESL essay	Number of turns on native essay

Group 1 (4 members)	12 turns
	By readers:
	  John: 2
	  Lucy: 6
	  Tom: 3
	By writer:
	  Maznah: 1
		7 turns
		By readers:
		  John: 2
		  Lucy: 2
		  Maznah: 1
		By writer:
		  Tom: 2

Group 2 (4 members)	18 turns
	By readers:
	  Melissa: 5
	  Jack: 4
	  Linda: 5
	By writer:
	  Jose: 4
		17 turns
		By readers:
		  Melissa: 3
		  Linda: 5
		  Jose: 4
		By writer:
		  Jack: 5

Group 3 (3 members)	2 turns
	By readers:
	  Steve: 1
	  Tim: 1
	By writer:
	  Andreas: 0
		27 turns
		By readers:
		  Tim: 12
		  Andreas: 6
		By writer:
		  Steve: 9

of turns taken. However, what is interesting is that each ESL writer consistently took fewer turns than the native English speaker writer in the same group.[5] Note that both the native speaker and ESL groups exhibited some variation with respect to the number of turns taken as writers.

As readers, ESL students took more turns than they did as writers. The three ESL students took 11 turns, with an average of 3.66 turns per person. The native speakers as a group performed 13 reader roles (8 reader roles on ESL writing and 5 reader roles on native speaker writing) and took a total of 51 turns, with an average of 3.9 turns per person, quite close to the 3.66 average by the ESL students. What is worth pointing out is that the ESL students did not always take fewer turns when compared with their native speaker counterparts in the same group. Note that both the ESL and native speaker groups demonstrated a range in terms of the number of turns taken as readers (1 to 6 for the ESL readers and 1 to 12 for native speakers).

When turn-taking behaviors were inspected in terms of initiations, it was found that non-native speakers did not initiate interaction and discussion of their own essays or peer essays. All discussions were initiated by a native speaker, and in one case, a native speaker writer, Steve (Group 3), initiated discussion of his own essay by inviting feedback "Okay, go ahead, tear my paper apart." When turn-taking behaviors were examined in terms of interruptions, it was found that, as readers, non-native speakers were more likely to be interrupted when providing feedback. The following is an example from Group 1.

NON-NATIVE SPEAKER READER
(MAZNAH, FROM MALAYSIA): Actually, when I first read your introduction, I wondered what the essay is about. Then, I go to the main part, then I realize you (interruption occurred)

WRITER (TOM): This is kind of in the middle . . .

NON-NATIVE SPEAKER READER
(MAZNAH): Okay. (Giggled, did not continue)

In the excerpt above, the non-native speaker reader, Maznah, seemed to be ready to point out a problem she perceived, that the introduction of the essay did not provide a clear direction for the reader. Her turn, however, was interrupted by the writer, and once interrupted, Maznah gave up her turn, the only turn she took. Similar interruptions occurred in Group 2, as shown in the following example. Here, the students were discussing an essay on learning styles.

NON-NATIVE SPEAKER READER
(JOSE, FROM SPAIN): What's your, um, learning style? Is it the converger?

WRITER (JACK): Yeah, I am a converger, supposedly, whatever that means.

NON-NATIVE SPEAKER READER (JOSE): Okay.

WRITER (JACK): Uh, I just, I think pretty much I mix different styles.

NON-NATIVE SPEAKER READER (JOSE): Also you are talking about converger and (interruption occurred)

WRITER (JACK): Yeah, in that paragraph, I am just listing the different types of learning styles.

NON-NATIVE SPEAKER READER (JOSE): Oh, yeah, what (interruption occurred)

WRITER (JACK): And then at the end I just say, I describe my own.

NON-NATIVE SPEAKER READER (JOSE): Oh, it looks good to me.

In this exchange, the non-native speaker, Jose, started by asking Jack's learning style and appeared to be prepared to point out something ("Also you are talking about converger and") when he was interrupted by Jack, who explained what he had been doing ("Yeah, in that paragraph, I am just listing the different types of learning styles."). Jose tried to resume the turn ("Oh, yeah, what") but was interrupted again ("and then at the end I just say, I describe my own"). After the second interruption, Jose gave up his turn by saying "Oh, it looks good to me." An examination of Jose's written comments revealed that Jose did not think everything was okay and thought that Jack ought to focus on his own learning style more. In the above excerpt, Jose seemed to be trying to convey this point to Jack, but after being interrupted, he gave up his turn and wrapped up the discussion.

Only in one instance did a non-native speaker writer, Jose, interrupt a native speaker reader. The difference in this case was that once interrupted, the native speaker, Jack, was able to resume his turn. Again, the essay being discussed was on learning styles.

> **NON-NATIVE SPEAKER WRITER (JOSE, FROM SPAIN):** How do I do that? Teaching styles?
>
> **NATIVE SPEAKER READER (JACK):** Yeah, how do you adapt to other teaching styles? Um, you talked about your specific learning style but what about other types of learning styles? What are (interruption occurred)
>
> **NON-NATIVE SPEAKER WRITER (JOSE):** I thought we didn't have to talk about others' learning styles.
>
> **NATIVE SPEAKER READER (LINDA):** That's what I thought too.
>
> **NATIVE SPEAKER READER (JACK):** That's interesting. I thought he (the instructor) was talking about learning styles, teaching styles, how you adapt.

Here, the non-native speaker, Jose, interrupted Jack before he could finish his question ("what are"). But unlike the non-native speakers who tended to give up, Jack tried to justify his comment ("that's interesting . . . "). Jack's justification then spurred a discussion about the nature of the assignment.

An interesting phenomenon was that turns taken by all non-native speakers when functioning as readers tended to occur at the end of the discussion, after the native speakers had taken their turns to convey feedback. This was true even in Group 3, in which the ESL student, Andreas (from Greece), took more turns than the other two ESL readers, and there seemed to be less pressure to compete for turns because there was only one other reader in the group. But still all turns Andreas took occurred after the native speaker reader, Tim, had completed all his turns. A related observation was that when functioning as readers, the ESL students tended to direct their turns exclusively to the writer. The native speakers, compared to the ESL students, were more likely to direct their turns to other readers. This was reflected in discussions of native speaker writing where two native speakers functioned as readers (e.g., Groups 1 and 2). When the native speaker readers were negotiating a point, the ESL students stayed out of the discussion.

Question 2. What are the language functions of native and non-native speakers' utterances during peer response?

A total of 145 language functions were identified for the three groups. The distribution of language functions across the three groups is presented in Table 2. As shown in Table 2, there is some variation across groups in terms of the number of language functions performed. For example, Group 2 produced more than twice as many functions (63) as Group 1 (26).

The number and type of language functions were then inspected according to writer and reader roles. Table 3 summarizes the number and type of language functions performed by the native and non-native speakers when acting as writers. As shown in the table, the three ESL students performed a total of 6 (4 responding, 2 eliciting) functions, compared to 16 functions performed by the three native speakers (7 responding, 2 eliciting, 7 clarifying). The fact that the non-native speaker in Group 3, Andreas, did not participate

TABLE 2.   Number of Language Functions Performed by Native and Non-native Speakers during Peer Response

Group	Number of language functions on ESL essay	Number of language functions on native essay
Group 1 (4 members)	15 functions By readers: John: 2 Lucy: 9 Tom: 3 By writer: Maznah: 1	11 functions By readers: John: 2 Lucy: 5 Maznah: 2 By writer: Tom: 2
Group 2 (4 members)	32 functions By readers: Melissa: 9 Jack: 13 Linda: 5 By writer: Jose: 5	31 functions By readers: Melissa: 9 Linda: 11 Jose: 6 By writer: Jack: 5
Group 3 (3 members)	18 functions By readers: Steve: 6 Tim: 12 By writer: Andreas: 0	38 functions By readers: Tim: 17 Andreas: 12 By writer: Steve: 9

in the discussion of his own essay and therefore did not perform any language functions certainly contributed to this gap. As writers, both the ESL students and the native speakers performed the responding function. For example, Steve (Group 3) responded to Tim's suggestion by saying "I think I can do that." However, only the native speaker writers (and all of them) performed the clarifying function. For example, Tom (Group 1) clarified what he wrote about by providing information about the situation ("We were in this place and my mom and I had a deal"). Only one ESL student, Jose (from Spain), and one native speaker, Steve, performed the eliciting function (two in each case). Jose elicited feedback by asking "how do I do that?" after receiving suggestions for revision, and Steve performed two eliciting functions consecutively at the beginning of the discussion of his paper:

STEVE: Okay, go ahead, tear my paper apart.

TIM: Alright.

STEVE: What did you guys think?

Table 4 presents the number and types of language functions performed by native and non-native speakers when functioning as readers. As readers, the ESL students performed 20 functions, 7 functions per person on the average, while the native speakers performed a total of 103 functions, approximately 8 functions per person (103 functions over 13 reader roles). These

TABLE 3.   Number and Type of Language Functions Performed by Native and Non-native Speakers when Functioning as Writers

Group	Responding	Eliciting	Clarifying	Total
Non-native speakers				
Group 1 (Maznah)	1	0	0	1
Group 2 (Jose)	3	2	0	5
Group 3 (Andreas)	0	0	0	0
Non-native speaker total	4	2	0	6
Native speakers				
Group 1 (Tom)	0	0	2	2
Group 2 (Jack)	2	0	3	5
Group 3 (Steve)	5	2	2	9
Native speaker total	7	2	7	16

numbers suggested that the ESL and the native speakers performed more comparably when acting as readers in terms of the number of idea units generated. Although the ESL students generally did not perform more functions than native speakers, they did not invariably perform fewer functions either.

A sharper contrast emerged between the native and non-native speakers when the types of language functions produced were examined. It is obvious from Table 4 that the types of language functions performed by the non-native speakers were more limited. The language functions performed by the non-native speakers fell under the categories of announcing, reacting, questioning, advising, and justifying, with announcing and questioning being the two major functions. Fourteen out of the 20 functions (70% of the functions) identified for the ESL students belonged to announcing (30%) and questioning (40%). Native speakers, on the other hand, performed the full range of functions, with "reacting" (22%), "advising" (24%), and "announcing" (17%) as the most frequently occurring, although not every student performed all types of functions. Note that the following functions were performed by native speaker readers exclusively: confirming, pointing, hedging, elaborating, and eliciting. Native speaker readers reacted more to peer writing (e.g., "That's pretty good and I like it") and advised more on peer writing (e.g., "I thought you should tell about the teacher a little more"). While only one non-native speaker, Andreas (from Greece), advised (e.g., "Focus on the subject more"), native speakers performed this function almost always when responding to ESL and each other's writing. Non-native speakers, instead, tended to "announce" (e.g., "Actually when I first read your introduction, I wondered what the essay is about") or "question" (e.g., "What are their values?") when providing feedback. Comparing the types of language functions performed, it seemed that native speakers tended to provide suggestions more directly through advising while non-native speakers tended to point out (announcing) and imply (questioning) problematic areas.

Question 3. *What similarities and/or differences exist concerning native and non-native speakers' comments on different aspects in peer writing?*

TABLE 4. Number and Type of Language Performed by Native and Non-native Speakers when Functioning as Readers

Group	Pt	Ad	An	Re	Eli	Qu	Ela	He	Co	Ju	To
Non-native speakers											
Group 1 (Maznah)	0	0	2	0	0	0	0	0	0	0	2
Group 2 (Jose)	0	0	1	1	0	4	0	0	0	0	6
Group 3 (Andreas)	0	2	3	2	0	4	0	0	0	1	12
Non-native speaker total	0	2	6	3	0	8	0	0	0	1	20
Native speakers on ESL writing											
Group 1											
John	0	0	0	2	0	0	0	0	0	0	2
Lucy	2	1	1	2	1	2	0	0	0	0	9
Tom	0	1	1	1	0	0	0	0	0	0	3
Group 2											
Melissa	0	2	0	2	1	0	2	0	2	0	9
Jack	0	1	4	1	0	2	3	0	1	1	13
Linda	0	1	0	1	0	0	1	0	2	0	5
Group 3											
Steve	0	2	0	4	0	0	0	0	0	0	6
Tim	0	4	4	3	0	0	0	1	0	0	12
Native speakers on native writing											
Group 1											
John	0	0	0	1	1	0	0	0	0	0	2
Lucy	0	3	0	1	0	0	1	0	0	0	5
Group 2											
Linda	1	2	1	2	2	0	0	1	1	1	11
Melissa	1	2	2	2	0	0	0	2	0	0	9
Group 3											
Tim	0	6	4	1	0	3	3	0	0	0	17
Native speaker total	4	25	17	23	5	7	10	4	6	2	103

Pt = Pointing; Ad = Advising; An = Announcing; Re = Reacting; Eli = Eliciting; Qu = Questioning; Ela = Elaborating; He = Hedging; Co = Confirming; Ju = Justifying; To = Total.

This question was answered by examining written feedback participants provided on each other's writing. Table 5 presents the number of evaluative, global, and local comments native and non-native English speaking participants provided on the six essays, 3 ESL and 3 native. As shown in Table 5, the three non-native speakers provided a total of 13 written comments (4, 3, 6, respectively), 4.3 comments per person on the average. All their comments, except for one, were global. The native speakers provided a total of 72 comments, 5.53 comments per person on the average (72 comments over 13 reader roles). While native speakers provided somewhat more feedback, they did not necessarily provide more global comments. In fact, non-native speakers provided as many global comments as native speakers did. As a group, the ESL students provided 12 global comments, an average of 4 comments per

TABLE 5. Number of Evaluative, Global, and Local Comments provided by Native and Non-native Speakers

Group	Evaluative	Global	Local	Total
Non-native speakers				
Group 1 (Maznah)	0	3	1	4
Group 2 (Jose)	0	3	0	3
Group 3 (Andreas)	0	6	0	6
Non-native speaker total	0	12	1	13
Native speakers on ESL writing				
Group 1				
John	0	4	1	5
Lucy	1	3	2	6
Tom	0	3	2	5
Group 2				
Melissa	2	3	3	8
Jack	0	3	4	7
Linda	0	4	0	4
Group 3				
Steve	2	0	2	4
Tim	0	3	0	3
Native speakers on native writing				
Group 1				
John	0	4	2	6
Lucy	0	3	2	5
Group 2				
Melissa	2	7	0	9
Linda	2	3	3	8
Group 3				
Tim	0	2	0	2
Native speaker total	9	42	21	72

person, and the native speakers provided a total of 42 global comments, 3.23 comments on the average per person. Comparing the number of global comments each ESL student provided to that by his/her native English-speaking counterparts in the same group also suggested that the ESL students provided a rather similar amount of global feedback as the native speakers.

Compared to the ESL students, the native speakers provided more evaluative remarks and local comments on peer writing. Nine of the 72 comments made by native speakers were evaluative (12.5%) and 21 were local (29%). Native speakers wrote comments such as "Very good," "Run-on sentences," and "A couple of sentence fragments." In contrast, none of the non-native speakers provided evaluative feedback, and only one ESL student, Maznah (from Malaysia), provided local feedback dealing with word choice. She wrote down "A few word [sic], 'buck,' 'a ton'" as a suggestion for revision. Interestingly, while commenting on the local aspects in ESL writing, two of the native speakers indicated an understanding of the language difficulties experienced by second language learners. Lucy in Group 1 wrote that "Grammar was a bit of a problem—I think it just might be our screwy language—trying to learn it as a second language is quite difficult." Jack in Group 2 indicated to Jose that one of the weaknesses in his essay was run-on sentences and, in order to help Jose understand the nature of the problem, inserted a short but less than accurate explanation of run-on sentences as "too many ideas in one sentence or repeating self." The native speakers also provided corrections on peer drafts. The non-native speakers, however, did not offer corrective feedback on their peers' drafts.

An inspection of the global comments made by both native and non-native speakers revealed that the global comments tended to center on content. Often, students indicated a need for more information by making direct requests such as "Get more specific and describe" and "Tell more about how you feel about the teacher (personality)" or by raising questions that they felt the writers needed to address such as "What if the families are never home? If they work, who would take care of the elderly?" Only in one case did a non-native speaker out of all participants, Andreas, indicate that less detail would be more desirable (and he was right) by writing "not to give too many details for the trip but go earlier to the main idea." Organizational and rhetorical issues were rarely discussed, except in a couple of comments such as "The introduction seemed disjointed" and "you sound like you are talking to your best friend—who are you talking to, teens only?" One ESL student, Maznah, commented on the introduction of Tom's essay by writing "Introduction—I can't tell what kind of paper that I am reading . . . only after I go through the main point."

4. DISCUSSION AND CONCLUSION

This case study examined interaction and feedback in mixed peer response groups in mainstream freshman composition classes. The results indicated both similarities and differences between the native and non-native speaker participants with respect to their participation and feedback during peer response. As writers, the ESL students took fewer turns, responded to peer feedback, but did not clarify their writing for the readers. As readers, the ESL students generated a similar amount of oral feedback but had difficulties competing for turns and sustaining and regaining turns when interrupted. They also performed a narrower range of language functions and chose somewhat different strategies for conveying feedback. Similarities between the native and non-native speaker participants, however, were also observed. One was that the non-native speakers offered a similar amount of global feedback as the native speakers in the written mode of peer response. Another similarity was that neither the native speaker group nor the non-native speaker group actively performed the "eliciting" function. Given that eliciting feedback is considered a major role of the writer during peer response, it seems that native and non-native speaker students alike did not perform the writer role effectively.

put is/. small

This case study involved a small number of participants (11 students in 3 groups, each with an ESL student). Because of the very small sample, the average used to present the number of turns, language functions, and written comments could easily mask variability in both the native and non-native speaker groups.[6] Also, the non-native speakers were from different L1 backgrounds (two Europeans, one Asian), and it was possible that their L1s, gender, individual propensities, attitudes toward and experience with peer response and other factors affected their peer response behaviors. Given these limitations, and given the "hypothesis-generating" (Seliger & Shohamy, 1989; Wallace, 1998) nature of the case study approach adopted in this study, results presented above must be interpreted with care. Yet, in spite of the limitations, this study provides some potentially useful information concerning mixed peer response groups which merits discussion.

Results of the study indicate that, in mixed peer response groups, native and non-native speakers could focus on the peer response tasks at hand and provide one another with global feedback for revision. Nevertheless, the ESL students' participation in oral peer response was more limited than that of their native speaker counterparts. The fewer turns they took as well as the largely "responding" function they performed as writers suggest that the ESL students in this study were less in control of the discussions of their own writing, and, as a result, might not have benefited as much as they could have from oral response. Further, their efforts to contribute feedback seemed to be hampered by peer interruptions. These observations suggest that the ESL students were at somewhat of a disadvantage when interacting with the native speakers in oral response and raise some concerns about ensuring equality in mixed peer response groups. How do we implement peer response in the mixed group situation? What can we do to help ESL students become equal participants in mixed peer response groups? These questions deserve consideration when we use mixed peer response groups. Sommers and Lawrence's (1992) study found that peer response may not be equitable along gender lines in the L1 setting and indicated that "instructional guidance plays a vital role in creating or denying equality between males and females in peer response groups" (p. 32). Results of this study suggest that the issue of equal participation is worth attending to in mixed peer response groups as well.

online peer review

Findings of the present study also indicate that while their participation in the oral discussion of writing was more limited compared to that by native speakers, the ESL students were valuable contributors to peer response, particularly through providing written feedback. Concentrating on global aspects of writing is a major objective of peer response (e.g., Spear, 1988), and the ESL students in this study accomplished this important objective as much as the native speakers. That the ESL students were equally able to focus on the global aspects of writing perhaps should not come as a surprise. First, the ESL students may have already developed some "writing expertise" (Cumming, 1989), the underlying writing ability independent of L2 linguistic proficiency, through L1 writing and may have been able to apply this expertise to examining the global, non-language specific issues in their peers' writing.

Second, the ESL students may have felt more comfortable focusing on the global rather than the local, language-related issues in their peers' writing because of their own developing proficiency in L2. The fact that only one ESL student made one local comment on peer writing is perhaps indicative of this. The results of this study also shed some light on the value of written feedback in mixed peer response groups. In this study, written response allowed the non-native speakers an additional opportunity to convey feedback, suggesting that the written mode of peer response could be a particularly valuable tool for mixed peer response groups and could supplement oral response.

A couple of similarities and differences between results of this study and those of other studies are worth mentioning. The finding that the ESL students in the writer role tended to respond but not clarify is similar to that of Stanley's (1992) study, from which coding categories used in this study were adapted. In Stanley's study, responding was performed most frequently and clarifying least frequently by the group of ESL students comparable to those in this study (i.e., Stanley's control group that received a similar amount of instruction on peer response as the three ESL students in this study). The language functions performed by the ESL students in the reader role, however, were somewhat different in the two studies. In Stanley's study, reacting was performed most frequently by the comparable group of ESL students, followed by pointing, announcing, and advising. The three ESL students in this study, however, preferred questioning and announcing. This difference of course could reflect individual differences of the participants in these studies, yet, it is also possible that it reflects a change in how ESL students as readers responded to the context of peer response. In Stanley's study, the ESL students were critiquing fellow ESL students' writing, but in the present study, the ESL students were critiquing writing by native speaker peers. It is possible that different response contexts, a crucial element of which is the participants, could elicit different response behaviors and strategies from the ESL students. The language functions performed by the native speakers in this study cannot be easily compared with those of other studies because of the different methodologies and/or coding categories used in the studies. It would certainly be interesting to examine the response behaviors and strategies of native speakers in L1 versus mixed peer response groups.

It is somewhat premature to offer suggestions for teaching based on a study with a small number of participants. While sound pedagogical suggestions can only be made with a better understanding of peer response based on more studies, several issues may deserve writing teachers' consideration when employing mixed peer response groups. First, there appears to be the need to provide all students with guidance and instruction so that they can be more equal participants when engaged in oral response. Training for peer response so far tends to focus on what to critique (e.g., helping students focus on the important aspects of writing during peer response) and how to convey peer feedback (e.g., helping students develop, for example, politeness strategies). The findings of the present study suggest that in mixed group situations, it may be beneficial to address turn-taking behaviors to facilitate peer response discourse and maximize equal participation. For example, taperecordings of peer discussions could be made and students could be helped to become aware of their own turn-taking behaviors. It might also be worthwhile to help ESL students enhance pragmatic skills conducive to peer response (e.g., how to compete for turns). To help students better perform the writer role, teachers may consider assisting students to expand repertoire of feedback strategies and instructing them to clarify their intentions for and elicit feedback from their peers. The ESL students in particular could be assisted to become more active participants as writers so that they could play a more important role in the discussion of their own papers and benefit more from peer response. Last but not the least, teachers might not want to rely on a single mode of peer response. Combining oral and written response or alternating them perhaps would better allow native and ESL students to contribute to, and benefit from, peer response.

This study provides some preliminary data concerning interaction and feedback in mixed peer response groups. Given the increasing number of international students on US campuses and the place of peer response in undergraduate writing instruction, native and non-native interaction and feedback during peer response deserve further investigation. Future research could investigate the questions posed in this study with larger samples and/or different methodology. Future studies could also examine (a) native and ESL students' perceptions of each other's feedback, (b) the relationship between feedback generated during peer response and incorporation of the feedback in subsequent revisions (i.e., to what extent and how do native speakers use feedback provided by the ESL students and vice versa), (c) the impact of direct (e.g., through advising) versus indirect (e.g., through questioning) peer feedback on revisions, and (d) the impact of language background and gender on ESL participants' behaviors and strategies in mixed peer response groups. With a better understanding of these issues, writing instructors are in a better position to help both native and non-native speakers become more effective participants in peer response and promote learning through peer response.

NOTES

1. This is a revised version of a paper I presented in the colloquium entitled "Current peer review research in ESL writing" at the 34th TESOL Annual Convention. I would like to thank Diane Belcher, the co-editors of JSLW, and two anonymous reviewers for their insightful comments on the earlier versions of this paper.

2. Factors such as cognitive styles, personality, writing skills, and experience with peer response tasks can affect group status and interaction during peer response.

3. Pairs were not selected because the dynamics in pair interaction is generally considered different from that in small group interaction. Since small groups are generally recommended for peer response, and since groups, rather than pairs, were typically used in the two composition classes from which data were collected, only small groups consisting of 3–4 students were selected for examination.

4. Comments in which students evaluated specific aspects of writing were coded as "global" or "local" depending on what was being evaluated. For example, "I like the different points you made—price, quality, etc." was coded as a global comment as it evaluated the content of writing.

5. The number of turns taken by each ESL student was compared to that by the native speakers in the same group because different groups may have different group dynamics, and the behaviors of group members may be influenced by the dynamics of each group.

6. Note that there was a sharp contrast in Group 3 in which the ESL student did not take any turns as the writer while the native speaker writer took nine turns. This contrast in Group 3 contributed considerably to the gap between the native and non-native speakers. Without further evidence, it is difficult to say whether what happened in Group 3 is the norm or the exception.

REFERENCES

Allaei, S., & Connor, U. (1990). Exploring the dynamics of cross-cultural collaboration. *The Writing Instructor, 10*, 19–28.

Berg, C. E. (1999). The effects of trained peer response of ESL students' revision types and writing quality. *Journal of Second Language Writing, 8*, 215–237.

Berlin, J. (1987). *Rhetoric and reality: Writing instruction in American colleges, 1900–1985*. Carbondale, IL: Southern Illinois University Press.

Bruffee, K. (1984). Collaborative learning and the "conversation of mankind." *College English, 46*, 635–652.

Bruffee, K. (1993). *Collaborative learning: Higher education, interdependence, and the authority of knowledge*. Baltimore, MD: Johns Hopkins University Press.

Carson, J., & Nelson, G. (1994). Writing groups: Cross-cultural issues. *Journal of Second Language Writing, 3*, 17–30.

Carson, J., & Nelson, G. (1996). Chinese students' perceptions of ESL peer response group interaction. *Journal of Second Language Writing, 5*, 1–19.

Chaudron, C. (1983). *Evaluating writing: Effects of feedback of revision*. ERIC Document Reproduction Service No. ED 227 706.

Connor, U., & Asenavage, K. (1994). Peer response groups in ESL writing classes: How much impact on revision? *Journal of Second Language Writing, 3*, 257–276.

Coulthard, M. (1985). *An introduction to discourse analysis*. New York: Longman.

Cumming, A. (1989). Writing expertise and second language proficiency. *Language Learning, 39*, 81–141.

Davis, T. (Ed.) (1998). *Open Doors 1997/98: Report on international educational exchange*. New York: Institute of International Education.

Freedman, S. (1992). Outside-in and inside-out: Peer response groups in two ninth-grade classes. *Research in the Teaching of English, 26*, 71–107.

Gere, A., & Abbott, R. (1985). Talking about writing: The language of writing groups. *Research in the Teaching of English, 19*, 362–385.

Graner, M. (1987). Revision workshops: An alternative to peer editing groups. *English Journal, 76*, 40–45.

Hacker, T. (1996). The effects of teacher conferences on peer response discourse. *Teaching English in the Two-Year College, 23*, 112–126.

Hedgcock, J., & Lefkowitz, N. (1992). Collaborative oral/aural revision in foreign language writing instruction. *Journal of Second Language Writing, 1*, 255–276.

Herrington, A., & Cadman, D. (1991). Peer review and revising in an anthropology course: Lessons for learning. *College Composition and Communication, 42*, 184–199.

Johnson, D. (1992). *Approaches to research in second language learning*. New York: Longman.

Lockhart, C., & Ng, P. (1995). Analyzing talk in peer response groups: Stances, functions, and content. *Language Learning, 45*, 605–655.

Mangelsdorf, K., & Schlumberger, A. (1992). ESL student response stances in a peer review task. *Journal of Second Language Writing, 1*, 235–254.

Mendonca, C., & Johnson, K. (1994). Peer review negotiations: Revision activities in ESL writing instruction. *TESOL Quarterly, 28*, 745–769.

Nelson, G., & Carson, J. (1998). ESL students' perceptions of effectiveness in peer response groups. *Journal of Second Language Writing, 7*, 113–131.

Nelson, G., & Murphy, J. (1992). An L2 writing group: Task and social dimensions. *Journal of Second Language Writing, 1*, 171–193.

Nelson, G., & Murphy, J. (1993). Peer response groups: Do L2 writers use peer comments in revising their drafts? *TESOL Quarterly, 27*, 135–141.

Nystrand, M., & Brandt, D. (1989). Response to writing as a context for learning to write. In C. Anson (Ed.), *Writing and response: Theory, practice and response* (pp. 209–230). Urbana, IL: National Council of Teachers of English.

Seliger, H., & Shohamy, E. (1989). *Second language research methods*. Oxford: Oxford University Press.

Sommers, E., & Lawrence, S. (1992). Women's ways of talking in teacher-directed and student-directed peer response groups. *Linguistics and Education, 4*, 1–36.

Spear, K. (1988). *Sharing writing*. Portsmouth, NH: Boynton/Cook Publishers.

Stake, R. (1998). Case studies. In N. K. Denzin, & Y. S. Lincoln (Eds.), *Strategies of qualitative inquiry* (pp. 86–109). Thousand Oaks, CA: Sage Publications.

Stanley, J. (1992). Coaching student writers to be effective peer evaluators, *Journal of Second Language Writing, 1*, 217–233.

Villamil, O., & De Guerrero, M. (1996). Peer revision in the L2 classroom: Social–cognitive activities, mediating strategies, and aspects of social behavior. *Journal of Second Language Writing, 5*, 51–75.

Vygotsky, L. (1962). *Thought and language*. Cambridge, MA: MIT Press.

Vygotsky, L. (1978). *Mind in society: The development of higher psychological processes*. Cambridge, MA: Harvard University Press.

Wallace, M. (1998). *Action research for language teachers*. Cambridge: Cambridge University Press.

Wordshop Productions. (1991). *Beginning writing groups*. Tacoma, WA: Wordshop Productions.

Zhu, W. (1995). Effects of training for peer response on students' comments and interaction. *Written Communication, 12*, 492–528.

APPENDIX. SAMPLE RESPONSE SHEETS

1. Sample response sheet from a native speaker (Lucy)

Your Name_____ Date_____
Writer's Name_____
Teacher's Name_____
Section Number_____

As peer revision is an integral part of this class, it is essential that you provide your peers with thoughtful feedback on their writing. Try to give your peers as much feedback as you can. Note that specific comments and suggestions are always more helpful than general ones. Also note that providing feedback on peer writing constitutes an important part of your participation score for the course.

1. What are the strengths of this paper?
   I liked the part where you talked about your society in Malaysia compared to US society (respecting your elders). Use of statistics was good.

2. What are the weaknesses of this paper?
   Grammar was a bit of a problem—I think it might be our screwy language—trying to learn it as a second language is quite difficult.

3. What questions do you have after reading this paper?
   Is everything you know about nursing homes from research or do you know someone that this has happened/is happening to?

4. What are your suggestions for revision of this paper?
   Some of the wording sounds odd—I wrote stuff on your paper—just my own opinions.

   I liked your paper—good topic.

2. Sample response sheet from a non-native speaker (Andreas)

Your Name_____ Date_____
Writer's Name_____
Teacher's Name_____
Section Number_____

As peer revision is an integral part of this class, it is essential that you provide your peers with thoughtful feedback on their writing. Try to give your peers as much feedback as you can. Note that specific comments and suggestions are always more helpful than general ones. Also note that providing feedback on peer writing constitutes an important part of your participation score for the course.

1. What are the strengths of this paper?
   Describes their way and the place with every detail.
   I like the way you end the essay.

2. What are the weaknesses of this paper?
   He writes a lot about his trip and only a little about the subject.

3. What questions do you have after reading this paper?
   What make you stay and laugh in front of him.
   How did they feel in front of him.

4. What are your suggestions for revision of this paper?
   Not to give too many details for the trip but go earlier to the main idea.

11   *Understanding Critical Writing*

A. SURESH CANAGARAJAH

S o what happens to writing when you attach the word *critical* to it? Does anything happen at all? Is this another newfangled label that promotes a novel pedagogy or method for purely commercial reasons or other ulterior motivations without substantially affecting the writing activity? Or, on the other hand, is too much happening—far too much for our liking—shifting our attention to things unrelated to writing? Is this label bringing into composition something extraneous to the writing activity, such as political causes and social concerns that are the whims of one scholarly circle or the other? We in the teaching profession are rightly suspicious of anything that claims to be new, fashionable, or revolutionary nowadays.

For me, the label *critical* brings into sharper focus matters that are always there in writing. It develops an attitude and a perspective that enable us to see some of the hidden components of text construction and the subtler ramifications of writing. We gain these insights by situating the text in a rich context comprising diverse social institutions and experiential domains. In doing so, the label also alerts us to the power—and dangers—of literacy. Texts can open up new possibilities for writers and their communities—just as illiteracy or ineffective writing can deny avenues for advancement. Writing can bring into being new orientations to the self and the world—just as passive, complacent, or mechanical writing parrots the established view of things (which may serve the unfair, partisan interests of dominant institutions and social groups). Indeed, the text is shaped by such processes of conflict, struggle, and change that characterize society. By connecting the text to context (or the word to the world), the critical perspective enables us to appreciate the complexity of writing and address issues of literacy that have far-reaching social implications.

From *Critical Academic Writing and Multilingual Students*. Ann Arbor: U of Michigan P, 2002: 1–22.

DEFINING THE CRITICAL

Before I spell out how *critical* redefines writing, we should consider briefly the currency of the label itself. We have by now come across critical theory, critical thinking, critical pedagogy, critical ethnography, critical linguistics, critical discourse analysis, and even critical classroom discourse analysis—just to mention a few.[1] We can of course go on attaching this label to any field we want because there is something predictable and distinctive that happens when we do so. It is natural for us to think of *uncritical* as the opposite of this label. But it is unfair to say that those who don't practice a critical approach are choosing to be apathetic or naive. There are good reasons why someone may choose to adopt an alternative approach. Indicative of these more serious motivations are terms like *objective, detached, disinterested, pragmatic, formalistic,* and *abstract.* These adjectives are less pejorative antonyms for the term *critical.*

To understand the ways these terms relate to each other, we need to take a brief detour through history. The Enlightenment movement of seventeenth-century Europe has much to do with the values attached to these terms. Taking pride in adopting a more rational, systematic, and scientific approach to things, the movement initiated radical changes in many domains of inquiry. Its effects are still there in certain traditions of the study of writing. In order to understand writing, the movement would have said, we need first to identify and demarcate the object of our analysis—the text. We should separate the "text-in-itself" from other related activities and domains so that it can speak for itself. For example, the writer's intentions, feelings, values, and interests should be separated from the text. Neither is the text the reader's processing of it in terms of his or her intentions, feelings, values, and interests. Also, the scholar must see to it that he or she doesn't bring any biases or predisposition to the analysis. This disinterested attitude was considered favorable to letting the object speak for itself. At its best, the study of the text could be undertaken without any involvement of the scholar by employing pre-designed procedures and methods. As a culmination of the Enlightenment tendency, Structuralism took the scholar further inside the isolated text. It claimed that if one entered the core of the text, cutting through the superficial clutter of content, meaning, and surface structural variations, one would discover the basic underlying rules that account for the text's universal laws of production and reception. This attitude encouraged an abstract and formalistic approach. Schools as diverse as New Criticism in literature, text linguistics in discourse analysis, and the "current traditional" paradigm in rhetoric display such an approach today. Literacy instruction, influenced by this tendency, has been formalistic, skill driven, and product oriented.

The cultivation of such an empirical perspective on texts was certainly productive in many ways. It brought a clarity, discipline, and rigor to the descriptive activity. Getting the predisposition of human subjects muddled in the analysis, or getting distracted by superficial variations, can be misleading. The approach certainly generated important insights into certain general properties of textuality and literacy. But there is also something lost in this type of approach. For the sake of analytical convenience we are deliberately simplifying the disposition and implications of texts. The text becomes more and more isolated, detached, abstract, and generic. The values that inform its structure and form are ignored. It becomes empty of content, losing its complexity and depth. With the decontextualized approach, the influences of social conditions and cultural diversity on text construction are lost. The ways in which texts are shaped by, and in turn shape, sociopolitical realities are obscured. Much of this happens because the text has become static, passive, and one-dimensional. Writers and readers themselves become automatons who employ predesigned formal procedures with detachment to generate texts. All this amounts to adopting an innocence and complacency toward the literate activity. As a corrective, the critical approach grounds the text in the material world to orientate to its troubling social functions, the value-ridden nature of its constitution, and the conflicting motivations behind its production and reception.

Now let's return to our original question: how does the critical orientation redefine writing? We may summarize the shifts in perspective in the following manner.

- *From writing as autonomous to writing as situated.* The production of texts is not an end in itself. We don't write simply to produce a text—and leave it at that. We produce texts to achieve certain interests and purposes. Furthermore, after a text is produced, it gets used in unanticipated ways. Launched into the public world, it takes a life of its own and effects results and processes totally unanticipated by the writer. Therefore, texts not only *mean* but *do*. Their functionality goes to the extent of reconstructing reality, rather than simply reflecting reality. We need to inquire what the word does to/in the world.

- *From writing as individualistic to writing as social.* For many of us, the stock image of writing is that of the lonely writer locked away in his small apartment (in crowded New York City) or a cabin (in the quiet woods of New England) pouring his thoughts on paper under mysteriously received inspiration. But writing is not a monologue; it is dialogical. One has to take account of the audience (implicitly or explicitly) while writing. This may involve a set of intended audiences, but it also involves an ever-expanding unintended audience (stretching limitlessly across time and space). In constructing a text, a writer is conducting a conversation with all this diversity of readers. This process is different from the definition of it we get from communication theory—which is often diagrammed as follows: writer → text → reader (or speaker → words → listener). Writing is not a one-way transmission of ideas, nor are constructs like *writer* and *text* autonomous. The writer's "intentions" and "thoughts" are considerably influenced by the expectations, norms, and values of the audience (or community). The text itself then becomes a *mediated* construct—one that is shaped by the struggle/collaboration/interplay between the writer, reader, and the community for thought. We have to become sensitive to how the text embodies the influences of this social interaction.

- *From writing as cognitive to writing as material.* For many, writing is a purely mental activity of putting down on paper the relevant ideas, words, and information that one has the capacity to generate. They view writing as a play between the mind and the text for meaning, order, and coherence. But there are many material resources required to do writing. At the simplest level, one needs a pencil, pen, typewriter, or computer to compose one's thoughts. Which of these one uses is often decided by one's economic status. Each of these instruments presents different levels of advantage to the writer. Furthermore, one needs to be privileged to devote the time required for writing. Writers also need the means to tap necessary resources from publishers, libraries, media industries, and the market. The text is shaped out of a negotiation of these constraints and resources. How these material factors impinge upon the text requires examination.

- *From writing as formal to writing as ideological.* Another commonsense assumption is that one only needs grammar, structure, and rules to construct a text. These are treated as abstract, value-free features of textual form. But writing is more than language or structure. It is also a representation of reality, an embodiment of values, and a presentation of self. Form itself is informed by diverse conventions of textuality, values of appropriacy, and attitudes to style. If writing is not just rules but how to use those rules—that is, for what purpose and with what attitude—then this is a contentious area of cultural difference and ideological preference. One has to consider what values are implied by the form and whether textual norms can be modified to represent alternate values.

- *From writing as spatial to writing as historical.* For many, the text (once produced) is an inert object that occupies a space. It is how words populate five pages, structured in a seamless manner, that is treated as the concern of writers and readers. But the text has evolved through time. While the writing was being done, the writer took care of many other responsibilities in his or her everyday life. There were many false starts and failed attempts. There were many visions and revisions of what the writer wanted to say. There were collaborations and conflicts around the evolving text. The changing social conditions of the community and the personal fortunes of the writer also shape the text. After being produced, the text continues to live in history, being decoded differently according to differing social conditions. The text then is not a seamless whole that stands static through reading and writing. How it is shaped by the disjunctions, fissures, struggles, and conflicts during its construction and reception needs attention.

If we can summarize all these differences in one simple slogan, the shift is from writing as an *object* to writing as an *activity*. In integrating the text into the flow of sociohistoric currents and understanding it as one more purposive activity we do in everyday life, writing becomes not a product but a practice. It is in perceiving writing as a situated, mediated, dynamic social activity that the work of critical practice begins. We cannot stop with charting the internal linguistic structures and rhetorical patterns of the text. We have to also interrogate the values and ideologies that inform the text; the ways in which the external contexts of production and reception shape the text; the prospects for human possibilities to be limited or expanded by the text; and the ways in which the unequal status and differing identities of writers (and readers) affect the constitution of the text. In short, we begin to see how writing is implicated in social conflict, material inequality, cultural difference, and power relationships. In critical writing, students would become sensitive to these factors. They would wrestle with textual constraints, tap the available material resources, and negotiate the conflicting discourses in their favor to communicate effectively. In teaching critical writing, instructors have to make students aware of these diverse constraints and possibilities as they strive for a representation of knowledge that is emancipatory and empowering.

The orientations listed earlier differ from the perspectives of some other current schools of thinking that may employ similar constructs in their definitions. For example, that writing should be contextualized is widely held by many schools these days. But for some, contextualizing the text means seeing the specific details/words/images in terms of the total framework of the text. Or it can mean seeing the details in terms of rhetorical/genre conventions. But this sense of context is still "internal" to the text. I have articulated an ever-widening context that expands beyond the writer/reader and the community to historical and social conditions. On the other hand, even when social context is acknowledged by some schools, it is treated as lying outside the text; it doesn't affect the text's very constitution. Furthermore, theorizing the politics of writing has become fashionable in many circles today—especially among those influenced by poststructuralist and postmodernist perspectives. However, here again, politics is defined in terms of discursive and linguistic issues only, leaving more recalcitrant material factors out of consideration. This orientation explains the trend in Western academic circles toward celebrating the rhetorical activity of interpreting the tensions within the text to show how ideological struggle is manifested there. The poststructuralist schools perceive language as one of the tools that sustain inequality and domination at the microsocial level; therefore, deconstructing the written text to expose the tensions therein is treated as equal to bringing the whole unfair social edifice crumbling down. Though I acknowledge the importance of language and discourse in reflecting/sustaining/enforcing inequality, I still feel that the historical and material dimensions of power have to be addressed in their own terms. Therefore my perspective on writing brings together text-internal and text-external factors, discursive and historical forces, linguistic and social considerations.

ORIENTATING TO THE MULTILINGUAL WRITER

I have been talking of the writer in very generalized terms up to this point. It is time now to give flesh and blood to the type of writers this book is concerned with. The pedagogical context assumed in this book is the teaching of English for speakers of other languages (ESOL). The ESOL student community includes those who are learning English as a second language—in other words, those living in former British colonies such as India, Nigeria, and Jamaica and those linguistic minorities living in the traditionally English-speaking countries of Canada, the United States, and Britain, all of whom actively use English as an additional language in social and educational life.

These are largely bilinguals. Included in this group are speech communities for whom English has become considerably "nativized." Through a long history of interaction, English has now become locally rooted, accommodating lexical, grammatical, and discoursal features from native languages. While some of these speakers would consider English their native language (i.e., speaking English as their first or sole language), they will still face challenges in using the "standard" English dialects (of the Anglo-American variety) treated as the norm for academic writing. Therefore they should also be considered bidialectals who have to shift from one variant of English to another in their writing.

These groups (largely ESL) differ from those who learn English as a foreign language (EFL). In many parts of the contemporary world, English is an indispensable auxiliary language for a variety of specialized purposes. In addition to being proficient in the vernacular, and perhaps in some regional or colonial languages (French in Vietnam, Dutch in Indonesia, Portuguese in Brazil), students from these communities will still have some competence in English. This circle is largely multilingual, speaking English as a third or fourth language. However, the traditional distinction between EFL and ESL contexts is becoming fluid these days as English attains the position of a global language.[2] It is becoming indispensable for almost everyone in the postmodern world to hold some proficiency in English and use it for a variety of purposes in their everyday life. Despite the varying levels of linguistic competence possessed by the different ESOL subgroups identified earlier, in practicing academic writing in English they have to all acquire new discourses and conventions and represent their identities in novel ways.[3]

Do these students require a different teaching approach from those used for L1 students? To address this question clearly we have to first ask how ESOL and L1 student communities are different. (By "L1 students" I am referring here to those who are "traditionally native" in English, largely monolinguals, coming from the former colonizing communities that still claim ownership over the language.) It has become pedagogical common sense to distinguish these groups in terms of linguistic difference. ESOL teachers have treated multilingual students as strangers to English and thus aimed to develop their grammatical competence in order to facilitate their academic writing. But this approach is misdirected. We must note that many of these students have some competence in one or more dialects of English—sometimes speaking their local variants of English "natively." There is also widespread proficiency in specialized registers in English—such as the language of computers, technology, academia, and the professions (e.g., legalese, journalese). Moreover, writing involves not just grammatical competence. Therefore, different pedagogies are not warranted based purely on differences in grammatical proficiency.

Teachers have also focused on the cultural difference between both student groups. Apart from the larger differences in beliefs and practices, there can be more specific differences related to literacy. The genres and styles of communication, the practices and uses of literacy, and the attitudes and processes in composing can be different. The popularity of approaches like contrastive rhetoric explains the importance given by teachers to cultural differences in text construction. But even this mustn't be exaggerated too much. After the colonial experience, European culture has left an indelible mark on many local communities (see Canagarajah 1999b; Pennycook 1994). The general trend of globalization in the contemporary world has also resulted in the spreading of Anglo-American values and institutions worldwide. More relevant to our discussion, literacy has spread to such levels that we don't have any "pure" oral communities to speak of today. Even the communities that didn't have a written script have developed one through the help of missionary enterprises (though some of this resulted from the motivation of teaching the Bible).

In general, it is becoming more and more difficult to "essentialize" students in ESOL—that is, to generalize their identity and character according to a rigidly definable set of linguistic or cultural traits. We are unable to define them in ways that are diametrically opposed to the language and culture of L1 students. ESOL students are not aliens to the English language or Anglo-American culture anymore. The hybridity that characterizes communities and individuals in the postcolonial world complicates some of the easy distinctions teachers are used to making about ESOL students. In fact, it is difficult now to speak of uncontaminated "native" cultures or "vernaculars," as many communities have accommodated foreign traditions and practices through a history of cultural interaction and adaptation (see Appadurai 1996). Students in ESOL bring with them a mixture of local and Western linguistic/cultural characteristics, and we shouldn't assume that they all require an "introduction" to the English language and Anglo-American culture.

These qualifications don't mean that ESOL students are not different from L1 students but that "difference" has to be redefined in more complex terms. We have to move away from easy stereotypes about them. The fact that ESOL students display hybrid multicultural, multilingual tendencies doesn't make them the same as L1 students. Hybridity doesn't preclude questions of sociocultural uniqueness. These students may display conflicting attitudes toward the various cultures that make up their subjectivity. They may in fact suspect—and resist—their "Anglo-American" legacy, which has the potential to dominate or suppress their more "indigenous" side. They may also display a different subject position in terms of cultural identity. Their preferred choices of community solidarity and cultural identities have to be respected. While most ESOL students occupy a largely unequal status, as colored individuals from periphery communities, L1 students occupy a privileged position. The latter's cultural identity enjoys the power of dominant communities from the geopolitical center, providing a head start on the linguistic and cultural capital necessary for success in the contemporary world. Hybridity shouldn't be taken to mean, therefore, that issues of power and difference are irrelevant in today's world. Some postmodernist scholars have mistakenly assumed that the reality of cultural and linguistic mixing has defeated the designs of imperialistic forces. Nor should we assume that trends toward hybridity and globalization lead to a homogeneous world where difference doesn't matter anymore.[4] In fact, these trends have inspired minority communities to celebrate their differences and develop their local knowledge and identities. Therefore, despite certain obvious signs toward homogeneity through forces of technology, multinational companies, market forces, and the media, we cannot say that difference has been eradicated altogether. Issues of power and difference have simply become more subtle and dispersed.

––––––––––

The more important consideration in critical writing is not difference per se but the attitudes we adopt toward difference. We have a long history in our profession where the linguistic/cultural difference of multilingual students has been treated as making them limited and deficient in their writing ability. Their distance from the English language and Anglo-American culture has been treated as depriving them of many essential aptitudes required for successful academic literacy practices. Some have gone further to stigmatize multilingual writers as illogical in thinking and incoherent in communication, by virtue of their deficient L1 and native culture. Consider a summary of the many differences discovered between L1 and L2 writers from empirical studies by Silva (1993).

> "L2 writers did less planning, at the global and local levels" (661).
>
> "L2 writers did less goal setting, global and local, and had more difficulty achieving these goals" (661).
>
> "Organizing generated material in the L2 was more difficult" (661).
>
> "Transcribing in the L2 was more laborious, less fluent, and less productive" (661).
>
> "Pauses were more frequent, longer, and consumed more writing time" (662).
>
> "L2 writers wrote at a slower rate and produced fewer words of written text" (662).
>
> "L2 writing reportedly involved less reviewing" (662).
>
> "There was evidence of less rereading of and reflecting on written texts" (662).[5]

We shouldn't be surprised that L2 students fall short when L1 writing is treated as the norm or point of reference. It is important therefore to examine the assumptions and attitudes with which our research is conducted. Though it must be acknowledged that ESOL students would practice English academic writing in the L1 context and cannot escape from the norms of the dominant linguistic circles, we must still ask: How would our interpretation differ if we understood the composing strategies of ESOL students in terms of their own cultural frames and literacy practices?

Adopting a perspective that takes the students' own frames of reference seriously is the *relativistic* orientation, distinct from the *normative* approach described earlier. It is important to take the students' own explanations and orientations into account, situated in their own cultural and linguistic traditions, to explain their writing practices. This way we are able to understand that there are good reasons why they do what they do. Although this attitude is more egalitarian, differing from the "deficit" perspective described earlier, it doesn't go far enough in providing dignity to multilingual students. Their perspectives are seen as being shaped by their respective cultures and languages, requiring inordinate effort to reorientate to other discourses. Even well-meaning scholars sympathetic to minority cultures sometimes theorize the competence of ESOL students in condescending terms. For example, some have argued that since students from Asian communities prefer nonlinear styles of thinking, they shouldn't be imposed upon to adopt the explicit forms of logic and reasoning of Anglo-American communities (see Fox 1994).[6] If these students fail in English literacy, this is explained as resulting from the fact that they are strangers to the established discourses of the academy. (And, displaying a trace of ethnocentrism, these scholars judge literacy skills according to Anglo-American rhetorical traditions anyway.) Such an attitude is to orientate toward difference as a problem all over again. Sometimes this can take a deterministic bent. The cultural uniqueness of students is treated as *preventing* them from becoming successful writers in English, trapping them into their respective cultural/linguistic worlds.

If *difference-as-deficit* and *difference-as-estrangement* are somewhat limiting perspectives on multilingual writers, an attitude that gives them more complexity is one that I call the *difference-as-resource* perspective. Multilingual students do — and can — use their background as a stepping-stone to master academic discourses. Their values can function as a source of strength in their writing experience in English, enabling them to transfer many skills from their traditions of vernacular communication. Even in cases where the connection is not clear, it is important for teachers to consider how the vernacular influence can be made beneficial for their writing experience rather than functioning in negative, unpleasant, or conflictual ways. Such an attitude will involve teachers orientating to their students differently. We should respect and value the linguistic and cultural peculiarities our students may display, rather than suppressing them. We should strive to understand their values and interests and discover ways of engaging those in the writing process. In doing so, we should be ready to accept the ways in which academic texts and discourses will be creatively modified according to the strengths brought by the students. Academic literacy should adopt a bilateral process — in other words, not only should students be made to appreciate academic discourses but the academic community should accommodate alternate discourses.

———

Having examined our *attitudes* toward the linguistic/cultural difference of multilingual students, we have to briefly consider the *approach* we should adopt to relate their background to academic writing practice. It is not surprising that the attitudes discussed earlier have brought forth different approaches to teaching writing. There is no need to discuss the unfairness of the *conversion* approach, informed by the deficit attitude, which posits that multilingual students have to permanently move away from their indigenous discourses to superior English-based discourses. An approach that has been more respectable in this regard is what I call the *crossing* model, informed by the relativistic attitude. According to this approach, teachers attempt to build bridges to help multilingual students move from their local literacy practices and cultural frames toward academic/English discourses (and vice versa). Though students may shuttle between academic and home settings, in this approach there is a clear-cut difference between the academic and vernacular literacies. Students have to keep their discourses from home at home and enter into academic discourses with a new sense of self and reality. Students are asked to adopt different roles and identities as they move between the home and school. They have to remember that in each context (or community) there are different values, knowledge, discourses, and styles practiced. So they have to develop the facility to switch discourses in contextually relevant ways as they cross boundaries.

Although this approach devises a way to develop respect for both the academic and nonacademic discourses, there are certain problems with it. It creates an either/or distinction between academic and vernacular literacies. Text construction in both traditions is treated as mutually exclusive. It also imposes a split subjectivity on multilingual students — they are asked to be different persons in different communities/contexts. However, there is an increasing body of research that suggests that minority students don't want to suppress or abandon their vernacular cultures when they practice academic writing.[7] They want to bring their preferred values, ideologies, and styles of writing into English literacy. Students cannot be expected to leave behind their identities and interests as they engage in the learning process. What I call the *negotiation* model requires that students wrestle with the divergent discourses they face in writing to creatively work out alternate discourses and literacies that represent better their values and interests. In some cases this means appropriating the academic discourse and conventions in terms of the students' own backgrounds. It can sometimes mean a creative merging of conflicting discourses. It shouldn't be surprising that the texts of multilingual students are somewhat different — they are embodiments of the unique voices and identities of the students. This approach also tackles some of the power conflicts experienced by multilingual students. Practicing academic discourses according to the established conventions (as defined by the dominant social groups) would involve endorsing the values and interests these conventions are informed by. If these values are unfavorable for multilingual students, or if they don't favor emancipatory interests, these writers are going to give life to the oppressive ideologies of the dominant groups. Appropriating academic discourses in their own terms would enable students to reconstruct established textual practices and infuse them with oppositional values and meanings. This is a way of eventually resisting the dominant ideologies and interests that inform academic literacy. There is therefore a critical edge in the negotiation model, while the crossing model (at its best) simply takes the established conventions and knowledge of each context/community for granted in a noncommittal way. Teachers and students who practice the negotiation model would tend to subscribe to the difference-as-resource attitude articulated earlier.

WRITING IN AN IMPERIALISTIC LANGUAGE?

Before I conclude these preliminary statements of intent, I need to adopt a position on one more matter. This is the question of the English language. To the extent that we are talking about academic writing in English, there are issues of linguistic imperialism that need to be addressed. Is it proper to encourage and facilitate the use of a language that is tainted with a history of global domination, colonizing other languages and communities with its values? There is no need to prove here that the English language does have a domineering status in the academy and society.[8] What is important, once again, are the attitudes and approaches to be adopted toward this language.

There is an important strand of thinking among some third world scholars that local communities should have no truck with English. We may call this the *separatist* orientation.[9] Treating languages as embodying partisan values, these scholars hold that English will condition our thinking and limit the meanings we may want to express in our writing. They would therefore think of English as muting any oppositional perspectives one may bring to knowledge creation in academic writing—and, in fact, as leading to the reproduction of Eurocentric values and thinking in the local communities. For them, the medium is the message. Opposed to them are the *universalists*, who believe that language is simply a neutral medium that one can use for whatever messages one may want to convey.[10] For the latter, the mind of the writer transcends language to freely employ any grammatical system desired. Some in this camp go further to argue that English has attained the position of a universal language that has accommodated values from different communities and lost its imperialist character.[11]

I hold that while each language is indeed ideological in representing partisan values and interests (being by no means neutral), it is not impossible to negotiate with language to win some space for one's purposes. It appears to me therefore that while the separatists are a bit too cynical, the universalists are complacent. While the former are too deterministic, the latter are romantic. Though we are all ideologically conditioned, human subjects do enjoy some relative autonomy from social institutions and discourses to conduct critical, independent thinking. English itself is becoming hybridized, embodying grammatical features, lexical items, and discourse conventions from a variety of communities. Through such processes of nativization, formerly colonized communities are appropriating the language and making it their own—thus making English a suitable medium for their values and interests. Consistent with my view expressed earlier on culture, the so-called alien language can also become a *resource* for oppositional and critical purposes. It is possible in critical writing for multilingual students to tap the resources of English and use it judiciously to represent the interests of their communities. An uncritical use of the language, on the other hand, poses the threat of making the individual and the community prone to domination. I would give this critical approach the same label I gave earlier for dealing with cultural difference — the *negotiation* model.[12] ESOL writers have to be made reflexively aware of the medium they are using, developing a critical understanding of its potentialities and limitations as they appropriate and reconstruct the language to represent their interests.

ON ADOPTING IDEOLOGICAL COMMITMENTS

There are important reasons why I am stating my position up front on some of the controversial questions affecting ESOL writing. It is the view of critical theorists that there are no positions of absolute neutrality available for anyone on any issue. Everything is value ridden and ideological. It is important therefore to be frank about the position one holds on social and educational matters. Making one's assumptions explicit can help one to examine one's ideological positions critically and adopt stances that favor more emancipatory, egalitarian, and empowering interests. Practicing a critical pedagogy would involve instructors being similarly clear about their values, positions, and interests as they engage in teaching writing. Apart from adopting emancipatory agendas in their teaching activity, this would also enable them to examine and refine their ideologies in relation to the conditions confronted in the classroom and the challenges posed by the students. Pretending to be neutral or hiding one's ideological stances is counterproductive, as such practices will lead both to surreptitiously imposing one's values on the students and to limiting one's own development into deeper social awareness.[13]

Needless to say, all this doesn't mean that any ideology is acceptable in the classroom. The purpose of acknowledging one's ideological stance is to frankly examine whether it furthers the interests of justice and equality for all. If teachers recognize that their ideological leanings lead to unfair outcomes, they should have the integrity to revise their beliefs. Even in cases where one may be convinced that one's ideology is the most liberating system of belief, one should have the humility to respect the values of students, engage with them frankly, and negotiate differences in favor of developing beliefs and practices that ensure the well-being of everybody.

Acknowledging one's values shouldn't be taken to mean that one holds rigidly to one's position in the face of conflicting evidence and deepening political understanding. One should be open to developing more humane and progressive positions based on increasing knowledge and changing social conditions. Adopting a critical orientation doesn't mean being dogmatic. It is possible to admit one's tentative position on something while being open to further developing one's awareness. In fact, what is "politically correct" in writing pedagogy has been changing over time, based on new research knowledge and social awareness. For example, during the 1980s the relativistic positions articulated earlier—that is, the difference-as-estrangement attitude and the crossing model—were held by many critical pedagogues (including me) as offering the best recourse for the conflicts faced by multilingual students.[14] This was certainly a more enlightened perspective compared to the deficit approach, as it respected the vernaculars and indigenous cultures of minority students and acknowledged their right to maintain them. But with additional research showing the dissatisfaction of minority students in adopting a split personality as they switch discourses and identities, and the understandable social consequences stemming from the complacency of a relativistic orientation, we have had to adopt more critical positions. Moreover, acknowledging one's position on some of these fundamental theoretical issues doesn't solve all the pedagogical questions one has to face in the classroom. Similarly, how one's positions are to be realized in writing will take different forms in different rhetorical contexts. There are many different methods and strategies that may be adopted to achieve the negotiation model and the difference-as-resource orientation articulated earlier. Between holding a standpoint and practicing it in the classroom (or practicing it in writing) there is a huge divide that needs to be imaginatively bridged.

THE CHALLENGE

Given the general orientation to multilingual students and their writing activity articulated earlier, how can we summarize the challenges we face in teaching critical writing? Here are some of the concerns:

- Whereas students are generally taught to take the established genre rules and literacy conventions for granted in constructing texts to suit different rhetorical situations (often with the assumption that these are value-free rules or neutral frameworks that we can use to articulate any message we want), critical writing involves examining the values and interests assumed by these rules. We should teach students not to treat rules of communication as innocent or indisputable but to negotiate for independent expression by reframing them in suitable ways. They have to ask: How did these rules come into being? Whom do these rules favor? What possibilities and limitations do these rules pose for critical expression? What alternatives are available?

- Whereas students are generally taught to use established knowledge already available in texts, critical writing involves interrogating received knowledge and reconstructing it through the writing process. All knowledge should be treated as "interested." Multilingual students have to question the dominant knowledge constructs in the academy, in addition to critically engaging the knowledge traditions they bring from their local communities as they make a space for oppositional knowledge that favors wider emancipatory and democratic interests.

- Whereas students are generally taught academic writing as a detached activity of expressing publicly verifiable knowledge in a balanced and logical way through conventional rules, critical writing encourages a personal engagement in the writing process. One should reflexively explore one's identity, consciousness, and values during text construction not only to make a textual space for one's voice but also to challenge dominant knowledge constructs according to one's personal location.

- Whereas writing is generally taught as an acquiescent activity of assuming a preexisting reality within which the text takes its place, critical writing involves interrogating the dominant conception of reality and changing it to create more democratic possibilities. In order to do so, students have to be taught to treat texts as not only reflecting but constituting reality. Apart from being instrumental in transforming realities, texts may themselves represent new realities.

- Whereas students are generally taught to treat the language of written communication (including registers, styles, and codes of that genre) as an abstract structure or system, critical writing involves interrogating the language for the ways in which it represents its own values and sometimes suppresses divergent messages. Students have to negotiate the ideologies informing the English language as they appropriate it to represent their interests and values in their writing, using language in creative new ways to struggle for alternate expression. Bilingual writers have the further task of finding appropriate ways of accommodating the strengths they bring from their nativized Englishes and vernaculars as they struggle for a voice that suits their values and interests in academic texts.

In one sense, these are perhaps the common issues facing all students in academic writing. But since multilingual students bring with them identities, values, and discourses from multiple communities, the challenges they face in practicing this writing are more complex. Their acquaintance with oppositional intellectual traditions and worldviews can also function as an advantage. These traditions hint of alternate ways in which knowledge and society can be reconstructed.

NOTES

1. While the first few terms here are well known, the final three—especially those that concern our profession relatively more closely—may sound strange. For publications that employ these labels, see Fowler and Kress 1979 for *critical linguistics;* Fairclough 1995 for *critical discourse analysis;* and Kumaravadivelu 1999 for *critical classroom discourse analysis.*

2. For a perspective on the need to reconsider these traditional distinctions, see Nayar 1997.

3. The new realizations about linguistic identity create a need for new terminology. In referring to students and teachers in second-language programs, I will use the term *ESOL* except when I make a specific point about the ESL/EFL situation or the L1/L2 distinction. Though this label is awkward, especially when it is used as an adjective to qualify teachers and students, it has been used in these contexts in the professional literature for a long time (see Canagarajah 1993; Harklau 2000). The term *ESOL* enables me to side step the question of whether the subjects are balanced bilinguals or not and of whether they are using English as a second language, a foreign language, or a nativized language.

4. For a debate on this issue in the pages of the *ELT Journal,* see Rajagopalan 1999 and Canagarajah 1999a.

5. These are culled from a review article on L2 writing research by Silva (1993). We must note that Silva is only reporting the findings of studies made by others and is not personally responsible for the findings represented in the article.

6. Since Fox adopts this view specifically in the case of Japanese students, see Kubota 1999 to understand why such generalizations fall short of capturing the complexity of Japanese cultural thought processes.

7. See Canagarajah 1997 for an ethnographic study where minority students (consisting of bilingual and bidialectal students) resist the notion of switching identities in different communities. They negotiate ways of infusing their values into mainstream discourse.

8. See Phillipson 1992 for an articulation of the linguistic imperialism thesis. For debates that slightly modify Phillipson's thesis, without denying the power of English, see Pennycook 1994 and Canagarajah 1999b.

9. See Ngugi 1986 for a forceful argument favoring this position.

10. See Achebe 1975 for an articulation of this position.

11. See Kachru 1986 for the notion of English as "an unmarked code" in formerly colonized communities. Crystal (1997) too presents the position of English as a value-free global language.

12. See Canagarajah 1999b for a detailed exposition of this approach.

13. There are of course many intermediary positions on ideology. For example, Santos (1993) in composition scholarship and Rajagopalan (1999) in ELT pedagogy argue that power is real but that it can be kept out of writing activity or the classroom. In saying this, they excuse teachers from having to commit themselves to any ideological position.

14. See Bizzell 1982 and Rose 1989 for progressive compositionists who have articulated this position.

WORKS CITED

Achebe, C. 1975. *Morning yet on creation day*. London: Heinemann.

Appadurai, Arjun. 1996. *Modernity at large: Cultural dimensions of globalization*. Minneapolis: University of Minnesota Press.

Bizzell, P. 1982. Cognition, convention and certainty: What we need to know about writing. *PRE/TEXT* 3:213–43.

Canagarajah, A. S. 1993. Critical ethnography of a Sri Lankan classroom: Ambiguities in opposition to reproduction through ESOL. *TESOL Quarterly* 27 (4): 601–26.

——. 1997. Challenges in English literacy for African-American and Lankan Tamil learners: Towards a pedagogical paradigm for bidialectal and bilingual minority students. *Language and Education* 11 (1): 15–36.

——. 1999a. On EFL teachers, awareness, and agency. *ELT Journal* 53 (3): 207–14.

——. 1999b. *Resisting linguistic imperialism in English teaching*. Oxford: Oxford University Press.

Crystal, David. 1997. *English as a global language*. Cambridge: Cambridge University Press.

Fairclough, Norman. 1995. *Critical discourse analysis: The critical study of language*. London: Longman.

Fowler, Roger, and Gunther Kress. 1979. Critical linguistics. In Roger Fowler, B. Hodge, G. Kress, and A. Trew, eds., *Language and control*, 185–213. London: Routledge.

Fox, Helen. 1994. *Listening to the world: Cultural issues in academic writing*. Urbana, Ill.: National Council of Teachers of English.

Harklau, Linda. 2000. "From the 'good kids' to the 'worst' ": Representations of English language learners across educational settings. *TESOL Quarterly* 34 (1): 35–68.

Kachru, Braj B. 1986. *The alchemy of English: The spread, functions and models of non-native Englishes*. Oxford: Pergamon.

Kubota, Ryuko. 1999. Japanese culture constructed by discourses: Implications for applied linguistics research and ELT. *TESOL Quarterly* 33 (1): 9–35.

Kumaravadivelu, Braj. 1999. Critical classroom discourse analysis. *TESOL Quarterly* 33 (3): 453–84.

Nayar, P. B. 1997. ESL/EFL dichotomy today: Language politics or pragmatics? *TESOL Quarterly* 31 (1): 9–37.

Ngugi wa Thiong'o. 1986. *Decolonizing the mind: the politics of language in African literature*. London: Currey, Heinemann.

Pennycook, Alastair. 1994. *The cultural politics of English as an international language*. London: Longman.

Phillipson, Robert. 1992. *Linguistic imperialism*. Oxford: Oxford University Press.

Rajagopalan, Kanavilli. 1999. Of EFL teachers, conscience, and cowardice. *ELT Journal* 53 (3): 200–206.

Rose, Mike. 1989. *Lives on the boundary*. New York: Penguin.

Santos, Terry. 1993. Ideology in composition: L1 and ESL. *Journal of Second Language Writing* 1 (1): 1–15.

Silva, Tony. 1993. Toward an understanding of the distinct nature of L2 writing: The ESL research and its implications. *TESOL Quarterly* 27 (4): 657–78.

12 Should We Invite Students to Write in Home Languages? Complicating the Yes/No Debate

JANET BEAN, MARYANN CUCCHIARA, ROBERT
EDDY, PETER ELBOW, RHONDA GREGO, RICH
HASWELL, PATRICIA IRVINE, EILEEN KENNEDY,
ELLIE KUTZ, AL LEHNER, AND PAUL KEI MATSUDA

What i be talking about
can be said in this language
only this tongue
be the one that understands
what i be talking about

       – LUCILLE CLIFTON, "DEFENDING MY TONGUE"

And now my tongue's use is to me no more
Than an unstringed viol or harp,
Or like a cunning instrument cas'd up
Or being open put into his hands
That knows no touch to tune the harmony.

       –SHAKESPEARE, *RICHARD III*

Increasingly students enter our writing classrooms with a mother tongue that is not the English or standardized English in which they will be expected to produce most or all of their public and academic writing. We believe that for most writers, informal exploratory writing helps to generate ideas and leads to stronger final drafts. But is the process of writing towards a final draft in standardized English always aided by informal writing and early drafting in standardized English? To become accomplished writers in standardized English, must students work within at least an approximation of that variety of English throughout their composing process? Must their mother tongue be of no more use to them than "an unstringed viol" in this enterprise? Can we validate language minority students' languages and identities at the same time we help them learn the dominant variety of English? Are there contexts and circumstances in which we might encourage

From *Composition Studies* 31.1 (2003): 25–42.

our students to draw on a home language or mother tongue as they generate ideas and compose early drafts?

These are questions that we sought to explore in a July 2002 symposium. The authors represent the fields of composition, second language acquisition, sociolinguistics, and literacy studies. We met for a week of intensive work at the University of Massachusetts in Amherst and shared our research, our experiences, and our thinking. We brought to this exploration our prior study of relevant issues in our individual research. We also brought our experiences working with linguistically diverse students in a variety of settings: teaching writing to students who speak a variety of English not dominant in the U.S. (such as African American Vernacular English), to international and immigrant students learning English as a second language, to students in other countries learning English as a foreign language, to students in countries where most people share a vernacular that is not widely accepted as a written language, and to mixed classes that include representatives of all these groups. We recognized different purposes in our teaching—purposes that reflected our different contexts. But we shared an interest in helping all our students to produce effective and appropriate writing in English for academic contexts and purposes. And we shared several assumptions: we see all writing as taking place within a particular social context and believe that writers are affected by the ways in which they are positioned in that context; we think that writers will feel more confident as language-users when their home language is valued and respected; and we want the writers in our classrooms to write from a position of strength and with a belief in their own competence.

In our symposium, we figured out fairly quickly that the question was not so much *whether or not* to invite students to write in a mother tongue different from standardized English, but rather, *when and under what conditions* might it make sense to do so? Of course there are many conditions in which it doesn't make sense to invite a home language. But we could see that there are at least a few limiting contexts in which it probably does make sense—for example for purely private exploratory writing or for comparing the grammar or rhetoric of a home language with standardized written English. In short, we seek to get away from the kind of yes/no, either/or debate that simplifies what is actually a complex matter. We saw the need to frame the question in a more empirical and human way and pay closer attention to differences—differences among classrooms, among larger contexts, among writing tasks, and among individuals.

We have been influenced by a helpfully persistent tradition of advocacy and research on the use of home languages. For example, Paulo Freire's work with adult literacy shows us the power of using the language of lived experience. Geneva Smitherman's research shows how rhetorical features of African American Vernacular English (AAVE) served to improve the scores of student papers on NAEP exams. Both Smitherman and Lisa Delpit suggest the benefits for AAVE students of starting writing tasks in AAVE and then revising to the dominant variety of English. (For recent research on writing in AAVE, see Gilyard and Richardson, and also Elbow "Inviting.")

And we have a concrete, first hand reason for rejecting the claim that it *never* makes sense to invite students to write in home languages. One of the authors, Patricia Irvine, during two years of teaching at the College of the Virgin Islands, invited students in both basic and honors first-year writing classes to write some pieces in Caribbean Creole English. In this context, standardized English was very much the goal. Students in these classes did much better than other students in the remedial writing program on exit exams in standardized English (Irvine and Elsasser; Elsasser and Irvine). Of course, writing in Creole was not the only feature that led to these students' success in standardized English. The concrete conditions that Irvine and Elsasser found and the practices they used were complex and situated. In short, their work didn't demonstrate that it's always good to invite writing in a home dialect of English, but it did convince us that it's not always *bad* to do so.

This paper is an account of our shared explorations and of our efforts to name some important variables or criteria that bear on the question of whether or not to invite students to write in a home dialect or language. We offer our conclusions in the form of a list of variables to consider. As you'll see, this list won't serve as a calculus for producing neat answers for every teaching situation by checking off boxes. In a single teaching situation, one variable may dispose towards inviting a home language while another variable disposes against it; and sometimes a single criterion is ambiguous in its force (Anderson and Irvine). There are no easy answers; so too, not every author agrees with every detail of the discussions that follow.

FIRST VARIABLE: *Are we inviting students to write in a home language or in a home dialect?*

We often find ourselves stressing what might be called an obvious or common sense view, namely that it makes more sense to invite writing in a dialect of English than in an entirely different language:

- Students who write in a dialect of English can usually retain more words and syntactical constructions from their drafts when they revise into standardized English than from drafts in a different language. Thus, dialect writers will seem better able to harness the strengths of voice as they revise into standardized English.

- Dialects of English are often more heavily stigmatized than languages other than English: native speakers of Japanese, Russian, or Khmer are unlikely to feel that there is something bad or stupid or defective about their home language, whereas these are exactly the feelings engendered in many speakers of dialects of English like AAVE, Caribbean Creole, or Hawai'i Creole English. When a dialect or language is stigmatized, student speakers are particularly likely to benefit from having it honored by the invitation to use it in writing. (More about stigmatization in a later section.)

Nevertheless, we sometimes question whether it makes sense to distinguish between writing in a home dialect and writing in a home language (or if it is even possible):

- It's not easy to distinguish definitively between languages and dialects. Dialects or varieties of a language can be considered languages with distinct rules of their own (see Palacas on AAVE as a distinct language). And how "close" a dialect or language is to standardized English can depend on context.

- Stigmatization is not restricted to dialects of English. Contact varieties of languages like the Spanish widely used in New York and the Southwest are liable to be heavily stigmatized (Kells; Kells, Balester, and Villanueva).

- There is research showing that the use of L1 by ESL and EFL students may help in fluency, organization, elaboration, and retrieval of ideas during L2 composing (see Friedlander for a review; see also Auerbach; Kobayashi and Rinnert; Woodall).

- Students can develop and experience their voice on paper in exploratory writing or first drafts, even when they use a language entirely different from English.

- The very sense of closeness that students often feel between a standardized variety of English and other varieties of English can lead them to retain words or grammatical forms from their home variety drafts—without realizing that these words or forms might be inappropriate in standardized English or else mean something different from what the writer intended. (For example, Shondel Nero has pointed out that the phrase "talking to a girl" in Caribbean Creole English may imply having sex with her.) Of course similar misunderstandings can sometimes also happen between different languages, especially with English loan words that have changed their meaning in the context of other languages. (For example, a Japanese speaker might look at a skinny person and say "he is smart" because the English loan word *smart* [smaat] has come to mean "slender" in Japanese.)

It would be useful to have more research and experimentation about the significant differences between writing in a home language and writing in a home dialect.

SECOND VARIABLE: *What kind of writing is the goal?*

Certain kinds of writing lend themselves more readily than others to the use of a home language or dialect. For example, many teachers ask for exploratory writing that's not to be developed any further because the goal is simply to help students think about a reading or prepare for a discussion. Sometimes this writing is not intended for the eyes of others—or even discarded; sometimes it is for sharing orally in pairs or small groups or sharing with the teacher—but not for response. The goal of such writing is not to create a product but rather to help students think something through or explore their reactions—though it may be intended to lay seeds for a product. Mother tongue writing also makes more obvious sense for pieces meant to convey personal experience such as personal essays, memoir, fiction, and poetry.[1]

But writing in a home language or dialect makes little sense when students have no chance to revise and the piece must be in standardized English.

This is common in exam situations. Also, there are many situations that call for simple informal writing that is not worth taking the trouble to revise, for example writing directions to a friend for something one understands well or writing a note to the teacher giving a straightforward reason why one must miss class.

For pieces of writing in an academic or formal register, it would also seem to make little sense to use a home language or dialect. But if an academic or formal writing task is sufficiently important to warrant extensive revising, many teachers do, in fact, routinely make use of a home dialect for the early stages. That is, there is nothing remarkable about starting off academic or formal writing tasks with freewriting. And freewriting usually involves the use of a more or less oral home dialect that differs from standardized written English. Even students who grew up with the mainstream variety of English cannot be said to have standardized written English as a mother tongue. The distance between these two dialects is illustrated by the difference between freewriting and careful writing.

THIRD VARIABLE: *Who is the audience?*

Many teachers have found it appropriate to invite students occasionally to work on pieces of writing in a home language for readers who are speakers of that language: perhaps family members, friends, or even a local employer. Teachers who make this invitation are usually seeking to increase students' ownership and investment in writing and also trying to give them a more palpable experience of a basic principle of rhetoric: audience and purpose determine genre *and* language choice. Such writing occasions might well propel students to go on and revise and copyedit in their home language. This activity will help them take more ownership of the copyediting process too. If a teacher doesn't know the home language or is not experienced in the home dialect, that teacher will be in the interesting and fruitful position of having less knowledge and authority about the language being used than the student has.

FOURTH VARIABLE: *What is the political or psychological context for an invitation to write in a home language — particularly with regard to stigmatization and identity?*

It can never be easy to decide whether to invite students to write in their home language. But if that home language is not stigmatized — as is usually the case for, say, Russian-, Cambodian-, or Japanese-speaking students in an English classroom (inside or outside the U.S.) — that decision, however uncertain, can be made on comparatively straightforward, pragmatic linguistic and pedagogical grounds. If, in contrast, the home language is highly stigmatized, then the context becomes incredibly vexed and dangerous and a teacher's decision can only be made with enormous uncertainty and humility. We spent much of our Symposium time discussing the issue of writing in stigmatized home languages, but we ended up mostly with questions to ask, not answers.

Is the home dialect or language looked down on in the larger community? Does the emphasis on standardized English tend to carry for these students the implication that their home dialect or language is bad, broken, stupid (or, as in some ESL/EFL classes, is the home language explicitly prohibited)? Does it feel to students that if they adopt English or the dominant variety of English, they are in danger of losing their present identity or becoming different people? And how much is the very existence of their home dialect or language threatened by the dominance of standardized English? There are subtle gradations here from little or no stigmatization (as with many ESL or EFL students), to small or moderate stigmatization (as experienced by many U.S. speakers of some Southern dialects of English), to extreme stigmatization (as experienced, say, by most speakers of AAVE or Southwestern and Puerto Rican forms of Spanish).

Our already-complex discussions were further complicated by those from our group who teach in historically Black colleges or in classrooms with large proportions of AAVE students and students with other highly stigmatized languages. We started with a predisposition to assume that when a home language is stigmatized, we have all the more reason to try to build a safe place for its use. After all, how can students prosper as writers and thinkers if they can only write in a language they are liable to experience as an enemy language—a language tending to destroy their own language? Irvine and Nan Elsasser managed to create these productive conditions, but the success of their students depended on lots of conditions that need exploring (more below); they didn't just say, "Let's write in Creole."

Even if an invitation to write in a mother tongue is *intended* as an invitation to an easier, freer, safer, more intimate and natural fount of language and thinking, it's not clear that speakers of stigmatized languages can necessarily *experience* the invitation this way:

- Will it really be easy and safe? Just because a first language is intimate or close, that doesn't necessarily make it easy or safe. Extreme intimacy can even make the language more dangerous to use—especially in a public setting.

- What about double consciousness? Or what if a student's private consciousness is more oriented to (say) African American language and culture and his or her public consciousness is more oriented to white mainstream culture?

- Where does any particular individual student with a stigmatized home language (e.g. AAVE or Spanglish) find himself or herself in relation to the political and literary history of the larger group of writers and public figures using that language?

- And what if the distinction between "home language" and standardized English (one we find ourselves building on here) is not so clear cut? What about the traditions of mixing, interlanguage, hybrid discourse, and code switching? Keith Gilyard's autobiography shows that code switching was a natural part of his home discourse; for some students an interlanguage or hybrid language seems to be the writing dialect that feels natural; some students grow up with many dialects or languages and can't name one as their "home" or "mother" tongue. (Anzaldúa; see Gutierrez et al. on "hybrid language" within "third spaces" as "zones of development.") An invitation to use a home language will be experienced differently depending on all these factors.

On top of these questions come other hard ones: how do institutional policies push standardization at the expense of diversity? How often do we as English teachers participate—even if unconsciously—in the stigmatization of home languages? (See, for example, Ball and Lardner on the persistence of negative attitudes about African American Vernacular English.) And how often does stigmatization from the outside lead students to *internalize* these attitudes and sincerely devalue or even condemn their own home language (see Lippi-Green on this phenomenon with AAVE and Kells on Southwest varieties of Spanish and Spanglish)? The more we work in this area, the more we see that feelings about language tend to be deeper and more explosive than feelings about ideas.

In the end, we find ourselves trying to figure out what would be involved in constructing a *context of respect*—within a larger context of disrespect. We think we see the main elements in the rich and complicated way Irvine and Elsasser slowly and carefully invited their students in the Virgin Islands to write in Creole. The stigmatization of that language was pervasive and intense. But they got a respected linguist from the College—notably one who was a native speaker of Creole—to make a presentation to the students showing them that Creole is a full and sophisticated language, not "broken" or "defective" in any way. They also devoted important time to comparative study of the syntax and lexicon and *politics* of Creole and standardized English in the Virgin Islands. Thus, on the occasions when students wrote in Creole, they did so with a rich and thorough meta-understanding of how language issues play out in the culture. The honors students were hesitant at first to have their Creole writings published: their academic knowledge that Creole is a complete and valid language conflicted with their social knowledge that they could be stigmatized for writing in Creole. Students learned about how Creole and other stigmatized languages came to be devalued—how the groups speaking them had lost a political struggle. Some students wrote in Creole partially as resistance to linguistic domination.

And what about *mixed* classrooms? Irvine and Elsasser's Caribbean students were all native speakers of the Creole, but mixed classrooms are probably more common in the U.S. When speakers of nondominant versions or English or non-English languages are in the minority (especially if the languages are stigmatized), they are liable to feel unsafe using their home language. Yet on the other hand, many classrooms look and sound more uniformly mainstream than they actually are: Students whose language does not mark them as different from their mainstream classmates may in fact have grown up with dialects or languages that are different—often stigmatized.

Such students are often grateful to explore the issue of writing in a mother tongue. (On the issue of mixed classrooms, see Matsuda and Silva.)

Eleanor Kutz, another co-author, describes a different path to a culture of respect. She shows how we can invite students themselves to explore the different discourse contexts in which they participate, and to bring their home languages and dialects into the English writing classroom as part of their study (Kutz). Such work allows all learners to recognize the discourse competence they use when speaking for familiar purposes in familiar communities and to gain a meta-level sense of how insiders to any setting develop ways of communicating that are appropriate to its shared purposes. There is also some evidence that if we help second-language writers focus more on how they move into new discourse contexts, they can apply to their writing more effective discourse-level strategies (such as how to place themselves within a conversation) rather than applying only limited language-learning strategies (such as how to fix lexical and syntactic errors). While such work invites students to write *about*, rather than *in* their home languages and dialects, it can also make space for students to reflect on how their work in a new discourse can benefit from drawing on the resources of home language or dialect.

FIFTH VARIABLE: *What is the learning goal for writing on this particular occasion: practicing for* future *fluency in standardized English or drafting for a* present *text in standardized English that captures the student's richest thinking and strongest voice?*

A teacher who takes future fluency as the sole exclusive goal is likely to decide that students should *always* compose in standardized English—and simply accept the price that must be paid for working exclusively on this goal: a considerable delay not only in comfort and fluency of language but also in richness and complexity of thinking. But many teachers insist that fluency is not the only goal and want, for example, to give students the experience of being able to call on their richest thinking and widest range of imaginative and linguistic distinctions. For this, it will make more sense to invite students to start off writing such a piece in their home language or dialect. Many fluent writers treasure the striking experience of being hit by new ideas right in the midst of putting down words. For most people, this experience comes more often in low stakes writing where one can put down words quickly without always planning them in advance. A home language is likely to facilitate this kind of *cognitive* fluency. (Note, too, that many students who study English as a foreign language have a chance to write in their home language outside of their English class—whereas many students who speak a stigmatized dialect have no other chances to write it.)

So if, for example, students have to write a high stakes essay for some kind of assessment and there is extensive time for re-drafting and revision, or an essay or autobiography for admission to some program or for a job, Irvine and Elsasser's experience (and some of our own) suggests that students may turn out a better final product in standardized English when they do lots of drafting and exploratory writing first in their home dialect or language. Of course this advantage holds only when other conditions or variables are favorable. Irvine and Elsasser's students needed to pass an essay test in standardized English. Nevertheless those researchers believe that they helped their students become more successful in standardized English by setting up *some* occasions for writing in Caribbean Creole—so that students could learn to take the rhetorical purposes for any written language into account.

SIXTH VARIABLE: *How much trust is there between students and teacher?*

Often, students can more easily trust a teacher who is a native speaker of the dialect or language in question—or a teacher who shares their race, ethnicity, and class. This issue is particularly important in the case of vernacular dialects such as AAVE or Caribbean Creoles. Such dialects, almost by definition, are media of intimacy: "mother tongues" used in the family and in-groups. Some students are liable to feel it inappropriate or even offensive to use a "home language" in the impersonal market place of the classroom. Irvine and Elsasser were white outsiders to the Virgin Islands and not experienced with Creole. They had to work hard to establish a climate of trust—and got a lot of benefit from bringing a local linguist and several local Creole writers to the class. Eileen Kennedy, in a study of Caribbean students, shows how her invitations to use a vernacular dialect went unheeded until she created more intimacy by speaking and writing about her own dialectal history and sharing more of her life with her students. At this point, students started experimenting with their vernacular, and the whole climate of the class became much closer. In ESL or EFL classrooms, a teacher whose home language is not English is likely to have valuable insights to share with students about the process of learning English—and is sometimes granted special credibility on those grounds. However, teachers who speak English as their mother tongue are sometimes granted more authority because they are insiders to the target language and culture, especially in EFL settings. Native and nonnative-English speakers bring different yet complementary strengths to the classroom (Matsuda and Matsuda).

SEVENTH VARIABLE: *Is the home dialect or language commonly used for writing?*

Does it have a settled orthography? Can the teacher provide readings in the home language? Are the students comfortable reading and writing in their home dialect or language?—or even able to read or write at all? The more these questions can be answered "Yes," the easier it is likely to be for students to write in their home dialect or language. Yet even though students in the College of the Virgin Islands had never written in Creole, and there was no settled orthography at that time for their varieties of Creole, nevertheless Irvine and Elsasser invited some writing in it for audiences outside the classroom. They gave students the problem of working out issues of orthography for a collaborative writing project in Creole. This served as a powerful meta-lesson about the nature of language standardization, not only in their own language for indigenous Creole genres and purposes, but also in standardized English for academic purposes.

Even if students have written rather little in *any* language—as is the case with some ESL students even in college classrooms—a case could be made for inviting some writing in that home language or dialect. For when such students try to write in standardized English, they face a double hurdle: an unfamiliar language and an unfamiliar medium. We noted from some of our own informal experiments in teaching that students *can* get comfortable writing in a language "by ear"—even when they are not literate in it or there is no official orthography. Indeed, an official orthography sometimes makes writers worry about spelling.

EIGHTH VARIABLE: *What is the process by which students move from exploratory writing or early drafts in a home dialect or language to revised and final versions in standardized English: word-for-word translating or more global rewriting/revising?*

This question is particularly important for students writing in a completely different language from English. The problems caused by translation are obvious and have often been noted:

> First, [translating] does not solve the problem that students are not able to fully and fluently express their ideas in English, a task they will be asked to perform throughout their school years. Second, having students use one language to negotiate the other can limit their opportunities of learning to express their ideas in English, reduce authentic reasons for using English, and diminish their felt need to learn to express their ideas in English. (Miramontes, Nadeau, and Commins 43)

Further, Kobayashi and Rinnert argue that, "The extensive use of translation may hinder second-language writing fluency and delay the development of an awareness of the expectations of a second-language audience" (205). Also, of course, word-for-word translating often leads to words and syntax that are inappropriate or wrong for L2.

But students can get the benefits of writing in a home language and still avoid the problems of direct translation. Peter Elbow worked with a woman who spoke Puerto Rican-based Spanish. She was not highly literate in her mother tongue, but she found it a great relief to write in it and found she could write many more thoughts and much more quickly. When she translated directly from her Spanish, she ran into the obvious problems of false cognates and inappropriate syntax for English. But when she put her Spanish text completely aside (after looking it over) and set herself the task of revising or rewriting—*composing explicitly in English* on the basis of it—she was able to call on the richer thinking and subtler distinctions she had produced thanks to her home language. In this revising task, she was working in standardized English—trying to use its lexicon and syntax. Of course she experienced the frustration of having more complex and subtle meanings in mind that were difficult for her to render in English, but at least she *had* that rich content driving her, and so she had a good incentive to stretch her use of English.

If this rewriting/revising approach proves beneficial in further research and classroom trials, it will yield a point of strategic leverage: when students compose in a language other than English and then rewrite/revise wholly in English—not seeing the lexicon and syntax of their home language and not trying to stay tied to it—they will get a double benefit: the benefit of composing or inventing in their home language, but also the benefit of *composing again in English* and thus practicing and developing a kind of syntactic fluency in the target language. This approach thus cuts through the over-simple either/or choice about whether to compose in standardized English or some other language: students can practice composing in both languages. Every time they go through this process, it will be a good occasion for reflecting on the contrasting resources of each language and the discourse or culture it tends to carry.

NINTH VARIABLE: *Who chooses whether to write in a language different from standardized English — the student or the teacher (or the institution)?*

We suspect most readers would agree that students should not be forced or even pressured into this option. Thus we stress our word *invite.* And we have seen a variety of good reasons for student reluctance, resistance, or refusal: some may not want to use a home language for *any* classroom task; some may not want to use it for academic rhetorical tasks that feel impersonal, abstract, and alien to home rhetorical traditions; some may not want to use it because they want practice in producing or generating standardized English (and are willing to pay the price of reduced comfort, fluency, and power in generating); and some may feel that they have too few allies in the class and so will need to use vernacular dialect only for private writing (if at all). In addition, sadly, a few won't want to use their home dialect because they have been taught to disapprove of it as a second-rate or broken language (just as Jesse Jackson called Ebonics "trash talk"). We can hope to chip away at this misconception, but we agree that even here, the student must retain choice.

But if choice is important, then we note this: in most classrooms, *students now have no choice.* That is, in most classrooms where the dominant variety of English is the norm, students feel it is wrong to write in a different dialect or language.

A TENTH AND FINAL VARIABLE: *The teacher's own beliefs or convictions, the variable that usually plays the biggest role in classrooms.*

In our hope of making this essay useful to all readers, whatever their attitudes toward the use of home languages or dialects, we have tended to frame our discussion pragmatically—almost as though the only reason to invite students to write in a home language is in order to improve their writing in standardized

English. But that's far from the whole story for us — especially when it comes to nondominant varieties of English. We take linguistic richness and bilingualism as values in themselves (Haswell). We sense the danger that standardized English will drive out other varieties of English — as it is putting pressure on other languages around the globe (Skutnabb-Kangas). Also, American academic discourse has a powerful ability to assimilate and neutralize other discourses and dialects (Dobrin). We believe that more work is needed in order to invite language minority students into higher education, and that towards this end it is important to honor the legitimacy and linguistic sophistication of all languages and dialects. Thus we affirm the 4C's statement on "Students' Rights to Their Own Language" (Committee) and the Linguistic Society of America's "Statement on Language Rights."

Turning again to our classrooms, then, we'd argue that even if *most* writing must end up in the dominant version of written English, it still makes good pedagogical and human sense occasionally to invite speakers of non-standardized varieties of English and speakers of languages other than English to write something in their home language that they do *not* turn into standardized English: a finished, revised, copy-edited, cherished piece in the student's home dialect or language. It's best when this piece is published in a class publication — just as regular student essays in standardized English are often published in the classroom (Elbow "The Role of Publication"). Furthermore, it will sometimes make sense for students to experiment with "writing back" — transforming their pieces in standardized English into versions in a home language: neither one privileged, neither one devalued.

Widespread change in classroom practices will require widespread change in teacher beliefs (Lehner). But there are reasons for hope. The rise of "world Englishes" around the globe is causing diverse varieties of English to be widely used, published, and sanctioned, thereby creating contexts in which the idea of a "standard English" is recurrently questioned and critiqued. (But obviously it's a problem when any version of English serves to undermine a local indigenous language.) The history of the Middle Ages and the Renaissance shows how stigmatized varieties of Latin came eventually to flower as Romance languages were recognized as legitimate for writing and publication. There is more and more publication of writing in nondominant varieties of English (see Elbow, "Vernacular"). Furthermore, the standardized variety of English and the conventions of academic discourse are gradually evolving as members of the academic world become increasingly diverse, both linguistically and culturally (Matsuda).

As we try to pull together what we have learned, we conclude that an invitation to write in a home dialect or language should be offered with:

- respect for the complexities of the invitation;
- respect for the many good reasons students might have for declining the objection (see variable #9);
- help for students in learning about the home language and the politics around it;

- awareness of institutional complicity in stigmatizing of the dialect;
- awareness of all that we teachers don't know and must try to learn about the vexedness of writing in a stigmatized dialect or language.

---

what i be talking about
can be said in this language
only

Lucille Clifton's poem sets the essential dilemma not just for us but for an enormous number of teachers: what someone from one culture is thinking may not be fully sayable in the language of another culture. By inviting home languages in classrooms dominated by standardized English, we seem to be pursuing an impossible goal. What shall we do? Throw up our hands and say "Write only what you can think in the new language"? This is not something we are willing to do. Just because a goal is impossible doesn't mean that there's no difference between getting closer to it and giving up. Besides, should we refrain from helping people write things in the language that fits them best, just because English is not right for expressing some of those things? Shall we decide not to read Homer unless we read Greek? Nevertheless, the essential dilemma remains and it explains why our essay is driven more by questions than answers.

Thus we have committed ourselves to further work on this perplexing issue—thinking, experimentation, and research. Please read our essay as a plea for more experimentation and research from you; contact any of us with what you can discover.

NOTE

1. A vernacular dialect usually appears first as quoted speech in published fiction, memoir, and poetry. From there it spreads to narrators of whole works. ("Alice Walker's . . . subject . . . writes herself to a personal freedom and to a remarkable level of articulation in the dialect voice in which Hurston's protagonist speaks" [Gates 169].) Then it spreads, as might be expected, more widely to nonfiction.

WORKS CITED

Anderson, Gary, and Patricia D. Irvine. "Informing Critical Literacy with Ethnography." *Critical Literacy: Politics, Praxis and the Postmodern*. Ed. Peter McLaren and Collin Lankshear. New York: SUNY Press, 1993. 81–104.

Anzaldúa, Gloria. *Borderlands /La Frontera: The New Mestiza*. San Francisco: Spinters-Aunt Lute, 1987.

Auerbach, Elsa Roberts. "Reexamining English Only in the ESL Classroom." *TESOL Quarterly* 27.1 (1993): 9–32.

Ball, Arnetha, and Ted Lardner. "Dispositions toward Language: Teacher Constructs of Knowledge and the Ann Arbor Black English Case." *College Composition and Communication* 48.4 (1997): 469–85.

Clifton, Lucille. "defending my tongue." *Quilting: Poems 1987–1990*. Rochester, NY: BOA Editions, Ltd., 1991.

Committee of the Conference on College Composition and Communication. "Students' Rights to Their Own Language." *CCC* 25.3 (1974): 1–18.

Delpit. Lisa. "Ebonics and Culturally Responsive Instruction." *Rethinking Schools* 12.1 (Fall 1997): 6–7.

Dobrin, Sidney. "A Problem in Writing (about) 'Alternative Discourse'." *ALT DIS: Alternative Discourse and the Academy*. Portsmouth NH: Boynton/Cook-Heinemann, 2002. 45–56.

Elbow, Peter. "Inviting the Mother Tongue: Beyond 'Mistakes,' 'Bad English,' and 'Wrong Language.'" *JAC* 19.2 (Spring 1999): 359–88.

——. "The Role of Publication in the Democratization of Writing." *Publishing with Students: A Comprehensive Guide*. Ed. Chris Weber. Portsmouth NH: Boynton/Cook-Heinemann, 2002.

——. "Vernacular Englishes in the Writing Classroom: Probing the Culture of Literacy." *ALT DIS: Alternative Discourses and the Academy*. Ed. Christopher Schroeder, Patricia Bizzell, and Helen Fox. Boynton/Cook-Heinemann, 2002. 126–38.

Elsasser, Nan, and Patricia Irvine. "English and Creole: The Dialectics of Choice in a College Writing Program." *Harvard Educational Review* 55.4 (1985): 399–415. Rpt. in *Freire for the Classroom*. Ed. Ira Shor. New Jersey: Boynton/Cook-Heinemann, 1987.

Freire, Paulo. *The Pedagogy of the Oppressed*. Trans. Myra Bergman Ramos. New York: Seabury, 1968.

Friedlander, Alexander. "Composing in English: Effects of a First Language on Writing in English as a Second Language." *Second Language Writing: Research Insights for the Classroom*. Ed. Barbara Kroll. New York: Cambridge UP, 1990. 109–25.

Gates, Henry Louis Jr. *The Signifying Monkey: A Theory of African-American Literary Criticism*. New York: Oxford UP, 1988.

Gilyard, Keith. *Voices of the Self: A Study of Language Competence*. Detroit: Wayne State UP, 1991.

Gilyard, Keith, and Elaine Richardson. "Students' Rights to Possibility: Basic Writing and African American Rhetoric." *Insurrections: Approaches to Resistance in Composition Studies*. Ed. Andrea Greenbaum. Albany, NY: SUNY Press, 2001. 37–51.

Gutierrez, Kris D., Patricia Baquedano-Lopez, and Carlos Tejeda. "Rethinking Diversity: Hybridity and Hybrid Language Practices in the Third Space." *Mind, Culture, and Activity* 6.4 (1999): 286–303.

Haswell, Richard. "Enter Double-Talk, to Hisses." Unpublished essay.

Irvine, Patricia, and Nan Elsasser. "The Ecology of Literacy: Negotiating Writing Standards in a Caribbean Setting." *The Social Construction of Written Communication*. Ed. B. Rafoth and D. Rubin. Norwood, NJ: Ablex, 1988. 304–20.

Kells, Michelle Hall. "Linguistic Contact Zones: An Examination of Ethnolinguistic Identity and Language Attitudes." *Written Communication*. 19.1 (January 2002): 5–43.

Kells, Michelle Hall, Valerie Balester, and Victor Villanueva eds. *In-Siting Literacy: Latino/a Discourses and Teaching Composition as Social Action*. Portsmouth, NH: Heinemann/Boynton-Cook, 2003.

Kennedy, Eileen. "Writing in Home Dialects." Unpublished essay.

Kobayashi, Hiroe, and Carol Rinnert. "Effects of First Language on Second Language Writing: Translation versus Direct Composition." *Language Learning* 42.2 (1992): 183–215.

Kutz, Eleanor. "From Outsider to Insider: Studying Academic Discourse Communities across the Curriculum." *Crossing the Curriculum*. Eds. R. Spack and V. Zamel. Mahwah NH: Lawrence Erlbaum, 2004. Also *Exploring Literacy*. New York: Longman, 2004.

Lehner, Albert J., Jr. *Bilingual Students, Writing, and Academic Discourse: An Interpretive Inquiry of University Writing-Across-the-Curriculum Instructors*. Unpublished doctoral dissertation, Department of English as a Second Language, University of Hawai'i at Manoa. Honolulu, HI, 2001.

Linguistic Society of America. January 1997. LSA Resolution on the "Oakland Ebonics" Issue. <http://www.LSADC.org/ebonics.htm>.

Lippi-Green, Rosina. *English with an Accent: Language, Ideology and Discrimination in the United States*. London: Routledge, 1997.

Matsuda, Aya, and Paul Kei Matsuda. "Autonomy and Collaboration in Teacher Education: Journal Sharing among Native and nonnative English-Speaking Teachers." *CATESON Journal* 13.1 (2001): 109–21. Rpt. in *Learning and Teaching from Experience: Perspectives on Nonnative English-Speaking Professionals*. Ed. Lia Kamhi-Stein. Ann Arbor: U of Michigan P, 2004. 176–89.

Matsuda, Paul Kei. "Alternative Discourses: A Synthesis." *ALT DIS: Alternative Discourse and the Academy*. Portsmouth NH: Boynton/Cook-Heinemann, 2002. 191–96.

Matsuda, Paul Kei, and Tony Silva. "Cross-Cultural Composition: Mediated Integration of US and International Students." *Composition Studies* 27.1 (1999): 15–30.

Miramontes, Ofelia, Adele Nadeau, and Nancy L. Commins. *Restructuring Schools for Linguistic Diversity: Linking Decision Making to Effective Programs*. New York, NY: Teachers College P, 1997.

Nero, Shondel J. *Englishes in Contact: Anglophone Caribbean Students in an Urban College*. Cresskill, NJ: Hampton P, 2001.

Palacas, Arthur L. "Liberating American Ebonics from Euro-English." *College English* 63.3 (Jan 2001): 326–52.

Skutnabb-Kangas, Tove. *Linguistic Genocide in Education – or Worldwide Diversity and Human Rights?* Mahwah, NJ: Lawrence Erlbaum, 2000.

Smitherman, Geneva. " ' The Blacker the Berry, the Sweeter the Juice': African American Student Writers." *The Need for Story: Cultural Diversity in the Classroom and Community*. Urbana IL: NCTE, 1994. 80–101. Rpt. in *Talkin That Talk: Language, Culture and Education in African America*. NY: Routledge, 2000.

Woodall, Billy R. "Language Switching: Using the First Language While Writing in a Second Language." *Journal of Second Language Writing* 11.1 (2002): 7–28.

Rethinking
Curriculum Design

Introduction to Part Four

The presence of second-language writers in composition courses not only affects classroom makeup but also compels composition instructors to reconsider their teaching strategies. The stakes of reexamining curricula become even higher when increasing cultural and linguistic diversity in classrooms is matched by the proliferation of different kinds of texts — both print and electronic — that students and teachers encounter and produce. This section approaches growing challenges of placement, course construction, and assignment design. The four essays included here ask compositionists to reconsider current practices in light of the complexity and diversity of each context.

In "Cross-Cultural Composition: Mediated Integration of U.S. and International Students," published in 1999, Paul Kei Matsuda and Tony Silva argue that the placement options available for second-language students are often inadequate. In many cases, students are either placed in second-language-dedicated sections of first-year composition where they are "segregated from the rest of the campus community," or they are placed in sections where they sink-or-swim, frequently with inexperienced instructors (p. 247 in this volume). Neither of these options provide opportunities for either second-language or NES students to develop communication skills necessary for the demographic and economic shifts of a globalizing world and workforce. Matsuda and Silva propose a third choice: a cross-cultural first-year composition course. In their course, which enrolled both NES and second-language students, they challenged students to reflect on diverse language practices and to interact with others from diverse language backgrounds, both in the classroom and around campus. The result was a course environment that appeared to make second-language students more comfortable speaking and writing in the presence of native English speakers while increasing NES students' awareness of and empathy with language learners.

In their 1995 article, "Designing and Assessing Effective Classroom Writing Assignments for NES and ESL Students," Joy Reid and Barbara Kroll argue that, in most courses across the curriculum, "academic writing is a form of testing" (p. 261), since students are evaluated largely based on their writing. Reid and Kroll present and analyze a variety of writing assignments they consider effective and ineffective. They discover that many assignments disadvantage second-language writers by being too vague or too broad in scope and by using concepts or language unfamiliar to them. These problems in assignment design may lead to several common problems that are often blamed on students, such as time mismanagement, unsupported generalizations, and even plagiarism. Reid and Kroll suggest that teachers make their criteria for successful writing more explicit; that they consider the social, cognitive, and affective factors that bear on their students' performance; and that they design assignments — from the writing prompt through the grading standards — that "bias for the best" by challenging students without overwhelming them (p. 263).

Ann Johns, in her 1999 article, "Opening Our Doors: Applying Socioliterate Approaches (SA) to Language Minority Classrooms," advocates teaching second-language writers following an approach that foregrounds literacy in context. As an alternative to what Johns views as still common expressivist pedagogies, which focus on developing students' individual voices regardless of particular contexts, SA emphasizes for students the social nature of all of the texts they encounter. Starting with texts of various kinds in students' first languages, Johns proposes leading students through discussions of how and why the texts appear the way they do and to what particular needs they respond. Then, she encourages students to "expand their genre repertoires" (161) in order to apply their developing analyses to more academic genres. But rather than training them simply to replicate academic forms, Johns's approach begins and ends with students' own abilities as language analysts and researchers. Students bring their various experiences in their primary languages and cultures into the SA classroom, and they leave the classroom as researchers who ask questions about textual expectations and use their research skills to achieve social purposes with their own writing. Johns is convinced that students should not be locked into preoccupations with individual expression or a focus on error — both common approaches in many second-language classrooms — but they should instead be mentored into applying and developing their language abilities in a variety of contexts.

In "The Impact of the Computer in Second Language Writing," first published in 2003, Martha C. Pennington argues that writing teachers cannot afford to ignore advances in computer technology. For Pennington, the relevant question writing instructors must ask is not whether their students will use word processors, e-mail, discussion and news groups, chat, and the World Wide Web, but how their use may help or hinder writing development. Pennington provides a useful overview of research on the role of the computer in second-language writing instruction, noting that, despite some mixed results, students generally react positively to the increasing presence of computers in academic situations. In fact, Pennington observes that computers may be of particular benefit to second-language learners because they seem to reduce some of the burdens those students encounter in writing words on paper and revising drafts. But the effects of the computer are, of course, not limited to students: Pennington notes that teachers, themselves, are more frequently turning to computers and computer networks as sources of information, facilitators of community (as in Listservs like TESL-L and SLW.CCCC), and storage media for corpora of language use. While she sounds a note of caution about the persistent lack of access to computers in many areas, Pennington is optimistic about the potential of computer technologies to expand students' writing opportunities and expand teachers' knowledge bases.

All of these articles argue provocatively about how composition courses may be redesigned to provide effective writing instruction for the full range of culturally and linguistically diverse students who enroll in them and for the full range of genres student writers use. As more and more classrooms come to resemble Matsuda and Silva's experimental one by default, the insights provided by these articles will become even more relevant.

13 Cross-Cultural Composition: Mediated Integration of U.S. and International Students

PAUL KEI MATSUDA AND TONY SILVA

Working at the turn of the millennium, writing teachers and writing program administrators are facing, among many others, two important challenges. The first is to provide an appropriate instructional environment for all types of students, as the student population at many university campuses is becoming increasingly diverse and international. According to the Institute of International Education, international student enrollment reached 481,280 in the 1997–98 academic year and is continuing to increase (Desruisseaux A66). At Purdue University, there are currently 3,266 international visa students, including 1,296 undergraduate students (Patterson 3). About 9% of 35,000 undergraduate and graduate students at our campus are international students, most of whom speak English as a second language (ESL). In addition, there is a growing number of ESL students who are permanent residents or naturalized citizens of the United States. The presence of these ESL students requires special attention from teachers and administrators because, while ESL writers are similar in many ways to their native English speaking (NES) counterparts, there is also a number of significant differences that make working with them challenging for many writing teachers who have traditionally had few opportunities to learn how to teach second language writers.[1]

The second challenge is to provide educational opportunities in which students can prepare themselves for an increasingly internationalized world. In "Fads and Fashions on Campus: Interdisciplinarity and Internationalization," Craufurd D. Goodwin suggests that

> almost all college graduates today are required by circumstances to understand the world. Whether they become businesspersons, engineers, journalists, public officials, or enter almost any other occupation, they will be faced inevitably over their life spans with a host of people and things that are not American. To the degree that they remain unfamiliar with this "difference," they will be unable to cope. Indeed, recognizing this reality ahead of their teachers, students (both American and foreign)

From *Composition Studies* 27.1 (1999): 15–30.

have formed one of the most strenuous forces pressing for the introduction of international material into the curricula of the liberal arts college and the professional schools. They demand that you prepare them for a world they will face that is already highly diverse and is becoming more so. (78)

Compared to the first challenge, the second one may seem less immediate. Nevertheless, it is an important concern for those involved in higher education — including writing teachers and administrators — because, as Goodwin points out, "so many of the problems that we face today within the United States are multinational in their origin and solution," and "if we are to attack these problems through research, and as citizens, we must understand other places and other peoples" (78).

One of the ways in which we have responded to these challenges is to offer what we call a cross-cultural composition course, which is designed to integrate U.S. and international students and is taught by an instructor who is prepared to address the needs of both groups of students.[2] Our goal in this essay is to consider this cross-cultural composition course as an alternative placement option that can provide an effective learning environment for ESL writers as well as a way of promoting international and intercultural understanding for both U.S. and international students.

CROSS-CULTURAL COMPOSITION AS A PLACEMENT OPTION

One of the most important reasons for creating our cross-cultural composition course is to offer an environment which is less threatening to ESL writers than existing placement options while providing an optimal learning opportunity for all students involved. Traditionally, the discussion of placement options for ESL students has often been cast in terms of the binary opposition between "mainstreaming" and "segregation" of ESL writers — that is, either integrating ESL students into "regular" first-year composition or basic writing courses, which are designed primarily for students who are proficient in spoken English (Roy, "Alliance," "ESL"), or separating them into special ESL sections of composition courses with or without credit (Braine; Nattinger). Although both approaches have some advantages, each of them falls short of providing for the needs of ESL writers in different ways. (For a comprehensive overview of placement options, see Silva, "An Examination.")

From the perspective of the administrator, integrating ESL writers into existing writing courses, including both mainstream sections of composition and basic writing, has a definite economic advantage. These courses require no additional resources for developing a new program, for hiring or preparing ESL writing teachers, or for administering a new program. From the perspective of ESL writers, however, it is essentially a sink-or-swim approach. Some students fare well in this situation or may even enjoy the challenge; to others, however, it means "farewell" — many students withdraw from these courses or receive failing grades.

Some ESL students tend not to do well in mainstream courses partly because many of them feel intimidated by their NES peers who are obviously more proficient in English and comfortable with the U.S. classroom culture. In an examination of students' attitudes toward and their performance in ESL and mainstream sections of an introductory composition course, Braine reported that students "expressed their fear and embarrassment about speaking up in mainstream classes" (100). That is, some ESL students were not able to ask questions or participate in discussions as fully as they wished to because they anticipated negative reactions from their classmates and teachers. The problem, however, was not all in ESL students' heads; the lack of awareness and sensitivity towards their needs among some NES students and teachers also added to the difficulty that ESL students faced. Braine found that the ESL students in his study often withdrew from mainstream classes because they "did not feel 'comfortable'":

> Many [ESL] students stated, generally, the [NES] students did not help them or even speak to them in class and that the teacher did little to encourage communication. During peer review of papers in groups, these students felt that the [NES] students were impatient with them, and one [ESL] student said that he overhead a [NES] student complain to the teacher about her inability to correct the numerous grammatical errors in [the ESL student's] paper. (98)

In an ethnographic study of ESL high school students, Harklau also observed that class discussion in the mainstream classroom may be dominated by NES students. ESL writers are often silenced not only because of their language difficulties, but because of negative reactions from both the teacher and NES classmates who may be oblivious to their special needs. Integrating ESL students into mainstream courses could be more appropriate if all composition teachers were prepared to teach ESL writing; however, as many ESL specialists have pointed out, teachers of mainstream classes in many cases are not prepared to work with ESL writers effectively (Atkinson and Ramanathan; Kroll; Matsuda, "Situating"; Roy, "ESL"; Silva, "An Examination").

A common solution to this problem is to create ESL sections of the composition course. In Braine's study, a majority of the ESL students who enrolled in a mainstream section of the first-semester composition course indicated that they would have preferred to have taken ESL sections while 95% of ESL students who took ESL sections of first-semester composition were satisfied with the course. Most of the students in the study explained that they felt "'comfortable' or 'at ease' in the ESL classes." One of the reasons for students' preference for ESL composition was that it did not make ESL students feel "self-conscious of their accents," thus allowing them to have "more confidence to ask questions of the teacher and to take part in class discussions" (97).

ESL sections of composition courses are not without their problems, however. Because students in ESL composition courses are segregated from the rest of the campus community on the basis of their linguistic backgrounds, some faculty may see the course as remedial and thus somehow less rigorous than the "regular" composition course. Similarly, ESL students may come into the ESL composition course with the expectation that, because it is designed specifically for ESL students, it is somehow "easier" than "regular" sections of composition courses. Some advanced ESL students may also feel that ESL sections do not provide a sufficient challenge, although ESL sections are often as demanding as, if not more demanding than, "mainstream" sections of composition courses. Another limitation of ESL composition is that it does not provide ESL students with the opportunity to work with NES writers. Preparing ESL students to work with NES writers is important because, once they complete the composition requirement, they will no longer have the luxury of being in an ESL section of, for instance, a history or sociology course. They must eventually face the challenge of working — and in some cases competing — with their NES peers. However, courses that separate ESL students may not be able to prepare them sufficiently in this respect.

An alternative to this integration/separation binary is to provide a mediated integration of NES and ESL writers, and the cross-cultural composition course can be a way of accomplishing this goal. Unlike mainstream writing courses, cross-cultural composition courses can create an ESL-friendly learning environment both because ESL students are no longer minorities in the classroom and because the teacher is prepared to work with both NES and ESL writers. Being ESL-friendly, however, does not necessarily mean being conflict-free. Rather, the cross-cultural composition course creates what Mary Louise Pratt calls "contact zones," or "social spaces where cultures meet, clash, and grapple with each other, often in contexts of highly asymmetrical relations of power" (34) because it encourages ESL students as well as NES students to foreground difference in order to explore the "ground rules for communication across lines of difference and hierarchy that go beyond politeness but maintain mutual respect" (40). In other words, it can create a "shared discourse community" (Matsuda, "Contrastive Rhetoric" 54) within which ESL students can openly negotiate how they relate to NES students rather than hide behind the comfort of ESL sections or conceal their cultural and linguistic backgrounds in an effort to conform to the expectations of teachers and students in mainstream courses. Furthermore, by deliberately integrating NES and ESL students, this course also allows them to see one another as "complementary resources" (Healy and Hall 21; see also Patthey-Chavez and Gergen; Silva "Examination").

In the next section, we will consider these claims by describing a section of the cross-cultural composition course taught at Purdue University during the Fall semester of 1997. Our goal in describing the projects and activities is not to prescribe a pedagogical package to be adopted uncritically; rather, we hope to illustrate how this placement option might work and to offer examples of pedagogical strategies that are designed to help students critically reflect on the implications of linguistic and cultural diversity.

A CROSS-CULTURAL COMPOSITION COURSE

At Purdue University, the cross-cultural composition course is offered as an equivalent of the first-semester introductory composition course. To achieve a mediated integration of NES and ESL writers, this course is designed to enroll more or less equal numbers of U.S. and international students. The section offered in Fall 1997 consisted of 20 first-year management students—including 8 native and 12 non-native speakers of English—who signed up voluntarily in consultation with their academic advisors. The group included 14 males and 6 females and represented a range of linguistic and cultural groups. Students came from various native-language backgrounds, including English (10), Hindi (1), Indonesian (5), Korean (2), Pakistani (1), and Spanish (1). The group included two Indian students who had a strong background in the English language; one of them was a permanent resident of the United States who was raised in a suburb of New York City, and the other, a British national, had graduated from a U.S. high school. One of the Korean students also was a graduate of a U.S. high school. Most of the U.S. citizens—with the exception of the Hispanic student from Puerto Rico—said they came from relatively small Indiana communities, where "multiculturalism did not exist" (Nicole, Reflective Commentary, December 12).[3]

Since its inception in 1993, the cross-cultural composition course has been staffed by instructors with theoretical and practical preparation in teaching ESL and writing as well as experience in teaching both ESL and mainstream sections of introductory composition courses. (See Reichelt and Silva for a description of the genesis of the course.) The syllabus and course projects are designed by individual instructors so that their interests, experience, and areas of expertise are reflected in the way the course is taught. The instructor for the Fall 1997 section was Paul Matsuda, a non-native speaker of English who had previously taught cross-cultural communication and foreign language courses. Consequently, he developed writing projects that were designed to focus more explicitly on cross-cultural issues than did his predecessors. Rather than seeing the cross-cultural component merely as a "dividend" (Silva, "Examination" 40), Paul made it a central focus of the course by developing writing projects in which students inquired into cross-cultural issues.

WRITING PROJECTS AND ACTIVITIES

Writing tasks for this section included weekly journals and five major writing projects. One of the elements that seemed to contribute to the success of this class was the cross-cultural journal, which has always been a key element of the course. Each week, students submitted a one- or two-page journal entry, in which they described and reflected on their cross-cultural experiences. From the students' perspective, this activity served at least three purposes. First, it provided a way of reflecting on thoughts and experiences related to cross-cultural communication. Second, students used the journal as a way of communicating insights—gained through in- or out-of-class cross-cultural interactions and experiences—to the instructor and their classmates. Third, it served as an invention heuristic; that is, it allowed students to record their reactions to certain issues for later reflection and development in one of the writing projects. From Paul's perspective, the activity provided a way of understanding students' levels of cross-cultural awareness and development as well as an opportunity to provide comments to encourage further reflection.

When the semester started, most of the students—both U.S. and international—seemed to be relatively unaware of the importance of cultural differences and their implications for communication and cross-cultural understanding. For this reason, discussions in the course during the first few weeks focused on raising awareness of cultural differences, allowing students to generate significant understanding of other cultures and accepting their practices before judging them. The first writing project, a cultural profile, was designed to facilitate this process. In this project, students were first asked to form groups of three, with each student representing a different cultural group. They then interviewed one another to learn as much as they could about cultural practices that were different from their own. Students were asked specifically to identify those practices that involved "dissonance" (Lauer 91) or "productive conflict" (Jarratt 118), which served as starting points of inquiry. Some examples of the cultural practices students discussed were arranged marriage in countries such as India and Japan, the status of women in Indonesia, and the use of physical punishment by teachers in Korea. After identifying dissonance, students interviewed each other further to develop a better understanding of the cultural practice in its broader social and cultural contexts. Based on their interviews, each student wrote an exploratory essay and made a brief oral presentation to share the insights gained through this project.

The second project focused on an aspect of cross-cultural communication that is important but often overlooked: nonverbal communication. To understand how different cultural groups used and interpreted nonverbal cues, students observed interactions among a group of people with similar linguistic and cultural backgrounds. For this project, students were asked to find a partner who came from a background that was different from her or his own. There were four reasons for making this project a collaborative one. First, it would provide students an opportunity to get to know someone from another linguistic or cultural background well. Another reason was that it would allow students to learn from each other's style and process of writing. The third reason was to provide students with an opportunity to experience the complexity of co-authorship and to reflect on the subject position of the author/researcher. The fourth, and most important, reason was that it would help students to contribute different perspectives on what they observed. For example, Nathan, a U.S. student, and Stephanie, an Indonesian student, observed a group of Indonesian students meeting regularly for lunch in the student union. Since Nathan did not understand the Indonesian language, he concentrated on describing nonverbal behavior—which was more transparent to the Indonesian student—while Stephanie acted as a cultural informant. In the texts that were produced collaboratively, students described various uses of nonverbal behavior and discussed their significance. Once again, insights from the observation project were shared through oral presentations, which were more formal than those for the previous project.

The third project involved survey research. By the time the second project was completed, students had become aware of many cross-cultural issues that affected them in significant ways. For instance, some students began to discuss issues such as the forming of racial cliques and the international students' participation in discussions and activities in various classes. One of the most interesting discussions was about international students' use of their first language in the presence of students from other linguistic backgrounds. Through journal sharing and in-class discussions, students found that there were various views as to whether speaking a language in front of people who did not understand it was appropriate and how often and why it occurred. To answer some of the questions that arose from these discussions, students conducted surveys. At the beginning, Priya, an ESL student from India with a strong English background, insisted that international students should try to speak English when they are in the United States. To understand why ESL students speak their native language in public, she proposed to survey bilingual international students. In her research, Priya found out that international students "do not choose to speak their native language" but "only use it out of necessity; when speaking English becomes difficult" (Priya, Project 3, Evaluation Version, October 29). This research helped to change her attitude, as she later wrote:

> When I hear a group of students speaking another language, it does not bother me as much as it did before. I realize now why they do it and how hard it is for them to always speak English and still send a clear message. (Priya, Reflective Commentary, December 12)

She was not the only one who was affected by this research. It also helped NES students to understand the difficulty that ESL students experienced and caused ESL students to realize the implications of speaking their native language in public.

Through the first three writing projects as well as class discussions, students had gained many valuable insights into cross-cultural communication. In the fourth project, students were asked to share those insights with people outside of the classroom community. The main goal of this project was to help students to become sensitive to the use of genre and audience in constructing arguments. To identify a viable topic, students reviewed all of their journal entries and writing projects, highlighting parts of the text that seemed promising. A few students chose to write flyers for bulletin boards and room doors in the residence hall, but most of them wrote letters to the editor of the campus newspaper, two of which were published.

For the final project, students were asked to demonstrate their development as writers and cross-cultural communicators by compiling a cross-cultural portofolio. The cross-cultural portfolio consisted of a cover letter, revisions of two of the writing projects, all versions of all writing projects (as well as written feedback from the instructor and classmates), all journal entries, and a reflective commentary. The last item, the reflective commentary, was the most challenging part of this project. Students were asked to demonstrate what they had learned by describing it or by referring to specific parts of their texts. For students, it provided an incentive for reviewing their work and for reflecting on their accomplishments. For Paul, it was a way of assessing students' work as well as the effectiveness of the course in addressing students' needs as writers and cross-cultural communicators. What follows is a consideration, based on students' perceptions, of the course's effectiveness in providing an ESL-friendly environment as well as in promoting cross-cultural learning.

AN ESL-FRIENDLY ENVIRONMENT

At the beginning of the semester, Park, a student from Korea, approached Paul Matsuda, the instructor, to ask whether it would be possible to do well in a class with so many NES students. In his reflective commentary, which was written at the end of the semester, Park reflected on his initial concerns:

> I was always worried about how I can get a good grade in the English course because I should study English with American students. Obviously, they speak and write better than I do. This fact really has depressed me. (Park, Reflective Commentary, December 12)

Park was not alone with this concern. Lia, an Indonesian student, wrote that she was "worried and afraid" when she came into the class on the first day: "Worried because I thought that I could not follow the class, and afraid because I was in the class of so many Americans with their ability in writing" (Lia, Reflective Commentary, December 12).

These comments resemble those made by ESL students who were enrolled in mainstream composition courses in Braine's study. As the semester progressed, however, students in the cross-cultural composition course were able to overcome the initial fear of being in the same class with NES students. Three weeks into the course, Stephanie, another student from Indonesia, explained in her journal how activities in the course were helping her to become more comfortable in working with other students:

> Things are getting better now. It is hardly that I can not understand what other people say. Although there are still some troubles on speaking and understanding other people, it surely is getting better. These week we talked and interviewed friends in class in order to get to know each other better. . . . What we've done is one way to make the class get to know each other, understand who your friends are, how they'd like to be treated. I am surely going to like this class. (Stephanie, Journal #2, September 12)

Lia also indicated in her reflective commentary that she became increasingly comfortable as a result of class interactions: "As soon as I knew my friends [in this class], I became more and more confident in expressing my thought, whether through my writing, or in front of the whole class." She attributed these changes to "the class's environment and atmosphere" which "helped us a lot in interacting with other students." She explained:

> The teacher gives us a freedom to utter our feeling and thoughts about things that are discussed in class. This is especially important for me because I am not used to expressing my feelings in front of the class. (Lia, Reflective Commentary, December 12)

Park also learned to turn his initial anxiety into a productive tension, which enabled him to learn from his U.S. classmates:

> . . . as time went by, I figured out that only the progress of English skill does not mean everything in the course. It means, I should acquire the writing skill that can be understood by Americans. Therefore, I should get the feedback from American students. Even though I can write well in Korean, Americans sometimes cannot understand my paper. So, I have tried to read paper of other American classmates so that I can understand their culture and thoughts. (Park, Reflective Commentary, December 12)

Although Park learned to cope with his U.S. classmates, he was not as successful in speaking up in class as Lia. In his own words: "one thing that I did not do well in this course is that I did not speak up in class. I need to talk with other students to share opinions" (Park, Reflective Commentary, December 12). However, he did speak up in class occasionally, and when he shared his thoughts on the difficulty of speaking a second language, other students were supportive. One of the U.S. students, Dave, even wrote an extensive response in his journal, which he read to the class:

> Park said that he had trouble communicating with Americans and did not participate much in many of his classes. At first he thought that it was the Americans' fault. He thought that the Americans did not want to communicate with him because of his nationality, and they would make fun of him if he tried to explain his thoughts during a class discussion. But then he made a statement that I had never really thought about, but I agreed with it 100 percent. He said that it was not the Americans' fault; he needed to put the blame on himself.
>
> I think this is a great realization, and this holds very true with college freshman, no matter what country you are from. Often times Americans even feel uncomfortable talking to international students. They do not feel superior to international students, they just feel as if international students might not care what they think or might not fully understand them. But what everyone needs to realize is that everyone else is basically in the same boat. We are all experiencing a very new and exciting experience in our lives. So I think a great place to start would be for all of us to take a look in the mirror and think to ourselves, "Maybe this is where the problem begins." Yes, some American students do make an effort to talk to international students, and some international students do make an effort to talk to American students. But when it is all laid out on the table, most nationalities are intimidated to talk to someone outside

of their own cultural background. So my main point of this journal is that I think we would all get along much better if we stopped blaming others for the lack of communication, and started blaming ourselves. (Dave, Journal #8, October 27)

Park's initial contribution as well as Dave's response contributed to a better understanding of different perspectives that U.S. and international students brought to the classroom on this issue. It also helped the members of the class to construct new insights into the bilateral nature of cross-cultural communication. The opportunity to gain this kind of cultural insight is another unique advantage of the cross-cultural composition course.

OPPORTUNITIES FOR CROSS-CULTURAL LEARNING

The dialogue between Park and Dave, which helped to heighten students' cross-cultural awareness, is but one example of how this course can help to promote international understanding, as Nathan, a U.S. student, observed:

It seemed that everyone became more conscious [of cultural issues] as our class advanced to greater levels in our writing projects. . . . People in class began to understand the feelings and views of each other from the start of the class and have been analyzing these issues ever since. (Nathan, Reflective Commentary, December 12)

In fact, students came to regard the cross-cultural component of this course to be a valuable part of their educational experience. Dave wrote, for instance: "This class has definitely enhanced my writing ability, but I do not think that was the greatest benefit I have received from this class."

The greatest benefit I received from this course was indeed being educated to be a cross-cultural communicator. I come from a fairly small town and a very small high school. Students with different cultural backgrounds really did not exist. I had never thought about what it would be like to be in a strange country, away from your friends and family, and not knowing the cultural norms of the people around you. But now I have worked in groups with international students, one-on-one with international students, and just socially interacted with international students. I have realized that after I put our cultural differences aside, it is actually quite easy for me to communicate with international students. (Dave, Reflective Commentary, December 12)

Jenny, who at the beginning of the semester was "very unsure about this class" because she had "never had an opportunity or option to associate with international students," came to enjoy working with international students. As she wrote:

Not only have I learned a lot in this class but this class has also helped me to correspond and befriend many international students. I not only have been given a chance to converse with international students but I have also learned a lot about many different cultures. (Jenny, Reflective Commentary, December 12)

For project 4, in which students were asked to share their insights in a public forum, Ryan, another U.S. student, chose to write a letter to the editor of the campus newspaper arguing that a "multi-cultural class" such as cross-cultural composition should be required for all students. In this letter, which was later published, he wrote: "Once I was there I quickly realized that it was even more different than I had expected. Suddenly, I felt as if I were in another country. I was the minority." He continued:

> I have never been in a situation where I was outnumbered by people from another race. This class makes one stop to think about how he or she treats minorities. It also helps American students to realize how it would feel to be studying in a foreign country. (Ryan, Project #4, Evaluation Version, November 17)

These students from small Indiana communities were not the only ones who saw the benefit of cross-cultural interactions, as Ramya, an Indian student from New York, suggests:

> I am originally from a suburb right outside of what is probably the most culturally diverse city in the world, New York City. So what could I possibly learn from a group of international students and a group of freshmen from Midwest? I'm sure they would have some good insight, but nothing I haven't heard before, right? I was totally wrong. (Ramya, Reflective Commentary, December 12)

Likewise, international students who were experiencing cross-cultural communication on a daily basis were also able to gain some useful cross-cultural insights from this course.

> Then I met friends in my English class and we discussed some cultural differences that we have. That was fun. It is interesting to know that there are other ways of life, they have positive facts that I should consider, beside all the way of life that I have right now. By getting to know other cultures, I can have more respect to other people because now I can understand who they are and the cultural background that they grew up with. (Stephanie, Journal #1, September 5)

As students' comments indicate, this course was able to meet the goal of providing a learning environment where ESL students can feel comfortable and where all types of students can increase their cross-cultural awareness. To borrow Jenny's words, "this class [was] a benefit to all who enrolled in it" (Jenny, Reflective Commentary, December 12).

IMPLEMENTING CROSS-CULTURAL COMPOSITION

As we have suggested, the mediated integration of U.S. and international students in a cross-cultural composition course can be an effective way of addressing the needs of both NES and ESL students. To develop cross-cultural composition courses successfully, two issues need to be addressed: staffing and the placement procedure.

First, to provide effective instruction for both U.S. and international students, the cross-cultural composition course should be taught by an instructor who is prepared to work with both NES and ESL writers. At Purdue, we are fortunate to have a pool of instructors who meet these criteria because our department offers graduate programs in both Rhetoric and Composition and Second Language Studies. In many cases, however, it is difficult to find instructors who have backgrounds in both first- and second-language writing because these two professions have traditionally been separated institutionally (Matsuda, "Composition," "Situating"). Composition teachers who are interested in teaching this course might wish to familiarize themselves with issues surrounding second language writing by attending presentations and workshops on ESL writing at CCCC or by reading introductory textbooks for ESL writing teachers such as Dana Ferris and John Hedgcock's *Teaching ESL Composition* and Ilona Leki's *Understanding ESL Writers*. Alternatively, the course can be team taught by one instructor with a background in composition and another with an ESL background. Having instructors from two different professional backgrounds can help to ensure that the course is informed by developments in both fields. In addition, it can provide an opportunity for teachers to enhance their professional preparation through collaboration. The team teaching approach can be further strengthened by having one native and one non-native speaker of English because they tend to have different strengths and perspectives that can complement one another.

Second, to maintain a balanced enrollment of the two types of students, a special placement procedure may need to be established. As Reichelt and Silva have described, the initial attempt to offer this course in Spring 1993 was unsuccessful because, although letters were sent out to faculty advisors from various departments in the previous Fall, not enough students signed up to justify a section. However, the School of Management saw cross-cultural composition as a way of increasing cross-cultural awareness and expressed their interest in the course for some of their students during the following semester. For this reason, placement of students into cross-cultural composition is coordinated by academic advisors in the School of Management and is currently designated for management students only.

Our experience suggests that the cross-cultural aspect of this placement option can be especially valuable at institutions where linguistic and cultural diversity is not prevalent. At some institutions, where the student population is already diverse, it may not be necessary to integrate students by creating a special placement option. Yet, even in those cases, some of the projects that we have discussed here may be useful. By foregrounding cross-cultural issues in the classroom, teachers can help already culturally-aware students to further develop their cross-cultural understanding, as Ramya's comments quoted earlier suggest. In emphasizing the benefits of cross-cultural composition over other options, however, we do not mean to suggest that it should replace other placement options completely. Since some students may prefer mainstream or ESL sections, cross-cultural composition should be offered as an alternative option.

NOTES

1. Ilona Leki's *Understanding ESL Writers* provides a useful overview of characteristics of ESL writers for writing teachers. For a systematic review of the distinct nature of second language writing, see Silva, "Differences," "Toward."

2. In this article, we define *U.S. students* as U.S.-born students as well as naturalized citizens and permanent residents of the United States. The term *international students* refers to non-U.S. citizens who are on student visas. In the context of our institution, this distinction generally coincides with the ESL/NES distinction; however, it is important to note that some U.S. students are ESL writers and that some international students are NES students.

3. All student names in this article are pseudonyms. Student texts quoted here come from the Fall 1997 section of the cross-cultural composition course and are unedited. The sources of student texts (indicated in parentheses) include weekly journal entries and writing projects as well as reflective commentaries, in which students considered their development as writers and cross-cultural communicators.

REFERENCES

Atkinson, Dwight, and Vai Ramanathan. "Cultures of Writing: An Ethnographic Comparison of L1 and L2 University Writing/Language Programs." *TESOL Quarterly* 29 (1995): 539–568.

Braine, George. "ESL Students in First-Year Writing Courses: ESL Versus Mainstream Classes." *Journal of Second Language Writing* 5 (1996): 91–107.

Desruisseaux, Paul. "2-Year Colleges at Crest of Wave in U.S. Enrollment Foreign Students." *Chronicle of Higher Education* 11 Dec. 1998: A66–68.

Ferris, Dana, and John Hedgcock. *Teaching ESL Composition: Purpose, Process, and Practice*. Mahwah, NJ: Erlbaum, 1998.

Goodwin, Craufurd D. "Fads and Fashions on Campus: Interdisciplinarity and Internationlization." *The Academic's Handbook*. Ed. A. Leigh Deneef and Craufurd D. Goodwin. 2nd ed. Durham, NC: Duke UP, 1995. 73–80.

Harklau, Linda. "ESL Versus Mainstream Classes: Contrasting L2 Learning Environments." *TESOL Quarterly* 28 (1994): 241–272.

Healy, Pamela, and Barbara Jean Hall. "From Separation to Integration: Accessing Students' Complementary Resources." *College ESL* 4.1 (1994): 20–27.

Jarratt, Susan C. "Feminism and Composition: The Case for Conflict." *Contending with Words: Composition and Rhetoric in a Postmodern Age*. Ed. Patricia Harkin and John Schilb. New York: MLA, 1991. 105–123.

Kroll, Barbara. "Teaching Writing IS Teaching Reading: Training the New Teachers of ESL Composition." *Reading in the Composition Classroom: Second Language Perspectives*. Ed. Joan Carson and Ilona Leki. Boston: Heinle & Heinle, 1993. 61–81.

Lauer, Janice M. "Writing as Inquiry: Some Questions for Teachers." *College Composition and Communication* 33 (1982): 89–93.

Leki, Ilona. *Understanding ESL Writers: A Guide for Teachers*. Portsmouth, NH: Boynton/Cook, 1992.

Matsuda, Paul Kei. "Composition Studies and ESL Writing: A Disciplinary Division of Labor." *College Composition and Communication* 50.4 (1999): 699–721.

——. "Contrastive Rhetoric in Context: A Dynamic Model of L2 Writing." *Journal of Second Language Writing* 6 (1997): 45–60.

——. "Situating ESL Writing in a Cross-Disciplinary Context." *Written Communication* 15 (1998): 99–121.

Nattinger, James R. "Second Dialect and Second Language in the Composition Class." *TESOL Quarterly* 12 (1978): 77–84.

Patterson, Amy. "International Enrollment Increases." *Purdue Exponent* 20 Nov. 1997: 3.

Patthey-Chavez, G. Genevieve, and Constance Gergen. "Culture as an Instructional Resource in the Multiethnic Composition Classroom." *Journal of Basic Writing* 11.1 (1992): 75–96.

Pratt, Mary Louise. "Arts of the Contact Zone." *Profession 91* (1991): 33–40.

Reichelt, Melinda, and Tony Silva. "Cross-Cultural Composition." *TESOL Journal* 5.2 (1995–1996): 16–19.

Roy, Alice. "Alliance for Literacy: Teaching Non-Native Speakers and Speakers of Nonstandard English Together." *College Composition and Communication* 35 (1984): 439–448.

——. "ESL Concerns for Writing Program Administrators: Problems and Policies." *Writing Program Administration* 11 (1988): 17–28.

Silva, Tony. "An Examination of Writing Program Administrators' Options for the Placement of ESL Students in First-Year Writing Classes." *Writing Program Administration* 18 (1994): 37–43.

——. "Differences in ESL and Native-English-Speaker Writing: The Research and Its Implications." *Writing in Multicultural Settings*. Ed. Carol Severino, Juan C. Guerra, and Johnnella E. Butler. New York: MLA, 1997. 209–210.

——. "Toward an Understanding of the Distinct Nature of Second Language Writing: The ESL Research and Its Implications." *TESOL Quarterly* 27 (1993): 657–677.

14

Designing and Assessing Effective Classroom Writing Assignments for NES and ESL Students

JOY REID AND BARBARA KROLL

Writing is essentially a social act: It takes place in specific contexts, and the situation for writing influences its purpose. Writing tasks differ in the purposes that call them into being and the audience(s) for whom they are intended, from grocery lists to published research reports, from letters to friends to assembly directions for a bicycle, from mystery novels to commercial advertisements. Academic (school) writing as prepared by U.S. college and university students is much narrower in scope but not without its own set of complexities and variables. Students may be asked to summarize a journal article in a biology class, write a persuasive proposal for a business class, do a literary analysis for an English class, or complete a research paper for a geology class — all in the same semester.

Formal school writing differs from most nonacademic writing tasks because the social context is unusual: The writing is not voluntary, the topics are usually assigned, and the written products are evaluated. The audiences and purposes for school writing are thus unique. The audience is usually limited to the person (the teacher) who also **designs, assigns,** and **assesses** that writing. To complicate the writing situation, the teacher-audience also faces unusual social interactions in her or his responses to and evaluation of student writing. Teachers often play several roles, among them coach, judge, facilitator, expert, responder, and evaluator as they offer more response and more intervention than an ordinary reader (Anson, 1989; Elbow, 1993; Freedman & Sperling, 1985; Johnson, 1992; Moxley, 1989, 1992; Radecki & Swales, 1988). Thus, the relationship between the writer and the reader differs from that of most other socially situated writing. Instead of an expert-to-novice relationship or a colleague-to-colleague relationship between the writer and the reader (as in "real" writing–reading events), the relationship is skewed: novice-to-expert, with the expert (teacher-reader) assessing the novice (student-writer) in ways that have consequences for the writer's life.

From *Journal of Second Language Writing* 4.1 (1995): 17–41.

The purposes of school writing tasks also differ from those of nonacademic writing. Both native English speakers (NESs) and English as a second language (ESL) writers understand, perhaps better than their teachers, that the primary purpose of academic writing assignments is not to inform, persuade, or entertain the teacher. From the student-writer's perspective, the purpose of writing assignments is to **demonstrate** understanding of the assignment in ways that the teacher-reader already anticipates (Belanoff, 1991; Horowitz, 1991; Popken, 1989). Although some writing assignments direct students to offer their opinions and support those opinions with various pieces of evidence, this student-writer "participation," especially in general education (or lower division) academic classes, does not usually inform or educate the teacher. Rather, teacher-evaluators are often familiar with the quality and quantity of available evidence; their role, then, is to assess the ways in which student-writers employ and arrange that support.

In other words, academic writing is a form of testing. Instead of testing class content or communication skills by multiple choice or true–false formats, writing assignments ask students to "perform," to demonstrate their knowledge and skills by composing and presenting written material. And like all tests, the completed writing assignment will be assessed. Criteria for evaluation of these writing "tests" differ according to the class (e.g., has the student assimilated the content of the course? synthesized concepts? arranged evidence appropriately? used language skillfully?), and the criteria for evaluation may be overt, covert, or even unconscious. But whatever the assessment criteria, teacher-evaluators expect students to fulfill those criteria, and they will judge the written product accordingly. Students know that academic writing tasks are tests: They almost invariably ask "What does [the teacher] want?" They realize that despite whatever "audience" may be assigned ("Write this essay for a classmate/the student newspaper/the President of the U.S."), the specter of the teacher-evaluator remains the "real" and most important audience, and the purpose of their writing is to demonstrate their ability to produce what the teacher expects for a certain grade. Consequently, designers of writing "prompts" (i.e., assignments that "prompt" students to respond in writing) should consider the purpose(s) for the prompt, the parameters and constraints of the assignment, and the way(s) in which the product will be evaluated. As Alice Brand (1992) states:

> Faculty have a right to expect competent writing. But they cannot expect competent writing when the prompts themselves are carelessly prepared. They cannot expect writing to be an accurate reflection of content knowledge or of higher-order thinking when the written assignments lack essential information or provide too much, are unclear or contradictory, are vague or picayune. (p. 157)

Because academic writing assignments can influence the lives of the students they test, all of these assignments should be designed and evaluated as carefully as any other test of student skills. This article discusses a range of issues in the design and assessment of classroom writing assignments given by teachers in courses across the U.S. college/university curriculum. In related work published in the *Journal of Second Language Writing*, we presented a framework designed to discuss the development of prompts for large-scale testing purposes (Kroll & Reid, 1994), and we will use categories from that framework to discuss the preparation and design of writing tasks administered by individual instructors in courses within the English/writing curriculum and in a variety of academic content courses. Finally, we will analyze successful and unsuccessful writing assignments and offer suggestions that will enable teachers to design and assess effective essay assignments.

DESIGN GUIDELINES

In general, effective writing assignments, whether for large-scale testing or within the U.S. academic classroom, must fulfill the testing expectations of the teacher-evaluators while at the same time be as fair as possible to the students: What is being tested? Why? In what specific ways? Have students been sufficiently prepared for the task(s)? An effective academic writing assignment should be clear, appropriate, and sound pedagogically; it should offer student-writers, whether NES or ESL, the best possible opportunity to demonstrate their strengths and to learn from their writing (Basham & Kwachka, 1991; Carlson, 1988; Cox, 1988; Hamp-Lyons, 1991b; Hamp-Lyons & Mathias, 1994; Larson, 1986). The effects of a writing task should be twofold: to measure student skills and to provide a learning opportunity for the writers (Ferris, 1994; Hamp-Lyons, 1991a; McKay, 1989; Walvoord, 1986; White, 1992). That is, students should "write-to-learn"; cognitive change and growth—education—should occur as a direct result of the writing task. Furthermore, writing assignments can define the emphasis and structure of a course because they reflect some of the values held by the teacher (Larson, 1986; Silva, 1993; Walvoord & McCarthy, 1991).

Teacher-designers of classroom writing prompts must therefore consider more than the general academic reasons for an assignment; they should ask themselves a series of questions to identify the contextual considerations which determine how best to shape a writing assignment that will serve both the teacher and the student most successfully (Figure 1). These questions, which we developed from our original framework (Kroll & Reid, 1994), demonstrate the social, cognitive, and affective aspects of student-writers as well as the global course/program objectives that teacher-designers should consider. For example, the complexity of a writing assignment, and even the amount and kind of detail in the instructions for the writing task will depend on such variables as the age and experience of the students (traditionally aged freshmen? second semester senior business majors?), the level of the class (an undergraduate general education class? a graduate seminar?), and even the individual learning styles and levels of motivation of the student-writers. Fortunately, most classroom teachers have substantial knowledge about and insights into their students' needs and limitations—the **classroom context**. Thus, teachers can design assignments that will "bias for the best":

FIGURE 1.   Contextual Considerations in Assigning Writing[1]

- For what reason(s)/purpose(s) will the writing be assigned?
- How will the assignment fit into the immediate context, and how in the overall objectives of the class? That is, how authentic is the prompt?
- In what ways will the content of the prompt be accessible to students as it integrates classroom learning with long-term goals?
- Who are the students who will be responding to the assignment, and what are their needs?
- How will the writing processes engage the students and further their knowledge of the content and skills being taught?
- What knowledge should the students be "demonstrating" in their written product?

They stretch the students without overwhelming them and provide students with significant learning experiences.

In addition to focusing on individual student factors and classroom objectives, teacher-designers are aware that an effective writing assignment should:

- be contextualized and authentic—it should be closely linked to classroom work, and students should be able to see the relationship of the assignment to both the class objectives and their "real world" future work (Canale & Swain, 1980; Frey & Ross, 1991; Leki & Carson, 1994; Paulson, 1992).

- be based on accessible content—it should tap into the existing background knowledge of the student-writers so that they can link old knowledge with new (Bereiter & Scardamalia, 1984, 1987; Carrell, 1983; Clayton, 1993; Newell & MacAdam, 1987).

- be engaging—the task(s) should involve the students, and the product should be of interest to the teacher-reader as well (Conlon & Fowles, 1987; Sudlow, 1991; Thorne, 1993).

- be developed in tandem with appropriate evaluation criteria, that reflect course goals (Allaei & Connor, 1990; Hamp-Lyons, 1994; Paulson, 1992; White, 1994).

In our earlier work analyzing the process of designing effective writing prompts for the assessment of writing per se, we suggested that test developers need to consider and control six critical categories: contextual variables, content variables, linguistic variables, task variables, rhetorical variables, and evaluation variables (Kroll & Reid, 1994). In Figure 2, we modify some of the descriptions of these categories in order to demonstrate how our earlier framework can be adapted to serve teachers in all disciplines as they shape writing assignments for their courses.

The last variable, apprising students of the evaluation criteria for a writing assignment, is perhaps the least well-developed criterion in prompt design. Yet it is integral to the process; only if the students fully understand how the "test" will be evaluated can they take responsibility for their own writing and learning. The more specific these criteria, the clearer the assignment

FIGURE 2.   Assignment Design Guidelines

Context
    place of writing task in <u>course objectives</u>, curriculum or long-term program goals
    student capabilities, <u>limitations</u>, learning objectives
    criteria/<u>reasons</u> for the assignment
    <u>authentic</u>/real-life context

Content
    <u>accessible</u> to all student writers, culturally and otherwise
    <u>authentic audience</u> and purpose(s)
    appropriately "rich" (for example, to allow for <u>multiple approaches</u>)

Language
    instructions
      <u>comprehensible</u>
      as brief as clarity allows
      <u>unambiguous</u>
    prompt
      vocabulary and syntax appropriately simple or complex
      <u>transparent</u>
      easy to interpret

Task(s)
    appropriately focused to accomplish within external parameters
    (for example, time constraints)
    further students' knowledge of classroom content and skills
    allows students to "demonstrate" their knowledge
    engaging, interesting, <u>involving</u>

Rhetorical specifications
    clear direction concerning shape and format(s)
    instructions concerning register and tone (i.e., audience relationships)
    adequate <u>rhetorical cues</u>[2]

Evaluation
    assesses what is being taught
    <u>clear, specific, unambiguous criteria</u> articulated to student-writers

---

objectives will be for the students, thereby reducing student beliefs that the real criteria for "good" writing (as evidenced by a final grade) are a mystery, that the teacher knows the "secrets" of good writing but will not share those secrets, and that students must therefore guess "what the teacher wants." Overt evaluation criteria can also assist teachers in their assessment processes. As Hamp-Lyons (1991a) as well as other researchers have demonstrated, without articulated scoring criteria, teacher-evaluators often apply "implicit criteria," using unarticulated and perhaps unconscious biases (toward, for example, article usage or neatness) as the basis for their assessment (Davis, Scriven, & Thomas, 1987; Greenberg, 1981; Huot, 1990; Mendelsohn & Cumming, 1987; Sweedler-Brown, 1993). To avoid such covert bias, writing assignments and evaluation criteria should be given in written form as well as orally.

A written set of assessment criteria can be designed to be handed out with a writing assignment; the criteria sheet can also be used as the cover sheet for the product that results from the assignment, and it then functions as an assessment guide as the teacher reads the paper. Appendix A demonstrates two rather generic cover sheets that can be adapted for a variety of writing tasks: the first identifies a variety of text properties that can be assigned weighted numerical values, depending on the context. The second, for an Advanced Composition course, concentrates on writing skills (although content is evaluated through the criteria of development, purpose, and audience). Appendix B demonstrates a more specialized cover sheet, this one for a problem–solution essay, in which points are given for the successful fulfillment of specific criteria that include both content and writing skills and that are specifically identified to the student-writer. In content courses across the curriculum, such specific evaluation criteria can accompany each writing assignment.

SUCCESSFUL PROMPTS

Below are several prompts from classes across the curriculum at three state universities. Because each of the prompt assignments in this article is taken out of the <u>classroom context</u>, it is difficult to fully examine the effectiveness of the writing assignment within the course objectives, the place of the writing task in the course, and the individual needs of the student-writers. We have, however, developed and/or collected these assignments from individual students over a period of two decades and have received written and oral feedback from students concerning the assignments discussed. We therefore believe that the following prompts have been analyzed with all available information and that they adequately control for the variables outlined previously (Figures 1 and 2) in ways that maximize students' ability to complete the assignments successfully. After each prompt is a brief analysis of the qualities that make the assignment effective; specific criteria from Figures 1 and 2 are underlined.

1. Freshman Composition

The following assignment has been used by both authors, with both NES and ESL writers, with substantial success. Usually, the assignment was given <u>more than midway through the composition class</u>, when the sense of classroom community (and its accompanying mutual trust and respect) had been established and developed, after the student-writers had been trained in the roles and benefits of group work, and during the time the students were being taught the writing skills of analysis and the use of evidence for support of their opinions.

Women's/Men's Roles

Imagine that you have two weeks to live as a person of the opposite sex. That is, if you are female, imagine you have two weeks to be a male; if you are male, imagine that you have two weeks to be female. Think of the differences in social roles, everyday life, and feelings that you might have. Use some of the questions below to begin pre-writing.

A. What about your life would be better? Try to list at least 3 things.
B. What about your life would be worse? Try to list at least 3 things.
C. What about your life would not be changed? Try to list at least 3 things.
D. What would you most enjoy being able to do in those two weeks that you can't do now? Describe 1 thing in detail.
E. What would you least enjoy having to do in those two weeks that you would probably have to do? Describe 1 thing in detail.

Write a 2–3 page (typewritten, double-spaced) essay in which you discuss the roles of women and men, using your pre-writing and personal observations to support your opinions. Your audience will be a classmate of the opposite sex with whom you will discuss your idea and who will review your essay drafts with you. Your final draft (and all your preliminary work for this assignment) is due on November 14th.

Your essay will be graded on the following criteria:

Organization	30%
Content	50%
Mechanics	20%

Analysis.   The <u>language</u> of the prompt and instructions was simple and direct; students understood immediately (though some were initially skeptical about the assignment). The <u>reasons</u> for the assignment were to (a) give the students an opportunity to use their own experience, memories, and observations to gather easily <u>accessible content</u> ("data"), and (b) then have the students organize and present their opinions and evidence in ways that would fulfill the parameters of the assignment. In-class discussion and organizational techniques and the use of evidence (<u>rhetorical specifications</u>) were integral to the writing process; peer review groups and at least one student–teacher conference were also part of the ongoing assignment.

The <u>evaluation criteria</u>, while not as detailed in the prompt as they might be, were part of previous assignments; however, students knew that in addition to the criteria listed, their essays would have a cover sheet like the second example in Appendix A. They were, therefore, well aware of the evaluation criteria for the course at the time in the semester. The resulting papers demonstrated that students were <u>interested and involved in the tasks</u>, that they were able to understand and address the tasks with success, that they used a <u>variety of approaches</u> to present their opinions and evidence, that they were able to discuss and review their partners' drafts, that their feedback on the drafts assisted the partner-writers, and that students could muster available evidence and present their opinions effectively.

2. Second-Year Biology Course

This hour-long midterm examination was used by a biology instructor who was committed to the concept of writing across the curriculum (WAC) and who designed this prompt with the students' learning experiences in mind. The results proved to be very successful; both NES and ESL students were able to <u>demonstrate their knowledge</u> and at the same time be creative in their responses.

> You are the only doctor in a small, rural town. People of all ages begin coming into your clinic with the following symptoms:
>
> | | |
> |---|---|
> | headache | fever of 102 degrees Fahrenheit |
> | aches in joints | swelling in the abdomen |
>
> The people in the village are not familiar with the germ theory of disease, and they are very frightened. Write an explanation of the disease process for these people.

Analysis.   First, the <u>context</u> of this prompt was clear for undergraduate students who had been studying the theory of contagion: They understood the reasons for the test, they knew they had been studying the disease process in class, and they prepared accordingly. The <u>language</u> of the instructions and the prompts was relatively simple, brief, and unambiguous; even students with limited English language skills who had studied for the test understood the instructions and the task. The major <u>reason</u> for the assignment was to give students the opportunity to demonstrate and apply their knowledge in a specific, nonclassroom situation; moreover, the task was both narrow enough for students to respond to adequately in the time period and "rich" enough to allow the teacher-evaluator to discriminate between effective and ineffective responses. In addition, all students (who studied) had equal access to the <u>content</u> of this prompt, and the <u>rhetorical specification</u> ("Write an explanation") was simple but effective; it cued students to shape their responses.

While <u>evaluation criteria</u> for the examination were not specifically stated, we assume that students who took this test at midsemester knew the general parameters of the assignment and the assessment criteria on which they would be evaluated, namely, on their demonstrated knowledge about the disease process and their ability to effectively fulfill the assignment.[3]

Finally, the greatest strength of this prompt was, we think, the <u>authentic audience and purpose</u> that provided a provocative "frame" or scenario for student writing. The assigned persona of being the "only doctor in a small, rural town" <u>involved the students</u> both personally and professionally. However, not all simulated scenarios are as effective as this one; often, the more detail that is provided, the more complex the scenario, and the less successful the prompt (Brand, 1992; Redd-Boyd & Slater, 1989; Smith et al., 1985). An example of how students do not appreciate assignments that are too confining is provided by Steinberg (1980), who notes:

> It was clear that the students were moving from amusement to annoyance when one day about mid-semester I came into the room at the beginning of the hour and saw on the board something like the following: "Write an explanation of a one-armed paper-hanger who is allergic to paste about how he can paper the room while standing on one foot without harming the newly shellacked floor." (p. 166)

3. Second-Year Genetics Laboratory Report

Sophomores in a large lecture-based genetics class received this exercise in their laboratory section. ESL students in that laboratory section reported that they understood the assignment (though they were initially "shy" about fulfilling it) and that their laboratory teaching assistant helped them individually with some vocabulary in the prompt.

- Purpose: This laboratory exercise and the subsequent report are intended to permit you to compare actual data obtained from the class, and a data sample of your own, with theoretical values, obtained from the development of Punnett squares.
- Procedure:
    (a)   A data collection sheet will be passed around each laboratory group. You should answer each question (e.g., your blood type, do you possess a widow's peak, or dimples, attached or free ear lobes, etc.). You will also be provided with an individual collection sheet. Note that at the bottom of the sheet is an area regarding color perception. Following your instructor's directions, complete this section of your sheet. Remove it at the broken line and turn it in before the end of the period. All of the data for the entire class will be pooled and provided to you at the next laboratory period.
    (b)   Before the next period, obtain an independent sample of your own from about 35 persons OTHER than members of the class—for example, your dormitory group, a club, or just the first 35 persons you encounter on campus. Select any TWO traits from the data collection sheet (additional traits are not necessary). NOTE: Retain your tally sheet and include it as an appendix with your report.
- Report: The report should include the following sections:
    (a)   Introduction—the purpose of the study
    (b)   Material and methods—how were the data obtained?
    (c)   Observations—the actual data
    (d)   Discussion—develop Punnett squares for each of the following, and each should be included in your report: a dihybrid cross, a sex-linked trait, and a multiple-allele system.

Analysis.   The report for this genetics class required actual student fieldwork that integrated class learning and application: to invest time and energy collecting data and then to report that data in an organized (and expected) way. The <u>classroom context</u> was clear and the audience was <u>authentic</u>: Students practiced what they had been learning, and the results <u>interested</u> both the individual students and the instructor. The data were equally <u>accessible</u> to every student; one particular strength of the assignment was the <u>language</u> of the directions for collecting the data (the <u>content</u> of the report), which was <u>transparent</u> and <u>unambiguous</u>. The language for the actual assignment of the report was more complex for the uninitiated, but students had learned vocabulary such as "dihybrid cross" and "multiple-allele system" previously during the class.

For this assignment, <u>evaluation criteria</u> were implicitly included in the <u>rhetorical specifications</u>; the instructor assessed how effectively student-writers communicated their data in a report format (with introduction, materials, observations, and discussion sections), and how successfully they "develop[ed] Punnett squares" for each of the categories. In other words, the instructor assessed what had been taught.

4. Third-Year Introduction to Linguistics Course

This short essay assignment was given to a class of varied student backgrounds: undergraduate and graduate students, linguistics majors and minors, education students, and others. The assignment came near the end of an academic semester; students and teacher had established the <u>context</u> of a classroom community.

> Date Due: November 14, 19____
>
> Write an essay of approximately 500 words (2 typed pages, double-spaced) in which you discuss how one or two concepts or principles you learned about linguistics or about the English language in the first 10 weeks of this course either (1) particularly interested or intrigued you, (2) surprised you, or (3) appear to you to have potential usefulness in a present or future career choice. Do not include any material you have studied for your group project presentation.
>
> In your discussion, identify not only the linguistic learning that took place but explain your reaction to that learning. This paper is not meant to be a summary or review of the semester but a discussion of one or two issues only.
>
> Your essay will be evaluated on the basis of its manifestation of linguistic awareness and correct understanding of linguistic concepts, along with its demonstration of such features of standard academic English as good organization and control over language.
>
> Your essay should be typed or prepared on a word processor using double spacing and printed on white bond paper. Proofread and correct any typing mistakes. Do not put your paper in any kind of binder or folder; simply staple the pages together.
>
> Remember: No late homework assignments will be accepted.

Analysis. Although the assignment seems a bit abbreviated, the teacher and students had ample opportunity to discuss the assignment and to negotiate information not mentioned in the prompt (e.g., specific "concepts or principles"). Note that the teacher asked students to choose their topics (<u>content</u>) individually, referred to other assignments ("Do not include material studied for your group presentation"), indicated what the assignment was *not* ("a summary or review of the semester"), and helped students to narrow their topics ("a discussion of one or two issues only").

The <u>rhetorical specifications</u> and <u>evaluation criteria</u> occupied half of the prompt and constituted its greatest strength for this analysis. Students learned the parameters and constraints of the assignment ("2 typed pages, double-spaced" and stapled), and they learned how they would be <u>assessed</u> (linguistic awareness, standard academic English, good organization, and language control). Papers resulting from this assignment demonstrated that both NES and ESL graduate and undergraduate students were able to <u>access</u> the directions and write appropriate, high-quality responses.

5. Urban Water Management Graduate Course

The <u>classroom context</u> for this graduate research paper prompt differed from the previous examples. First, it is apparent from the due dates (in a semester system) that this assignment was given near the beginning of a graduate seminar and that it would be a major part of the course and the course grade. Second, the participants in this class were all graduate students in the field of water management. Third, the assignment required more than a written account; students would also do an oral presentation—the language, audience, and purpose of which no doubt differed from the written paper.

> A major part of the class effort will be directed toward a research paper and oral presentation. The goals of the exercise are: First, you will study a particular topic of interest in enough detail to become an expert; second, you will convey to the class in the form of a summary abstract and a brief oral presentation the most important aspects of the subject you chose.
> Due dates:
>
> *February 10:* Submit a one-page proposal for your topic, with objectives and scope of the paper. I will comment on them and return.
>
> *March 31:* Submit a one-page summary abstract of your paper and oral presentation. Include any diagram that may help illustrate your topic as part of the one page. These will be collected, assembled, printed, and distributed to the class as reference material.
>
> *April 7:* Oral presentations begin. I will provide a schedule and copies of the abstracts. Each oral presentation will last 5–10 minutes, including questions. We will schedule about 4 per class period. We will arrange to have an overhead projector or a slide projector if you request one in advance.
>
> *April 24:* Written papers due. They should be well presented in a format similar to that you would use for a journal article submission. This means: clear, objective, good presentation of facts; a conclusion; and references. Length should be about 5–10 pages, single-spaced equivalent.

Analysis.   Notice that this was not as detailed an assignment as would be necessary for an undergraduate, nonmajor class. The assignment did not, for example, detail the overall organization of the "proposal"; rather, it indicated the expected sections, the "objectives and scope of the paper." Nor did it describe the instructor's expectations concerning the "summary abstract"; as part of the classroom context, the graduate students should already have known the parameters and the constraints, the rhetorical specifications, and the language expected in this part of the assignment. In addition, students did not have an opportunity for "multiple approaches" to the prompt; rather, the <u>rhetorical specifications</u> were relatively rigid. However, since the purpose of this assignment was not to discriminate between effective and ineffective lower division writing, for example, but rather to develop a community of learning among senior colleagues, multiple approaches was not an important criterion.

On the other hand, the assignment itself was <u>directly related to course objectives</u> and to the students' professional futures: The <u>purposes</u> of the assignment were to assist students in becoming "experts," using their expertise to inform others in the class and learning to write an article suitable for submission to a journal in their major field. Moreover, the process outlined in the assignment provided students with essential deadlines and instructor support ("I will comment on [the proposal]").

The most specific directions in this assignment concerned the format and <u>rhetorical expectations</u> of the final paper. Graduate students in the class needed to investigate or refresh their knowledge of the format(s) for "journal article submission," and their papers were evaluated on "clear, objective, good presentations of facts, a conclusion, and references."

For the ESL students in the class, the <u>language</u> of this assignment was not as clear as it might have been; for example, they professed some confusion about the amount of required material. In particular, the second sentence ("The goals . . .") should probably have been rewritten into two or three clearly detailed sentences. However, these ESL students reported that the negotiation necessary to decipher this sentence did take place in class.

UNSUCCESSFUL PROMPTS

The following prompts also are authentic writing assignments from a variety of U.S. college/university classes across the curriculum. Again, we have collected these assignments from our NES and ESL students over two decades of teaching, eliciting both verbal and written student input about the prompts. So, while we cannot speak to the exact classroom context for each assignment, we have asked students in the represented classes about their responses to the prompts, and in some cases we have seen the drafts of those responses. Our investigations demonstrated that, because these prompts were poorly designed, they caused difficulties for students in the classes. While the prompts often exhibit several problems simultaneously, this section will evaluate only the major problems of each prompt. The first three assignments are examples of the flaw most often found in problematic writing assignments: They are too broadly focused for successful student writing within the classroom context in which they were assigned; in terms of the design guidelines, their <u>content</u> is flawed. The next two prompts present <u>classroom context</u> problems, particularly in the areas of prompt relevance and understanding of student capabilities and learning objectives. The last prompt poses the more visible problem of <u>language</u> difficulties and misunderstandings for ESL students. The analysis following each prompt is based on student input as well as on the guidelines for effective assignment design (Figures 1 and 2); we have underlined criteria from Figures 1 and 2.

Flawed Content

1. Freshman Political Science Course. We have numerous prompts from this class, brought to us by angry NES and overwhelmed ESL students over a period of years. All of the prompts present the same major problems, which are the result of a departmental policy to hire undergraduate students, many not even political science majors, to run discussion sections for the large-lecture format of the class and then to "design" a research paper assignment. Because these discussion leaders lack teaching and prompt-design experience and expertise, they tend to write the most global prompts possible (under the mistaken assumption of "the bigger the better") and then to assess the resulting papers arbitrarily. Assigned just after midterm for an end-of-term due date, none of the prompts considers the <u>limitations</u> of freshmen concerning library use, synthesis of substantial amounts of material, and the presentation of material about which they have very little background knowledge or experience.

> The purpose of this paper is to examine the origins and results of Soviet control and influence in the Soviet satellites of Bulgaria, Czechoslovakia, East Germany, Hungary, Romania, and Poland, as well as the current reforms and their implications. Your paper must be 6–10 double-spaced, typewritten pages. The written quality of your paper will be graded. This will include the use of proper grammar, correct punctuation, spelling, and word usage as well as the citation of references and the inclusion of a bibliography in the proper form.

Analysis. The major problem with this assignment was in the <u>content</u> of the assignment itself: The focus of the assignment was broad enough for a book (at least) rather than being "appropriately focused to accomplish within the external parameters of the task" (Figure 2). That is, 6 to 10 pages provided freshman writers only with an experience in frustration: Most began as novices in the topic, and as they gathered information, they found extraordinary quantities of material that needed to be read, analyzed, and synthesized. In fact, the assignment contained nearly 20 separate tasks, at least one third of which could each fill 10 pages of a research report. Since the students had to comment on origins, results, current reforms, and implications of the reforms in five "satellites" in 10 pages, the resulting research papers could not help but descend into gross generalizations with virtually no evidence; plagiarism occurred as students struggled to fulfill the expectations of the evaluators. Instead of having room to develop an argument and to gather and arrange persuasive evidence, student-writers tried to cram short responses to all of the tasks into the paper in order to fulfill the unrealistic demands of the assignment.

Especially for freshmen, designing assignments with framed/constrained content, clear objectives, and rhetorical cues can give the student-writers substantial assistance. With this assignment, how could the student-evaluator help but be disappointed in the results? Furthermore, while the evaluation criteria were given generally, ESL students reported that the student-instructor did not clearly define such instructions as "bibliography in the proper form."

2. Freshman Music Class Research Paper.   This was the first writing assignment given in the class, during the second week of class. The course, a "cultural context" requirement, is frequently taken by first-semester freshmen and by newly admitted ESL undergraduates. Given this classroom context, we were not surprised when puzzled NES and ESL students arrived at the university Writing Center and in our offices almost immediately. We advised the students to ask the instructor specific questions.

> You will write a 3–5 page research paper on a **musical topic**. The purpose of this assignment is to familiarize you with music resources in the library. You must cite at least three different sources found in the library in your paper. This paper must be typed and double-spaced. The paper is worth a maximum of 60 points. It is due Nov. 6.

Analysis.   While the language of the instructions and the prompt for this research paper were clear, the content for the paper was vague, especially for a first-semester freshman audience. For example, students had no framework for choosing a viable topic that they could write about satisfactorily in 3 to 5 pages (Rap? The use of the violin in Broadway musicals? Seventeenth century Baroque music? How Bach's life affected his composing? Elvis?). Perhaps because the stated objective of the prompt was to "familiarize students with music resources in the library," the instructor felt that the topic did not matter (i.e., any topic would do). However, because no specific rhetorical specifications or evaluation criteria were given, students could not guess "what the teacher wanted," nor could they assume that their choice of topic would not influence their grades.

In response to student questions about the topic, the instructor later added this sentence to the prompt: "Subjects for this paper are limited to subjects found in the *New Groves Encyclopedia of Music*, which will provide a good bibliography."

3. Third-Year Business Course.   This writing assignment, given during the last quarter of the course in a class for management majors, caused special problems for ESL students, whose major-field background knowledge was culturally different from the NESs in the class. For example, "performance appraisal" is a culturally bound concept and a form for that appraisal completely "foreign." Moreover, even though the NESs had a better grasp of the jargon and the instructor's expectations, they still had difficulty interpreting the assignment.

> Create two performance appraisal forms based on your knowledge of the process. Each form should contain performance dimensions relevant to the position under consideration. The forms should utilize appropriate behavioral anchors for each dimension being measured. A generic form may not be used.

Analysis.   Even within the context of the class, this prompt is vague, full of jargon, and directionless. Unfortunately, the instructor in this class felt that this written prompt was self-explanatory, and so did not discuss the assignment with the students. Among student questions were the following: Why are we doing this? (learning/teaching objectives). What does [the instructor] want? (evaluation criteria). What form for the appraisal should I use? What form, if not "generic," may be used? (rhetorical specifications). When is the due date? The length? (instructions). What is the "position under consideration"? (language).

Note that while the problems with the content of this prompt are completely clear to us (and to other nonbusiness instructors), we believe that prompt designers in all fields regularly write prompts that seem to the instructor to be crystal clear, while students (and other nonspecialized audiences) reading the prompt flounder.

Flawed Classroom Context

1. Freshman Astronomy Course.   The following assignment, given near the end of a course for "extra credit," smacks of elementary school "book reports." It was, unfortunately, given as a "special" assignment in order to "bring up" the grade of an ESL student who was failing the class. However, the ESL student had never written such a report and so had little rhetorical information or perspective about the topic.

> Do a report on an astronomer who is currently living or has lived in the past 100 years. The report should consist of 4 or 5 typed pages and should be well written and well researched.

Analysis.   The most important problem with this prompt is that it lacks crucial information about the classroom context for the task. What was the purpose of the assignment? What was the place of this writing assignment within the objectives of the freshman astronomy course? What was being tested? Was a biographical narrative (perhaps a summary of a single book or book chapter) a "report"? In what ways did this prompt consider student needs and potential for learning? What did the student learn doing this assignment? In addition, what did the instructor use as evaluation criteria: What did he or she consider "well written" and "well researched"?

2. Second-Year History of Science Course.   This assignment was given just before the midterm of the semester to a class of nonscience and science majors in order to fulfill an "intensive writing" component for the class. Clearly, the content of the task is too broad and unfocused for more than a cursory response ("examining Western culture before, during, and after *Origin of the Species*"!). But, in addition, student complaints highlighted the relationship between content and classroom context in prompt development. In particular, an ESL student in the class spent an inordinate amount of time during the semester working to fulfill the assignment, slighting other parts of the class (and other university classes) to complete the paper, and thus hurting, rather than helping, his course grade.

> Write a 7–10 page paper with at least 7 different sources on the social, political, philosophical, and religious consequences of Darwinism. This paper should place Darwin's theory in its cultural context, examining Western culture before, during, and after the *Origin of Species*. How did people react to the theory? Why did they react to it?

Analysis.   The scope of this course involved centuries of scientific discoveries. While Darwin occupied a section of the course, class reading and discussion (and other forms of testing) encompassed only 2 weeks of the semester. Students who immersed themselves in this writing project later learned that the paper represented only a fraction of their course grade, an imbalance that was neither written nor discussed in class. In addition, the reason/purpose for this task was unclear: What was the teacher "testing"? Finally, there were no evaluation criteria, nor was there guidance about the rhetorical specifications. And, if these aspects of the assignment were given to the students orally, the ESL students in the class did not comprehend them.

Flawed Language

Many writing prompts contain problems for students because their language is idiomatic and/or culturally vague. That makes them especially challenging for ESL students. For example, in one economics class, the assignment stated: "The paper should be chosen in consultation with the instructor with a rough outline submitted by the 10th week of the course." ESL students misunderstood this sentence, thinking they should conference with the instructor only after they had written an outline and during the 10th week of class. Thus, they missed the early opportunity to discuss their topic with the instructor, alienated that instructor by not coming in for the early conference, and arrived at the conference in the 10th week of class with an outline (and, clearly, a chosen topic) in hand.

In the writing assignment below, the boldfaced words and phrases presented comprehension problems for ESL writers as well as NESs.

1. Second-Year Adult Education Course.   This assignment was given during the first week of class, before students had learned about the instructor's expectations or about the content of the course. It was an ongoing assignment, to be worked on throughout the course and handed in at the end of the semester.

> Every member of the class identifies something that he or she wants to learn about this semester. The assignment involves (1) writing up a plan by which you will learn this new thing, and (2) keeping a diary as you go about the process of learning. (The diary should include insights you get about the **nature of learning** in general as well as specific thoughts regarding your own learning.) Write a descriptive statement (**of whatever length**) that summarizes how you believe you learn best when you have something you want to learn about.

Analysis.   Although most of the students in this class were education majors, both NES and ESL students had trouble defining the "nature of learning," and they could not determine what length the final statement should be. However, initially, no student asked the instructor about the specifics of the assignment. As the semester progressed, and the sense of classroom community grew, students asked questions about the assignment and negotiated the specifics.

In a writing-across-the-curriculum survey of important criteria for course success (Leki & Carson, 1994), 91% of the ESL students rated "figuring out the assignment" 6th out of 25. Because effective writing assignments must be accessible to all the students in college/university courses, and because those students are becoming increasingly ethnically diverse, it is imperative that teacher-designers focus on precision in the language of writing assignments. For ESL students, the problem is more severe; they need more clarity of language, more background information, and more specified teacher expectations (Raimes, 1985; Reid, 1993; Silva, 1993).

ASSESSING NEWLY DESIGNED PROMPTS

Topics for large-scale writing tests are often widely pretested and evaluated one or more times to assure their viability as testing measurements (Conlon, 1980; Conlon & Fowles, 1987; Kroll, 1990; Stansfield, 1986). This rigorous process can be duplicated in a variety of ways on a smaller scale to assess the clarity, accessibility, and potential effectiveness of newly designed classroom prompts. Most formally, the teacher can collect writing samples on the new prompt from a population of students who are similar to the intended student-writers. For example, instructors at one campus can pretest a prompt from another campus as an in-class writing assignment. The instructor might ask students to respond to the prompt and then evaluate the prompt with those students: Did you understand the language of the direction and/or the prompt? Was it interesting? Difficult? Were you able to begin writing immediately? Were you able to finish? What would you do differently if you had more time? The purpose of such an exercise for the pretest class might be

(a) to increase students' knowledge of responding to prompts, (b) to evaluate student in-class writing skills, and/or (c) to teach students to evaluate prompts in light of specific academic purposes and audiences. Following this discussion, the instructor can pass along copies of the student essays and comments to the prompt designer on the other campus.

Specific guidelines for assessing a prompt's effectiveness in individual classroom assignments, for NES and ESL writers, include attention both to the prompt and to the written responses. Prompts that work well are likely to yield affirmative responses to the following questions:

- Did the prompt discriminate well among the "pretest population"?
- Were the products easy to read? Easy to evaluate?
- Were students able to write to their potential?

On the other hand, the following questions suggest ways to focus the analysis when it appears that there is some problem with the initial responses to the prompt:

- Is the context of the prompt
  - irrelevant to the course and/or to the students?
  - unreasonable, considering the students' capabilities and learning objectives?
- Is the content
  - too broad to be accomplished within the assignment parameters?
  - outside the expertise, experience, or research ability of the student-writers?
- Is the language of the instructions or the prompt
  - too simple or too complex?
  - culturally biased?
  - too abstract or philosophical?
  - unacademic or otherwise inappropriate?
- Are the responses
  - trite?
  - highly emotional?
  - similar?
  - misleading or confusing?

It is also possible to "pretest" a newly designed prompt intended for classroom use in less formal ways. Teacher-designers might ask their current classes to read, discuss, and evaluate the prompt, to begin to write the prompt as an in-class assignment (either individually or collaboratively), and then to discuss the strength and weakness of the prompt. Or the teacher might ask a colleague to write the assignment and then discuss the expectations about the prompt in light of the colleague's response. Or, most easily and perhaps more efficiently, teacher-designers might write a response themselves and then analyze the response:

- Did I accomplish what I expected my students to do?
- What problems did I encounter?

- What can I predict will be difficult for my students?
- Will I be able to fairly evaluate a set of class essays on this topic?

CONCLUSION

This article uses the many stages in the process employed by writing test developers to select prompts for administration to large numbers of students as a backdrop for discussion of general and specific guidelines for developing and evaluating writing assignments (prompts) in individual courses. In a large-scale examination, there is little or no room for negotiation of the content, wording, or format of the prompt. Therefore, test developers must closely control all six of the critical variables we have identified (contextual variables, content variables, linguistic variables, task variables, rhetorical variables, and evaluation variables). Although classroom teachers have more room for negotiation of the prompt with their students, to be fair to their students and to provide them opportunities to both learn from their writing experiences and demonstrate knowledge and understanding of material, teachers should be no less rigorous in their preparation of course writing assignments.

School-assigned writing is performance-based testing. Teacher-readers who are honest in viewing the intentions of their classroom-based writing assignments understand that, in broad terms, they assign writing for the underlying **purpose** of testing the student at one or more levels. If most formal school writing is a form of testing, then the assignments for such writing should be as carefully designed as any test. And given the "mainstream" approach to college/university teaching in the U.S. (i.e., having NES and ESL students in the same classes), particular attention to prompt design is essential for success of ESL (and other ethnically diverse) students (Clarke, 1994). Given the importance that writing tasks can have for the student-writers, the casual assigning of an essay within the framework of a course may therefore be as irresponsible as thoughtlessly pulling a math or science multiple-choice test from someone else's file and hoping that it "works."

Presumably, teachers in composition classes help to train their students to go through a number of stages to complete the writing assignments they receive (e.g., oral discussion, library research, thinking, reading, outlining, drafting, collaborating, revising, and editing), and teachers across the curriculum expect their students to be "fluent" in those steps and processes that will serve them best in completing writing assignments for their courses. Yet, unless all writing assignments are carefully designed, both NES and ESL writers face frustration and wasted effort as they prepare those assignments, and teacher-evaluators may encounter disappointing results. In short, "wherever writing is integral to instruction, both teaching and learning across the subject areas stand to benefit from the careful design of writing assignments" (Brand, 1992, p. 156).

NOTES

1. We have underlined key words and phrases that we use in our analysis of writing prompts later in this article.

2. In the following example, from the third-year agriculture course hour-long examination, students are cued (in boldface) to organize and present their material and ideas; the cuing words provide organizing principles for student-writers and suggest a sequence of tasks that will result in the expected product.

> As a manager of a cattle operation, you have found Brucellosis in your herd. **Explain** the means of eradicating this disease and **describe** the ways of preventing its recurrence. **Explain how** each of these is effective.

3. Note that the teacher assessment of in-class test writing differs somewhat from evaluation of assignments that are prepared outside of class; in general, grading criteria are based more on the demonstration of assignment content and less on rhetorical specifications (Popken, 1989).

REFERENCES

Allaei, S.K., & Connor, U.M. (1990). Exploring the dynamics of cross-cultural collaboration in writing classrooms. *The Writing Instructor, 10,* 19–28.

Anson, C. (Ed.). (1989). *Writing and response: Theory, practice and research.* Urbana, IL: NCTE.

Basham, C., & Kwachka, P. (1991). Reading the world differently: A cross-cultural approach to writing assessment. In L. Hamp-Lyons (Ed.), *Assessing second language writing in academic contexts* (pp. 37–49). Norwood, NJ: Ablex.

Belanoff, P. (1991). The myth of assessment. *Journal of Basic Writing, 10,* 54–66.

Bereiter, C., & Scardamalia, M. (1984). Knowledge telling and knowledge transforming in written composition. In S. Rosenberg (Ed.), *Advances in applied linguistics* (pp. 142–175). New York: Cambridge University Press.

Bereiter, C., & Scardamalia, M. (1987). *The psychology of written composition.* Hillsdale, NJ: Lawrence Erlbaum Associates.

Brand, A.G. (1992). Drafting essay assignments: What the disciplines can learn from direct writing assessment. *Issues in Writing, 4,* 156–174.

Canale, M., & Swain, M. (1980). Theoretical bases of communicative approaches to second language teaching and testing. *Applied Linguistics, 1,* 1–47.

Carlson, S. (1988). Cultural differences in writing and reading skills. In A. Purves (Ed.), *Writing across language and cultures: Issues in contrastive rhetoric* (pp. 227–260). Newbury Park, CA: Sage.

Carrell, P.L. (1983). Background knowledge in second language comprehension. *Language Learning and Communication, 2,* 25–34.

Clarke, M.A. (1994). "Mainstreaming" ESL students: Disturbing changes. *College ESL, 4,* 1–19.

Clayton, T. (1993). Using background knowledge to stimulate composition in Malay students. In M.N. Brock & L. Walters (Eds.), *Teaching composition around the Pacific Rim: Politics and pedagogy* (pp. 48–60). Bristol, England: Multilingual Matters.

Conlon, T. (1980). *Suggestions for writing essay questions.* Princeton, NJ: Educational Testing Service.

Conlon, T., & Fowles, M. (1987). *Guidelines for developing and scoring free-response tests.* Princeton, NJ: Educational Testing Service.

Cox, G.H. (1988). Designing essay assignments. In F.V. Bogel & K.K. Gottschalk (Eds.), *Teaching prose: A guide for writing instructors* (pp. 87–113). New York: Norton.

Davis, B.G., Scriven, M., & Thomas, S. (1987). *The evaluation of composition instruction* (2nd ed.). New York: Teachers College Press.

Elbow, P. (1993). Ranking, evaluating, and liking: Sorting out three forms of judgment. *College English, 55,* 187–206.

Ferris, D. (1994). Rhetorical strategies in student persuasive writing: Differences between native and non-native speakers. *Research in the Teaching of English, 28,* 45–65.

Freedman, S., & Sperling, M. (1985). Teacher-student interaction in the writing conference: Response and teaching. In S. Freedman (Ed.), *The acquisition of written language: Revision and response* (pp. 106–130). Norwood, NJ: Ablex.

Frey, O., & Ross, M.E. (1991). Writing is more than words. In K.H. Adams & J.L. Adams (Eds.), *Teaching advanced composition: Why and how* (pp. 267–282). Portsmouth, NH: Boynton-Cook Heinemann.

Greenberg, K. (1981). *The effects of variations in essays questions on the writing performance of CUNY freshman.* New York: New York Instructional Center.

Hamp-Lyons, L. (1991a). Issues and directions in assessing second language writing in academic contexts. In L. Hamp-Lyons (Ed.), *Assessing second language writing in academic contexts* (pp. 323–337). Norwood, NJ: Ablex.

Hamp-Lyons, L. (1991b). The writer's knowledge and our knowledge of the writer. In L. Hamp-Lyons (Ed.), *Assessing second language writing in academic contexts* (pp. 51–68). Norwood, NJ: Ablex.

Hamp-Lyons, L. (1994). Interweaving assessment and instruction in college ESL. *College ESL, 4,* 43–55.

Hamp-Lyons, L., & Mathias, S.P. (1994). Examining expert judgments of task difficulty on essay tests. *Journal of Second Language Writing, 3,* 49–68.

Horowitz, D. (1991). ESL writing assessments: Contradictions and resolutions. In L. Hamp-Lyons (Ed.), *Assessing second language writing in academic contexts* (pp. 71–85). Norwood, NJ: Ablex.

Huot, B. (1990). Reliability, validity, and holistic scoring: What we know and what we need to know. *College Composition and Communication, 41,* 201–213.

Johnson, H. (1992). Fossilizing. *ELT Journal, 46,* 180–189.

Kroll, B. (1990). Understanding TOEFL's Test of Written English. *RELC Journal, 22,* 20–33.

Kroll, B., & Reid, J. (1994). Guidelines for designing writing prompts: Clarifications, caveats, and cautions. *Journal of Second Language Writing, 3,* 231–255.

Larson, R.L. (1986). Making assignments, judging writing, and annotating papers: Some suggestions. In C.W. Bridges (Ed.), *Training the new teacher of college composition* (pp. 109–116). Urbana, IL: NCTE.

Leki, I., & Carson, J. (1994). Students' perceptions of EAP writing instruction and writing needs across the disciplines. *TESOL Quarterly, 28,* 81–101.

McKay, S. (1989). Topic development and written discourse accent. In D. Johnson & D. Roen (Eds.), *Richness in writing: Empowering ESL students* (pp. 253–262). New York: Longman.

Mendelsohn, D., & Cumming, A. (1987). Professors' ratings of language use and rhetorical organization in ESL composition. *TESL Canada Journal, 5,* 9–26.

Moxley, J. (1989). Responding to student writing: Goals, methods, alternatives. *Freshman English News, 17,* 3–11.

Moxley, J. (1992). Teacher's goals and methods of responding to student writing. *Composition Studies/Freshman English News, 20,* 17–33.

Newell, G., & MacAdam, P. (1987). Examining the source of writing problems: An instrument for measuring topic specific knowledge. *Written Communication, 9,* 156–174.

Paulson, D. (1992). *Assessment of FL learners' writing ability: Formulation of tasks and evaluation.* (ERIC Reproduction Service No. ED 342 249)

Popken, R. (1989). Essay exams and papers: A contextual comparision. *Journal of Teaching Writing, 8,* 51–65.

Radecki, P.M., & Swales, J. (1988). ESL student reaction to written comments on their written work. *System, 16,* 366–365.

Raimes, A. (1985). What unskilled ESL students do as they write: A classroom study of composing. *TESOL Quarterly, 19,* 229–258.

Redd-Boyd, T., & Slater, W.M. (1989). The effects of audience specification on undergraduates' attitudes, strategies and writing. *Research in the Teaching of English, 23,* 77–108.

Reid, J. (1993). *Teaching ESL writing.* Englewood Cliffs, NJ: Regents-Prentice Hall.

Silva, T. (1993). Toward an understanding of the distinct nature of L2 writing: The ESL research and its implications. *TESOL Quarterly, 27,* 657–677.

Smith, W.L., Hull, G.A., Land, R.E.J., Moore, M.T., Ball, C., Dunham, D.E., Hickley, L.S., & Ruzich, C.W. (1985). Some effects of varying the structure of a topic on college students' writing. *Written Communication, 2,* 73–89.

Stansfield, C. (1986). A history of the Test of Written English: The developmental year. *Language Testing, 3,* 224–234.

Steinberg, E.R. (1980). A garden of opportunities and a thicket of dangers. In L.W. Gregg & E.R. Steinberg (Eds.), *Cognitive processes in writing* (pp. 156–168). Hillsdale, NJ: Erlbaum.

Sudlow, M. (1991). *The test of a topic: Satisfying three audiences – Writers, readers, and score users.* Paper presented at the annual meeting of the National Council on Measurement in Education, Chicago.

Sweedler-Brown, C.O. (1993). The effects of ESL errors on holistic scores assigned by English composition faculty. *College ESL, 3,* 53–67.

Thorne, S. (1993). Prewriting: A basic skill for basic writers. *Teaching English in the Two-Year College, 20,* 31–36.

Walvoord, B.E. (1986). *Helping students write well: A guide for teachers in all disciplines* (2nd ed.). New York: Modern Language Association.

Walvoord, B.E., & McCarthy, L.P. (1991). *Thinking and writing in college: A naturalistic study of students in four disciplines.* Urbana, IL: NCTE.

White, E.M. (1992). *Assigning, responding, evaluating* (2nd ed.). New York: St. Martin's Press.

White, E.M. (1994). *Teaching and assessing writing* (2nd ed., rev. ed.). San Francisco: Jossey-Bass.

APPENDIX A

Textual Features Evaluation Criteria

Assignment-Based Criteria
    fulfills the goals stated for the assignment   _____
    looks like the assigned writing (summary? research?
      report?)   _____
Content-Based Criteria
    substantive   _____
    shows understanding of key concepts   _____
    includes original insights and synthesis   _____
Presentation/Organization-Based Criteria
    paper follows through on what the introduction sets out   _____
    paper is sequenced in a clearly discernible and
      appropriate way   _____
    parts of the paper are well-connected to each other
      (coherence)   _____
    source materials are cited appropriately and integrated
      with the text   _____
Language-Based Criteria
    grammar and usage   _____
    sentence structure and variety   _____
    vocabulary   _____

Evaluation Cover Sheet for
Advanced Composition Course

Essay Title: _____

	Strengths	Problem Area
Purpose and audience		
Focus		
Development		
Organization		
Grammar/Sentence Structure		

  Suggestions for revision:

  Writer's plans for revision:

APPENDIX B

Problem-Solving Evaluation Criteria for
Undergraduate Critical Reading and Writing Class

	Points	Earned (+ comments)
Problem: Show that a problem exists and needs attention. This may involve identifying the causes for and the effects of the problem. Be specific. Include details, examples, and facts.	20	
Solution: Propose solution(s) for the problem. This is your chance to convince your audience that you know what will solve or reduce the problem. Justify your solution(s) with reason and evidence. Remember to give details, facts, and examples.	30	
Key Elements: Use at least one of the following where appropriate: • Evaluate alternative solutions • Show that your solution meets certain criteria: feasibility, cost, effectiveness, legality • Answer possible objections • Suggest implementation or call for action	25	

Overall Effectiveness:

	Points	
• Creativity, style, and audience-voice agreement	10	
• Organization. Essay should be four pages, including an introduction and a conclusion	5	
• Mechanics: correct grammar, spelling, and punctuation	5	
• Pre-writing: include a rough draft with comments from the drafting workshop	5	
Total	100	**Final Score** _____

15 Opening Our Doors: Applying Socioliterate Approaches (SA) to Language Minority Classrooms

ANN M. JOHNS

Throughout *Generation 1.5 Meets College Composition* (Harklau, Losey, & Siegal, 1999), contributors have spoken of the special characteristics and needs of language minority students in English-medium colleges and universities. Caught among different worlds, these students require pedagogies that will assist them in sorting out their languages and cultures and in approaching new, and often foreign, literacy demands with strategies for success. In my view, it is the responsibility of composition instructors to help these students acquire a literacy strategy repertoire and develop the confidence that enables them to approach and negotiate a variety of literacy tasks in many environments. However, it appears that many composition instructors do not view these goals as their responsibility. Instead, they turn their classes inward, toward the students themselves and away from the literacy lives that have constructed, or will construct, them.

Expressivist and personal identity approaches to teaching, perhaps the most inward-looking, still predominate in many classrooms.[1] In these approaches, the focus is almost exclusively on developing individual voice and identity, personal interests, and personal meaning making, generally through a limited number of pedagogical and literacy genres, such as the personal essay or works of literature. The expressivist experience is undoubtedly a pleasure for some students[2] because much of what they write is considered successful and interesting by their composition teachers. However, their very success and pleasure can present problems later, as Leki (1995) pointed out:

> if writing successes come too easily, they may be insufficiently challenging to serve the purpose of giving students writing experiences they can later refer back to in attempting to address tasks across the curriculum. Although the [composition] class should no doubt be a psychologically nurturing place, surely being a safe refuge is not enough. (p. 256)

From *Generation 1.5 Meets College Composition: Issues in the Teaching of Writing to U.S.-Educated Learners of ESL*. Ed. Linda Harklau, Kay M. Losey, and Meryl Siegal. Mahwah, NJ: Erlbaum, 1999: 119–42.

In other parts of the world, such as among Australian genre theorists and literacy teachers, expressivist and personal identity approaches are viewed as damaging to the language minority student. Martin (1985), one of the major Australian theorists, contended that many types of identity-based, student-centered classrooms do not assist the culturally and linguistically diverse students to understand literacy practices in the world around them. Thus, these classrooms "[promote] a situation in which only the brightest, middle-class monolingual students will benefit" (Martin, 1985, p. 61). Christie (1993) spoke of these approaches as "cruelly unfair" to language minority students (p. 100) because they are not encouraged to examine the unfamiliar social and rhetorical contexts in which they will be attempting to succeed while working within their second or third languages and cultures.

What I advocate is something quite different from personal identity and expressivist approaches, resembling, but not duplicating, Australian curricula. I call it a socioliterate approach (SA).[3] SA is based on the contention that texts are social; important written and spoken discourses are situated within specific contexts and produced and read by individuals whose values reflect those of the communities to which they belong. The principal focus in an SA is not on the individual and his or her identity or meaning making as separate from culture, language, and context, but on understanding how all of us are shaped by the social nature of language and texts. Certainly students understand, at some level, texts' social nature, and the purposes of SA classes are to bring this understanding to the forefront and to encourage student flexibility and creativity in negotiating and processing texts in new social settings.

How might an SA classroom be organized? First of all, the teacher provides leadership, because the teacher has both expertise and years to his or her advantage. The teacher sets goals for students, makes a variety of assignments that encourage an understanding of the social construction of texts, and promotes text analysis and peer review in light of the social forces that surround the particular discourses at issue. Students read and write texts in more than one genre,[4] preferably a variety of texts from genres that are familiar and unfamiliar. Throughout the class, students are encouraged to bring texts from their first languages and cultures and to discuss the nature and purposes of these texts in light of the social environments in which they have been produced.

What kinds of texts do language minority students bring to class? Some bring flyers in English and their home languages that they find at the grocery store, the laundromat, or in their siblings' schools. These flyers are then analyzed for their purposes (e.g., to inform, invite, make a claim, promote a candidate), for their uses of language, for their layout, and for how the visual presentation is organized to meet the writer's purposes. Using flyers, students can discuss reader and writer's roles and values, context, and the effect that particular texts from the genre have on them and their families within their own communities. Other students bring their favorite magazines, such as *Low Rider*, which include a number of accessible texts for analysis: letters to the editor, editorials, feature articles, and advice columns. These common magazine genres are then compared with comparable texts in magazines directed to other populations. In some classes, students draw from their previous literacy experiences by bringing texts that have influenced their literacy lives.[5] They bring papers they have written for classes in high school, or books they read as children. All of these texts are viewed as social, influencing the students' literacy theories and approaches to reading and writing.

Instructors can also bring examples of their own writing to demonstrate the importance of social factors in the construction of texts. Huckin (1997), for example, used a letter he wrote to a state legislator, and this elected official's standard and inappropriate response, as texts for analysis of roles, language and the uses of power, and purposes and contexts for writing. Throughout his classroom analysis, Huckin spoke of the ways in which style, format, and text organization are employed by both reader and writer in attempting to achieve their ends.

After students have examined familiar or teacher texts, they can work on a variety of reading and writing tasks to expand their genre repertoires. If the class consists of undergraduates who will be processing pedagogical genres, students can study and write various types of summaries and abstracts.[6] They can also write short timed essays to very specific prompts, much like those required in discipline-specific classes[7] (Horowitz, 1986). Students can bring readings or papers from other classes to compare them for a number of features. In addition to using the standard pedagogical genres, instructors can ask students to write a memo to a faculty member discussing why they want to drop a class or were late turning in an assignment. Students can write letters to the editor of the college newspaper and be awarded a high grade if their letters are published. It is important to note that in a socioliterate class, students often analyze a number of texts from the target genre before beginning their writing processes. This analysis, of both text-external and text-internal features, assists students in understanding that no text is autonomous and that the various textual elements are influenced by social and personal factors.

Throughout the class, students are asked to draft and redraft their papers, peer reviewing each other's work in light of social and linguistic factors. Students also pay close attention to their strategies for literacy practices: for deconstructing prompts, for approaching timed and process writing of various types, for understanding roles and purposes as readers and writers, and other factors.

Reflection is essential to student internalization of the social and personal factors influencing text processing for a particular genre. In my classes, for example, students have to take timed tests as the final examination. Before the final, they are administered practice exams that somewhat approximate the real test. Because timed tests are central to their academic progress, I encourage students to reflect critically on their strategies for writing under pressure and other factors influencing their success. Here, for example, is a comment by a Chinese American student about her reaction to and planning for the prompt on a timed practice examination:

> The practice exam has a good topic. However it seems that people need
> to take some time to really understand what the question is. I took about

ten minutes to understand the question and spent another ten minutes to think my essay contents. Even though the topic was great, I misunderstood the question. I wrote another thing which seems not the main point of the question.

A Vietnamese American student compared the two practice examinations that she was administered, discussing how the topic of an examination prompt influences her writing success:

> I have took two practice exams, and both of them left me two different impressions. First at the early exam, the question came out with a description and explain a favorite person. I was totally not interested because I did not have any favorite friend. Conversely, the second one was more interesting which was mentioned about living in several places. It was related closely to a real life so it made me more easier to write and demonstrate my writing skill.

Another student, from the large, local Chaldean community, was annoyed by what he saw as the superficial nature of the topic in the practice examination, and his written response was unsuccessful because of this annoyance:

> I was surprised by the question. I thought that they would bring something more sophisticated and more complex. The subject was too wide and big to write about in the first place. [Because of this] I got confused about how much should I write about, and what exactly to focus on.

In addition to examining their strategies for approaching particular genres and comparing topics for assigned writings, students are asked to reflect on organization, language, values, and other social features of the texts they read and write. Students are also asked to compare texts within a genre for a number of features, so that they could understand that texts within a genre can—and often do—vary considerably depending on a number of factors such as context, content, and reader and writer roles (see, e.g., Johns, 1997, pp. 20–37).

The purposes of an SA are for students to free themselves of their sometimes limited theories of pedagogical and other genres, to analyze and value the genres from their first cultures, to approach all texts as socially constructed, and to reflect on their experiences with text processing.

Some Goals for a Socioliterate Classroom

What are the specific goals of a socioliterate classroom, and how can they be realized? Below, I outline and discuss these goals in some detail.[8]

Goal 1: Draw from Student Knowledge of Genres and Apply That Knowledge to Analysis and Critique of Known and New Texts

Our language minority students already know a great deal about socially constructed discourses, and, as the contributors to Murray's volume entitled *Diversity as Resource: Redefining Cultural Literacy* (1992) pointed out, the students themselves are valuable resources in teaching and learning. A central element of socioliterate classrooms is student discussion of familiar texts from their languages and cultures. Through this discussion, students recognize the conflicts and convergences among some first culture texts – and with those in the majority academic culture. What they know about the social construction of texts can, and should, provide topics for discussion and student research.

Goal 2: Perpetually Revise Theories of Genre

One possible liability of an SA is that students will (again) attempt to discover a simple text template for certain common genres. This is a major problem for more traditionally taught students who may believe that every paper should look like a five-paragraph essay.[9] In our classes, we need to expose students to more than one text from a genre, therefore demonstrating that texts with the same name, and thus within the same genre category (e.g., "essay," "research paper," "lab report") tend to differ in various ways – because the situations in which the texts are produced are considerably different.[10] In a useful discussion of this important feature, Berkenkotter and Huckin (1995) spoke of "centripetal forces" that contribute to text conventions within a genre that are carried across situations – and "the centrifugal forces" that force changes in content, reader and writer roles, use of language, or other features. One example of these influences can be found in a pedagogical genre called *the summary*. Although we know that a summary is a shorter version of the original, and that in many cases, the summarizer is encouraged to combine sentences and ideas in the final product, the other conventions of summarizing depend on the particular rhetorical situation in which the literacy event is taking place. When interviewing a faculty member from philosophy, for example, I discovered that there are specific ways to summarize texts from his disciplinary canon. Because of this, he devotes considerable time in his first-year classes to modeling the construction of summaries and he requires summarizing on every examination. His summaries are considerably different from those assigned by a history professor with whom I work. She is most interested in a single sentence summary of the argument, followed by analysis or critique.

Goal 3: Assess, Expand on, and Revise Strategies for Approaching Literacy Tasks

No doubt many composition instructors devote considerable time to discussion of varying strategies for reading and writing. It is important to ask questions in which students distinguish among strategies, such as "What strategies did you use to approach this assignment? How were these strategies different from – or the same as – strategies that you attempted for our previous assignment?" In this way, students begin to understand what the research on good writing tells us: Individual processing of texts is complex and strategies may differ considerably from task to task. From this discussion of strategies, teachers can point out that there is no one "writing process"; instead, there are a myriad of processes depending on the importance of the text to the writer, his or her purposes and roles, the audience, the task, the topic and the context (see, e.g., Prior, 1995). If we provide our students with assignments that vary in terms of task complexity and constraints, context, roles, purposes, genre and other features, they will have an opportunity to reflect on the differences in their strategies—and on what does and does not work when approaching different types of literacy tasks.

Goal 4: Develop Abilities to Research Texts, Tasks, Roles, and Contexts

If language minority students are to be successful in the many, unpredictable, and foreign environments in which they will be attempting to read and write texts, they must become researchers, constantly asking good questions of texts, tasks, and themselves. The last question most discipline-specific faculty want to hear from a student about an assignment is "What do you want?" However, there are many other ways to approach what faculty have assigned that are productive for students. Students can ask to look at a paper written by a successful student in the past; they can bring their drafts of a paper to the professor in order to elicit his or her comments; they can ask how the professor might approach the assignment. And they can also negotiate assignments to fit their needs and interests (see, e.g., Leki, 1995). A number of writing problems faced by language minority students are related to independent reading of assigned texts,[11] as some of the contributors to the Carson and Leki (1993) volume entitled *Reading in the Composition Classroom* pointed out. There are a number of identified reading strategies, of course, outlined in texts for teachers (see, e.g., Davies, 1995; Feathers, 1993; Grellet, 1981). These can and should be discussed and practiced in our classrooms. And, as researchers of disciplinary practices, our students can pose questions to the faculty member who made a reading assignment: "How would you read this assignment?" "What kinds of notes do you take when you read?" or "What will we be asked to do with this reading?"

Goal 5: Cultivate a Metalanguage about Texts and Textual Experiences

One of the most challenging aspects of teaching language minority students is that although they may be completely bilingual and biliterate, they may not have the metalanguage necessary to discuss texts. Unless we share a language about their texts and can discuss the grammar and lexicon in some way, we operate at a distinct disadvantage. Thus, a class goal should be to encourage student development of a metalanguage in which they can discuss the language of their texts, by using handbooks or by developing, within the class, their own terms to discuss the language, structure, and social purposes of texts.

Using Socioliterate Practices in the Classroom

What happens when we attempt to use an SA? In this section I discuss a few assignments from a class in which I attempted to follow the goals just listed.

The class was a remedial or developmental course for students who had not passed the lower division writing competency examination at the university. The 25 students, all language minority, had been educated in U.S. high schools and, in most cases, community colleges. They had been in the United States for a minimum of 4 years although most had been in the country much longer. About 15 spoke Vietnamese, but others spoke Spanish, Arabic, or Southeast Asian. The students had a variety of majors, with a preponderance in technology and business. Marketing, engineering, computer science, and nursing were the most popular. Not surprisingly, none had chosen a major in the social sciences or humanities. Thus, the content of many of the typical English as a second language (ESL) or composition texts was unfamiliar—and sometimes not very interesting—to them.

Administratively, these remedial classes are organized in the following manner: The instructor is free to use any textbook or approach available until the last 2 weeks of class, at which time, the students purchase a required pamphlet of readings on a single topic, such as overpopulation. The information from that pamphlet provides the basis for the timed essay examination administered during the final examination week. Students pass the class if they complete the classwork and pass the holistically scored final examination with a composite of eight or more (two scorers, each using a 1 to 6 rubric much like those employed by the Educational Testing Service). If the students' instructors believe that a student has not been appropriately graded by the finals scorers, they may appeal the final examination score using texts written during the semester.

In a class such as this, which seems to be typical of many remedial classes throughout the country, the instructor and the students are in a bind: The students are anxious to pass the final examination so that they can proceed with their academic work,[12] yet the teacher knows that the composition class may provide one of the students' few formal experiences with writing instruction. How can we assist these language minority students to acquire some of the tools that they need to approach any writing task, yet provide sufficient practice in the timed composition class essay to insure that students pass the final examination?

After I discussed my research on problems students from science and technology disciplines face when confronting final examinations developed by English teachers (Johns, 1991), the class and I decided to treat their entire experience as a laboratory for the study of the social construction of texts and the ways in which individuals might process or evaluate them. Like all texts, the final examination essay is socially constructed: There are teacher/grader and student roles, one of which predominates; there are certain types of prompts, most of which are quite open-ended (see the students' comments on the practice essay); and there is a preference among graders, whatever they might claim, for a five-paragraph essay form. Because of the pressures on the students to pass the final, the class and I studied features of the final graded writing, emphasizing the particular values of the audiences who would be grading the texts,[13] the constraints of the context, and the possible topics. We also talked about their writing: the ways in which to make arguments, writing strategies, and other factors that influence success. And we practiced timed writing with typical prompts — frequently.

However, my principal mission was to prepare students for writing for a number of occasions beyond the final, particularly for analyzing writing situations that they might confront in the university and in their professional lives. In addition to buying a grammar reference textbook, the students were asked to subscribe to *Newsweek*[14] because it provided a number of current topics and a variety of genres to study and emulate.[15] Students used the magazine readings to construct texts of a variety of types for a number of audiences. They also drew from *Newsweek* sources as data for their argumentation, a very important skill in academic writing (see Carson, Chase, Gibson, & Hargrove, 1992). At one point, the students decided to write a letter to the *Newsweek* editor because they were displeased with the particular construction of Asian culture within one of the articles. After this decision was made, we spent considerable time studying various letters to the editors for their organization, argumentation, and use of language. Students reflected on the nature of these letters with each other and in writing. Then, we talked at some length about audience: how they might write a letter that would appeal to both the general audience of the magazine and the editors who made publishing decisions. It became very clear to the class that their letters to the editor might take a position that was unusual or adversarial. Thus, they would have to assume very different roles from those they were required to take, as students, in the final examination. The letter to the editor was one of their favorite assignments. When I asked the students at the end of the semester to discuss the assignments that they liked the best, a Vietnamese American responded in this way:

> One of the assignments I like the best is to write a letter to the editors of *Newsweek* magazine. That was the first time I've ever wrote to magazine editors. If felt so interested. . . . By writing to them, I can judge the information from the article as well as telling my opinion about it.

Sometimes, the students experimented with roles and purposes of writers that were very different from those in their own lives. When the Hale-Bopp suicides occurred near us in San Diego and the articles about this event appeared in *Newsweek*, I gave students the opportunity to imagine that they were one of the cult members and explain to their parents why they had joined. This was an interesting assignment for the students, for most would never consider joining this cult. In fact, like many language minority students, they were very close to their parents and felt that they should do nothing that might offend them or lose their face in the community. Nonetheless, when asked about his favorite assignment, a Vietnamese American student said the following:

> My favorite was writing to explain to my parents why I joined the cult. I had fun in writing this informal letter because I had to play a role of a person who believe in their causes and purposes. On the other hand, I was not at all interested in joining because I think that the people were making a desperate attempt to belong to something. I had to put aside my beliefs in order to write and to read the [*Newsweek*] article for important beliefs and pretend to believe in them.

However, the absolute class favorite and best-written assignment during the semester was a serendipitous one. The new president of the university was planning to visit our department, Rhetoric and Writing Studies, and the students and I viewed this occasion as an opportunity for writing something that might have a direct impact on their lives. Thus, we decided together on a memo. The students began by researching the new president's public speeches and comments, principally because they wanted to understand his values and interests so that they could make the best impression. I provided information about the conversations he was having with various stakeholders in the college community in which I was taking part. Throughout, the student interest in understanding the president as audience, and what he knew and valued, remained high.

In addition to exploring the issue of audience, the students felt that it was important to examine their roles and purposes as writers, particularly how their memos could have the most impact. We talked about the fact that when writing the president, it is very important that they make themselves understood. As a result, this was the best paper for most of the students in the class, although they had very little time to revise.[16]

After considerable discussion of their audience and writer roles, purposes, and responsibilities, the students began to consider how the memo should be structured. Although they knew the basic conventions of the memo form, they were concerned with what topics they might include and in what order. Together, we negotiated this move structure: first, to introduce themselves and talk briefly about their backgrounds, because the president is very interested in maintaining diversity on the campus.[17] Second, the students would write about their personal goals, and, third, they would make some suggestions for improvements to the campus. The students agreed that the final, short paragraph should say something positive so that the president would finish reading the memo "with a good feeling."

In the paragraph on "improvements," many of the students discussed the examinations, suggesting that they not be tested in formal, timed situations, and arguing that they were much better writers when they had real audiences and purposes and time to plan their texts.[18] Here is a text portion from a Vietnamese American student:

> My name is . . . and I am a junior at SDSU after I transfer from El Camino College in Los Angeles. My major is pre-nursing and I am a

bilingual student who just came here for about five years. I am attending in SDSU because I want to complete my education in order to have a better job to take care of my family. Right now, I am a full-time students and a full-time worker which is very stressful time for me.

Dr. Johns asked us to tell you what we think SDSU's future goals should be. Here are my suggestions:

- Making[19] a lower-division writing competency test more fairly by giving students more time. We cannot write a complete formal essay in a short time.

- Let students take major courses before passing the test. By doing that way, the students do not feel bored and have more opportunity to move up.

- SDSU should have a writing center so students can come up when they need help.

Thank you for taking your time to read this memo. I hope that SDSU will be much better in the next 10 years.

But other students had different agendas. Here is the text of a memo from a Spanish speaker in the class:

I would like to introduce myself, I am an ESL student, Spanish being my first language. This is my second semester in SDSU, at this moment I am a junior Electrical Engineering student. I transferred from Southwestern College which is located in Chula Vista. I decided to come to SDSU because it is close to my home, it is affordable, and it has a good reputation.

The reason of seeking a higher education is because I want to be of help to my community. I want to have my own business in the community and to develop electronic equipment.

SDSU can make my goal and the goal of all engineering students easier by improving the engineering facilities. The major problem at this time is the computer lab in the engineering building.[20] It has computers that are very old and slow. They are of GGMKZ, also the computers are in terrible shape. If you just go and use them for five minutes, you will find out what I really mean.

Other than this little problem, SDSU is a great university.

These memos were given to the president when he visited our department. A few weeks later, he wrote a memo to my class, thanking them for their comments. A second memo was to me, asking for a two-page position paper on the testing requirements at SDSU and discussing whether our testing discourages language minority students from applying.

CONCLUSION

No doubt the composition of many classes for language minority students is similar to the one described here: The students are Americans and they have been educated in the public school and college system.[21] Yet they are considered remedial in that the students have not mastered the grammar of standard academic English. The curriculum for these classes is fairly open, but the final examination is a timed composition class essay.

What I argued here is that these language minority students need a class that takes an outward-looking, Socioliterate Approach. First, students need to be encouraged to discuss what they already know about the social construction of texts and the interactions of readers and writers. When they prepared the memo to the president, for example, they were very wise about his role and what would be most appealing to him. Second, students need to discuss at some length how many features of texts influence readers: language, careful editing, text layout, and other factors. Because I have attempted to learn several languages (Spanish, Swahili, Chinese, and Arabic) after passing the Critical Period, I am very sympathetic with the fact that our language minority students may never attain perfect grammar in their writing. And, in my view, that is all right. However, they need to know what kinds of texts should be error-free and work with a proficient monolingual English speaker to correct any minor errors they may have.

If we take the attitude that students may go elsewhere to have small errors corrected, then we can concentrate on other issues: reader and writer roles and purposes, the ways language can be used to achieve ends with particular readers, and contexts for reading and writing. On the other hand, if we become fixated on making our students discover their personal identities, or feel good, then other goals, much more important to their future lives, will be neglected. A socioliterate classroom attempts to focus first on the big picture: the context of the text to be processed and the social forces influencing it. However, it does not neglect the student as a social being, one who understands and processes texts within a variety of social contexts.

NOTES

1. Although expressivism was most popular in the 1960s, it appears to be making a comeback in various forms in composition classrooms. At a recent College Composition and Communication Conference, the number of papers devoted to writer identity, expressivism, and composition as therapy far outnumbered papers in which an epistemic voice was discussed (MacDonald, 1998).

2. Although it may be very difficult for others. In a useful article on personal voice, Ramanathan and Kaplan (1996) argued that "voice . . . [is] largely a culturally constrained notion, relatively inaccessible to students who are not full participants in the culture within which they are asked to write" (p. 22).

3. See Johns (1997) for a much more complete discussion.

4. *Genre* is defined in a number of ways. Here is my definition: "complex, evolving mental abstractions held by individuals within communities or larger cultures who share social and textual experiences" (Johns, 1997, p. 22).

5. See chap. 8 of Johns (1997).

6. Ratteray (1985) contended that there are at least six different types of academic summaries that vary in terms of organization and content.

7. I use the term *discipline specific* rather than content based for nonliteracy classes. Literacy classes should be, by their very nature, cross-disciplinary.

8. See Johns (1997) for a more thorough discussion of these goals and suggestions for pedagogical approaches to realize them.

9. Some of my students from high school and community college classes have been told just how many sentences should be in the introduction, what the topic sentences in each of the internal paragraphs should look like, how a conclusion should be formed, and so forth. They have

rigidly followed an essay template over and over in their composition classes, and they find it very difficult to break from it to produce papers in other genres.

10. In an interview with a finance instructor, my colleagues and I discovered that he referred to analyses of law cases as "essays." In my view, this is not helpful to students; however, naming of every pedagogical paper "an essay" is very common in discipline-specific classrooms.

11. Many first- and second-year students at colleges and universities have had few chances to do independent reading, especially of expository prose. In California and a number of other states, most of the high school reading is of literature and it is completed within the students' classes.

12. On campus, students are forbidden to take certain classes until they have met the lower division writing requirement.

13. Most, of course, are middle-aged, liberal, U.S.-born, monolingual women. The students have difficulty writing for this audience, particularly because the graders do not represent a discipline with which they can identify (see Johns, 1991).

14. The total cost for 10 weeks was $12, which was cheaper than most textbooks.

15. The students also studied the genres of their own preferred magazines, as noted earlier.

16. In two cases, I used this paper in the appeals process for those students who failed the final examination. And it was successful!

17. Currently, the San Diego State campus is 50% non-White. Of this group, about 35% of the students are language minority. However, because the campus is popular, its leadership has decided to raise its entrance requirements and phase out remedial classes, including ESL. These moves will undoubtedly have considerable impact on language minority students, who often need a bridging literacy class to assist them in succeeding in university classes.

18. As the results of this memo demonstrated.

19. This student was also taking a business writing class and he knew that important points in memos to busy people need to be highlighted in some way.

20. Although many students on campus have their own computers, some language minority students, who tend to come from lower income families, do not. If we are going to attract and keep these students, we need good computers on campus.

21. A very good publication discussing the complexity of the language minority student population in California, and their English skills, is *California Pathways: The Second Language Student in Public High Schools, Colleges and Universities*. Browning, Brinton, Ching, Dees, Dunlap, et al. (1997), published by CATESOL.

REFERENCES

Berkenkotter, C., & Huckin, T. N. (1995). *Genre knowledge in disciplinary communication: Cognition/culture/power*. Hillsdale, NJ: Lawrence Erlbaum Associates.

Browning, G., Brinton, D., Ching, R., Dees, R., Dunlap, S., Erickson, M., Garlow, K., Manson, M., Poole, D., & Sasser, L. (1997). *California pathways: The second language student in public high schools, colleges, and universities*. Glendale, CA: California Teachers of English to Speakers of Other Languages.

Carson, J. G., Chase, N., Gibson, S., & Hargrove, M. (1992). Literacy demands of the undergraduate curriculum. *Reading Research and Instruction, 31*, 25–50.

Carson, J. G., & Leki, I. (Eds.). (1993). *Reading in the composition classroom: Second language perspectives*. Boston: Heinle & Heinle.

Christie, F. (1993). The "received tradition" of literacy teaching: The decline of rhetoric and the corruption of grammar. In B. Green (Ed.) *The insistence of the letter: Literacy studies and curriculum theorizing* (pp. 75–106). London: Falmer Press.

Davies, F. (1995). *Introducing reading*. London: Penguin.

Feathers, K. M. (1993). *Infotext: Reading and learning*. Markham, Ontario: Pippin.

Grellet, F. (1981). *Developing reading skills: A practical guide to reading comprehension exercises*. Cambridge, England: Cambridge University Press.

Harklau, L., Losey, K. M., & Siegal, M. (Eds.). (1999). *Generation 1.5 meets college composition: Issues in the teaching and writing to U.S.-educated learners of English.* (pp. 159–171). Mahwah, NJ: Lawrence Erlbaum Associates.

Horowitz, D. M. (1986). Essay examination prompts and the teaching of academic writing. *English for Specific Purposes, 5*, 107–120.

Huckin, T. (1997, March). *Discourse analysis and literacy education*. Presentation at the Conference on College Composition and Communication, Phoenix, AZ.

Johns, A. M. (1991). Interpreting an English competency examination: The frustrations of an ESL science student. *Written Communication, 8*, 379–401.

Johns, A. M. (1997). *Text, role and context: Developing academic literacies*. New York: Cambridge University Press.

Leki, I. (1995). Coping strategies of ESL students in writing tasks across the curriculum. *TESOL Quarterly, 29*, 235–260.

Martin, J. (1985). *Factual writing: Exploring and challenging social reality*. Oxford, England: Oxford University Press.

MacDonald, S. P. (1998, April). *Critiquing the critiques of epistemic voice*. Presentation at the Conference College Composition and Communication, Chicago, IL.

Murray, D. E. (Ed.). (1992). *Diversity as resource: Redefining cultural literacy*. Alexandria, VA: Teachers of English to Speakers of Other Languages.

Prior, P. (1995). Redefining the task: An ethnographic examination of writing and response in graduate seminars. In D. Belcher & G. Braine (Eds.), *Academic writing in a second language: Essays on research and pedagogy* (pp. 47–82). Norwood, NJ: Ablex.

Ramanathan, V., & Kaplan, R. B. (1996). Audience and voice in current L1 composition textbooks: Some implications for L2 writers. *Journal of Second Language Writing, 5*, 21–33.

Ratteray, O. M. T. (1985). Expanding roles for summarized information. *Written Communication, 2*, 257–272.

16

The Impact of the Computer in Second-Language Writing

MARTHA C. PENNINGTON

The computer in its many guises as writing tool and communications medium is changing the way we interact with information and with each other. Whether in the form of a word processor installed on a personal computer (PC), a group of PCs inked in a computer lab or a university network, or the Internet connecting people and electronic information sources around the globe, the computer is having a profound effect on literacy practices in the present age. It is, at the same time, contributing to an ongoing expansion of information and communication resources that has put English in the hands of more and more people around the globe.

These trends have created a great demand for literacy in English as a second language (ESL) as well as for literacy in computer writing tools, issues that are sometimes hard to separate. Many of our literacy practices in education, work, and social life have moved off the page and onto the screen: more and more people are doing the majority of their writing and reading on computer and transmitting messages electronically rather than on paper (Warschauer, 1999).

As the communicator of the present day and especially of the future is inevitably linked to electronic media, those charged with instructing ESL students in writing cannot afford to remain outside these developments, teaching without regard to the communication technologies that are increasingly at the center of their students' world; teachers should be prepared to bring computers into the center of their own pedagogical practice. The modern ESL writing teacher needs to understand the nature of electronic writing media, the kinds of impacts these media have on students' writing, and the ways they can best be employed in the teaching of writing. This chapter aims to raise the awareness of ESL writing teachers regarding electronic writing media, their effects on ESL writers, and their pedagogical applications, beginning with a review of some critical issues in word processing and then moving on

From *Exploring the Dynamics of Second Language Writing*. Ed. Barbara Kroll. Cambridge, UK: Cambridge UP, 2003. 283–310.

to networking, hypermedia, and the use of the Internet as a research tool/assistant for writers.

WORD PROCESSING

The basic writing tool provided by the computer is a word processor, with most word processors including a spellchecker and many including a grammar checker as well. Most people agree that word processors are useful for writing because they facilitate the mechanical processes of putting words on paper; revising text by substitutions, deletions, additions, and block moves; and producing attractive and readable finished copy. The word processor is not only a convenient tool combining an automated typewriter, editor, and printer; it is also a composing medium that with time and practice can significantly change the writer's process and product. Many studies have shown that beyond their facilitating effects, word processors have an impact on student writers' attitudes, the characteristics of their texts, their revising behavior and the attention they pay to form and mechanics, and the order and the type of writing activities in which they engage (for reviews and discussions of research, see Bangert-Drowns, 1993; Cochran-Smith, 1991; Pennington, 1996b, 1996c, 1999a, 1999b; Snyder, 1993).

Student Attitudes

Most students have a good initial reaction to the computer and feel that it can help them in their work, though some users, especially older students, may be uncomfortable with the technology or may even be "computer-phobic." Another minority of users may have their enthusiasm dampened if they experience technical problems early on, have difficulty typing or mastering computer commands, or have limited access to computers and to experienced users who can offer assistance when things go wrong. As a result, a few who try word processing will give up in frustration. Typically, however, after a period of weeks or months spent improving their keyboarding skills, most students persist and become regular computer users.

The mechanical capabilities of a word processor are especially valuable in a second language (L2) context, where the physical processes of putting words on paper and revising text to a finished product, and the cognitive processes underlying these, are more effortful and less automatized (Jones & Tetroe, 1987) than when writing in the first language (L1). Not only the actual capabilities of the machine but also the students' view of these as helpful for their writing are significant for L2 writers, who may, even more than inexperienced L1 writers, lack confidence in their writing ability (Betancourt & Phinney, 1988). Word processors can relieve the anxiety some L2 writers feel about writing the L2 script, about producing academic work in their L2, and about writing in general (Pennington, 1999a; Phinney, 1989).

Many studies conducted with L2 writers report positive attitudes associated with word processing (e.g., Neu & Scarcella, 1991; Pennington & Brock,

1992; Phinney, 1991; Phinney & Mathis, 1990). For example, in their comparison of word processing and pen-and-paper composing in English by Turkish university students, Akyel and Kamisli (1999) report that the use of the computer improved student attitudes toward writing and built up their confidence. In a longitudinal investigation of a group of mature ESL writers in Hong Kong who were able to use the computer as much or as little as they wished in their written work for a course (Rusmin, 1999), the majority of the students were positive toward the computer and adopted it for their writing from the beginning of the term or increasingly as the course progressed. On the basis of the different patterns of attitudes and computer use, Rusmin (1999) classified the 27 students in the class into six categories, which she labeled "devotees," "enthusiasts," "rededicateds," "positives," "converts," and "skeptics," categories that may be applicable to a host of students in a wide variety of locales.

Textual Properties

Also related to attitude is self-consciousness. The student writer working in a computer medium is led to write in a less self-conscious way and with greater engagement, thus writing with a freer mind and less "rewriting anxiety." As a result, the student's greater involvement may lead him or her to write for longer periods of time and produce longer texts. Several studies with L2 writers (e.g., Brock & Pennington, 1999; Chadwick & Bruce, 1989; Pennington & Brock, 1992) document that longer texts are a general effect of word processing.

In addition to the production of longer texts, the physical easing of the writing process that results in a less constrained, more relaxed writing process may produce texts that are in a sense also "more relaxed." Written products generated on a word processor "are often unconstrained and experimental, being more likely to be in a non-generic form that sometimes amounts to what has been called 'train of thought' or 'spaghetti writing' — long strings of loosely connected strands of ideas" (Pennington, 2000, p. 14). In some cases, computer-produced text represents an unfinished, intermediate work that given sufficient time for continued development will result in a high-quality product (Pennington, 1996b, 1996c). In other cases, it may represent a new type of work, as when writing in hypertext — for example, for a Web page or in an e-mail context.

Revision Strategies and Accuracy Concerns

Surface-level editing for spelling and mechanics is encouraged in a word processing environment, where the small size of text visible on one screen may engender an especially focused type of revision at word, phrase, and sentence level (Pennington, 1996b, 1999b). At the same time, the ease with which individual words can be searched and whole sections of text deleted, added, or moved suggests that word processing may have value as a macro-level revision tool. Rather than being a separate activity following the generation of a draft, revision in a computer context is closely linked to text generation. Pedagogical intervention aimed at increasing students' awareness of and ability to apply revision strategies in their own writing (e.g., Steelman, 1994) has demonstrated the value of the computer medium for helping learners increase the type and depth of their revisions.

In other research, L2 writers have been found to revise more when writing with a computer than when writing by traditional means (e.g., Chadwick & Bruce, 1989; Li & Cumming, 2001; Phinney & Khouri, 1993); to revise more dynamically and continuously (Phinney & Khouri, 1993); and to spend more time revising in a computer context, where they may "continue revising after planned changes [have] been made" (Phinney & Khouri, 1993, p. 271). Writers also make more revisions beyond the surface level. There is some evidence that word processing is more effective in stimulating meaning-level revision when aligned to a process approach to writing (Daiute, 1985; Susser, 1993) than when used without process support or with other computer writing aids such as grammar checkers (Brock & Pennington, 1999; Pennington & Brock, 1992). The research thus supports an approach that teaches the writing process in the context of learning to write and revise using a word processor.

Implications for Planning

In pen-and-paper composing, writers often spend a lot of time in intensive planning before writing to avoid making mistakes or changing their minds about what they want to say and then having to undertake the tedious chore of rewriting or recopying text already written down. Under such conditions, pen-and-paper writers may habitually write a paper without any revision or with only a minimum amount of revision to avoid producing more than one draft. In sharp contrast to this paper-based mode of composing, the automated text-generation and revision tools provided on computer, coupled with the malleability of text on screen or disk, encourage a very different computer-based writing mode (Bernhardt, Edwards, & Wojahn, 1989; Haas, 1989; Williamson & Pence, 1989). In a contrasting "computer writing style," the writer generally begins writing immediately, soon after a topic is decided — or even before it is decided.

Instead of writing to fit a plan, computer writers plan as they are writing (Haas, 1989), an effect also documented for L2 writers (Akyel & Kamisli, 1999; Li & Cumming, 2001). Planning thus becomes more of a middle stage than a beginning stage activity, and the time and intensive cognitive activity that would have been involved in pre-planning is instead involved in writing itself. The sharp division of composing into the three stages of planning, writing, and revising breaks down in a computer context, in which planning as well as revision occurs as part of the writing process. In the computer-engendered approach to writing, cognitive effort is distributed throughout the writing process and writing is developed more on the basis of concrete text already generated than on an abstract plan; this procedure would seem to be especially valuable for L2 writers, who have less cognitive capacity available for writing than do L1 writers.

Weighing the Advantages and Disadvantages

In spite of the obvious advantages of the computer over pen-and-paper writing in terms of automation, flexibility, and cognitive demands, the results of research on the quality of writing produced in a computer context are not all favorable, as only some studies have yielded positive effects for student compositions produced by word processing in contrast to pen and paper (see Pennington, 1996b, 1996c, 1999a, 1999b, for reviews). A mixed pattern of findings can be seen in the L2 literature: In some studies, word processing gave writers an advantage in terms of writing quality (e.g., Lam & Pennington, 1995; McGarrell, 1993), while in others, word processing gave no advantage over pen and paper (e.g., Benesch, 1987; Chadwick & Bruce, 1989).

These mixed results from individual studies have often been used to caution teachers against an easy acceptance of word processing; however, three summative (meta-analytical) reviews of research results comparing word processing to pen-and-paper composing have demonstrated an advantage for computer-produced over pen-produced text in terms of traditional measures of writing quality (Bangert-Drowns, 1993; Roblyer, Castine, & King, 1988; Schramm, 1989). In addition, most studies showing negative results for word processing were carried out from the late 1970s to the mid 1980s, and some of the negative findings may have been related to the characteristics of early word processors, subjects' unfamiliarity with computers, the context of research, or the ways in which effects were measured in these early studies. Teachers are therefore cautioned against placing too much weight on the older studies of word processing; they are advised instead to base their decisions about computer use on more recent findings and the accumulated comparative evidence, which generally show a positive impact of word processing on students' writing. At the same time, teachers should always keep an eye out for the latest trends in computer use and research findings, bearing in mind that the focus and the results of research are likely to change as the context for writing on computers also changes — from word processed compositions to e-mail and Web pages.

As in all other cases in which new technologies or teaching approaches are introduced, teachers' and learners' behavior is dictated by their knowledge and understanding of the innovation. As students learn how to apply their word processing capabilities in their writing, they are likely to develop positive attitudes toward the computer writing medium and the context of writing, which may in the case of L2 writers extend also to their attitudes toward the English language. When the learners' knowledge and attitudes are favorable, that is, when their "cognitive-affective response" to word processing is positive, in the process of learning about the medium they will gradually experience effects on their writing behavior of three types (Pennington, 1996b, 1996c, 1999a, 1999b):

FIGURE 1.   The Positive Path in Computer Writing Effects

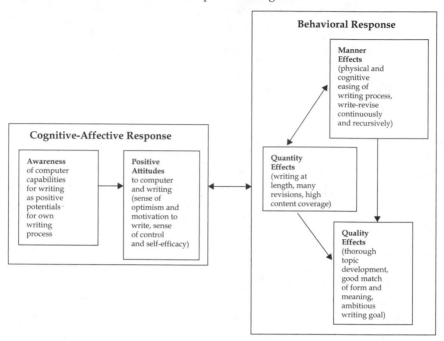

Adapted from Pennington 1999a, p. 283. Used with permission from Swets & Zeitlinger.

> *Manner Effects.* A sense of the ease of writing and revising in a fluid writing process involving continuous and recursive write-revise cycles
>
> *Quantity Effects.* Writing for extended periods of time, producing long texts with much content and many revisions
>
> *Quality Effects.* Writing to a high standard in terms of topic development, formal characteristics, and writing goal

Given enough time and favorable circumstances for learning, these three types of effects, represented in Figure 1, may ultimately result in high-quality written products.

Under less favorable conditions, learners may not experience a positive cognitive-affective response to word processing if they have low awareness of computer potential that can help them in their writing, if they are intimidated by the computer or find it difficult to use, or if they experience frequent mechanical breakdowns. Consequently, under such conditions, their behavioral response is essentially the opposite of the learners' response found in more positive circumstances. This negative response consists of

> *Anti-Manner Effects.* A sense of the difficulty of writing and revising, reinforcing a one-shot linear plan-write process
>
> *Anti-Quantity Effects.* Limited time spent writing, producing short texts with restricted content and few revisions

FIGURE 2.   The Negative Path in Computer Writing Effects

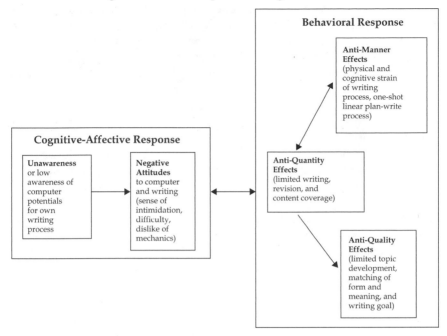

Adapted from Pennington 1999a, p. 285. Used with permission from Swets & Zeitlinger.

Anti-Quality Effects. Writing to a minimal standard in terms of topic development, formal characteristics, and writing goal

These three types of behavioral effects, illustrated in Figure 2, represent disfavoring conditions that predict poor written products.

Whatever the research findings, the inevitable presence of word processors in L2 contexts and in the future of most of our students is undeniable, and any teacher who ignores this reality is avoiding a responsibility to teach to student needs.

NETWORKING

Another way in which ESL writing teachers find that computers can play a key role in instruction is when they have the opportunity to teach in or have their students participate in a networked environment. A local area network (LAN or intranet), such as in a computer lab, or a wide area network (WAN), such as the Internet or World Wide Web, makes it possible to extend the computer writing environment by linking student writers to other people with whom they may interact to develop their writing. Through a computer network, students' computers may be linked to those of their teachers as well as other students as a way to develop collaborative work or to gain input on their writing other than by face-to-face interaction (Bruce, Peyton, & Batson, 1993;

Bruce & Rubin, 1993; Mabrito, 1991; Palmquist, 1993). All types of network arrangements have the potential for motivating L2 students to write and to revise in response to a real audience, for helping them to gain more input on their writing, for encouraging them to experiment in their writing, and for empowering them to seek out the resources they need for developing their ideas.

Within a computer network, students may participate in such novel activities as online feedback on classmates' work or "team editing" (Kaufer & Neuwirth, 1995) as well as the sending and receiving of e-mail "letters" or other sorts of messages (Howard, 1992). Where the students' computers are linked in a network, the potentials for collaboration and participatory interaction are increased (Warschauer, 1997). Some of this collaboration and interaction takes place around the computer; but increasingly it takes place in cyberspace, with the interactors being physically removed — often at great distances — from one another. As a result, the writer may be encouraged to experiment with ideas and with language because of the risk-free social access afforded by electronic connectivity. At the same time networks bring writers together to increase shared knowledge and produce collaborative work, they also seem to help student writers to create an individual voice. Moran and Hawisher (1998) observe that writers can use online space to create alternative selves and to experiment with roles that they might not assume in face-to-face interaction.

E-mail Exchanges

In a departmental or university-wide network, writing teachers can use e-mail to contact their students, and students can have easy access to their teachers to ask questions about their work and to receive feedback on drafts. As a further advantage, e-mail aids students working together on team projects to fulfill written assignments (Hoffman, 1996). With a university-wide network, L2 students can be linked to L1 partners or more experienced L2 students on campus (Nabors & Swartley, 1999). With Internet access, L2 students can participate in information exchange with sister classes and e-mail partners overseas (Sayers, 1989; Slater & Carpenter, 1999; Woodin, 1997), such as via the International Tandem Network (available at: http://www.slf.ruhr-uni-bochum.de/email/stats-eng.html) or via the Intercultural E-mail Classroom Connections (IECC) service (http://www.teaching.com/iecc/). Woodin (1997) points out that in providing an opportunity for real communication one-on-one with speakers of the target language, e-mail functions "as a bridge between the language classroom and the natural setting. There is the opportunity for contact with a variety of native speakers, but from within the safety of one's own environment" (p. 31). In either type of partnering arrangement, the e-mail contact may allow writers to obtain information or input from a real audience in relation to their written assignments. Or the contact with other communicators over a network may itself function as stimulation for students' writing.

Lists, Newsgroups, and Bulletin Boards

An additional possibility is to join a group that communicates by e-mail through a discussion list. Within each of these lists, many of which are available via Listserv, there is a wide range of topics that subscribers may access or participate in. Lists often serve the purpose of providing specialized information or the answers to questions in a field. For example, students or teachers might request information about language teaching from the ESL list, TESL-L (listserv@cunyvm.cuny.edu); about teaching ESL on a network from NETEACH-L (listserv@raven.cc.ukans.edu); or about linguistics, language acquisition, or a specific language such as English from the applied linguistics list, LINGUIST (listserv@tamvm1.tamu.edu). Such specialized lists can be used to locate experts and other sources of information in a specific field or on a specific topic. They also often serve the purpose of debating issues, generating different points of view, and comparing different (well-known or unknown) people's information or points of view. Windeatt, Hardisty, and Eastment (2000) have activities for introducing students to discussion lists and for setting up an electronic list.

A newsgroup is a group of users networked by e-mail for specialized discussions through a service called Usenet, which has newsgroups of various kinds for different countries, such as in the UK (http://www.usenet.org.uk/) or Norway (http://www.usenet.no/). A bulletin board is like a list except that instead of receiving information via e-mail, the user goes to a specific Web site to read messages posted on the bulletin board. Bulletin boards thus allow for individual access to information and individual choice as to whether and when to participate. Students might visit bulletin boards as part of Internet searches (see Windeatt, Hardisty, & Eastment, 2000, for suggestions). A bulletin board can also be set up for a specific class or group of students (e.g., at a site called BeSeen, http://www.beseen.com/board/index.html), as a way to encourage their independence, full participation, and sharing of information. Bulletin boards are also of value to teachers for sharing resources and expertise and for building a sense of community. For example, in a study of students in a TESOL (Teachers of English to Speakers of Other Languages) methods course interacting on a World Wide Web bulletin board, Kamhi-Stein (2000) found that the electronic medium encouraged participants to take responsibility for learning both collectively and individually, as shown by a high level of student-led interaction, collaborative learning, and equal participation by native and non-native students alike.

Synchronous Communication: Chat, MUDs, and MOOs

In addition to the asynchronous, or saved and time-delayed transmission of messages via e-mail and e-mail lists, networked communication includes several types of synchronous, or nearly immediate, real-time communication. One interactive writing program, *Daedalus Interchange* (Daedalus, Inc.), allows students in a networked class to send a message related to a writing task to other students simultaneously. Teleconferencing and videoconferencing, though not widely used in instruction, are other examples of synchronous communication. An increasingly popular type of program is text-conferencing software, most commonly in the form of Internet relay chat (IRC) programs, such as *Microsoft Chat* (Microsoft Corp.) or *mIRC* (available free at: http://www.mirc.com/), which makes it possible for participants to have an online discussion or "chat" by typing at the computer keyboard while others who are also logged on to the same site can watch the interaction evolve. There are many open IRC "chat rooms," and a closed chat room can also be set up for selected participants.

An advantage is the equality of the interaction, as every participant has the same chance to initiate a topic and/or to respond to another's turn. There is also the possibility of any number of people composing input at the same time. These discussion programs therefore offer possibilities for expanding student writers' ability to gather and refine their ideas in interaction with others. They can also, like e-mail and other forms of networked communication, stimulate creativity and personalization. There are some disadvantages, however, as Windeatt, Hardisty, and Eastment (2000) observe:

> Unfortunately, the more people join in a "chat," the more disjointed the discussion is. In addition, the contributions to the discussion are often short and people tend to use abbreviations, and make a lot of typing mistakes. Nevertheless . . . IRC can be useful for discussion among a small number of people, especially as the discussion can be "logged," i.e., a copy can be saved on disk, to look at more carefully later. (p. 113)

Such functions have utility for writing, for example, in interacting about ideas for writing and giving feedback on writing, and in general, for establishing and maintaining contact with a community of writers not only in a networked classroom but also beyond the confines of a classroom. Note, however, that IRC software (unlike, for example, the *Daedalus* package) is not specifically designed for composing-related use and in fact seems to promote a type of spontaneous playfulness that encourages the breaking of conventions.

Two additional types of synchronous communication are MUDs (multi-user domains) and MOOs (multi-user domains, object-oriented). Like text-conferencing, these involve multiple users interacting online by going to a specific Web site and typing information on a keyboard. Rather than chat sites, these are Internet-based specialized environments or virtual worlds where participants can interact with each other or access information. Unlike chat rooms, in which the interaction exists only as long as users remain online, these environments are structured to have continuity of characters, spaces (e.g., "rooms"), and objects from one session to another.

A MOO is similar to a simulation in which participants interact online. Since participants are generally linked from all over the globe, a MOO can be seen as a type of "global village" in which students can be linked with an international group of participants as resources for their ideas and their writing. MOO interactions have the special characteristic that users can assume one or more imaginary identities and keep their real identity hidden, thus encouraging playfulness and experimentation. MOO interactions may therefore have some value in stimulating student writers to develop ideas and "freeing" them to experiment with different authorial voices and writing styles.

An example of a MOO that incorporates properties of other sorts of Web sites is schMOOze University (http://schmooze.hunter.cuny.edu:8888/), which is described on the opening page of the Web site as

> a small, friendly college known for its hospitality and the diversity of the student population . . . established as a place where people studying English as a second or foreign language could practice English while sharing ideas and experiences with other learners and practitioners of English. Students have opportunities for one-on-one and group conversations as well as access to language games, an online dictionary, virtual stockbroker and many language games.

The schMOOze University Web site includes an introduction to the MOO environment and the schMOOze University, a Virtual English Language Center, Internet TESL Journal pages for ESL students, a collaborative MOO project, teacher discussions on NETEACH-L, and a link to Dave's ESL Café (an ESL Web site run by Dave Sperling, an ESL instructor based in the United States).

Expanding Peer Response

Communication in a networked environment can change some of the dynamics of peer feedback sessions as found in traditional classrooms (discussed by Ferris, 2003). Sullivan and Pratt (1996) discovered that the communication that occurred as peer feedback over the computer network was of a type that might have been especially valuable for students in improving their writing. They summarize some of the contrasts as follows:

> [Face-to-face peer] discussions were often filled with personal narratives (students focusing on themselves rather than the task at hand) and short interjections of agreement (uh-huh) or repetition . . . [whereas, over the network] . . . the responses followed a pattern that consisted of a positive comment about the essay followed by one or more suggestions for revision. (p. 499)

Moreover, the networked feedback from more than one student tended to reinforce the same points and the same suggestions for revision, thereby perhaps focusing the writer's attention on certain points for revision. However, in a study carried out with EFL writing students in Hong Kong, Braine (2001) reports that the feedback given in a networked environment did not result in better written texts. He found that final draft essays written by students who engaged in traditional face-to-face classroom peer interaction received higher holistic scores and showed greater gains than final drafts written by students who carried out peer discussions via a LAN (Braine, 2001, p. 283). Thus, networking student writers electronically does not guarantee better writing.

Changing Patterns of Communication

There is some evidence that more focused use of language is a general effect of networked communication: "With more opportunities and different opportunities to negotiate input in a computer environment come not only a greater quantity of language, particularly, the second language, but also more focused, explicit, and specific uses of language" (Pennington, 1996a, p. 2). This is probably because the relatively "cueless environment" (Spears & Lea, 1992) of the computer context makes it necessary to invoke the context of the speech event more explicitly than would be required in face-to-face communication. In a study of ESL learners exchanging information by e-mail in Canada, Esling (1991) found that "in the initial exchange of notes, the communication is characterized by revelation of information about local setting which would not normally be exchanged but which would rather be taken for granted and left unsaid in face-to-face conversation" (pp. 126–127). A similar finding is reported by Nabors and Swartley (1999) in a study in which e-mail partners were provided for ESL students on an American university campus. Thus, the relatively cueless environment, coupled with the anonymity and ease of communication in an electronic network, may promote both a more content-rich and a more individual and creative form of writing.

Discourse Implications

Writing over a network can add real audiences, input, and motivation to write; also, the online context changes the writing task to one that has some of the attributes of spoken interaction. Thus, for example, Nabors and Swartley (1999) found that the ESL e-mail penpals in their study used a range of strategies to build a relationship with their partner, many of which, such as giving personal information and sharing feelings, are also common in face-to-face relationships. As Moran (1995) notes: "E-mail is, simultaneously, the most intimate and the most public form of correspondence" (p. 16). In consequence, discourse produced in an e-mail context shares characteristics with both personal and professional letters, as well as with some speech genres, particularly, public interviews (Collot & Belmore, 1996). At the same time, based on its unique contextual attributes, e-mail communication appears to be evolving as a new genre, which Baron (2000) describes as a "creole" that merges some properties of both speech and writing. The e-mail context may therefore contribute to improving the student's fluency and willingness to write even as it contributes to a breakdown of established writing conventions and genres. This breakdown of conventions appears to be even greater in synchronous network communication.

HYPERTEXT / HYPERMEDIA

Another development of import to writers is the possibilities for creating hypertext, a computer tool for building "layered text":

> Like Chinese boxes, text can be nested within text, and huge texts can reside within tiny fragments. With the combination of both hierarchical subordination and lateral links from any point to any point, hypertext offers greatly expanded possibilities for new structures characterized by layering and flexibility. (Bernhardt, 1993, p. 164)

In hypertext, writers create "mosaics of information" (Marcus, 1993) made up of chunks of information arranged on computer "pages." These chunks of information, which may be textual, visual, auditory, or any combination of these, are connected by electronic links in a Web page format. Users are then free to create their own paths to negotiate the information from one part of the screen to another or from one screen to another.

The possibility of linking a chunk of text to another to create "information layers" encourages a new mode of "layered thinking" and "layered composing." Because of its nonlinear properties, "hypertext . . . may help support an enriched network of thoughts and associations that assists writers to explore and develop their ideas, thereby enhancing the cognitive potentials of [the computer]" (Pennington, 1996b, p. 23). The possibility of combining chunks of text with "sound bites," "video bites," and other "media chunks" adds creative potential for illustrating written work while also encouraging the creation of new modes of presentation using text, other visual media, and sound media. When all these potentials are combined with Internet access, the computer offers a distributed set of links and a highly creative, all-purpose hypermedia or multimedia communication tool.

WEB PAGES AND WEB SITES

The World Wide Web (generally referred to as "the Web") is a sector of the Internet made up of linked hypertext sites that can be accessed by mouse clicks. A Web browser such as Internet Explorer or Netscape Navigator is needed to read Web pages. Web searches can be conducted online using search engines such as Google (http://www.google.com/) and AltaVista (http://www.altavista.com/), which, among other things, allow the user to type in a word or phrase to find Web pages that contain all or some of the desired words or that match these most closely. Web pages can be created using various tools and then put up on a local-area network or placed on a public drive. Software such as Microsoft Inc.'s FrontPage or Macromedia's Dreamweaver will allow a teacher to manage a Web site (and also to author Web pages). In addition, Windeatt, Hardisty, and Eastment (2000) have a Web site linked to their book with useful information for teachers regarding Web pages and anything to do with the Internet (available via the Oxford Teachers' Club at http://www.oup.com/elt/global/teachersclub/). Another useful resource is the WebCT (World-Wide-Web Course Tools) program (available at: http://www.webct.com/) used by Kamhi-Stein (2000) in her TESOL teacher education course. It offers Web-based bulletin board systems, group presentation and chat areas, conferencing tools, and e-mail.

Increasingly, hypermedia tools and the Web are defining new domains of communication and literacy, including a new emphasis on visual and combined-media literacy (Kress, 1998), extending to new dimensions some of the more conventional reading and writing connections important to L2 students (see Grabe, 2003). An investigation comparing texts written by L2 French students in pen-and-paper, word processing, and hypertext modes (Marcoul & Pennington, 1999) found that the latter medium, when aligned to a student newspaper Web site, sparked students' creativity and drew their attention to visual aspects of design at the same time that it drew their attention away from surface correction of language. Interestingly, although the students in the Marcoul and Pennington (1999) study made fewer surface revisions, they made more content and paragraph-level revisions in hypertext than in the other two modes. This comparative study of writing media suggests that having students write in hypertext for a Web page may encourage them to spend more time refining their texts in terms of content and organization of information at the same time that it encourages them to focus on other aspects of presentation that take time away from the writing process per se.

In the instructional project investigated by Marcoul and Pennington (1999), readers could interact with student creators of Web pages to add comments to their text and to visit the links that writers had created to their Web pages. In this way, readers interacted with writers by collaborating in the ongoing development of texts and by exploring a part of the writer's world. The interactive creation of text, which is greatly facilitated by network and Web-based communication, is a major area of literacy innovation that has value for L2 writers.

In a study that involved Web explorations by junior high school students in Mexico, Romano, Field, and de Huergo (2000) report on the students' engagement with knowledge outside their community, including their engagement with the English language, finding "a strong tendency for Web literacy and literacy in English to converge, becoming nearly one and the same" (p. 204). An investigation by Lam (2000) of the e-mail and text-conferencing chat activities of a Chinese adolescent immigrant to the United States revealed that "the English he controlled on the Internet enabled him to develop a sense of belonging and connectedness to a global English-speaking community" (p. 476). In a discussion of Web communication in Australia, McConaghy and Snyder (2000) stress the interaction of local and global knowledge and perspectives that result from this type of communication. As they conclude:

"Perhaps, in the final analysis, the possibilities for engaging the local in the global through the World Wide Web represent the new medium's greatest potential" (McConaghy & Snyder, 2000, p. 89).

THE INTERNET AND WORLD WIDE WEB AS RESOURCES

The Internet and World Wide Web provide students access to electronic resources online that may be helpful for their writing, such as journals, library catalogs, topical databases, search services, and resources on English language. Most journals' Web sites give access to contents and abstracts and in some cases, to articles in past issues. Bibliomania (http://www.bibliomania. com/) is a resource for searching reference materials and works of fiction, drama, poetry, and religious texts. Project Gutenberg Electronic Library (http://promo.net/pg/index.html/) offers free download of a variety of electronic texts, and Kidon Media-Link (http://www.kidon.com/medialink/) provides links to Web editions of thousands of newspapers. Online dictionaries are available for English and other languages at http://www.dictionary.com/, a Web site that includes a language discussion forum, *Roget's Thesaurus*, and writing resources such as grammar, usage, and style guides, including some for writing on the Internet. Many grammar references are also available online, such as Charles Darling's Guide to Grammar and Writing (http://cctc2. commnet.edu/grammar/), and Professional Training Company's Good Grammar, Good Style TM Archive (http://www.protrainco.com/grammar.htm). The text by Windeatt, Hardisty, and Eastment (2000) contains a variety of structured activities for students to learn how to negotiate the Internet and to use different types of resources available on the World Wide Web, such as English language stories, films, and new sources.

The Web is also an excellent resource for teachers, offering quick access to professional organizations such as TESOL (http://www.tesol.org/) and IATEFL (the International Association of Teachers of English as a Foreign Language) (http://www.iatefl.org/); teaching materials and articles, such as those through ERIC Educational Resources Information Center (http://www.askeric.org/); online journals, such as the monthly *Internet TESL Journal* (http://www.aitech.ac.jp/~iteslj/), and the quarterly *TESL E-J* (http://www-writing.berkeley.edu/TESL-EJ/); teaching sites, such as the Beaumont Publishers' Virtual Learning Community site for K–12 projects (http://www.cyberjourneys.net/), the English Through the Internet projects of Elaine Hoter (http://web.macam98.ac.il/~elaine/eti/), the Email Projects Home Page by Susan Gaer (http://www.otan.us/webfarm/emailproject/email. htm), and the Linguistic Funland TESL Page (http://www.linguisticfunland. com/tesl.html/), a rich site including everything from listings of job opportunities and graduate programs in TESL to teaching and testing materials and services for students. There are also useful individually-sponsored Web pages with information oriented toward teaching English as a second language, such as those of Dave Sperling (http://www.eslcafe.com/), Ruth Vilmi (http://www.ruthvilmi.net/hut/), or Mark Warschauer (http://www. gse.uci.edu/markw/).

In addition, a good annotated compilation called "Internet Projects for Learners and Teachers of English" is available at http://www.wfi.fr/volterre/inetpro.html/.

Other electronic resources include concordancing programs, such as TACT (available at http://tactweb.humanities.mcmaster.ca/) or Athelstan, Inc.'s MonoConc (available at http://www.athel.com/); these allow student writers and their teachers to search their own or others' texts for the occurrence and contexts of specific words or phrases. With Internet access, they can search online corpora such as the British National Corpus Online (available at http://www.hcu.ox.ac.uk/bnc) and find out about others, such as those listed at the University of Lancaster UCREL (University Centre for Computer Corpus Research on Language) Web site (http://www.comp.lancs.ac.uk/computing/research/ucrel/corpora.html). There are also online resources for preventing and detecting plagiarism, such as Plagiarism.org (http://www.plagiarism.org/) and the Indiana University Writing Resources Web page (http://www.indiana.edu/~wts/wts/plagiarism.html).

POTENTIALS AND ISSUES

The computer offers a wide variety of literacy and communication tools that may assist more people to achieve literacy in one or more languages than ever before. At the same time, "the result of writing in an electronic medium may not be the written products of a pen-and-paper age but more ephemeral forms of *think-text* and *talk-text*" (Pennington, 2000, p. 21). In addition, in the contexts of computer-mediated communication, writing is moving in the direction of, on the one hand, a more social construction of the activity and interactivity of writing and, on the other, a more media-saturated construction of text as existing within a rich nexus of other resources.

The value of the computer for the L2 writer is considerable for helping to automate the production and revision of text, to encode ideas, and to spark and energize the writing process. With the additional resources of networking and hypermedia, it offers a veritable banquet of media and communication options. Figure 3 summarizes some potentials of the computer to aid L2 student writers.

In addition, as Warschauer (2000b) notes, computer media empower students and give them greater control over their own learning, thus increasing their *agency*:

> Agency is really what makes students so excited about using computers in the classroom: the computer provides them a powerful means to make their stamp on the world. Think, for example, of the difference between authoring a paper (i.e., writing a text for the teacher), and authoring a multimedia document (i.e., creatively bringing together several media to share with a wide international audience), and even helping to author the very rules by which multimedia is created. . . . By allowing and helping our students to carry out all these types of authoring—toward fulfilling a meaningful purpose for a real audience—we are helping them exercise their agency. The purpose of studying English is

FIGURE 3.   Computer Potentials for L2 Writers

Computer assistance in the way of mechanical tools and an environment to

   help with writing, revising, and dissemination of text

Increased writing *efficiency and effectiveness*

Increased *motivation*

Increased *amount of writing*

More *effective use of language*

Creative potential

Interactivity and collaboration

New *modes and genres* of writing

Flexibility of access to tools, texts, helps, and partners

Expanded access to writing resources, information, and the world

thus not just to "know it" as an internal system, but to be able to use it to have a real impact on the world. (p. 7)

At the same time the computer offers all of these potentials to student writers, certain issues of literacy on the computer remain to be resolved, as summarized in Figure 4.

Those of us involved in teaching L2 writing can help to ensure computer access for all to avoid a division of the world into computer "haves" and "have-nots" that Warschauer (2000a) terms the "digital divide."

At the same time, we need to consider what effective limits might be on students' computer access, so as to keep work on the computer from taking up too much of their time and attention and from replacing human contact. There are also issues we need to address about how to assess the new types of work produced in computer contexts, such as group-produced essays, Web pages, and the illustrated texts and texted illustrations made possible by multimedia and hypertext. It is also important to consider what values should be stressed in evaluating students' computer-produced work. For example, should originality be emphasized over correctness and quality of layout emphasized as much as quality of content and linguistic form? Finally, there are important matters we need to consider about whether and how to control students' use of others' work and "unsuitable information" (e.g., pornography or violent material) available electronically.

FIGURE 4.   Issues of Literacy on Computer

Access

> How to ensure computer access for all?
>
> What (if any) is a reasonable limit to computer access?

Assessment

> How to assess group-produced essays?
>
> How to assess writing in hypertext/Web pages?
>
> How to assess illustrated text/texted illustrations?

Control

> How/whether to keep students from "using" the work
>
> of others available on Internet?
>
> How/whether to keep students from "surfing" the net
>
> to find "inappropriate" material ?

Issues of access and control in computer contexts are matters that we in ESL need to be concerned about. As observed by Hawisher and Selfe (2000):

> The Web is a complicated and contested site for postmodern literacy practices. This site is characterized by a strongly influential set of tendential cultural forces, primarily oriented toward the values of the white, western industrialized nations that were responsible for designing and building the network and that continue to exert power within it. Hence, this system of networked computers is far from world-wide; it does not provide a culturally neutral conduit for the transmission of information; it is not a culturally neutral or innocent communication landscape open to the literacy practices and values of all global citizens. But the site is also far from totalizing in its effects . . . , [as] [t]he Web also provides a site for transgressive literary practices that express and value difference; that cling to historical, cultural, and racial diversity; and that help groups and individuals constitute their own multiple identities through language. (p. 15)

How we make use of computer potentials with our L2 learners and how we resolve the issues surrounding the use of electronic media are matters of great interest and concern. Even more important than how these matters are resolved is that we take an active role in computer-affected outcomes, that we are directly involved in resolving computer issues and deciding the best ways to make use of computer potentials for our own population of students, that is, L2 writers. In the present day, no ESL teacher can afford to remain on the sidelines of these developments, which have transformed and are continuing to transform literacy, language, and all communication in very significant ways.

REFERENCES

Akyel, A., & Kamisli, S. (1999). Word processing in the EFL classroom: Effects on writing strategies, attitudes, and products. In M. C. Pennington (Ed.), *Writing in an electronic medium: Research with language learners* (pp. 27–60). Houston: Athelstan.

Bangert-Drowns, R. L. (1993). The word processor as an instructional tool: A meta-analysis of word processing in writing instruction. *Review of Educational Research, 63,* 69–93.

Baron, N. S. (2000). *Alphabet to email: How written English evolved and where it's heading.* London: Routledge.

Benesch, S. (1987). *Word processing in English as a second language: A case study of three non-native college students.* Paper presented at the conference on College Composition and Communication, Atlanta, GA. (ERIC Document No. ED 281383)

Bernhardt, S. A. (1993). The shape of text to come: The texture of print on screens. *College Composition and Communication, 44,* 151–175.

Bernhardt, S. A., Edwards, P. G., & Wojahn, P. R. (1989). Teaching college composition with computers: A program evaluation study. *Written Communication, 6,* 108–133.

Betancourt, F., & Phinney, M. (1988). Sources of writing block in bilingual writers. *Written Communication, 5,* 461–478.

Braine, G. (2001). A study of English as a foreign language (EFL) writers on a local-area network (LAN) and in traditional classes. *Computers and Composition, 18,* 275–292.

Brock, M. N., & Pennington, M. C. (1999). A comparative study of text analysis and peer tutoring as input to writing on computer in an ESL context. In M. C. Pennington (Ed.), *Writing in an electronic medium: Research with language learners* (pp. 61–94). Houston: Athelstan.

Bruce, B., Peyton, J. K., & Batson, T. (Eds.). (1993). *Network-based classrooms: Promises and realities.* New York: Cambridge University Press.

Bruce, B. C., & Rubin, A. (1993). *Electronic quills: A situated evaluation of using computers for writing in classrooms.* Hillsdale, NJ: Lawrence Erlbaum.

Chadwick, S., & Bruce, N. (1989). The revision process in academic writing: From pen and paper to word processor. *Hongkong Papers in Linguistics and Language Teaching, 12,* April, 1–27.

Cochran-Smith, M. (1991). Word processing and writing in elementary classrooms: A critical review of related literature. *Review of Educational Research, 61,* 107–155.

Collot, M., & Belmore, N. (1996). Electronic language: A new variety of English. In S. Herring (Ed.), *Computer mediated communication: Linguistic, social, and cross-cultural perspectives* (pp. 13–28). Philadelphia: John Benjamins.

Daiute, C. (1985). *Writing and computers.* Reading, MA: Addison-Wesley.

Esling, J. H. (1991). Researching the effects of networking: Evaluating the spoken and written discourse generated by working with CALL. In P. Dunkel (Ed.), *Computer-assisted language learning and testing: Research issues and practice* (pp. 111–131). New York: Newbury House/ HarperCollins.

Ferris, D. (2003). Responding to writing. In B. Kroll (Ed.), *Exploring the dynamics of second language writing* (pp. 119–140). Cambridge, UK: Cambridge University Press.

Grabe, W. (2003). Reading and writing relations: Second language perspectives on research and practice. In B. Kroll (Ed.), *Exploring the dynamics of second language writing* (pp. 242–246). Cambridge, UK: Cambridge University Press.

Haas, C. (1989). How the writing medium shapes the writing process: Effects of word processing on planning. *Research in the Teaching of English, 23,* 181–207.

Hawisher, G. E., & Selfe, C. L. (2000). Introduction: Testing the claims. In G. E. Hawisher & C. L. Selfe (Eds.), *Global literacies and the World-Wide Web* (pp. 1–18). London: Routledge.

Hoffman, R. (1996). Computer networks: Webs of communication for language teaching. In M. C. Pennington (Ed.), *The power of CALL* (pp. 55–78). Houston: Athelstan.

Howard, T. (1992). WANs, connectivity, and computer literacy: An introduction and glossary. *Computers and Composition, 9(3),* 41–57.

Jones, S., & Tetroe, J. (1987). Composing in a second language. In A. Matsuhashi (Ed.), *Writing in real time: Modelling production processes* (pp. 34–57). Norwood, NJ: Ablex.

Kamhi-Stein, L. D. (2000). Looking at the future of TESOL teacher education: Web-based bulletin board discussion in a methods course. *TESOL Quarterly, 34,* 423–455.

Kaufer, D. S., & Neuwirth, C. (1995). Supporting online team editing: Using technology to shape performance and to monitor individual and group action. *Computers and Composition, 12,* 113–124.

Kress, G. (1998). Visual and verbal modes of representation in electronically mediated communication: The potentials of new forms of text. In I. Synder (Ed.), *Page to screen: Taking literacy into the electronic era* (pp. 53–79). London: Routledge.

Lam, F. S., & Pennington, M. C. (1995). The computer vs. the pen: A comparative study of word processing in a Hong Kong secondary classroom. *Computer-Assisted Language Learning, 7,* 75–92.

Lam, W. S. E. (2000). L2 literacy and the design of the self: A case study of a teenager writing on the Internet. *TESOL Quarterly, 34,* 457–482.

Li, J., & Cumming, A. (2001). Word processing and second language writing: A longitudinal case study. *International Journal of English Studies, 1(2),* 127–152.

Mabrito, M. (1991). Electronic mail as a vehicle for peer response. *Written Communication, 8,* 509–532.

Marcoul, I., & Pennington, M. C. (1999). Composing with computer technology: A case study of a group of students in computer studies learning French as a second language. In M. C. Pennington (Ed.), *Writing in an electronic medium: Research with language learners* (pp. 285–318). Houston: Athelstan.

Marcus, S. (1993). Multimedia, hypermedia and the teaching of English. In M. Monteith (Ed.), *Computers and language* (pp. 21–43). Oxford: Intellect Books.

McConaghy, C., & Snyder, I. (2000). Working the Web in postcolonial Australia. In G. E. Hawisher & C. L. Selfe (Eds.), *Global literacies and the World-Wide Web* (pp. 74–92). London: Routledge.

McGarrell, H. M. (1993, August). *Perceived and actual impact of computer use in second language writing classes.* Paper presented at the Congress of the Association de Linguistique Appliquée (AILA), Frije University, Amsterdam.

Moran, C. (1995). Notes toward a rhetoric of e-mail. *Computers and Composition, 12,* 15–21.

Moran, C., & Hawisher, G. E. (1998). The rhetorics and languages of electronic mail. In I. Snyder (Ed.), *Page to screen: Taking literacy into the electronic era* (pp. 80–101). London: Routledge.

Nabors, L. K., & Swartley, E. C. (1999). Student email letters: Negotiating meaning, gathering information, building relationships. In M. C. Pennington (Ed.), *Writing in an electronic medium: Research with language learners* (pp. 229–266). Houston: Athelstan.

Neu, J., & Scarcella, R. (1991). Word processing in the ESL writing classroom: A survey of student attitudes. In P. Dunkel (Ed.), *Computer-assisted language learning and testing: Research issues and practice* (pp. 169–187). New York: Newbury House/HarperCollins.

Palmquist, M. E. (1993). Network-supported interaction in two writing classrooms. *Computers and Composition, 10,* 25–57.

Pennington, M. C. (1996a). The power of the computer in language education. *The power of CALL* (pp. 1–14). Houston: Athelstan.

Pennington, M. C. (1996b). *The computer and the non-native writer: A natural partnership.* Cresskill, NJ: Hampton Press.

Pennington, M. C. (1996c). Writing the natural way: On computer. *Computer Assisted Language Learning, 9,* 125–142.

Pennington, M. C. (1999a). The missing link in computer-assisted writing. In K. Cameron (Ed.), *CALL: Media, design & applications* (pp. 271–292). Lisse: Swets & Zeitlinger.

Pennington, M. C. (1999b). Word processing and beyond: Writing in an electronic medium. In M. C. Pennington (Ed.), *Writing in an electronic medium: Research with language learners* (pp. 1–26). Houston: Athelstan.

Pennington, M. C. (2000). Writing minds and talking fingers: Doing literacy in an electronic age. In P. Brett (Ed.), *CALL in the 21st century* [CD-ROM]. Whitstable, UK: IATEFL.

Pennington, M. C., & Brock, M. N. (1992). Process and product approaches to computer-assisted composition. In M. C. Pennington & V. Stevens (Eds.), *Computers in applied linguistics: An international perspective* (pp. 79–109). Clevedon, UK: Multilingual Matters.

Phinney, M. (1989). Computers, composition, and second language teaching. In M. C. Pennington (Ed.), *Teaching languages with computers: The state of the art* (pp. 81–96). La Jolla, CA: Athelstan.

Phinney, M. (1991). Word processing and writing apprehension in first and second language writers. *Computers and Composition, 9,* 65–82.

Phinney, M., & Khouri, S. (1993). Computers, revision, and ESL writers: The role of experience. *Journal of Second Language Writing, 2,* 257–277.

Phinney, M., & Mathis, C. (1990). ESL student responses to writing with computers. *TESOL Newsletter, 24(2),* 30–31.

Roblyer, M. D., Castine, W. H., & King, F. J. (1988). *Assessing the impact of computer-based instruction: A review of recent research.* New York: Haworth.

Romano, S., Field, B., & Huergo, E. W. de. (2000). Web literacies of the already accessed and technically inclined: Schooling in Monterrey, Mexico. In G. E. Hawisher & C. L. Selfe (Eds.), *Global literacies and the World-Wide Web* (pp. 189–216). London: Routledge.

Rusmin, R. S. (1999). Patterns of adaptation to a new writing environment: The experience of word processing by mature second language writers. In M. C. Pennington (Ed.), *Writing in an electronic medium: Research with language learners* (pp. 183–227). Houston: Athelstan.

Sayers, D. (1989). Bilingual sister classes in computer writing networks. In D. M. Johnson & D. H. Roen (Eds.), *Richness in writing: Empowering ESL students* (pp. 120–133). New York: Longman.

Schramm, R. M. (1989). The effects of using word-processing equipment in writing instruction: A meta-analysis. (Doctoral dissertation, Northern Illinois University, 1990). *Dissertation Abstracts International, 50,* 2463A.

Slater, P., & Carpenter, C. (1999). Introducing e-mail into a course in French as a second language. In M. C. Pennington (Ed.), *Writing in an electronic medium: Research with language learners* (pp. 267–283). Houston: Athelstan.

Snyder, I. (1993). Writing with word processors: A research overview. *Educational Research, 35,* 49–68.

Spears, R., & Lea, M. (1992). Social influence and the influence of the "social" in computer-mediated communication. In R. Spears & M. Lea (Eds.), *Contexts of computer-mediated communication* (pp. 30–65). New York: Harvester Wheatsheaf.

Steelman, J. D. (1994). Revision strategies employed by middle level students using computers. *Journal of Educational Computing Research, 11,* 141–152.

Sullivan, N., & Pratt, E. (1996). A comparative study of two ESL writing environments: A computer-assisted classroom and a traditional oral classroom. *System, 24,* 491–501.

Susser, B. (1993). ESL/EFL process writing with computers. *CAELL Journal, 4(2),* 16–22.

Warschauer, M. (1997). Computer-mediated collaborative learning: Theory and practice. *Modern Language Journal, 81,* 470–481.

Warschauer, M. (1999). *Electronic literacies: Language, culture, and power in online education.* Mahwah, NJ: Lawrence Erlbaum.

Warschauer, M. (2000a). Language, identity, and the internet. In B. Kolko, L. Kakamura, & G. Rodman (Eds.), *Race in cyberspace* (pp. 151–170). London: Routledge.

Warschauer, M. (2000b). The death of cyberspace and the rebirth of CALL. In P. Brett (Ed.), *CALL in the 21st century* [CD-ROM]. Whitstable, UK: IATEFL.

Williamson, M. M., & Pence, P. (1989). Word processing and student writers. In B. Britton & S. M. Glynn (Eds.), *Computer writing environments: Theory, research, and design* (pp. 93–127). Hillsdale, NJ: Lawrence Erlbaum.

Windeatt, S., Hardisty, D., & Eastment, D. (2000). *The internet.* Oxford: Oxford University Press.

Woodin, J. (1997). E-mail tandem learning and the communicative curriculum. *ReCALL, 9(1),* 22–33.

Responding to and Assessing Second-Language Writing

Introduction to Part Five

How composition teachers respond to and assess student writing may say more about their pedagogy than even syllabi or assignments do. The articles in this section critically examine how the assessment of writing reflects teachers' positioning of second-language students in relation to their NES peers, and suggest productive and ethical ways to respond to second-language writers' texts.

The section begins with Robert E. Land Jr. and Catherine Whitley's landmark essay, "Evaluating Second Language Essays in Regular Composition Classes: Toward a Pluralistic U.S. Rhetoric." Land and Whitley argue that many evaluation practices in composition courses set unrealistic and unattainable goals for second-language writers—namely, to produce texts that emulate those produced by NES peers. Pointing to research that shows that second-language readers tend to rate second-language texts more highly than do NES readers, Land and Whitley challenge composition instructors to adopt the expectations of second-language readers, whose wide-ranging rhetorical experiences may predispose them to recognize the sophistication of second-language texts. Thus, they challenge instructors to take seriously composition studies' nominal embrace of multiculturalism and linguistic diversity by learning from their diverse students.

Carol Severino, in "The Sociopolitical Implications of Response to Second Language and Second Dialect Writing," picks up Land and Whitley's implication that the ways in which instructors respond to second-language writing entail implicit sociopolitical agendas. In this article, published in 1993, Severino draws from her wealth of experiences working with second-language writers as a university writing center director to argue that responses to second-language texts are directly related to readers' stances on whether and how much the student writers of those texts should assimilate into U.S. cultures. Echoing the framework for approaches to difference that Canagarajah lays out in part three (see p. 210 in this volume), Severino describes a range of stances readers can take in relation to a second-language student's writing: separatist, accommodationist, and assimilationist. Separatists do not give direct instruction on how writers should change their texts, but instead—as Land and Whitley do—attempt to help students preserve their differences from the perceived U.S. mainstream. At the other end, assimilationists regard linguistic diversity as "errors" or evidence of first language "interference," and advocate helping students eliminate such "deficiencies." In the middle of this spectrum is the accommodationist stance, which holds that second-language students "can be both *a part of* mainstream society and *apart from* it" (p. 338). Accommodationist readers would draw their students' attention to the options they have in negotiating possible responses to rhetorical situations through their writing.

Donald L. Rubin and Melanie Williams-James's "The Impact of Writer Nationality on Mainstream Teachers' Judgments of Composition Quality" (1997) presents research on how teachers' perceptions of students' ethnolinguistic identities can influence evaluation. In their analysis of responses by NES instructors to texts variously attributed to U.S., European, and Asian students, Rubin and Williams-James were surprised to find that their participants did not, in general, rate the second-language writers lower than the NES writers; in fact, they gave the papers attributed to Asian second-language writers the highest overall ratings in the study. Based on their findings, Rubin and Williams-James caution composition instructors to avoid grading solely on the number of surface errors, and stress the importance of providing written commentary on the strengths of a text, not just its weaknesses.

Pat Currie, in "Staying Out of Trouble: Apparent Plagiarism and Academic Survival," points to how instructors' responses might unexpectedly shape student writing. Originally published in 1998, Currie's article draws from a case study of "Diana," a native speaker of Cantonese, who had been writing in Canadian educational institutions for three years prior to the study. As the case study progresses, Diana increasingly borrows text from readings in her management course to use in her own writing, as part of her effort to "stay out of trouble." To the extent that Diana's teaching assistant (TA) rated her writing higher and higher as Diana integrated more and more copied text, Currie believes that the TA reinforced Diana's apparent plagiarism. Currie draws on critical reappraisals of the complexities of "plagiarism" to argue that second-language students' copying—rather than representing laziness or a lack of academic engagement—is often evidence of those students' attempts to acquire the vocabulary and conventions of their target disciplines. Students often must do this for themselves in the absence of explicit instruction about how disciplines create and use texts.

Dana Ferris and Barrie Roberts's "Error Feedback in L2 Writing Classes: How Explicit Does It Need to Be?" directly addresses effective ways for teachers to respond to surface-level features of second-language students' writing. In this article, originally published in 2001, Ferris and Roberts examine the effect of different methods of error response on the editing processes of second-language writers. They found that the second-language writers who participated in the study were better able to self-edit when their texts were marked for errors or when they were specifically coded by error type than when they were given no feedback. Moreover, Ferris and Roberts did not find that students edited better in response to specific error coding than to simple marking of errors, which may indicate that teachers do not need to take the time to code errors. However, they suggest that coding texts may have the pedagogical benefit of reducing student frustration.

The articles in this section raise a number of critical questions for instructors who are reconsidering assessment and response in light of the presence of second-language writers in their courses. How explicit do instructors need to be about generic conventions? About rhetorical preferences? Intertextual practices? Surface-level editing? How can instructors interrogate their assumptions about who second-language writers are and who they should become? Can second-language writers' diverse linguistic experiences inform new assessment standards and practices? And, since writing assessment frequently occurs outside of composition courses, what are the implications for those instructors? Exploring these and other questions raised by awareness of students' linguistic and cultural diversity will lead to more equitable and enriched pedagogy, not only for second-language students, but for all students.

17

Evaluating Second-Language Essays in Regular Composition Classes: Toward a Pluralistic U.S. Rhetoric

ROBERT E. LAND JR. AND
CATHERINE WHITLEY

How we go about empowering English as a second language (ESL) students when they enter regular college composition classes in the United States is determined by our response to two questions: What do we wish them to be empowered to do, and for whom are they being empowered? Our first response to these questions (a traditional, nominal one) is that we wish ESL students to acquire enough facility with standard written English (SWE) to succeed in school and in the workplace for their own benefit and, second, especially in the case of the large numbers of ESL students who are immigrants to this country, for the benefit of our society. To achieve these goals, we need to emphasize grammatical and syntactic correctness and, certainly at the college level where students are called upon to use written communication in a variety of disciplines and for a variety of purposes, we need to emphasize the larger rhetorical conventions of academic writing. Although, as Raimes (1986) notes, we have problems of implementation even in separate ESL classes, we have at hand the means of establishing programs to meet these goals.

Our nominal goal of helping students avoid linguistic disenfranchisement seems, at first glance, both pragmatic and responsible. However, the prevalent methods of evaluating writing—especially in classes where ESL students compete directly with native speakers (NSs) and where instructors have little or no training in teaching second language (L2) learners—suggest that we don't wish ESL students to attain only a "facility" with written English; instead, we expect them to become entirely fluent in English, a goal different in nature and implication from our purported one. The discrepancy between our purported and apparent goals for instructing ESL students emerges in our standards of evaluation as a hidden agenda—that is, an agenda that is rarely made known to the students whose writing is being evaluated and one that is seldom clear to the evaluator (see Sommers, 1982; Zamel, 1985). Thus, even when an ESL writer produces an error-free composition in

From *Richness in Writing: Empowering ESL Students*. Ed. Donna M. Johnson and Duane H. Roen. New York: Longman, 1989. 284–93.

English, a hidden agenda leads the evaluator to find fault with other formal features. Our research (Land and Whitley, 1986) suggests that the text features influencing English NS readers most negatively are the ESL students' patterns of organization, patterns established in what Purves (1986) calls "rhetorical communities" where ESL students learned their native language. At present, our understanding of the cultural determination of rhetorical patterns is limited, although investigations like those by Purves (1986), Hinds (1983), and Kaplan (1983) are extending these limits. We probably know too little about the mechanisms of our own preferred rhetorical patterns, let alone about those that ESL students bring with them, to establish programs aimed at reifying "ours" by isolating and eliminating "theirs" from their written English. But even if such knowledge were available, our efforts at making ESL students entirely fluent would almost certainly fail.

To be truly "fluent," our ESL students would have to be able to produce essays in English that were not only grammatically and syntactically, but also rhetorically indistinguishable from those written by their NS peers. But, as Haugen (1986) points out, even writers who are isolated for years from their first language (L1) culture produce texts in their L2 which carry noticeable L1 features; and most of our ESL students maintain strong associations with members of their L1 rhetorical communities. The distinct world views of these communities influence members' thoughts, actions, and, consequently, their patterns of communication for many generations (see, e.g., Giordano, 1976; Havighurst, 1978; McGoldrick, 1982). "English only" movements and literacy crises notwithstanding, we can neither legislate nor educate away culturally determined rhetorical differences in writing.

To enable ESL students to write English with "facility," we should, of course, pay special attention to teaching the linguistic conventions of SWE. We may also be able to teach them how to use some of SWE's rhetorical conventions. But such instruction may not be an end in itself. In the United States, SWE rhetorical conventions generally emphasize strong sentence-to-sentence connections, resulting in "linear" prose (see Kaplan, 1966), and a deductive logical arrangement that satisfies what Lakoff and Johnson (1980) call our "objectivist myth." But there are many patterns of cohesion, other logics, other myths through which views of the world may be constructed (see Knoblauch and Brannon, 1984). In teaching SWE rhetorical conventions, we are teaching students to reproduce in a mechanical fashion our preferred vehicle of understanding.

As MacCannell and MacCannell (1982) note, "culture that reproduces itself as a series of endless mirrorings, yet adds nothing to either the original 'natural culture' or the original 'image' of it, is literally the death of culture" (p. 28). Elsewhere they stress that "the heart of cultural evolution . . . begins with a production and proceeds to a reproduction that is not a simple doubling but a reflection at a higher power" (p. 26). In this view, we are encouraging our ESL students to contribute to the death of our culture: Their textual productions are simply to mirror, in their use of our rhetorical tradition, an experience that might be entirely foreign to them. We are not asking ESL writers to add to our culture from their own storehouses of experience; the sense is that our culture has reached the end of its evolution: There's nothing more to add. Trying to teach ESL students to reproduce SWE rhetoric may be not only likely to fail, but even if it were to be successful, it would be a pyrrhic victory.

Thus, we must change the way we read, respond to, and evaluate ESL writers' work at all stages of its development. If we fail to do so, our composition courses will be as retributive as they are instructive. If we wish to admit rhetorical concerns openly to our system of evaluation (thus unmasking the hidden agenda), if we believe that concerns of "correctness," content, and rhetoric are inseparable, then we must learn to recognize, value, and foster the alternative rhetorics that the ESL student brings to our language. In this chapter, we argue for such an approach, one that will not only empower students to succeed in school and at work, but will also free them to incorporate their own forms of logic into their writing, to the potential benefit of our language and culture.

RHETORICAL DIFFERENCES

No one who has ever read through a stack of compositions written by native and nonnative speakers needs to consult research to confirm that there are differences. Differences in the number of surface errors made by ESL students are obvious to teachers and have been well documented by researchers (Ahrens, 1984; Fein, 1980; Kroll, 1983). But error is not the only difference between texts written by ESL students and their NS peers. Even with error removed from all essays, researchers (McGirt, 1984; Whitley, 1984) have found that NS readers give higher scores to papers of NSs than to those written by ESL students. Clearly, other important differences exist.

Most of the research designed to find these important differences has focused on patterns of organization. Some of this research, following the work of Halliday and Hasan (1976), has focused on contrasting cohesive ties and drawing conclusions about textual cohesion from analysis of the ties, or from global measures of cohesion, or both (Connor, 1984; Land & Whitley, 1986; Lindsay, 1984; Scarcella, 1984). Along with more general investigations of differences (Hinds, 1983; Kaplan, 1966; Purves, 1986), these studies taken as a whole demonstrate fairly clearly that ESL writers connect their ideas differently than do NS writers. They demonstrate as well that these differences in organization are, at least in part, the result of ESL students' membership in distinct rhetorical communities and not necessarily the result of inadequate mastery of U.S. English. Finally, they demonstrate that these organizational differences are partly responsible for ESL students' essays being judged by NS readers as inferior to native speakers' essays.

One of the questions we have asked in our research (Land & Whitley, 1986) is whether or not the L1 status of readers would affect their perceptions of batches of student essays sampled from freshman composition classes where about half the students were nonnative speakers of English. We found, predictably, that U.S.-born NS readers rated the papers of ESL writers lower than the papers of NS students. But we also found that readers whose L1 was not English (our sample included native speakers of German, Spanish, and Japanese) rated essays from both ESL and NS students as being of about equal quality. Data from analytic rating scales revealed that the differences in perceptions of quality were probably the result of differences in perceptions of organization: The U.S.-born NS readers marked down ESL essays for what they perceived as problems of organization; readers whose L1 was not English did not mark down ESL texts for organization. In this respect our results mirror the language-specific research of Hinds (1983), who found that native English speaking readers rated the organization of English translations of Japanese newspaper articles lower than Japanese speaking readers rated the originals.

From our results we concluded that either our English NNS readers have lax standards and can't tell a poorly organized essay from a well organized one or they can accommodate to more kinds of rhetorical patterns than can NS readers. Because both groups of readers agreed on the ratings of NS essays, and because both groups were sampled from our pool of experienced teachers of freshman writing, we opted for the second conclusion. We believe that our bilingual and multilingual readers' experience with different kinds of texts used in different cultures allow them to adapt to and value writing that employs varying rhetorical organizations.

READERS READING

Any reader confronting any text faces it with a preconceived set of expectations; as Iser (1976/1978) and Carrell (1982) note, the reader comes to a text armed with the sum of previous reading experiences. The reader and the text interact in the process of reading. The wandering viewpoint is a means of describing the way in which the reader is present in the text. This presence is at a point where memory and expectation converge, and the resultant dialectic movement brings about a continual modification of memory and an increasing complexity of expectation. These processes depend on the reciprocal spotlighting of the perspectives, which provide interrelated backgrounds for one another. The interaction between these backgrounds provokes the reader into synthesizing activity (Iser, 1976/1978). The expectations of a teacher of writing in the United States would be based upon the grammatical, syntactic, and rhetorical conventions of SWE, expectations which the student essay should trigger and bring into play, thus beginning the dialectic movement. For instance, the presence of an identifiable, analytic thesis sentence signals a certain rhetorical pattern and allows the reader to begin building a set of expectations specific to that particular text. The reader remembers the thesis, moves on, and expects to find its promise fulfilled.

Because ESL readers seem to find organization in ESL texts—texts that NS readers judge to be poorly organized—perhaps they have a wider and more varied set of expectations when they come to a text, expectations resulting from a wider and more varied reading experience. As Purves (1986) has shown, "good" student writers from different countries (students selected by their own instructors as being exemplary), when asked to write an essay on the same topic, write those essays in different rhetorical modes that vary in stance, descriptive quality, and levels of abstraction and concreteness. He notes that "the fact that the compositions come from 'good' students suggests that these students have learned and are applying the norms of their rhetorical community" (Purves, 1986, p. 43); these students have learned to conform to the expectations of the community in which they find themselves. Likewise, the ESL readers have negotiated between the norms of their native communities and the one in which they find themselves; these readers recognized the SWE patterns of organization in the NS essays.

If every time we face a student paper we do so with the expectations of SWE firmly in mind, and we expect to find a linear, deductive argument, our experience of reading ESL students' essays will be different from our experience of reading NS students'. Most ESL students, even those in "regular" (i.e., linguistically heterogeneous) college writing classes, have not learned to use the organizational patterns of U.S. academic prose. This does not mean they are "bad" writers or that their essays are "badly organized"; it could mean that they are very skillfully manipulating patterns of organization that we don't recognize. A reader with expectations shaped by SWE will not interact successfully (in Iser's terms) with such essays; ESL writers' essays will not trigger dialectic movements because they do not fulfill the reader's expectations.

If the "wandering viewpoint" is a way to describe the way in which the reader is present in the text, then a reader with SWE expectations continues to wander rather aimlessly in a text by an ESL writer because the reader cannot recognize the signposts left by the writer. (For instance, we have found that ESL writers tend to use a few distantly separated cohesive ties as a way of establishing coherence, something very uncommon in their NS peers' work.) Readers should allow themselves to be lost for a while, for readers who suspend judgment and thus become accustomed to recognizing a wider variety of rhetorical modes, will begin to alter their expectations, to widen them, a process which will ultimately permit them to interact with more types of texts, thereby enriching their reading processes.

In contrast, readers who rigidly insist on finding a set of distinct expectations met in every encounter with student writing squelch in themselves responses to different approaches to presenting and receiving ideas; in effect, they suppress new information. SWE, as a set of conventions, is itself a rigid and rather artificial stratum of English if, as Bakhtin (1975/1981) describes, all national languages are stratified into social dialects, characteristic group behavior, a professional jargon, generic languages, languages of generations and age groups, tendentious languages, languages of authorities, of various circles, and of passing fashions, languages that serve the specific sociopolitical purpose of the day (pp. 262–263). In this view, SWE is just a particular stratification of English, the one privileged by and identified with academia, a sublanguage which, by its nature, is sociopolitical.

In demanding that ESL students write SWE and use a deductive, linear argument, we are asking them to situate themselves within a particular sociopolitical context, and we respond to and judge their writing according to how accurately they are able to do so. If students are not natives of this culture they will be less likely to signal satisfactorily to us, the readers, their understanding of their position within the English language as a sociopolitical construct; even if their writing is in more or less error-free English, they will still be writing according to the norms of their native communities. By asking these students to use our signals according to our expectations, we are not taking language to be "a system of abstract grammatical categories"; instead, we are at least implicitly understanding "language conceived as ideologically saturated, language as world view" (Bakhtin, 1975/1981, p. 271). We require our ESL students to share and reproduce in their writing our world view, one to which they are, of course, alien. Such instruction is composition as colonization.

CHANGING THE WAY WE READ, RESPOND, AND EVALUATE

In general we would argue that all teachers should become more like the ESL readers in our study; that they acquire the ability to suspend judgment, to allow the piece of writing at hand to develop slowly, like a photographic print, shading in the details. But what does this mean in practice? It may mean that teachers with ESL students should become familiar with rhetorical traditions their students bring with them (see Reid, 1989). It certainly means that we need to consciously suppress our desire to label ESL writers' work as "out of focus" or "lacking in organization."

In our regular freshman writing classes, for example, assignments written by writing program directors are given to the teachers to be distributed. These assignments often require the ESL students in these classes, many of whom are U.S. residents who have spoken English for five or fewer years, to use conventional SWE structures such as thesis paragraphs. The ESL students comply, at least superficially, with these conventions. Eventually, however, usually in the second or third paragraph, ESL students return to the organizational conventions of their native rhetorics. This return does not go unnoticed; based on our examination of hundreds of marked essays, when ESL students stop consciously attending to the formal concerns of SWE patterns and begin focusing on what they have to say, teachers begin to note "problems" of clarity, focus, and organization. We would argue that it is here, at this point of departure from SWE expectations, that readers should suspend judgment and read on for meaning. After reading the entire text, a teacher might suggest that the introductory thesis paragraph is superfluous, instead of noting that the rest of the essay doesn't live up to the promise of the introduction. Or the teacher might suggest alternatives to seemingly disembodied topic sentences, alternatives that would meet the obligation of teaching the student how to produce passable prose that would not be dismissed, out of hand, by less open readers. In some cases, the teacher might not know how to respond to the text except by asking lots of questions about what the student was trying to say. In some situations we have known exactly where to help our ESL students; in others we have had only very vague ideas.

Perhaps the most common specific deviation from SWE expectations that we find in ESL students' papers is what seems like redundancy. Sometimes students seem to repeat themselves pointlessly or they seem to argue the same point in slightly different ways, paragraph after paragraph, each paragraph a modest addition or alteration of given information. We have chosen a similar structure for this chapter; we have argued for the same point, "that teachers should change the way they evaluate ESL writers' papers," in several ways. We hope our readers will be generous and recognize that we do so by trying to appeal separately to logic, the "facts" of research, the "authority" of theory and, finally, to our own personal experience—all of which are fairly standard "artistic" and "inartistic" proofs of Western classical rhetoric, although it might have been more traditional for us to have outlined our plan earlier in the text. More generosity is often needed when we read our students' texts.

One helpful strategy for reading seemingly redundant essays is to use a form of "topical structure" analysis like the one Connor and Farmer (1985) suggest as a revision strategy for writers. In its simple form, one circles, during the second reading, all of the grammatical subjects of all the independent clauses. Rereading the list of subjects can lead readers to revisions of their initial understanding of the essay as patterns of meaning that were not at first evident are revealed. Often the subjects seem to operate as higher-order cohesive devices. For example, one student (whose essay we used in our research) used thunder, or a variant thereof, as the subject of three very distantly removed sentences in his essay on the possibility of afterlife. Of course this bit of imagery stood out and it was fairly easy to recognize that the repetition seemed to operate as a device connecting distinct parts of his essay, but this was an essay that NS readers scored low because of its poor organization and that ESL readers scored high and found to be acceptably organized. Now, when we receive a paper like that one, we usually recognize its structure; we no longer make comments about its organization.

Conclusion

Research suggests that evaluative focus on sentence-level mechanics may be a waste of the teacher's time (Robb, Ross, & Shortreed, 1986) and confusing and even harmful to students (Land & Evans, 1987; Zamel, 1985). Thus, against all the forces that seem to keep our attention riveted on surface concerns, good pedagogy demands that we respond to larger features of our students' texts. As we learn to rid ourselves of surface-level tunnel vision, we will have to struggle against the forces that can lead us to rigid, oversimplified notions of how essays should be structured: rhetoric-level myopia.

Assuming that our responses to students' essays are intended to inform them in specific ways about how to make those pieces of writing (or the next ones) better, we can ask students to add to, delete from, or alter the paper; or we can let students know that they should keep up the good work. We have argued that teachers of ESL students should broaden their concept of what constitutes "good work" and that they should not automatically request additions of SWE features and deletions and modifications of everything else. In the end, because ESL texts customarily contain a lot of the "everything else," such practices should cut down on the amount of marking teachers feel they must do. At first (and even much later, especially when faced with high stacks of papers in the wee hours), reading "interactively" is hard work. It would be easy, in the midst of trying to figure out a particularly puzzling text, to dismiss the whole project as idealistic, impractical, or stupid and to return to the more comfortable, familiar mode of reading with narrow SWE rhetorical expectations.

To do so would be to ignore what is happening to our culture and our language: they are becoming more pluralistic, not coincidentally with the rise of English as the world language. If we are indeed part of a culture which admits change, this change will obviously appear at the linguistic level because one's epistemology underlies one's language. When our language changes, it is a sign that our way of thinking has changed. Unless we want to institute a structure like the Academie Française or the British Royal Academy, we have no choice but to recognize and examine the changes that are happening daily everywhere in order to see what we think now.

REFERENCES

Ahrens, C. D. (1984). *Comparing composition skills of native and non-native born students at the junior high school level.* Unpublished master's thesis, University of California at Los Angeles.

Bakhtin, M. M. (1981). *The dialogic imagination* (C. Emerson & M. Holquist, Trans.; M. Holquist, Ed.). Austin: University of Texas Press. (Original work published 1975.)

Carrell, P. (1982). Cohesion is not coherence. *TESOL Quarterly, 16*, 479–488.

Connor, U. (1984). A study of cohesion and coherence in ESL students' writing. *Papers in Linguistics: International Journal of Human Communication, 17*, 301–316.

Connor, U., & Farmer, M. (1985, April). *The teaching of topical structure analysis as a revision strategy: An exploratory study.* Paper presented at the annual meeting of the American Educational Research Association, Chicago.

Fein, D. (1980). *A comparison of English and ESL compositions.* Unpublished master's thesis, University of California at Los Angeles.

Giordano, J. (1976). Community mental health in a pluralistic society. *International Journal of Mental Health, 5*, 5–15.

Halliday, M. A. K., & Hasan, R. (1976). *Cohesion in English.* London: Longman Group, Ltd.

Haugen, E. (1986). Bilinguals have more fun! *Journal of English Linguistics, 19*, 106–120.

Havighurst, R. J. (1978). Structural aspects of education and cultural pluralism. *Educational Research Quarterly, 2*, 5–19.

Hinds, J. (1983). Contrastive rhetoric: Japanese and English. *Text, 3*, 183–195.

Iser, W. (1978). *The act of reading: A theory of aesthetic response.* Baltimore: Johns Hopkins University Press. (Original work published 1976)

Kaplan, R. B. (1966). Cultural thought patterns in intercultural education. *Language Learning, 16*, 1–20.

Kaplan, R. B. (1983). Contrastive rhetoric: Some implications for the writing process. In A. Freedman, I. Pringle & J. Yalden (Eds.). *Learning to write: First language/second language* (pp. 138–161). New York: Longman.

Knoblauch, C. H., & Brannon, L. (1984). *Rhetorical traditions and the teaching of writing.* Upper Montclair, NJ: Boynton/Cook.

Kroll, B. (1983). Levels of error in ESL composition (Doctoral dissertation, University of California at Los Angeles, 1982). *Dissertation Abstracts International, 43,* 3307A–3308A. (University of Southern California Micrographics No. 2898A)

Lakoff, G., & Johnson, M. (1980). *Metaphors we live by.* Chicago: University of Chicago Press.

Land, R. E., & Evans, S. (1987). What our students taught us about paper making. *English Journal, 76*(2), 113–116.

Land, R. E., & Whitley, C. (1986, April). *Influences of second-language factors on the performance of freshman writers.* Paper presented at the annual meeting of the American Educational Research Association, San Francisco.

Lindsay, D. B. (1984). *Cohesion in the compositions of ESL and English students.* Unpublished master's thesis, University of California at Los Angeles.

MacCannell, D., & MacCannell, J. F. (1982). *The time of the sign: A semiotic interpretation of modern culture.* Bloomington: Indiana University Press.

McGirt, J. D. (1984). *The effect of morphological and syntactic errors on the holistic scores of native and non-native compositions.* Unpublished master's thesis, University of California at Los Angeles.

McGoldrick, M. (1982). Ethnicity and family therapy: An overview. In M. McGoldrick, J. K. Pearce, & J. Giardano (Eds.), *Ethnicity and family therapy* (pp. 3–30). New York: Guilford.

Purves, A. C. (1986). Rhetorical communities, the international student, and basic writing. *Journal of Basic Writing, 5,* 38–51.

Raimes, A. (1986). Teaching ESL writing: Fitting what we do to what we know. *The Writing Instructor, 5,* 153–166.

Reid, J. M. (1989). English as a second language composition in higher education: The expectations of the academic audience. In D. M. Johnson & D. H. Roen (Eds.), *Richness in writing: Empowering ESL students* (pp. 220–234). New York: Longman.

Robb, T., Ross, S., & Shortreed, I. (1986). Salience of feedback on error and its effect on EFL writing quality. *TESOL Quarterly, 20,* 83–93.

Scarcella, R. (1984). How writers orient their readers in expository essays: A comparative study of native and nonnative English writers. *TESOL Quarterly, 17,* 165–187.

Sommers, N. (1982). Responding to student writing. *College Composition and Communication, 33,* 148–156.

Whitley, C. (1984). *Error, content, and grading: ESL vs NES.* Unpublished manuscript, University of California at Irvine.

Zamel, V. (1985). Responding to student writing. *TESOL Quarterly, 19,* 79–101.

18

The Sociopolitical Implications of Response to Second-Language and Second-Dialect Writing

CAROL SEVERINO

INTRODUCTION

Toward the conclusion of "Ideology in Composition: L1 and ESL," after portraying the first language (L1) field as expressly political and the second language/English as a Second Language (L2/ESL) field as non- or apolitical, Terry Santos (1992) speculates about whether L2/ESL studies will follow L1 composition studies in articulating a similar ideological stance. Although the political implications of L2/ESL teaching are not yet clearly and frequently articulated, they are more evident than has been heretofore suggested. Both inside and outside the university, ESL teaching abounds with ideological undertones, overtones, and arguments, which, as Johns (1990) recommends, need to be brought out in the open—the primary goal of this article. To accomplish this goal, I first discuss the ideological implications of ESL teaching in general and then develop a "continuum of sociopolitical stances" toward response to second language and second dialect writers and their writing. I then apply the continuum of stances to actual and alternative responses to three writers from different cultural and language backgrounds to illustrate on a practical level the political nature of ESL instruction.

THE POLITICS OF ESL INSTRUCTION

The political dimensions of ESL pedagogy are evident in many contexts, both academic and nonacademic. On a university level, ESL curricula such as English for Academic Purposes (EAP) and English for Specific Purposes (ESP) are not simply pragmatic as Swales (1990) suggests, but imply an acculturative ideological stance—the desirability of assimilating quickly into academic, corporate, and U.S. mainstream cultures. In other words, the implications of an EAP or ESP curriculum are ideological, but the ideology can be construed as more conservative and assimilative to the status quo, not radical and challenging to it, as the pedagogies advocated by the L1 composition scholars Santos (1992) mentions purport to be. Expressivist L2 writing

From *Journal of Second Language Writing* 2.3 (1993): 181–201.

pedagogies emphasizing personal experience, growth, and discovery also have assimilative and Americanizing implications, especially for international students whose home cultures are more oriented to the group rather than to the individual (Leki, 1992). Emphasizing individualism in writing pedagogy is a particularly Western, or more specifically, American, cultural and political bias; it is neither ideologically neutral nor culturally universal. Politics also surface when ESL teachers are reluctant to engage in discussions of world politics with students from the wealthy and influential upper classes of their native countries—"the educational and economic elite of the world," as Johns (1993) characterizes them. These teachers fear the classroom tension and discomfort which might result when students disagree with them and with one another about how nations should be governed. How can the sources of such tension be characterized in any way but political?

Outside the university, the political implications of ESL teaching are even more evident. In community-based ESL programs in large U.S. cities, the dynamics of the curriculum are more obviously assimilative and conservative in ideology; such programs promise immigrants and refugees that learning English will increase their chances of acquiring jobs and the good life. Auerbach and Burgess (1985) have shown that ESL "survival approach" curricula common in these programs often encourage passive and subservient social roles in relation to employers, health professionals, and agency bureaucrats: "Language functions in most survival texts include asking for approval, clarification, reassurance, permission, and so on, but not praising, criticizing, complaining, refusing, or disagreeing" (p. 484). James Tollefson (1989) in his book *Alien Winds: The Reeducation of America's Indochinese Refugees* describes how the ESL curricula of the refugee programs follow the tradition of the Americanization movement by communicating to refugees that their ability to solve economic and social problems depends on their cultural and economic assimilation. Tollefson points out that in contrast to the post-World War I Americanization programs in which immigrants were taught to make sandwiches and pies and salute the flag, today's ESL texts "focus instead on the ethos of the consumer society. Rather than didactic patriotism, texts teach economic patriotism—the importance of proper market behavior and of accepting the principle of starting at the bottom of the employment ladder" (p. 57).

In the recent Amnesty Program for undocumented workers, ESL pedagogy was also reminiscent of the Americanization described in *The Education of Hyman Kaplan* (Ross, 1937), although the political circumstances of this recent wave of immigrants were more threatening to them; to avoid deportation, undocumented workers learned English while studying pro-U.S. versions of civics and history from materials produced by the Immigration and Naturalization Service. The students prepared for test questions such as "What were the 13 colonies?" and "How many stripes are on the U.S. flag?" (Wolfram, 1992).

Many ESL teachers resisted the propagandistic features of the ideological ESL/Amnesty curriculum and encouraged their students to do likewise; they developed a counter-ideology of resistance modeled on the problem-posing pedagogy of Paulo Freire (1972), Ira Shor (1987), and Henry Giroux (1983) and specifically adapted to ESL instruction by Nina Wallerstein (1983) — to think critically about what they are learning and about their economic and linguistic situations, to choose, as Wolfram (1992) says, the relationship they want to have with the dominant culture in which they find themselves. The very circumstances of these students' ESL classes — learning the host's language in the host's country in hopes of increasing their economic status — are manifestly political. As Tollefson (1989) demonstrates, it is often the case that U.S. policies in their native countries have contributed to their immigration to the U.S. in the first place. In fact, the ascendance and dominance of English, contributing to the proliferation of ESL or English as a Foreign Language (EFL) programs both in the U.S. and abroad, is obviously political, thus causing the situation of *any* ESL student in *any* classroom inside or outside a university to be ideologically charged. To use Frederick Erickson's (1984) terms, the "micropolitics" of the ESL teaching/learning situation inevitably reflect the "macropolitics" of the world situation.

BLURRING OF L1 AND L2 DEMOGRAPHICS AND PEDAGOGIES

Santos (1992) predicts that L2 pedagogical literature may gradually become more expressly political, for as the demographics of the college population change, it becomes more difficult to separate L1 from L2 pedagogy. Indeed, the fields are becoming closer as classrooms become more multicultural and ESL students become harder to distinguish from non-ESL students. Ann Johns (1993) recently described a proposal at one California state institution to combine L1 and L2 writing instruction into one Department of Rhetoric and Writing Studies. Increasing numbers of college students, especially in California, New York, Illinois, Texas, and Florida, were born in countries such as Mexico, El Salvador, Korea, Vietnam, The Philippines, or China, but have received much if not most of their education in the U.S. Years of a U.S. education, including years in Intensive College English and ESL, do not guarantee native-speaker proficiency; how then are these second-generation immigrants grouped — with L1 or L2 students?

Sorting and classifying students and disciplinary subfields can become hairsplitting. For example, if the students just described are fairly fluent, conversant English *speakers*, but not fluent English *writers*, are they L1 or L2? And what about the large population of bilingual Puerto Rican students raised in New York or Chicago who are speakers of a dialect similar to African-American English Vernacular? Are they L1, L2, or Standard English as a Second Dialect (SESD)? And how much should it matter how teachers label various types of ESL students?

What should matter is not how teachers label fields and students, but how they teach them, especially how they respond to students' writing. My argument is that whatever our responses to their writing are, they have sociopolitical implications, some more subtle than others, that need to be brought out in the open and examined. To support this argument, I use three case studies to analyze actual and alternative responses to the writing of three college students from different linguistic and academic backgrounds— an L2/ESL international student, a bicultural ESL student, and an L1 (SESD) student. This analysis of actual practices helps counteract the tendency toward vagueness of much ideological L1 composition theory which is hard to translate into everyday teaching situations (Santos, 1992), as well as the tendency of ESL pedagogy toward pragmatism without acknowledging ideology (Johns, 1993; Santos, 1992).

THREE STANCES TOWARD RESPONSE TO WRITING

In my analysis, I argue that all teachers and tutors, consciously or subconsciously, have a *stance toward response* to all writing, in this case, second language and second dialect writing. This stance, or, as Louise Wetherbee Phelps (1989) calls it, the "deep structure of response to writing," is determined by a complex of many factors, some more influential than others, in different situations. One factor is how the teacher's own L1 and L2 writing has been responded to by English and foreign language teachers. Other influential factors are the pedagogy of the overall writing/language program, the demands of a particular writing assignment, and the needs of the writers and their linguistic and academic situations—their own ideas and feelings about what features constitute helpful responses to their writing. Also, factors such as whether international students will be returning to the native country or going onto the U.S. job market affect the way a teacher responds to them and their writing.

Teachers' stances are also determined by an even weightier factor— their general political attitude, or their *ideology*, as James Berlin (1988) would say, toward international students and dialect speakers. Specifically, this political attitude or ideology of response is about the issue and extent of acculturation—how much and how quickly or even *if* teachers think second language and second dialect students should assimilate culturally, socially, and linguistically into the U.S. corporate and academic mainstreams, and how much of their cultural and language patterns they can and should retain. Related to the degree of acculturation assumed desirable by writing teachers, three stances for responding to writing are posited: *separatist, accommodationist,* and *assimilationist.* These stances comprise a continuum of response represented by the broken line (----) in Table 1.

Models representing different stances toward social, cultural, and linguistic assimilation have been developed in ethnic studies, sociolinguistics, and L1 composition. In ethnic studies, the conflict between the assimilationist, or melting-pot, model and the model of cultural pluralism to explain immigration and assimilation patterns in the U.S. (Chametzky, 1989–90) has been explored by historians Nathan Glazer and Daniel Moynihan (1963) in their classic work *Beyond the Melting Pot: The Negroes, Puerto Ricans, Jews, Italians, and Irish of New York City* and by Milton Gordon (1964) in *Assimilation in American Life.* In sociolinguistics, more than 20 years ago, different stances toward

TABLE 1. A Continuum Representing Sociopolitical Stances toward Response to Second Language and Second Dialect Writing

>---

	Sociopolitical Stance		
	Separatist	*Accommodationist*	*Assimilationist*
1) Attitude about cultures	Independent cultures	Intersecting cultures	A blended U.S. culture
2) Attitude about differences	Ignore differences	Explain differences	Correct differences
3) Public policy examples	"Students' Right to Their Own Language" (1974)	1979 Ann Arbor Decision	"English Only" Movement
4) Student case-study examples	Michael	Susan	Takaro

linguistic assimilation by teachers and administrators were addressed by Ralph Fasold and Roger Shuy (1970) in their preface to *Teaching Standard English in the Inner City*. They contrasted three pedagogical approaches to the dialect differences of African-American students: eradication, biloquialism, and appreciation of dialect differences. Min-Zhan Lu (1992) has examined the differences between acculturative, assimilationist, and accommodationist L1 composition pedagogies and how they have been articulated in relation to the basic writers who entered City University of New York through Open Admissions; she then proposes a fourth alternative—a "pedagogy of struggle."

Two features on the Table 1 continuum distinguish the stances from one another: (a) the attitude toward culture contact, and (b) the attitude toward linguistic differences. I define the first stance, *separatism*, as the belief that cultures, languages, and dialects in contact should be able to exist almost independently—unaffected, untainted by mainstream cultures, languages, and dialects. The second more compromising position of *accommodation* is the belief that second language and second dialect speakers can be both *a part of* mainstream society and *apart from* it, retaining to some extent their culture and language. The third position is *assimilation*—the stance that everyone should blend into the mainstream or melting pot. Table 1 must be thought of as a continuum because those involved with L1/L2 writing are likely to fall somewhere in between the categories or may even occasionally change response stances.

These stances, if contemplated apart from the continuum, might seem like a set-up for the classic "critical" L1 composition essay in which three views are laid out, and one of them, usually the third, is obviously the most correct, thereby pointing the finger at those who subscribe to the first and second views. However, following Fasold and Shuy (1970), I believe that valid political and pedagogical arguments exist for each stance, arguments I hope to explain fairly, although my preference is for the accommodationist view, as theirs is for biloquialism.

Assimilationist Stance

The most extreme assimilationist response to second language or second dialect writing would be to encourage the student to write linear, thesis-statement and topic-sentence-driven, error-free, and idiomatic academic English as soon as possible. The goal is to smoothly blend or melt into the desired discourse communities and avoid social stigma by controlling any features that in the eyes of audiences with power and influence might mark a writer as inadequately educated or lower class. The assimilationist position on what Bruce Horner (1992) calls the "sociality of error" is conservative. Linguistic differences would be regarded as "errors" or instances of L1 "interference" — cultural or linguistic—to be eliminated.

At their best, assimilationist responses are practical, bottom-line acknowledgments of the realities and demands of academic and corporate discourses, in short, what many students (and their parents) assume they are paying for when they sign up for an L1 or L2 course. At their worst, a disproportionate attention to form and convention over meaning and message either inadvertently or purposely disparages students for the language, skills, and culture they bring with them into the classroom/writing center. Sensitive, moderate assimilationist responses are savvy about discourse conventions, the job market, and promotions; insensitive, extremist ones put students and their cultures down and aim to eradicate linguistic and cultural differences.

Separatist Stance

In contrast, the most extreme separatist view holds that assimilationist responses are unjust and colonialistic and that language minorities should not have to change or adapt in order to gain educational and economic rights and opportunities. Like those who advocate the third approach described by Fasold and Shuy (1970), which they call "appreciation of dialect differences," separatists believe that the society and the class of employers or educators that disparage and discriminate against ESL and SESD speakers should be challenged and changed, not the ESL and SESD speakers themselves or their discourses. Separatists want to preserve and celebrate linguistic diversity, not eradicate it.

Language policy statements and movements illustrate how the stances and the continuum function. Separatists were more influential in the 1960s and 1970s as shown by the position statement, "Students' Right To Their Own Language" (1974), of the Conference on College Composition and Communication (CCCC). For this reason, the CCCC's statement is placed toward the left on the Table 1 continuum. The 1979 Ann Arbor Court Decision, which held that teachers of Vernacular Black English speakers must educate themselves about their students' language and use this knowledge of language contrasts to teach standard English, is placed in the middle of the continuum, where sociolinguistics argue it belongs, not at the separatist end where the media placed it (Farr, 1980). The ideologically conservative "English Only" Movement is placed at the right (Auerbach, 1992).

At their best and in the most ideal contexts, separatist responses, in emphasizing meaning and ignoring formal differences, permit the ESL or SESD writer to work on fluency, development, and communication, freed from what might be distractions and constraints, such as attention to word endings and spelling. Separatists read ESL texts generously, with a "cosmopolitan eye" (Leki, 1992); they are accepting of different culturally influenced logics and rhetorical patterns. As Land and Whitley (1989) say, such readers of ESL writing "allow the piece of writing at hand to develop slowly, like a photographic print shading in the details" (p. 290). At their worst, separatist responses, forgiving or applauding deviations from Standard English rhetorical and grammatical patterns, inevitably set students up for a shock when the next teacher, tutor, or employer they encounter tends toward an assimilationist stance.

Accommodationist Stance

An accommodationist stance, like Fasold and Shuy's (1970) biloquialism, often called the "compromise" position (Farr, 1990), includes students not giving up their home oral and written discourse patterns in order to assimilate, but instead acquiring *new* discourse patterns, thus enlarging their rhetorical repertoires for different occasions. In the best of all possible accommodationist worlds, patterns are only gained, not lost; true bi- or tri- or even multilingualism and culturalism would be the ideal, a stance embodied in Lisle and Mano's (1997, pp. 12–26) "Embracing a Multicultural Rhetoric." At their best, accommodationist responses are comprehensive and rhetorical, emphasizing that certain discourse features are appropriate or inappropriate for certain occasions. At their worst, they are longwinded, laden with conditions, and hard to process. Accommodationists tell students that in certain more informal situations, certain features, like lack of idiomatic English for ESL students and lack of past tense or third-person-singular-present tense markers for SESD speakers are acceptable, but in certain more formal situations, they are unacceptable. "It all depends on how much like a native speaker you want to sound," teachers tell ESL students. "It all depends on what kind of an impression you want to make on whom," teachers tell SESD speakers. At their worst, the accommodationists' conditions, contexts, and qualifications may sound like double-talk that may confuse more than help the students; with their explanations they might even help themselves more than students as the accommodationists literally talk themselves into feeling better for not Americanizing ESL students or forcing African-American students into standard English and out of their spoken dialect. Sensitive accommodationists are, according to their name, accommodating of both linguistic differences and societal conventions. Insensitive accommodationists are overexplainers, whose own agenda, shared by many separatists, to rid themselves of any association with academic or linguistic assimilation or colonization, can overwhelm their teaching of writing.

RESPONSES TO THREE WRITERS

The enactment of these stances will be demonstrated in actual and optional responses to the writing of three students: (a) Takaro, an international student from Japan, a senior in his mid-20s who is planning to become a teacher of Japanese in the U.S.; (b) Susan, an 18-year-old freshman who immigrated with her family from Korea at age 11 and is embarking on a liberal arts education; and (c) Michael, an African-American student in his 20s, a janitor for the university, enrolled in the university's evening program. Takaro had been referred to the writing center by International Student Services; Susan, by her classroom teacher; and Michael, by a friend.

I will describe to you the ways I responded to Takaro's, Susan's, and Michael's texts, all of which were written at the beginning of the semester in and for the writing center, not for a grade or a class, but for written and verbal responses to help them improve as writers. After these introductory assignments, however, students can receive help with any of their academic papers for any graded course. The center's pedagogy, in keeping with the writing and speaking courses it also serves, is rhetorical; writers write to communicate rather than to demonstrate proficiency, and meaning/content/ideas are more important than the formal features of grammar and mechanics, although the latter considerations cannot be ignored, especially when they interfere with the message conveyed. This writing center operates more like an independent study course than a drop-in center; students commit themselves to coming to the center twice a week and work with the same teacher throughout the semester.

The sample texts of all three students are political in content: Takaro's is about the tragedy of a Japanese-American bilingual after WWII, Susan's is about her "binationality" possibly preventing her from acquiring "A Sense of Place," the title of her assignment, and Michael's is about the Nazi invasion of The Netherlands, the setting for *The Diary of Anne Frank*, the book he chooses to discuss. Such emotionally, culturally, and politically charged themes, common in the texts of writing center students, international students, and basic writers, demand responses that are content-based. Not to address the substance of the students' accounts of political and personal tragedy is reminiscent of the caricature of the insensitive elementary-school teacher who responded to the written sentence "Yestrday my sistr was hit by a truk" by correcting the student's spelling.

The ways I responded all tend toward accommodationist on the Table 1 continuum, although my responses to Michael veered more closely to separatist than my responses to Takaro and Susan. With Takaro, I tended more toward assimilationist (see Table 1). I will also suggest alternative responses that are more separatist and more assimilationist to these three students' texts. Using my own interactions with students rather than those of other teachers has both disadvantages and advantages; in these combination self and case studies, the objectivity that is lost is compensated for by the opportunity for "thick" description (Geertz, 1973) of and critical reflection about the texts and responses to them.

Takaro

Takaro wrote "Futatsu no sokoku" (Appendix A) in 1 ½ class periods. His essay is strikingly relevant to the present discussion in its powerful depiction of the conflicts of a bilingual/bicultural interpreter. In response to a previous assignment to describe his reading interests, Takaro had written that he had recently stayed up all night to finish the book *Two Motherlands*. I asked him for his next assignment to write about the book and why it was important to him. When he finished his piece up to the completed sentence of line 40, he called me over to tell me that he did not consider himself finished because he had not yet told how he felt about the book; he said he wanted to do that the next lab period.

My response to the text that he handed me was as follows: I sat down and with the paper between us, I read it aloud rhetorically with feeling and meaning like a reader. In this expressive oral reading, I did not stumble or do doubletakes over nonidiomatic phrases, inconsistencies in tense, or the *l* and *r* errors, and I supplied the missing articles myself. If there was an emotional section, I reacted the way I actually felt. Because I had never seen Takaro's essay or read the book before, it was all new and news; to use James Kinneavy's (1971) term, this discourse had "surprise value." Of course, I was shocked upon reading that the main character, Kenji, committed suicide and stopped reading to react accordingly. Then Takaro and I briefly discussed the dilemma of being caught between two worlds, two nonaccommodating ones.

At Takaro's next lab period, the following week, he took about 20 minutes to write the last three sentences (line 40, "This novel is . . .") about what the book meant to him. Again, I read these lines as an interested reader. When I looked a bit puzzled afterwards, he showed me the Japanese characters he had written at the top of the original page and explained how their meaning was ambiguous; they could be translated two ways into two "ancestral lands" *or* two "nations." As Takaro says, being caught between two nation states or two governments or political entities destroyed Kenji, not being caught between two cultures.

Had I been more separatist, I might have adopted a "hands off formal features" (verbs, wording, spelling) policy and stopped responding right there. Rhetorically reading for meaning would have been enough; after all, Takaro's discourse is not only comprehensible, but powerful, rich, and interesting. I could have ignored its various levels of L1 transfer—cultural, syntactic, and phonological. That is, Takaro's conclusion could be an instance of cultural transfer—a writer from a reader-based rhetoric of Japanese (Hinds, 1987) expecting an English-speaking reader from a writer-based rhetoric to understand the ambiguity of "Two Motherlands" without further explanation. Syntactic transfer is evident in the missing articles and the nonidiomatic phrasing, and phonological interference in the confusing of *l* and *r*, resulting in "interigence" (line 19) and "corapse" (line 23). However, the grammar, wording, *l–r*, and other spelling (pronunciation) problems were not serious enough to interfere with the communication of Takaro's summary and evaluation of *Two Motherlands*.

After doing an error analysis, I discovered that Takaro's most common error was inconsistency of tense. He had two problems with articles and six spelling mistakes—two, as mentioned, from phonological interference. Five problems were in wording/phrasing, some more "global" (causing some cognitive strain to a native speaker) than others (Burt & Kiparsky, 1972). As separatist arguments go, systematically addressing these errors (first the puzzling conclusion, then verbs, wording, articles, and spelling) could stifle Takaro's desire to write further on this topic and others; such a systematic response would change/interfere with his linguistic choices, some of which resulted in "interlanguage" features (Selinker, 1972) which actually contribute to the charm and uniqueness of Takaro's discourse. Such changing and editing often results in what L1 theorists Brannon and Knoblauch (1982) call "appropriation" of the students' texts (158), often construed as an act of academic/linguistic colonization. If the recommended pedagogical technique of "reformulation" of L2 texts by L1 writers (Cohen, 1983) became more widespread, it could also become an assimilationist appropriation of students' texts.

However, as an accommodationist wanting Takaro to add as native-as-feasible English discourse to his repertoire, and responding to Takaro's requests for detailed corrections, I read the entire paper aloud *again* to help Takaro *edit* it. The more assimilationist option would have been to dispense with a rhetorical reading and do only the second reading to edit. When I read Takaro's paper aloud this second time, I read it more slowly and with less feeling, pausing a few seconds before reading a problematic feature. Takaro had a pen in his hand, and with the pause hints and possibly having remembered the changed features from my previous oral reading, he caught most of the verb/tense problems himself. I helped him correct the five phrasing problems and read the smoothed out phrases aloud in context a few more times so that they would sound natural and he might later have an auditory memory of these phrases—for example, "he had a lot of problems with the camp authorities" (line 15). My last comment to him was the situation-based advice typical of the accommodationist, that is, that one's rhetoric depends on the occasion. If Takaro were writing the paper for a class, he would have to explain in the *paper* what he told me orally about the ambiguity of the Japanese words and characters to make sure his ending had the proper impact. The common spelling errors that even native speakers make, like "exsistence" (line 31) and "goverments" (line 42), I ignored to focus on the more important areas.

Susan

Susan, the second student, is not an international student like Takaro, but immigrated from Korea at the age of 11 with her family. She is a good example of someone who is neither L1 nor L2, but close to bilingual. She attended a U.S. junior high and high school in a school system with an excellent reputation for its rhetorically based language arts programs. Susan had also been through the university's ESL program. However, her fluency in speaking English is far ahead of her fluency in reading and writing, as can be seen from her brief piece responding to a writing center assignment called "A Sense of Place" which asks students to recall in detail a place that is important to their emotional development (see Appendix B).

As with Takaro's paper, my first response was rhetorically based, but in the form of written marginal and end comments that simulated a conversation. I wrote the comments rather than reading aloud and commenting orally as with Takaro's essay because Susan had not completed the piece until the very end of the lab period. To Susan's comment that she did not have a significant place "to show the part of me," which at the time struck me as sad and self-deprecatory, I wrote what I thought was an up-beat comment—that maybe her significant place was here in the Midwest. In retrospect, I realize this comment could be interpreted as a kind of push toward stronger emotional identification with the U.S., in other words, toward assimilation. It seems that Takaro, Takaro's subject Kenji from *Two Motherlands*, and Susan all have one foot in each land.

My other marginal comment is a "me-too" comment, common in responses in the center and writing/speaking program that train teachers to respond to the discourse as an act of meaning-making. I asked why in the U.S., the game is called "Red Light, Green Light" and in Korea, "Red Light, Blue Light." My two endnotes are also me-too comments focused on childhood games ("Playing with friends under the street lights is a great memory"), but the second endnote, after proposing the topic of "the midwestern place" for the next writing, introduces an error pattern intimately attached to meaning that I wanted her to work on in the following session ("Is there a special place in the midwest that you can write about today? Also, we could edit this paper for tenses to make sure it shows your games happening in the past").

I chose tense/time as a focus because it seemed like the easiest feature to work on successfully, and it was the most frequent error, as in line 13 ("want" vs. "wanted" and "should come" vs. "had to come") and line 24 ("tomorrow" vs. "the next day"). Susan had one article problem ("*the* part of me" vs. "*a* part of me" in line 5) and a faulty word form (the adverb "well" instead of the adjective "good" in line 29). During the next session, after we chatted briefly about childhood games, I reiterated the point about happenings in past time, and had Susan read the paper aloud slowly, pausing where something did not sound right, so she could make corrections. She did experience dissonance when reading over a few features and proceeded to correct them herself with a bit of prompting. In the first two lines, for example, she deleted the words that did not belong — both instances of the word "in" (lines 1 and 2). She also added words that were missing — "little *girl*" (line 3) and "close *enough*" (line 6).

Another assimilationist response could have been to circle all the errors and/or correct them myself, which would backfire and contradict the assimilationist goal to write in standard English as soon as possible, because Susan would not be participating in the process of finding and correcting problems. A more separatist response would have been to avoid mentioning matters of form such as tense and omitted words, in the interest of working on Susan's fluency and development, clearly the discourse level she needed to address first. Yet I was concerned about Susan's fitting into her English class and therefore veered to the right on the response continuum. In the course of the semester, I discovered she was unsure about when and how to use relative clauses. In Korean, relative clauses are used before rather than after the head noun as they are in English (Celce-Murcia & Larsen-Freeman, 1983).

Michael

The third student is Michael, a man in his 20s who, when he finishes his shift as a janitor for the university, attends a freshman English class. (When the writing center teacher who enrolled Michael asked him if he had ever worked in the writing center, he said yes, that he had cleaned the writing center many times.) Trained as a welder in a high-school vocational program, but unable to afford the equipment to go into business for himself, he is now exploring the option of a college education. In high school, he had done very little writing. His piece, like Takaro's, is also a response to my request to choose a favorite book and write about why it is important to him. Michael chose *The Diary of Anne Frank* (see Appendix C).

When I read this piece (Michael was not present), like the teachers in Shaughnessy's (1977) basic writing program, I was temporarily "stunned" by the sheer quantity of errors. My error analysis revealed, however, that most of Michael's problems (16 of the 26 errata) are in spelling. It could be that, from lack of school writing experience, he had missed or forgotten some spelling and grammar rules—dropping *e* before adding *-ing*, when and how to form the possessive with *s*, homophones ("their" vs. "there," "hole" vs. "whole," "passed" vs. "past"), and when to terminate sentences (lines 1, 14). Some of the spelling problems may result from his pronunciation, especially of word endings and beginnings ("survie" vs. "survive," "abanded" vs. "abandoned," "lone" vs. "alone," "hiden" vs. "hiding"). Another error, the verb/tense problems ("troop was," "want" vs. "wanted"), may also result from the carryover from dialect features; in African-American English Vernacular, it is not necessary to mark plural or past with *-s* or *-ed* or other endings, because one can tell from context whether the speaker means past or plural, with words such as *yesterday* or *many* (Labov, 1972).

I might have been tempted to begin explaining to Michael the rules he had forgotten, the obvious assimilationist response. A more extreme assimilationist response would also include telling Michael that books, unlike movies, do not contain "footage" (line 2), and that in Standard English "bad" does not mean "good" like it does in African-American English Vernacular, and that therefore he should change these lexical items, thus encouraging him to remove features of his personal voice from the text. An accommodationist may have commented on "footage" and the two meanings of "bad," but not demanded the changes.

In keeping with the center's pedagogy, I responded to his piece as an act of communication, which it was, rather than as a demonstration of how well Michael knew and/or could apply the rules. In light of Michael's situation as a returning student just beginning to articulate his ideas in writing and considering the serious content of the piece, I decided also to veer toward separatism with a solely content-based response. In later lab sessions, however, I had Michael start a list with his spelling problems, explained some rules of spelling and tense, and taught him to use the word processor and the spell check.

On this piece, I wrote three marginal comments and one end comment. My first comment was "I like the way you say actual 'footage' as if it were a movie." In my next comment, I told him about dramatic and film versions of the Anne Frank story. The third was a me-too comment about my own fears of facing this kind of adversity. The end comment, like my response to Susan, responds to signs of negative self-image about a lack of memory or concentration (line 26): "You *did* manage to remember quite a bit of this, Michael—a very powerful and dramatic book that should always be read as a reminder of what humans have done to one another."

Because of a heightened awareness of race and class differences in the U.S., most discussions of response to SESD writing such as Michael's, in teachers' lounges, newspaper columns, and L1 literature, have been more volatile and more manifestly political than discussions of responses to ESL writing. For example, Allen Ballard (1973), a former head of the Search for Education, Elevation and Knowledge (SEEK) Program at the City College of New York, chided the young white radical teachers in Mina Shaughnessy's basic writing program for their hands-off (what I am calling "separatist") policy on the different grammatical features of the texts of African-American students. Accusing these teachers of not correcting features because they bore the guilt of white racism, he urged an assimilationist stance that would result in the eradication of SESD traces in the writing of African-American students. Like many educators and parents, he does not want African-Americans to be left behind due to the discrimination they might face from potential employers and the mainstream public because of the potentially stigmatizing features of their language. A separatist response to this common position, reflected in the CCCC's statement ("Students' Right to Their Own Language," 1974) is that employers and the public must be encouraged by the English-teaching community to *change* their attitudes and biases and regard content and deep structure, not form and surface structure, as the bases of communication. This ongoing discussion of the appropriate stance to SESD writing, too complex to retrace here, periodically resurfaces in the media as a "literacy crisis" and in the L1 literature as a reaction to the media's crisis-fabricating.

[handwritten annotation: disagree — does he want to be in the world writing standard English or not?]

THE POLITICS OF RESPONSE TO WRITING

The issues surrounding response to the (L1) texts of SESD writers like Michael are politically charged with questions of identity, autonomy, and opportunity, but as I have shown, response to L2/ESL texts, such as those by Takaro and Susan, has political implications as well; the nature of a particular response to a text and a writer suggest a stance toward linguistic and cultural assimilation. Indeed, the entire ESL teaching/learning endeavor, both inside and outside the university, is as politically charged as L1 teaching/learning; it is just that the sociopolitical implications need to be openly articulated and discussed, as I have begun to do. ESL teachers need to be aware of the politics of their stances toward ESL writers and realize that a continuum of choices is available to them. They can choose responses based not only on the L2 development of ESL students, but also on the kinds of political messages their responses invariably suggest to students—messages about acculturation. Because it is impossible to separate language issues from their political contexts, and because the international and national "macropolitics" affect the "micropolitics" of the relationships among teacher, student, and text, it is important for L1, L2/ESL composition, or any endeavor concerned with English language teaching to acknowledge and make explicit the sociopolitical implications of response to writing.

REFERENCES

Auerbach, E. (1992). Review: The challenge of the English Only movement. *College English, 54,* 843–851.

Auerbach, E., & Burgess, D. (1985). The hidden curriculum of survival ESL. *TESOL Quarterly, 19,* 475–495.

Ballard, A. (1973). *The education of black folk.* New York: Harper & Row.

Berlin, J. (1988). Rhetoric and ideology in the writing class. *College English, 50,* 477–494.

Brannon, L., & Knoblauch, C. (1982). On students' rights to their own texts: A model of teacher response. *College Composition and Communication, 33,* 157–166.

Burt, M., & Kiparsky, C. (1972). *The gooficon: A repair manual for English.* Rowley, MA: Newbury House.

Celce-Murcia, M., & Larsen-Freeman, D. (1983). *The grammar book: An ESL/EFL teacher's course.* New York: Newbury House.

Chametzky, J. (1989–90). Beyond melting pots, cultural pluralism, ethnicity — Or, deja vu all over again. *MELUS, 16,* 3–38.

Cohen, A. (1983). Reformulating compositions. *TESOL Newsletter, 17,* 4–5.

Erickson, F. (1984). School literacy, reasoning, and civility: An anthropologist's perspective. *Review of Educational Research, 54,* 525–546.

Farr, M. (Ed.). (1980). *Reactions to Ann Arbor: Vernacular Black English and education.* Arlington, VA: Center for Applied Linguistics.

Farr, M. (1990). Dialects, culture, and teaching the English language arts. In J. Jensen, J. Flood, D. Lapp, & N.J. Squire (Eds.), *Handbook of research in teaching the English language arts* (pp. 365–371). New York: Macmillan.

Fasold, R.W., & Shuy, R.W. (1970). *Teaching standard English in the inner city.* Washington, DC: Center for Applied Linguistics.

Freire, P. (1972). *Pedagogy of the oppressed.* New York: Herder & Herder.

Geertz, C. (1973). *The interpretation of cultures.* New York: Basic Books.

Giroux, H. (1983). *Theory and resistance in education.* South Hadley, MA: Bergin & Garvey.

Glazer, N., & Moynihan, D.P. (1963). *Beyond the melting pot: The Negroes, Puerto Ricans, Jews, Italians, and Irish of New York City.* Cambridge, MA: MIT Press.

Gordon, M. (1964). *Assimilation in American life.* New York: Oxford University Press.

Hinds, J. (1987). Reader vs. writer responsibility: A new typology. In U. Connor & R.B. Kaplan (Eds.), *Writing across languages: Analysis of L2 text* (pp. 141–152). Reading, MA: Addison-Wesley.

Horner, B. (1992). Re-thinking the "sociality" of error: Teaching editing as negotiation. *Rhetoric Review, 11,* 172–199.

Johns, A. (1990). L1 composition theories: Implications for developing theories of L2 composition. In B. Kroll (Ed.), *Second language writing: Research insights for the classroom* (pp. 24–36). Cambridge: Cambridge University Press.

Johns, A. (1993). Too much on our plates: A response to Terry Santos' "Ideology in Composition: L1 and ESL." *Journal of Second Language Writing, 2,* 83–88.

Kinneavy, J. (1971). *A theory of discourse.* New York: W.W. Norton.

Labov, W. (1972). *Language in the inner city: Studies in the Black English vernacular.* Philadelphia: University of Pennsylvania Press.

Land, R., & Whitley, C. (1989). Evaluating second language essays in regular composition classes: Toward a pluralistic U.S. rhetoric. In D. Johnson & D. Roen (Eds.), *Richness in writing: Empowering ESL students* (pp. 284–293). New York: Longman.

Leki, I. (1992). *Understanding ESL writers: A guide for teachers.* Portsmouth, NH: Boynton/Cook.

Lisle, B., & Mano, S. (1997). Embracing a multicultural rhetoric. In C. Severino, J. Guerra, & J. Butler (Eds.), *Writing in multicultural settings* (pp. 12–26). New York: Modern Language Association.

Lu, M.Z. (1992). Conflict and struggle: The enemies of pre-conditions or basic writing? *College English, 54,* 887–913.

Phelps, L. (1989). Images of student writing: The deep structure of teacher response. In C.M. Anson (Ed.), *Writing and response* (pp. 37–67). Urbana, IL: National Council of Teachers of English.

Ross, L. (1937). *The education of Hyman Kaplan*. New York: Harcourt Brace.

Santos, T. (1992). Ideology in composition: L1 and ESL. *Journal of Second Language Writing, 1,* 1–15.

Selinker, L. (1972). Interlanguage. *International Review of Applied Linguistics, 10,* 209–231.

Shaughnessy, M. (1977). *Errors and expectations: A guide for the teacher of basic writing*. New York: Oxford University Press.

Shor, I. (1987). *Critical teaching and everyday life*. Chicago: University of Chicago Press.

Students' right to their own language. (1974). *College Composition and Communication, 25,* 1–18.

Swales, J.M. (1990). *Genre analysis: English in academic and research settings*. New York: Cambridge University Press.

Tollefson, J.W. (1989). *Alien winds: The reeducation of America's Indochinese refugees*. New York: Praeger.

Wallerstein, N. (1983). *Language and culture in conflict: Problem-posing in the ESL classroom*. Reading, MA: Addison-Wesley.

Wolfram, R. (1992). Toward a feminist shift in the ESL classroom. In M. Hawthorne & T. Williams (Eds.), *Essays by the feminist foreign language teaching collective*. Unpublished collection.

Appendix A

The Writing of Takaro, an International Student

"Two Motherlands"

1   "Futatsu no sokoku"
2   "Two mother lands" is the most impressive novel I've
3   read recently. The scenes are U.S., the pacific islands,
4   and Japan. The main character is Kenji Amou, who is a
5   second generation Japanese immigrant. He was born in
6   California, and his parents send him to Kagoshima, Japan,
7   where they came from, for learning Japanese spirit and
8   culture. So, Kenji became a complete bilingual. This
9   character put him in a difficult situation in coming war
10   between U.S. and Japan. Kenji got a job at a local
11   Japanese news paper for Los Angels area, but the war broke
12   out and he was sent to a kind of concentration camp only
13   because he is a Japanese though he has an American
14   citizenship. However, his attitude is always reasonable
15   though he made a lot of dispute with the camp authorities.
16   A U.S. interigence officer sees through his talent and
17   reliability, and persuaded Kenji to join the U.S.
18   military as a Japanese teaching instructor, translator,
19   interpretator, and interigence officer.
20   He is distressed about what his identity is and he
21   joins the U.S. army after all. He knows Japan will lose
22   sooner or later, he wanted to prevent Japan from its total
23   corapse. He was assigned to the front of Pacific islands,
24   and then, after the victory of the U.S., goes to Japan as
25   a monitor of the translation of the Tokyo trial, which
26   judges war criminals. From Kenji's view, this trial is
27   not fair, and the American authority who occupies Japan
28   try to use this trial politically to carry out the
29   occupation. Kenji's distress and fatigue make him kill

30 himself, at last.
31   The existence of such Japanese-Americans are not known
32 well. Their role during the war was tremendous because
33 they are the bridge and they know both sides. This
34 extreme situation is not occuring in today's U.S.-Japan
35 relation, but I guess some element is existing all the
36 time. The concept or notion of "nation states" separate
37 the people and their thoughts. The nations' borderlines
38 are clearly on the map, but actually today's big
39 multinational enterprises activity is crossing those lines
40 all over the world. This novel is tragic because the
41 main characters so clinged the notion of "nation" or "two
42 governments." I prefer the word "mother land" to "state."
43 This novel's title, two mother lands" don't tear him
44 apart, but "two states" do.

Appendix B

The Writing of Susan, an Immigrant Student

"A Sense of Place"

1   My native soil could be Korea since I was born in
2   there and raised in there; a beginning of my childhood.
3   Since I was a little, I haven't been to any places except
4   around seoul, and mostly around my neighborhood. I don't
5   have a significant place to show the part of me. Maybe I
6   haven't paid close attention to where I was and how
7   it might have affected me.
8   I lived in a neighborhood with a lot of kids around my
9   age. Without very much separation between boys and girls,
10 we all gathered around and played active games, like hide
11 and seek, tag, blue light, red light etc.
12   Usually our playing time was set, after dinner.
13 Around that hour everybody who want to play should come
14 out by the post, which was close to my house. I remember
15 with my brothers, I used to hurry up with the meal to be
16 on time for a game. Even though, it was pretty dark, the
17 electric light on the top of the post helped us to see
18 where we were going. We could not go very far, for the
19 safety that we always drew the line to never go over that
20 line or else one is out of the game.
21   Each game, we had a policy, but it was fair enough to
22 enjoy the game.
23   After the game, everybody would go back home and ready
24 for school tomorrow.
25   The reason we set the time of playing at night was,
26 everybody would be free by then. Finish school work or

27 other things during the day and enjoy the free time after
28 dinner while adults watched television for themselves. It
29 was a pretty well neighborhood.

Appendix C

The Writing of Michael, a Standard English as a Second Dialect Student

The Diary of Anne Frank

1   The Ann Frank Diary was a good book to read, it contain
2   actall footage of what happen when Ann Frank lived in
3   Germany. It was war time when Hitler and his troops where
4   at war. Ann Frank and her people were helled against
5   their will and could not be seen or troop was going to
6   caputure as prisinor. Ann and her family were hiding in
7   an atic of an abanded building that had allready been
8   bomb. While the was going on, Ann would always listen to
9   the radio to hear what Hitler was saying to the people.
10   Ann knew that Hitler was a bad person and that he
11 would use people and his own family to get what he wants.
12 Ann was always thinking about hope, praying that his would
13 all come to an end. The people that Ann was with took in
14 as their own they had a son named Peter and everyday Ann
15 and Peter would talk about the way things were. Ann lost
16 her family so she really did not have any place to go.
17 But when Peters family took her in she had better relief
18 of haveing people around her because she thought she was
19 really going to be lone and would not have any person or
20 place to turn to. Ann and Peter got to know each other so
21 well that they began liking each other. Since war was
22 upon them started keeping a Diary and she would put down
23 every thing, that happened she even put Peter and his
24 family their. Ann was a very bright girl she would tell
25 stories to keep things off your mind. She knew games that
26 past the time away. I really do not remember the rest,
27 but, I do know that Anns Diary was found and a publisher
28 took the Diary and made a book out of it.
29   The hole book was effective because she was writing
30 about her being in hiden. She lost her family, before
31 Peter took her in she thought she was going to die because
32 she couldn't get food and she did not know how to servie
33 in a war. The book made me think, what if I was in her
34 place, how strong would I be, would I servie. Ann Franks
35 Diary was one bad book that I really like.

19

The Impact of Writer Nationality on Mainstream Teachers' Judgments of Composition Quality

DONALD L. RUBIN AND
MELANIE WILLIAMS-JAMES

F or many postsecondary ESL teachers, the ultimate mark of success is to see their students integrate with no disadvantage into mainstream English instruction classes (Land & Whitley, 1989). Indeed, some intensive English programs may evaluate their effectiveness in part by tracking the passage of their "graduates" through regular (i.e., non-ESL) writing classes. And yet many ESL teachers figuratively hold their breath as they release their students into that mainstream. Often their trepidation is not a matter of doubting their students' abilities. Instead, ESL teachers fear that their students are stepping into an environment which has little time, little expertise (see Clair, 1995), and perhaps too little interest in supporting nonnative English Speaking (NNES) students (Braine, 1994). Some ESL educators fear that too often NNES students experience loss of confidence and an increase in alienation in mainstream English composition classes (see Silva, 1994; Zamel, 1995).

Were writing assessment somehow a value-free endeavor, were it a matter of measuring easily verifiable indices of performance, then perhaps ESL professionals would have less justification for their fears. But writing assessment is notoriously nonsystematic. A considerable body of research in that tradition documents the rather erratic responses to student writing of both English L1 teachers (Huot, 1993; Rafoth & Rubin, 1984) and ESL teachers (Vaughan, 1991, Zamel, 1985).

Teachers' ratings of student writing can be influenced by extraneous individual differences like students' names (Braddock, Lloyd-Jones & Schoer, 1963) and students' physical attractiveness (Seligman, Tucker & Lambert, 1972). Composition assessment is also influenced by cultural identity factors like students' ethnic background (Piché, Rubin, Turner & Michlin, 1978) and speech style (Seligman et al., 1972). Studies of written language and attitude indicate that teachers tend to assign lower quality ratings to papers they believe have been written by members of low prestige social groups.

From *Journal of Second Language Writing* 6.2 (1997): 139–53.

In short, writing assessment is extremely vulnerable to well-known teacher expectancy effects. Teacher expectancy effects have been well documented as a pervasive phenomenon in public school classrooms (Dusek & Joseph, 1985), but post-secondary teachers are by no means immune (Allen & Niss, 1990).

Teachers are often acutely aware of their susceptibility to unreliability in classroom writing assessment. Some teachers, therefore, are most comfortable when they are engaged in the relatively concrete task of identifying surface errors in writing conventions. Previous research confirms that when mainstream teachers assess NNS writing, they are liable to base their grades on the incidence of mechanical errors, and ignore strengths in broader rhetorical features (Sweedler-Brown, 1993). Perhaps they suppose they can be more objective when marking errors than when responding to holistic aspects of composition quality.

Research in error detection, however, suggests that this supposition is mistaken. Even error detection appears to be subject to teacher expectancies. Williams (1981) demonstrated that individuals vary in their tolerance for various violations. One person's egregious desecration is another's minor irritation (Vann, Meyer & Lorenz, 1984). Moreover, the salience of mechanical errors can be hard for teachers to resist. Rafoth and Rubin (1984) found that teachers tend to react to weak content by evaluating mechanical errors more harshly, and even when teachers are told to ignore mechanics and to focus instead on content in their evaluations, it can be difficult for them to do so. Zamel (1985) similarly concluded that even after the introduction of progressive process-centered writing pedagogies, teachers of ESL "attend primarily to surface-level features of writing and seem to read and react to a text as a series of separate sentences or even clauses" (p. 86), yet they can be inconsistent in their patterns of error detection and marking. The treatment of error among teachers of mainstream composition is likewise nonsystematic; some fail to recognize common errors, and others are prone to attribute error to constructions which in fact are quite correct (Greenbaum & Taylor, 1981).

As Hull (1985, p. 165) observes, "Most of the controversy surrounding correctness in writing has finally to do with power, status, and class. . . ." Propriety in language usage has historically been associated with moral virtue (Finegon, 1980). Writing assessment that separates the linguistically elect from the heathen serves a social gatekeeping function. It is quite possible, therefore, that raters attribute lower composition quality in general, and higher error rate in particular, to persons from low prestige groups (Piché, Rubin, Turner & Michlin, 1978). Addressing the situation of ESL students in regular composition classes, Land and Whitley (1989, p. 285) claim that "even when an ESL writer produces an error-free composition in English, a hidden agenda leads the evaluator to find fault with other formal features." On the other hand, some evidence indicates that when raters do *not* know the language background of writers — that is when they are artificially precluded from exercising differential expectancies — similarly prepared NNS and native English speaking (NES) writers are evaluated similarly by ESL and mainstream composition teachers alike (Brown, 1991; Song & Caruso, 1996).

The teacher expectancy model, then, predicts that teachers will devalue even adept NNS's compositions based on negative stereotypes of NNS English language proficiency. A rival model, articulated by Janopoulos (1992, 1995) predicts the opposite, however. This alternate view suggests that teachers will bend over backwards and make extra allowances for NNS's composition difficulties. In particular, this model postulates that teachers regard errors in grammar and mechanics as less serious when committed by NNSs, and that teachers deliberately overlook interference at the level of code in order to ascertain meaning in NNS writing.

Empirical support for this position is limited, however. Santos (1988) found that faculty in various disciplines claimed to look beyond error in reading papers by NNS students, but this was in the limited context of judging error gravity. Song and Caruso (1996) similarly conclude that English faculty (as compared to ESL faculty) give greater weight to organizational and rhetorical features than to language propriety when rating NNS's writing. Their research design, however, did not ascertain whether raters *ascribed* NNS or NES identity to the papers they read. Moreover, since only a single student paper represented, for example, an ESL composition with strong development but poor language mechanics, it is possible that the study's conclusions about the differential weighting English teachers accord to development versus language could be an artifact of the particular paper sampled.

Janopoulos (1992) asked faculty from a variety of disciplines to rate the academic acceptability of isolated sentences, each containing one of twelve types of error. In some cases the sentences were represented as having been written by NNSs; in other cases, the self-same sentences were represented as having been written by NESs. In this way the study's design renders it possible to disambiguate effects due to the student/writer's language identity from those due to idiosyncratic qualities of the papers sampled. Faculty were indeed more tolerant of five of the twelve error types when the sentences were associated with NNSs, as compared to when associated with NESs. On the other hand, only faculty in the social sciences were overall more tolerant of NNS errors; humanities faculty—presumably including faculty teaching first-year composition—manifested no such extra allowance. No previous research has in a parallel fashion examined teachers' responses to differentially identified NNS and NES papers in the context of more naturalistic grading of complete compositions.

The present research addresses these issues by examining the responses of mainstream English composition instructors to writing samples attributed to ESL writers. Instructors rated and graded compositions, and also wrote comments on the papers. The student authors of the compositions were identified either as (1) U.S. citizens—NESs, (2) Northern Europeans—native speakers of Danish, or (3) Asians—native speakers of Thai. Given the greater homophily (Dodd, 1991) between Anglo Americans and Northern Europeans, relative to Asians, we expected that instructors would give lower evaluations to the essays attributed to Thai writers. We expected also that raters would detect more errors among these Asian writers than among the Danes or the U.S. writers.

METHODS

Participants

Participants — that is the mainstream teachers who served as readers and evaluators in this study — were graduate teaching assistants in departments of English at four U.S. universities (one located in the Midwest, one in the Southeast, and two in the Mid-Atlantic region). Methods of soliciting participation varied among the institutions; in some cases experiment packets were simply placed in instructors' mailboxes. In other cases the director of composition made a direct appeal for volunteers. In all, 33 usable responses were returned. All participants were native speakers of English. Fifty-four percent of the respondents were female. Members of the sample reported an average of about 13.5 classes (quarters or semesters) of teaching experience (s.d. = 12.25). They ranged from beginning graduate teaching assistants to relatively experienced adjunct instructors.

Since there is some reason to believe that readers' own cultural backgrounds and contact with non-native speakers can influence their ratings (Hamp-Lyons, 1991; Land & Whitley, 1989), we inquired about the number of ESL students each instructor had taught, and we also inquired about instructors' knowledge of languages other than English. A single participant reported proficiency in a non-European language, 15% reported no foreign language proficiency at all, 39% reported proficiency in one European language, and another 42% reported proficiency in two languages. Twenty-one percent of the respondents indicated that they never see any ESL students in their writing classes. Forty-five percent stated that they typically have one or two ESL students in their composition classes.

Stimulus Materials

Essays.   Stimulus essays were produced by modifying a set of six papers that had been written by NESs in a statewide writing proficiency test for college juniors. All of the essays addressed the same topic (course distribution requirements), and all had been passing papers rated at about mid-range. Essays were typed. Before reading and evaluating the essays, participants read the writing prompt which elicited the papers and a page-long description of the criteria used in the statewide test from which these papers were drawn.

We intruded six types of errors into each of the essays. Based on findings regarding perceived error gravity (Vann et. al, 1984), we selected two types of errors to represent each of high, medium, and low salience. The error types were, respectively, (1) word order reversals, (2) wrong tense, (3) wrong preposition, (4) lack of pronoun/antecedent agreement, (5) minor spelling errors—mainly homonym confusions, and (6) omitted articles. Each essay contained these same errors at the same rate of occurrence. To determine an appropriate frequency for intruding these errors, we doubled the normative error rate among native speakers (Connors & Lunsford, 1988). The resulting overall error rate was five errors per hundred words. The first and last sentence of each essay was left error-free, with errors roughly distributed throughout the remainder of the papers. A copy of one of the six stimulus papers thus constructed appears in the Appendix.

It is worth noting that participants in this study in fact detected the intruded errors in approximately the same order of frequency as would be predicted by Vann et al.'s order of error gravity: wrong word order, 58.5%; wrong tense, 51.3%; preposition error, 44.1%; pronoun error, 41.6%; low gravity spelling error/homonym confusion, 50.4%; article error, 39.3%.

Fabricated Writer Profiles. Writer nationality—U.S. English speaker, Dane or Thai—was attributed to essays by means of fabricated student record sheets. We deliberately selected Danes to represent Northern Europeans and Thais to represent Asians for the very reason that these nationalities are unlikely to engender nongeneralizable nation-specific stereotypes (as might, say, Germans and Japanese).

Participants read a student record sheet immediately preceding each essay in the rating task. The record sheets indicated the stimulus students' names (e.g., "Erik Grundtrigian" for the Dane, "Rutai Chaichongrak" for the Thai, and "Ray Wilkinson" for the U.S. NES), home high schools (e.g., "Westwood Austin, TX" for the U.S. NES; "Sukhothai Bangkok, Thailand" for the Thai; and "Tinbjergskole Copenhagen, Denmark" for the Dane), and TOEFL scores (the latter only in the case of the Thai and Danish student profiles). Two fictional students from each of the three nationalities were created in this fashion, for a total of six student profiles. To strengthen the perceptual salience of these constructed ethnolinguistic identities, participants were required to physically copy the fictional students' names on their rating sheets.

A scale ("The writer is minority culture student/person of color . . . dominant culture student/white-Euro") was included in the questionnaire to determine the success of this experimental manipulation of writer ethnicity. Results indicated that manipulated writer ethnicity did register on the participants as intended. The Thai writers were judged significantly more minority-like ($F_{2,177} = 37.17$; $p < .001$; $M = 1.77$), relative to the U.S. writers ($M = 4.10$) and the Danes ($M = 4.72$). The latter two did not significantly differ from each other on this social perceptual dimension.

Each participant, then, encountered six papers representing two of each of three nationalities. A total of 198 ratings were thus conducted. To avoid confounding essay text with nationality, we nonsystematically rotated the assignment of student profiles to compositions. The order of presentation of the essays was also nonsystematically rotated.

Measurement

Evaluation Scales. The rating instrument employed in this experiment was developed for use in the same state-wide writing examination that yielded the stimulus writing samples. The instrument consists of ten 4-interval Likert type scales assessing: (1) central idea, (2) style, (3) organization, (4) major points, (5) evidence, (6) details, (7) writing conventions, (8) transitions, (9) tone, and (10) expression. These ten items were summed into a single scale with internal consistency reliability (Cronbach's alpha) of .94. In addition, participants assigned a single letter grade (A–F) to each paper. They also rated the purported writer along several semantic differential scales. For the purposes of this paper, we report results for judgements reflecting (1) overall writing proficiency, (2) intelligence, (3) socioeconomic status, and (4) minority culture identity. The entire rating instrument is reproduced in the Appendix.

Coding Teacher Comments and Markings. Participants were asked to mark the six papers themselves as they "normally would mark and comment upon a class writing assignment." The resulting marginal, interlinear, and end paper markings were coded for the following features (1)–(6) identification of instances of the six intruded error types, (7) other elements corrected, (8) number of elements signaled merely by some graphic means (circles, underlines, or check marks, for example), (9) number of words in positive or encouraging marginal comments, and (10) number of words in negative or discouraging marginal comments. The fact that all participants wrote comments—sometimes effusively, always in role as appropriate for the stimulus students' classroom teacher—we take as informal evidence that the manipulated writing samples appeared quite natural to them. A randomly selected subsample of 16 marked papers was independently coded by a second coder. For all ten types of notations inter-rater reliability (correlation or percent of agreement, as appropriate) was over .91.

Analysis

Two primary sets of statistical analyses were conducted. The first set of analyses examined differences in the average ratings or error detection rates corresponding to each of the three nationalities of writers. Three separate 3×2 repeated measures multivariate analyses of variance (MANOVAs) were run. For each MANOVA, the repeated measure of interest is NATIONALITY at three levels (Thai, Dane, American). The other repeated measure is REPLICATION at two levels (i.e., two different compositions were nonsystematically assigned to each of the three nationalities). Significant MANOVA effects were followed-up by corresponding univariate analyses of variance (ANOVAs). The rationale for the multivariate analyses is to reduce the rate of spuriously significant results that can occur when highly intercorrelated variables are analyzed separately. One MANOVA examined the cluster of three writing quality indices: composite composition quality measure, overall grade assigned, and judged writing proficiency. The second MANOVA examined the cluster of the six error detection rates corresponding to the six types of intruded errors. A third MANOVA examined the cluster of four types of teacher comments and markings (i.e., other elements corrected, graphic markings, positive marginal comments, and negative marginal comments).

The second statistical approach used multiple linear regressions to determine how well error detection rates (treated as predictor variables) could explain variance in composition quality ratings (criterion variables, i.e., composite quality ratings, overall grade assigned, and judged writing proficiency). These regressions were run separately for each of the three composition quality dependent variables and also within each level of attributed nationality (i.e., Thai, Dane, U.S.). By running the regressions separately for each level of nationality, it was possible to determine whether raters were employing similar or dissimilar evaluation models for NNSs and NESs.

RESULTS

The MANOVA of six types of intruded errors revealed no statistically significant main or interaction effects. The MANOVA of four other types of teacher comments/markings indicated a significant multivariate effect only for replication (i.e., between the two Danish or the two Thai or the two U.S. students writers; $F_{6,184} = 7.28$, $p < .01$), which is of no practical interest, especially as no interaction with nationality emerged. That is, the statistically significant main effect for replication can only be interpreted as an idiosyncratic artifact of the particular student papers sampled; some quite naturally engendered more comments than others. The lack of an interaction between replication and nationality is reassuring; it means that the finding of practical importance here (in this case similar numbers of comments across all three nationalities) can be generalized across papers, and is *not* an artifact of the particular writing samples we selected. Consequently no univariate analyses were performed on these variables.

The MANOVA of the three writing quality indices indicated a single multivariate main effect for nationality ($F_{6,184} = 4.33$, $p < .01$). The follow-up univariate ANOVAs of the nationality factor revealed an effect only on the composite composition quality scale ($F_{2,188} = 3.40$; $p < .05$). Post hoc comparison among cell means (Student-Neumann-Keuls procedure) revealed that writers identified as Thai received higher ratings ($M = 25.44$) than those identified as NES ($M = 22.38$). The Danish writer was not judged differently than either the Thai or the American ($M = 24.09$). No statistically significant effects emerged in the follow-up univariate ANOVA of rated writing proficiency nor of overall grade assigned.

To identify factors that influenced writers' judgements of student writing, regressions were run for each of the three indices of evaluation: (1) perceived writing proficiency, (2) grade assigned to the paper, and (3) composite composition quality ratings. The regressions were run separately for each attributed nationality. These regressions are summarized in Table 1.

TABLE 1.   Summary of Regression Analyses (Run Separately for
Each Nationality)

Nationality	Predictors	beta	F Value	Partial R^2	Cum. R^2
A.	Criterion Variable: Writing		Proficiency		
Thai	Pronoun Error	−1.34	8.50	0.13	0.13
Dane	-none-				
U.S.	-none-				
B.	Criterion Variable: Grade		Assigned		
Thai	Pronoun Error	−1.90	5.53	0.09	0.09
Dane	-none-				
U.S.	Other Notations	−10.53	8.99	0.13	0.13
C.	Criterion Variable: Composition	Quality	Scores		
Thai	Pronoun Error	−4.72	5.82	0.09	0.09
Dane	Tense Error	−4.23	4.15	0.06	0.06
U.S.	Pronoun Error	−4.33	10.11	0.14	0.14
	Other Notations	−24.34	9.52	0.12	0.26

Table 1 indicates, when rating the overall writing proficiency of Thai writers, instructors were significantly affected by the number of pronoun errors they detected. The negative Beta-weight indicates an inverse relation between these variables. This single predictor accounted for 13% of the variance in writing proficiency judgements. No additional predictor was statistically significant. None of the predictor variables entered the regression equations for U.S. or Danish students when the criterion was overall writing proficiency.

When the criterion variable was the grade assigned to the stimulus essays, instructors' ratings of Thai writers were again significantly predicted by the number of pronoun errors detected by those instructors. Pronoun errors detected accounted for nine percent of the variance for this criterion variable and the negative Beta-weight again indicates an inverse relation. None of the predictor variables significantly predicted grades when the composition was attributed to a Danish writer. On the other hand, when the essays were attributed to U.S. writers, the number of other notations (praise, questions, suggestion) accounted for 13% of the variance among grades assigned. The frequency of these comments was inversely related to grade.

When the composite of composition quality ratings served as the criterion variable, scores for the Thai-written papers were again significantly predicted by the number of pronoun errors identified. Nine percent of the variance was accounted for in this case, and the negative Beta-weight again indicates an inverse relation between predictor and criterion. Only a single variable, the number of verb tense errors identified, predicted quality ratings of the papers attributed to the Danish writers. This error type, also inversely related to quality ratings, accounted for six percent of the variance. For U.S. writers, the frequency of pronoun errors entered the regression equation at the first step. It accounted for 14% of the variance in judged composition quality. Number of other notations entered the equation at the second step. It accounted for an additional 12% of the variance. Both of these variables stood in inverse relation to quality judgements. No other variables were significant predictors.

DISCUSSION

This study was designed to investigate the impact of student nationality on mainstream English teachers' evaluations of writing quality. Based on most previous research, the expectation was that the writing of NNSs would be judged most stringently, and that raters would be most likely to notice mechanical errors in the writing of NNSs. Moreover, it was anticipated that the students who were least homophilous with the U.S. instructors (i.e., the Southeast Asians as opposed to the Northern Europeans) would suffer the most in that regard.

The picture that emerges from the study of composition evaluations is complex, however, and mainly contrary to our expectations. English instructors did *not* react more harshly to papers written by NNS writers. In fact, on the one index which revealed statistically significant differences (the composite composition quality scale), the Asian NNS writers were judged superior to the U.S. NES writers. (The Northern European NNSs were ranked intermediately, but not significantly different than either Americans or Thais.)

One explanation for the elevated writing scores for Asian students may be that in the context of error-laden papers, U.S. writers were being judged especially harshly; they should have known better. Another explanation is that English instructors were aware of their potential bias against ESL writers. As a corrective, they were compensating for that proclivity with extra lenience. This would be an instance of the "bending over backwards" phenomenon that has sometimes been observed in other evaluation tasks. For example, when judging the liability of a physically unattractive defendant in a mock court case, jurors were told *not* to be negatively biased by the defendant's physical appearance. As a result of this warning, they tended to be more lenient with the unattractive defendant than they were with a physically attractive defendant (Sigall & Ostrove, 1975).

Our expectations about error identification were likewise not confirmed. While no previous studies directly examined this exact phenomenon, related research and theory suggested that teachers might be more primed to notice errors when they appear in the writing of ESL students, as compared to the writing of NESs. In fact, MANOVA results indicated no such differences.

That is not to say teachers engaged in the same evaluation processes when reading papers written by native and non-native English speakers. The regression results imply different bases for their ratings. Overall, it appears that judgements of NES-written papers were justified in a richer and more complex fashion. This greater complexity in evaluation was manifest in the use of marginal comments—either positive or negative, in the use of graphic signs like circling or arrows, and in teachers' corrections of other elements of the compositions. While the absolute number of these marginal and interlinear notations did not differ according to student nationality, it was only for

NES writers that those notations manifest any significant correlations to instructors' perceptions of composition quality. That is, a NNS student's paper might bear relatively many teacher notations or relatively few, and this would give no clue as to the teacher's overall assessment of the writing quality. But for NES writers, a significant but inverse relation between teachers' comments and ratings was evident.

It is important to note that these results do indeed warrant the queasiness many U.S. students feel when they see copious teacher comments on their papers. The more comments teachers wrote, the lower the grade they assigned. Why might this be so? Perhaps teachers feel a need to defend giving a poor grade, whereas they suspect that students who receive high grades will be pleased enough with the grade and will not demand any justification. Alternatively, it may be that teachers can articulate easily enough the deficiencies of a piece of work, but they lack much vocabulary for describing strengths.

In rating papers attributed to Asian (Thai) writers, according to all three indices of writing quality, teachers' judgements were most strongly affected by the number of pronoun errors they detected. In assigning composition quality ratings to the Northern European (Danish) writers, teachers were most strongly influenced by the number of tense errors they detected. It is difficult to know why these errors in particular—and not some more grievous error like word order violations—had such perceptual salience in this study. That may very well be an idiosyncratic artifact of the specific manipulation in this experiment.

One generalization does seem warranted by these patterns by which NNS papers were rated: Judgements of the quality of NNS papers—to the degree these judgements could be predicted by the variables investigated in this study—were solely related to instructors' detection of surface error. Although instructors were not more prone to find surface error in NNS writing, what error they did find they used as the exclusive basis for their evaluations of ESL students in particular.

One promising direction for additional research in this area would combine the controlled experimental approach we have employed in this study with the think-aloud procedures used by Vaughn (1991) and Huot (1993). By using these techniques in conjunction, one could ascertain the actual impact of error identification on evaluation and attempt to explain that impact according to each raters' own phenomenology of error (Williams, 1981). Another issue that bears investigation pertains to differing judgmental processes that instructors use in holistic assessment, relative to more analytic assessment. In the present study, when a composite of analytic scales was used to index composition quality, a greater proportion of the variance was explained, relative to when more holistic grades served as criterion variables. In other studies, however, holistic ratings have been more susceptible to extraneous influence and analytic scales less so (e.g., Song & Caruso, 1996). In this study, moreover, we surveyed only mainstream English teachers. It would be valuable to determine the degree to which writing instructors with more experience reading NNS composition (i.e., ESL teachers) converge with mainstream teachers of writing in the evaluation processes in which they engage. More-over, this study deals only with teachers' responses to surface error in writing. NNS writing also varies from NES writing along a number of broader rhetorical or discourse-level dimensions (e.g., indirectness, politeness, explicitness; see Purves & Purves, 1986). A subsequent study might investigate how teachers assess divergent rhetorical patterns when they are variously attributed to writers of different nationalities.

Limited though the present study is, it points toward some important instructional practices vis a vis our evaluation of student writing. First, the results of this study caution us to beware the apparently persistent tendency to base our grades and evaluations on surface error. We should avoid basing grades on surface error for at least two reasons: (1) obviously competence in writing is a great deal more than avoiding errors, and (2) we are in any event very erratic at detecting errors. Second, the results of this study caution us to attend to our use of comments in our responses to student writing. We ought not reserve our most extensive comments just for poorly written work. To the contrary, we must cultivate at least an equally rich vocabulary to help us reinforce for students what they have done well. Finally, this study cautions us to examine the bases we use for assessing NNS writing as compared to NES writing. If we do ultimately decide to use different evaluation criteria for the two populations, that decision ought to be based on principle and not on any reflexive tendency to attend mainly to surface errors when responding to the writing of NNSs.

REFERENCES

Allen, B.P., & Niss, J.F. (1990). A chill in the college classroom? *Phi Delta Kappan, 71,* 607–609.

Braddock, R., Lloyd-Jones, R., & Schoer, L. (1963). *Research in written composition.* Champaign, IL: National Council of Teachers of English.

Braine, G. (1994). Starting ESL classes in freshman writing programs. *TESOL Journal, 2*(3), 22–25.

Brown, J.D. (1991). Do English and ESL faculties rate writing samples differently? *TESOL Quarterly, 25,* 587–604.

Clair, N. (1995). Mainstream classroom teachers and ESL students. *TESOL Quarterly, 29,* 189–196.

Connors, R., & Lunsford, A. (1988). Frequency of formal errors in current college writing, or Ma and Pa Kettle do research. *College Composition and Communication, 39,* 395–409.

Dodd, C. (1991). *Dynamics of intercultural communication,* 3rd ed. Dubuque, IA: Wm C. Brown.

Dusek, J.B., & Joseph, G. (Eds.). (1985). *Teacher expectancies.* Hillsdale, NJ: Erlbaum.

Finegon, E. (1980). *Attitudes toward English usage: The history of a war of words.* New York: Teachers College Press.

Greenbaum, S., & Taylor, J. (1981). The recognition of usage errors by instructors of freshman composition. *College Composition and Communication, 32,* 169–174.

Hamp-Lyons, L. (1991). Second language writing: Assessment issues. In B. Kroll (Ed.), *Second language writing: Research insights for the classroom* (pp. 69–87). Cambridge, UK: Cambridge University Press.

Hull, G. (1985). Research on error and correction. In B.W. McClelland & T.R. Donovan (Eds.), *Perspectives on research and scholarship in composition* (pp. 162–184). New York: Modern Language Association.

Huot, B.A. (1993). The influence of holistic scoring procedures on reading and rating student essays. In M. Williamson & B. Huot (Eds.), *Validating holistic scoring for writing assessment* (pp. 206–265). Cresskill, NJ: Hampton Press.

Janopoulos, M. (1992). University faculty tolerance of NS and NNS writing errors: A comparison. *Journal of Second Language Writing, 1,* 109–121.

Janopoulos, M. (1995). Writing across the curriculum, writing proficiency exams, and the NNS college student. *Journal of Second Language Writing, 4,* 43–50.

Land, R., & Whitley, C. (1989). Evaluating second language essays in regular composition classes: Toward a pluralistic U.S. rhetoric. In D. Johnson & D. Roen (Eds.), *Richness in writing* (pp. 284–293). White Plains, NY: Longman.

Piché, G.L., Rubin, D.L., Turner, L.J., & Michlin, M.L. (1978). Teachers' subjective evaluations of standard and black nonstandard English compositions: A study of written language and attitudes. *Research in the Teaching of English, 12,* 107–118.

Purves, A.C., & Purves, W.C. (1986). Viewpoints: Cultures, text models, and the activity of writing. *Research in the Teaching of English, 20,* 174–197.

Rafoth, B.A., & Rubin, D.L. (1984). The impact of content and mechanics on judgments of writing quality. *Written Communication, 1,* 446–458.

Santos, T. (1988). Professors' reactions to the academic writing of nonnative-speaking students. *TESOL Quarterly, 22,* 69–90.

Seligman, C.R., Tucker, G.R., & Lambert, W.E. (1972). The effects of speech style and other attributes on teachers' attitudes toward pupils. *Language in Society, 1,* 131–142.

Sigall, H., & Ostrove, N. (1975). Beautiful but dangerous: Effects of offender attractiveness and nature of the crime on juridic judgement. *Journal of Personality and Social Psychology, 31,* 410–414.

Silva, T. (1994). An examination of writing program administrators' options for the placement of ESL students in first year writing classes. *Writing Program Administration, 18* (1&2), 37–43.

Song, B., & Caruso, I. (1996). Do English and ESL faculty differ in evaluating the essays of native English-speaking and ESL students? *Journal of Second Language Writing, 5,* 163–182.

Sweedler-Brown, C.O. (1993). ESL essay evaluation: The influence of sentence-level and rhetorical features. *Journal of Second Language Writing, 2,* 3–17.

Vann, R., Meyer, D.E., & Lorenz, F.O. (1984). Error gravity: A study of faculty opinion of ESL errors. *TESOL Quarterly, 18,* 427–440.

Vaughan, C. (1991). Holistic assessment: What goes on in the raters' minds? In L. Hamp-Lyons (Ed.). *Assessing second language writing in academic contexts* (pp. 111–126). Norwood, NJ: Ablex.

Williams, J. (1981). The phenomenology of error. *College Composition and Communication, 32,* 152–168.

Zamel, V. (1985). Responding to student writing. *TESOL Quarterly, 19,* 79–101.

Zamel, V. (1995). Strangers in academia: The experiences of faculty and ESL students across the curriculum. *College Composition and Communication, 46,* 506–521.

APPENDIX

Sample Stimulus Essay

College courses offer a wide variety of information. It may be a first time in student's life that they are exposed to different culturals, religions, or lifestyles in general. College allows one the opportunity by learning more about themselves with presenting them these alternatives. Although the ultimate goal of attending a university is to prepare you for a later career, I feel that the courses a student take should not be limited to a specific field.

Learning is a step in self-improvement. The more you having to learn, the better person you will be. Allowing science major to take a variety of classes, in addition to the specific classes for his or her major, will greatly enhance his or her general education.

College is the time with one's life when the future is like an open book. It's a time when you are exposed to a variety of experiences that can help fill those "blank pages." By having a larger variety of information to choose from, you will be able to more likely successfully pick ultimate career choice.

I felt that college's need to continue with having set classes or general education program that each student must take to reach their undergraduate requirements, in addition to having the specific career classes. The more a student can learn is more advantages that student will be exposed to. Deciding to attend by a university, in the pursuit of a degree, a person is consciously making the decision to be more "educated" than the average person. This education should know no limits or boundaries, they should be allowed to explore a wide range of interests. That person who knows may discovered a subject matter or topic that never they knew even existed. That is why I feel that the courses a student takes should definitely not just be limited to his or her future occupation.

Composition Evaluation Form

Student's name: _____

Circle the appropriate number to indicate your evaluation of the composition.

The **CENTRAL IDEA** is:
unclear   1   2   3   4   very clear

The **STYLE** is:
not effective   1   2   3   4   very effective

The **ORGANIZATION** is:
inadequate   1   2   3   4   very good

The **MAJOR POINTS** are:
undeveloped 1   2   3   4   very developed

The **EVIDENCE** is:
vague   1   2   3   4   very detailed

The **DETAILS** are:
uninteresting 1   2   3   4   very interesting

The **CONVENTIONS OF WRITTEN LANGUAGE** are:
unsophisticated 1   2   3   4   very sophisticated

The **USE OF EFFECTIVE TRANSITIONAL DEVICES** is:
inadequate   1   2   3   4   very good

The maintenance of a **CLEAR & EFFECTIVE TONE** is:
inadequate   1   2   3   4   very good

The **EXPRESSION OF IDEAS** is:
inadequate   1   2   3   4   very good

The **OVERALL GRADE** should be:
A A– B+ B B– C+ C C– D+ D D– F

The **STUDENT/WRITER** is:

reliable	1	2	3	4	5	6	7	unreliable
good writer	1	2	3	4	5	6	7	bad writer
intelligent	1	2	3	4	5	6	7	unintelligent
high socioeconomic status	1	2	3	4	5	6	7	low socioeconomic status
minority culture student (person of color)		1	2	3	4	5	6	7	dominant culture student (white/Euro)

20 Staying Out of Trouble: Apparent Plagiarism and Academic Survival

PAT CURRIE

Recent discussions in second language writing and sociolinguistics have focused on the issue of plagiarism by nonnative English speaking (NNES) students in academic settings. As we have learned from these discussions, plagiarism is a complex issue, embedded in social, cultural, and political matrices (Scollon, 1995) and rife with tensions (Pennycook, 1996).

One tension stems from the failure of the traditional and oversimplified view of plagiarism to account for the layers, complexities, and ambiguities embedded in the production of text (Scollon, 1995). Scholars from both first (L1) and second language (L2) domains (e.g., Bakhtin, 1986, as cited in Cazden, 1993; Cazden, 1993; Hull & Rose, 1989; Pennycook, 1994, 1996; Scollon, 1994, 1995) have pointed out how much we all "borrow from existing texts, how much we depend on membership in a community for our language, our voices, our very arguments" (Hull & Rose, 1989, p. 152). They argue that the intertextuality of discourse renders it difficult indeed for any writer to be the sole originator of his or her words or ideas.

A second tension is that the traditional view of plagiarism is ideological: it unjustifiably elevates a Western concept to the status of norm (Pennycook, 1994, 1996; Scollon, 1995) and privileges a "concept of the person established within the European Enlightenment" (Scollon, 1995, p. 3). From this position of "ideological arrogance" (Scollon, 1994, p. 45), the traditional view neither acknowledges practices it sees as outside the norm nor accords validity to other, different understandings of text, memorization, and learning (Pennycook, 1996). Other, power-related tensions also exist. Pennycook (1996), for example, speaks of an academic double standard: one for novices seeking to participate in disciplinary communities, another for those who have already arrived.

Nor are such tensions unfamiliar to our students. Even as they are being actively socialized into their various disciplinary communities and encouraged

From *Journal of Second Language Writing* 7.1 (1998): 1–18.

to assume the appropriate discourses (Bartholomae, 1985; Scollon, 1995), they are charged with displaying the required mastery in their own words (Pennycook, 1994, 1996; Sherman, 1992).

Further tensions lie in the distinction between borrowing actual words and borrowing ideas, where students must disambiguate the "unclear relationship between originality in thought and originality in words" (Pennycook, 1994, p. 282).

According to both first and second language writing researchers, tensions can derive from discrepancies between students' academic workloads and their still developing linguistic and cognitive resources (Britton, Burgess, Martin, McLeod, & Rosen, 1975; Campbell, 1990; Mohan & Lo, 1985; Pennycook, 1994). Caught between the two, student writers may be unable either to produce a mature, skilled synthesis of the ideas of others, or to attend simultaneously to all the demands of a complex writing task (Campbell, 1990).

Other tensions surface as students attempt to cope with intellectual contexts from which they are both linguistically and culturally distant (Ballard & Clanchy, 1991; Bloch & Chi, 1995; Garrow, 1991; Hull & Rose, 1989; Johns, 1991) and where they are "more likely to face obstacles than those who have already mastered the 'code' " (Shaughnessy, 1977, p. 13). As a case in point from first language composition, Garrow (1991) has speculated that plagiarism was, at least in part, Martin Luther King's way of coping with a discourse with which he did not feel comfortable and an "intellectual setting in which he might well have felt like an outsider" (p. 90). For their part, second language students can be "expected to produce high-quality research papers in a language they have barely mastered" (Bloch & Chi, 1995, p. 238). Current research suggests that in attempting to be perceived as belonging to and competent in academe, students may fall back on what they consider to be a "safe strategy" (Garrow, 1991), as they opt for a more correct, more appropriate, more academic discourse (Campbell, 1990; Bloch & Chi, 1995; Hull & Rose, 1989; Scollon, 1995). In Campbell's (1990) study, for example, copying was the major strategy for both L1 and L2 university students writing from sources.

Non-Western students may experience particular tensions between the Western view of plagiarism and what has for them been a valuable and effective "way of learning" (Pennycook, 1996, p. 225). Further, as Pennycook (1994, 1996; and indirectly, Deckert, 1993) has observed, while such students are often aware of the issues of textual borrowing, they are frequently unsure about the rules governing plagiarism and how to avoid it. In such cases, copying reflects less an intentional violation of a cultural code than a survival measure in the face of perceived difficulties or deficiencies.

Pennycook (1994, 1996) cautions us to avoid oversimplifying the issue of plagiarism or castigating particular cultures for practices which have served their members well, especially since it is only recently in Western culture that those practices have changed. He urges us instead to "attempt to understand plagiarism in general as an umbrella term for a complex set of different issues" (Pennycook, 1994, p. 282) and to scrutinize our own academic contexts

for ways they might exclude even as they include those attempting to participate in the various disciplinary communities.

This study looks under the umbrella of "apparent plagiarism" as it shaded
one second language writer—Diana—in a university content course. Following Pennycook (1996), the study examines her copying relative to her particular academic context, her task, her developing English language abilities, and
her general learning processes.

METHODOLOGY

This case study was part of a larger examination of disciplinary expectations
and evaluation (see Currie, 1990, 1993, 1994). Over the term, I interviewed
Diana weekly, immediately after her seminar meetings and after she had received her graded assignments for the course. She allowed me to copy those
assignments as well as her notes and preliminary drafts. Every week as well,
my research assistant interviewed the teaching assistant (TA). Several times
before and after the term, I interviewed the course professor, who agreed to
grade and comment on the assignments for the purposes of the study, a task
he would not normally have undertaken. The substantive comments on Diana's assignments that appear in this paper come directly from those interviews and my own analysis.

BACKGROUND

To understand Diana's copying, it is necessary first to understand her position relative to the context in which she copied: the structure and demands of
the course and her interaction with the TA.

Context and Task

The context in this study was a one-semester course in Management and Organizational Behaviour (OB 210), a core course in the Bachelor of Commerce
(B.Com.) program in the School of Business at Carleton University in Ottawa,
Canada. The class met twice weekly for a one-hour lecture, given by the professor, and once for a one-hour seminar session for each group of 15 students,
led by a TA. The primary objective of the course was for the students to learn
basic OB concepts and use them to analyze organizational problems, a goal
which entailed learning the specialized language necessary for oral and written discussion. To this end, the students wrote 9 weekly assignments of approximately 2½ pages each, based on both case studies in the text and "live"
organizations with which they were familiar. To write, the students had to analyze the problems and use the data to carry out other operations such as causal
analysis, classifying, and resolving an issue. In terms of cognitive demands, the
assignments varied considerably: some required careful, fine-grained analysis;
others, only superficial application of the concepts; still others required short,

factual answers (for a full description of the activities and genres required, see Currie, 1993). The TAs were to act as "coach" in the trial-and-error process, leading seminar discussions; grading the assignments, which accounted for 30% of the final grade; and providing oral and written feedback on them to the students. The TAs, who were also responsible for 15% in seminar participation marks, were thus responsible for 45% of the final grade.

Diana

The student I followed in OB 210 was Diana, a native speaker of Cantonese. Since arriving in Canada from Macau three years prior to the study, she had completed Grade 13 (in Ontario, equivalent to the first year of university) and the first two years of her Bachelor of Commerce program. Her academic average was approximately C/C+, with grades ranging from A to D. While a TOEFL score of 590 three years earlier had exempted her from ESL classes, she had taken two Business Writing courses, where she had achieved final grades of C and C+.

WRITING THE ASSIGNMENTS

To understand Diana's copying, it is also necessary to examine her difficulties as she attempted to deal with the tasks demanded in her OB context. To pass the course and stay in the B.Com. program, Diana needed a minimum of C–. In reality, however, she wanted more than a C–; at least a C, or "better, C+."

Early in the term, her goal appeared to be in jeopardy, the result of serious difficulties writing the assignments. Some of these problems she identified on her own; others were pointed out by the TA; still others emerged from my analysis of the data and the comments of the professor. While I have separated the difficulties for the purposes of discussion, I am not suggesting that they were unrelated; on the contrary, I believe they were inextricably intertwined.

First of all, Diana had difficulty meeting what the TA termed the "presentation" aspects of the assignments. From the beginning, Diana had been anxious lest her English writing skills disadvantage her. Specifically, she was concerned about "[her] grammar, . . . clarification, and . . . conciseness of sentence," and what an earlier instructor had called her "awkward sentences," concerns which were realized when the TA handed back the first assignment.

Assignment 1 required a six-dimensional structural analysis of a live organization using concepts provided on a handout. Based on the results of her analysis, Diana was to rate each dimension as high/medium/low/nonexistent in her organization and provide detailed support for each rating. The following excerpt, which illustrates her writing at the beginning of the course, is taken from this first assignment:

> Headquarter usually is the main decision-maker but under certain circumstances the General Manager can have the right of making his own

decision. This decision-making is not violated against the goal of Holiday Inn. It is important for Holiday Inn to maintain his image of being the friendly hotel in town. Formalization still plays an important role. There are rules, procedures, planning and budgeting which indirectly keep the functional managers coordinate horizontally across departments.

In her feedback, the TA, a former English Literature major, had made few substantive comments. She had, however, corrected over 20 errors and "awkward phrasings" and requested a meeting with Diana to discuss her writing. The feedback at the meeting taught Diana that she needed to write more clearly, more accessibly: "I try to simplify the sentence, to clarify the ideas, and everything will get better later."

A second major difficulty lay in the readings she was required to do in order to write. While it is unclear whether her problems were reading-based or language-based (Alderson, 1984), she reported great difficulty managing the lengthy text (approximately 40 to 50 pages per week) and the new, specialized vocabulary:

> I had to read over the chapters and then—the input, what's the input? . . . I tried to think it over and over, and later I talked with some of my friends who are doing the same assignments, 'Do you know what means by the input?'

The resulting confusion (see also Spack, 1997), which she attributed to her second language skills, led her to bluff her way through the writing:

> Maybe I am not sure of what is in the chapter, but I try to tell myself I know everything. . . . Maybe [native English speakers] understand the chapter right away so they can write the words they want. . . . I try to pretend I know the stuff so I try starting the work. It's not the right way to go.

Another obstacle involved the ways of reasoning required to complete the assignments. Diana experienced particular difficulty with the fundamental conceptual activity (Currie, 1993) of the course—applying the concepts to analyze. She often failed to separate the concepts into their component parts and use each one to tease out the relevant organizational information. This problem, which was likely exacerbated by her reading difficulties, persisted throughout the course, as illustrated by her comments late in the semester:

> I didn't get everything right away; for example, at first I miss the part about analyze the decision process so I just stuck with which decision model fit the decision. And later on when I read the question over I said, 'Oh, first we have to analyze the decision process before we apply the model'.

A second reasoning task Diana found difficult was that of resolving issues. This task entailed procedures such as analyzing all available options, stating her warrant (Toulmin, Rieke, & Janik, 1979), and arriving at an unequivocal decision—procedures neither explicitly taught in the course nor reflected in her argumentation. While it is likely that her reasoning was impeded by her inability to cope with the text and her lack of procedural knowledge, it is also possible that at least part of the difficulty stemmed from her cultural distance from a Western education. Research (for example, Ballard & Clanchy, 1991; Matalene, 1985) suggests that Chinese education does not typically require students to take a stance (Ballard & Clanchy, 1991), but rather to find a way to harmonize the various alternatives (Matalene, 1985). Whatever the reason, Diana intensely disliked choosing between options: "I hate to be put in the middle of two alternative."

It is also possible that at least part of her difficulty resulted from the lack of explicit guidance in the expected ways of reasoning and writing, a condition not uncommon in academe (Hymes, 1980; Johns, 1990; Langer, 1992). For instance, while Assignment 1 had been designed to model analysis, this intention was never explicitly articulated to the students. Other expectations were left unstated because of the professor's inability to articulate tacit knowledge. For example, when asked how the students were to learn how to select the appropriate concepts to apply in any given situation, the professor replied that he doubted he could explicitly teach this skill: "I don't know that I can teach them to do it. I just know that I *can* do it."

Showing considerable insight, Diana saw her difficulties as having less to do with the writing *per se*, than with the problem-solving it entailed:

> It's only when you understand what you are planning to write then you can write it fluently. But if you are not sure of your ideas, for sure you will get stuck by the time you go halfway through the assignment. I don't think it's the drafting that bothers me; it's figuring out the answer.

Unfortunately, while she sensed the existence of tacit expectations, she attributed her inability to intuit them not to her second language proficiency or her status as a novice in the community, but rather, to her lack of *intelligence*:

> If you're very bright it's easy to get an A. You can read through the mind of the professor. Otherwise you stay at B+ or whatever. That will be the best grade you can get.

Finally, Diana faced significant problems managing her workload. By the time she submitted Assignment 2 in Week 4, she was spending disproportionate time and effort on OB 210 and facing "stress and pressure from the other course." Thus by Week 4, Diana's position was indeed precarious: she was confused by the text, her writing was lowering her grades, and she was jeopardizing her other courses.

TEXTUAL BORROWING AS SURVIVAL STRATEGY

To understand Diana's response to her position, it is also useful to understand the strategies she had used up to that time. An early interview revealed what appears to have been her overall approach to academic study—and thus, in a sense, her overarching strategy for survival—staying out of trouble:

> I just avoid making mistakes to make them angry. You know, some pro-
> fessors they try to tell after the mid-term during the final, avoid doing
> that and avoid doing this. That's all I can tell myself.

If she just could keep her head down and not attract the attention of the TA,
she could survive and pass the course.

In conjunction with this approach, she had also employed a number of
more specific strategies. She had sought the help of friends to clarify
prompts, explain readings, and solve problems (see also Leki, 1995); she had
attempted to accommodate the TA's explicit demands (Leki, 1995; Spack,
1997) for accessibility with a purpose statement, shorter paragraphs, and
numbered answers; during seminar sessions she had listened carefully in order to compare her ideas with those of her seminar colleagues. She had also
compared her grades with theirs, discovering that her sevens were below
their eights and nines. Clearly these strategies were not working as she had
hoped.

In Week 5, Diana reported being hopeful that she could "show [the TA]
some changes." My analysis suggests that by the time she wrote Assignment
3, the "changes" were the result of a newly-adopted strategy—copying from
the course text. While she had copied only a few phrases for the first two assignments, by Assignment 3 she was copying extensively, a practice she continued for all but one of the remaining assignments.

A number of features characterized her copying. First, perhaps because
of her difficulties managing lengthy text, Diana appeared to make use of
point form items in lists and tables which she then combined into full sentences. As well, she copied partial and entire sentences, and even whole paragraphs, often from separate sections of the text, slightly paraphrasing them
and occasionally adding details specific to her own organization. The following excerpt from Assignment 3 illustrates her early technique (the original is
on the left; Diana's answer on the right):

The organization and its parts in-teract with each other. Conflict will oc-cur over products but will be resolved in the interests of the organization. — Daft, 1983, p. 105	The organization and its units in-teract functionally. Conflict may occur but will be resolved in the interest of Acme.

For Assignment 4, from which the following excerpt is taken, she copied
approximately one-third of the paper:

In a functional organization struc-ture, activities are grouped together by common function from the bottom to the top of the organization. . . . The dis-tinctive feature of **functional structure** is that people and activities are grouped by resources. . . . The func-tional structure is most effective when	the environment is stable, and when technology is relatively routine with low interdependence across functional departments. . . . Employees are ex-posed to a range of functional activities within their departments. — Daft, 1983, p. 231–232

Holiday Inn is a functional organization where activities are grouped by common function from the bottom to the top. Employees and activities are grouped by resources. Each functional department provides resources. The functional structure is most effective when the environment is stable and low interdependence across functional department. Employees are exposed to a range of functional activities within their departments.

For Assignment 8, Diana copied approximately three-quarters of the paper, patching together sentences and parts of sentences from seven different pages in the chapter. The excerpt below also illustrates a development in her syntactic fluency: several times she altered verb phrases as if to suggest that what she was describing represented the reality within her live organization rather than the general situation in the course text:

Certain rights, responsibilities, and prerogatives accrue to top positions. . . . People throughout the organization accept the legitimate right of top managers to set goals, make decisions, and direct activities. . . .

(Daft, p. 383)

Control of decision premises means that top managers place constraints on decisions made at lower levels. . . . An additional way to influence decision premises is . . . through the control of information. Information flows continuously. . . . By carefully controlling this information, the manager has a major source of power. Information can be released to define the decision premises for other people. . . . Managers can use their central position to built alliances and loyalty, and hence be in a position to wield substantial power in the organization.

—Daft, 1983, pp. 386–388

They had certain rights, responsibilities, and prerogatives accruing to their positions. Most of all the organization accepted the legitimate right of top managers to set goals, make decisions and direct activities. The project managers placed constraints on decisions made at lower levels. Besides they also controlled the flow of information which could be released to define the decision premises for other people. Also, the project managers used their central positions to build alliances and loyalty, and hence wield substantial power in the organization.

It is difficult to read the juxtaposed texts without realizing the extraordinary time, effort, and patience it must have taken for Diana to struggle through the reading, find precisely those phrases or sentences that met her needs in terms of content and generality, and then weave them together, using still-developing syntactic skills, into what she hoped would bring her an acceptable grade. And yet, when she spoke later of changing her approach, she referred to her need to write the assignments more "efficiently." For Diana, despite the enormous time and effort involved, copying meant saving time.

In the end, how successful was Diana's copying? Did it help her achieve her goal? The short answer is yes. From Assignment 3 onwards, when she began copying substantially, the lowest mark Diana received for any assignment was 8 on 10. Her final mark for the assignments was 23.9 out of 30, or 79% — a B+, what she had considered the best grade possible without reading the professor's mind. What she had done, in fact, was to accommodate the explicitly stated demands of the TA for more accessible, less awkward text that contained the appropriate disciplinary terminology. While the TA continued to mention several on-going problems (for example, occasional failures to understand or apply the concepts and a lack of elaboration), by the end of the course she viewed Diana's performance as having steadily improved throughout the term. She spoke warmly — and unwittingly accurately — about her progress:

> [Diana's] writing style has drastically improved. She sort of developed her own style. It's a very kind of descriptive literary style, but not fuzzy because of that. I enjoy reading her papers more and more. Of any of [the three NNESs in the study], she has improved the most. . . . She's gaining confidence, and I think her linguistic skills are improving. Also, in last week's oral work in class she handled herself very well in terms of confidence and expressing herself.

Not once did the TA suggest that she had noticed similarities between Diana's assignments and the course textbook.[1] A number of explanations can be offered here: a busy academic schedule involving courses and TA responsibilities that mitigated against a close reading of the text; a focus on textbook content rather than particular words; a reliance on the Instructor's Manual for solutions; a sincere belief in Diana's improvement, both written and oral; and perhaps, too, the desire to see her own efforts as instrumental in Diana's growth. It is also possible that she did, in fact, note the similarities, but decided against opening that particular Pandora's Box. Her grades as well as her comments in the interviews, however, suggest that for her, Diana was a success story, both conceptually and linguistically.

Thus, there were indeed "many complex things going on behind the surface phenomenon of apparent plagiarism" (Pennycook, 1996, p. 225–226), things which involved her task, her context, her language proficiency, and her learning processes. Her task involved extensive reading, learning new concepts and terminology, carrying out complex cognitive operations, a knowledge of several genres, and the ability to write clearly and smoothly. These expectations existed in a context with very little explicit guidance about the more substantive matters of analysis and argumentation, a situation which can perhaps be viewed as exemplifying unintentional, but nonetheless "exclusionary" (Pennycook, 1994, p. 281) academic practices, which may disadvantage many NNESs by "assum[ing] a set of cultural norms [they] do not have" (Ramanathan & Kaplan, 1996, p. 23). What explicit demands there were, however, Diana did her best to accommodate.

Moreover, the disparity between her developing language and academic skills and the level she needed to accomplish her task successfully may have created a cognitive overload that left her scrambling to write the assignments. If copying is, as has been suggested, a natural stage in the progression toward full synthesizing ability (Britton et al., 1975; Campbell,

1990), it is possible to view Diana's behavior as simply a natural consequence of her developing proficiency; in short, a way to manage, and one
which in Chinese culture might have been a mark of scholarly achievement
(Bloch & Chi, 1995).

For Diana, copying represented a way of achieving one goal explicitly
encouraged by the TA—learning the terminology of the OB community:

> Usually I stick to the book because they give you a better expression of
> what you're supposed to say. Usually you would say "department" but
> in the book they say "unit" and that will give you another terminology,
> so you won't just stay with certain areas. You try to expand your knowl-
> edge of what actually in society the people are using the term.

Interview data further suggest that Diana saw this learning as unattainable
by any other means:

> I like to stay with the terms that is written from the book. That's how I
> got to make use of the terms. . . . The point is if I keep on using the lan-
> guage that never be ours in the book then I will never be able to learn
> the more specific terms.

Additionally, copying allowed her to "enact" (Scollon, 1995, p. 215; see
also Ivanič, 1994) the role of competent OB student, to stay out of trouble,
and to pass the course. For scholars such as Cazden (1993), Scollon (1995),
Pennycook (1996), and Hull and Rose (1989), such a move would be neither
exceptional nor exceptionable, but rather an instance of the social purposes
implicit in the construction of text:

> A fundamental social and psychological reality about discourse—oral or
> written—is that human beings continually appropriate each other's lan-
> guage to establish group membership, to grow, and to define themselves
> in new ways. (Hull & Rose, 1989, p. 151)

Such were the goals that Diana, with her own "understandings of text and
language" and her own "approaches to learning" (Pennycook, 1996, p. 226)
was attempting to achieve.

As Scollon (1995) has argued, "the construction of identities in discourse
is a process of mutual interactive negotiation" (p. 15). In this case, the TA and
Diana actively negotiated the language and the identity Diana would assume
in her assignments, the choice facilitated by Diana's own understandings of
texts and language. As Ivanič (1994) has pointed out, much of the power in
such negotiations lies with the instructor: the student's anticipation of what
that instructor will "value and reward" (p. 8) can exert enormous pressure on
the student's discursive choices. I suggest that given her focus on presentation and terminology and her control of almost half the final grade, the TA,
albeit unintentionally, reinforced Diana's reliance on copying (see also Spack,
1997). What I am arguing here is that Diana copied not with the intent to violate Western cultural norms, but rather with the intent to learn, to keep her
head down, and to pass the course. She achieved her goals: her final grade
in OB 210 was C+—more than enough to pass the course and stay in the

program, from which she graduated one year later. While copying was, if neither appropriate nor justifiable in a Western academic context, it was at least understandable: it enabled her to manage an array of variables—task, context, current knowledge, language abilities, and learning—in a way that for her was, at least in this one context, acceptable.

It is significant that on the one occasion when Diana had no need to copy, she did not. As noted earlier, not all assignments were equally cognitively demanding. Perhaps the least demanding of all was Assignment 7, based on her "live" organization: the analysis was superficial, the reading minimal, and the choice of content largely her own. It was, as another second language student described it, "common sense." Moreover, the prompt provided a transparent framework for both problem-solving and narrative writing. Two questions will illustrate: "Describe a change that occurred in your organization" and "Who was pushing for the change?" A brief excerpt from her paper, graded 9 out of 10, illustrates how well she could control the discourse when she knew what she wanted to say:

> Particularly the Accounting Department found the need for this change to occur. As the manager recognized that they did not have an efficient system in controling Accounts Payable and Accounts Receivable. Accounts Payable related to the difficulty of keeping up-to-date records to ensure correct payments of accounts. Accounts receivable related to the inefficiency of keeping customers' accounts up-to-date and not knowing status of outstanding receivables and difficulties in controlling customer credit. Those were the serious problem that pushed for this change.

Diana's comments on this paper emphasize the ease and fluency with which she wrote when she knew the answer:

> Every time I try to emphasize this point. If I know what I want to write that will be very easy and straightforward to do. If I don't, then I will have to make up something or whatever to answer the question. That means to force myself to answer the question, by not knowing the right answer; that is, to fill up the space but not the right words. It's only I know the stuff, no matter it's given me four nights, it is very easy to write out the stuff.

CONCLUSIONS AND IMPLICATIONS

Diana's story supports Pennycook's notion of the complexity of the whole issue of textual borrowing. If we assume that this issue is equally multidimensional for other second language writers, any attempt to deal with "apparent plagiarism" needs to incorporate at least three features.

First, we need to inform our students about the dangers of plagiarizing (Pennycook, 1996; Sherman, 1992)—the possibility of reprimands, course failure, and even expulsion, depending on the policies of the particular institution. Further, to help them develop some of the necessary skills to synthesize source material (Campbell, 1990; Spack, 1988, 1997), we need to give them opportunities to write from sources (Campbell, 1990; Spack, 1988, 1997) along with instruction in citation, paraphrase (Campbell, 1990; Sherman, 1992), and effective reading strategies (Spack, 1988, 1997). As Campbell (1990) points out, one benefit of such classroom instruction might be an increase in self-confidence and less reliance on copying.

Yet, such approaches alone fail on at least two counts: first, they fail to acknowledge both the ambiguity surrounding textual borrowing—the fuzziness of the concept itself and how difficult it is to identify (Pennycook, 1994, 1996; and indirectly by Deckert, 1993)—and the language abilities of our student writers. The letter below, written by one of my introductory EAP students, exemplifies such uncertainty and ambiguity. He knows he lacks the lexical fluency required by the task and that the best words have already been taken by the original writer (Spack, 1997). Further, he cannot distinguish between the borrowing of words and the borrowing of ideas (Pennycook, 1996; Spack, 1997), and he worries that his essay will end up being little more than a string of quotation marks and parentheses:

> I read a book talking about what is called plagiarism which I'm very much concerned with. The problem is I'm not be able to distinguish when it is plagiarism and when it isn't. I'm totally aware that when I recite something, which is not mine, from the text book, I'm supposed to give the writer credit, in other word I will put the recitement in the quotation mark, and this is applied even in the case I just recite the author's idea (paraphrase: I'm not sure this is right or wrong). However, when I getting deeper in the definition of plagiarism, I become totally confused. I'll make this claim clearer by showing some examples. For instance, so far, I've been going on the aboriginal people issue, and I've found out that I might write down the author and the book's name all over of my essay. Why? Because all the information I've acquired is not mine; I've known by reading the text book. For Ex: If you asked my what the main purpose of the Whites when they've done all kinds of mistreatment against the natives, I would say that because the whites want to "Civilized" the natives. Trouble is arising here: Since the word civilized is from the book and I do not have other alternative vocabulary. Second Example, I'd say in my essay that the natives came from Asia about 50,000 years ago, should I put (give) credit for the author? Third Example, I'd talk about all kind of problem that the natives 've encountered resulting from the government's bad policies, should I say this is taken out from the text. Finally, my essay is covered with only quotation marks or this ( ) signs [parentheses]. Please explain me to overcome this problem.

Although he wants to stay within the bounds of his new academic system, he does not know where they are. Nor could I articulate them explicitly in ways that would have been wholly satisfactory to me, fully comprehensible to him, or entirely transferable to other academic contexts.

Second, appeals for a "cultural syllabus" and practice in paraphrase fail to acknowledge both the "fundamentally different attitudes toward text" (Pennycook, 1996, p. 227) our students may bring to the classroom and the learning power they have afforded. It is very doubtful that any appeals would have dissuaded Diana from the copying that enabled her to learn, to stay out of trouble, and to pass the course. To promote the necessary understanding—theirs and ours—the classroom needs also to include discussions of the varying cultural notions of "authorship, authority, and plagiarism" (Pennycook, 1996, p. 227), as they are historically embedded in our cultures (for a full discussion of these issues, see Pennycook, 1996; Scollon, 1995).

Third, Diana's experiences suggest that any attempt to discourage plagiarism amongst our students must include a greater understanding of their tasks and contexts and how their past strategies have contributed to their earlier successes. We cannot ask them to reject something without helping them find other means to replace it, and only when we understand their attitudes and strategies can we begin to help them adapt those strategies in ways acceptable to Western institutions. Copying, for example, might prove a useful early step in the composing process, a way for them to develop a felt sense of written English, or as for Diana, a vehicle for learning the language and conventions they are attempting to appropriate. The "free-wheeling pedagogy of imitation" advocated by Hull and Rose (1989, p. 151) might provide a beneficial preliminary stage in the development of a more mature ability to synthesize or appropriate the words and ideas of others.

Given their cultural remove from Western academic institutions, our students need more than an admonishment about plagiarism. Neither a cultural syllabus nor a general purpose approach to EAP speaks, for example, to Diana's lack of procedural knowledge for problem-solving (Currie, 1993) or to her unfamiliarity with the argumentation (Johns, 1988, 1995) demanded by her disciplinary community. We need at least to try to raise "sociocultural and textual awareness" (Johns, 1995, p. 185) of what they are encountering in their other courses. Following Johns (1990) and Braine (1988), we can teach our students ethnographic techniques (Johns, 1990) to help them examine various aspects of their disciplinary communities, including, for example, the genres of argumentation (Johns, 1990, 1995), article introductions (Swales, 1990; Swales and Feak, 1994), and the conceptual activities required in order to write (Currie, 1993). Using their own essays as bases for interviews with their professors, students might investigate the textual practices of their own courses.

All such exploration necessarily entails learning from our students the kinds of difficulties they face in their Western academic institutions, working with them to forge appropriate responses, and asking them to evaluate our attempts in the classroom. For example, research into student perceptions of how effective we are (Kanno & Applebaum, 1995; Leki & Carson, 1994, 1997; Spack, 1997) has all pointed to the need to provide greater intellectual challenge in the ESL/EAP classroom, a conclusion strongly supported by Diana's situation in OB 210. It is time to take our students' advice, to provide texts and tasks that require increasingly indepth levels of complexity and engagement (Leki & Carson, 1994, 1997) along with the scaffolding for developing the necessary skills, strategies, and self-confidence in their own abilities.

Insofar as research in both L1 and L2 composition has uncovered a number of previously tacit expectations (for example, Bazerman, 1992; Currie, 1990, 1993, 1994; Johns, 1986, 1990, 1991, 1995; Odell, 1992; Ramanathan & Kaplan, 1996; and Swales, 1990), further collaborative exploration of this nature appears promising. This OB professor's inability to articulate tacit knowledge is not uncommon, but perhaps reflects what Langer (1992) suggests may be in fact a "general failure by both scholars and practitioners to clarify and articulate those rules of argument and evidence in ways that enable [them] to think about what they're teaching" (p. 83). Such a failure cannot but impede the participation in the academic enterprise of second language and other non-mainstream students (Ramanathan & Kaplan, 1996). To continue to search for ways to articulate more clearly disciplinary expectations and conventions is a worthwhile endeavor. To continue to guard the tower (Maimon, 1983) is to jeopardize the culturally-distanced student, regardless of his or her language.

Finally, there is a need to work toward making our university colleagues aware of the different cultural attitudes toward textual ownership and textual borrowing, in order that, when confronted with "apparent plagiarism," they will be better equipped to address it from a perspective of inter-cultural understanding.

ACKNOWLEDGMENTS

I would like to thank Ellen Cray for her valuable insights on earlier versions of this paper, as well as Ilona Leki, Tony Silva, and the three anonymous *JSLW* reviewers for their helpful suggestions as I prepared the manuscript. I am also grateful to the Carleton University ALS graduate students for their questions and comments, the TA, my eloquent EAP student, and especially, Diana. This research was funded in part by a grant from the Graduate Studies and Research Office of Carleton University.

NOTE

1. By the time I discovered the copying, the TA had finished her MA and left to work in Papua, New Guinea.

REFERENCES

Alderson, J. C. (1984). Reading in a foreign language: A reading problem or a language problem? In J. C. Alderson & A. H. Urquhart (Eds.), *Reading in a foreign language* (pp. 1–27). London: Longman.

Ballard, B., & Clanchy, J. (1991). Assessment by misconception: Cultural influences and intellectual traditions. In L. Hamp-Lyons (Ed.), *Assessing second language writing in academic contexts* (pp. 19–35). Norwood, NJ: Ablex Publishing.

Bartholomae, D. (1985). Inventing the university. In M. Rose (Ed.), *When a writer can't write: Studies in writer's block and other composing-process problems* (pp. 134–165). New York: Guilford.

Bazerman, C. (1992). From cultural criticism to disciplinary participation: Living with powerful words. In A. Herrington & C. Moran (Eds.), *Writing, teaching, and learning in the disciplines* (pp. 86–98). New York: Modern Language Association.

Bloch, J. & Chi, L. (1995). A comparison of the use of citations in Chinese and English academic discourse. In D. Belcher & G. Braine (Eds.), *Academic writing in a second language: Essays on research and pedagogy* (pp. 231–274). Norwood, NJ: Ablex Publishing.

Braine, G. (1988). A reader reacts. . . . *TESOL Quarterly, 22,* 700–702.

Britton, J., Burgess, T., Martin, N., McLeod, A., & Rosen, H. (1975). *The development of writing abilities* (pp. 11–18). Houndmills, Hampshire, U.K.: Macmillan.

Campbell, C. (1990). Writing with others' words: Using background reading text in academic compositions. In B. Kroll (Ed.) *Second language writing: Research insights for the classroom* (pp. 211–230). Cambridge: Cambridge University Press.

Cazden, C. B. (1993). Vygotsky, Hymes, and Bakhtin: From word to utterance and voice. In E. A. Forman, N. Minnick, & C. A. Stone (Eds.), *Contexts for learning: Sociocultural dynamics in children's development* (pp. 197–212). Oxford: Oxford University Press.

Currie, P. (1990). Argument and evaluation in organizational behaviour: Student writing in an introductory course. In S. Anivan (Ed.) *Language Teaching Methodology for the Nineties* (pp. 127–142). Singapore: SEAMEO Regional Language Centre.

Currie, P. (1993). Entering a disciplinary community: Conceptual activities required to write in one introductory university course. *Journal of Second Language Writing, 2,* 101–117.

Currie, P. (1994). What counts as good writing? Enculturation and evaluation. In A. Freedman & P. Medway (Eds.), *Teaching and learning genre* (pp. 63–79). Portsmouth, NH: Boynton/Cook Publishers, Heinemann.

Daft, R. L. (1983). *Organization theory and design.* St. Paul, MN: West Publishing.

Deckert, G. D. (1993). Perspectives on plagiarism from SL students in Hong Kong. *Journal of Second Language Writing, 2,* 131–148.

Garrow, D. J. (1991). King's plagiarism: Imitation, insecurity, and transformation. *The Journal of American History, 20,* 86–92.

Hull, G., & Rose, M. (1989). Rethinking remediation: Toward a social-cognitive understanding of problematic reading and writing. *Written Communication, 6,* 139–154.

Hymes, D. (1980). *Language in education: Ethnolinguistic essays.* Washington, DC: Center for Applied Linguistics.

Ivanič, R. (1994). I is for interpersonal: Discoursal construction of writer identities and the teaching of writing. *Linguistics and Education, 6,* 3–15.

Johns, A. M. (1986). Coherence and academic writing: Some definitions and suggestions for teaching. *TESOL Quarterly, 20,* 247–265.

Johns, A. M. (1988). The discourse communities dilemma: Identifying transferable skills for the academic milieu. *ESP, 7,* 55–60.

Johns, A. M. (1990). Coherence as a cultural phenomenon: Employing ethnographic principles in the academic milieu. In U. Connor & A. M. Johns (Eds.) *Coherence in writing: Research and pedagogical perspectives* (pp. 209–226). Alexandria, VA: TESOL.

Johns, A. M. (1991). Interpreting an English competency examination: The frustrations of an ESL science student. *Written Communication, 8,* 379–401.

Johns, A. M. (1995). Teaching classroom and authentic genres: Initiating students into academic cultures and discourses. In D. Belcher & G. Braine (Eds.), *Academic writing in a second language: Essays on research and pedagogy* (pp. 277–291). Norwood, NJ: Ablex Publishing.

Kanno, Y., & Applebaum, S. (1995). ESL students speak up: Their stories of how we are doing. *TESL Canada Journal, 12,* 32–49.

Langer, J. A. (1992). Speaking of knowledge: Conceptions of understanding in academic disciplines. In A. Herrington & C. Moran (Eds.), *Writing, teaching, and learning in the disciplines* (pp. 69–85). New York: Modern Language Association.

Leki, I. (1995). Coping strategies of ESL students in writing tasks across the curriculum. *TESOL Quarterly, 29,* 235–260.

Leki, I., & Carson, J. G. (1994). Students' perceptions of EAP writing instruction and writing needs across the disciplines. *TESOL Quarterly, 28,* 81–101.

Leki, I., & Carson, J. G. (1997). Completely different worlds: EAP and the writing experiences of ESL students in university courses. *TESOL Quarterly, 31,* 39–69.

Maimon, E. P. (1983). Maps and genres: Exploring connections in the arts and sciences. In W.B. Horner (Ed.), *Composition and literature: Bridging the gap* (pp. 110–125). Chicago: University of Chicago Press.

Matalene, C. (1985). Contrastive rhetoric: An American writing teacher in China. *College English, 47,* 789–808.

Mohan, B. A. & Lo, W. A-Y. (1985). Academic writing and Chinese students: Transfer and developmental factors. *TESOL Quarterly, 19,* 515–534.

Odell, Lee (1992). Context-specific ways of knowing and the evaluation of writing. In A. Herrington & C. Moran (Eds.), *Writing, teaching, and learning in the disciplines* (pp. 86–98). New York: Modern Language Association of America.

Pennycook, A. (1994). The complex contexts of plagiarism: A reply to Deckert, *Journal of Second Language Writing, 3*, 277–284.

Pennycook, A. (1996). Borrowing others' words: Text, ownership, memory, and plagiarism. *TESOL Quarterly, 30*, 201–230.

Ramanathan, V., & Kaplan, R. B. (1996). Audience and voice in current L1 composition texts: Some implications for ESL student writers. *Journal of Second Language Writing, 5*, 21–33.

Scollon, R. (1994). As a matter of fact: The changing ideology of authorship and responsibility in discourse. *World Englishes, 13*, 33–46.

Scollon, R. (1995). Plagiarism and ideology: Identity in intercultural discourse. *Language in Society, 24*, 1–28.

Shaughnessy, M. (1977). *Errors and expectations: A guide for the teacher of basic writing.* New York: Oxford University Press.

Sherman, J. (1992). Your own thoughts in your own words. *ELT Journal, 46*, 190–198.

Spack, R. (1988). Initiating ESL students into the academic discourse community: How far should we go? *TESOL Quarterly, 22*, 29–51.

Spack, R. (1997). The acquisition of academic literacy in a second language: A longitudinal case study. *Written Communication, 14*, 3–62.

Swales, J. M. (1990). *Genre analysis: English in academic and research settings.* Cambridge: Cambridge University Press.

Swales, J. M., & Feak, C. B. (1994). *Academic writing for graduate students: A course for nonnative speakers of English.* Ann Arbor: The University of Michigan Press.

Toulmin, S., Rieke, R., & Janik, A. (1979). *An introduction to reasoning.* New York: Macmillan.

21
Error Feedback in L2 Writing Classes: How Explicit Does It Need to Be?

DANA FERRIS AND BARRIE ROBERTS

INTRODUCTION

There are many elements and characteristics of student texts that determine their overall quality, and no experienced L2 writing instructor would argue that the number of linguistic errors made by students represents the sum total of a text's merit or a student's ability. Even so, few experts on L2 writing would argue with the propositions that written accuracy is important to students in many contexts and that students themselves want and expect feedback on their written errors from their teachers (Ferris, 1995b; Ferris, Chaney, Komura, Roberts, & McKee, 2000; Hedgcock & Lefkowitz, 1994; Leki, 1991; Radecki & Swales, 1988; Rennie, 2000; Truscott, 1996). Nonetheless, issues surrounding how, and even whether, to give L2 students feedback on their written errors continue to be a source of interest and debate among researchers, instructors, and students (Ferris, 1999a; Truscott, 1996, 1999). Only a few available studies have explicitly examined differences in accuracy and writing quality between students who have received error feedback and those who have not, and these have reported conflicting results (Fathman & Whalley, 1990; Kepner, 1991; Polio, Fleck, & Leder, 1998; Semke, 1984). However, in other studies which have examined student progress in written accuracy over time, researchers have typically found that writers who received feedback on their errors showed improvement, which in some cases was statistically significant (Chandler, 2000; Ferris, 1995a, 1997; Ferris et al., 2000; Frantzen, 1995; Lalande, 1982; Robb, Ross, & Shortreed, 1986; Sheppard, 1992). This evidence, while not conclusive as to the ultimate success of error feedback in helping students to improve their writing, at minimum supports further investigations into the nature and effects of teacher error correction. Such research can and should include both studies of short-term effects of error correction on student revision (i.e., from one draft of a paper to the next) and longitudinal analyses of the effects of error feedback on student accuracy over time. Though some have argued that only longitudinal designs have merit in investigating these issues (Truscott, 1996, 1999), the examination of student processing of error

From *Journal of Second Language Writing* 10.3 (2001): 161–84.

feedback under controlled conditions provides information that can subsequently be applied to the study of longer-term student progress.

One issue about which there is little existing evidence is the level of explicitness that is required for error feedback to help students. Specifically, when teachers mark student errors, do they need to indicate the type of error (wrong verb tense, omitted obligatory article, run-on, etc.) the student has made, or is it adequate for the teacher to simply underline or circle an erroneous form, leaving it to the student to diagnose and correct the problem? For pedagogical purposes, this is an important question because labeling errors by type or category may well be more time-consuming for teachers than just indicating that an error has been made. More significantly, there is a much greater chance that the teacher will mislabel an error if s/he is identifying it by type rather than simply locating it for the student.

In a previous study (Ferris et al., 2000), we noted that our subjects, who were primarily long-term immigrants at a U.S. university, were nearly as successful in self-editing errors when they were marked but not coded as when they were labeled with a specific error code from a standard list of 15 error types. However, this finding, though interesting, was somewhat incidental to the design of the study and represented only a small proportion (about 10%) of our larger sample of over 5700 marked errors. Thus we decided to investigate further in a controlled experimental study with a similar student population which specifically targeted the issue of coded versus uncoded feedback. In addition, we added a "no-feedback" control group for comparison purposes. Our study was guided by the following four research questions:

1. Are there differences in student ability to self-edit errors across feedback condition (codes, no codes, no feedback)?

2. Are there differences across error type in student ability to self-correct?

3. What are student views about their own grammar needs and feedback preferences, and how do these correspond to their textual data?

4. How does prior knowledge of grammar terminology and error types factor into students' ability to process feedback and self-edit their texts?

BACKGROUND

Does Error Feedback Help Student Writers to Edit Their Texts Successfully?

Several studies have examined the effects of error feedback on student ability to edit their papers from one draft to the next. In an experimental classroom study, Fathman and Whalley (1990) found that students in two feedback groups who received error feedback had significantly fewer grammatical errors on a revised draft than groups who received only content feedback or no feedback at all. In a study of university-level Spanish language students, Frantzen and Rissell (1987) found that students were able to edit 93% of errors marked in various linguistic categories during a 10-min. in-class editing session. Ferris (1997), using a longitudinal design, reported that verbal feedback on error patterns (i.e., brief explanations provided in endnotes) combined with in-text underlining of examples of these error types led to successful revisions in 73% of the cases. Finally, in our previous study (Ferris et al., 2000; see also Chaney, 1999; Komura, 1999), we found that students were able to successfully edit about 80% of the errors marked by their teachers.

What Are the Effects of Differing Teacher Feedback Strategies?

One distinction that has been made in the literature is between direct and indirect teacher feedback (Bates, Lane, & Lange, 1993; Ferris, 1995c; Ferris & Hedgcock, 1998; Hendrickson, 1978, 1980; Lalande, 1982; Walz, 1982). *Direct feedback* is given when the teacher provides the correct form for the student writer; if the student revises the text, s/he needs only to transcribe the correction into the final version. *Indirect* feedback occurs when the teacher indicates in some way that an error exists but does not provide the correction, thus letting the writer know that there is a problem but leaving it to the student to solve it. Second language acquisition theorists and ESL writing specialists alike argue that indirect feedback is preferable for most student writers because it engages them in "guided learning and problem solving" (Lalande, 1982), leading to reflection about linguistic forms that may foster long-term acquisition (James, 1998; Reid, 1998b).[1] Error correction researchers who have examined the effects of these two contrasting types of feedback have reported that indirect feedback helps students to make progress in accuracy over time more than direct feedback does (Ferris et al., 2000; Ferris & Helt, 2000; Lalande, 1982) or at least equally as well (Frantzen, 1995; Robb et al., 1986).

If indirect feedback is preferable in most cases (with the possible exceptions of student writers at lower levels of L2 proficiency or for certain complex, idiosyncratic types of errors), the question then arises as to how explicit indirect feedback should be in order to give students enough direction to self-correct their errors. As noted by various writing experts, options for teachers range from very explicit feedback (marking an error at its exact location in the text and labeling it with a code or verbal cue, such as "VT," "wrong verb tense," or "use past tense") to placing a checkmark in the margin to let the writer know that there is an error somewhere in that line of text, but leaving it to the student to find, diagnose, and repair the problem (Bates et al., 1993; Ferris, 2002; Hendrickson, 1980; James, 1998; Lalande, 1982; Reid, 1998b; Walz, 1982).

In a study by Robb et al. (1986), 134 Japanese EFL college students were assigned to one of four feedback groups: (1) direct feedback; (2) coded in-text feedback; (3) uncoded in-text feedback; and (4) marginal feedback about the total number of errors per line. Five student texts per student produced over a 9-month academic year were analyzed on a set of measures designed to assess "accuracy, fluency, and complexity," and the authors report no significant differences across the four treatment groups on any of the measures. They conclude that "less time-consuming methods of directing student attention to surface errors may suffice" (1986, p. 91).

It has been argued that because EFL and/or international students may have both different motivations for L2 writing and different experiences with learning English, the types of grammar feedback appropriate for them may be different from what is helpful for immigrant student writers, who are primarily "ear learners" (Reid, 1998a) and whose knowledge of English comes primarily from unconscious acquisition processes rather than from formal grammar teaching (Ferris, 1999b). In a study of mostly immigrant student writers at a U.S. university (Ferris et al., 2000; Ferris & Helt, 2000), we examined the types of grammar feedback given by three instructors to 92 ESL writers, assessing the effects of the teacher feedback both on short-term next-draft revisions and the long-term progress made by students in overall written accuracy from the beginning to the end of the semester. The teachers in the study agreed to give indirect, coded feedback to their students on the second draft of each of four out-of-class essays, using a list of 15 standard error categories and codes. However, when we analyzed the data, we found that the teachers actually adhered to this system for only 41% of the errors they had marked, providing direct feedback on over 45% of the marked errors, indirect, uncoded feedback in 5.6% of the cases, and corrections marked with a code not on the standard list 4.4% of the time. Because of this range of responses, we were able to assess the effects of these different marking strategies on students' short-term edits and long-term progress in written accuracy. We found that students made correct revisions 77% of the time when they received indirect feedback with codes from the standard list but were nearly as successful (75%) when the feedback had either nonstandard codes attached or even no codes at all. Students were even successful in making corrections in 62% of the (relatively rare) instances in which the attached codes were judged by the researchers as being inaccurate! These results led us to speculate that these immigrant student writers were simply using the teacher feedback as a cue that an error had been made and applying their own acquired competence to self-correct mistakes, and that the error type codes were not necessary and perhaps not even being utilized by the student writers in revision. This finding stood in direct contrast to the intuitions of the teachers and students in the study, who clearly indicated in interviews and written surveys that they felt that error codes were necessary for students at this level of proficiency (high-intermediate, two semesters below college composition). However, because these uncoded or nonstandard coded marks comprised only about 10% of the sample and because they occurred incidentally, we felt that it would be helpful to follow up with an experimental design which controlled this particular variable (coded versus uncoded indirect feedback) to see whether our findings and the findings of Robb et al. (1986) would hold with this immigrant population. In addition, we added a "no-feedback" control group, which was not part of either of the previous two studies, to the design, just as in Fathman and Whalley (1990).[2] We felt that this was a necessary step to ensure that students' success ratios in editing could be attributed to their feedback condition and not to other factors. Thus, we examined the effects of these differing treatments on short-term editing success (Research Question 1).

How Do Different Error Categories Respond to Treatment?

One of Truscott's (1996) well-taken criticisms of teacher error correction practices is that instructors and editing texts or checklists treat different linguistic categories (lexical, syntactic, and morphological) as being equivalent, when in fact they represent separate domains of knowledge that are acquired through different stages and processes. Truscott's assertion is supported by the findings of prior studies of error correction. In all instances, when specific categories of written error were targeted for feedback and analysis, there were significantly different rates of student achievement and progress across error types (Chaney, 1999; Ferris, 1995a; Ferris et al., 2000; Ferris & Helt, 2000; Frantzen & Rissell, 1987; Lalande, 1982; Sheppard, 1992). In addition, in the study which preceded this one, we examined the larger subcategories of "treatable" and "untreatable" error, as discussed in Ferris (1999a),[3] finding that teachers were more likely to give indirect feedback to treatable errors and direct feedback to untreatable errors, and that these patterns affected both short- and long-term student progress (Ferris et al., 2000). Thus, in this study, we examined the differences in student editing success ratios across five major categories of error — verbs, noun endings, articles, word choice, and sentence structure — and also examined errors and revisions across the treatable/untreatable dichotomy (Research Question 2).

What Are Student Preferences Regarding Error Feedback?

Previous studies of student writers' views toward error feedback (Ferris, 1995b; Ferris et al., 2000; Hedgcock & Lefkowitz, 1994; Komura, 1999; Leki, 1991; Roberts, 1999) have consistently reported that L2 student writers want, expect, and value teacher feedback on their written errors. In several of these studies, students have also indicated that they prefer indirect feedback with error codes or labels attached over either direct teacher correction or errors being simply marked but not labeled (Ferris et al., 2000; Komura, 1999; Leki, 1991; Rennie, 2000). However, with the exception of the study by Ferris et al. (2000) (see also Komura, 1999), expressed student preferences have not been connected explicitly to patterns seen in student texts. Thus, in addition to examining textual data, we felt it important to investigate student attitudes and preferences about error feedback and their own assessment of their weaknesses in writing (Research Question 3). We did this for the purpose of triangulating our data collection, but also because students' attitudes and preferences have unfortunately been a neglected piece of information in many previous error correction studies and reviews (Ferris et al., 2000; Reid, 1998b).

How Does Students' Formal Knowledge of Grammar Terms and Rules Affect the Feedback and Revision Process?

Finally, survey and interview data from our previous study suggested that students struggled with applying teacher feedback to their writing because they were unfamiliar with the grammatical rules and terminology connected with the 15 error categories on our list (see Ferris, 1995b; Lee, 1997). As noted by Ferris and Hedgcock (1998), "When giving feedback on student errors, teachers also need to take into account their students' backgrounds, especially their previous English language instruction" (206). We therefore developed a "Grammar Knowledge Pretest" as an attempt to discover what students already knew about the five categories of error we had targeted for the study and to relate these objective test results to error patterns actually observed in student texts (Research Question 4).

In summary, our study builds on and adds to the previous research base on error correction in L2 writing in the following ways: (1) It examines the short-term effects of differing levels of explicitness in indirect feedback given to immigrant student writers, comparing the two feedback treatments (coded and uncoded) with a control group of writers who received no feedback at all; (2) it specifically relates what students say about their grammar needs and feedback preferences to their written texts; and (3) it connects students' prior knowledge of the error types and categories targeted for analysis to their written production and self-editing success ratios.

METHOD

Setting and Subjects

The student subjects, as in our previous study, came from ESL classes at the Learning Skills Center at California State University, Sacramento, a large U.S. university. Forty-four of the students were enrolled in three sections of LS 86, a three-unit composition class two semesters below the freshman composition level. Two of the three sections were taught by one of the researchers (the second author), and the third section was taught by another instructor who had been involved in the earlier study and who agreed to cooperate with us. The remaining 36 students were enrolled in LS 6B, a voluntary one-unit "Grammar for Writers" tutorial which met for 2 hours per week for 6 weeks.[4] They represented six different tutorials taught by graduate student interns in the MA TESOL program at the university. These interns were supervised by the other researcher (the first author). Thus, 72 ESL students and 8 teachers were involved in the data collection process.

Demographic information collected from all of the students indicated that the vast majority (82%) were immigrant students and that the largest first language groups were Southeast Asian (55%) and Chinese (12%). The grammar knowledge pretest scores were significantly higher for the LS 6B group than for the LS 86 group. However, the normalized error totals on the diagnostic essays were not significantly different between the two groups. Thus, the LS 6B group apparently had more prior knowledge of the grammatical terms and categories focused on in the study, but they were equivalent to the LS 86 group in overall written accuracy at the start of the study.

Treatment

Both sets of students wrote an in-class, 50-min diagnostic essay during the first week of class. Though the two classes wrote on different essay topics, in both cases students were given a short reading and asked to respond to a question raised by the reading by giving their opinion and supporting it. The researchers took the handwritten essays and word-processed them to make it easy to obtain word counts for normalizing purposes and also so that the papers would be easier to work with during both editing and analysis. We made no changes to the student texts as we typed them.

The different classes were randomly assigned to three treatment groups according to their "feedback condition." Group A, the "codes" group, had all instances of errors in five categories underlined and coded by the two researchers (see Table 1 for a detailed description of the five categories).[5] In addition, we merged several smaller error types from the previous study into the larger categories. Group B, the "no codes" group, had all errors in the same five categories underlined but not coded. The control group (C) simply had their typed papers returned to them with no error markings. One LS 86 class was assigned to each of the three groups, three of the six LS 6B tutorial groups were assigned to Group A, and the other three LS 6B groups were assigned to Group B. In all, there were 28 subjects in Group A, 25 in Group B, and 14 in Group C.[6]

Approximately 2 weeks after the diagnostic essays had been written, the students received their word-processed and marked (if applicable) papers back. They were given a cover sheet with instructions (see Appendix A.3) and were asked to spend exactly 20 min. self-editing their essays. They were told that this was an editing exercise that would help them with required in-class essay examinations and that they would receive a report on how well they did within 2 weeks (see Appendix A.4 for report form). Students wrote in corrections by hand on the typed, double-spaced texts, and they were immediately collected by the teachers and given to the researchers.

TABLE 1.   Description of Error Categories Used for Feedback and Analysis

Verb errors	All errors in verb tense or form, including relevant subject–verb agreement errors.
Noun ending errors	Plural or possessive ending incorrect, omitted, or unnecessary; includes relevant subject–verb agreement errors.
Article errors	Article or other determiner incorrect, omitted, or unnecessary.
Wrong word	All specific lexical errors in word choice or word form, including preposition and pronoun errors. Spelling errors only included if the (apparent) misspelling resulted in an actual English word.
Sentence structure	Errors in sentence/clause boundaries (run-ons, fragments, comma splices), word order, omitted words or phrases, unnecessary words or phrases, other unidiomatic sentence construction.

In addition to the in-class writing, feedback, and editing cycle, students completed a "Grammar Knowledge Questionnaire" and a "Grammar Knowledge Pretest" prior to receiving their marked diagnostic essays. Copies of both instruments are included in Appendix A. Both were completed in class during a 10–20 min period, with the classroom instructors encouraged to answer any questions about the instructions and procedures. The five-item questionnaire asked students about their prior experiences with English grammar instruction, about their own assessments and the opinions of previous English teachers about problems with English grammar in their writing, and about the ways in which they preferred to receive feedback about their errors.

The pretest consisted of three sections, all with items related to the five major error categories targeted for feedback and analysis. In the first section, students examined individual sentences that each contained one error. They had to find the error and label it with one of the five error categories from a key. In the second and third sections, students referred to an excerpt from a student essay in which six errors were underlined and numbered. In the second section, they had to label each marked error from one of the five categories. In the third section, they had to suggest a correction for the error. There was a total of 18 points on the test (six items in each section), with the first being the most difficult because subjects had to both find errors themselves and label them, the second part being a bit easier because errors were underlined for them, and the third part being the easiest because they had only to suggest corrections, not find or label the errors by category.

Analysis

After typing up the student texts, the two researchers met to mark a sample of the student texts using the five error categories. Interrater reliability calculations showed that we had achieved over 95% agreement on both the total errors marked and on the assignment of errors to specific categories, so we divided up the rest of the papers and marked them individually. After the students had completed the in-class editing exercise, we met again to mark the changes made by the students as "correct" or "incorrect/no change." This time we achieved almost 99% agreement on the subsample of papers we both analyzed. When we had completed the analysis, we used this information to complete Student Report Forms, which were returned as promised to the students. We obtained word counts for each student text by using our word processors (Word 97), and used the word counts to calculate normalized error scores, following the procedure suggested by Biber, Conrad, and Reppen (1998).[7]

The responses to the Grammar Knowledge Questionnaire were collated, and totals and percentages calculated. The Grammar Knowledge Pretest was corrected by the researchers using a standard answer key, with some latitude given for alternate responses in the third section (in which they suggested corrections).[8] Statistical procedures used to analyze all of the data included descriptives (frequencies, percentages, means, and standard deviations),

ANOVAs and *t* tests (to assess differences across classes and treatment groups), and correlations (to examine relationships among pretest scores and textual data). SPSS Version 9.0 for Windows was used for all statistical tests.

RESULTS

Errors Marked

Diagnostic essays from 67 subjects were marked and analyzed for all instances of errors in the five categories described in Table 1. The results, shown for all subjects, for the two different classes (LS 86 and LS 6B), and for the three treatment groups, are shown in Table 2.

The greatest number of errors was observed in the verb category, followed by, respectively, sentence structure, word choice, noun endings, and articles. Though there were no significant differences between the LS 86 and LS 6B classes in total number of errors, there were significant differences in the verb and article categories. It should also be noted that, although the LS 6B students made fewer total errors, they had higher mean error counts in the word choice and sentence structure categories (i.e., the "untreatable" categories that may reflect acquired competence rather than formal learning), possibly because a higher proportion of them were international students who may have had limited prior opportunities for exposure to English outside the language classroom. Other than the verb category, there were no significant differences across the three feedback treatment groups. Scheffé post hoc comparisons (not in the table) showed that all significant differences were between the control "no feedback" group and the other two feedback groups. Table 2 also shows that the control group made noticeably more errors in the noun ending and word choice categories, even with normalized error counts. Thus, it is possible that this group was weaker to start with as to grammatical accuracy. This is a key issue to keep in mind in interpreting the findings of this study.

Errors Self-Corrected by the Students: Effects of Feedback Treatment

Table 3 shows the percentages of errors successfully corrected in the different categories. Percentages were derived by dividing the number of errors corrected by the number of errors marked (with all counts normalized as previously described).

It is immediately evident that both groups which received error feedback substantially outperformed the control, "no feedback" group. This finding is thus very similar to that reported by Fathman and Whalley (1990). Even allowing for the fact that the control group students made more errors to begin with (Table 2), the differences in editing success are quite striking. In contrast, there were no statistically significant differences in editing success ratios between the "codes" and "no codes" groups, though the "codes" group had higher percentages for correction on all categories except articles.[9]

TABLE 2. Errors Marked—Means/S.D.s

Group	Verbs	Nouns	Articles	Word choice	Sentence structure	Total
All subjects (N = 67)	9.74/7.40	5.23/4.17	2.36/1.97	7.50/4.44	8.78/5.57	33.6/13.8
By class						
LS 86 (N = 39)	11.9/8.3*	5.7c/4.24	1.9/1.6**	6.75/3.36	8.08/4.33	34.2/12.7
LS 6B (N = 28)	6.8/4.6*	4.45/4.01	3.0/2.3**	8.51/5.51	9.74/6.89	32.7/15.4
By feedback treatment						
Codes (N = 28)	7.8/6.0[a]	4.8/4.2	2.4/2.0	7.7/4.2	8.7/5.1	31.5/11.6
No codes (N = 25)	9.2/5.1[a]	4.5/4.2	2.2/2.2	8.1/5.3	8.7/6.6	32.7/16.0
No feedback (N = 14)	14.9/10.8[a]	7.5/3.6	2.5/1.5	6.0/3.0	9.2/4.8	39.4/13.2

The average number of words per text was 356. Error counts have been normalized by dividing number of errors by number of words and multiplying by a standard, which was set at 350 (see Biber et al., 1998).

*t test results: P < .005.
**t test results: P < .05.
[a] ANOVA results: P < .009.

TABLE 3. Percentage of Errors Corrected[a]. Essay 1

Group	Verbs (%)	Nouns (%)	Articles (%)	Word choice (%)	Sentence structure (%)	Total (%)
All subjects (N = 67)	56	58	60	53	47	53
Codes (N = 28)	69	79	69	63	53	64
No codes (N = 25)	64	64	71	55	52	60
No feedback (N = 14)	14	8	25	31	23	18

For all categories, ANOVA results across treatment groups were significant at $P < .005$. Post hoc comparisons (not in table) showed that the "no feedback" group differed significantly from the other two groups in all categories. There were no significant differences in any category between the "codes" and "no codes" groups.

[a]Percentages = number of errors corrected divided by number of errors marked (all counts normalized as described in previous table).

Effects of Error Type on Self-Editing Success

In general, it can be observed from Table 3 that all five error categories were reasonably amenable to student self-editing. For all subjects, the success ratios ranged from 47% (sentence structure) to 60% (articles). This is an important finding because it suggests that indirect feedback can even help students to self-edit idiosyncratic errors such as word choice and sentence structure. It has been previously suggested that because such errors are not rule-governed, students may be helped more by direct feedback in these cases (Chaney, 1999; Ferris & Hedgcock, 1998; Hendrickson, 1980). However, a careful reading of Table 3 presents a somewhat more complicated picture. The two groups which received error feedback had noticeably higher success ratios in the three "treatable" categories (verbs, noun endings, and articles) than in the "untreatable" word choice and sentence structure categories. In contrast, the "no feedback" group was *more* successful in editing word choice errors than any other type, and their success rate in editing sentence structure errors was better than for either verbs or noun endings.

To examine these findings more closely, we did a statistical reanalysis of the data, combining error correction totals for verbs, noun endings, and articles into a larger "treatable errors" category and the word choice and sentence structure totals into an "untreatable" variable. The results of this analysis are shown in Table 4.

Our reanalysis shows that there was a statistically significant difference in students' ability to edit treatable and untreatable error types. However, the major differences are caused by the "sentence structure" category. The *t* test results comparing correction success between treatable errors and word choice errors were nonsignificant. This suggests that some "untreatable" errors may be more so than others — specifically, complex sentence structure problems versus single-word errors. Further, as already noted, the "no feedback" control group was relatively successful (31%) in catching word choice errors by themselves on second reading. Word choice errors in L2 student texts often

TABLE 4. Treatable vs. Untreatable Error Categories

Category	Mean (%)	S.D.	t*	df	Significance
All treatable	57	0.29			
All untreatable	50	0.22	2.02	50	.048
Word choice	54	0.28	−0.569	51	.572 (n.s.)
Sentence structure	46	0.28	−2.67	50	.01

Percentage of errors corrected.

"Treatable" is a combined variable consisting of normalized error counts for verb, noun, and article errors. "Untreatable" combines word choice and sentence structure error counts.

*t scores are for differences between the "all treatable" and three "untreatable" categories.

cause serious comprehensibility problems. However, these data suggest that they may be more amenable to student self-editing without feedback than other types of errors, even "treatable" ones such as verb tense.

Questionnaire Responses

Sixty-three of the 72 subjects completed the Grammar Knowledge Questionnaire. The results are summarized in Table 5.

The majority of the students (82%) said they had prior English grammar instruction "a lot" (30%) or "sometimes" (52%). No respondent claimed to have "never" had English grammar instruction. Most students said that either in an English teacher's opinion and/or in their own view, they had problems with verbs (81%), word choice (68%), or sentence structure (68%). On the other hand, only about one-third of the students said that they had serious problems with noun endings or article usage. These perceptions about their grammatical strengths and weaknesses apparently were quite accurate, matching up consistently with error patterns found in their diagnostic essays (see Table 2). A majority of the students (56%) said that their grammar problems were very serious and really hurt their writing. However, a significant minority (24%) responded either that their grammar problems were, in their opinion, not serious (10%) or that other issues (writing, organization) were more important to them (14%). As to feedback preferences, no respondent said that s/he did not want any error correction (the "treatment" received by Group C). The most popular feedback choice (48%) was for the teacher to mark the error and label it with an error code (i.e., the treatment received by Group A in this study), followed by having the teacher correct all errors for them (31%). Only 19% said that having errors marked but not labeled by error type (the Group B treatment) was preferable to other feedback methods.

Pretest Scores

Fifty-eight of the 72 subjects completed the Grammar Knowledge Pretest. The results for all subjects are summarized in Table 6. The average score for all subjects was 9.34 out of a possible 18 points. The data for the LS 86 students confirm the intuition that the first part was the most difficult and the third part was

TABLE 5.   Grammar Knowledge Questionnaire Responses ($N = 63$)

Question	Frequency	Percent
1: Prior grammar instruction		
a lot	19	30
sometimes	33	52
very little	11	18
never	–	–
2/3: Types of grammar problems identified		
Verbs		
No	12	19
Yes	51	81
Noun endings		
No	41	65
Yes	22	35
Articles		
No	40	63.5
Yes	23	36.5
Word choice		
No	20	32
Yes	43	68
Sentence structure		
No	20	32
Yes	43	68
4: Seriousness of grammar problems in writing		
Serious	35	56
Not serious	6	10
Other issues more important	9	14
Not sure	13	20
5: Error feedback preferences		
Don't correct	0	0
Correct most serious	1	2
Circle errors	12	19
Circle & label error type	30	48
Correct all errors	19	31

the easiest. However, the LS 6B data showed a reverse trend—the students in this group actually scored higher on the first two parts (in which they had to label errors by category) than on the third part, in which they had to supply correct forms for the errors. It is possible that these differences occurred because the LS 6B group had a higher proportion of international students, who likely had a stronger background in formal grammar terminology but possibly less of an acquired sense of what "sounds" right than the immigrant students largely represented in LS 86 (Ferris, 1999b; Reid, 1998a). While we do not have

TABLE 6.   Pretest Results by Class: Mean/Standard Deviation

Test portion	LS 86 (N = 41)	LS 6B (N = 29)
Pretest, Part A (6 points)	2.05/1.83*	4.00/2.07
Pretest, Part B (6 points)	2.90/1.79*	4.34/1.49
Pretest, Part C (6 points)	3.51/1.14	3.93/1.10
Pretest totals (18 points)	8.34/3.10*	12.28/2.88

Differences between the two class groups:
*t test results: $P < .001$.

adequate background information on all subjects to confirm this speculation, the fact that the LS 6B students scored higher overall on the pretest (totals and all three subsections) than the LS 86 students also suggests that their prior formal knowledge of English grammar was greater. However, there were no significant differences in pretest scores across the three feedback treatment groups.

Correlations between Pretest Scores and Textual Variables

Finally, to assess the relationship between students' prior knowledge of the grammatical terms and categories we had targeted, the texts they produced, and their success on the self-editing task, we examined correlations between pretest scores and number of errors "marked" (by the researchers) or "corrected" (by the students), again working with normalized error counts as previously described. The correlations are shown in Table 7.

Table 7 shows that there was little relationship between the student writers' formal knowledge as measured by the pretest and the different errors they produced. The only significant correlation was in the "total errors marked" category, and that was barely so at $P = .04$. On the other hand, four

TABLE 7.   Correlations between Pretest Score and Text Variables

Variable	Correlation with pretest total score	Significance
Verbs — marked	−.221	.08 (n.s.)
Noun endings — marked	−.197	.12 (n.s.)
Articles — marked	.088	.49 (n.s.)
Word choice — marked	−.071	.58 (n.s.)
Sentence structure — marked	−.167	.91 (n.s.)
Total errors marked	−.252	.04
Verbs — corrected	.405	.001
Noun endings — corrected	.358	.005
Articles — corrected	.114	.41 (n.s.)
Word choice — corrected	.252	.04
Sentence structure — corrected	.030	.82 (n.s.)
Total errors corrected	.285	.02

out of six of the "corrected" variables were significantly correlated to the pretest scores. This suggests that formal knowledge may have come specifically into play at the editing phase, in which students were asked to focus specifically on correcting errors they had made (and in the case of the two groups which received feedback, they actually had information about exactly where to look). This finding is reminiscent of Krashen's (1982) Monitor Hypothesis, which suggests that formal learning primarily has an "editor" function which operates when learners are intentionally focused on form, when they know the rule involved, and when they have sufficient time to reflect on and apply their knowledge. However, it may also be the case that the Grammar Knowledge Questionnaire, which contained only 18 items, was not detailed or extensive enough to isolate differences in subjects' prior formal knowledge and its relationship to the accuracy of their texts and their ability to self-edit their writing.

CONCLUSION

Summary of Results

Research Question 1 asked about the effects of different error feedback treatments on students' ability to self-edit their texts. We found substantial, highly significant differences in our subjects' editing outcomes between the two feedback groups and the no-feedback group (Table 3). On the other hand, there were no significant differences in editing success between the group that received coded feedback and the group that simply had errors underlined. We also looked at the effects of specific error types on students' ability to utilize feedback for editing. Our subjects made the most errors in verbs, followed by sentence structure, word choice, noun endings, and articles (Table 2). They were more successful in editing errors in the "treatable" category (verbs, noun endings, and articles) than the "untreatable" types (word choice and sentence structure; see Table 3). However, they were much more successful in coping with word choice problems than sentence structure errors (Table 4). It was also notable that the no-feedback control group was more successful in finding and correcting word choice errors than any other error category.

We also examined the relationships between students' self-assessments of their own writing problems, their preferences about error correction (Table 5), and their prior knowledge about specific grammar problems and the texts they produced (Tables 6 and 7). Despite the report of 82% of respondents that they had had prior grammar instruction "a lot" or "sometimes," their pretest scores were fairly low (averaging a bit over 9 correct out of 18 possible points). Students also reported that their major areas of weakness were in verbs, sentence structure, and word choice; as already noted, these were the top three patterns of errors found in their actual texts, suggesting that their own perceptions about their writing problems were quite accurate. No student said that they did not want errors corrected by their teacher. The most popular error correction technique among the questionnaire respondents was for the teacher to mark errors and label them with a code (the treatment given to Group A in this study). On the grammar knowledge pretest, we found that the scores were highest for the third subsection, in which students merely had to suggest corrections for errors underlined in a student text but did not have to label them by error category. We found little relationship between pretest scores and the errors actually made by students in their texts, but their formal knowledge appeared to come into play most significantly during the follow-up self-editing exercise.

Implications

Our findings are similar to those of Ferris et al. (2000) and Robb et al. (1986) in that there did not seem to be an immediate advantage to more explicit (coded) indirect feedback for the student writers in this study. Thus, if teachers' primary goal in giving error feedback is to give students cues so that they can self-edit their papers most successfully, it may be adequate at least with some student populations to locate errors without labeling them by error type. This is good news in that marking errors in this way may be faster and easier for teachers, and, more importantly, it reduces the possibility that instructors themselves will make errors while correcting.

It is possible that using a consistent system of marking and coding errors throughout a writing class, paired with mini-lessons which build students' knowledge base about the error types being marked, might yield more long-term growth in student accuracy than simply underlining or highlighting errors. Though the results of this study and the previous two all suggest that a less explicit marking technique may be equally effective in the short-run, this strategy may not give adequate input to produce the reflection and cognitive engagement that helps students to acquire linguistic structures and reduce errors over time (James, 1998; Lalande, 1982; Reid, 1998b). To assess this issue fairly, a longitudinal study is needed which carefully examines classroom instruction and other variables and assesses student progress in accuracy over time.

The finding that students in the no-feedback control group were less successful in self-editing their own texts was not terribly surprising and was similar to the result reported by Fathman and Whalley (1990). In both studies, while students in the no-feedback group were able to catch some of their own errors, they had far less success in doing so than the groups which received feedback on their errors (see Table 3 in this paper and Table 1, p. 183, of Fathman and Whalley's study). Fathman and Whalley note that while students were able to significantly improve their content simply by rewriting even without feedback, "students made significant improvement in grammatical accuracy in revisions only when teachers provided feedback on grammar errors" (1990, p. 183). The students in the present study made a lot of grammar errors — an average of 33.6 errors in the five categories examined in texts that averaged 350 words, or nearly 1 error for every 10 words of text

(Table 2). Without feedback, the control group was able to catch only about six errors on the average (Table 3). While it could be argued that students should be given the chance to edit their own work without feedback so that they can develop independent self-editing skills, at this level of instruction such an approach might prove ineffective in helping students to reach accuracy levels that would enable them to pass the course and might thus be extremely frustrating to the students.

Furthermore, the possibility of student frustration with less explicit error marking strategies is one of which teachers also need to be aware. In this study and the one which inspired it (Ferris et al., 2000), students clearly favored the more explicit (coding) approach. In the previous study, both students and teachers expressed the opinion that simply locating errors was not adequate for students at this level of L2 proficiency. However, in both studies, the textual evidence did not support the subjects' perceptions or preferences. If teachers choose to give students less explicit feedback on their errors, they may need to be prepared to explain and defend this strategy, and perhaps even demonstrate its effectiveness to students by means of a self-editing exercise like the one described in this study.

Another option for writing instructors to consider is whether or not indirect feedback is appropriate for complicated and idiosyncratic errors in sentence structure. As shown in Tables 3 and 7, students were less able to edit such errors successfully than the other four categories. On the other hand, the differences in editing success ratios across categories, while noticeable, were not enormous (the success rate for sentence structure was 47% for all subjects, compared with a range of 53–60% for the other four categories). The students who received indirect feedback on these errors (Groups A and B) were able to self-edit over half of them. In sum, while the sentence structure category appears to be the most problematic of the five for student self-editing, teachers may wish to at least give student writers an opportunity to self-correct such errors via indirect feedback before providing any direct correction. Similarly, these mostly immigrant subjects did surprisingly well at self-correcting word choice errors, even those who received no feedback at all. Teachers of similar students may wish to exploit their ability to catch such errors without intervention by specifically discussing them with students and suggesting some strategies for finding and correcting word choice errors and avoiding them in the future.

While teacher response to student writing can and should cover a variety of concerns, including students' ideas and rhetorical strategies, error correction and improvement of student accuracy continue to be serious issues for both teachers and students in L2 writing classes. It is therefore important for researchers and writing experts to identify issues, feedback strategies, and techniques for helping students to help themselves through various types of research designs. Though this study, examining primarily a controlled experimental feedback treatment, obviously has its limits, it nevertheless provides specific evidence that can help teachers weigh some of their feedback options more carefully. Clearly, it also raises further questions for future investigations on this topic. It is to be hoped that researchers will continue to pursue this research agenda for the benefit of teachers and students alike.

NOTES

1. In a parallel line of research looking at "focus-on-form" in oral L2 production, similar issues, such as recasting student utterances, helping students to "notice" errors by means of feedback, and the feasibility of learner self-correction, have been examined. See Doughty and Williams (1998) for an excellent collection of papers examining focus-on-form research.

2. In a study by Lee (1997), 149 EFL college students in Hong Kong were divided into three feedback groups: (1) errors underlined; (2) checkmarks in the margin indicating error-free lines of text; and (3) no error feedback at all. The researcher found that students in Group 1 were significantly more able to correct errors than students in the other two groups. However, in this study students were editing a text that they had not themselves written, so its comparability to the others discussed in this section is questionable.

3. Ferris (1999a, p. 6) describes "treatable" errors as those that "occur in a patterned, rule-governed way," and "untreatable" errors as those for which "There is no handbook or set of rules students can consult to avoid or fix those types of errors." She comments that she uses a combination of "strategy training and direct correction" to help her students with untreatable errors.

4. Some students were enrolled in both courses. Only their LS 86 data were used for the study.

5. These five categories were chosen and operationalized based on information from our previous study (Ferris et al., 2000), in which we utilized 15 error categories but found the marking system too cumbersome for both teachers and students (Roberts, 1999). The five categories used here represent the five most frequent error types found in a sample of 5707 errors analyzed in texts by 92 ESL writers in the same setting (Chaney, 1999).

6. It was deemed too intrusive to the goals of the LS 6B tutorial program (which in contrast to the semester-long LS 86 was only 6 weeks long) to have a third of the students assigned to a no-feedback group. Thus, only LS 86 students served as controls.

7. This procedure consists of dividing the error counts (for each separate category and for the total errors) by the number of words in the text and then multiplying them by a standard number representing the average number of words in each text in the whole sample. In this case, the number used was 350 words.

8. All alternate responses were discussed and agreed upon by the two researchers as being either appropriate substitutions or incorrect.

9. We repeated the treatment at the end of the semester for the LS 86 students on their Practice Final essay ($N=35$), keeping students in the same three treatment groups. We had identical findings: The control group was substantially less successful in editing than the other two groups, and there were no significant differences between the two groups that did receive feedback.

REFERENCES

Bates, L., Lane, J., & Lange, E. (1993). *Writing clearly: Responding to ESL compositions.* Boston: Heinle & Heinle.

Biber, D., Conrad, S., & Reppen, R. (1998). *Corpus linguistics: Investigating language structure and use.* Cambridge: Cambridge University Press.

Chandler, J. (2000, March). *The efficacy of error correction for improvement in the accuracy of L2 student writing.* Paper presented at the AAAL Conference, Vancouver, BC.

Chaney, S. J. (1999). *The effect of error types on error correction and revision.* MA thesis, Department of English, California State University, Sacramento.

Doughty, C., J. Williams (Eds.) (1998). *Focus on form in classroom second language acquisition.* Cambridge: Cambridge University Press.

Fathman, A., & Whalley, E. (1990). Teacher response to student writing: Focus on form versus content. In B. Kroll (Ed.), *Second language writing: Research insights for the classroom* (pp. 178–190). Cambridge: Cambridge University Press.

Ferris, D. R. (1995a). Can advanced ESL students be taught to correct their most serious and frequent errors? *CATESOL Journal, 8* (1), 41–62.

Ferris, D. R. (1995b). Student reactions to teacher response in multiple-draft composition classrooms. *TESOL Quarterly, 29,* 33–53.

Ferris, D. R. (1995c). Teaching ESL composition students to become independent self-editors. *TESOL Journal, 4* (4), 18–22.

Ferris, D. R. (1997). The influence of teacher commentary on student revision. *TESOL Quarterly, 31,* 315–339.

X Ferris, D. R. (1999a). The case for grammar correction in L2 writing classes: A response to Truscott (1996). *Journal of Second Language Writing, 8,* 1–10.

Ferris, D. R. (1999b). One size does not fit all: Response and revision issues for immigrant student writers. In L. Harklau, K. Losey, & M. Siegal (Eds.), *Generation 1.5 meets college composition* (pp. 143–157). Mahwah, NJ: Lawrence Erlbaum Associates.

Ferris, D. R. (2002). *Treatment of error in L2 writing classes.* Ann Arbor, MI: University of Michigan Press.

Ferris, D. R., Chaney, S. J., Komura, K., Roberts, B. J., & McKee, S. (2000). *Does error feedback help student writers? New evidence on the short- and long-term effects of written error correction.* Manuscript submitted for publication.

Ferris, D. R., & Hedgcock, J. S. (1998). *Teaching ESL composition: Purpose, process, & practice.* Mahwah, NJ: Lawrence Erlbaum Associates.

Ferris, D. R., & Helt, M. (2000). *Was Truscott right? New evidence on the effects of error correction in L2 writing classes.* Paper presented at the AAAL Conference, Vancouver, B.C.

Frantzen, D. (1995). The effects of grammar supplementation on written accuracy in an intermediate Spanish content course. *Modern Language Journal, 79,* 329–344.

Frantzen, D., & Rissell, D. (1987). Learner self-correction of written compositions: What does it show us? In B. VanPatten, T. R. Dvorak, & J. F. Lee (Eds.), *Foreign language learning: A research perspective* (pp. 92–107). Cambridge: Newbury House.

Hedgcock, J., & Lefkowitz, N. (1994). Feedback on feedback: Assessing learner receptivity to teacher response in L2 composing. *Journal of Second Language Writing, 3,* 141–163.

Hendrickson, J. M. (1978). Error correction in foreign language teaching: Recent theory, research, and practice. *Modern Language Journal, 62,* 387–398.

Hendrickson, J. M. (1980). The treatment of error in written work. *Modern Language Journal, 64,* 216–221.

James, C. (1998). *Errors in language learning and use: Exploring error analysis.* London: Longman.

Kepner, C. G. (1991). An experiment in the relationship of types of written feedback to the development of second-language writing skills. *Modern Language Journal, 75,* 305–313.

Komura, K. (1999). *Student response to error correction in ESL classrooms.* MA thesis, Department of English, California State University, Sacramento.

Krashen, S. D. (1982). *Principles and practices in second language acquisition.* Oxford: Pergamon Press.

Lalande, J. F., II (1982). Reducing composition errors: An experiment. *Modern Language Journal, 66,* 140–149.

Lee, I. (1997). ESL learners' performance in error correction in writing: Some implications for college-level teaching. *System, 25,* 465–477.

Leki, I. (1991). The preferences of ESL students for error correction in college-level writing classes. *Foreign Language Annals, 24,* 203–218.

Polio, C., Fleck, C., & Leder, N. (1998). "If only I had more time": ESL learners' changes in linguistic accuracy on essay revisions. *Journal of Second Language Writing, 7,* 43–68.

Radecki, P., & Swales, J. (1988). ESL student reaction to written comments on their written work. *System, 16,* 355–365.

Reid, J. (1998a). "Eye" learners and "ear" learners: Identifying the language needs of international student and US resident writers. In P. Byrd, & J. M. Reid (Eds.), *Grammar in the composition classroom: essays on teaching ESL for college-bound students* (pp. 3–17). Boston: Heinle & Heinle.

Reid, J. (1998b). Responding to ESL student language problems: Error analysis and revisions plans. In P. Byrd, & J. M. Reid (Eds.), *Grammar in the composition classroom: Essays on teaching ESL for college-bound students* (pp. 118–137). Boston: Heinle & Heinle.

Rennie, C. E. (2000). *Error correction in ESL writing: Student views.* MA thesis, Department of English, California State University, Sacramento.

Robb, T., Ross, S., & Shortreed, I. (1986). Salience of feedback on error and its effect on EFL writing quality. *TESOL Quarterly, 20,* 83–93.

Roberts, B. J. (1999). *Can error logs raise more than consciousness? The effects of error logs and grammar feedback on ESL students' final drafts.* MA thesis, Department of English, California State University, Sacramento.

Semke, H. (1984). The effect of the red pen. *Foreign Language Annals, 17,* 195–202.

Sheppard, K. (1992). Two feedback types: Do they make a difference? *RELC Journal, 23,* 103–110.

Truscott, J. (1996). The case against grammar correction in L2 writing classes. *Language Learning*, 46, 327–369.

Truscott, J. (1999). The case for "the case for grammar correction in L2 writing classes": A response to Ferris. *Journal of Second Language Writing, 8*, 111–122.

Walz, J. C. (1982). Error correction techniques for the foreign language classroom. *Language in Education, Theory, and Practice*, No. 50. ERIC Document Reproduction Service No. ED 217704.

APPENDIX A. INSTRUMENTS USED IN DATA COLLECTION

A.1. Grammar Knowledge Questionnaire

1. In English classes you have taken before, have you ever learned any English grammar rules or terms (noun, verb, preposition, etc.)? Circle one answer.
   (a) Yes, a lot
   (b) Sometimes
   (c) Very little, or never
   (d) Not sure

2. Has an English teacher ever told you that you have problems with any grammar rules? Please circle any specific problems that a teacher has told you about.

   None   Nouns – plural endings   Articles   Verb tenses
   Verb forms   Subject–verb agreement   Word choice   Sentence structure

3. In your own opinion, what problems do you have with using English grammar in your writing? Circle all problems that you think you have.

   None   Nouns – plural endings   Articles   Verb tenses
   Verb forms   Subject–verb agreement   Word choice   Sentence structure
   Don't know

4. Please circle ONE statement which BEST describes how you feel about your English grammar:
   (a) My English grammar problems are very serious and really hurt my writing.
   (b) Although I don't know much about English grammar, it's not a serious problem for me.
   (c) English grammar is not really a serious issue for me. Other writing issues are more important.
   (d) I'm not really sure whether English grammar is a problem for my writing.

5. In your opinion, what is the best way for me to give feedback about your grammar errors in your writing? Please circle ONE statement only:
   (a) Don't correct my grammar. Let me try to correct my errors myself.
   (b) Only correct the most serious errors.

    (c) Circle my errors, but don't correct them for me.

    (d) Circle my errors and tell me what type of error it is (verb tense, word choice, etc.).

    (e) Correct all of my errors for me.

A.2. Grammar Knowledge Pretest

A. Each of the sentences below has an error in it. Using the terms from the KEY below, match the error type with each sentence. [Each sentence has only one error, and you will not use any error type more than once.]

Error Type Key:

1. Noun ending (plural or possessive) missing or wrong
2. Article or determiner missing or wrong
3. Verb tense wrong
4. Verb form wrong
5. Wrong word
6. Sentence structure error

1. _____ I didn't buy the car because I didn't wanted to spend so much money.
2. _____ We all rushed to help because my uncles house was on fire.
3. _____ I didn't worry about my English. Now, I understood how important it is.
4. _____ I looked at all of the cars and picked up the one I wanted.
5. _____ For immigrants there always something that makes them live unhappily in this country.
6. _____ When you are student, you always have to study hard.

B. In the student essay excerpt below, there are six errors marked. Using the same KEY that you used for Part A above, identify each error type and suggest a correction.

"College Pressures"

I need to disagree with Zinsser when he states, "Professors who actually like to spend time with students don't have much time to spend." I $\underset{1}{\text{noticed}}$ that most professors try to spend as much time as possible with their students. I have seen many $\underset{2}{\text{professor}}$ who sometimes are willing to stay half an hour after the class is over to explain to students any misunderstanding they might have $\underset{3}{\text{on}}$ the material the professor is teaching.

When I think of peer pressure I see it more as an encouragement for me to succeed in a class. But Zinsser states peer pressure is a disadvantage to a student. I disagree with him completely. When one of my peers receives a higher grade than I do most of the time it does not make me feel jealous or

feel <u>pressure, instead</u> it makes me understand that if I try just a little harder that I
could do just as well as the other students. <u>Most of friends</u> who I have classes with
never <u>have rub</u> in my face that they did better than me.

A.3. Editing Exercise Cover Sheets

Teacher feedback on your grammar errors: correction codes (Group A)

To the Student: Using the codes listed below, I have marked errors in the
five categories listed. Please go through your paper and try to make as many
corrections as you can, using the codes to help you understand what the
error is.

Code	Meaning
V	error in verb tense or form
NE	noun ending (plural or possessive) missing or unnecessary
Art	article or other determiner missing or unnecessary or incorrectly used
WW	wrong word or word form
SS	sentence structure: missing or unnecessary words; wrong word order; run-ons and sentence fragments

Diagnostic essay editing exercise (Group B)

Instructions: Please carefully reread the diagnostic essay you wrote in
class and typed in lab (attached). I have marked errors that I have found.
Please try to correct them. If you find any other errors that I have not
marked, you may correct those as well. You will have 20 min. to make the
changes.

Please write changes either above the word(s) or in the margins. Please
write as clearly as you can. You will receive a report in a couple of weeks
about how well you did!

Diagnostic essay editing exercise (Group C)

Instructions: Please carefully reread the diagnostic essay you wrote in
class and typed in lab (attached). If you find any errors in grammar, spelling,
word choice, or punctuation, please correct them. You will have 20 min. to
make the changes.

Please write changes either above the word(s) or in the margins. Please
write as clearly as you can. You will receive a report in a couple of weeks
about how well you did!

A.4. Student Report Form: Diagnostic Essay Editing Exercise

Student Name: _____

LS 86/6B Section: _____

Error type	Number of errors	# you corrected
Verb tense/form incorrect		
Noun endings missing, unnecessary, or incorrect		
Articles/determiners missing, unnecessary, or incorrect		
Word Choice or word form incorrect		
Sentence structure: missing or unnecessary words, word order; fragments; run-ons; comma splices		
Totals		

ADDITIONAL READINGS

SITUATING SECOND-LANGUAGE WRITING WITHIN COMPOSITION STUDIES

Matsuda, Paul Kei. "Composition Studies and ESL Writing: A Disciplinary Division of Labor." *College Composition and Communication* 50.4 (1999): 699–721.

——. "Process and Post-Process: A Discursive History." *Journal of Second Language Writing* 12.1 (2003): 65–83.

——. "Situating ESL Writing in a Cross-Disciplinary Context." *Written Communication* 15.1 (1998): 99–121.

Santos, Terry. "Ideology in Composition: L1 and ESL." *Landmark Essays in ESL Writing.* Ed. Tony Silva and Paul Kei Matsuda. Mahwah, NJ: Erlbaum, 2001. 159–72.

Silva, Tony. "Toward an Understanding of the Distinct Nature of L2 Writing: The ESL Research and Its Implications." *Landmark Essays on ESL Writing.* Ed. Tony Silva and Paul Kei Matsuda. Mahwah, NJ: Erlbaum, 2001. 191–208.

Silva, Tony, and Ilona Leki. "Family Matters: The Influence of Applied Linguistics and Composition Studies on Second Language Writing Studies — Past, Present, and Future." *Modern Language Journal* 88.1 (2004): 1–13.

SECOND-LANGUAGE WRITERS: DEFINITIONS AND COMPLEXITIES

Goldstein, Lynn. "Comments on Awad El Karim M. Ibrahim's 'Becoming Black: Rap and Hip-Hop, Race, Gender, and Identity and the Politics of ESL Learning.'" *TESOL Quarterly* 34.4 (2000): 739–44.

Matsuda, Paul Kei. "Basic Writing and Second Language Writers: Toward an Inclusive Definition." *Journal of Basic Writing* 22.2 (2003): 67–89.

Rodby, Judith. "Contingent Literacy: The Social Construction of Writing for Nonnative English-Speaking College Freshman." *Generation 1.5 Meets College*

Composition: Issues in the Teaching of Writing to U.S.-Educated Learners of ESL. Ed. Linda Harklau, Kay M. Losey, and Meryl Siegal. Mahwah, NJ: Erlbaum, 1999. 45–60.

Spack, Ruth. "The Rhetorical Construction of Multilingual Students." *TESOL Quarterly* 31.4 (1997): 765–75.

Shifting Our Theoretical Framework

Atkinson, Dwight. "On Peter Elbow's Response to 'Individualism, Academic Writing, and ESL Writers' by Vai Ramanathan & Dwight Atkinson." *Journal of Second Language Writing* 9.1 (2000): 71–6.

Casanave, Christine Pearson. *Controversies in Second Language Writing: Dilemmas and Decisions in Research and Instruction.* Ann Arbor: U of Michigan P, 2003.

Elbow, Peter. "Individualism and the Teaching of Writing: A Response to Vai Ramanathan and Dwight Atkinson." *Journal of Second Language Writing* 8.3 (1999): 327–38.

Ivanič, Roz, and David Camps. "I Am How I Sound: Voice as Self-Representation in L2 Writing." *Journal of Second Language Writing* 10.1/2 (2001): 3–33.

Kubota, Ryuko, and Al Lehner. "Toward Critical Contrastive Rhetoric." *Journal of Second Language Writing* 13.1 (2004): 7–27.

Matsuda, Paul Kei. "Contrastive Rhetoric in Context: A Dynamic Model of L2 Writing." *Journal of Second Language Writing* 6.1 (1997): 45–60.

Ramanathan, Vai, and Robert B. Kaplan. "Genres, Authors, Discourse Communities: Theory and Application for (L1 and) L2 Writing Instructors." *Journal of Second Language Writing* 9.2 (2000): 171–91.

Rethinking Curriculum Design

Braine, George. "A Study of English as a Foreign Language (EFL) Writers on a Local-Area Network (LAN) and in Traditional Classes." *Computers and Composition* 18 (2001): 275–92.

Holten, Christine. "Charting New Territory: Creating an Interdepartmental Course for Generation 1.5 Writers." *CATESOL Journal* 14.1 (2002): 173–89.

Hyland, Ken. "Genre-Based Pedagogies: A Social Response to Process." *Journal of Second Language Writing* 12 (2003): 17–29.

Pennington, Martha, ed. *Writing in an Electronic Medium: Research with Language Learners.* Houston: Athelstan, 1999.

Swales, John M. *Genre Analysis: English in Academic and Research Settings.* Cambridge, UK: Cambridge UP, 1990.

RESPONDING TO AND ASSESSING SECOND-LANGUAGE WRITING

Byrd, Patricia, and Gayle Nelson. "NNS Performance on Writing Proficiency Exams: Focus on Students Who Failed." *Journal of Second Language Writing* 4.3 (1995): 273–85.

Byrd, Patricia, and Joy Reid. *Grammar in the Composition Classroom: Essays on Teaching ESL for College-Bound Students.* New York: Heinle and Heinle, 1998.

Crusan, Deborah. "An Assessment of ESL Writing Placement Assessment." *Assessing Writing* 8.1 (2002): 17–30.

Ferris, Dana R. "The Case for Grammar Correction in L2 Writing Classes: A Response to Truscott (1996)." *Journal of Second Language Writing* 8.1 (1999): 1–11.

——. *Response to Student Writing: Implications for Second Language Students.* Mahwah, NJ: Erlbaum, 2003.

——. *Treatment of Error in Second Language Student Writing.* Ann Arbor: U of Michigan P, 2002.

Goldstein, Lynn M. "For Carla: What Does the Research Say about Responding to ESL Writers." *On Second Language Writing.* Ed. Tony Silva and Paul Kei Matsuda. Mahwah, NJ: Erlbaum, 2001. 73–89.

——. "Questions and Answers about Teacher Written Commentary and Student Revision: Teachers and Students Working Together." *Journal of Second Language Writing* 13.1 (2004): 63–80.

——. *Teacher Written Commentary in Second Language Writing Classrooms.* Ann Arbor: U of Michigan P, 2005.

Johns, Ann M. "Interpreting an English Competency Examination: The Frustrations of an ESL Science Student." *Landmark Essays on ESL Writing.* Ed. Tony Silva and Paul Kei Matsuda. Mahwah, NJ: Erlbaum, 2001. 117–35.

Liu, Jun, and Jette G. Hansen. *Peer Response in Second Language Writing Classrooms.* Ann Arbor: U of Michigan P, 2002.

Truscott, John. "The Case against Grammar Correction in L2 Writing Classes." *Language Learning* 46.2 (1996): 327–69.

——. "The Case for 'The Case against Grammar Correction in L2 Writing Classes': A Response to Ferris." *Journal of Second Language Writing* 8.2 (1999): 111–22.

WRITING ACROSS THE CURRICULUM (WAC)

Beer, Ann. "Diplomats in the Basement: Graduate Engineering Students and Intercultural Communication." *Transitions: Writing in Academic and Workplace Settings.* Ed. Patrick Dias and Anthony Pare. Cresskill, NJ: Hampton Press, 2000. 61–88.

Bloch, Joel, William Condon, Dona Hickey, Paul Kei Matsuda, Leland McCleary, Sarah Rilling, and Mike Palmquist. "Academic.Writing Forum: Connecting WAC and ESL?" *Academic.Writing* (2001). 12 Oct. 2005 <http://wac.colostate.edu/aw/forums/fall2001/>

Braine, George. "When Professors Don't Cooperate: A Critical Perspective on EAP Research." *English for Specific Purposes* 20 (2001): 293–303.

Flowerdew, John, and Matthew Peacock, ed. *Research Perspectives on English for Academic Purposes.* New York: Cambridge UP, 2001.

Grobman, Laurie. "Beyond Internationalization: Multicultural Education in the Professional Writing Contact Zone." *Journal of Business and Technical Communication* 13 (1999): 427–48.

Hyland, Ken. *Disciplinary Discourses: Social Interactions in Academic Writing.* Ann Arbor, U of Michigan P, 2004.

Janopoulos, Michael. "Writing across the Curriculum, Writing Proficiency Exams, and the NNS College Student." *Journal of Second Language Writing* 4.1 (1995): 43–50.

Johns, Ann M. "ESL Students and WAC Programs: Varied Populations and Diverse Needs." *WAC for the New Millennium, Strategies for Continuing Writing across the Curriculum Programs.* Ed. Susan H. McLeod, Eric Miraglia, Margot Soven, and Christopher Thaiss. Urbana, IL: NCTE, 2001. 141–64.

——, ed. *Genre in the Classroom: Multiple Perspectives.* Mahwah, NJ: Erlbaum, 2001.

——. *Text, Role, and Context, Developing Academic Literacies.* New York: Cambridge UP, 1997.

Leki, Ilona. "Coping Strategies of ESL Students in Writing Tasks across the Curriculum." *TESOL Quarterly* 29.2 (1995): 235–60.

——. "Pretty Much I Screwed Up: Ill-Served Needs of a Permanent Resident." *Generation 1.5 Meets College Composition: Issues in the Teaching of Writing to U.S.-Educated Learners of ESL.* Ed. Linda Harklau, Kay M. Losey, and Meryl Siegal. Mahwah, NJ: Erlbaum, 1999. 17–43.

——, *and Joan G. Carson.* "Students' Perceptions of EAP Writing Instruction and Writing Needs across the Disciplines." *TESOL Quarterly* 28 (1994): 81–102.

Matsuda, Paul Kei, and Jeffrey Jablonski. "Beyond the L2 Metaphor: Towards a Mutually Transformative Model of ESL/WAC Collaboration." *Academic.Writing* 1 (2000). 12 Oct. 2005 <http://wac.colostate.edu/aw/articles/matsuda_jablonski2000.htm>.

Santos, Terry. "Professors' Reactions to the Academic Writing of Nonnative-Speaking Students." *TESOL Quarterly* 22.1 (1988): 69–90.

Spack, Ruth. "Initiating ESL Students into the Academic Discourse Community: How Far Should We Go?" *Landmark Essays on ESL Writing.* Ed. Tony Silva and Paul Kei Matsuda. Mahwah, NJ: Erlbaum, 2001. 91–108.

Vann, Roberta, Daisy Meyer, and Frederick Lorenz. "Error Gravity: A Study of Faculty Opinion of ESL Errors." *TESOL Quarterly* 18.3 (1984): 427–40.

Wolfe-Quintero, Kate, and Gabriela Segade. "University Support for Second-Language Writers across the Curriculum." *Generation 1.5 Meets College Composition: Issues in the Teaching of Writing to U.S.-Educated Learners of ESL.* Ed. Linda Harklau, Kay M. Losey and Meryl Siegal. Mahwah, NJ: Erlbaum, 1999. 191–209.

Zamel, Vivian. "Strangers in Academia: The Experiences of Faculty and ESL Students across the Curriculum." *College Composition and Communication* 46.4 (1995): 506–21.

Zamel, Vivian, and Ruth Spack, ed. *Crossing the Curriculum: Multilingual Learners in College Classrooms.* Mahwah, NJ: Erlbaum, 2004.

Zhu, Wei. "Faculty Views on the Importance of Writing, the Nature of Academic Writing, and Teaching and Responding to Writing in the Disciplines." *Journal of Second Language Writing* 13.1 (2004): 29–48.

SECOND-LANGUAGE READING AND WRITING

Belcher, Diane, and Alan Hirvela, ed. *Linking Literacies: Perspectives on L2 Reading-Writing Connections.* Ann Arbor: U of Michigan P, 2001.

Carson, Joan G., and Ilona Leki, ed. *Reading in the Composition Classroom: Second Language Perspectives.* Boston, MA: Heinle and Heinle, 1993.

Ferris, Dana R., and John Hedgcock. *Teaching ESL Composition: Purpose, Process, and Practice.* Mahwah, NJ: Erlbaum, 2004.

Hyland, Ken. *Genre and Second Language Writing.* Ann Arbor: U of Michigan P, 2004.

Hyon, Sunny. "Genre in Three Traditions: Implications for ESL." *TESOL Quarterly* 30.4 (1996): 693–722.

Koda, Keiko. *Insights into Second Language Reading: A Cross-Linguistic Approach.* Cambridge Applied Linguistics Series. New York: Cambridge UP, 2004.

Kroll, Barbara, ed. *Second Language Writing: Research Insights for the Classroom.* New York: Cambridge UP, 1990.

Li, Shuyun, and Hugh Mumby. "Metacognitive Strategies in Second Language Academic Reading: A Qualitative Investigation." *English for Specific Purposes* 15.3 (1996): 199–216.

Paltridge, Brian. *Genre and the Language Learning Classroom.* Ann Arbor: U of Michigan P, 2001.

Silva, Tony, and Paul Kei Matsuda, ed. *Landmark Essays on ESL Writing.* Mahwah, NJ: Erlbaum, 2001.

——. *On Second Language Writing.* Mahwah, NJ: Erlbaum, 2001.

Writing Centers

Blau, Susan, and John Hall. "Guilt-Free Tutoring: Rethinking How We Tutor Non-Native-English-Speaking Students." *The Writing Center Journal* 23 (2002): 23–44.

Bruce, Shanti, and Ben Rafoth, ed. *ESL Writers: A Guide for Writing Center Tutors.* Portsmouth, NH: Boynton/Cook Heinemann, 2004.

Harris, Muriel. "Cultural Conflicts in the Writing Center: Expectations and Assumptions of ESL Students." *Writing in Multicultural Settings.* Ed. Carol Severino, Juan C. Guerra and Johnnella E. Butler. New York: MLA, 1997. 220–33.

——, **and Tony Silva.** "Tutoring ESL Students: Issues and Options." *College Composition and Communication* 44.4 (1993): 525–37.

Healy, Dave, and Susan Bosher. "ESL Tutoring: Bridging the Gap between Curriculum-Based and Writing Center Models of Peer Tutoring." *College ESL* 2.2 (1992): 25–32.

Powers, Judith K. "Rethinking Writing Center Conferencing Strategies for the ESL Writer." *The Writing Center Journal,* 13.2 (1993): 39–47.

——, **and Jane V. Nelson.** "L2 Writers and the Writing Center: A National Survey of Writing Center Conferencing at Graduate Institutions." *Journal of Second Language Writing* 4.2 (1995): 113–38.

Thonus, Terese. "Tutors as Teachers: Assisting ESW/EFL Students in the Writing Center." *The Writing Center Journal* 13.2 (1993): 13–26.

——. "What Are the Differences? Tutor Interactions with First- and Second-Language Writers." *Journal of Second Language Writing* 13.3 (2004): 227–42.

Weigle, Sara Cushing, and Gayle L. Nelson. "Novice Tutors and Their ESL Tutees: Three Case Studies of Tutor Roles and Perceptions of Tutorial Success." *Journal of Second Language Writing* 13.3 (2004): 203–55.

Williams, Jessica. "Tutoring and Revision: Second Language Writers in the Writing Center." *Journal of Second Language Writing* 13.3 (2004): 173–201.

——, **and Carol Severino.** "The Writing Center and Second Language Writers." *Journal of Second Language Writing* 13.3 (2004): 165–72.

Writing Program Administration

Braine, George. "ESL Students in First-Year Writing Courses: ESL versus Mainstream Classes." *Journal of Second Language Writing* 5.2 (1996): 91–107.

——. "Starting ESL Classes in Freshman Writing Programs." *TESOL Journal* 3.4 (1994): 22–25.

Haswell, Richard H. "Searching for Kiyoko: Bettering Mandatory ESL Writing Placement." *Journal of Second Language Writing* 7.2 (1998): 133–74.

Roy, Alice M. "Alliance for Literacy: Teaching Non-Native Speakers and Speakers of Nonstandard English Together." *College Composition and Communication* 35.4 (1984): 439–48.

——. "ESL Concerns for Writing Program Administrators: Problems and Policies." *Writing Program Administration* 11.3 (1988): 17–28.

Silva, Tony. "An Examination of Writing Program Administrators' Options for the Placement of ESL Students in First Year Writing Classes." *Writing Program Administration,* 18.1/2 (1994): 398–428.

Williams, Jessica. "ESL Composition Program Administration in the United States." *Journal of Second Language Writing* 4.2 (1995): 157–79.

AREAS FOR FUTURE RESEARCH

Atkinson, Dwight. "Writing and Culture in the Post-Process Era." *Journal of Second Language Writing* 12.1 (2003): 49–63.

Casanave, Christine Pearson. "Looking Ahead to More Sociopolitically-Oriented Case Study Research in L2 writing Scholarship (But Should It Be Called 'Post-Process'?)." *Journal of Second Language Writing* 12.1 (2003): 85–102.

Ferris, Dana. "The 'Grammar Correction' Debate in L2 Writing: Where Are We, and Where Do We Go from Here? (and What Do We Do in the Meantime . . . ?)." *Journal of Second Language Writing* 13.1 (2004): 49–62.

Kubota, Ryuko. "New Approaches to Gender, Class, and Race in Second Language Writing." *Journal of Second Language Writing* 12.1 (2003): 31–47.

Matsuda, Paul Kei, A. Suresh Canagarajah, Linda Harklau, Ken Hyland, and Mark Warschauer. "Changing Currents in Second Language Writing Research: A Colloquium." *Journal of Second Language Writing* 12.2 (2003): 151–79.

Matsuda, Paul Kei, and Tony Silva, ed. *Second Language Writing Research: Perspectives on the Process of Knowledge Making.* Mahwah, NJ: Erlbaum, 2005.

Santos, Terry, Dwight Atkinson, Melinda Erickson, Tony Silva, and Paul Kei Matsuda. "On the Future of Second Language Writing: A Colloquium." *Journal of Second Language Writing* 9.1 (2000): 1–20.

Singh, Parlo, and Catherine Doherty. "Global Cultural Flows and Pedagogic Dilemmas: Teaching in the Global University Contact Zone." *TESOL Quarterly* 38.1 (2004): 9–42.

Warschauer, Mark. "The Changing Global Economy and the Future of English Teaching." *TESOL Quarterly* 34.3 (2000): 511–35.

Yoon, Hyunsook, and Alan Hirvela. "ESL Student Attitudes toward Corpus Use in L2 Writing." *Journal of Second Language Writing* 13.4 (2004): 257–83.

You, Xiaoye. "The Choice Made from No Choice: English Writing Instruction in a Chinese University." *Journal of Second Language Writing* 13.2 (2004): 97–110.

ABOUT THE EDITORS

Paul Kei Matsuda is Assistant Professor of English and the Director of Composition at the University of New Hampshire, where he teaches various writing courses as well as graduate courses in composition, rhetoric, and applied linguistics. Since 1998, he has been chairing the CCCC Committee on Second Language Writing. With Tony Silva, he has cofounded and chairs the Symposium on Second Language Writing, a biennial gathering of second-language writing specialists from around the world, and coedited *Landmark Essays on ESL Writing* (2001), *On Second Language Writing* (2001), and *Second Language Writing Research: Perspectives on the Process of Knowledge Construction* (2005). With Kevin Eric DePew, he has edited a special issue of the *Journal of Second Language Writing*. Matsuda has published in journals such as *Academic. Writing, Computers and Composition, College Composition and Communication, Composition Studies, International Journal of Applied Linguistics, Journal of Basic Writing, Journal of Second Language Writing,* and *Written Communication*. Access his Web site at http://matsuda.jslw.org/.

Michelle Cox is a doctoral candidate studying in Composition Studies at the University of New Hampshire, where she teaches first-year composition, technical writing, and introductory literature courses. Along with Virginia Taylor, she chaired the 2004 Graduate Student Conference on Second Language Writing. She has presented at CCCC and the National Writing Across the Curriculum Conference, and currently serves on the CCCC Committee on Second Language Writing. Much of her research explores the complex interplay between social context, learning, and writing. Her dissertation, "When the Workplace Is on Campus: Learning to Write for a University Speech Language Clinic," follows five graduate students as they negotiate the complex and sometimes contradicting demands of writing for an on-campus speech-language clinic, a space where academic and workplace activity systems and genres systems overlap.

Jay Jordan is a doctoral candidate studying Rhetoric and Composition at the Pennsylvania State University. His research interests include second-language writing, technical and computer-mediated communication, writing program administration, and sociolinguistics. He is especially interested in the interactions of diverse language speakers in composition courses. He has published in the 2004 TESOL collection, *Gender and English Language Learners*, and has forthcoming articles in *College English* and *Rhetoric Review*. His dissertation, "ESL, 'Comp,' and Composition: Terms, Assumptions, Implications, and New Practices for Native and Non-native English-Speaking Students," will present a critical review of how the field of composition has positioned ESL students relative to native speakers of English as well as a grounded analysis of ESL students' interactions with their native-speaking peers. He has presented at CCCC and is a member of the CCCC Committee on Second Language Writing.

Christina Ortmeier-Hooper is a doctoral candidate in Composition Studies at the University of New Hampshire, where she teaches first-year composition, ESL, advanced composition, technical writing, and teacher education courses. Her research interests include second-language writing, teacher education, and immigrant literacy. She has published in *TESOL Journal* and has presented her work at CCCC, NCTE, and TESOL. She currently serves on the CCCC Committee on Second Language Writing. Her dissertation follows the experiences of five U.S. resident second-language writers in public high schools. The study explores students' complex responses to their identities as second-language writers and the social influences that play a role in their approaches to academic writing.

ACKNOWLEDGMENTS (*continued from page iv*)

Janet Bean et al. "Should We Invite Students to Write in Home Languages? Complicating the Yes/No Debate." *Composition Studies*, Volume 31, Number 1, Spring 2003. © 2003. Reprinted by permission.

Linda Lonon Blanton. "Classroom Instruction and Language Minority Students: On Teaching to Smarter Readers and Writers." From *Generation 1.5 Meets College Composition Issues in the Teaching of Writing to U.S.-Educated Learners of ESL*. Linda Harklau et al. Copyright 1999. Reprinted by permission of Lawrence Erlbaum Associates.

A. Suresh Canagarajah. "Understanding Critical Writing." From *Critical Academic Writing and Multilingual Students* by A. Suresh Canagarajah. © 2002. Reprinted by permission of the University of Michigan Press.

"CCCC Statement on Second Language Writing and Writers." From *College Composition and Communication* 52:4, June 2001. Copyright © 2001 National Council of Teachers of English. Reprinted with permission.

Yuet-Sim D. Chiang and Mary Schmida. "Language Identity and Language Ownership: Linguistic Conflicts of First-Year University Writing Students." In *The Teaching of Writing to U.S.-Educated Learners of ESL*." Reprinted by permission of Lawrence Erlbaum Associates.

Pat Currie. "Staying Out of Trouble: Apparent Plagiarism and Academic Survival." From *Journal of Second Language Writing*, vol. 7. Reprinted with permission from Elsevier.

Dana Ferris and Barry Roberts. "Error Feedback in L2 Writing Classes: How Explicit Does It Need to Be?" © 2001. Reprinted with permission from Elsevier.

Linda Harklau. "From the 'Good Kids' to the 'Worst': Representations of English Language Learners across Educational Settings." In *Tesol Quarterly* by Linda Harklau. Copyright © 2000 by Tesol, Inc. Reproduced with the permission of Tesol, Inc. in the format Textbook via Copyright Clearance Center.

A. M. Ibrahim. "Becoming Black: Rap and Hip-Hop, Race, Gender, Identity, and the Politics of ESL Learning." From *Tesol Quarterly* by Awad El Karim M. Ibrahim. Copyright © 1999 by Tesol, Inc. Reproduced with the permission of Tesol, Inc. in the format Textbook via Copyright Clearance Center.

Ann M. Johns. "Opening Our Doors: Applying Socioliterate Approaches (SA) to Language Minority Classrooms." From *Generation 1.5 Meets College Composition: Issues in the Teaching of Writing to U.S.-Educated Learners of ESL* edited by Linda Harklau, Kay M. Losey, and Meryl Siegal. Copyright © 1999. Reprinted with permission of Lawrence Erlbaum Assoc.

Robert E. Land, Jr. and Catherine Whitley. "Evaluating Second Language Essays in Regular Composition Classes: Toward a Pluralistic U.S. Rhetoric." From *Richness in Writing: Empowering ESL Students* by Donna M. Johnson and Duane H. Roen, Editors. Copyright © 1989 by Pearson Education. Reprinted by permission of the publisher.

Paul Kei Matsuda. "Second Language Writing in the 20th Century: A Situated Historical Perspective." From *Exploring the Dynamics of Second Language Writing* edited by Barbara Kroll. Copyright © 2003. Reprinted with permission of Cambridge University Press.

Paul Kei Matsuda and Tony Silva. "Cross-Cultural Composition: Mediated Integration of U.S. and International Students." From *Composition Studies*, Volume 27, Number 1, 1999. Copyright © 1999. Reprinted by permission.

Martha C. Pennington. "The Impact of the Computer in Second Language Writing." From *Exploring the Dynamics of Second Language Writing*. Copyright © 2003. Reprinted by permission of Cambridge University Press.

Vai Ramanathan and Dwight Atkinson. "Individualism, Academic Writing, and ESL Writers." From the *Journal of Second Language Writing*, vol 8. Reprinted with permission from Elsevier.

Joy Reid. "'Eye' Learners and 'Ear' Learners: Identifying the Language Needs of International Student and US Resident Writers" (Chapter One). From *Grammar in the Composition Classroom, Essays on Teaching ESL for College-Bound Students*, 1st Edition by Joy Reid. Copyright © 1988. Reprinted with permission of Heinle, a division of Thomson Learning: www.thomsonrights.com. Fax: 800-730-2215.

Joy Reid and Barbara Kroll. "Designing and Assessing Effective Classroom Writing Assignments for NES and ESL Students." From the *Journal of Second Language Writing*, Volume 4 by Joy Reid and Barbara Kroll. Copyright © 1995. Reprinted with permission from Elsevier.

Donald L. Rubin and M. Williams-James. "The Impact of Writer Nationality on Mainstream Teachers' Judgments of Composition Quality." From the *Journal of Second Language Writing*, Volume 6 by Donald L. Rubin and Melanie Williams-James. Copyright © 1997. Reprinted with permission from Elsevier.

INDEX